INTERNATIONAL JOURNAL OF
PSYCHOANALYTIC PSYCHOTHERAPY

International Journal of Psychoanalytic Psychotherapy

Edited by ROBERT LANGS, M.D.
and the Editorial Board

Volume Six
1977

JASON ARONSON • NEW YORK

JOURNAL POLICY

All manuscripts should be submitted in triplicate and double-spaced on white bond paper. The title page of each article must contain the author's full name and address, academic affiliation, date of submission, and a 150-page word summary of the article's contents. Charts and tables must be on separate pages, keyed to the manuscript. Headings, which should be brief, follow the style used in this Journal. Footnotes and references, also following the style of the Journal, should be listed separately triple-spaced at the end of the article.

Submit all manuscripts to Robert J. Langs, M.D., 425 East 58th Street, New York, New York, 10022.

SUBSCRIPTION INFORMATION

Standing orders and back orders of all or individual volumes of the Journal are available at twenty dollars per volume. Address orders to Jason Aronson, Inc., Order Department, 59 Fourth Avenue, New York, New York, 10003.

ISBN: 0-87668-282-4

Library of Congress Catalog Number: 75-648853

Managing Editor—John Woodside

First Paper Prize

The 1977 First Paper Prize has been awarded to Dr. Donald B. Nevins for his paper *Adverse Response to Neuroleptics in Schizophrenia*. We have been most gratified by the many excellent manuscripts recieved in response to this award and shall offer it again for the 1978 Annual. In addition, we continue to welcome original contributions related to all aspects of psychoanalysis and psychoanalytic psychotherapy.

ROBERT LANGS, M.D.
for the Editorial Board

Contributors

CARL P. ADATTO, M.D. is a clinical professor of psychiatry at the Louisiana State University Medical School, New Orleans, and a training and supervising analyst at the New Orleans Psychoanalytic Insitute.

K. H. BLACKER, M.D. is clinical professor of psychiatry and associate dean for hospital educational affairs, University of California School of Medicine at Davis. He is on the faculty of the San Francisco Psychoanalytic Institute and a member of the American Psychoanalytic Association.

ARNHILT BUELTE is codirector of the Center for Parents and Children and on the board of directors of Child Development Research.

THEODORE L. DORPAT, M.D. is clinical professor in the Department of Psychiatry and Behavioral Sciences at the University of Washington School of Medicine, and a training and supervising psychoanalyst at the Seattle Psychoanalytic Institute.

DEAN P. EYRE, M.R.C.PSYCH. qualified as a psychoanalyst with the British Psycho-analytical Society. He is medical director of a child guidance clinic in London and in private practice as a psychoanalyst.

WILLIAM N. EVANS graduated from the British Psychoanalytic Society and has been on the teaching staff of the Albert Einstein College of Medicine and Brookdale Hospital.

DAVID B. FEINSILVER, M.D. is a staff psychiatrist at Chestnut Lodge, Rockville, Maryland, and in private practice. He is a candidate at the Washington Psychoanalytic Institute and was formerly at the Center for Studies of Schizophrenia, National Institute of Mental Health.

RICHARD P. FOX, M.D. is associate adjunct professor in the Department of Psychiatry and Human Behavior of the University of California at Irvine and an advanced candidate in the Los Angeles Psychoanalytic Institute.

STEPHEN A. FRANKEL, M.D. is on the faculty at Children's Psychiatric Hospital, the Department of Psychiatry, University of Michigan Medical Center.

PETER L. GIOVACCHINI, M.D. is clinical professor in the Department of Psychiatry at the University of Illinois College of Medicine and is in private psychoanalytic practice in Chicago. He is a member of the editorial board of the *International Journal of Psychoanalytic Psychotherapy,* a fellow of the American Psychiatric and Orthopsychiatric Associations, and a member of the American Psychoanalytic Association.

HENRIETTE T. GLATZER, Ph.D. is President of the American Group Psychotherapy Association. She is training and supervising analyst at the Post Graduate Center for Mental Health and has been clinical assistant professor of psychiatry at Albert Einstein College of Medicine and on the faculty of Adelphi College.

ENRIQUE GUARNER, M.D. is on the graduate faculty at the University of Mexico and at the Universidad Iberoamericana in Mexico City. He is also a consultant in the adolescent department of the Mexican Institution for the Assistance of Childhood and head of the Scientifica Comissión at the Asociación Mexicana de Psicoterapía Psicoanalítica.

JAMES W. HAMILTON, M.D. is associate professor of psychiatry, Medical College of Wisconsin.

MARDI J. HOROWITZ, M.D. is professor of psychiatry and director of the Psychotherapy Evaluation and Study Center, Langley Porter Institute, University of California, San Francisco; he is also on the faculty of the San Francisco Psychoanalytic Institute.

JUDITH S. KESTENBERG, M.D. is clinical professor of psychiatry and training analyst for parents and children at the Down State Medical Center in Brooklyn, as well as on the medical staff of the Long Island Jewish-Hillside Medical Center. She is also codirector of the Center for Parents and Children and on the board of directors of Child Development Research.

M. MASUD R. KHAN, M.A. is a member of the British Psychoanalytical Society. He is editor of the *International Psycho-Analytic Library;* co-redacteur etranger de la *Nouvelle Revue de Psychoanalyse;* and director, *Freud Copyrights.* He is also associate editor of *The International Journal of Psycho-Analysis* and *The International Review of Psycho-Analysis.*

STEVEN T. LEVY, M.D. is director of outpatient psychiatry at Grady Memorial Hospital, where he teaches and supervises in the areas of psychotherapeutic technique and psychoanalytic theory. He is an assistant professor of psychiatry at the Emory University School of Medicine and a candidate at the Columbia University Psychoanalytic Clinic for Training and Research at Emory.

MARGARET I. LITTLE, M.R.C.S., M.R.C. PSYCH. has been associated with the Tavistock Clinic, where she was assistant medical officer of Brooke House, and with the London Clinic of Psycho-Analysis, where she supervised training for over twenty years. She is a member of the British Psycho-Analytic and International Psycho-Analytic Associations.

W. W. MEISSNER, S.J., M.D. is associate clinical professor of psychiatry at the Harvard Medical School, Boston, Massachusetts, chairman of the faculty at the Boston Psychoanalytic Institute, and staff psychiatrist at the Massachusetts Mental Health Center in Boston and the Cambridge Hospital, Cambridge, Massachusetts.

RICHARD L. MUNICH, M.D. is an assistant clinical professor of psychiatry at Yale University and unit chief at the West Haven Veterans Administration Hospital. He was formerly clinical director of the Yale Psychiatric Institute and is currently a candidate at the Western New England Institute for Psychoanalysis.

WAYNE A. MYERS, M.D. is a clinical assistant professor of psychiatry at the Cornell University Medical Cneter. He is a member of the New York Psychoanalytic Society and Institute, the American Psychoanalytic Association, the International Psycho-Analytic Association, and a Fellow of the American Psychiatric Association.

DONALD B. NEVINS, M.D. is assistant clinical professor in the Department of Psychiatry at the University of California School of Medicine, San Francisco, and is in private practice in Kentfield, California. He is a clinical associate at the San Francisco Psychoanalytic Institute and a consultant in psychiatry at both Letterman Army Medical Center, San Francisco, and the California Department of Vocational Rehabilitation.

LEON J. SAUL, M.D. is emeritus professor of psychiatry, Medical School of the University of Pennsylvania; on the honorary staff, Institute of Pennsylvania Hospital; and emeritus training analyst, Philadelphia Psychoanalytic Institute.

JOSEPH E. SCHWARTZ, M.D. is a candidate in psychoanalysis at the Boston Psychoanalytic Society and Institute. He is on the active training staff in the Department of Psychiatry of the Massachusetts General Hospital, a clinical instructor in psychiatry at the Harvard Medical School, and a clinical assistant professor of psychiatry at the Tufts University School of Medicine.

HANNA SEGAL, F.R.C. PSYCH. is currently engaged in private psychoanalytical practice, as well as training, supervising and teaching at the British Psycho-Analytical Society. She is visiting professor of the Freud Memorial Chair, University College, London, 1977/1978.

AUSTIN SILBER, M.D. is clinical associate professor in the Department of Psychiatry and for many years supervised psychotherapy at the State University Alcohol Clinic at the Downstate Medical Center in Brooklyn. He is a training and supervising analyst for the Downstate Psychoanalytic Institute. He is active on committees of the Downstate Psychoanalytic Institute and the American Psychoanalytic Association.

JOSEPH W. SLAP, M.D. is clinical professor at Hahnemann Medical College where he is active in the residency training program and in the Section of Psychosomatic Medicine and Liaison Psychiatry. He is also a consultant at the Philadelphia State Hosptial.

WILLIAM HURT SLEDGE, M.D. is a major in the United States Air Force and teaches at the USAF School of Aerospace Medicine at Brooks Air Force Base, Texas; his present paper is based on work while a postdoctoral fellow and member of the Behavioral Sciences Track of the Yale University School of Medicine, Department of Psychiatry.

SILAS L. WARNER, M.D. is instructor in psychiatry, Medical School of the University of Pennsylvania; associate psychiatrist, Institute of Pennsylvania Hospital; consultant in psychiatry, Swarthmore College; and a member of the Philadelphia Psychoanalytic Society.

Table of Contents
International Journal of
Psychoanalytic Psychotherapy
Volume 6, 1977

Severe Psychopathological States

General Clinical Issues

Contents

INTERNATIONAL JOURNAL OF
PSYCHOANALYTIC PSYCHOTHERAPY

Transference Phenomena in Initial Interviews

CARL P. ADATTO, M.D.

Transference phenomena can be used effectively in pursuing diagnostic and therapeutic aims in initial interviews. Theoretical and clinical aspects of transference phenomena are discussed with special reference to preformed transference expectations, the dynamic and genetic aspects of transference, the differentiation of transference phenomena from transference and the transference neurosis, and their relevance to other analytic data. A case is presented, and two transference phenomena in the initial interviews are traced through later stages of the analysis; their origins and multiple determinants are demonstrated.

Initial interviews with patients seeking psychoanalysis are crucial in determining diagnosis and recommendations for therapy. They offer a unique opportunity to experience and examine in action important aspects of the patient's psychopathology to be analyzed in later sessions. The psychoanalyst is interested in determining the nature of the unconscious conflicts and psychodynamics and to this end assesses various aspects of the patient's mental functioning. The complexity of this assessment has been outlined by Anna Freud (1965) and subsequently elaborated in diagnostic profiles for all age groups (A. Freud et al. 1965, Laufer 1965, Meers 1966).

The aim of this presentation is to discuss the nature and relevance of transference phenomena in initial interviews. Understanding these phenomena helps the analyst determine analyzability and prepare for the continuation of an analysis that might begin in the initial interviews. The examination of transference phenomena is of special interest because of the uniqueness of transference as a vehicle for expressing and revealing the patient's conflicts, and its potential for examination in the immediacy of the analytic setting. Ultimately, the analysis of the transference becomes one of the central foci of the analytic work.

Rather than cover the entire topic of transference and its manifestations, an attempt will be made to illustrate the value of paying attention to these phenomena during the course of initial interviews, which last from one to several sessions. Use will be made of a clinical example in which initial transference phenomena were traced and identified as transference later in the analysis. Defenses, character traits, memories, dreams, fantasies, and other important areas of the patient's mind expressed or revealed during initial interviews will not be dealt with, except in passing, so as to highlight the nature and significance of transference phenomena.

TRANSFERENCE AND TRANSFERENCE PHENOMENA

Freud (1905) defined transferences as "new editions or facsimiles of the impulses or phantasies which are aroused and made conscious during the progress of the analysis; but they have this peculiarity, which is characteristic for their species, that they replace some earlier person by the person of the physician. To put it another way: a whole series of psychological experiences are revived, not as belonging to the past, but as applying to the person of the physician at the present moment" (p. 116). To meet the requirements that a given phenomenon is transference requires that present attitudes toward the analyst must be connected to unconscious impulses or fantasies specifically related to some person in the patient's early life. Since it is not possible to fulfill these requirements during initial interviews, one must be content to hypothesize that certain phenomena potentially represent transference.

Rapaport (1944) distinguished between transference phenomena, which are ubiquitous and seem analogous to transference, and transference proper, which he defines as a theoretical explanatory construct inferred from the analytic setting. A phenomenon that, at first, seems transference, may later be identified and utilized predominately as some other psychological construct. In actuality, many kinds of psychic phenomena are in evidence simultaneously during any time of a patient's presentation, and offer different paths to reach the common unconscious mental activity from which they arise.

INITIAL INTERVIEWS

The literature on initial interviews (Deutsch and Murphy 1955, GAP 1961, Gill et al. 1954, Saul 1957) and on assessing analyzability (Guttman 1960), usually touch upon the transference or the analyst-patient interaction as a source of material. Rappaport (1960) considers it important to gauge transference potentials in preparing a patient for analysis. Rosen (1958) comments on the historical development of the psychoanalytic point of view in initial interviews. Difficulties are encountered by the analyst interested in obtaining transference information while maintaining a stance that will not interfere with its development, or with the analysis as a whole. Freud noted: "Lengthy preliminary discussions before the beginning of the analytic treatment, previous treatment by another method and also previous acquaintance between the doctor and the patient who is to be analyzed, have special disadvantageous consequences for which one must be prepared. They result in the patient's meeting the doctor with a transference attitude which is already established and which the doctor must first slowly uncover, instead of having the opportunity to observe the growth and development of the transference from the outset" (1913, p. 125). Despite taking precautions, patients have preformed transferences upon presenting themselves for initial interviews. Kubie stated in regard to transference: "It begins even when a patient starts to consider being analyzed, indeed before he has even met his analyst, with his dim fantasies of what the analyst is going to be like" (1950, p. 58).

In a large sense, all transferences are preformed. Those that occur in relationship to the analyst prior to, or during, the initial interviews have special relevance by providing clues to the possible nature of the transferences and conflicts. Preformed transference fantasies are usually revealed through the patient's expectations of how the analyst might react to him or how he might help him.

Part of the problem of studying initial transference phenomena can be approached by distinguishing the dynamic from the genetic aspects of transferences, as well as transference from the transference neurosis. The genetic aspects of transference, the origins of both the unconscious fantasies and the attitudes toward the infantile objects, are established through intensive analytic work. The dynamic aspects of transference, on the other hand, are readily accessible and subject to mutual examination by analyst and patient. What is meant by *dynamic* is the clinical manifestations of the play of psychic forces emerging from the conflicts as observed and inferred by the analyst in his direct interaction with the patient. The patient usually has little awareness of the significance of this information he communicates and expresses to the analyst, or of how it is related to his unconscious or past.

Transferences can be observed and identified starting in the early months of analysis and are manifested in relationship to people other than the analyst. The transference neurosis, a current version of the infantile neurosis centrally related to the analyst, usually becomes clearly evident only following a sustained period of analysis of the transference and defenses. Its manifestation varies in degree and in intensity (Adatto 1971). The transference neurosis is not observed during initial interviews nor, as a rule, during the beginning phases of an analysis.

CASE ILLUSTRATION

The following patient illustrates two major transference phenomena during the initial interviews.

A thirty-seven-year-old man came for analysis in an acute anxiety state growing out of a marital discord. Several months earlier he had an argument with his wife during which she was openly hostile to him for the first time during their nine-year marriage. This episode precipitated doubts about himself and his goal of always trying to be "good and do what is right." He described a feeling of having his bubble burst. Following this incident he became more anxious and sleepless and attempted various ways to resolve his problem. When he developed an acute anxiety state several days previously, he talked to a friend who recommended that he consult a psychoanalyst.

He opened the first session stating that it was very difficult for him to seek help from anyone because he had always been self-sufficient, and that he came only because his distress had grown unbearable. In a rapid and organized way he volunteered his life history. He came from an impoverished background and worked his way through school, attending college on an athletic scholarship. It was not possible to depend on his parents' help, because what little financial or emotional support he could get from them was always the basis for argument. He was ashamed of his father's lowly occupation and felt that his hypochondriac mother always demanded that he be good according to her standards. In college, he felt relief for the first time in his life, as though released from prison. After that he rarely went home or had much contact with his parents. Upon graduating from college he became a professional athlete and shortly afterwards married. Several years later, he left his athletic career, enrolled in law school, and graduated high in his class. He then entered the practice of law and became an immediate success. On several occasions during the interview he emphasized he had always been highly successful in anything he undertook.

Sometime during the latter part of the visit he visibly sank into the chair and reported that the mere act of talking to me gave him immediate relief. He felt this was due to his doing something constructive about his problem and also that he sensed that I understood him. After telling me this he straightened up again and said that depending on me for help would be of no use since he would see that as a weakness in himself (first transference phenomenon). There was close connection of the sequence of associations describing his home life, his successes, his sense of relief, then of caution in seeing me. I asked him if it were possible that he saw coming to see me as being similar to visiting his parents. He initially rejected this possibility by saying that I was totally different from his parents and that he came to see me because he considered me a success, and not a failure like his parents. After a short reflective pause, he laughed and said: "I guess I still hope Mother and Dad can do something for me." Next he turned his attention to his wife and his disappointments over her letting him down and related in detail several sexual affairs he had over the past two years. It surprised him that he could talk so freely about these affairs, and as he did he realized that his anxiety had started long before the precipitating episode with his wife.

During the next two meetings he again sank back into the chair and associated freely about present and past events in his life. He expressed how relieved he was now that he was seeking help and he described me as a friendly ally; however, an element of cautiousness prevailed. When analysis was recommended during the third interview he accepted and stated that he was glad I understood his plight and was willing to work with him. *He then revealed a fantasy to me which he had prior to coming to my office and again upon meeting me: I would not accept him as a patient because I would feel that he was exaggerating his problems and that I would be critical of him* (second transference phenomenon). Not until that time did he give any indication he was uncertain that I might not accept him as a patient. He said that the experience reminded him of his high school coach who always expected him to play whether or not he were injured; to do otherwise would be weak. Months later in the analysis this experience was specifically related to how his mother would treat him when he was sick or injured. She would accuse him of pretending that he was sick or exaggerating an injury, so that he could stay home. During early adolescence, he ignored a broken hand for a week; he finally asked for treatment when his hand was so swollen that he could not write with it.

During the first several months of analysis he was enthusiastic about his insights, especially about how he tried to be good and please people as a way of getting what he wanted from them and avoiding criticism. There was elaboration of the sketchy history he had presented during his first interview. He recognized that he had learned to use his skills and intellect in the service of certain traits prominent during his athletic career. At that time he was free in his use of physical aggression and was popular. Usually he would shake hands with his rivals after a game because he wanted them to like him. He would take extraordinary risks, prevail because of his skill and strength, and rarely complain. After several years in the professional ranks he incurred a severe injury which required surgical treatment. He could have returned as an active player the following season but he decided, since he might not continue to be a star athlete, to quit athletics and enter law school. As he related his decision, he boasted, "I knew I could beat them in the courtroom, too."

During the early part of the analysis he considered me only an ally and apparently exempted me as a target of his aggression. Then he began to complain that I was not helping him enough, because his marital problems were still unresolved and he was beginning again to experience increased anxiety. At first he denied his rather obvious displeasure with me, explaining that he understood analysis took a long time and recognized that he was impatient. This was interpreted as a denial of anger toward me associated to my not giving him relief, despite his attempts to be a cooperative and pleasant patient. A few days later he openly became angry at me while I was attempting to understand his being late for an appointment. He viewed my analytic activity as prying, and accused me of being petty and critical. After the outburst, he acknowledged that he considered coming to analysis as an interference in his life and that he, indeed, was angry at me. A conflict emerged centered around not being fed by his mother and, recently, his wife. Relief was associated to a feeling of both oral and sexual satisfaction. As homosexual derivatives began to appear, he veered off in other directions; this theme reappeared and was worked out at length in the latter part of the analysis.

Several weeks later he reported a dream: "I was in your office, but it looked different. You seemed disinterested and bored and I wondered what was wrong. There were some small farm implements in the corner of your office and I wondered if you needed them in your work as an analyst." He was puzzled by the dream; with some sense of certitude he identified the affect he attributed to me as his own, and then seemed to ignore further analysis of the dream. When I commented that he failed to associate to the farm implements and their relationship to me, he grew irritated and accused me of being self-centered and not letting him analyze his dreams in his own way. I ventured that his reaction might be considered as reluctance to deal with something important that emerged in the dream. After a tense pause, he said "You don't stay down when I put you down—you don't seem afraid of me." Following a short silence, he mused about the farm implements, recalling that when he was four or five years old his father had farmed for several years. It was a difficult period for the family; the father was doing poorly financially, and the mother, following the birth of his sister, had become withdrawn. As a result of these circumstances, the father gave up farming and returned to the city to seek a job for himself and medical help for his wife.

He stated that the feeling he had at that time in his life was similar to the feeling he remembered having during the first interview, in which he expressed the necessity of helping himself. Also, he recalled that when I connected the hesitancy to get help from me as being similar to going home, he experienced a sense of relief, but was ashamed to convey that to me at the time. Later in the analysis he recognized that the problem was not only a hesitancy to get help, but also a fear of reviving an old feeling of depression and the sense of helplessness in reaching his mother. Much further in the analysis, the oedipal aspects of this memory emerged. Rivalry with, and defeating of, the father, along with extensive castration anxiety, became an important aspect of the transference.

Not too long after the analysis of the dream he began to demonstrate a growing transference neurosis. He felt relatively free of anxiety and symptoms except in relation to me and coming to analysis. His relationship with his wife changed after he analyzed some of the maternal connections to her. In addition, he was able to analyze his relationship to his son and daughter, especially his identification with them as objects of maternal indifference. As he regressed more into the transference neurosis, he felt trapped; nevertheless, he maintained good analytic capacity.

DISCUSSION

In retrospect, the analysis of this patient began during the first interview, and the interpretation of a transference phenomenon had the effect of analyzing a resistance to being analyzed. Later this phenomenon was verified as being transference through analysis of the connection to an early period in his life related to his parents and conflicts surrounding them and through the tying together of past and present affect. The second transference phenomenon became evident when, after being offered psychoanalysis, the patient revealed a preformed fantasy that he would not be acceptable as a patient. The fantasy, at first associated to a coach, later was connected to infantile transferences.

It is important to recognize that focusing on the transference phenomena does not do justice to the complexity of the analytic data worked with during the first interviews. Waelder's concept of multiple function (1936) alerts one to the need to appraise psychic phenomena from many points of view. For instance, the unfolding of defenses and character traits was also of significance during the initial interviews. The presenting character traits of being an independent and good person were already in a state of disequilibrium when he came for analysis. The patient himself connected his anxiety to these traits, opening the way for further exploration during the interview. The interpretation of the first transference phenomenon covered not only potential transferences, but also had the effect of interpreting the denial of his conflict related to considering analysis. Following the interpretation he amended the time of appearance of his presenting anxiety, and connected this with earlier sexual affairs. Thus, the mobilization of his unconscious conflicts took many forms.

The transference phenomena themselves contained multiple transference determinants. The conflict about returning home was initially related to both his father and mother. The dream associating my office to the family home of his earlier years led to fantasies and recollections of his father's failures and difficulties, his mother's depression, and the birth of his sister. Considerable analysis was necessary to work out the complex origins of each of these relationships and how they emerged in the current transferences, both with me and others. Multiple layers of transference were also in evidence in regard to the fantasy he had that I would not accept him as a patient. The first connection was to a coach, and later to his mother. Sharp memories of his wanting to stay at home with his mother, and being rejected by her, opened up an even more intense transference connected to rivalry with his father and the accompanying castration anxiety.

Preformed transference expectations are important leads to the status of transferences; they are also sources of resistance which interfere with the unfolding of the transference. This patient was able to begin the analysis of his preformed fantasy only after initial resistances were worked with and after an agreement was made to undertake analysis. One could speculate that if this fantasy had not been brought into the analytic setting, the patient might have continued to use it as part of the defensive constellation around his presenting conflicts. The differentiation of conscious, preformed transference phenomena from those that are out of awareness and emerge in the analysis has limited conceptual value. Both types were present in this patient, and were traced to their sources in the unconscious transferences and fantasies. As the analysis progressed, the initial transference phenomena, while acting as points of reference in the analysis, became relatively unimportant as the transferences and the transference neurosis were analyzed.

The transference phenomena in this patient were manifestly dynamic in character; they were identified by the interplay of psychic forces inferred from the conflicts revealed in the immediacy of the analytic setting. The dynamics of the first phenomenon were inferred from verbal associations, shifts in affect (feeling of relief, then tension and anxiety), and from nonverbal expressions (bodily posture in the chair and facial expressions). Some genetic connections were present (references to father and mother in the associations to the first phenomenon), but were considerably distant from the infantile period. Transferences in this patient were analyzed in the confluence of present and past, as evidenced in the analysis of the dream.

The transference neurosis, which developed after the analysis was well under way, carried the highest degree of relevance of all the transferences. It emerged as a result of the unconscious conflicts becoming relatively freed from their defenses, and was more or less contained in the analytic setting. Following the analysis of the initial transference phenomena and early transferences, the transference neurosis became apparent and was characterized by the patient's symptoms and anxiety becoming more centered in the analytic relationship than in his everyday life and relationships. For this patient, the transference neurosis became a major source of identifying and resolving the patient's core conflicts.

The patient illustrated is not unusual in regard to initial transference phenomena. Practically all patients give evidence of such phenomena, even though at times they are difficult to identify.

Some patients reveal initial fantasies only after a prolonged period of analysis. A patient, after an early summer consultation, started her analysis following the summer holidays. Prior to the beginning of the summer at the end of the first year of analysis, she became depressed. She then revealed that she had a fantasy that, because of some catastrophe, the analyst would not return from his summer vacation to start the analysis. This fantasy occurred prior to her consultation, when she herself knew that she wanted to begin analysis and knew that she would wait until the fall to begin. Soon she associated to her parents leaving on a prolonged trip one summer when she was about eight years old; at that time, she fantasized that because of a catastrophe they would not return. Still later this fantasy was connected to her mother's absence from home to give birth to her brother during the summer of her fourth year. The transference fantasy set in motion an anniversary-like reaction, and she was able through this route to begin to understand some of the destructive conflicts related to her mother.

Absence of reference—direct or indirect—to the analyst is worthy of note in itself. A patient began an analysis with apparent disregard for the analyst as a person. When confronted with this early in the analysis, the patient dismissed the analyst as a mere "instrument" to help him resolve his difficulties. An attempt to analyze this view of the analyst was met with "You're a doctor, not a friend or relative" and "I expect you to be totally objective." While these remarks in themselves were revealing, they were not analyzable early in the analysis. After about two years of analysis he was able to understand some of the significance of his concept of the analyst as an instrument. Anatomical connections were the first made, followed by an eroticized transference related to the father. The initial phenomenon, while ultimately leading to transference, was primarily ego defensive.

Another patient began her analysis with an open transference phenomenon. She stated early during the initial interview that the analyst reminded her of her maternal uncle who was a physician. With great ease she associated to her mother and the maternal side of her family. They were the ones who were kind and lovable; her father and his relatives were cold and distant. The openness of the transference phenomenon and the associations of the analyst to the mother and her relatives was, in itself, a resistance which only could be analyzed after a period of analysis. The apparent genetic connections were incomplete because the initial reactions turned out also as a defense against attachment to her father.

Technical management of initial transference phenomena is a complex issue. To adequately cover this issue one must deal with the general topic of analytic technique, which is outside the scope of this presentation. However, certain principles can be stated. Brenner, in referring to the long-prevailing technical rule that transference manifestations are analyzable only when they are clearly in the service of resistance, stated that "transference should be dealt with and interpreted like anything else in the analytic material: that is, as it appears and in accordance with its importance at the moment relative to other material" (1969, p. 337). This principle can be applied to transference manifestations in initial interviews. Transference phenomena are but one aspect of the patient's data that are of special interest to the analyst. They are kept in perspective to other analytic data and are subject to the basic principles of analytic technique. Trial interpretations of various kinds, including transference interpretations, are often useful in initial interviews to help determine analyzability or any aspect of the diagnostic assessment. For the most part transference phenomena need not be interpreted, but should be explored and stored for further reference.

SUMMARY

Transference phenomena, clinical manifestations that potentially represent transferences, constitute one of the major areas for exploration during initial interviews because of their special relevance to unconscious conflicts and the possibility of their being examined by both analyst and patient in the immediacy of the analytic setting. They often take the form of preformed transference expectations which are conscious and begin before the patient first visits the analyst; more often, they are out of awareness and surface throughout the analysis, beginning with the initial interviews. Considerable analytic work is necessary before one can verify, through genetic connections, that these dynamic phenomena are transference proper; even more analysis is required before the transference neurosis becomes evident. By subjecting transference phenomena at the outset to the basic principles of psychoanalytic technique, both diagnostic assessment and the beginnings of a potential analysis are served simultaneously.

REFERENCES

Adatto, C. P. (1971). Developmental aspects of the transference neurosis. In *Currents in Psychoanalysis*, ed. I. M. Marcus, pp.337-360. New York: International Universities Press.
Brenner, C. (1969). Some comments on technical precepts in psychoanalysis. *Journal of the American Psychoanalytic Association* 17:333-352.
Deutsch, F., and Murphy, W. F. (1955). *The Clinical Interview*. New York: International Universities Press.

Freud, A. (1965). *Normality and Pathology in Childhood: Assessments in Development.* New York: International Universities Press.

Freud, A., Nagera, H., and Freud, W. E. (1965). Metapsychological assessment of the adult personality: the adult profile. *The Psychoanalytic Study of the Child* 20:9-41.

Freud, S. (1905). Fragment of an analysis of a case of hysteria. *Standard Edition* 7:7-122.

——— (1912). The dynamics of transference. *Standard Edition* 12:99-108.

——— (1913). On beginning the treatment (further recommendations on the technique of psycho-analysis). *Standard Edition* 12:123-144.

GAP (1961). *Reports in Psychotherapy: Initial Interviews.* Report no. 49 Vol. 4, Part 1, 437-458. New York: Group for the Advancement of Psychiatry.

Gill, M., Newman, R., and Redlich, F. C. (1954). *The Initial Interview in Psychiatric Practice.* New York: International Universities Press.

Guttman, S. A. (1960). Criteria for analyzability (panel report). *Journal of the American Psychoanalytic Association* 8:141-151.

Kubie, L. S. (1950. *Practical and Theoretical Aspects of Psychoanalysis.* New York: International Universities Press.

Laufer, M. (1965). Assessment of adolescent disturbances: the application of Anna Freud's diagnostic profile. *The Psychoanalytic Study of the Child* 20:99-123.

Meers, D. R. (1966). A diagnostic profile of psychopathology in a latency child. *The Psychoanalytic Study of the Child* 21:483-526.

Rapaport, D. (1944). The scientific methodology of psychoanalysis. In *The Collected Papers of David Rapaport,* ed. M. M. Gill, pp. 165-220. New York; London: Basic Books, 1967.

Rappaport, E. A. (1960). Preparation for analysis. *International Journal of Psycho-Analysis* 41:626-632.

Rosen, V. H. (1958). The initial psychiatric interview and the principles of psychotherapy: some recent contributions. *Journal of the American Psychoanalytic Association* 6:154-167.

Saul, L. J. (1957) The psychoanalytic diagnostic interview. *Psychoanalytic Quarterly* 26:76-90.

Waelder, R. (1936). The principle of multiple function: observations on over-determination. *Psychoanalytic Quarterly* 5:45-62.

Countertransference Aspects of Pharmacotherapy in the Treatment of Schizophrenia

STEVEN T. LEVY, M.D.

Emphasis is placed on largely unconscious aspects of the therapeutic relationship which determine the inappropriate or untimely use of psychotropic drugs, particularly on the therapist's response to the regressive modes of relating and sharing emotional experience which characterize therapeutic work with schizophrenic patients. Case examples illustrate the use of drugs to establish interpersonal boundaries, to disavow frightening feelings within the self, and to renounce forbidden regressive pleasures—thus defending against the regressive pull of the developing symbiotic relationship. The effect of postpsychotic depression on the therapeutic relationship is explored with regard to the dynamics of psychotropic drug usage in treatment.

It is not the purpose of this paper to question the value of psychotropic agents in the treatment of schizophrenia. There are many studies which demonstrate the effectiveness of phenothiazines and related drugs in the management of psychotic patients. The relative merits of pharmacotherapy versus both supportive and insight-oriented psychotherapies, both alone and in combination with drugs, have been extensively investigated (see especially May 1968, 1971, Feinsilver and Gunderson 1972, Grinspoon, Ewalt, and Shader 1972, Karon and Vanden Bos 1972, Davis 1975). That no consensus among investigators has been reached is in part due to difficulties in controlling for variables both within and across studies. I believe that for certain patients, a psychoanalytically oriented, investigative psychotherapy, with the goal of increased self-understanding and personal growth, can be successful even in the face of vulnerability to psychotic disorganization (Levy, McGlashan, and Carpenter 1975). It is the treatment of such cases which is the subject under discussion here, particularly as it relates to the concomitant use of psychotropic drugs.

During the course of therapeutic work with schizophrenic individuals, therapists are often confronted with feelings within themselves which lead them, for reasons largely outside their awareness, to consider using pharmacologic agents. This is in contrast to the consciously planned use of medication as an adjunct to insight psychotherapy. Whenever medications are used during psychotherapy, their meaning and usefulness to patient and therapist must be continuously scrutinized to prevent medications becoming a vehicle for the unconscious avoidance of the therapeutic task (Ostow 1962, Linn 1964, Langs 1973). In my own work, as well as in supervising the work of others, I have found that at certain junctures during therapy with schizophrenic patients, a consideration of adding or changing drugs becomes an almost predictable event which signals a disruptive but not necessarily detrimental alteration in the therapeutic relationship. Inexperienced therapists, in particular, are prone to use the complex controversies around what constitutes the best treatment for schizophrenia to justify using or changing drugs at this point, and suddenly question whether initial therapeutic hopes and goals were realistic given such severely impaired patients.

The following clinical vignette illustrates how the issue of medications may enter the treatment situation and result in the therapist not responding appropriately to the patient.

Case 1

Miss A , a twenty-three-year-old single woman, was evaluated and referred for time-limited psychoanalytic psychotherapy with an advanced psychiatric resident. The following information is abstracted from the intake worker's case summary. Miss A complained of feelings of "deadness" and "vagueness," insomnia, and trouble organizing her thoughts. She had recently worked as a waitress, having dropped out of college due to feelings of anxiety, confusion, and inability to concentrate. Within a year of dropping out of school and returning home to live with her mother, Miss A had a psychotic episode for which she was hospitalized for seven months. After discharge, she moved to another city, because living with her family was thought by the hospital staff to be too stressful.

Miss A was one of six children, whom she described as "scattered all over the country." Her parents, both educators, were divorced when she was eleven years old. After that time, the patient lived with her mother and rarely saw her father. The evaluation report ended with the following statement: "The patient feels badly about her inability to function at a higher level. She is frustrated at her difficulty in communicating but, in fact, expresses her feelings quite well. She has been on a variety of drug regimens, none of which were helpful."

The therapist, Dr. T, reported that, even prior to beginning the treatment, he felt anxious about working in psychoanalytic psychotherapy with a severely impaired patient who had recently been psychotic. Miss A arrived at her first session dressed boyishly, without make-up, looking somewhat unkempt. She began by relating that she had "cracked up" while away at college. She dropped out of school and was admitted to a hospital in her home town. Miss A then added that she didn't "focus on one thing a lot." She described her current living arrangement with a girlfriend. She next detailed some of her family history and mentioned her parents' divorce. This was followed by a long pause. The therapist had not said anything yet, and reported that the patient seemed very anxious about his listening quietly. In fact, Dr. T attributed the long pause to his inability to think of what to say after her "giving a history."

Miss A now became somewhat agitated and said that she knew treatment would go badly, that she couldn't think properly, that she had really been in need of treatment for a long time, but that now it was too late. She said rather dispairingly that she used to function well prior to her crack up. Dr. T asked what she meant by "crack up" and she responded by saying that she felt foolish and was thinking about her friend sitting in the waiting area. She next said, "You're not going to get anywhere this way." Dr. T replied that he heard Miss A saying she would waste his time.

He reported in supervision that he said this under the impact of the patient's anxiety, which he described as unbearable. When asked how this made him feel, he said he felt somewhat paralyzed, dissatisfied with his comments as well as with his silence. In fact, he hadn't meant to say that the patient might waste his time. He had actually wanted to make an empathic remark about her concerns that treatment might not help her. He admitted that his comment related to his wondering at this time whether this way of treating her was appropriate. He thought that he should stop groping around and put her on medicine.

He asked the patient whether she had been on drugs in the past. Miss A replied that she hadn't been honest in talking about herself. She didn't live away from home while at college. She commuted every day from home to school, a one hundred mile trip. She couldn't leave home; couldn't leave mother. She next added that she had been seeing a psychologist while at school and had asked for medicine. She next recounted several of her experiences with medication. She told Dr. T that medicines made her numb and she wished Dr. T would talk more. She paused and then said she thought Dr. T has his own problems.

During this session, the therapist experienced the patient as frightening and unbearably anxious. He felt much the way she did, not being able to collect his thoughts or respond appropriately. He wondered whether it was too late and thought about medication. The patient recognized his difficulties, told him that medicines didn't help, and said that what she needed was talk. The next several sessions were occupied with both the patient and the therapist trying to be more comfortable with each other. The patient repeatedly both asked for drugs which would make her feel better and said that the people she knew who had been on medication for long periods looked hollow. She seemed to have taken in the therapist's ambivalence about drugs and was working this over internally.

Dr. T, after exploring his reactions in supervision, told the patient that medications had not helped her in the past and that he thought working on her problems by talking together would be more helpful. Miss A looked relieved and described her current life as "being on the outside looking in. But I do it, I don't let things register." Dr. T asked her to elaborate on not letting things register. She responded, "Yes, because it doesn't matter. There has to be like a frame of reference—something to refer back to. Something that you're going to stay with. Ask me another question. See, the thing I have in my head, I have like a dialogue. Your inner voice; but it's not there to refer back to. It's just not there. It's just a whiny, irritating, little——"

We see in this vignette how the therapist used the issue of medication to deal with his own anxieties. The patient's immediate response to the therapist's introducing medication into the therapeutic field is to confess her dishonesty; next she provides information that drugs do not help, and finally points out that she wants the therapist to help her by talking. In subsequent sessions, the patient is preoccupied with medicines. She has incorporated the therapist's ambivalence and works to create a more helpful treatment relationship. In psychotherapy with schizophrenics and to a lesser degree with neurotic individuals, the patient is prone to take in relatively sick aspects of the therapist (Searles 1958, Langs 1976) and to make curative efforts on his behalf (Little 1951, Searles 1975, Langs 1975a, 1975b, 1976).

When the therapist resolved his ambivalence about being able to treat the patient and made a clear statement to her, the patient was obviously relieved and commenced to describe with greater detail and clarify aspects of her inner experience. Her comment about the need for "a frame of reference— something to refer back to" describes what she needs the therapist to provide if she is to stay with the work. I believe she correctly perceived the therapist's ill-timed and anxiety-ridden introduction of the medication issue as a threat to the therapeutic frame which required immediate restorative efforts (Langs 1975b).

SYMBIOTIC RELATEDNESS
AND THE THERAPEUTIC RELATIONSHIP

The nature of the relationship between schizophrenic patient and therapist regularly takes on a particular cast which recapitulates a pathologically extended, unsuccessfully mastered, phase of early development commonly referred to as the symbiotic phase. The role and importance of symbiosis in normal and pathological development has been extensively explored by Mahler (1968). In this paper, I use symbiotic relatedness to refer to the patient-therapist relationship when it is characterized by a severe degree of loss of self-object differentiation reflecting a significant diffusion of ego boundaries between patient and therapist. This boundary diffusion greately facilitates projective and incorporative modes of identification which come to dominate the treatment relationship (see especially Klein 1946, Heimann 1955, Malin and Grotstein 1966, Langs 1976).

It is most important to remember that, in therapeutic work with adult schizophrenics, symbiotic relatedness exists simultaneously with less regressive modes of relating. Symbiosis is a childhood phenomenon which cannot be totally replicated in adulthood. The nonpsychotic part of the adult schizophrenic patient (Katan 1954, Bion 1957) is available to perceive and respond to both the patient's and the therapist's participation in the regressive exchange and merging of feelings and ideas. Symbiotic relatedness is at times experienced by both patient and therapist as terrrifying, and at other times as comforting and gratifying (Searles 1961). The patient needs a therapist who can shift back and forth between symbiotic relatedness and a more mature, better differentiated patient-therapist relationship, even if the patient himself is not as readily able to make these shifts. Incapacity to accept the patient's symbiotic mode of relatedness deprives the patient of the opportunity to resolve important early fixations (Little 1957, Searles 1961). However, the therapist must ultimately be able to use the nonsymbiotic aspects of the relationship to understand the patient and correctly formulate and interpret the unconscious meanings of the patient's experiences and fantasies.

The therapist's need to shift back and forth between symbiotic modes of relatedness and a more detached, analytic position, relates to the meaning of countertransference in the treatment of schizophrenic patients. Kleinian analysts, particularly Winnicott (1949), Little (1951, 1957), and Heimann (1950), point out the special importance of countertransference problems in work with schizophrenics. Countertransference is seen by these authors as a legitimate, and at times exclusive means of understanding the patient. I disagree that what these authors describe should be called countertransference in the same sense as the more traditional view of countertransference—

that is, the interference of the therapist's unconscious needs and conflicts with his ability to understand and treat the patient.

Reich (1960, 1966) has clarified the relationship between empathy and countertransference in a manner which seems useful in this connection. She conceptualizes empathy as a series of transient identifications with the patient which the therapist employs in understanding the patient's experience. These consciously intended trial identifications must be distinguished from the therapist's unconsciously determined identifications and projections. The latter represent countertransference problems in the therapist, in that they interfere with, rather than promote, empathic understanding. This is not to say that more classically defined countertransference problems cannot be used, if carefully analyzed, to aid in the therapeutic work. However, the focus is then on clarification and understanding of unconscious fantasies and attitudes rather than on the mere experience of mutual incorporations and projections. The shifts back and forth between symbiotic relatedness and a more objective analytic positon in work with schizophrenic patients is related to Reich's concept of trial identification. When the therapist is not in conscious control of these shifts, or fears losing his control over them, the search for countertransference problems is warranted.

Proper understanding of aspects of symbiotic relatedness within the therapeutic relationship helps to clarify the complex interaction between psychotherapy and drug therapy in question here. The manner in which the therapist is drawn into a symbiotic relatedness, at times against his will and outside of his awareness, will be described below. Schizophrenic patients and their therapists, in the course of their work together, come to share many ideas and feelings which seem to obscure and at times obliterate their interpersonal boundaries. Both parties, in effect, become caught up in the confusion and tragedy of psychosis. Elements of symbiotic relatedness can be observed even in the earliest meetings between patient and therapist. It is during this early phase of treatment that the therapist most often begins to wonder about medications. The patient, long accustomed to the intrusion of primitive ideas into his thinking and interpersonal relationships, especially with equally, if less obviously, disturbed family members, begins to stir up feelings in the therapist for which the latter feels totally unprepared.

Searles (1959a) has discussed aspects of this process as "the effort to drive the other person crazy," and has clarified much about its motivation and mechanisms. The therapist may begin to experience many of the patient's psychotic ideas and disturbing affects as his own. Schizophrenic patients readily project their own distortions, feelings, and conflicts into the therapist. In addition, such patients are very quick to respond, usually in an exaggerated way, to correctly perceived areas of conflict in their therapists. This can be a particularly unnerving experience for therapists unaccustomed to working with schizophrenic patients. In my experience, the therapist's use of pharmacologic intervention at this time represents an unconscious attempt to firmly localize in the patient both that which has been projected into the therapist by the patient (Grinberg 1962), as well as those conflicts within the therapist accurately perceived and accentuated by the patient. The prescribing of medicines is then used as tangible evidence of the interpersonal boundaries between patient and therapist, repudiating any shared ideas and feelings which reveal a growing symbiotic relatedness with its regressive pull on both participants.

The fact of their own readiness to be drawn into symbiotic modes of relating comes as a great surprise to most therapists as they begin work with schizophrenic patients. It is usually thought that, for nonpsychotic individuals, the ideas, affects, and modes of relating characterizing both preverbal developmental periods and psychotic states are deeply repressed and unavailable to consciousness without considerable effort. On the contrary, the ease with which new parents, for instance, enter into nonverbal, intense, and mutually gratifying relationships with their infants serves as evidence that relatively well-adjusted individuals, given the right circumstances, have easy access to regressive modes of relating.

In therapeutic work with schizophrenic patients, however, the appearance of symbiotic trends is often an unexpected development, particularly early in the course of treatment. Therapists may find themselves harboring murderous and sadistic thoughts toward patients and important people in their patient's lives, without recognizing that this represents an incorporation of their patients' own hostility and sadism. Therapists may spend sessions daydreaming, only half-listening or half-heartedly trying to engage withdrawn or mute patients. This usually reflects the therapist's defensive flight from the patient's frighteningly aggressive or even more frightening needful and loving impulses. Therapists of schizophrenic patients often entertain the idea that they are able to read their patients' minds. Patients wishing to be magically understood may suggest this by leaving out pertinent parts of a train of thought and then accepting whatever the therapist fills in regardless of its accuracy. Such patients may adopt the therapist's manner of speech and thought, leading the therapist to feel he completely understands and can even anticipate the patient's train of thought; Deutsch (1942) describes related phenomena in her discussion of the "as if " personality.

Case 2

Miss R, a twenty-eight-year-old, single woman, was referred by her former therapist because he felt that therapy had come to a standstill, that the patient tended to act out in a bizarre manner, and that the patient needed a therapist with more experience in working with schizophrenic patients. The patient had been very attached to her former therapist and resented being transferred to a new doctor. She began treatment by describing her withdrawal from the world. She no longer had friends, hated her parents, spent hours staring at the walls of her room, and spoke of her life as empty. During the first six months of twice weekly psychoanalytic psychotherapy, she became progressively more withdrawn during sessions, rarely showing much enthusiasm about any ideas which she grudgingly admitted to having during the hours. One exception arose when she spoke of her horse, of which she was passionately fond. She described her horse as the only thing to which she felt close, and believed that she completely understood what her horse was thinking and feeling. She treated the therapist as an unwelcome intruder but unfailingly attended sessions. "Only my horse means anything to me." She rarely responded to what the therapist said and spoke little of herself, taking the view that the therapist already understood her completely. She elaborated occasionally on a point he brought up in a way which seemed to complete his thoughts, but then would fall silent or report that she was daydreaming about riding her horse. Mostly she said nothing at all, and after a while the therapist found himself falling in with the patient's silence.

During these silences, the therapist would often daydream about the patient and her family. The patient described her mother as depressed, overtly intrusive, and controlling. She portrayed her father as perpetually angry and uninterested in her mother. She was disgusted with her father because he was, in her eyes, "too seductive" toward her. She felt uncomfortable around him because he was always embracing her, his hands straying toward her breasts and genitals. During one particular session, the patient and therapist had been sitting quietly for thirty minutes. The therapist remembered feeling extremely angry about the patient's father during this silence. He recalled his fantasy of exposing this father, a prominent and respected community leader, as a "disgusting, incestuous fraud." The patient commented at this point, suddenly breaking the silence and startling the therapist with her rare verbalization, that she wished the hour would end so she could get to the stables. The therapist remarked angrily that someday she would have to give up this horse of hers, that people also had something to offer. The patient again fell silent. The therapist thought it ridiculous to feel jealous "toward the patient's horse." He thought the therapy was going nowhere, that "nothing was happening." He decided the patient needed medication to "help get things moving."

This brief clinical illustration illustrates the means by which the therapist takes in the patient's problems. The therapist felt disgusted, murderous, jealous, and ridiculous, while the patient, having emptied these feelings into the therapist, sat quietly wishing to be riding in the country. In supervision, the therapist was able to understand that his wish to medicate arose not from a desire to get things going in the patient, but to stop things from going in himself. The therapist had incorporated the patient's conflicts, experiencing them as his own. He felt out of control, unable to step back from the therapeutic interaction and objectively evaluate what was happening in order to interpret to the patient the feelings she felt unable to contain. His wish to medicate reflected his countertransference inability to use the projective-incorporative process as a means of understanding because he was unable to shift back to a more objective analytic position.

REGRESSIVE GRATIFICATION

An important issue to consider in understanding countertransference problems and the use of drugs during psychotherapy with schizophrenic patients is the gratification, often not immediately obvious, which is a part of psychosis and symbiotic relatedness. There can be no question that psychosis and the modes of interpersonal interaction characterizing the relationships of schizophrenic individuals must be viewed, at least from the angle of adaptation to society at large, as maladaptive and tragic. However, elements of symbiosis as a severely regressive process are also deeply satisfying and thus tenaciously maintained (Searles 1959b, 1961). This is true for schizophrenics and pertinent to our discussion, for their therapists as well. To return to an earlier analogy, parents of infants regularly greet the milestones of development, (communicative use of language, etc.) with nostalgic sadness, recognizing each developmental achievement as a harbinger of the end of very special rewards and gratifications which are only reluctantly relinquished as separation-individuation proceeds. The prolonged use of baby-talk by parents after the child is available for more meaningful communication supports this notion. As treatment begins with schizophrenic patients, and particularly as therapists struggle to make emotional contact with difficult to reach patients, they discover to their surprise formerly repudiated regressive yearnings in themselves which their patients are all too ready to gratify.

Case 3

A supervisee reported, somewhat hesitatingly, that he secretly looked forward to his therapy hours with a particularly regressed schizophrenic patient. He had agreed to include this patient in a caseload of primarily neurotic and borderline individuals with considerable trepidation, recognizing that work with this patient would be difficult and demanding. He reported, however, that after the restrained and often tedious hours with his better integrated patients, he found himself enjoying the no-holds-barred encounters which his schizophrenic patient demanded of him. While the therapist often ended these therapeutic hours feeling drained and confused, he nevertheless enjoyed and valued these experiences, much to his own surprise. He recognized these crazy hours as a rare opportunity for him to experience ideas and feelings within himself from which he felt cut off in other settings.

He reported that he often thought about medicating his patient, several times made a decision to do so, but never seemed to find an opening. It gradually became clear during supervision that his wish to medicate the patient arose from guilty feelings about enjoying his patient's engaging him in primitive modes of relatedness. Using drugs was a means of disturbing the symbiosis, communicating to the patient that this craziness has got to stop. By doing so the therapist was hoping to renounce in himself gratifying aspects of symbiotic relatedness about which he felt guilty. His reluctance to in fact medicate the patient is evidence of just how powerful are the gratifications inherent in the regressive relationships formed with schizophrenic patients. It further became clear that, in wishing to treat the patient with drugs, the therapist was treating what he viewed as his own craziness manifest in his enjoyment of his patient's bizarre and uninhibited mode of relationship.

The therapist's fear and guilt concerning gratifying aspects of symbiotic relatedness are common motives for introducing phenothiazines during psychotherapy. Drugs may also be used for the opposite reason, to perpetuate symbiosis. Searles (1959b) has noted that in long-term psychoanalytic psychotherapy with chronically psychotic patients, therapists must be wary of blocking their patients' movement away from undifferentiatedness and toward increased personality integration, due to the therapist's unconscious wish to maintain the rewards of symbiosis. Here drugs are used to block the patient's growth in a variety of ways. Medication may represent an abandonment of hope about increased self-understanding through insight, a communication to the patient that his impulses are too dangerous to express without being dampened by drugs, or a warning to the patient that changes he is making are intolerable to the therapist. A third possibility needs mention here, namely that drugs may be withheld when their use would be appropriate. This often happens to keep the patient disorganized and thus maintain regressive gratifications. At other times, the therapist may inappropriately withhold drugs in order to join the patient in splitting off the patient's bad self and denying its existence, particularly its aggressive components. In summary, drugs may be inappropriately used or inappropriately withheld to maintain or repudiate regressive gratifications, depending on the therapist's countertransference response to his involvement in regressive forms of relatedness.

POSTPSYCHOTIC DEPRESSION

An important clinical phenomenon pertinent to the dynamics of psychotropic drug usage with recovering psychotic patients is the syndrome referred to as postpsychotic depression (PPD). The PPD syndrome was found to occur in as many as 50 percent of recovering schizophrenic patients in a recent study (McGlashan and Carpenter 1976a; for a review of the literature about PPD, see McGlashan and Carpenter 1976b). In this syndrome, the patient, who while psychotic seems particularly alive, fascinating, and accessible to influence, perhaps excessively so, gradually becomes withdrawn, stubbornly uncommunicative, monotonous, and painful to be with during therapeutic sessions. The therapist who begins work with an acutely psychotic patient is often surprised and dismayed by the appearance of severe depressive symptomatology and is frequently moved to consider using psychotropic drugs at this juncture in therapy.

The dynamics active in therapists confronted with the appearance of severe depressive symptoms following an acute psychotic episode are illustrated in the following vignette:

Case 4

The therapist reported to the author his work with a twenty-two-year-old man who had recently experienced his first psychotic episode, which lasted approximately six months. Therapy began while the patient was still psychotic and actively involved with feelings of extraordinary intellectual and physical endowment. He saw himself as a champion scientist, athlete, and lover, and he regaled his therapist with the details of his grandiose ideas.

The therapist, while anxious about his inexperience in doing psychoanalytic psychotherapy with schizophrenic individuals, spoke of his work with enthusiasm and guarded optimism. He expressed both surprise and pleasure at his growing rapport with a patient whom he would heretofore have viewed as incomprehensible and too impaired to enter into a therapeutic alliance. As treatment proceeded, the patient began to express wonder and astonishment at the therapist's own unique qualities, his great perceptiveness, patience, and wisdom. The therapist, while made uncomfortable by the transference idealization and feeling somewhat apprehensive about the patient's reactions should he fail to live up to the patient's expectations, reported on his work with interest and affective involvement.

After about three months, the therapist began a supervisory hour by reporting that he was having particular difficulty with another patient with whom he had been working for some time. He noted that therapy with his schizophrenic patient had settled down and was proceeding in an orderly and comfortable manner. After hearing something of the current problems with his troublesome patient, I requested that we return to the therapist's work with the case we had previously been discussing, suspecting that the introduction of troublesome material from work with a new patient represented a commentary on even more troublesome developments in work with the previous patient. In fact, what was hidden behind "proceeding in an orderly and comfortable manner" was painfully tedious and often discouraging work with a depressed, withdrawn, almost mute patient who seemed to be mourning the loss of his omnipotent psychotic feelings. The therapist, who had come to share in a real way the patient's former psychotic ideas and feelings, was himself discouraged, resentful, and feelings hopeless about recapturing the excitement that had been part of the treatment process while the patient was closer to psychosis. In fact, he had changed the patient's phenothiazine to an "activating" phenothiazine, and had added an antidepressant to the drug regimen.

Without commenting on the psychopharmacological soundness of such a decision, some discussion of the psychological forces effecting this decision is warranted. In reviewing with the therapist his reactions to the patient's postpsychotic depression and his thoughts about why he chose to avoid further exploration of therapeutic problems with this patient in supervision, the following themes emerged.

First, the therapist's conviction that he could help the patient was built on shaky ground. He was much influenced by the attitudes of many that schizophrenic individuals are irretrievably impaired and doomed to chronic emotional desolation. For the therapist, the appearance of the patient's feelings of emptiness with the gradual abandonment of protective narcissistic fantasies confirmed his worst fears of an irreversible progression toward burnt-out, chronic schizophrenia. In fact, the therapist admitted that he had, at times, covertly supported and encouraged the patient to maintain his omnipotent ideas in hopes of forestalling what seemed like the inevitable appearance of painful depressed feelings in both himself and his patient.

A second theme which emerged concerns the character of the depression which often follows psychosis. In exploring why the therapist felt disinclined to use supervision to help him deal with the depression which had come to characterize the treatment, the therapist noted that some of his reluctance was related to ambivalent feelings about using drugs in this case. He had the distinct feeling of "treating myself rather than the patient." He noted that his patient failed to take the familiar demanding posture of other depressed patients he had treated, and in fact, tended not to complain so much as wish to be left alone. The therapist felt he was intruding on the patient, that he was more upset at the end of each session than the patient, and that his patient had somehow tricked him into believing he could be of help. (No doubt he had similar feelings toward his supervisor for encouraging him to treat this schizophrenic patient.)

The therapist had prescribed the drugs to define who was in distress and to allow himself to feel he was doing something useful for the patient. The therapist was fearful he might otherwise attack the patient for not establishing the kind of relationship he had hoped would follow after the mutual excitement of psychosis. The patient's need to keep the therapist at a distance was experienced by the latter not as an outgrowth of the patient's previous overly close, confusing, anxiety-ridden relationships with deeply disturbed and intrusive parents, but rather as a rejecting, depriving act on the patient's part. The therapist in retrospect viewed his own prescribing of medicines at this point as a disguised, hostile, rejecting, counter-attack, which he felt his patient and his supervisor would interpret as an abandonment of a psychotherapeutic, investigative stance.

The patient accepted the prescriptions from the therapist without comment. He missed the next session, his first absence since beginning therapy. Upon his return, he began describing his troubles at home. His mother had put him out of the house and he spent the night with his father, whom mother had divorced ten years earlier. He said he didn't feel at home in either mother's or father's house. He couldn't look people in the eye and tell them how he felt without getting scared. He felt it was hard to talk to his mother because she never believed him and was always preoccupied with her own feelings. He said he didn't know whether "talk therapy" was for him. His mother couldn't understand him and nagged him about getting a job. She felt that the patient's coming to see the therapist was "no indication of illness." He reported missing the session because he was job hunting. He asked his mother to come in his place. "She's a talker." Next he mentioned how different he was from his brother. The patient's mother was always comparing him to his more outgoing brother. She accused the patient of being lazy like his father. After a pause, the patient asked the therapist how the medicines worked. He hadn't filled the prescriptions but was meaning to.

The patient responded to the untimely offer of drugs by talking about being misunderstood by his mother. People kept wanting him to be something he wasn't, more talkative, more outgoing. Mother couldn't understand because her feelings got in the way. He felt put out. We see that the patient correctly perceived the therapist's distress and many of his reasons for prescribing drugs. While not expressed directly, his perceptions were communicated as displaced observations about people in his family.

Eventually the therapist came to understand the patient's depressive withdrawal as a needed retreat which gave him time to bear the pain of having had a severe psychotic break, to slowly relinquish very important grandiose views of himself, and to partially disengage himself from very destructive family interactions. The patient felt his wishes for personal growth dangerous and, by his withdrawal, was preserving a much needed therapeutic relationship, albeit at a distance greater than seemed comfortable for the therapist. Young therapists generally underestimate their importance to their schizophrenic patients, particularly when the latter are withdrawn and depressed. In this case, the therapist felt that one reason he had put the patient on medication was to justify meetings which the patient was more than willing to attend anyway. This clinical example, while it by no means exhausts the list of dynamic factors which determine the nature and timing of pharmacological interventions during postpsychotic depression, does illustrate many salient issues which complicate psychoanalytic psychotherapy with recovering schizophrenic individuals.

CONCLUSIONS

The introduction of drugs of proven value in the management of psychotic decompensations requires an integration of pharmacologic and psychotherapeutic treatment modalities which is far from complete. Factors other than sound clinical and pharmacological judgment contribute to decision-making about prescribing psychotropic drugs in the setting of psychoanalytic psychotherapy with schizophrenic patients. Of particular importance in this regard are the nature and intensity of shared emotional experiences characteristic of work with these patients. The therapist, partly due to the patient's own mode of relating and partly due to the therapist's genuine wish to make contact with and understand his difficult-to-reach patient, reaches deep into his own regressive and largely repudiated store of feelings, memories, and modes of relating, for a common ground upon which to establish a relationship based upon shared experience. Kernberg (1975) refers to an analogous process in work with borderline patients as empathic regression.

As discussed earlier, trial identifications play an important role in this empathic process. The therapist's difficulty in negotiating the shifts back and forth between these trial identifications and a more objective, analytic position, results in many of the disturbing feelings leading to the unnecessary or untimely use of drugs. The schizophrenic patient's ability to rapidly establish a mode of relatedness characterized by intense and ubiquitous projective and incorporative identifications often leaves the therapist unable to determine the origin of his own thoughts and feelings. The therapist's unconscious attempts to deal with this problem by prescribing drugs is a form of countertransference frequently observed in work with schizophrenic patients. The widely accepted appropriateness of using antipsychotic agents in this patient group makes this form of countertransference problem particularly likely to occur. As illustrated in the clinical material, the therapist may use the prescribing of drugs as a concrete enactment of establishing interpersonal boundaries, a disavowal of frightening feelings, a guilty renunciation or secret fostering of forbidden regressive pleasures, or a means of establishing control over a seemingly uncontrollable situation. The frequency with which psychotropic agents are used during the course of psychoanalytic psychotherapy with schizophrenic patients, when contrasted with the paucity of information in the scientific literature about the interaction of these different modes of treatment, points out the need for continued analytic investigation of the psychological determinants which play a decisive role in the nature, timing, and outcome of this interaction. This discussion will hopefully lead to further investigation and debate about this important and little studied clinical problem.

REFERENCES

Bion, W. R. (1957). Differentiation of the psychotic from the non-psychotic personalities. *International Journal of Psycho-Analysis* 38:266-275.

Davis, J. M. (1975). Overview: maintenance therapy in psychiatry, I. Schizophrenia. *American Journal of Psychiatry* 132:1237-1245.

Deutsch, H. (1942). Some forms of emotional disturbances and their relationship to schizophrenia. *Psychoanalytic Quarterly* 11:301-321.

Feinsilver, D. B., and Gunderson, J. G. (1972). Psychotherapy for schizophrenics—is it indicated? a review of the relevant literature. *Schizophrenia Bulletin* 6:11-23.

Grinberg, L. (1962). On a specific aspect of countertransference due to the patient's projective identification. *International Journal of Psycho-Analysis* 43:436-440.

Grinspoon, L., Ewalt, J. R., and Shader, R. I. (1972). *Schizophrenia, Pharmacotherapy and Psychotherapy*. Baltimore: Williams and Wilkins.

Heimann, P. (1950). On countertransference. *International Journal of Psycho-Analysis* 31:81-84.

——— (1955). A combination of defense mechanisms in paranoid states. In *New Directions in Psycho-Analysis*, ed. M. Klein, P. Heimann, and R. E. Money-Kryle, pp. 240-265. London: Tavistock Publications.

Karon, B. P., and VandenBos, G. R. (1972). The consequences of psychotherapy for schizophrenic patients. *Psychotherapy: Theory, Research and Practice* 9:111-119.

Katan, M. (1954). The importance of the nonpsychotic part of the personality in schizophrenia. *International Journal of Psycho-Analysis* 35:119-128.

Kernberg, O. F. (1975). *Borderline Conditions and Pathological Narcissism*. New York: Jason Aronson.

Klein, M. (1946). Notes on some schizoid mechanisms. *International Journal of Psycho-Analysis* 27:99-110.

Langs, R. (1973). *The Technique of Psychoanalytic Psychotherapy*. Vol. 1. New York: Jason Aronson.

——— (1975a). The patient's unconscious perception of the therapist's errors. In *Tactics and Techniques in Psychoanalytic Therapy*, vol. 2, ed. P. Giovacchini. New York: Jason Aronson.

——— (1975b). The therapeutic relationship and deviations in technique. *International Journal of Psychoanalytic Psychotherapy* 4:106-141.

——— (1976). *The Bipersonal Field*. New York: Jason Aronson.

Levy, S. T., McGlashan, T. H., and Carpenter, W. T., Jr. (1975). Integration and sealing over as recovery styles from acute psychosis: metapsychological and dynamic concepts. *Journal of Nervous and Mental Diseases* 161:307-312.

Linn, L. (1964). Use of drugs in psychotherapy. *Psychiatric Quarterly* 38:138-148.

Little, M. (1951). Counter-transference and the patient's response to it. *International Journal of Psycho-Analysis* 32:32-40.

—— (1957). "R"—the analyst's total response to his patient's needs. *International Journal of Psycho-Analysis* 38:240-254.

McGlashan, T. H., and Carpenter, W. T., Jr. (1976a). An investigation of the postpsychotic depressive syndrome. *American Journal of Psychiatry* 133:14-19.

—— (1976b). Postpsychotic depression in schizophrenia. *Archives of General Psychiatry* 33:231-239.

Mahler, M. (1968). *On Human Symbiosis and the Vicissitudes of Individuation*. Vol. 1. Infantile Psychosis. New York: International Universities Press.

Malin, A., and Grotstein, J. (1966). Projective identification in the therapeutic process. *International Journal of Psycho-Analysis* 47:26-31.

May, P. R. (1968). *Treatment of Schizophrenia*. New York: Jason Aronson.

—— (1971). Psychotherapy and ataraxic drugs. In *Handbook of Psychotherapy and Behavior Change: An Empirical Analysis*, ed. A. E. Bergin and S. L. Garfield. New York: J. Wiley.

Ostow, M. (1962). *The Use of Drugs in Psychoanalysis and Psychotherapy*. New York: Basic Books.

Reich, A. (1960). Further remarks on countertransference. *International Journal of Psycho-Analysis* 41:389-395.

——(1966). Empathy and countertransference. In *Annie Reich: Psychoanalytic Contributions* pp. 344-360. New York: International Universities Press, 1973.

Searles, H. F. (1958). The schizophrenic's vulnerability to the therapist's unconscious processes. In *Collected Papers on Schizophrenia and Related Subjects*, pp. 192-215. New York: International Universities Press.

—— (1959a). The effort to drive the other person crazy—an element in the aetiology and psychotherapy of schizophrenia, In *Collected Papers*, pp. 254-283.

—— (1959b). Integration and differentiation in schizophrenia: an over-all view. In *Collected Papers*, pp. 317-348.

—— (1961). Phases of patient-therapist interaction in the psychotherapy of chronic schizophrenics. In *Collected Papers*, pp. 521-559

—— (1975). The patient as therapist to his analyst. In *Tactics and Techniques in Psychoanalytic Therapy*, vol. 2, ed P. Giovacchini. New York: Jason Aronson.

Winnicott, D. W. (1949). Hate in the countertransference. *International Journal of Psycho-Analysis* 30:69-75.

Countertransference

HANNA SEGAL, F.R.C.PSYCH.

Countertransference can be used as an instrument in understanding the patient's projective identification. An analogy for the patient/therapist interaction is found in Bion's model of the infant's communicating by projection in to the breast and the mother as containing and modifying such projections. The particular countertransference problems created by patients who have been objects of massive parental projections are examined. In such cases the patient's projections induce in the analyst diverse experience of past helplessness in relation to projections.

As psychoanalysis developed what were originally seen as obstacles in the psychoanalytic process have become new tools in the psychoanalytic practice when understood. The outstanding example, of course, is transference, at first considered a major obstacle in psychoanalytic treatment, then later realized as the very fulcrum of the psychoanalytic situation. The same applies to our changing views on countertransference: first seen as a neurotic disturbance in the analyst, preventing him from getting a clear and objective view of the patient, it is now increasingly recognized as a most important source of information about the patient, as well as a major element of the interaction between patient and analyst. In her 1950 paper, a pioneering paper on the subject, Paula Heimann draws attention to the fact that, though not recognized as such, countertransference had always been a guide in psychoanalytical work. She suggests that Freud's discovery of resistance was based on his countertransference, his feeling that he was meeting a resistant force in the patient. Once our attention is drawn to it, this view of countertransference seems almost obvious.

To take a single example, I have a patient who evokes in me a whole gamut of unpleasant feelings. It would obviously be very foolish of me to ignore these feelings or consider them my own neurotic reactions, since this patient's principal complaint is her terrible unpopularity. Obviously, the way she

Presented at the Symposium on Countertransference at the English Speaking Conference in London 1975.

affects me is a function of her psychopathology—a function of utmost importance to her, and one which it is crucial for us to understand.

This view of countertransference as a function of the patient's personality is not however universally accepted. It is still often contended that ideally countertransference should be eliminated, though it is recognized that in practice this might not be possible. On the other hand, the view of countertransference as an important part of the psychoanalytical process is widely recognized. The literature on the subject is far too vast to discuss in this short paper, but to mention only a few, there are papers on the subject by Money-Kyrle (1956), Leon Grinberg (1962), Winnicott (1949), and a book by Heinrich Racker (1968). Many authors simply take countertransference for granted and describe the uses they put it to, as Bion (1967) does in his accounts of his work with psychotics.

Our changing views on countertransference are in part related to changes in our views on transference. Originally, the analyst was seen as a mirror *on to* which the patient projects his internal figures and to whom he then reacts. As Enid Balint put it succinctly in a paper recently read in the British Society: "We now have a more three-dimensional view of the transference." We do not think of the patient projecting *on to*, but rather *in to* the analyst. This view assumes that transference is rooted in primitive preverbal infantile experience and is consistent with the Kleinian concept of projective identification. We see the patient not only as perceiving the analyst in a distorted way, reacting to this distorted view, and communicating these reactions to the analyst, but also as doing things to the analyst's mind, projecting *in to* the analyst in a way which affects him.

We are all familiar with the concepts of acting in, which can happen in quite a gross way; I speak here, however, not of gross acting in, but of something constantly present—a nonverbal constant interaction in which the patient acts on the analyst's mind. This nonverbal activity takes many forms. It may be underlying and integrated with other forms of communication and give them depth and emotional resonance. It may be the predominant form of communication, coming from preverbal experiences which can only be communicated in that way. Or it may be meant as an attack on communication; though when understood, even this can be converted into communication. Of course, all communication contains elements of desire for action. We communicate in order to produce some effect on the other person's mind, but the degree to which action, nonverbal or even apparently verbal (using words to act rather than to communicate), occurs varies enormously from situation to situation and patient to patient. As a general rule, the nearer we are to the psychotic processes, the more acting in takes precedence over symbolic or verbal communication. By action, I specifically mean here action on the analyst's mind. If we look at transference in this way, it then becomes quite clear that what Freud describes as free-floating attention refers not only to intellectual openness of mind, but also to a particular openness of feelings—allowing our feelings, our mind to be affected by the patient to a far greater degree than we allow ourselves to be affected in normal social intercourse, a point stressed by Paula Heimann (1950).

By speaking of these free-floating feelings in the analyst am I saying that there is no difference between transference and countertransference? I hope I am not saying anything of the kind, because at the same time the analyst is opening his mind freely to his impressions, he has to maintain distance from his own feelings and reactions to the patient. He has to observe them, to conclude from them, to use his own state of mind for the understanding of his patient and at no point be swayed by it. The analyst's capacity to contain the feelings aroused in him by the patient can be seen as an equivalent to the function of a mother containing the infant's projections, to use Bion's model (1967). Where the parents reacts instinctively, however, the analyst subjects his state of mind to an examination—a reflection, albeit, much of the time preconscious.

In the past we have thought of an ideal analyst as cold, objective, having no feelings, etc. Am I presenting here in the analyst's perfect containment, a similarly unattainable ideal? I think so indeed. This would be an idealization of the analyst's capacity. In fact, this capacity for containment can be breached in many ways. There is a whole area of the patient's pathology (I am ignoring for the moment the analyst's pathology) which specifically aims at disrupting this situation of containment: such as, invasion of the analyst's mind in a seductive or aggressive way, creating confusion and anxiety, and attacking links in the analyst's mind. As with anything else, we have to try to turn this situation to good account and learn about the interaction between the patient and ourselves from the very fact that our containment has been disturbed. It is from such disturbances in the analyst's capacity to function that one first gets an inkling of such psychotic processes as, for instance, attacks on links, again a subject with vast literature.

There is a particular countertransference difficulty (described also by Grinberg 1962, as projective counter-identification) produced by some patients who, as infants, have been themselves subjected to heavy parental projections. I shall give an example here from the second session with a patient—a mild example of the kind of thing I have in mind. In the first session the patient had spoken about the various ways in which she felt she had been a great disappointment to her parents and to herself. In the next session, she seemed extremely depressed, spoke in a hardly audible voice and went on at fairly great length describing how terrible she felt. She was depressed, she felt dead, terribly weak, she had an awful headache, perhaps it was due to her period which was about to start. The session went on for a time and I felt unduly affected by it. I wondered if I had done something wrong in the previous session. I felt helpless and terribly eager to understand her. In answer to a query on my side, the patient said that, no, she did not usually have headaches with her periods, but her mother had that symptom. I knew that the patient at that point was identifying with her mother, but somehow this knowledge did not help and I felt that there would not be much point in interpreting it to her. I was more puzzled by my own overreaction and slowly came to realize that I now felt that I was a disappointment to both her and to myself. I was in the position of a helpless and rather bewildered child, weighed down by projections coming from a depressed mother, and it was an interpretation emphasizing that aspect which produced a change in the situation.

Later on the patient related that she had perfect pitch but that though she was trained and encouraged and apparently gifted enough to become a soloist, she could never do it and so had specialized as an accompanist. When she was a child her mother sang and she used to accompany her on the piano. It seemed to me that this patient had developed perfect pitch for her mother's depression and found a way of getting on with her some of the time, but only as an accompanist. I also understood that my quite unwarranted concern in the second session that I did not understand my patient perfectly arose because somehow she managed to make me feel right at the start that I must now be the child with perfect pitch. I shall return to the problem of the perfect pitch. This situation can be compared and contrasted with a much more violent though similar one.

To return to the patient who complains of unpopularity, this patient can considerably disrupt my capacity to function. The experience of closeness with her is an experience of almost unceasing discomfort or pain. She evokes anxiety, confusion, guilt, anger, irritation; occasions on which I feel more relaxed are dangerous, I am immediately and unexpectedly assaulted in some way or other. Her stream of accusations is almost incessant. This patient is the child of parents who had hated one another at the time of her birth. So far as I can reconstruct, she was flooded from the start by her mother (an anxiety neurotic) with extreme anxiety and with the hatred derivative of her hatred for the father. The father, on the other hand, a near psychotic, flooded her with either aggressive accusations or gross sexuality. After she was older and her parents divorced, she describes how her father would pour accusations and complaints about her mother at her by the hour and how, when she was with her mother, the mother on a few occasions pinned her to the armchair and made her listen to violent attacks on the father. This later situation probably reproduces what was originally a nonverbal but violent experience of projection from both parents. In the countertransference it may be this experience that she tries to inflict on me often with success. I frequently feel with her that I am pinned into my armchair and must listen to violent outpourings of accusation against some third person: I feel attacked, I do not want to hear them and cannot defend myself against them. The experience is not that of a parent bombarded by infantile projection, but of an infant bombarded by overpowering projections, often beyond its understanding. This lends to the countertransference feelings of a particular kind of helplessness, and there is always a danger of reacting by withdrawal, omnipotence, hatred of the patient, etc.—in other words, of mobilizing our infantile defenses against helplessness. We are all familiar of course with patients reversing roles and putting us in the position of helpless child. But here I think is an infrequent added dimension—projection of the situation of being a helpless infant being projected in to. This patient is a borderline, and this particular method of projecting infantile experiences in to her analyst may be what protects her from psychosis.

The situations of the two patients may be compared and contrasted. From this patient it is exceedingly difficult to obtain any kind of nondestructive communication. In defending herself against projections, she projects violence and in turn experiences her objects as projecting it back in a vicious circle of increasing distress and violence. The first patient, the one with perfect pitch, had obviously developed some kind of satisfactory communication with her mother, albeit, one based on a split, and at the cost of her own personality (being an accompanist).

But I know her perfect pitch will cause other big problems. One is her expectation, which will be projected in to me, that I also should have perfect pitch (hence my discomfort in the second session). Secondly, she is already showing signs of her perfect pitch in relation to me. In the third session she spotted some minor change in my expression—one unnoticed by other patients. If we think of the transference/countertransference situation as an interaction, we must take into account that the patient's perceptions of us are not all projections. Patients do, indeed, react to aspects of our personalities, changes of mood, etc., whether these are a direct response to their material or come from some other source, and patients with perfect pitch present a particular problem that way. I think this perfect pitch is a function of the patient's dependence. It is the extremely dependent patient that develops an unusual sensitivity to the slightest change in the analyst's attitude. Usually, the pitch is only selectively perfect. We are all familiar with the misleading perfect pitch of the paranoid patient, who most correctly perceives anything negative and is totally blind to any evidence of positive attitudes, or with that of the depressive patient, who is most sensitive to any sign of weakness or illness. Be that as it may, one must be aware of the patient's pitch, or responsiveness to what comes from us, and not deny it in ourselves. I am not advocating here breast beating or confession of countertransference, just awareness of the nature of the interaction and recognition of it in the interpretation.

Of course, all this is easier said than done. I have noticed that when people speak of transference they recognize, of course, that the major part of the transference is unconscious, whereas, when speaking of countertransference, they apparently speak as though countertransference referred only to the analyst's conscious feelings. Of course the major part of the countertransference, like the transference, is always unconscious. What we do become aware of is conscious derivatives. The way I visualize it is that at the depth at which our countertransference is, say, in a good functional state, we have a double relation to the patient. One is receptive, containing and understanding the patient's communication; the other active, producing or giving understanding, knowledge, or structure to the patient in the interpretation. It might be analogous to the breast as containing and the nipple as feeding, or to the maternal/paternal functions. This does not exclude our own infantile experience, since our capacity to perceive and contain infantile parts of the patient depends on our capacity to contain the infant part of ourselves. We must not, however, equate that analytical function with the parental function. We give over part of our mind to this experience with the patient, but we also remain detached from it as professional analysts, using professional skills to assess the interaction between the patient and the parental parts of ourselves. In other words, we are deeply affected and involved but, paradoxically, uninvolved in a way unimaginable between an actual good parent and a child. When our countertransference works that way, it gives rise to a phenomenon called empathy or psychoanalytic intuition or feeling in touch. It is a guide to understanding. When breaches in this attitude occur, we become aware of disruption in our analytical functioning, and we must in turn try to understand the nature of the disruption and the information it gives us about our interaction with the patient. When such disruptions occur, there is always an internal pressure to identify with our countertransference, and it is very important to be aware that countertransference is the best of servants but the worst of masters and that the pressure to identify with it and act it out in ways either obvious or very subtle and hidden is always powerful.

Countertransference has become a very abused concept and many analytical sins have been committed in its name. In particular, rationalizations are found for acting under the pressure of countertransference, rather than using it as a guide to understanding. I often find myself telling supervisees that countertransference is no excuse; saying that the patient projected it in to you or he made you angry or he put you under such seductive pressure must be clearly recognized as statements of failure to understand and use the countertransference constructively. I do not contend here that we must, or indeed, can be perfect, merely that we will not learn from our failures unless we clearly recognize them as such.

REFERENCES

Bion, W. R. (1967). *Second Thoughts*. London: Heinemann.

Grinberg, L. (1962). On a specific aspect of countertransference due to the patient's projective identification. *International Journal of Psycho-Analysis* 43:436-440.

Heimann, P. (1950). On countertransference. *International Journal of Psycho-Analysis* 31:81-84.

Money-Kyrle, R. E. (1956). Normal countertransference and some of it deviations. *International Journal of Psycho-Analysis* 37:360-366.

Racker, H. (1968). *Transference and Countertransference*. London: Hogarth.

Winnicott, D. W. (1949). Hate in countertransference. *International Journal of Psycho-Analysis* 30:69-74. Reprinted in *Collected Papers*, pp. 194-203. New York: Basic Books, 1958.

On Neutrality

THEODORE L. DORPAT, M.D.

The various meanings of *neutrality* are traditionally assigned either to the psychoanalytic model, which developed within psychoanalysis, or to the natural science model whose meanings and methods were imported from the observational methods of natural science. The rules of abstinence and anonymity and the analyst's respect for the patient's autonomy are the principal distinctly psychoanalytic meanings of neutrality. These are discussed and illustrated by case examples. Psychoanalytic neutrality is founded upon and regulated by ethical principles of truthfulness, personal freedom, and the analyst's caring commitment to the patient. The natural science model includes the inhibition of the analyst's affective reactions, the attitude of impersonal detachment, and the requirement that the analyst's evaluations and interpretations be value-free. It is neither possible nor desirable for analysts to adopt the neutral attitudes and techniques of the natural science observer.

Many of the central conceptual terms of psychoanalysis do not have unitary or generally accepted meanings (see Leites 1971). Like many other psychoanalytic terms (ego, transference, etc.), the word *neutrality* has different meanings in different contexts. As Wittgenstein (1953) emphasized, the same word may have different meanings and, in fact, words gain meaning by their *use* in language. The meaning is the use. In this study of neutrality I have examined the different meanings of the term by studying the contexts in which it is used.

In psychoanalytic literature there is much confused counsel and dispute over the ambiguous concept of neutrality and the related technical rules for conducting analysis. There is disagreement over whether the analyst should be neutral at all times or neutral only in response to the patient's transference to the analyst. Glover (1955) thought that the idea of the analyst's complete neutrality was something of a myth. Phrases such as *compassionate neutrality* (Greenson 1958) and *benevolent neutrality* (Laplanche et al. 1973) are hardly unambiguous and indicate the need for a more searching examination of the concept of neutrality and its meanings and function in the psychoanalytic situation.

Disagreement even exists on whether analytic neutrality is necessary or desirable. Some analysts have considered neutrality an essential aspect of psychoanalytic technique. Gill said, "Psychoanalysis is that technique which, employed by a neutral analyst, results in the development of a regressive transference neurosis and the ultimate resolution of this neurosis by the techniques of interpretation alone" (1954, p. 775). Others have attacked the principle of neutrality as tantamount to a failure of commitment or involvement with the patient. Hammet (1965) described neutrality as "habitual noninvolvement," claiming that adherence to the rule of neutrality and the proscribing of affect on the part of the therapist limit the effectiveness of analytic therapy, that contemporary training in the technique of psychoanalytic therapy placed heavy emphasis on neutrality and the mirror analogy with the result that psychoanalytic therapists tend to become impersonal, detached, and uninvolved with their patients. Hammet argued for commitment to the patient and to the treatment. In his view, affect must flow from therapist to patient and vice versa.

Stein responded to Hammet's article, and correspondence between the two was published. Stein said, "The candidate now is encouraged not to be neutral but rather to serve as the model of a highly interested, sympathetic observer and participant in the search for that *objectivity* which will reveal psychic reality with a minimum of distortion, and thus allow the more efficient recognition of 'external' reality in the broadest sense. The neutral, noncommitted analyst is no analyst at all" (1966, p. 880).

Much of the apparent disagreement about the use of neutral techniques has arisen because various authors use the term in different ways. Terminological and semantic issues need to be distinguished from substantive issues. Some analysts continue to search for consensus and specificity of meaning in psychoanalytic terms when, in fact, there often is none. This state of conceptual confusion and ambiguity derives in part from a failure of analysts to organize, systematize, and clarify their concepts and their conceptual language (see Leites 1971).

NEUTRALITY AND THE RULE OF ABSTINENCE

The rule of abstinence and other fundamentals of psychoanalytic technique were laid down by Freud (1912a, 1912b, 1913, 1914, 1915) over fifty years ago and still serve as the basis for psychoanalytic practice. Freud first elucidated the abstinence requirement in "Observations on Transference Love" where he said, "The treatment must be carried out in abstinence" (1915, p. 165). His only use of the term *neutrality* was in connection with his recommendation that analysts abstain from gratifying the patient's transference wishes. "In my opinion, therefore, we ought not to give up the neutrality toward the patient, which we have acquired through keeping the countertransference in check" (1915, p. 164).

There are two related meanings to the rule of abstinence. The first is that the analyst ought to refrain from offering extraanalytic gratifications, and the second is that the analyst should not gratify the patient's transference wishes. Extraanalytic gratifications which extend beyond the appropriate boundaries of the patient-therapist relationship are detrimental to the maintenance of the therapeutic alliance and to the patient's search for constructive change. The neutral therapist restricts his interventions to those activities such as questions, clarifications, and interpretations designed to enlighten the patient. Interactions between analyst and analysand are limited to the consultation room and to those activities required for the therapeutic task. Social contacts or conversation between the analyst and patient outside the consultation room should be minimized. The restriction on extraanalytic gratifications is best accomplished by adherence to the ground rules of analysis and by maintaining the boundaries of the patient-therapist relation (see Langs 1975b, for a discussion of the ground rules and boundaries of the patient-therapist relation).

Freud indicated that the abstinence rule refers not simply to sexual abstinence but to the denial of transference gratification generally. "Nor do we mean ... simply refraining from sexual intercourse.... As far as his relations with the patient are concerned, the patient must be left with unfulfilled wishes in abundance. It is expedient to deny him precisely those satisfactions which he desires most intensely and expresses most importunately" (1919, pp. 162, 164).

Technical rules of abstinence and anonymity are intended to preserve a relatively uncontaminated field for the interpretation and mastery of transferences. In the handling of these transferences, the main strength of the analyst's position lies in the fact that whatever transference demands are made upon him and whatever roles are ascribed to him, he does not satisfy those demands or play those parts. In my opinion, two of the main criteria of a true analytic situation are, first, accurate and empathic interpretation and, second, maintenance of neutrality on the analyst's part.

Even seemingly slight deviations from the abstinence principle can disrupt an analysis and impair the therapeutic alliance. The analysis of a young woman with a hysteric character disorder went well until the sixth month when she provoked the analyst into a teasing, sarcastic comment. For the next few days, the analysis floundered; she became more anxious, drank excessively, and had nightmares. The analyst wondered if his teasing remark had evoked her disturbance. He said, "You experienced my remark of last Wednesday as teasing and sarcastic. What is there about teasing that disturbs you?" She then revealed her mutually teasing relationship with her father, a relation which had unconscious erotic overtones and which had excluded her mother. The analyst's teasing comment meant for her a repetition of her unconsciously incestuous relation with her father. By working through the events in the analysis that had disturbed her and analyzing what teasing meant to her, the traumatic break in the analysis was repaired and the therapeutic alliance restored.

A number of compelling reasons have been advanced by Searles (1965), Stone (1961), and others for rejecting the inclusive rule that the analyst should be neutral at all times and in all ways. There are acceptable and even necessary interventions in analysis which cannot be categorized as neutral. The rule of abstinence excludes the gratification of extraanalytic wishes and the patient's transference wishes. It does not forbid all kinds of gratification. The analyst should distinguish between the patient's reasonable demands to be understood and related to as a fellow human being and the unreasonable, irrational, infantile demands that persistently press upon him with great force. Normal human needs for empathy should be gratified, whereas infantile transference demands should be met with neutrality. The analyst is repeatedly confronted with the analysand's wishes for transference gratifications through attempted seductions, aggressive demands, and manipulations as the patient attempts to involve the analyst in a repetition of his infantile object relations.

In the case of narcissistic personality disorders, neutrality has a somewhat different meaning than in the transference neuroses. During the analysis of patients with narcissistic personality disorders, the analyst should not act the part of the patient's undeveloped psyche which the patient is projecting upon him. In patients with mirror transferences, the rule of abstinence prohibits the analyst from direct gratification of the patient's need for praise and admiration. With patients who develop an idealizing transference, this means not playing the part of the idealized or omnipotent object. The rule of abstinence applies not only to libidinal kinds of gratification but also to the gratification of needs for moral directives and guidance. These admonitions are probably not needed for most psychoanalysts, since analysts, unlike therapists who practice one of the various kinds of supportive or inspirational therapies, seldom act out the part of the omnipotent self-object. As Kohut (1971) has explained, the more common technical error involves the interruption of the expression and understanding of narcissistic transferences by interpretations of such transferences as defensive or unrealistic.

Many therapists are unaware of the deleterious effects of coopting the ego or superego functions of patients with narcissistic personality disorders. One of the most common such mistakes is the analyst's appropriation of the patient's reality-testing function. The opening phases of a masochistic woman's analysis went favorably as she began regressing in the analysis and expressing her fears that the analyst would punish her. The analyst repeatedly interpreted her fears as distortions of reality and as unrealistic. The patient felt humiliated. She withdrew and the analysis was derailed. The interpretations about her being unrealistic led her to lose confidence in her own capacities for reality-testing. Having her fears called distortions meant for her that she was going crazy.

In taking over the patient's reality-testing function, the analyst had failed to respect the patient's autonomy. (More will be said later about the neutrality principle of respecting the patient's autonomy.) Also, the analyst unwittingly aborted the emergence and expression of an idealizing transference, because his interventions were similar to her preconscious fantasies of an omnipotent parent who would think for her. Finally, his interpretations about her distortions interrupted the analytic regression. She became more anxious and defensively vigilant as her attention turned from her feelings and fantasies toward the tasks of reality-testing.

One guide in helping the analyst maintain a neutral attitude, and one which does not interfere with the expression of the transference, has to do with not challenging the genuineness of the patient's love for the analyst. This injunction applies to both object-libidinal transferences and narcissistic transferences in which the analyst is loved as a need-gratifying agent. Freud wrote, "We have no right to dispute that the state of being in love which makes its appearance in the course of analytic treatment has the character of a 'genuine love'" (1915, p. 168). The maintenance of the analytic role requires being neutral about the transference love—that is, not being disparaging about it or interpreting it as unrealistic. Kohut (1971) warned that the same tactful understanding and caution about interpreting libidinal transferences as unrealistic or ungenuine applies to the analysis of the need-fulfilling (self-object) transferences in psychoanalysis of the narcissistic personality disorders.

NEUTRALITY AND THE RULE OF ANONYMITY

Although not all analysts use the term *neutrality* to mean the rule of anonymity, most analysts hold that they are related issues. The rule of anonymity was first enunciated by Freud when he pointed out the requirement for the analyst to maintain his anonymity in order for the patient to resolve the transference. "The doctor should be opaque to his patients and, like a mirror, should show them nothing but what is shown to him" (1912b, p. 118). Concerning anonymity there is general agreement that the analyst should, at most times, be like a relatively blank screen. This does not mean that he should be cold, aloof, or indifferent. It does mean that he should not intrude his private life, values, or needs onto the patient. The analyst withholds information about himself, his family, his interests, opinions, and his personal reactions to the analysand.

A number of writers have warned against the literal, unvarying, and inclusive employment of the abstinence and anonymity principles (Glover 1955, Stone 1961, Greenson 1958). According to Calef (1967), the mirror analogy is often mistaken to mean passivity and inactivity. Excessive frustration and anonymity may produce interminable or interrupted analyses. Others have pointed out the dangers of superfluous deprivations (Stone 1961, Glover 1955, Fenichel 1941, Bibring 1935, Menninger et al. 1937). Stone argued against the widespread tendency toward an overly literal carrying out of neutrality. "The tendencies I have in mind are the withholding or undue limitation of certain legitimate and well-controlled gratifications, which can provide a palpably human context for the transmission of understanding, which is, by general agreement, the central function of the analyst" (1961, p. 108).

Neutral technique precludes interventions in which the therapist employs such moral directives as prohibitions, injunctions, or limit-setting. Moral directives risk cutting short the development and working through of transference, because to some extent the analyst is playing the part of the superego or the parental ego. Such techniques tend to encourage reenactment rather than remembering. Setting limits on the patient's behavior and giving moral directives should be kept to a minimum and used only in emergencies. As emergency measures they may be employed when the patient's cognitive capacities and impulse controls are impaired by such factors as drugs or acute psychoses or when the patient's life or someone else's life is endangered by the patient.

Analytic neutrality does not mean, however, indifference to or noninvolvement with the destructive aspects of acting-out behavior. The analyst should first attempt to deal with acting out by interpreting the motives, defenses, conflicts, or other relevant aspects of the behavior. If meaningful and effective interpretive work cannot be accomplished, then the therapist should confront the patient with the destructive implications and consequences of the acting out. Several analysts have recommended the occasional use of limit-setting and moral prohibition in the treatment of acting-out patients (see Hoedemaker 1960, Menninger and Holtzman 1973). Menninger held that a therapist's moral convictions play a significant part in his therapy. According to him, analysts who adopt a *laissez faire* philosophy in regard to their patient's outside behavior are engaging in a practice which is dangerous to their patients. He proposed a neutral attitude toward the patient's ideas and fantasies. If, however, the fantasies approach enactment and if the acting out is destructive to the patient or others, he recommended that the analyst express disapproval. Some nonanalyst psychotherapists opposed psychoanalytic neutrality and advocated making moral directives to patients (see Mowrer 1961, London 1964).

Unwarranted and arbitrary directives and limit-setting can prevent the working through of the patient's transference or bring about the formation of what Langs (1975a, p. 78) called a misalliance. Both unfortunate consequences of arbitrary directives occurred in the analysis of a young married, professional man with a lifelong history of alternating periods of compliance and rebellion toward authority figures who unconsciously represented his authoritarian father. In the second year of his analysis, he talked with the analyst about his plan to seek marital therapy for his wife and himself from another therapist. The analyst's first mistake was to not explore with the patient the meaning and purpose of the wish to see a marital therapist. He abruptly forbade the patient to go to a marital therapist, and interpreted the patient's wish to see another therapist as a defensive need to displace his feelings for the analyst onto someone else. The patient compliantly agreed, and the next day he reported having a dream in which he was sitting in the front seat of an automobile driven by the analyst. His associations to the dream centered around two preconscious themes: one theme was a need to be close to the analyst and the other was some vague fear of being controlled. The analyst interpreted the wish for closeness as a need for the analyst's approval, but he ignored the patient's fear of being controlled. The dream image of the analyst driving the car represented the patient's fear that the analyst was controlling the patient's life, and the dream symbolized the patient's need for reassuring closeness to defend against his anxiety and anger over being controlled by the analyst. His anger was evoked by the analyst's arbitrary prohibition against his plan to obtain marital therapy.

The analyst's antianalytic limit-setting tactic of forbidding marital therapy replicated the patient's relationship with the stern father. In this way, the patient's early relation with his father was repeated rather than remembered and mastered. Through this and similar interactions a misalliance formed in which the analysand was defensively compliant with the controlling analyst. The patient used compliance to repress his angry, competitive feelings for the analyst, and the analysis entered a prolonged stalemate.

Neutrality rules of abstinence and anonymity apply not only to the verbal content of the analyst's interventions but also to his nonverbal affective communications. The principles of psychoanalytic neutrality cover the analyst's attitude as well as the manifest content of his interventions. One of the more insidious infringements of the neutrality principle occurs when the analyst' so-called interpretations are actually disguised directives. These are interventions where the verbal content is nondirective and neutral, but the analyst expresses himself in an authoritarian and imperative tone of voice. In these double-bind messages the analysand is more apt to hear and respond to the nonverbal imperative tone than to the verbal communication. The authoritarian and controlling character traits of such therapists are unconsciously discordant with explicit adherence to neutrality rules.

An analyst who prided himself on his neutral interpretations had a group of patients with stalemated analyses. The verbal content of his interpretations was scrupulously neutral, but his nonverbal affective communication was often contemptuous and depreciative. In his interpretations of an obsessive patient's intellectualization defense, the analyst's attitude and tone of voice expressed the following: "You should be ashamed for intellectualizing." The patient felt humiliated and became silent. Thereafter, he increasingly responded with uncontrolled defiance and compliance. Other patients reacted to the analyst's contemptuous attitude with intractable masochistic and paranoid behaviors.

NEUTRALITY AND THE ANALTYIC PROCESS

The analyst's neutrality plays a crucial role in achieving the goal of insight, because it is essential for the patient's awareness, expression, and working through of transferences. Transference interpretations provide the foundations for the analysand's structural changes. Macalpine (1950) indicated that the patient's transferences do not simply arise spontaneously in the psychoanalytic setting. Rather, psychoanalytic technique, of which the neutrality of the analyst is but one feature, creates an infantile setting. To this infantile setting the analysand adapts by a regression which allows for the emergence of transference.

Psychoanalytic neutrality facilitates transference by frustrating the patient's wishes for transference gratification and by providing the conditions for making it safe for the patient to experience and express his transferences. According to Freud (1919, p. 162-165) and Glover (1955, p. 167), neutrality (abstinence) is used to maintain the element of frustration, the original trigger impulse of the neuroses. Weiss (1971) challenged the traditional view that frustration plays a major role in bringing to consciousness warded-off impulses. He held that the emergence of new themes such as previously unacceptable impulses is causally connected to the analyst's neutral responses. It is not connected, according to Weiss, because neutrality frustrates the patient, but because the analyst's neutrality creates conditions which make it safe for the patient to bring the warded-off impulse to consciousness. In my opinion both factors (frustration and providing a safe environment) may play a role in facilitating the patient's awareness and mastery of transferences. In some cases, the frustration element appears most decisive, whereas in other instances, such as in the following vignette from Weiss, the safety element is paramount.

A patient described by Weiss wished to bring his homosexual impulse to the surface, not primarily to satisfy it but to master it. "He wished to bring it forth and *not* satisfy it in his relationship to the analyst. His bringing it to consciousness would be a step to mastering it only if the analyst would not reciprocate the patient's interest" (1971, p. 460). The patient then unconsciously set out to determine whether or not the analyst would reciprocate his interest. The patient's testing of the neutral analyst assured him that he could not seduce the analyst. Assured that it would be safe for him to experience his erotic interest, he lifted his defenses and permitted it to awareness. Patients such as this one may *wish* for what they do not *want*. The patient wanted mastery and understanding, not gratification of his wishes.

The analyst's neutral responses facilitate the patient's awareness of warded-off affects and thoughts by providing the environmental conditions for the patient to feel safe. The pathways to one's awareness are regulated by one's need to maintain a feeling of well-being. In a series of papers Sandler and Joffe (Sandler 1960, Joffe and Sandler 1968, Sandler and Joffe 1969) formulated the individual's attempt to attain or maintain an ideal state of well-being or safety as a basic regulatory principle. This principle is considered to be superordinate to both the pleasure principle and the reality principle.

Being neutral is sometimes defined as the technical precept whereby the analyst does not take sides or support either contesting side of a patient's psychic conflicts. The meaning was first formulated by Anna Freud (1946, p. 30); she recommended that analysts remain equidistant from all of the major structures, id, superego, and ego. Since the rule against taking sides in the patient's conflicts is subsumed under the rules of abstinence and anonymity, I will not further discuss this meaning of neutrality.

THE ANALYST'S
PROFESSIONAL ROLE REQUIREMENTS

The concept of the analyst's role is important in establishing the limits and guidelines for the analyst's transactions with analysands. Professional role requirements define the kinds of permissable activities and overt responses. The analyst's role may be defined as the structurally given demands (rules, expectations, responsibilities, and the like) associated with his position as an analyst. Neutrality rules of abstinence and anonymity are subsumed under the analyst's role requirements.

The rule of neutrality is only one of several rules governing the analyst's actions in the psychoanalytic situation. Langs (1975b) has discussed the ground rules and boundaries of the patient-therapist relationship. In addition to neutrality they include: setting fees and hours; the rule of free association; the absence of physical contact; and the exclusive one-to-one relationship with confidentiality. Langs explained how adherence to these ground rules furthers therapeutic progress and how deviations tend to impede the therapeutic process.

Stone (1961) has compared the analyst's role with that of the physician and teacher. Although most analysts are also physicians and although there are educative aspects of the psychoanalytic process, such aspects of the psychoanalyst's role functions are peripheral and secondary to his principal function and role as interpreter.

The analyst must have no other major goal than that of analyzing and interpreting the material presented to him. He does not attempt to guide or educate the patient. Freud (1912b) denounced "therapeutic ambition" and "educative ambition" and deemed it wrong to set a patient tasks such as collecting memories or thinking over some particular time of his life. The damaging effects of using educative methods in psychoanalytic therapy are illustrated in the following case of a college student who, early in analysis, was struggling with conflicts over dependency on her mother. After being involved in a serious auto accident, she talked anxiously about her conflict between disobeying or obeying her mother's prohibitions against driving with her reckless friends. The therapist responded to the patient's anxiety by explaining that the patient had several other options open to her such as going out with more cautious drivers or visiting, but not driving with, her reckless friends. This ostensibly helpful and educative intervention repeated the patient's relation with her over-protective mother. Disturbed by the analyst's remarks, the patient missed the next session. The analyst's antitherapeutic, educative intervention threatened the patient's efforts to achieve independence from her mother and interrupted the developing therapeutic alliance. Later, after the patient's anxious and angry reactions to the disruptive intervention were analyzed, the therapeutic alliance was restored.

In psychoanalysis as in other helping professions—teaching, medicine, psychiatry, social work, etc.—some distancing of the professional from his involvement with clients is essential to the success of the relationship. The development of a *professional attitude*, acquired in large measure from learning and adhering to the rules and role requirements of the analyst's profession, allows the analyst to take a certain distance from the patient and yet remain in touch with his own and the patient's feelings (see Sandler et al. 1973). Both analyst and analysand recognize that as persons they can establish a relationship with each other only through roles, and that the discipline, the therapeutic direction, and the adequacy of this professional association demands the principle of control provided by following their roles as analyst and analysand. Much acting in by analysands may be understood as transference-motivated efforts to manipulate the analyst to abandon his role and to provide transference gratifications (see Newton 1971).

When the analyst breaks neutrality rules or, in other ways deviates from his role as an analyst, he may unconsciously form with the patient a therapeutic misalliance. According to Langs (1975a, p. 78), therapeutic misalliances are interactions designed to undermine the goals of insight and structural change, or interactions designed to achieve symptom modification on some other basis. The analyst's failure to follow the rules of neutrality in the case of a narcissistic personality disorder created a therapeutic misalliance and prevented the conscious emergence of working through of an idealizing transference. A young attorney's sense of well-being and security depended on his attachment in reality or in fantasy to men whom he endowed with omnipotent powers of wisdom and masculine strength. One day the patient asked how long the analysis would last. The analyst answered with remarks about the average length of most analyses and a prediction about how long the patient's analysis would last. In the following years the same sequence was repeated several times with the patient asking and receiving an answer to his question about the duration of the analysis. The question arose from the patient's unconscious fantasy that the analyst possessed omnipotent power to predict the future. Another reason for the question was the patient's need for magical reassurance. Obtaining a prediction meant for him a guarantee by the analyst that he would successfully complete the analysis. By answering rather than analyzing the question, the analyst unconsciously acted out the omnipotent role attributed to him by the patient. A therapeutic misalliance was formed based upon the mutual acting out of the patient's unconscious fantasy that the analyst could predict the duration and guarantee the outcome of the analysis.

Thus far, I have emphasized the restraints, limits, and controls inherent in the analyst's role and the technical rules regarding neutrality. This emphasis should not be overstressed since the role-restraints provide the background for the patient's feeling of safety and the conditions for a more spontaneous expression of feeling and thought by the analysand and a more free access on the part of the analyst to the analysand's unconscious mental processes. Role requirements, such as neutrality, set limits on the analyst, but they also provide channels for an opening-up for the patient, a release of expression which is neither appropriate nor sanctioned in other interpersonal contexts.

THE NATURAL SCIENCE
MODEL OF NEUTRALITY

The psychoanalytic model of neutrality is fundamentally different from that derived from the natural sciences. Unfortunately, however, the natural science model of neutrality has often been applied to both psychoanalytic theory and practice. In psychoanalytic discourse there are three meanings of neutrality derived from the natural science model of neutrality which I will examine. They are (1) the inhibition of the analyst's affective reactions to the patient, (2) the attitude of impersonal or uninvolved detachment from the analysand, and (3) the ideal of value-free neutrality.

Neutrality and impersonal objectivity in natural science observation is required for the observer to guard against projecting onto the perceived any qualities, attitudes, etc. which are not actual qualities of the object. Acting in his role as a neutral observer, the natural scientist sets aside (suspends) his feelings and value judgments about the perceived object, so that he can focus his attention on observing some actual and publicly observable physical quality of the perceived object. As a neutral observer he restricts his relation to the perceived to that of observation, and he seeks to maintain an attitude of detachment and noninvolvement with respect to the object of observation. No one holds that the natural scientist can perfectly fulfill these methodological ideals of neutrality and impersonal objectivity. However much he seeks to suspend his feelings, values, and expectancies, they will affect his observations. Because of this the ideal natural science observer is not a man but a machine which will observe accurately without the interfering influence of human feelings and values. Indeed, today in most natural science research, machines have assumed the tasks of sensing or observing, measuring, and recording the physical qualities of the object being investigated.

Contrast the operational stance of the psychoanalyst with that of the natural science observer. Like the natural scientist the analyst is also influenced by his feelings, values, and personal reactions to his patients. But unlike the natural science observer, he does not attempt to suspend his affective reactions as interfering contaminants. On the contrary, as I will argue later, the analyst's affective reactions are essential data used to further his understanding of the patient.

Loewald (1960) argued that the neutrality of the analyst is different from the neutral attitude of the pure scientist toward his subject of study. According to him, the model of the relationship between a scientific observer and his subject of study is misleading and not useful as a model for the analytic relationship. Nielsen also has argued against the applicability and usefulness of the natural science model of neutrality for psychoanalysis. "Values are the motive force behind our investigations and our therapy, and they determine the direction of our efforts" (1960, p. 429).

NEUTRALITY AS INHIBITION OF AFFECT

There are several related versions of the prohibition against affective reactions on the part of the analyst. One is that the ideal therapist is unresponsive and unaffected by anything the patient says or does. Another commonly held rule opposes affective expression. During a case discussion an analyst said, "I try to be neutral about the patient. I remove any emotion from my voice when I talk to the patient." He could not, of course, remove any emotion from his speaking, since to talk without affect is impossible. But his attempt to speak without affect created a tone of voice which was stilted and mechanical. In talking this way he introduced an unnecessary and stultifying parameter. Hammet (1954), as noted above, criticized what he considered a general proscription of affect expression on the part of analysts.

Neutrality for some has meant a general rule against both experiencing and expressing the analyst's emotional reactions to the analysand. A more tolerant acceptance of countertransference and an understanding of its constructive aspects led to change in the former inhibition against affective reactions to the patient. In this paper I use the term *countertransference* in its broadest sense to designate the analyst's affective reactions to the patient. Kernberg (1965) and Sandler et al. (1973) discussed the different meanings of the word countertransference. Not all of the analyst's affective responses to their patients arise primarily in response to the patient's needs and transferences. Some of the analyst's reactions arise from his own unresolved conflicts and transferences.

Frequently in the history of science what at first was considered a troublesome and interfering phenomenon is later considered an important aspect of the problem being investigated. This occurred in psychoanalysis when transference was first discovered and, later, studied by Freud. Countertransference, at first considered an unwanted contaminant of the analytic process, is now being considered in the same light.

A growing appreciation has gradually developed of the positive value of recognizing and understanding the analyst's affective responses to the patient (see Heimann 1950). Countertransference is one of the analyst's instruments for facilitating perception of the analysand's present and past object relations. A sensitive awareness of one's incipient reactions to the patient leads to a richer and more subtle understanding of the patient's transference strivings (see Tower 1956, Stone 1961, Giovacchini 1975). Countertransference is considered something more than an obstacle to treatment, more than unresolved transference and resistance. Papers by Racker (1957), Weigert (1954), and others recognized the complex conscious and unconscious relations between analyst and patient and how the understanding of the analyst's emotional responses and countertransference may be used for understanding the analyst-analysand relationship in its real and its transferential aspects.

With the growing appreciation of the positive and constructive values of detecting and accepting countertransference and the less rigidly employed rules of abstinence and anonymity, there has been a gradual shift in the affective ambience of the analytic situation. The change seems one from an intellectually detached rapport to one of a sublimated, emotional closeness between the two partners, patient and analyst.

An analyst can engage in lively affective interchange with his patient and still be neutral. It is neither possible nor desirable for the analyst to repress or suppress his emotional reactions. The rules of abstinence and anonymity and the other analytic role requirements provide sufficient guidelines for affective interchange. Outward affective expressions are limited to those required for the analytic task.

NEUTRALITY AS IMPERSONAL DETACHMENT

The natural science observer's stance is one of noninvolvement and detachment from the objects of observation. A contrary situation obtains for the analyst who is involved and related to the analysand. This is not a matter of choice. I am not advocating a stance of involvement or relatedness as opposed to a position of noninvolvement. What I am asserting is that noninvolvement with the patient is, in principle, impossible. The analyst who seeks to be noninvolved and detached is actually carrying out a stultifying kind of involvement or relation with the patient.

One cannot *not* relate. It is impossible for two people who are together, analyst and analysand, to remain unrelated. My point is not the desirability of this or that kind of involvement or relation with the patient; rather, I am saying that everything we do or say with another person implicitly, if not explicitly, communicates some kind of relation. One of the fundamental concepts formulated by Watzlawick et al. (1967) about human communication is that "one cannot not communicate." They demonstrate that the nature of one's relation with another is continually being communicated in the affective expressions and somatic gestures of nonverbal communication. Schizophrenics tend to deny they are relating and to deny that they are communicating with others. Their denial is itself a type of communication, and their withdrawal is a kind of relating and a kind of communication.

Maslow (1969) argued for two kinds of objectivity: one impersonal, detached, and uncaring, and the other personal, caring and involved with the object. *Impersonal* objectivity is applicable to the natural science study of *things*, whereas *personal* objectivity obtains for the study of *persons*. With this type of noninterfering and nonpossessive personal objectivity, the analyst can be neutral and still care for the patient. Freud (1963, p. 113) noted that "listless indifference" by the analyst could bring about resistances in the patient. Kernberg argued that an important force in overcoming and neutralizing the destructive effects of the therapist's aggression and self-aggression is the capacity of the analyst to experience concern for the patient.

Concern, he said "does not mean abandonment of the analytic position of the analyst's neutrality" (1965, p. 52).

The neutrality and relative silence of the analyst is basically dissimilar in its meaning and function from the detached observing attitude of the natural science observer. There is a fundamental difference between the natural science observer and the psychoanalyst in their operational stance. The natural science observer takes the point of view of a detached spectator. Contrastingly, the analyst takes the point of view of the actor (the patient). This concept of the psychoanalytic method opposes the idea of those like Rangell (1975, p. 92) who wrote of the analyst's assuming the stance of a distanced or detached observer. Therapeutic employment of neutral attitudes and techniques should not include attitudes of detachment, indifference, or noninvolvement. In contrast to the impersonal objectivity of the natural science observer, the psychoanalyst's method implies relation and involvement.

A crucial aspect of the analyst-analysand relation is the analyst's respect for the analysand's autonomy. This aspect may be illuminated by Heidegger's concept of "letting be" or "let it be." "The freedom to reveal something overt lets what 'is' at the moment *be* what it is. Freedom reveals itself as the 'letting-be' of what is" (p. 305). Heidegger explained that the "letting be" of what-is does not refer to indifference or neglect but to the very opposite of them. To let something be is actually to have something to do with it. Letting-be means participating in the revealed nature of what-is. He wrote, "Freedom, so understood as the letting-be of what-is, fulfills and perfects the nature of truth in the unconcealment and revealment of what-is" (1968, p. 309).

The following vignette illustrates neutrality as "letting be." The patient was a thirty-four-year-old married intellectual. Prior to the hour in question, he had made some gains in overcoming an almost lifelong inhibition against writing and expressing himself. He obtained a job with some opportunity to write and give talks. A day after he had given a successful talk he came to the analytic hour tense and obsessed with fantasies of my punishing him. He recognized the transferential basis of these fears as he began to remember the beating his father had given him. Some of his associations alluded to the idea that he wanted something from me. I made an interpretation to the effect that although he feared I would punish him as his father had, he wished I would encourage him to express himself in writing and his talks. The patient was silent and then he laughed with obvious pleasure and relief. I asked what he thought the laugh meant. He said he was pleased by my attitude. "You leave everything as it is. You illuminate. You do not try to control or change anything." The patient's laughter expressed his relief and pleasure over understanding my neutrality and using it to affirm his success.

Neutrality has a positive as well as a negative meaning: it refers to what analysts *do* as well as what they do *not* do. In the present case vignette the negative side of neutrality meant that I was not going to control, punish, approve of, or change him. The positive aspect of my neutral attitude and technique concerned my recognition and acceptance of his autonomy. Analytic neutrality in the sense of "let it be" means that the analyst participates in revealing the truth about the patient without trying to change him.

The relief the patient gained from my interpretation stemmed from his fear of losing autonomy. He was as fearful of receiving approval as he was of being punished. At this juncture in the analysis, he was most anxious over losing his developing but precarious sense of autonomy. My active approval or encouragement of his recent successful performances would have aroused his fears that I would appropriate (as he felt his father did) his successes. I recognized his success, but I did not possess it. He then felt sufficiently safe to feel and to be successful for himself.

Some maintain that an attitude of neutrality should obtain only for analysis of neurotic patients, and that therapy of more severely ill patients must add supportive measures in which the analyst takes over ego functions and parental functions for the patient. I strongly disagree; respect for the patient's autonomy is an even more critical issue in the treatment of severely ill patients. Psychoanalysis or psychoanalytic psychotherapy of such patients is made difficult if not impossible when the analyst assumes and carries out parental functions or attempts to manage the patient's life. Flarsheim (1967) in "The Separation of Management from the Therapeutic Setting in a Paranoid Patient" recommended that psychoanalytic therapists refrain from assuming management functions for psychotic patients. He stressed the need for fostering the psychotic patient's autonomy and the importance of not usurping the patient's ego and superego functions. In the psychoanalytic therapy of psychotic or character disorders as well as of neurotic disorders, neutrality means the avoidance of a directive or parental role and respect for the patient's autonomy. Searles (1965) held that schizophrenic patients require the therapist's neutrality in order to master their basic ambivalence concerning individuation. Whether or not a neutral response is required depends on the therapist's intuitive appraisal of the patient's changing needs. At times, the schizophrenic patient requires an intense emotional responsiveness and at other times, according to Searles, he needs neutral and related responses of "inscrutability, imperturbability, and impassivity."

NEUTRALITY AS VALUE-FREE

The acrimonious arguments during the past several decades in science and philosophy about the concept of a value-free science have seldom distinguished the different ways in which the phrase *value-free* has been used. One meaning of value-free in psychoanalysis concerns the proscription against the analyst's imposition of his values upon the patient. Since this meaning falls under the rules of abstinence and anonymity, I will not discuss it further. Other meanings of value-free have to do with the *subject matter* of psychoanalysis and with psychoanalytic *methods* of description, explanation, and interpretation. In the following section I will argue that both the subject matter and the methods of psychoanalysis, unlike the natural sciences, cannot logically be free of values. Finally, I will discuss the ethical values of truthfulness, personal freedom, and a caring commitment to the patient implicit in the psychoanalyst's neutral attitudes and techniques.

Natural science deals with physical phenomena, which, by definition, are morally neutral and empty of intrinsic values. Psychoanalysis is concerned with emotions, conflicts, and ideals which are the very stuff of values. The subject matter of psychoanalysis is human *action*. Since the subject's actions are regulated by his values, the subject matter of psychoanalysis must include values. The concept of human action implies values. As used here the term *action* refers to meaningful behavior; it does not refer to motoric *movements*. According to Schafer (1976), action "is human behavior that has a point; it is meaningful human activity; it is intentional or goal-directed performances by people; it is doing things for reasons" (1976, p. 178). Meldon (1961) and Louch (1966) have provided philosophical studies of action concepts.

The concept of *action* most clearly distinguishes the mental or human act from inanimate *movement*. The same event may be described as an action by the psychoanalyst and as a movement by the natural scientist. A person's suicidal jump from a building is an action. The phrase "a falling body" describes the same event as a movement. A mechanical description of the muscle, bone, and arm activities, "rising arms," is a description of a movement, whereas the phrase "he raised his arm" is a description of an action. The psychoanalyst wants to know *why* the subject raised his arm, and the natural scientist wants to know *how* it rises. A mechanical account of movements does not give the kind of description or explanation of behavior the psychoanalyst is looking for.

In recent decades a number of analysts have persuasively argued that analysts should pay more attention to the investigation of values (Reid 1960, Ramzy 1965, Ginsburg 1950, Redlich 1960). Ramzy (1965) concluded that psychoanalysis—as a therapeutic technique, as a theory, and as a branch of science—is concerned with values. He opposed the self-imposed moratorium on the subject of values in psychoanalysis and proposed that psychoanalysis could become, not a value-creating, but a value-investigating science.

The recent and partial shift in psychoanalysis away from a position of value neutrality parallels and reflects a similar change in other fields of science. The traditional concept of science as free of values has been effectively challenged in recent decades by a number of scientists and philosophers (Bronowski 1964, Maslow 1969, Myrdal 1969, Polanyi 1964). In the past science was defined in terms of objectivity and detachment. The study of needs and values was turned over to nonscientific and nonempirical investigators. Many today reject the view of science as merely instrumental and unable to assist mankind in the study of its ultimate values and ideals. As a human enterprise and as a social institution, science has goals, ethics, morals, ideals—in a word, values—as Bronowski (1964) so convincingly and brilliantly demonstrated. Before Hiroshima, physicists also talked of a value-free science and of the need for scientists to avoid value judgments. Today, some physicists reject the ideal of a value-free science and many of them have become more acutely concerned with the moral consequences and implications of their work.

Many scientists now concede that the value-neutral (value-free) idea correctly applies to the observational methods designed by the natural sciences for the study of *things*. Value-neutrality does not and should not apply to all phases of scientific activities. The natural science model of neutrality is applicable and required in the hypothesis-testing (observational) phase of natural science research. It is not applicable to other phases of natural science research such as the creation and formulation of hypotheses.

Although most analysts now agree that values constitute a prominent part of the subject matter of psychoanalysis, few understand the fact that psychoanalytic methods of description, explanation, and interpretation inevitably involve value assessments. Analytic methods cannot logically be free of values, since these methods describe, explain, and interpret human action in value terms. The analyst's explanation of an action as due to a sexual wish is a value or moral explanation, because the desirability of the sexual object is the grounds for the action. In contrast, the terms used by the natural scientist for describing or explaining events are, like the subjet matter of natural science, free of values. Louch, using the word *moral* in a broad sense to mean values, said, "Explanation of human action is moral explanation. In appealing to reasons for acting, motives, purposes, intentions, desires, and their cognates, which occur in both ordinary and technical discussions of human doings, we exhibit an action in the light of circumstances that are taken to entitle or warrant a person to act as he does" (1966, p. 4).

Value-free for some psychoanalysts means making observations, evaluations, and interpretations free of values. This meaning of value-free stems from a confusion between the methodologies of natural science and psychoanalysis. The natural science observer suspends his value judgments about what he is observing in order that his observations may be unaffected by his values and may reflect the actual physical qualities of the perceived. Some psychoanalysts mistakenly seek to follow the method of natural science observation in this regard. The analyst assesses values not from the point of view of a detached (natural science) observer or from that of societal standards. He takes the perspective of the actor rather than the spectator. This requires empathic understanding of the patient's actions in the light of motives, desires, and intentions. There is a tendency among many psychoanalytic theoreticians and practitioners to think of values as subtle and dangerous obstacles to empathic understanding and interpretation. In their efforts to emulate and imitate the observational methods of the natural scientists, analysts have tried to set aside value judgments in their work with patients. However, value-free observation and assessment of human action is neither possible nor desirable. Psychoanalytic terms for describing, evaluating, and explaining human action imply value categories. According to Louch, "To identify a piece of behavior as an action is already to describe experience by means of moral concepts" (1966, p. 4).

In our reports and explanations of human actions, we use such terms as *adaptive* or *maladaptive, destructive* or *constructive, productive* or *nonproductive, appropriate* or *inappropriate*. These are all value judgments (value appraisals) to be sure, but they are also descriptive. The natural science observer correctly distinguishes between judgments of physical facts and jugdments of value. Acting in his role as a natural science observer, he suspends value judgments. The physical objects of his observation are free of intrinsic values. However, the distinction between judgments of value and judgments of fact does not obtain in the sphere of human action. In psychoanalysis and in our everyday relations with others we observe, describe, and explain *moral facts*. When we say that a person is acting cowardly, generously, defensively, adaptively, hatefully, etc., we are describing moral facts and we are making value appraisals.

My use of terms such as *value* (or *moral*) *appraisal, assessment,* or *judgment* does not imply approval, consent, or condemnation of the human action in question. These terms refer to strategies and categories of description and explanation. The word *judgment* is used here in the sense of assessment and evaluation rather than of legal, theological, or other kind of censure. Moral (value) assessment is not moral condemnation. The psychoanalyst's interpretations must necessarily include his value appraisals, but they can and should exclude moral directives and condemnation.

Value-free or morally neutral discussion or explanation of human action is logically impossible. Psychoanalysis and the social and behavioral sciences have in the past mistakenly maintained that they could investigate and explain human behavior in value-free terms. In so doing they mistakenly imitated the observational methods of the natural sciences. The position taken here is opposed to that of Hartmann (1960) and other analysts who have asserted that considerations of value should not be a source of concern for the analyst, and that value judgments are outside the analyst's scientific and thera-peutic roles.

Prominent sociologists, including Myrdal (1969) and Gouldner (1962), rejected the aim of a value-free sociology. They have argued that it is not possible for sociology to be value-free. According to Gouldner, the sociologist has a choice between an open and honest expression of his values and pursuing a "vain ritual" of moral neutrality "which because it invites men to ignore the vulnerability of reason to bias, leaves it at the mercy of irrationality" (1962, p. 212). Myrdal (1969) claimed that many social scientists, out of their fear of valuations, tend to speak of them "objectively." They attempt to objectify what is not, and cannot be, simply objective. He persuasively argues that a purely objective and value-free social science has never existed and can never exist.

Psychoanalysis, alongside the social and behavioral sciences, has maintained the myth that it *could* and *should* be value-free. Because of its adherence to this myth it has neglected the study of its own values and the place of values in the psychoanalytic process and technique. Again, I emphasize that the study of the analysand's values does not imply moral condemnation or consent. The rules of abstinence and anonymity provide sufficient restraints against destructive and authoritarian moralizing.

Psychoanalytic neutrality, in contrast to the natural science model of value-free neutrality, is based on fundamental principles of morality and ethics (see Shor 1961). The principles of psychoanalytic neutrality (the rules of abstinence and anonymity) are in part derived from, and more fully exemplify, Judeo-Christian and medical codes of ethics than they do the natural science methodologies of value-free neutrality and impersonal objectivity. Three values: the love of truth, the ethic of personal freedom, and the analyst's caring commitment to the patient, are implicit in the analyst's neutral attitudes and techniques. The importance of adhering to the ethical principles of truthfulness and personal freedom in the analytic situation was discussed by Freud in his writings on technique, especially in his discussion of the abstinence rule. (See Freud 1915, p. 164, and 1919, pp. 164-165.) A broader definition and formulation of neutrality principles include, in addition to abstinence and anonymity prohibitions, the following injunctions: the analyst should seek and speak the truth; he should have a caring commitment to the patient, and he should respect the patient's freedom.

Neutrality is required to maintain the preeminent value of truth in the analytic relationship and for the analysand's attainment of insight. Telling the truth about the patient to the patient is the analyst's major task, and his search for the truth about the patient guides and informs his interpretive work. Neutrality is usually defined negatively as in the prohibitions of the abstinence and anonymity rules. These prohibitions only make sense when coupled with the ethical injunctions mentioned above. The don'ts and do's belong together. For example, in dealing with the patient's transference, the analyst follows both the prohibition against gratifying the patient's transference wishes and the injunction which says that the analyst should tell the truth about the patient's transference. Freud summarized the analytic ethic of truthfulness: "And finally we must not forget that the analytic relationship is based on a love of truth—that is, on a recognition of reality—and that it precludes any kind of sham or deceit" (1937, p. 248). (See Ricoeur 1970, pp. 279-280, for a discussion of the relationship between the truthfulness ethic and psychoanalytic neutrality.)

As Freud (1915, p. 164) explained, the abstinence rule is required so that the patient may understand and master his transferences to the analyst. Neutrality and the goal of insight distinguish psychoanalytic therapy from other therapies. Psychoanalysis aims at character change through understanding, whereas most other therapies seek symptomatic change through various forms of moral, social, physical, or pharmacological manipulation. The issue here is not the efficacy but the ethical aspects of manipulative techniques. Behavior modification does work. So does torture. Behavior modification techniques are not new. Pain and pleasure evoking instrumentalities have been effectively used to manipulate people since the beginnings of recorded history.

Too often, in the manipulative therapies, short-term symptomatic gains are achieved at the cost of sacrificing the patient's long-term developmental potential. Manipulative therapies often bring about symptom relief through transference gratification. These techniques may relieve the patient's distress at the same time that the patient's infantile fixations are reinforced and his potentialities for future personal development are lessened. Witness the Veterans Administration's system for caring for service-connected psychiatric patients. One need not be an authority on learning theory, on conditioning, or on psychoanalysis to understand that awarding money to veterans for being sick helps to keep them sick.

Psychoanalytic neutrality is founded on the ethic of personal freedom; neutrality rules protect the patient's rights and capacities to understand and freely choose his own way of life. Rules of abstinence and anonymity safeguard the interests of the patient against antitherapeutic manipulations and encroachments by the analyst. The analyst's respect for the patient's autonomy assumes adherence to the ethic of personal freedom.

The analyst guards the patient's constructive use of free association by not guiding or controlling the direction of the patient's expressions. This attitude and technique was summarized by Freud: "It exposes the patient to the least possible amount of compulsion . . . that nothing will be introduced into it by the expectations of the analyst. It is left to the patient in all essentials to determine the course of the analysis and the arrangement of the material; any systematic handling of particular symptoms or complexes thus becomes impossible" (1925, p. 41).

Analysands are free to accept or reject the analyst and what the analyst says. The analyst renounces any actual power over the decisions of the patient, and he refuses to accept any responsibility for the patient's choices. The analyst's task is to analyze and interpret resistance and transference; it is not his role to educate, manipulate, or otherwise act upon the patient. Neutral attitudes recognize and respect the analysand's freedom. "After all," as Freud said, "analysis does not set out to make pathological reactions impossible, but to give the patient's ego *freedom* to decide one way or the other" (1923, p. 50).

The analyst's adherence to truthfulness in the pursuit of the patient's insight and his respect for the patient's freedom imply an ethical, caring commitment to the patient. A caring commitment enjoins the analyst to say and to do what is best for the patient's self-understanding and development within the limits prescribed by neutrality rules and the analyst's role requirements. The psychoanalyst's caring is not so much a feeling as it is an attitude and a commitment. Therapists cannot maintain and should not be expected to have any particular feeling or emotion for the patient. Feelings come and go; a commitment endures. A caring commitment, or "concern" as described by Kernberg (1965), helps the analyst overcome the disturbing countertransference feelings inevitable in all analyses. For the patient a caring commitment provides what Winnicott (1963) described in the metaphor of the "holding environment." I would like to stress that the caring commitment or holding environment are *implicit* in psychoanalytic neutrality and in other elements of classical psychoanalytic technique. The introduction of *explicit* caring expressions are, of course, under most conditions contrary to the rules of abstinence and anonymity.

Abstinence and anonymity rules and the values of truthfulness, personal freedom, and a caring commitment are strategies for the overall direction and regulation of the analyst's actions. These strategies are necessary but not sufficient regulations for the analyst's tactical decisions about when and how to intervene. Such tactical decisions are based upon his moment-to-moment empathic judgments about the patient-therapist relationship and the patient's transferences and resistances.

THE DEFENSIVE USE OF THE
NATURAL SCIENCE MODEL OF NEUTRALITY

The natural science model of neutrality and impersonal objectivity have long had a strong and persuasive influence, not only on the ideals and methods of various behavioral and social sciences, but also on our culture and on all levels of our educational system. In recent decades, a growing number of scientists and philosophers have argued against the mistaken and harmful application of natural science neutrality methods to diverse fields fundamentally different in origin from natural science (see Myrdal 1969, Polanyi 1964, Maslow 1969, Louch 1966, Hampden-Turner 1971).

A comprehensive examination of the scientific, philosophical, and sociological aspects of this issue is beyond the scope of this paper. I do wish to emphasize that the misapplication of the natural science model is of existential and practical, as well as theoretical, significance to psychoanalytic training and practice. Psychiatric and psychoanalytic educators constantly confront the difficult task of trying to reverse the deleterious effects of medical school education on the student's relations with patients. Medical school training tends to foster the misapplication of a natural science model of neutrality to the students' patient-physician relationships. By both precept and example, students are taught to set aside their feelings and values and to strive for a detached, observing relationship with the patient. Ernest Jones wrote about "the exceptional difficulty of teaching psychology to medical students, whose whole training strengthens their natural defence against facing deep emotions" (1959, p. 74).

In my experience, most medical students are less able to be empathic with others after medical school than before. Winnicott (1958, p. 116) also claimed that medical school does little to qualify the student in psychological understanding and it does much to disqualify him. Freud (1926) said that medical education gives doctors "a false and detrimental attitude" (p. 231) toward the field of the neuroses. There is considerable empirical evidence for the hypothesis that medical school training reinforces and supports the development of personality traits of emotional constriction and impersonal detachment (see Light 1975). Psychotherapists whose medical education has indoctrinated them with attitudes of affectlessness, impersonal detachment, and value-free neutrality often use these meanings of neutrality defensively to justify and rationalize their emotional unresponsiveness and their empathic failures.

Some psychiatrists whom I have seen in analysis or in supervision use such ideas of neutrality to deny their emotional alienation from their patients. Their defensive patterns of affective isolation and impersonal detachment from others had their roots in childhood development, but their professional training allowed them to strengthen and rationalize these attitudes as being scientific. The defensive use of neutral attitudes and techniques, especially those linked with the natural science model, allows the therapist to avoid the feeling of responsibility for whatever role the therapist or therapeutic situation has in evoking the patient's responses. The latter can be dismissed as transference.

REFERENCES

Bibring, G. L. (1935). A contribution to the subject of transference resistance. *International Journal of Psycho-Analysis* 17:181-189.

Bronowski, J. (1964). *Science and Human Values*. New York: Harper and Row.

Calef, V. (1967). Activity-passivity (panel report). *Journal of the American Psychoanalytic Association* 15:709-728.

Fenichel, O. (1941). *Problems of Psychoanalytic Technique*. Albany, New York: Psychoanalytic Quarterly.

Flarsheim, A. (1967). The separation of management from the therapeutic setting in a paranoid patient. *International Journal of Psycho-Analysis* 48:559-572.

Freud, A. (1946). *The Ego and the Mechanisms of Defence*. New York: International Universities Press.

Freud, S. (1912a). The dynamics of transference. *Standard Edition* 12:97-108.

——— (1912b). Recommendations to physicians practicing psycho-analysis. *Standard Edition* 12:109-120.

——— (1913). On beginning the treatment. *Standard Edition* 12:123-144.

——— (1914). Remembering, repeating and working-through. *Standard Edition* 12:145.

——— (1915). Observations on transference-love. *Standard Edition* 12:157-171.

——— (1919). Lines of advance in psycho-analytic therapy. *Standard Edition* 17:157-168.

——— (1923). The ego and the id. *Standard Edition* 19:19-27.

——— (1925). An authobiographical study. *Standard Edition* 20:7-70.

——— (1926). The question of lay analysis. *Standard Edition* 20:179-250.

——— (1937). Analysis terminable and interminable. *Standard Edition* 23:216-253.

——— (1963). *Psychoanalysis and Faith: The Letters of Sigmund Freud and Oskar Pfister*, ed. H. Meng and E. L. Freud. New York: Basic Books.

Gill, M. (1954). Psychoanalysis and exploratory psychotherapy. *Journal of the American Psychoanalytic Association* 2:771-797.

Ginsburg, S. (1950). Values and the psychiatrist. *American Journal of Orthopsychiatry* 20:466-478.

Giovacchini, P. L. (1975). Countertransference. In *Tactics and Techniques in Psychoanalytic Therapy*, vol. 2, ed. P. L. Giovacchini. New York: Jason Aronson.

Glover, E. *The Technique of Psycho-Analysis*. New York International Universities Press.

Gouldner, A. W. (1962). Anti-minotaur: the myth of a value-free sociology. *Social Problems* 9:199-213.

Greenson, R. R. (1958). Variations in classical psycho-analytic technique: an introduction. *International Journal of Psycho-Analysis* 25:200-201.

Hammet, V. B. O. (1954). A consideration of psychoanalysis in relation to psychiatry generally, circa 1965. *American Journal of Psychiatry* 122:42-54.

Hampden-Turner, C. (1971). *Radical Man*. Garden City, New York: Anchor Books.

Hartmann, H. (1960). *Psychoanalysis and Moral Values*. New York: International Universities Press.

Heidegger, M. (1968). *Existence and Being*. Chicago: Henry Regnery.

Heimann, P. (1950). On countertransference. *International Journal of Psycho-Analysis* 31:81-84.

Hoedemaker, E. D. (1960). Psycho-analytic technique and ego modifications. *International Journal of Psycho-Analysis* 41:34-46.

Joffe, W. G., and Sandler, J. (1968). Comments on the psychoanalytic psychology of adaptation, with special reference to the role of affects and the representational world. *International Journal of Psycho-Analysis* 49:445-454.

Jones, E. (1959). *Free Associations*. London: Hogarth.

Kernberg, O. (1965). Notes on countertransference. *Journal of the American Psychoanalytic Association* 13:38-56.

Kohut, H. (1971). *The Analysis of the Self.* The Psychoanalytic Study of the Child, Monograph 4. New York: International Universities Press.

Langs, R. (1975a). Therapeutic misalliances. *International Journal of Psychoanalytic Psychotherapy* 4:77-105.

——— (1975b). The therapeutic relationship and deviations in technique. *International Journal of Psychoanalytic Psychotherapy* 4:106-141.

La Planche, J., and Pontalis, J. B. (1973). *The Language of Psycho-Analysis.* New York: Norton.

Leites, N. (1971). *The New Ego.* New York: Jason Aronson.

Light, D. (1975). The impact of medical school on future psychiatrists. *American Journal of Psychiatry* 132:607-610.

Loewald, H. W. (1960). On the therapeutic action of psycho-analysis. *International Journal of Psycho-Analysis* 41:16-33.

London: P. (1964). *The Modes and Morals of Psychotherapy.* New York: Holt, Rinehart and Winston.

Louch, A. R. (1966). *Explanation and Human Action.* Berkeley: University of California Press.

Macalpine, I. (1950). The development of the transference. *Psychoanalytic Quarterly* 19:501-539.

Maslow, A. H. (1969). *The Psychology of Science.* Chicago: Henry Regnery.

Meldon, A. I. (1961). *Free Action.* London: Routledge and Kegan Paul.

Menninger, K. A., and Holzman, P. S. (1973). *Theory of Psychoanalytic Technique.* New York: Basic Books.

Mowrer, O. H. (1961). *The Crisis in Psychiatry and Religion.* Princeton: Van Nostrand.

Myrdal, G. (1969). *Objectivity in Social Research.* New York: Pantheon.

Newton, P. M. (1971). Abstinence as a role requirement in psychotherapy. *Psychiatry* 34:391-400.

Nielsen, N. (1960). Value judgments in psycho-analysis. *International Journal of Psycho-Analysis* 41:425-429.

Polanyi, M. (1964). *Personal Knowledge.* New York: Harper Torchbooks.

Racker, H. (1957). The meanings and uses of countertransference. *Psychoanalytic Quarterly* 26:303-357.

Ramzy, I. (1965). The place of values in psycho-analysis. *International Journal of Psycho-Analysis* 46:97-106.

Rangell, L. (1975). Psychoanalysis and the process of change: an essay on the past, present and future. *International Journal of Psycho-Analysis* 56:87-98.

Redlich, F. C. (1960). Psychoanalysis and the problem of values. *Psychoanalysis and Human Values*, ed. J. H. Masserman. New York: Grune and Stratton.

Reid, J. (1960). Values, truth and psychoanalysis. *Science and Psychoanalysis* 3:54-65.

Ricoeur, P. (1970). *Freud and Philosophy: An Essay on Interpretation.* New Haven, Connecticut: Yale University Press.

Sandler, J. (1960). The background of safety. *International Journal of Psycho-Analysis* 41:352-356.

Sandler, J., Dare, C., and Holder, A. (1973). *The Patient and the Analyst.* New York: International Universities Press.

Sandler, J., and Joffe, W. G. (1969). Towards a basic psychoanalytic model. *International Journal of Psycho-Analysis* 50:79-90.

Schafer, R. (1976). *A New Language for Psychoanalysis.* New Haven, Connecticut: Yale University Press.

Searles, H. (1965). The place of neutral therapist responses in psychotherapy with the schizophrenic patient. In *Collected Papers on Schizophrenia and Related Subjects.* New York: International Universities Press.

Shor, J. (1961). The ethic of Freud's psycho-analysis. *International Journal of Psycho-Analysis* 42:116-121.

Stein, M. H. (1966). Letters to the editor (response to V. B. O. Hammet's article, A consideration of psychoanalysis in relation to psychiatry generally, circa 1965, and Hammet's replies to Stein). *American Journal of Psychiatry* 122:830-833.

Stone, L. (1961). *The Psychoanalytic Situation*. New York: International Universities Press.

Tower, L. E. (1956). Countertransference. *Journal of the American Psychoanalytic Association* 4:224-255.

Watzlawick, P., Beavin, J. H., and Jackson, D. D. (1967). *Pragmatics of Human Communication*. New York: Norton.

Weigert, E. (1954). Counter-transference and self-analysis of the psycho-analyst. *International Journal of Psycho-Analysis* 35:242-246.

Weiss, J. (1971). The emergence of new themes, a contribution to the psychoanalytic theory of therapy. *International Journal of Psycho-Analysis* 52:459-467.

Winnicott, D. (1958). Through paediatrics to psychoanalysis. In *Collected Papers*. London: Tavistock.

——— (1963). Psychiatric disorders in terms of infant maturational processes. In *The Maturational Process and the Facilitating Environment*. New York: International Universities Press, 1965, pp. 230-241.

Wittgenstein, L. (1953). *Philosophical Investigations*. New York: Macmillan.

Monologue, Dialogue, and Soliloquy

DEAN P. EYRE, M.R.C.PSYCH.

Psychoanalytical therapy can be seen along developmental lines of three phases, the phases correlating with the early mother/child relationship which is reenacted in the transference relationship. At times one or the other of the phases can be totally permanent, but there can be alternation of the various phases both within a session and between sessions. Techniques implied for therapy are outlined and discussed, as the phases are explicated and related to Rickman's one-, two-, and three-or-more body relationships.

The human infant develops in stages, both physiological and psychological. Freud (1905) early detailed the stages of development along libidinal lines, bringing in the concept of object choice and direction of aims. Melanie Klein later developed these themes, particularly with reference to early object relationships.

In psychoanalytic therapy, we provide the patient a neutral setting with as few outside intrusions as possible, allowing him or her to have a live dream, that is, to make of the setting what the unconscious dictates. We can see three different phases which reenact in the transference the mother-child relationship of the early developmental stages—monologue, dialogue, and soliloquy. The phases correspond roughly to what Rickman (1957) has termed the one-body, two-body, and three-or-more body relationships. There is also an important phase intermediate between monologue and dialogue, which like the three main phases corresponds to early development. The different relational phases appear in varying degrees with all patients during therapy, and one or another may be totally prominent for long periods. Although there is eventually a progression to more mature phases, the possibility of return to earlier ones remains.

The first phase I call *monologue* and correlate it with the stage of fusion or union which first exists between mother and child (Winnicott 1971a, see also Mahler 1969). It corresponds to Rickman's one-body relationship, in which, as with early infantile omnipotence, there is not even awareness of another (see also Spitz 1965). Here between the first two main phases is an important intermediate one which I call the *fantasied transitional object phase*. In the second main developmental stage separation has occurred between mother and child, but the mother is still seen by the child as under omnipotent control. This stage corresponds to the *dialogue*, or two-body, phase. The phase implies, in Winnicott's terms (1971), relating to an object without formal acknowledgment that it has separate rights and wishes of its own. The last and final phase, *soliloquy* or three-or-more body, correlates with the third developmental stage, in which the infant separates from the mother and feels the mother-world no longer under omnipotent control. After destruction of the object (Winnicott 1971d), it is refound as an external object and both its positive and negative attributes acknowledged. External objects are seen here as introjects to build up a representational world (Sandler et al. 1963). It is my contention that these phases always appear in the relationship of patient, analyst, and analytic setting.

Lest it be thought that these concepts apply only to severe patients, I quote from Giovacchini: "At a recent workshop attended by experienced analysts representing over seven different psycho-analytic societies I asked if any one in our group had ever seen a patient who might be considered 'classical,' that is, one who met the criteria of analysability—a patient without a schizoid core whose problems were primarily at the oedipal level. Not one analyst reported ever having seen such a case" (1972, p. 8).

MONOLOGUE

The Shorter Oxford Dictionary defines monologue as "a scene in which a person of the drama speaks by himself, contrasted with chorus and dialogue." Freud refers to the oceanic feeling of an infant at the breast who "does not as yet distinguish his ego from the external world as the source of the sensations flowing in upon him. He gradually learns to do so, in response to various promptings" (1930). At this stage of functioning if the outside world becomes intrusive, or in Winnicott's (1971) terms, the breast that does instead of the breast that is, then the infant takes massive defensive action to protect the infantile ego, usually in the form of huge dissociations. Glover (1968) conceptualizes a nuclear development for the ego with various primitive nuclei coalescing and maturing to form the mature ego. However, with massive early dissociation, the ego nuclei do not coalesce and ego integration does not occur. Consequently, an ego nucleus or fragment of a nucleus matures in relationship to the outside world, but out of contact with the rest of the ego nuclei. The fragment, or ego nucleus, therefore acts the self in relation to the external world, while the rest of the nuclei remain at a primitive developmental level. Implications depend on the degree of intrusiveness by the anaclitic object and the consequent dissociation of the ego nuclei. Where this is very marked a large number of nuclei remain at a primitive developmental level and never undergo separation from the primary union with the mother.

Patients presenting this difficulty will, in therapy, be unaware of the significance of the therapist. The analyst will often feel an impersonal observer or feel treated by the patient as his or her robot. The ego nuclei fragment acting the self corresponds to Winnicott's false self (1960), and it is particularly here that Rickman's remarks on one-body psychology are applicable.

One-Person Psychology concerns itself with what goes on inside one person taken in isolation. It studies the neurological aspect of the mind, sensation, reaction time, learning and forgetting, memory, imagery, hallucinations, introspection, etc.—a very varied field. It is true that in the study of some of these phenomena an experimenter or observer is usually present, but with the present richness of imagination and ingenuity now given to the construction of apparatus of all kinds it would be possible for most of the experiments in this branch of psychology to be carried out, not to be sure designed, by a robot. Where for reasons of economy or of scientific curiosity an observer is used in place of a robot to carry out the routine of testing in the case of one-person psychology the relation between the observer and the person observed is reduced to a minimum. In situations where the responses of the subject of the experiment annoy the observer in one-person psychology the experimental situation is usually considered to be vitiated in some degree because only one person's responses are relevant to the problem being investigated. In the language of two- and three-person psychology the ego ideal of the observer in one-person psychology is a robot. The basis of the research is observation in the a-historical present, the 'here and now' of the laboratory. (1957, pp. 218-219)

People who function mainly at this level and present themselves for analysis often have the vaguest reasons—dissatisfaction with life or intellectual curiosity. In therapy there is an unawareness of the analyst as a person. The patients often seek to relate more to such inanimate objects as the time of the sessions or the physical characteristics of the room. Bick (1968) noted this in her infant observation: children undergoing trauma from a very intrusive world begin to relate more to inanimate objects than to the mother, to focus for instance, on bright lights. At the time of the electricity blackout one patient whom I had had in therapy said that he missed the overhead light, it was so friendly and reassuring, and he liked talking to it. Later, when I moved my consulting rooms, he would walk past the previous consulting rooms with sadness because the room which could be seen from the outside of the building, had been demolished for a large office. The sadness, he said, was for all the memories he had papered the room with. From the analyst's point of view, there is also the difficulty of reverie, and free floating attention. The countertransference feelings are those of being unnecessary as a person for the analysis. Interpretations are, as often as not, totally wide of the mark in content or timing or both. If free floating attention is attempted, there is often a sense of confusion, the feeling that the patient is involved in slang associations or coded information, the code as yet unrevealed to the analyst. The patient may give vast amounts of information which somehow never lives, no use can be made of it. The people discussed never seem real. The remarks of Rickman are again appropriate. The information is given out as though the patient is putting in a punch card for a computer. One patient said she could never tell me anything of importance when it just happened; she would have to savour it for a few weeks, and then when it meant nothing, she could tell me. With another patient this was so marked that interpretations made were greeted by silence and then by tears, because the interpretations seemed to her to have nothing to do with the ongoing material, and the patient felt continually misunderstood.

Case 1

The following more detailed material is from a woman in her late twenties. Miss A arrived by a very devious route, through a clinic, ensuring that no one had referred her directly. She said she was interested in analysis and wanted some experience of it. It was possible she might one day wish to apply for training herself. For the next two years she attended regularly and talked animatedly of her life, yet I felt I knew nothing more of her as a person than I had on our first meeting, and I felt no progress had been made. This prompted me to ask what she felt she was getting from her therapy. She became tearful and upset, fearing I had had enough and was going to throw her out. She began to talk about what she was doing in her therapy and her relationship with me. Over the next few months the following material emerged. "I was waiting for this session yesterday so much" (pulling at her fingers and hands). "I want to come more often" (at this time three times a week). "Otherwise the monologue inside my head gets monotonous, more than I can bear. I just have to get it out. I feel I will burst if I don't tell someone what is on my mind. I don't know what is on my mind, yes I do." At this point I made the interpretation that she seemed to record experiences in her life rather like a camera. She came to a session, used me as a projector and a screen (in an inanimate way), attempted to understand what occurred, and then took it back inside herself. She continued, relating her experiences since the last session, and then said, "I hope you don't mind the session, that it hasn't harmed you my gabbling on like this." I replied that my separate existence was not acknowledged: she seemed to use me as an extra sense organ such as another pair of ears. There seems a correlation with early ego development, in which the infantile ego is thought of as mainly a sensory apparatus.

Some sessions later she said, "I often think you make very stupid remarks, and then I have to keep reminding myself that you only know what I tell you and don't know everything I think."

She referred to an affair she had had: "I can't understand his not leaving his wife for me. I feel because I have made the decision that he should, he will. I can't believe that he thinks differently at all." Later in the session she added, "It's hard thinking of dialogue. After all you are just a disembodied voice. I find it hard to accept your ideas. After a period of time they come to mean something and then come to mean my thoughts. It is difficult this idea of becoming you, it's difficult this two-body relationship. I have to take some notice of what you say. You wouldn't talk off the top of your head, would you? It's what I call behavior conditioning. I know you won't agree. I come round to your way of thinking."

Two days later before the Christmas break she said, "I can't stand gaps. I have to have a handy male around. I can't even recognize the existence of a gap. Holidays are gaps. I can't tolerate it. It's a nightmare gap, a gap that goes on and on for ever." Her way of coping with gaps became clear some considerable time later when we resumed sessions after a summer break.

"I drew a portrait of you while you were on holiday. I'll show you. And then I thought it looked like me. I couldn't work out which one of us it was." The portrait turned out to be a torso with two large breasts, the right hand holding the right breast in a suggestive way, while the left hand held an erect penis. She said she couldn't work out whether it was she stimulating herself or was myself in some kind of feeding role. After Christmas she stated, "I talked and talked at home solidly for eight hours. I felt I fulfilled my obligations to talk, as in these sessions. I talked without any prospect of being listened to. My father never listened to me: he would just walk off in the middle of what I was saying." Two months later she added, "I don't see people as separate from me. I just love parts of them which seem to be attached to me. It's like the Greeks believed, at birth losing an identical part or whole of oneself and still looking for it. How wrong they were."

In this respect she had an unusual way of telling me of intercourse with someone. Her report would always be that she had screwed X last night. I pointed out to her the semantics of the word, the concept of the recipient and donor of the act. What she was attempting to convey, however, was her inability to conceive of the penis belonging to the male, that in fact it was part of her which she was using on him. This seems to relate to Spitz's concept (1955), the primal cavity. This patient could have no image of her vagina being a space or cavity which could receive an object, the penis; moreover, the penis was somehow fused into her without any interface between it and the walls of her vagina. She referred again to her broken affair. "I couldn't believe X could leave me because he was part of me. That was why I couldn't get angry with him. That would be to recognize him as a separate person. I can never think with my parents, whether they had me or I had them." I pointed out her coming to treat me. "Well," she said, "I think I had my mother, but you are giving me help. When I am on this couch I can never be sure which way gravity is." I interpreted this to her as whether she was dependent on me for treatment or I was dependent on her for treatment. Later she added, "It's so much easier to talk to you in the abstract," that is, in her mind, "than in the concrete." She found it easier to talk to me in her mind when she was not at a session. She related a dream that contained many secrets she could not remember. "I am not having a relationship here: I am just telling you lots of things."

This brought up the idea, which I put to her, that the most important of her relationships was her fantasy of me. Patients resort to such fantasies in moments of stress just as a child often grasps his or her transitional object at stressful periods. It is particularly common on a Monday or after a longer holiday break. One patient, referring to me, says that on Monday "I have Mondayitis, I am not myself, I am unable to work or say something of relevance." It turns out, however, that over the weekend she constructs a fantasy of me which she relates to, but on Monday she is faced with me in reality and the difficulty of equating the real me and all my failings with the fantasy me. Another patient says he would like my consulting room left open when I am away on holiday so he can keep on coming to the sessions; that is, he can keep on relating to his fantasy of me. This appears to be an intermediate step between monologue and dialogue, perhaps corresponding to some kind of internal, fantasied, transitional object such as an imaginary companion. This step seems always present. Another patient reported she had a fantasy relationship with me: the real one was unimportant. In this fantasy she would follow rules imposed on her by the fantasy me. She related all this to me in the sessions. Only after a long period of my interpreting the difference between her fantasy me and the real me did she begin to relate to me, relinquishing the internal fantasy me as being of less importance. As with the transitional object, however, she often harked back to this experience of being able to have these fantasies and remembered it in a fond and treasured way. Flaubert, in his novel *Madame Bovary,* instances this experience in Emma Bovary's life. He has her hunting a fantasy experience which can never be found in reality: "She was in love with Leon; and she sought solitude that she might revel in his image undisturbed. It marred the pleasure of her daydreams to see him in the flesh. The sound of his step set her trembling. In his presence her agitation subsided, leaving nothing but an immense astonishment that worked itself out in sadness" (p. 120).

The next step with Miss A was her appearing one day saying she was in financial difficulty; she would have to drop one session. Would I please tell her which one would be convenient? I said I wouldn't consider that but would adjust the fees downward to what she could afford. She was confused and perplexed. She had made up in her mind everything I would say, and I had not said it. She needed time to think. She agreed, after some sessions, to accept my offer, then stated she felt she could no longer regard me as a cardboard-cutout figure but would have to recognize me as a flesh and blood man. At this point, her analysis became alive, both for her and me. That is, she was able to take due cognizarce of the fact that she and I were not fused, that I was not simply an extra sense organ for her or her robot but that in actuality, I was a real person whom she had to relate to on this basis. I, for my part, felt her analysis came alive because I no longer felt or was treated by her as her robot.

Therapeutic implications for patients functioning in this phase are that all interpretations must be aimed at showing the patient the lack of separateness between himself and the therapist. Interpretation of anxieties, conflicts, etc., are politely listened to, but as the therapist and patient are fused, the patient simply regards them as part of him or herself and ignores them. Analysis of this sort can go on for years as the patient dutifully acts the part for the industrious analyst. There can be no ending to something that has never had a beginning, a point clearly explained by Winnicott (1960) in his paper "Ego Distortion in Terms of True and False Self."

DIALOGUE

The Shorter Oxford Dictionary defines dialogue as "a conversation between two or more persons, a colloquy, a talking together." It is my contention that a second way of using the analytical relationship is via dialogue and that this corresponds to the later phase in the development of the ego in which separateness has occurred between the mother and the child, but where the infantile ego has omnipotent control over the outside world. This phase being, as Winnicott (1971) described it, relating to the object though the object as yet is not conceived as having a separate life of its own. Rickman details this in two-person psychology:

We enter the psychological region of reciprocal relationships. In this it differs from one-person psychology but is linked with some if not all of the other psychologies. It studies the relation existing when two persons are in a more or less closed region and are tied to one another by simultaneously acting aims, tasks or needs. The example of two-body psychology which has proved of outstanding utility in both theory and practice is the psycho-analyst and his patient in the analytic transference situation, which is in one sense a closed region devoted largely but not exclusively to the study of a-historical events observed in the 'here and now.' The two psychologists who laid the foundations of this research are of course Freud and Ferenczi. (The transference phenomena seen in statu nascendi though originating in the past are noted by both analyst and patient in the present, and the counter transference phenomena are reckoned with by the observing analyst and frequently noted by the observant patient.) The analytic situation also gives insight into another occurrence of two-persons psychology in the mother-child relationship, particularly in the stages of the nursing couple and the sphincter interests which they share and dispute. (1957, p. 219)

Where does the difference lie between monologue and dialogue? It lies, I believe, in that between the nursing infant who is as yet unaware of the separateness of its mouth and the nipple and who has not yet begun to explore its own internal space, that is, its mouth cavity (Spitz 1955) and the infant who has made that step and now commands the nipple via gaze and other omnipotent thinking, to give it milk. This seems to relate to how often patients in this particular phase need to look at the analyst and control him with their gaze.

Case 2

A male patient in his thirties, married with a family, and highly successful in a professional career came to analysis after a breakdown. His general practitioner rang me and asked if I could take on a patient in a few months. There were explicit restrictions on the time of appointments, frequency, and place of meeting, which by chance I could fulfill. I heard nothing for six months, then the general practitioner rang me to ask if I remembered the person he had spoken of. I replied I had. The practitioner then related that the patient had refused to come, feeling that he was coping, though his headaches and back pain continued. On the previous night, however, the patient had suddenly begun shouting on the phone. After crying uncontrollably for some hours, he was finally quieted with a tranquilizer; he then agreed to come and see me. When he arrived he appeared neatly and correctly dressed for his profession, quietly spoken and polite. The one note of incongruity in such a well-dressed person was that for almost the whole interview, until he noticed it himself, his fly was completely undone. He gave me his history with a sense of despair and puzzlement and we made arrangements to meet and discussed times, fees, etc. Therapy proceeded and his depression lifted enough after three months for him to go back to work, but there remained a sense of puzzlement in him about my role. After a couple of years, he could relate this to his puzzlement at the age of six about the role or need for parents.

There was a marked compliance in his attitude toward me. He said I was his professional adviser in this matter and he must take my advice to continue his therapy or not, as his clients would also take his advice on what to do. During the first two years he continually complained that he wanted to stop, the times were difficult, etc. I said eventually that I thought his wishes were the reverse, that he would like me seven days a week if necessary, and could I tolerate and fulfill that sort of demand? The thought had crossed his mind, he said: he supposed it had been something like that, and his complaints about coming ceased. The notable thing about him was the way he made me focus on him in what he was saying, and how he somehow denied me the use of free floating attention and reverie.

The countertransference feelings during this phase of analysis concern the analyst's being required to stick to manifest content. Where there is an attempt at latent content interpretation, it is immediately challenged by the patient as invalid. Behind everything with this patient lay an intense control: he reported that thoughts would go through his mind like machine-gun fire, that he would then sift them, selecting what he felt interesting and appropriate and rejecting the rest. He feared his own thoughts might run out of control and therefore had to control mine. When he evacuated to America as a child, there had been bouts of night screaming, and later there was sleep-walking, and of course finally his breakdown before coming to therapy. He always dreaded what I was thinking, and if I was silent for some time he became uneasy, stopped talking, and looked often at me.

The following is rather typical material. After his talking for some time (I want some reaction now. It's your turn to say something. Why don't you react?), I asked if I had to say something all the time. He replied, "Well, yes. I talk, but after a while I want your reaction to it all. I want a dialogue." Again, in another session: "Why don't you say something? I have thrown several lines for discussion and you haven't said anything. I want your reaction. I don't want to do all the talking here like some soapbox orator. I want a discussion." It is relevant in this patient's history that up to the age of two he was looked after by a nanny. From two to six he was in America and did not see his parents in this time. On his return he was put into a boarding school until eighteen. Perforce, some of his ego nuclei had a precocious development after dissociation from the main core. These nuclei acted the part of the person while inside were kept all his feelings, emotions, and sensations of aliveness. These, on the one hand, were felt as a wished-for ideal self, alive, cheerful, gay, able to relate, yet on the other hand they were felt as a threat to him, a threat to his sanity and the whole structure of his personality. To reiterate because of early intrusiveness his ego nuclei had dissociated—one nucleus acting the part of the self in its orientation to the external world and as caretaker to the rest of the nuclei. There was, however, also a wish to leave this compliance. Hence free association meant for him not just destruction, in Winnicott's (1971) terms, of the external object. Since his dissociated ego nuclei had been and were still his external controlling object or caretaker, their destruction meant destruction of his present self. This state related to his strong, compulsive, suicidal feelings and wishes to run away, abandon everything, and find a new experience, that is, to his inner core of realness. He asked at times if it was not a dialogue we were supposed to be having and what was supposed to occur. One one occasion I said I felt one aspect of him was talking to another aspect of himself, perhaps an ideal aspect, and thinking about the divergence between the ideal and the real.

The implications in this phase are that although the patient recognizes and is aware of the separateness of himself and the analyst, he must nevertheless maintain omnipotent control over the analyst. He does this typically by indulging in questions and answers or technical discussions about analysis or other subjects. The analyst, on his part, must focus on this aspect and show the patient his need to control himself and the analyst, and his fear of losing control and going to pieces, of losing reality testing, and his intense fear of emptiness, of the absence of a representational world. Free association is felt here as very threatening and out of control. The actual step from dialogue to soliloquy is, however, a difficult one, as it involves the infant's destructing the anaclitic object again, so that it is no longer under omnipotent control (Winnicott 1971), but is available for use. It is precisely this enactment of the transference relationship that allows the patient to progress from a two-body to a three-or-more body relationship. The analyst allows and survives the patient's aggressive murderous attacks and is still there for the patient to use and introject into his internal world.

SOLILOQUY

The Shorter Oxford Dictionary defines soliloquy as "an instance of talking to or conversing with self or of uttering one's thoughts aloud without addressing any person." Rickman expresses this idea in his concept of three-body relationships. ."Investigations in the seemingly closed two-person relationship, however, disclose that it is not in fact closed; though there are only two persons shut up in one room there is forced on the attention of both of them that some of the patient's behaviour can only be explained by the fact that he cannot consider himself alone with his analyst but as acting as if the analyst's wife (or husband) were in the closed region too" (1957, pp. 219-220).

Rickman feels that the third and more-body relationship is due to the oedipus complex; I, however, believe it due to the setting up of an internal world with internal objects. It would seem, in reference to Winnicott's (1971d) work, that when the personality matures from relating to the object to using the object, not only is the object recognized as separate from the personality but it becomes available to be introjected, not into various structures of the psyche (superego, ego and id), but as a whole to build up the internal world From this process, develops the ideal self, an amalgam often at variance with the self. In this respect, patients who function in therapy mainly at the level of monologue or dialogue present with intense feelings of emptiness: that is, introjection has taken place only into the id, ego, and superego, but has not been used to build up an internal world. This area of functioning and the importance of its development (introjection to build up an internal world) seems to be what Sandler et al. (1963) discuss as the concept of the representational world. This phase of therapy usage can appear in most patients, as there will usually be some development of ego nuclei to this stage. The frequency of appearance depends on this development, and as therapy proceeds and there is a greater development in this area then soliloquy becomes the usual rather than the rare. However, the ability to return to other modes of usage as a defense remains. In this phase, the patient reflects on the tension and distance between his real self and his ideal self, the underlying cause as Sandler et al. (1963) pointed out of his psychic pain. When a patient is in this phase, the noticeable development is a lack of demand on our attention in either a positive or negative way. Free floating attention and reverie can be indulged in to the benefit of the patient and the understanding of a latent meaning in the overt material. The patient speaks to his internal ideal self, yet simultaneously observing himself and allowing the analyst to join as part of the audience.

Case 3

A male patient, some years in analysis, treated me in the early phase with a sort of curious disdain, not being able to decide where I fitted in to the analysis. Shortly after starting, he had a psychotic breakdown but continued with his analysis. After some years, he would talk and then demand that I talk or contribute something. At present he can talk of what he would like to be. He has achieved professional qualifications which he has found very difficult to identify with or have any sense of fulfillment in. The following is typical: "I feel sort of vague. I have little energy. I just want to do many more things. I would like to play squash, take up other interests, make something of my life, enjoy myself, go out with people as other people do." He was talking here to his ideal self and reflecting on the distance between it and his real self with resulting depression and psychic pain.

In another session he again talked on the same theme, his wishes and past memories. He suddenly said "Ouch!" and put his hands to his head. I asked what was wrong. He said, "I have such pain. There is such a discrepancy between that ideal person and what I am." He often talks of how friends and colleagues seem to enjoy life, have girl friends, and he somehow can't, though he wishes he could. In this state he can tolerate my silence and allow me to contribute when I feel there is something worthwhile to say without feeling he must challenge my ideas or wonder where I got them. For example, I was away one day and he missed a session. The next session he talked of his work, how much easier it would be if people told him things they know. I said that in other words people were withholding things from him. Perhaps he feels I withheld my attention and affection from him by being away as his mother was. He grinned and laughed, saying I twist things, but it was sort of like that. At one time making a simple interpretation from such latent material and linking it to his past would have been immediately challenged by his saying he could see no evidence for such a statement and wondering where had I got the idea? In other words, he was unable to tolerate my separate functioning.

Dream 1

Perhaps the most illustrative example of internal change accompanying the change in external relationship is from dream material. The following are two dreams from two different patients. The first, in therapy for two years, spent most of this time on the theme of separateness. She saw her friends as extensions of herself, me included. She had no need to tell me anything because I was part of her: I knew everything any way. However, recently there has been a change; I am separate, although there are often quick defensive reversions to more primitive forms of functioning. The following is a dream which she produced:

The dream began in a large room at the top of a grand house. I was with X and in a panic because I wanted three chapters of a book which was in a room downstairs. For some reason I was frightened to go down, but X could, and fetched the book for me. Then the room became a consulting room and I was lying on the couch during a session. I looked around and realized there was a third person in the room. Sitting by the window was a leering, demonic figure who I knew was *your* analyst. It seemed clear to me that he was supervising the session. Then it became an ordinary session, but with the couch at the opposite end of the room. I was upset and couldn't talk, and looked around at you for reassurance and comfort. The person I saw was an older man, very formally dressed, who I took to be you. When I woke up it was some time for me to realize that it had not been you but Dr. A.

We did quite a lot of work on the dream and at the end of the session I asked if she could write down the dream and give it to me. I did this because of my own interest in the dream, that I told her of, and because I felt this an important dream for her. The following was the result of this request. She agreed, but after some time the dream was still not written down. She said it was because she would have to use the words *I* and *you* in writing, which she couldn't face. Eventually she produced the dream, adding her associations although I made no mention of it in my request to her. She had regarded herself as the analyst. The following are *her* associations:

My disturbance at X's affair, which I couldn't face. The book links with a psycho-analytical textbook, the first three chapters of which had to be read for a seminar. The supervisor connects with having supper with my old boss, who clearly disapproved of my analysis and I was irritated by being perceived as purely a professional person. The dream was after a weekend at home with the whole family, when I had felt the urge to shout sexual obscenities, feeling angry about seeing myself as shut off from normal relationship. Dr. A was the senior analyst I first consulted.

As I had recorded these associations, she said that she had been home for the weekend, and it had been awful. Her mother had cried continuously, especially when she had the patient on her own, saying she was going to commit suicide. She had thought her mother near a psychotic breakdown. She had dined on Friday night with her old boss. I interjected "supervisor" at this point as in the dream. She said she never talked to her old boss about her analysis. She knew the woman was very antagonistic toward analysis and regarded it as an evil. I interjected again and said, "As a demon in the dream." In interpreting the dream to her, I reminded her of having talked on Friday about X, who was having a wild affair, and about her envy of X and wish to be like her. Somehow in the dream, she was talking to a supervisor inside herself which she wished to be, but which felt like a demon. This was the wished-for aspect of herself, able to do the things she wants instead of presenting a front for other people. She said yes, she felt like that. She felt like swearing at her mother and telling her what she thought. Then she remarked, "You were like Dr. A I had somehow elevated you." I suggested that my elevation to the status of Dr. A was a self-elevation to her ideal self. I reminded her of frequent references to doubts about me, whether I was adequate for her, whether I was a good enough analyst; of her comparing herself with various friends whom she felt had much better analysts, much more capable, etc. With this patient there has been a progression through the two various phases and the intermediate step of a fantasied transitional object. She had become aware of an intense fear of losing control, with identity loss consequent on growing separateness from me—mother. During these phases, weekends had been treated by complete denial of the break. Some weeks prior to this particular dream, however, she had been able to say on a Friday that she knew I would be there on Monday. In other words, she had been able to internalize me to a degree as a real figure.

Dream 2

The next dream is from a patient in therapy for three years. Most of the time the work had been at the monologue phase, but recently this had changed to the step intermediate between monologue and dialogue and had progressed occasionally to the soliloquy phase. She related the following dream. As with the previous patient I asked her, after some work in the session, if she would write it down, again for the same reasons. As with the previous patient she also included her associations, although again I had made no specific request for it. She also behaved as though she were the analyst and I the patient.

Related about one week after dreaming. Somehow I had become acquainted with a monkey-person who was a humanoid. Clothes and body were indistinct, but he was about three feet high with a vividly detailed monkey-face in a human head. He lived in a room and couldn't go out, do things or get to know people in the outside world because he wouldn't have been accepted and no one knew his capabilities. I don't remember any other people in the dream, how I met him or what way I learned more about him. I don't recall any conversation or activities in the room, but as I got to know him better his body grew up into a man's body in normal clothes. The image of a monkey's face became vague. I felt more and more convinced that he was basically human in a general way, yet specifically in intelligence. I felt concerned that he couldn't go out or be accepted as a human but never tried to do anything about it. The dream stopped when I was awoken after a rest period.

Her added associations were:

1. Three years ago during a sudden breakdown I spontaneously drew the junior psychiatrist dealing with me, but added a monkey's face,

hands, feet, and tail. For some reason the sketch was important to me and I kept it, and months later made a joke about it, that I had made a monkey of him.

2. One year after that I went back to a psychiatrist for further help and a week after I made a few idle sketch marks which just turned into a hairy human/monkey, who, like the first, was also scrunched up and worried looking like I felt inside.

The first association was made after relating the dream to Dr. Eyre, and he commented on making a monkey out of him. The second was finding the second sketch when I was looking for the first sketch to show him.

The point to be made about both these patients is that when I interpreted their dreams on the lines that they represented a growing internal world and hence separateness from me, both became very angry and upset. They came back several sessions running and gave their own interpretations to these dreams which they felt disproved what I had said. My interpretations produced in both a state of anxiety concerning the threatened loss of me, that is, to become separate *versus* a wish to revert to the form of functioning in which I was under omnipotent control.

SUMMARY AND DISCUSSION

It is the hypothesis of this paper that psychoanalytic therapy may be seen along developmental lines correlative to early infantile development and the psychopathology of the patient. The phases are reenacted in the transference relationship and may be enumerated as follows:

- *Monologue or a one-body relationship.*   Separateness in a mother-child relationship has not occurred for a large number of ego nuclei. The patient is unaware of the presence of the analyst as a separate person and treats him as though he were fused with him. Interpretations of anxieties or conflicts which do not take due cognizance of this involve the analyst and patient in an endless analysis. For the patient this functions as a defensive fantasy (Winnicott 1971c).

- *Intermediate phase or the fantasied transitional object stage.*   The most important relationship for the patient is to the fantasy of the analyst. It is the stage between fusion and full separateness. Interpretations must be aimed at the discrepancy between the patient's fantasied patient relationship to the fantasied analyst and the analyst as he is.

- *Dialogue or two-body relationship.* Separateness has occurred but the infant retains omnipotent control over the mother-world. This is reenacted in the transference relationship as the patient attempts to do the same to the analyst. Interpretations must be aimed at this respect of the relationship. The underlying fear of loss of control involves aggression and murder, loss of identity, and a fear of emptiness.

- *Soliloquy or three-or-more body relationship.* An anaclitic object has been destroyed (Winnicott 1971d) and refound but without the child's having omnipotent control over it. It is available for introjection to build up the internal world. Hence other figures can also be introjected.

All phases are present in varying degrees in therapy, alternation occurring within a session or between sessions. Reversion to earlier phases are particularly noticeable after stress, for instance weekends or holiday breaks. The most common reversion is seemingly to the intermediate stage of a fantasied transitional object stage.

REFERENCES

Bick, E. (1968). The experience of the skin in early object relations. *International Journal of Psycho-Analysis* 49:484-486.

Flaubert, G. (1857). *Madame Bovary.* Trans. A. Russell.

Freud, S. (1905). Three essays on the theory of sexuality. *Standard Edition* 7:125-248.

——— (1930). Civilization and its discontents. *Standard Edition* 21:59-148.

Giovacchini, P. (1972). *Tactical Approaches: An Overview in Tactics and Techniques in Psycho-Analytic Therapy.* London: Hogarth.

Glover, E. (1968). *The Birth of the Ego.* New York: International Universities Press.

Klein, M. (1975). *Envy, Gratitude and Other Works 1946-1963.* London: Hogarth and the Institute of Psycho-Analysis.

Mahler, M. S. (1969). *On Human Symbiosis and the Vicissitude of Individuation.* London: Hogarth and the Institute of Psycho-Analysis.

Rickman, J. (1957). Number and the human sciences. In *Selected Contributions to Psycho-Analysis*, ed. C. M. Scott. London: Hogarth.

Sandler, J., Holder, A., and Meers, D. (1963). The ego ideal and the ideal self. *Psychoanalytic Study of the Child* 18:139-158.

Spitz, R. A. (1955). The primal cavity. *Psychoanalytic Study of the Child* 10:215-240.

——— (1965). *The First Year of Life.* New York: International Universities Press.

Winnicott, D. W. (1960). Ego distortion in terms of true and false self. In *The Maturation Processes and the Facilitating Environment.* London: Hogarth, 1965.

——— (1971). *Playing and Reality.* New York: Basic Books.

On Guntrip's Analysis with Fairbairn and Winnicott

HENRIETTE T. GLATZER, Ph.D.
and WILLIAM N. EVANS

Guntrip's paper is an account of his analytic experience, first with Fairbairn and then with Winnicott. Although attempting to be objective, he cannot disguise the fact that he is frustrated and dissatisfied. He raises this question: "How complete a result does psychoanalytic therapy achieve?" The question Guntrip is, in effect, asking himself, is: "What went wrong?" We suggest the following points: The failure of both analysts to recognize a very specific form of resistance and to deal with an unusual transference situation. Fairbairn's insistence on giving oedipal interpretation to a patient who, as Winnicott recognized, did not have an oedipus complex. The failure of both analysts to recognize Guntrip's infantile megalomania; to expose his insistence that the blame for his neurosis must be attached to a "totally" bad mother; and the failure to recognize the intensity of his sibling rivalry. Psychoanalytic therapy is not merely "correct" interpretation and "correct" technique. It involves the interaction of two human beings. The countertransference of Fairbairn and Winnicott prevented their perceiving and dealing with the essential problem of this exceptionally gifted patient.

Guntrip sought analysis with Fairbairn in 1949 with a specific purpose, to break through a total amnesia for a severe trauma at the age of three and a half, related to the death of his younger brother, Percy: "There, I felt, lay the cause of my vague background experiences of schizoid isolation and unreality." His mother had told him that at the age of three and a half he had walked into a room and seen his brother, Percy, naked and dead on her lap. "I reached up and grabbed him and said, 'Don't let him go. You'll never get him back.' She sent me out of the room and I fell mysteriously ill and was thought to be dying." All memory of this event was completely repressed. If, Guntrip believed, this trauma could be broken through, then the true nature of his earliest relationship with his mother could be examined. Both analysts, Guntrip wrote, *"failed to resolve my amnesia for that trauma"* (1975, p. 146; Guntrip's italics).[1]

Prior to beginning his training analysis with Fairbairn, according to Guntrip, he was "psychoanalytically knowledgeable." He had studied under Flugel and was well versed in the literature. He had studied his dreams for two years, and had psychiatric experience as a staff member of a medical school. What is more, he had published his views on psychotherapy. Here was a highly sophisticated analysand. He deliberately chose Fairbairn as his analyst "because we stood philosophically on the same ground and no actual disagreements would interfere with the analysis."

One of the precipitating factors that drove him into analysis was his "mysterious exhausting illness." As a student, at the age of twenty-six, he formed a friendship with a fellow student "who was a brother figure to me." When his brother figure left college, Guntrip fell ill of the same mysterious exhaustion illness. Many years later this friend from his student days suddenly died and again Guntrip was seized by the same illness.

His mother revealed many confidences to him in his teens—for example, that she had breast-fed him because it would prevent another pregnancy. After Percy's death, she refused any further intimacy with her husband. All that she divulged seemed to confirm his image of the bad mother. She had refused to breast-feed Percy and he had died, and Guntrip's father attributed Percy's death to this refusal. In her guilt-ridden old age, she would say that she would never have had children as she did not understand, and could not be bothered with, them. As an aged widow—she told Guntrip—she had tried keeping a dog but could not stop beating him. "No wonder," Guntrip concludes, "I had an inner world of internalized, libidinally excited object relations."

It is our surmise that she probably meant every word. Consider the facts of her life as given by Guntrip. He described her as an overburdened "little mother" before she married, the eldest daughter of eleven children who had seen four siblings die. Mrs. Guntrip's mother was described as "a feather-brained beauty queen" who left her daughter to manage the household even as a schoolgirl. The daughter ran away from home at the age of twelve because she was unhappy, but she was brought back. Her main characteristic was a strong sense of duty and responsibility to her widowed mother and three younger siblings. These characteristics had impressed Guntrip's father so much that he proposed marriage, not realizing "that she had had her fill of mothering babies and did not want any more." On an intellectual level, then, Guntrip understood his mother's reluctance to have more children, but on an emotional level he exploited these confessions to demonstrate that his mother was not just a failure, but a "total" failure and a murderess as well.

Guntrip saw his father in a supporting role in his fight against his aggressive mother. "In all my years of dreaming he never appeared as other than a supportive figure *vis-a-vis* mother, and in actual fact she *never* lost her temper in his presence." (Guntrip's italics). On the whole he was a minor character in the drama. The arena was occupied by two contestants, Guntrip and his mother.

The first seven years of his life were very disturbed, he tells us. His mother suddenly weaned him and began a business of her own, and Guntrip was left to the care of an invalid aunt who lived with them. After the death of Percy and Guntrip's first illness, he was sent to a maternal aunt to recuperate. Both his analysts believed that he would have died had he not been sent away from his mother. No evidence was supplied for this conclusion. All memories had been repressed. The statements were based on the evidence of the sole witness: a guilt-laden mother.

Returning home at the age of three and a half, he spent the next year and a half waging an incessant battle, trying, as he puts it, "to coerce mother into mothering me by repeated petty psychosomatic ills, tummy-aches, heat spots, loss of appetite, constipation and dramatic, sudden high temperatures." His mother told him that the family doctor had said: "I'll never come to that child again. He frightens the life out of me with these sudden high temperatures and next morning he's perfectly well."

On moving to a larger school, when he was five, he changed tactics. His mother told him: "You began not to do what I told you." She flew into violent rages and beat him. When canes were broken he was sent out to replenish the supply. At seven he moved to a larger school and steadily developed interests of his own. At eight his mother, having known years of financial failure, was suddenly successful. She became less depressed and gave him all the money he needed. "Gradually I forgot not quite all the memories of the first seven years."

It was with this period of his life that Fairbairn's analysis dealt. "His broadly oedipal analysis of my internalized bad-object relations did correspond to an actual period of my childhood." But doubts about Fairbairn's analysis began to creep in. He "became convinced that this was keeping me marking time in a sadomasochistic inner world of *bad-object relations* with mother, as a defense against quite different problems of the period before Percy's death."

The third illness in 1957, following the death of this old college friend, now became the focal point of his analysis and just as some progress was being made, Fairbairn suddenly fell ill and nearly died. When he returned to work in 1959, he made a crucial interpretation, which we will comment on later. After that interpretation Guntrip started to phase out his analysis with Fairbairn and in 1952 began treatment with Winnicott, continuing until Winnicott died in 1968.

The Nature of the Resistance

To give an account of one's own analysis is a particularly difficult task, for large tracts of it fade from memory. The outstanding impression which remains is the impact of the analyst. But to ask for complete objectivity as well—particularly about subtleties of the transference—would mean standing right outside the analytic situation. And if that were done, it would no longer be analysis. Instead of being an ally in the therapeutic task, one would become an observer, necessarily disassociated from the therapeutic process: one cannot sit with the audience and be on stage at the same time.

How did Guntrip do it? The answer: he kept detailed records of every session with both his analysts. This is an unusual procedure and what is remarkable is that neither analyst recognized this as part of his resistance. Normally, analytic interpretations are assimilated and become part of one's being, and this is not altogether a conscious process. But if they are stored away in paper archives to be scrutinized at leisure, one has, in effect, disinvolved oneself from the analytic treatment. Winnicott commented that the written records constituted a link with the analyst. We contend that the written records constituted what Langs (1975a) aptly calls a *therapeutic misalliance*; by keeping the diary, he prevented the material being analyzed.

This unusual practice accounts, we believe, for the detachment that characterized Guntrip's account of his case history. For example, in describing his prolonged battle with his mother, he reported in this oblique way: "My mother told me, 'You began not to do what I told you.'" A child of five to seven conducting open warfare with his mother is old enough to have memories of his own and should not have to rely on hearsay. This period of his life was not adequately worked through in his analysis, for had it been, it would have evoked memories and, as a result, we would have a first-hand account. That is the reason, we believe, that in place of recollection, we have a reenactment of his quarrels with his mother in his relationship with Fairbairn. If, as Guntrip claimed, Fairbairn had really resolved the negative transference to his dominating mother, we would not have these records of theoretical altercation between analyst and patient in which the disputatious Guntrip always seeks to prove that he is right.

Here we come to the specific nature of Guntrip's resistance. In a perceptive paper, which in many ways anticipates the findings of Kohut (1971) and Kernberg (1975), Abraham described a particular form of narcissistic resistance which "has received little consideration in our literature, like so many questions of technique. . . . There are certain patients," he said, "who show a never-wearying readiness to be psychoanalyzed" but, he went on, this eagerness is nothing more than a pretended compliance, for analysis is an attack on their narcissism. They may differ in symptomatology, nevertheless, in their attitude to the psychoanalyst and to psychoanalysis "they all produced a certain number of characteristics with astonishing regularity. They expect from analysis interesting contributions to the autobiography they are writing. . . . They instruct the physician by giving him their opinion of their neurosis, which they consider a particularly interesting one, and they imagine that science will be especially enriched by their analysis." The result, said Abraham, "is that these narcissistic patients abandon the position of patient and lose sight of the purpose of their analysis" (1919, p. 304). Guntrip instructed his analysts in what they had to uncover, namely his trauma. And, both did his biding. He thus attempted, we would add, to establish a therapeutic misalliance (Langs 1975a). Guntrip's avowed motive in publishing the records of his sessions was the hope that they "may have both a theoretical and a human interest."

Another characteristic of these narcissistic patients, Abraham continued, is "that they are adept in turning analysis into a discussion with the analyst as to who is right" (1919, p. 307). Guntrip constantly suggested such opposition: "Fairbairn held that——" "My own view is——" He was critical of Fairbairn's *intellectually precise interpretations....* " I developed a double resistance to him consciously, partly feeling he was my bad mother forcing her views on me, and partly openly disagreeing with him on genuine grounds. I began to insist that my real problem . . . was mother's basic 'failure to relate at all' right from the start. But Fairbairn repeatedly brought me back to oedipal three-person libidinal and antilibidinal conflicts in my 'inner world,' Kleinian object splits and Fairbairnian ego splits." The academic debate between the two went on. Guntrip concluded that his analysis with Fairbairn was not a waste of time despite the fact that Fairbairn was "certainly wrong" in his diagnosis of Guntrip's psychopathology.

It follows that if such narcissistic patients feel they are better than their analyst there is obviously only one person who can conduct their analysis—themselves. They call it "auto-analysis," says Abraham and it "contains an obvious depreciation of the physician's powers. . . . They want to do everything by themselves." In fact, he went on to say, the analyst is a "hindrance" and "they are exceedingly proud of what they imagine they have achieved without his assistance" (1919, p. 307). This is an apt description of Guntrip. During Fairbairn's illness he conducted his own analysis. "Insights kept welling up at all sorts of times, and I jotted them down as they flowed with compelling intensity." These insights formed the basis of three papers which were elaborated into a book *Schizoid Phenomena, Object Relations and the Self.* "In two years they took me right beyond Fairbairn's halting point." Shortly before writing the account of his case history, Guntrip restudied the records of his analyses. "I was intrigued to see the light they cast on why my two analyses failed to resolve my amnesia for that trauma at three-

and-a-half, and yet each in different ways prepared for its resolution as a post-analytic development."

In the contest between himself and Fairbairn, Guntrip wrung concession after concession, until finally Fairbairn, in effect, conceded victory: "At last he began to accept in theory what he no longer had the health to cope with in practice. He generously accepted my concept of 'a regressed ego' split off from his 'libidinal ego.' " When Guntrip published this concept, Fairbairn wrote: "This is your idea not mine, original, and it explains what I have never been able to account for in my theory. Your emphasis on ego-weakness yields better therapeutic results than mine." In 1960, when Guntrip wrote a paper on this topic, Fairbairn wrote: "If I could write now, that is what I would write about." Guntrip concluded: "I knew my theory was broadly right for it conceptualized what I could not get analyzed. With great courage he [Fairbairn] accepted that."

Before Guntrip heard of Fairbairn he had written a book in which he stated that psychoanalytic theory "is not a purely theoretical but a truly personal relationship." Later, on reading the works of Fairbairn and realizing that his views were similar to his own, he chose Fairbairn as his analyst. But, very soon, he was complaining that Fairbairn did not have the capacity for natural "personal relations," precisely the complaint he had leveled against his mother: she could not "relate" to him. After the sessions Fairbairn and Guntrip discussed psychoanalytic theory "and I found the human Fairbairn as we talked face to face. Realistically, he was my understanding good father after sessions."

With Winnicott, the rivalry did not surface, but every so often we find Guntrip in the role of supervising analyst, carefully scrutinizing Winnicott's interpretations to make sure that they conformed to Guntrip's object relations theory. During the second session with Winnicott, speaking of Percy's death, Winnicott commented, "You accepted Percy as your infant self that needed looking after. When he died, you had nothing and collapsed." Guntrip was full of commendation: "That was a perfect object relationship interpretation, but from Winnicott not Fairbairn."

At one time Winnicott nearly failed the test. He wanted—and we think rightly—to get at Guntrip's infantile aggression, the baby's ruthlessness. But his patient thoroughly disapproved. Guntrip said, "This was Freud and Kleinian instinct theory, innate aggression." The implication was that Winnicott was back-sliding, for he "knew that Winnicott had moved far beyond Freud when I met him." At this point a comment is relevant. The theoretical discussions which Fairbairn held with Guntrip after the analytic discussions constituted what Langs has called a deviation in technique: "The therapist establishes and maintains the ground rules and boundaries of the therapeutic setting," and the manner in which the analyst lays down those ground rules "contributes to the nature of the analytic 'field' or 'screen'—the person with whom the patient interacts and onto whom he projects his intrapsychic fantasies." If there are deviations then "changes in the therapist's stance are essential to correct the detrimental consequences of such deviation and, further, it may prove virtually impossible to alter certain effects on the patient through any means" (1975b, p. 107).

After Fairbairn's return to work and the death of Guntrip's friend, Fairbairn made the crucial interpretation to which we have already referred: "I think since my illness I am no longer your good father or your bad mother, but your brother Percy, dying on you." Guntrip now suddenly saw the analytic situation "in an extraordinary light." He wrote Fairbairn a letter which he did not send. "I suddenly saw that I could never solve my problem *with* an analyst." He wrote: "I am in a dilemma. I have got to end my analysis to get a chance to finish it, but then I do not have you to help me with it." Here one sees first the omnipotent fantasy and then reality breaking in. Guntrip explained his dilemma thus: "Once Fairbairn had become my brother in transference *losing him* either by ending analysis myself or by staying with him till he died, would represent the death of Percy, and I would be left with a full scale eruption of that traumatic event, and no one to help me with it." One is left with the impression that Guntrip had this grandiose fantasy: the only person who could fully analyze Guntrip was Guntrip. Hence, the high importance of the recorded sessions. Guntrip had set his analysts a problem. Neither solved it. It was solved by the patient. On the night that Winnicott died, Guntrip began a series of dreams which continued night after night taking him back in chronological order right back through his life, till finally he sees his brother Percy "on the lap of a mother with no face, arms or breasts." He had lifted the amnesia by himself.

If we are correct in our assumption, then the omnipotent illusion could be worded thus: I do not need a mother to feed me. I have my own breast and can feed myself. Not only did Guntrip have the trauma of Percy's death and along with it the fantasy that his mother was a murderess, there was also a much earlier one—namely, giving up the irrational fantasy of megalomania when the infant is forced to adapt to reality. This, too, could have accounted for his "schizoid isolation and sense of unreality."

The Concept of the Bad Mother

What is outside is bad (Evans 1972, p. 185). This could be regarded as a terse summary of Freud's statements on the most primitive phase of human development in which the ego is disengaging itself from the external world (1930). "A tendency arises to separate from the ego everything that can be a source of unpleasure, to throw it outside and to create a pure pleasure-ego which is confronted by a strange and threatening outside" (1920, p. 67). In an earlier statement he phrased it thus: "The ego-subject coincides with pleasure and the external world with unpleasure" (1915a, p. 136). Ten years later in his paper *Negation* he gave this pellucid summing up: "At the very beginning, it seems, the external world, objects and what is hated are identical" (1925, p. 237). This antithesis Freud regarded as sovereign, and as creating for research "the basic situation which no efforts can alter" (1915a, p. 134).

From that major premise it follows that there can be no such thing as primary love. On this point Freud was emphatic: "Hate as a relation to objects is older than love" (1915a, p. 139). He then proceeded to explain why: it derives from the primitive ego's reactive rage to the deluge of the "out-pouring stimuli" from the external world after birth. In speaking of the ego's reaction to the outside Freud used such phrases as throwing outside and thrusting forth. Let us remind ourselves that an object is, literally, something that is thrust or thrown in one's way. Jacobson put it this way: "We remember that at first the child wants to take in what he likes and to spit out what he dislikes; to ascribe to his self what is pleasant and to the 'strange' outside object what is unpleasant. In other words, he tends to turn aggression toward the frustrating objects and libido toward the self" (1964, p. 56).

It may well be that the simplicity of this dichotomy has been obscured by the fact that Freud's statements about it were embedded in his disquisitions on such concepts as the constancy principle and later the death instinct and the Nirvana principle. But in his paper, *Formulations on the Two Principles of Mental Functioning* (1911), in which he first elaborated this theme, the darkness of this previous piece of intellectual shorthand, "ego-non-ego (external), i.e., subject-object" (1915a, p. 134) was illuminated by two examples of a situation in which the pleasure principle reigns supreme and the reality of the external world is excluded. These, curiously enough, were tucked away in a lengthy footnote (1911, p. 219).

The first is the nursing situation, assuming it is a good one. Freud did not say, however, that it is the prototype of a "physical situation which was the slave of the pleasure-principle: it is an approximation." His train of thought then becomes clearer. He gave a "neat example," as he called it, "of a psychical system shut off from the stimuli of the external world and . . . able to satisfy its nutritional requirements autistically." The example he gave was "a bird's egg with its food supply enclosed in its shell." All the mother has to provide is warmth. Freud then went on to say that a system living according to the pleasure principle "must have devices to enable it to withdraw from the stimuli of reality." These devices he called the "correlative of repression which treats internal, unpleasurable stimuli as if they were external" (1911, pp. 219-220). The prototype of the pleasure-principle is to be found in this self-contained existence where no stimuli from the outside can impinge.

Ferenczi, in his paper "Stages in the Development of the Sense of Reality," published two years later, seized on the implications of this "neat example." There *is*, he said in effect, a stage in human development that completely achieves a subservience to the pleasure-principle, not approximately, "but in actual fact and completely. . . . I mean," he went to say, "the period of life spent in the womb." At such a stage an "outer world" exists only in a very restricted degree. Compared with a foetus, "an intestinal worm has a good deal of work to perform in order," and here he referred to the reality principle, "to change the outer world in order to maintain itself." He contended: "If the human being possesses a mental life when in the womb, although only an unconscious one, . . . he must get from his experience the impression that he is in fact omnipotent." For what is omnipotence? "The feeling that one has all that one wants and that one has nothing left to wish for" (1951, pp. 218, 219). If one listens carefully to Ferenczi, he is not saying that omnipotence is having all one's needs met. It is much more. It is a state in which one does not *even need to need*. It is self-sufficiency.

A capital difficulty confronts us when we use sophisticated adult language to try and portray preverbal experience which, in its intensity, no speech nor language can convey. The inventiveness of creative genius can only hint at these "intimations of immortality." Ferenczi used the terms *infantile megalomania* and *omnipotence*; others speak of *narcissism* and *grandiosity*. *Self-sufficiency* is another term. But—and this was Ferenczi's conclusion— this state of primordial bliss, by whatever name it goes, is "at least . . . no empty delusion. . . . It is a state that once existed" (1951, p. 219). There can be no return.

And yet, Ferenczi said, this is exactly what the newborn wishes—to regain this state of "wishless tranquility" (p. 220). Nurses instinctively recognize this by providing an environment that resembles as closely as possible the one he has left. And the better the environment the greater the illusion, namely, that he is the magical provider of all his needs. As Freud put it, "To begin with the child does not distinguish between the breast and his own body. . . . The breast," he went on to say, "has to be separated from the body and shifted to the *'outside'* because the child so often finds it absent" (1931, p. 188; Freud's italics). The fiction of self-sufficiency, that the infant possesses the mother's breast, constitutes the first denial.

According to this argument, then, reality is always intrusive in that it intrudes into and disrupts the illusion of self-sufficiency. The clear implication of this first stage, the period of unconditional omnipotence, is that growing up is painful quite apart from the nature of the environment, as every adaptation to reality requires a gradual eschewing of self-sufficiency.[2] He has to recognize that he is dependent on a power outside himself that comes when it wants. "The outstretched hand must often be drawn back empty" (Ferenczi 1951, p.

226). In short, the first piece of reality the child has to learn is that one and one make two, and not one. And unless he gets that sum right he will never get anything right. The reason why mourning is a burden so grievous to bear is that one has to learn that one from two equals one. And if one found it hard to add, it becomes all the harder to substract. In discussing the first three subphases of the separation-individuation process, Mahler (1972) said, " 'Growing up' entails a gradual growing away from the normal state of human symbiosis, of 'one-ness with the mother.' This growing-away process is ... a life-long mourning process. *Inherent in every step of independent functioning is a minimal threat of object loss*" (1972, p. 333, Mahler's italics). And of the third phase she said, "The junior toddler gradually realizes that his love objects ... are separate individuals with their own individual interests. He must gradually and painfully give up his delusion of his own grandeur" (p. 338).

To sum up, the unconscious fiction of the frustrating outside is ineluctable and universal. It is the inevitable consequence of being born. Now the cardinal importance of Ferenczi's contribution is this: The reactive rage of the child to not being fed is not due merely to the fact that he is hungry; he is more likely to be depressed. The main cause of his anger is that his illusion of self-sufficiency is constantly being shattered. This then is the source of the rage which, inevitably, is projected on to the outside.

At the time Ferenczi wrote his paper, Freud had not developed his theory of an independent aggressive drive; as a result, Ferenczi underestimated the intensity of the infant's primal rage, which because of its physical helplessness and its lack of reasoning power, is projected. The recipient of these first projections will be the mother, for she is the representative of the outside. Anna Freud expressed a similar opinion. "The mother is merely the representative symbol of inevitable frustration in the oral stage, just as the father in the oedipal phase is the representative of inevitable phallic frustration which gives him his symbolic role of castrator. The new concept of the rejecting mother has to be understood in the same sense as the familiar older concept of the castrating father. . . . Even a most devoted mother finds it a difficult task to fulfill her infant's needs" (1954, p. 321).

The unconscious image of the mother that is formed in this early preoedipal period is of an all-powerful being who can give and take away and later prohibit and punish. In the triangular relationship of the Oedipus complex, rivalry is above all the hallmark. At this stage of development the father is now the dangerous all-powerful being. But the lineaments that his image bears are those that belonged to that of the preoedipal mother. The all-powerful father is but an ectype of which the preoedipal mother is the archetype. This stage of development is characterized by what Brunswick (1940) called the second great antithesis—phallic/castrated; here the image of the mother is passive and weak. In discussing the change from the preoedipal to the oedipal stage, Brunswick asserted that the boy, unlike the girl, makes no change of object. To be sure, the reality of the mother remains the same, but the image changes. "For whether the oedipal mother be regarded as sensual or tender—the things she is not are cruel and dangerous. These characteristics apply to the image of the mother which is formed in the very earliest stage of development" (Evans 1972, p. 83). From the moment the child is born the preoedipal mother is open to at least two reproaches. As she is the all-powerful giver she can by the same token be the great withholder for the simple reason, as Freud pointed out, that "Childhood love is boundless, it demands exclusive possession, it is not content with less than all" (1931, p. 231). It is fated, therefore, to be disappointed. Second, she will receive further calumnies when she has to train, discipline, and prohibit. Neurotically, the child will see every injunction as an imposition. Freud even went so far as to see the "germ of paranoia in the manifold restrictions which the physical care of the child necessitates (Freud 1931, p. 227). It is at moments of high conflict, when the child pits the whole of his forces against the maternal authority, that one sees the image of the bad mother in pure culture, as it were. If, in reality, the mother is loving and kind, it becomes increasingly difficult for the child to project the image of the bad mother on to her, and his position becomes increasingly untenable. When confronted with reality his guilt will intensify, resulting either in a change of behavior or an intensification of neurotic defenses. If the mother is in reality cruel and unreasonable she will tend to confirm the unconscious fantasies. But, however malevolent reality may be, it can never equal the fantasy images of the unconscious—compared with which, as Guntrip's teacher Flugel pointed out, "the parents' real tendencies to express anger or impatience sink into insignificance" (1945, p. 114). This distinction Guntrip never became aware of—namely, that between the unconscious image and the reality. To him the concept of the bad mother was not a fantasy, it was a living reality.

The Case History

For the first two and a half years of his life, Guntrip was an only child. Then his place as the object of his mother's care was usurped by the arrival of Percy. During this early preoedipal phase the relationship between child and mother is one of the utmost intensity. The omnipotent, infantile fantasy could be worded thus: "I must have mother all to myself alone. There must be neither brother nor sister, not even a father; just the two of us existing in a beatific symbiosis" (Evans 1975, p. 492). Hence, the inevitability of death wishes against younger siblings.

When Guntrip was three and a half, his brother Percy died. Guntrip could not tell us anything about his reactions, as they were completely repressed. It is hard to believe that in these two analyses the topic of sibling rivalry was not touched upon, for there was no shortage of evidence. Although he was able to see that Fairbairn was often his bad mother in the transference setting, he never saw him as a sibling rival. At the moment when Fairbairn made his "crucial interpretation," Guntrip decided to phase out of his treatment because in Fairbairn's frail state of health he could not have stood the full scale eruption of that traumatic event in the transference. We suggest that this was a complete rationalization. It was Guntrip who could not stand the eruption of the truth that it was he, Guntrip, who had wished the death of Percy; for then his mother would have been exonerated. When Guntrip's colleague left for the war, possibly to be killed, Guntrip fell suddenly ill with the same "exhaustion illness." He dreamt he saw a man in a tomb buried alive. The man tried to escape. "But I threatened him with illness, locked him up and got away quick." Next day he was better. Guntrip never realized that the dream was a confession and that his mysterious illness was a talion punishment. It is also possible that the man who fled could have been Guntrip himself fleeing from the death-trap of his analysis. During his auto-analysis prior to going to Fairbairn he recalled a "mysterious death-threat dream" which followed a visit at the age of six to visit his aunt who was thought to be dying. An invisible band of ectoplasm was tying him to a dying invalid. He knew that he would be absorbed into her. He fought and suddenly the band snapped "and I knew I was free."

As we see it, since Guntrip could not admit his unconscious wish to kill Percy—hence the intensity of the amnesia—he counter-attacked, marshalling the evidence to prove that his mother was the killer, "this woman who could not stand me as a live baby." This was another way of saying she wished him dead. In the dream series that followed Winnicott's death there was one dream in which his mother was portrayed as staring fixedly into space ignoring Guntrip and his brother Percy who was about a year old. She was not a woman but a grotesque monstrosity. He had lifted the amnesia and what is more he claims to have found the mother who existed before Percy died, the mother who not only failed to relate to him, but a "faceless" being "who totally failed to relate to both of us." He had proof in these dreams that his mother was completely bad. If his mother had not kept Percy alive, then he would suffer the same fate. This, he believed, was what caused him to collapse at the age of three and a half.

During his auto-analysis, prior to his analysis with Fairbairn, he dreamt of a savage woman attacking him, of a quiet friendly father supporting him, and of mysterious death threats. In 1970 he was told that he was overworked and that if he did not retire "nature would make me." He developed pneumonia and spent five weeks in the hospital. The consultant said: "Relax, you're too overactive." He had never linked the idea of "retirement" with the deep fear of losing his battle with the mother who wished "to crush his active self." But then he did. The image of the murderess pursued him to his dying day. After the death of Percy, Guntrip waged an unrelenting war on his mother, first with psychosomatic illness and then in open rebellion. The ostensible reason was to make his mother capitulate and relate to him. She did not, and young Guntrip withdrew his forces and the conflict was internalized. In the campaign that he waged against his mother, the father, whom Guntrip saw as supportive, was unwittingly an ally. In one revealing dream, he was being "besieged" by his mother and he said to his father, "You know I'll never give in to her. It doesn't matter what happens, I'll never surrender." His father agreed, "I'll go and tell her." He went and said to her, "You'd better give it up. You'll never make him submit." She then gave up. Here is an excellent picture of embattled omnipotence in which the child pits the whole of his psychic resources against the environment in an attempt to make it do his bidding. Consideration of this factor of omnipotence is completely missing in both analyses and according to Guntrip's version, there was no consideration of the fact that Guntrip might have provoked these beatings from his easily provoked mother. He portrayed himself as the innocent victim of unprovoked aggression.

In a criticism of Kohut, who had implicitly blamed a patient's mother for evoking her daughter's rage, Kernberg pointed out (and we think rightly) that by making such an interpretation "he was protecting the patient from a full examination of the complex origins of her own rage" (1975, p. 299). That identical criticism could be leveled against both of Guntrip's analysts.

Winnicott made an indelible impression on Guntrip. "He became a good breast mother to my infant self in my deep unconscious at the point where my actual mother had lost her maternalism and could not stand me as a baby any more." Guntrip has arrived home: "Here at last I found a mother who could value her child." It would seem that Winnicott was saying, As your mother deprived you so completely of love I will give you that love by being your good mother. Kohut comes very near agreeing to this role of the analyst: "Where a patient has not received the necessary approval from a depressive mother, the analyst must provide this approval as a 'corrective emotional experience'" (1971, p. 290). He qualifies this statement by saying this reluctant compliance with a childhood wish is not the true analytic aim, but mastery based on insight.

It is our view that it is not the function of an analyst to play the part of good mother, but rather to initiate and maintain a therapeutic alliance. Unless that alliance is maintained it is not possible to analyze *all* the images that are projected on to him, including the image of a good mother. The use of the words *good* and *bad* in psychoanalytic language is imprecise. In reality, of course, there are good and bad mothers, but in speaking of the unconscious image of good and bad, we mean one who is infinitely good and infinitely bad. Kernberg, for example, in speaking of the splitting activity pointed out that the external objects are divided into "all good" ones and "all bad" ones (1975, p. 29).

In this connection Strachey, devised the term *mutative interpretation*. How is one to break the "neurotic vicious circle," by which he meant the constant projection of archaic images onto the outside world? He pointed out that the analyst will inevitably have these archaic images projected onto him. The gradual distinction between the analyst as a fantasy object and a real figure is the work of the mutative interpretation "and it consists in a repeated process of introjections of imagos of the analyst—imagos that is to say of a real figure and not of an archaic and distorted projection" (1969, p. 290). Strachey was not denying the effectiveness of extratransference interpretations, but saying they are just "feeders" for the transference situation and so pave the way for the mutative interpretations whereby the inner world of dangerous images can be changed. If the images of the bad mother are seen as infantile projections, what is revealed is the mother as she is in reality with all her inevitable limitations as a human being. It may well be that because Guntrip saw his mother as totally bad, he saw Winnicott as infinitely good.

Guntrip had one hundred and fifty sessions with Winnicott. "But their value," he said, "was out of all proportion to their number." One reason why we believe Winnicott's analysis of Guntrip was more effective was that he intuitively saw that Guntrip's problem was essentially preoedipal, although he did not use the term. Twice he remarked to Guntrip, "You show no signs of ever having had an Oedipus complex." Freud (1931) criticized Deutsch on the grounds that she had not freed herself "from the endeavor to apply the Oedipal pattern to the pre-oedipal phase." The same criticism would apply to Fairbairn's neglect of the preoedipal factors which played such an important part in Guntrip's psychopathology. Brunswick was still more emphatic: "The phenomena of the pre-oedipal phase should be described in their own terms and not in terms of the Oedipus Complex" (1940, p. 297). Earlier, in her description of a case of paranoia, Brunswick had given a similar warning: "As a matter of fact, fixations at a pre-oedipal level are theoretically quite in order, so that there is no need to falsify clinical observations in order to explain it on the basis of pre-existing theory" (1929, p. 177). It may well be that in going beyond the oedipus complex some analysts may feel they are impugning an article of faith, as it were. One sees this dilemma in Fairbairn's statement that "the Oedipus Complex is central for therapy but not for theory."

Alliance and Misalliance

An analyst conveys much about himself by his bearing, his manner of speech, the set-up of his office, the atmosphere he creates. Fairbairn was notably aristocratic. Sutherland wrote of him: "He had a slightly formal air about him" (1965, p. 246). He lived in the country outside Edinburgh in the spacious old family house. The drawing room was furnished with valuable and beautiful antiques; a large antique bookcase filled most of one wall of the consulting room. Fairbairn sat in state behind a flat-topped desk in a high-backed plush-covered armchair. The head of the couch was in front of the desk. "Imposing" was Guntrip's description. "It struck me as odd for an analyst who did not believe in the 'mirror-analyst' theory." The atmosphere, we suggest, was not conducive to a therapeutic alliance. It was fear-inducing: "At times I thought he could reach over and hit me on the head." The atmosphere erected an artificial barrier in order to protect Fairbairn from too personal a relationship with the patient, making it easy, therefore, for Fairbairn to become a superego figure. "The negative transference" Guntrip said was fostered by Fairbairn's manner of speech—one which obviously irked Guntrip.

"Many deviations in technique are not undertaken primarily because of the patient's needs, but are rationalizations of the extensive countergratifications they offer the therapist" (Langs 1975b, p. 117). Guntrip and Fairbairn held similar theoretical views, and Guntrip notes Fairbairn's "isolation in Edinburgh, in the medico-religious-intellectual climate antipathetic to psychoanalysis" (1969, p. 314). How far were their theoretical discussions a gratification to the lonely Fairbairn who must have realized that he had an exceptionally gifted patient? For Guntrip they afforded an opportunity for that personal relationship he seemed to crave so deeply. Here he found "the natural warm-hearted human being behind the exact interpreting analyst." Fairbairn had two modes of speech, one for making interpretations and another for postanalytic discussions. But the result of this technical deviation on Guntrip was that he had two images of his analyst which were completely disparate and which were never subject to analysis.

By way of contrast Winnicott's office was "simple, restful in colors and furniture, unostentatious." Everything was carefully planned "to make the patient feel at ease." Guntrip was not ushered into a stately consulting room. "I would knock and walk in, and presently Winnicott would stroll in with a cup of tea in his hand and a cheery 'Hallo' and sit on a small wooden chair by the couch." The patient was allowed to sit on the couch or lie down or take any position that he wished. By way of contrast with Fairbairn, Winnicott had gone to great lengths to ensure that the atmosphere should be conducive to a therapeutic alliance. It might appear casual, but it was calculatedly casual.

At the end of each session Winnicott held out his hand for a friendly handshake. This gesture was to remind Guntrip that in his thousand sessions with Fairbairn they had never once shaken hands.

It would seem that Winnicott, too, realized that he had an exceptional patient, and analyst and patient seemed to have formed a *friendly* alliance.

Winnicott once said to Guntrip, "We differ from Freud. He was for curing symptoms. We are concerned with living persons, whole living and loving." On the record as it stands, the statements made by Winnicott to his patient precluded any possibility of analyzing his sibling rivalry and the underlying envy. "I'm good for you, but you're good for me. Doing your analysis is almost the most reassuring thing that happens to me. The chap before you makes me feel I'm no good at all. You don't have to be good for me. I don't need it and can cope without it, but in fact you are good for me." These comments and the following one by Winnicott demonstrate how the countertransference modified the psychoanalytic relationship with Guntrip.

Toward the end of his analysis with Winnicott, Guntrip had a sudden return of his habit of hard talking and Winnicott made an extraordinary statement: "I had to stand it while you were in labor being creative. . . . You are talking about 'object relating,' 'using the object.'. . . I couldn't have made the interpretation five years ago." It is as if Winnicott were metaphorically holding the child and saying in effect, "I am being that good mother you never had." Later, Winnicott gave a paper in this country on the use of an object. "Only an exceptional man could have reached that kind of insight." And, perhaps only an exceptional patient could have provided the material for it. There is a common fantasy according to Kernberg in narcissistic patients "that their analyst is the best that exists; they do not need to envy any other patients having another analyst; they are the only patient of the analyst, or at least the most interesting patient whom the analyst prefers above all others" (1975, p. 280). Winnicott gave Guntrip every opportunity to indulge in that fantasy.

Winnicott, said Guntrip, became the good mother, and he concluded that lacking a good parent "to find a genuine 'good object' in one's analyst is both a transference experience and a real life experience." Yet, playing the role of the good mother constitutes a deviation from the analytic role, and Guntrip's paper illustrates the consequences. As a result, Guntrip's essential problem, his narcissism and infantile megalomania, were never touched upon. We do not believe that it was enough for Winnicott to stand with Guntrip against his non-relating mother. To the very young child, the preoedipal mother, who is active and omnipotent, was perceived not as the mother who *could not*, but as the bad mother who *would not* keep him alive, just as she would not keep his brother Percy alive. The ogress fantasy must be dispelled, by means of the mutative interpretation. To protect the patient from his fantasy, or to guard against it, or circumvent it, is not part of the therapeutic contract.

In Guntrip's case, the analytic emphasis might have been shifted from the paralyzing effect of his murderess mother on him to a reality awareness of empathy for her schizoid illness. With this insight integrated through the traditional interpretive technique, he might have been able to experience himself as emotionally adequate so that neither Winnicott's death nor mother nature could again threaten his active self.

Unless this fixation on the bad mother image is worked through (Glatzer 1959, 1962, 1969) it is impossible for the patient to make a realistic appraisal of his mother. He remains constantly blaming, shifting the responsibility for his neurosis onto the mother and blinds himself to the fact that however bad she may have been, she could not have been without some redeeming quality.

Guntrip died before his paper was published, and it was written after the death of Fairbairn and Winnicott. It is regrettable that we cannot have their comments, for they might have cast a different light on Guntrip's case history.

NOTES

1. Unless otherwise noted all descriptions of Guntrip's analyses are cited from "My Experience of Analysis with Fairbairn and Winnicott," 1975.

2. Ferenczi regarded the stage of unconditional omnipotence as universal. This is in striking contrast to Winnicott's stance: "Omnipotence is *nearly* a fact of our experience" (1971, p. 11, italics added).

REFERENCES

Abraham, K. (1919). A particular form of neurotic resistance to the psycho-analytic method *Selected Papers on Psycho-Analysis,* pp. 303-311. London: Hogarth, 1949.

Brunswick, R. M. (1929). The analysis of a case of paranoia. *Journal of Nervous and Mental Diseases* 70:45-53.

———— (1940). The pre-oedipal phase of libido development. *Psychoanalytic Quarterly* 9:293-319.

Evans, W. N. (1953). Two kinds of romantic love. *Psychoanalytic Quarterly* 22:75-85.

———— (1972). The mother: image and reality. *Psychoanalytic Review* 59:183-199.

———— (1975). The eye of jealousy and envy. *Psychoanalytic Review* 62:481-492.

Ferenczi, S. (1951). *Sex in Psychoanalysis.* New York: Basic Books.

Flugel, J. C. (1945). *Man, Morals and Society.* London: Duckworth.

Freud, A. (1954). Psychoanalysis and Education. *The Writings of Anna Freud,* vol. 4, pp. 317-326. New York: International Universities Press, 1968.

Freud, S. (1911). Formulations on the two principles of mental functioning. *Standard Edition* 12:213-226.

———— (1915a). Instincts and their vicissitudes. *Standard Edition* 14:109-140

———— (1915b). The unconscious. *Standard Edition* 14:159-208.

———— (1920). Beyond the pleasure principle. *Standard Edition* 18:1-64.

———— (1925). Negation. *Standard Edition* 18:235-240.

———— (1930). Civilization and its discontents. *Standard Edition* 21:57-146.

———— (1931). Female sexuality. *Standard Edition* 21:215-220.

———— (1940). An outline of psychoanalysis. *Standard Edition* 23:139-208.

Glatzer, H. T. (1959). Notes on the pre-oedipal fantasy. *American Journal of Orthopsychiatry* 29:383-390.

———— (1962). Handling narcissistic problems in group psychotherapy. *International Journal of Group Psychotherapy* 12:448-455.

——— (1969). Working through in analytic group psychotherapy. *International Journal of Group Psychotherapy* 19:292-306.

Guntrip, H. (1969). *Schizoid Phenomena, Object Relations and the Self.* New York: International Universities Press.

——— (1975). My experience of analysis with Fairbairn and Winnicott. *International Review of Psycho-Analysis* 2:145-156.

Jacobson, E. (1964). *The Self and the Object World.* New York: International Universities Press.

Kernberg, O. (1975). *Borderline Conditions and Pathological Narcissism.* New York: Jason Aronson.

Kohut, H. (1971). *The Analysis of the Self.* New York: International Universities Press.

Langs, R. J. (1975a). Therapeutic misalliances. *International Journal of Psychoanalytic Psychotherapy* 4:77-105

——— (1975b). The therapeutic relationship and deviations in technique. *International Journal of Psychoanalytic Psychotherapy* 4:106-141.

Mahler, M. (1972). On the first three sub-phases of the separation-individuation process. *International Journal of Psycho-Analysis* 53:333-338

Strachey, J. (1969). The nature of the therapeutic action of psychoanalysis. *International Journal of Psycho-Analysis* 50:275-308

Sutherland, J. (1965). Obituary, W. R. D. Fairbairn. *International Journal of Psycho-Analysis* 46:245-247.

Winnicott, D. W. (1971). *Playing and reality.* New York: Basic Books.

Visual Imagery
and Defensive Processes

MARDI J. HOROWITZ, M.D.

The ideas and feelings that a patient usually avoids gain expression in therapy as words, images, or acts. The model presented of these representational systems conceptualizes defensive processes as information processing decisions at the boundaries of particular systems and describes in detail the cognitive maneuvers that regulate image formation. Specification of these operations allows for acute observation and selective wording of the interpretation and direction on the part of the therapist that may help a patient override unconscious defenses by conscious choice.

The use of images such as those in dreams and fantasies has always played a prominent role in psychoanalysis. More recently, image techniques have been widely used in different psychotherapies (Singer 1974). When therapists employ image techniques, they usually do so to alter the operation of defensive processes and promote expression of usually warded-off mental contents.

The rational use of such techniques should rest, ideally, on a theoretical model of the place of image formation in the spectrum of thought, and the operation of defensive processes in relation to this modality. The present paper offers such a model. After outlining the model, the paper will detail five types of image-formation inhibition and then describe both interpretive and directive interventions aimed at these inhibitions.

In the first era of psychoanalysis, interpretations were presentations to the patient of his or her own unconscious thoughts. Later, with the development of ego psychology, emphasis shifted to include the importance of interpreting defenses. As ego psychology continues to develop, interpretation aims not only at presentation of warded-off contents, and at confrontation with defense, but at drawing the attention of the patient to the cognitive maneuvers by which the defenses are accomplished.

When there is adequate evidence and the time is right, a therapist tells a patient that he is not thinking about a specific topic and explains why he is afraid to do so. *A cognitive interpretation extends such interventions. It tells the patient how he is going about not thinking the thought and shows him how he might think about the topic.* After presenting a model of the place of images in thought, we will examine such cognitive interventions in relation to inhibitions of the image system. It is through these various types of inhibition of all representational modalities that repression is accomplished. By drawing attention to the *specific site of inhibition* one gives the patient a conscious choice to alter what has been, up to that point, an unconsciously determined avoidance.

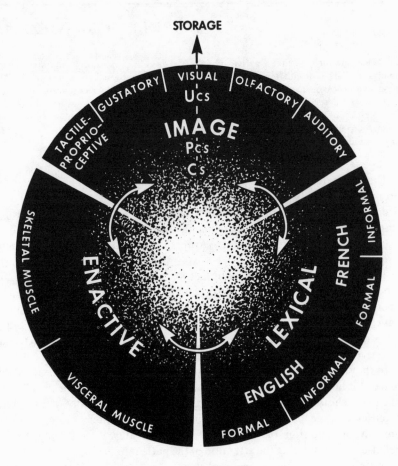

Figure 1

IMAGE FORMATION
AS A MODE OF REPRESENTATION

Modes available for the conscious expression of meanings include enactive, image, and lexical representations. In ordinary wakeful thought, these modes blend richly; reflective awareness seldom distinguishes one from another. This multimodal thought is symbolized, in figure 1, as the center of the sphere of attention. As the periphery is approached, there is less blending, and one may be aware that a train of thought is pictorial rather than verbal, is in auditory images rather than subvocal speech, or is a flow of word meanings without sensory qualities. Each mode has its own special utility and organizational properties as elaborated in table 1.

Table 1.
An Outline of Modes of Representation

Enactive Mode
Subsystems. Skeletal neuro-musculature. Visceral neuro-musculature.
Sample Organizational Tendencies. By directionality and force. By operational end-products.
Sample Statement. X does this.
Sample of Complex Units of Represented Information. Gestures. Facial expressions. Postures.

Image Mode
Subsystems. Visual. Auditory, Tactile-kinesthetic. Olfactory-gustatory.
Sample Organizational Tendencies. By simultaneous occurrence. By spatial relationships. By concrete categorization of similarities and differences.
Sample Statements. X is like this. X is like Y. X is there and Y is there. X and Y happen together. X does this to Y.
Sample of Complex Units of Represented Information. Introjects. Body images. Relationship between self and object.

Lexical Mode
Subsystems. (Different languages?)
Sample Organizational Tendencies. By sequentiality and linear structure. By abstract categorization.
Sample Statement. If X and Y then Z because X + Y→Z.
Sample of Complex Units of Represented Information. Phrases or sentences. Stories and histories.

Enactive thought depicts information in the form of trial actions, with minor tensing of muscles. The flow of enactive thoughts may be reflected in micromomentary gestures and facial expressions and competing action tendencies may be recognized (Haggard and Isaacs 1966).

Image thought allows continued information processing after perception and, as in dreams and daydreams, can lend a sensory configuration to emergent ideas and feelings.

In lexical thought the essential ingredients are word meanings and grammatical organization. Conceptualization, reasoning, and abstract generalization are most secure in this mode.

Each mode is composed of subsystems. Enactive systems may be organized by functional activities such as different work sets or sports. Image systems are divided by sensory modes: auditory, visual, olfactory, gustatory, tactile, and proprioceptive. The visual mode is the focus of this paper. The lexical system may be organized by different languages, each with a specific vocabulary and grammar.

When emergent ideas enter a system, the information may then be translated from one mode to another (indicated by arrows in Figure 1). Regulatory processes act at the system boundaries to inhibit or facilitate these entries and exits.

UTILITY OF THE VISUAL IMAGE SYSTEM

Visual images are private experiences, rarely communicated by pictorialization, more often communicated by translation into words. Perhaps because of the early development of image formation, before conscientiousness or superego formation, or perhaps because of the privacy inherent in this mode, images often carry into awareness ideas censored from lexical representation. Such properties lead to the extremes of image use noted in clinical settings: At times the spontaneous flow of images seems almost like a direct expression of unconscious thought, as suggested by Freud (1900) and later by Jung (1916) in explanation of his active imagination technique. At times reversion to images is a withdrawal from verbal communication, a form of resistance (Kanzer 1958).

Images of dreams and waking fantasies often carry the first awareness of a newly emergent theme. Other clinical observations have shown that it is in this mode that preverbal memories (Kepecs 1954) and unresolved traumatic episodes may reenter awareness after a long period of repression (Horowitz 1976, 1977). Even if a theme has not initially gained entry into awareness in image form, the extension of ideas into image form is often associated with intensified emotion. Images can depict the intensity of a wish or fear because they reveal particular actions between persons. Finally, image experiences, even of entirely internal origin, may have a quasi-perceptual quality which allows the person a sense of interaction with them, on an as-if-real basis. Common examples are experiences of introjective presences and temporarily restorative fantasies of missing objects, from the fantasy of food in a starving person, to the fantasy of a separated lover, to the imaginary companion of a lonely child.

If these are the utilities of image representation, what motivates therapists to use interventions that increase image formation rather than those that encourage the continued employment of lexical thought? The most common aim is to short circuit repression and elicit expression of warded-off ideas. The second most common aim is to short circuit the partial repression involved in the more complex defenses of isolation and undoing and thus uncover the emotion-arousing properties of thought.

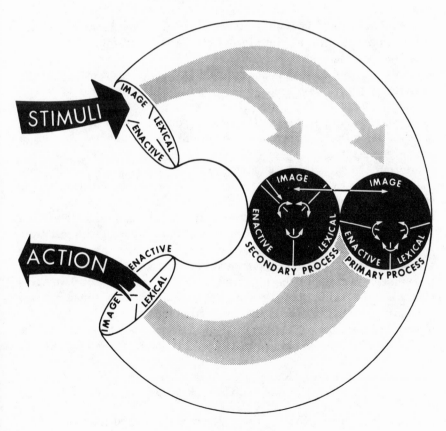

Figure 2

Most frequently, the material then expressed in image form is composed of traumatic memories, conflicted interpersonal fantasies, and disavowed but dynamically powerful self-images. It is the conflict between current conscious attitudes and the wishes and fears inherent in these emergent images that generates emotional responses to the images experienced. This conflict can then, hopefully, be worked through. As one step in working through such conflicts, image experiences are translated into word meanings. This extends awareness of meaning and alters the earlier state of censorship.

A MODEL OF THE IMAGE SYSTEM

Having described some of the properties of the image system, we may now consider a model of the system in order to focus on the possible sites for the accomplishment of defensive aims. Figure 2 provides a visual metaphor of such a model.

Stimuli enter the mind as information in the form of images. Eventually the information is transformed into the enactive and lexical forms suitable for usual interpersonal communication.

For a time, the process of image thinking may take place in separable trains of thought, organized by relatively primary process, and also secondary process, regulations. The same stimulus situation is thus simultaneously contemplated in different ways. Comparison, and even competition, among these ways then occurs prior to any conclusive interpretation of a stimulus or decision on action.

Information enters the visual system from at least four and probably five sources, as shown in figure 3. One source is perceptual input, including entoptic sensations. The second source is internal information, including both the schemata necessary to construct perceptual images and the storehouse of long term memory and fantasy. The third input is from codings retained from prior episodes, episodes retained in a kind of short-term or active memory with a property of recurrent representation. The fourth input is translation from thought cycles occurring in other modes. The hypothetical fifth source is from parallel image forming systems. Entry of information from a primary process type of image formation into an image system that has been regulated by secondary process is the instance of concern here. Defensive aims can be accomplished through the regulation of each of these forms of input.

DEFENSES AND THE PROCESS
OF WORKING THROUGH

Working through involves, in part, the recognition and reconciliation of discrepancies between reality and fantasy, between current possibilities and

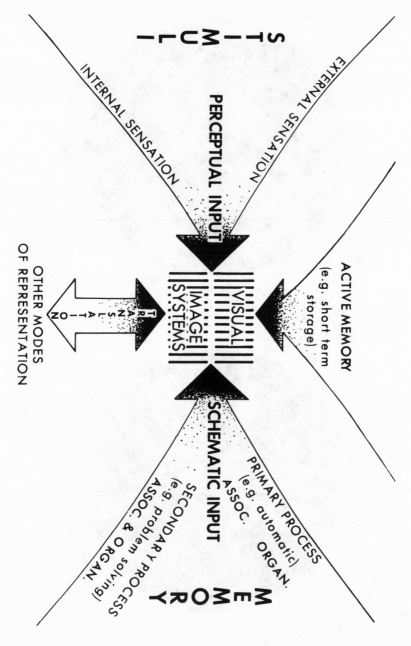

INTERNAL SENSATION

EXTERNAL SENSATION

PERCEPTUAL INPUT

STIMULI

OTHER MODES
OF REPRESENTATION

TRANSLATION

VISUAL IMAGE SYSTEMS

ACTIVE MEMORY
(e.g. short term storage)

SCHEMATIC INPUT

PRIMARY PROCESS
(e.g. automatic)
ASSOC. ORGAN.

SECONDARY PROCESS
(e.g. problem solving)
ASSOC. & ORGAN.

MEMORY

Figure 3

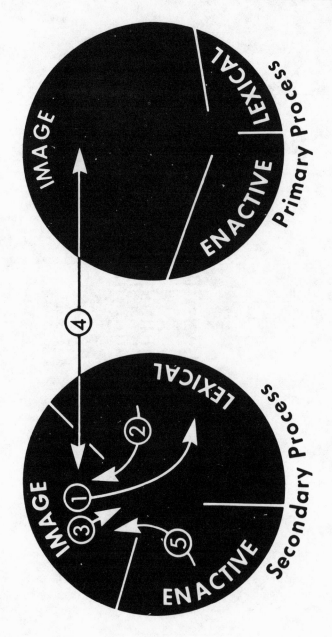

Figure 4

inner attitudes or aims. Recognition and confrontation means that ideas and feelings usually warded-off are now expressed within a safe and therapeutic relationship. This process requires change in defensive operations and, generally, a change in the inhibitory maneuvers that accomplish repression. The model of representational modes presented here illustrates sites where inhibitions prevent the free flow of information in the form of visual images. One may now consider therapeutic interventions aimed at alteration of such inhibitions. The presence of a therapeutic relationship will be assumed.

TECHNIQUES TO ALTER
INHIBITORY OPERATIONS

The five most frequent inhibitions of entry of information into the visual image system are illustrated in figure 4 as follows:

1. The failure to attach word labels to images.
2. The converse, which is avoidance of image associations to contents expressed in words.
3. Inattention to dim or fleeting image episodes.
4. The prevention of primary process or spontaneous flow types of image formation.
5. The nontranslation of enactive representations into imagery.

Overstated examples of interpretive and directive interventions are provided in table 2 (Horowitz 1977). These are illustrative only The directive remarks included in table 2 are comparatively gentle in that they suggest to the patient changes in the form of thought. In guided fantasy techniques and behavior therapy techniques, direction is more extensive, and specific contents to conceptualize are suggested. The choice of interpretive or directive intervention for a given type of inhibition, as well as the timing, dosage, and nuances of intervention, is dependent on the current state of transference and the potential for transference topics—a subject too broad for discussion here.

Without going too far into the choice of interpretation or direction, what can be said about the difference between these techniques for the same type of inhibition? The directive interventions are similar to those of a teacher. If the assumption of a developmental lag is indicated, that is, if the patient has not yet learned to make full use of various modes of thought, if inhibition has been in fact a long-standing limitation of cognitive style, then a simple directive statement may help the patient learn new ways of using thought processes. Interpretive remarks are, of course, also covert suggestions. The patient hears such remarks as implications that he ought to try doing what he is told he is avoiding. But interpretive remarks give more information and so require

Table 2. Defensive Inhibitions and Sample Interventions

Site of Inhibition	Sample of an Interpretive Intervention	Sample of a Directive Intervention
1. Images not associated with word meanings	"You do not let yourself describe those images you are having because you are afraid to think clearly about and tell me about those ideas."	"Describe your images to me in words." "Tell me what that image means."
2. Lexical representations not translated into images	"You do not let yourself think that idea visually because you are afraid of the feelings that might occur if you did."	"Let yourself think in visual images and report whatever you experience to me."
3. Vague images (preconscious) not intensified (conscious)	"You are afraid to let that fleeting image become really clear in your mind because you are afraid you will feel or act badly if you do."	"Try to hold onto those images and 'tune them up.'"
4. No cross translation between secondary process and primary process images	"You are afraid to let yourself have daydream images because you are afraid that bizarre ideas will take over and you will lose control!"	"Let yourself kind of dream about this right now."
5. Enactive representations not translated into images	"You are afraid to picture in your mind the implications of your present posture and facial expression; you are afraid the self image that would result would shame you."	"Try to picture yourself in your mind with that posture and expression on your face."

more inference of knowledge on the part of the therapist. If this information is accurate and well timed, interpretations place the patient in a position of greater control. He can consciously choose to continue or to set aside the inhibitory processes set in motion by unconsciously made decisions.

The errors possible in intervention by direction or interpretation also influence the therapist's choice of technical style. Directive intervention, especially the suggestion of particular contents in guided fantasy techniques, may put the patient in a passive position; the directive acts of the therapist provide a nidus of reality for the elaboration of a transference in which the therapist is like a parent telling the patient what to do and holding him responsible as he complies or stubbornly resists in an overt or covert manner. Interpretative interventions can provide erroneous information which the patient may either believe or use against the therapist. For example, when the therapist interprets a behavior as defensive when it is in fact due to a lack of regulatory capacity, the interpretation does not help the patient gain control over his thought process.

FACILITATIONS AND INHIBITORY FAILURES

The avoidance of images can be contrasted with the intrusion of images. Episodes of unbidden images are more complex because they may result from either active facilitation of failure of inhibition. An example of interpretation of facilitated imagery follows. Suppose the patient becomes flooded with emotion because he has formed vivid images of a painful memory. The therapist might then interpret the transference: "You are upsetting yourself by forming lurid images of that event because you hope I will be compelled to comfort you if I see you cry." While this is an ordinary transference interpretation, albeit without a link to an earlier figure, it also conveys information about how cognitive processes are used. This is contained in the phrase "by forming lurid images." Such information puts the patient in a slightly better position to exert conscious choice over ensuing thought process.

Such an interpretation would be inappropriate if the main reasons for the lurid images were failures of inhibition. In this context, directive remarks might help the patient gain control. "Please contemplate that idea in words. You feel sad remembering this event. What did it mean to you?" At times, therapists suggest even more dramatic shifts to other modes as a way to learn control, as when Beck (1970) showed a patient with intrusive images that he could stop these images by clapping his hands.

It would also be possible for the therapist to direct attention to another topic, or to stay on the same topic but suggest specific images, as is done in behavior therapy techniques. For example, in systematic desensitization, the therapist takes phobic imagery, assembles a hierarchy of images from least to most threatening, and tells the patient when to start an image, what to image, and when to stop. This maneuver teaches the patient control over image formation; if the therapist can tell him to start and stop, he can tell himself the same thing.

MORE COMPLEX DEFENSIVE OPERATIONS

Defenses such as undoing and isolation are more complex than repression because they involve multiple cognitive operations. A brief clinical vignette provides an illustration of the play of such defenses at the boundaries of representational systems.

> Early in a course of psychoanalytic psychotherapy, an obsessional man was describing a situation with his work supervisor and concealing from himself his hatred of this man.
>
> The supervisor gave the patient more work than he thought he could do. As he tried to describe his response, he oscillated between feelings of respect and feelings of dislike for the way his supervisor told him to try to take on more work. In a given sentence, he would add undoing clauses: He admired the firmness of the supervisor, but he didn't like being given more work; he ought to do more, but it irritated him to be told to; he respected the supervisor, but the supervisor was too authoritarian; he spoke up to the supervisor, but in a wishy-washy way, and so forth.
>
> The lexical system was the principal mode of representation here and lent itself to undoing because of its sequential organization. The therapist attempted to hold the patient to his irritation: Wasn't he saying that he did not like the supervisor when he gave him extra work?
>
> The patient complained of the way the therapist said "did not like." That wording was too strong, sometimes he did admire the supervisor, at other times he felt less respect. The patient fell silent for awhile, then reported the image of a door on which a red hot branding iron had just emblazoned an arrow. He could not think of what the image might mean, but felt vaguely frightened.

Reconsider the two states. In one the patient is thinking in words and communicating these mental contents. In the other, he has shifted to images, and for a time does not communicate. In the first state he manifests little emotion, in the second he reports feeling frightened. We know from other evidence that in both states he avoids clear depiction of himself as angry and destructive. In the lexical state he accomplishes this avoidance by using neutral words such as "respect" and "disrespect" and changing his way of ascribing even these mild attitudes to himself. The requirements of grammar fix the subject and object as self or other: He respects or does not respect the supervisor.

In contrast, in the image system, the impulses are rather clear: The door is burned by the forcefully assertive branding iron. The patient avoids thinking of himself as angry by leaving the self and object designation unstated. Symbols are present—the door, the arrow, the iron, burning; but he does not identify himself with any of them. Instead he is frightened. In his kind of image thinking, his position as the subject or object of action can remain unclear; he is either the injured door, and hence frightened, or the out-of-control injuring iron, and hence frightened that he might hurt someone else.

As he translates the images into words and thinks of possible meanings related to himself, he can still accomplish undoing by verbal juggling, by changing ideas from self as victim to self as aggressor, with a resulting cancellation of anger by fear and fear by anger. The end result is, of course, only a vague sense of guilt and self-doubt.

To recapitulate, a given defensive aim, such as undoing, can be accomplished differently in different systems of representation. Some information leaks through to each system, subject and object are designated, but several oppositional interactions are asserted in order to maintain the protective confusion. In the image system, the emotional quality of the contemplated action is made clear, but the self-designation such as victim or aggressor is left unclear. The separation of the modes accomplishes isolation of idea from affect. The therapist, however, does not have to segregate information from either system; it is possible to pick up the emotional clues from the images, and the ideational clues from the words. Information derived from both states can be put together, the defensive codes broken, and the underlying threat recognized.

Intervention to help the patient set aside defenses in order to expose and deal with this threat will be a much longer process. It will involve interpretation of what is warded off, the manner of warding off, and the various cognitive maneuvers used to maintain defense. Change in cognitive style will involve the patient's learning to put together information by using both representational systems, just as the therapist has done.

CONCLUSION

There are several modes for the representation of thought. Thinking usually combines and orchestrates these modes. But each mode has a particular utility and is regulated in different ways. In particular states, especially in conflict when emergent ideas and feelings are avoided by defensive operations, the modes may be experienced as separable vehicles for expressing meanings.

Defenses are accomplished by operations at the boundaries of each mode. An understanding of the cognitive process may help therapists choose interventions, either interpretive or directive, that are at the level of the patient's method of processing information. Such interventions may place a patient in a position of greater control, to the point that he can decide to experience thought in new ways—more consciously, expressively, and expansively.

REFERENCES

Beck, A. T. (1970). Role of fantasies in psychotherapy and psychopathology. *Journal of Nervous and Mental Diseases* 150:3-17.

Freud, S. (1900). The interpretation of dreams. *Standard Edition* 4/5:1-630.

Haggard, E. A., and Isaacs, K. S. (1966). Micromomentary facial expressions as indicators of ego mechanisms in psychotherapy. In *Methods of Research Psychotherapy*, ed. L. A. Gottschalk and A. H. Auerbach. New York: Appleton-Century-Crofts.

Horowitz, M.J. (1976). *Stress Response Syndromes.* New York: Jason Aronson.

——— (1977). *Image Formation and Cognition.* New York: Appleton-Century-Crofts.

Jung, C. G. (1916). *The Archetypes and the Collective Unconscious.* New York: Pantheon, 1959.

Kanzer, M. (1958). Image formation during free association. *Psychoanalytic Quarterly* 27:465-484.

Kepecs, J. G. (1954). Observations on screens and barriers in the mind. *Psychoanalytic Quarterly* 23:62-77.

Salzman, L. (1968). *The Obsessive Personality.* New York: Jason Aronson.

Singer, J. L. (1974). *Imagery and Daydream Methods in Psychotherapy and Behavior Modification.* New York: Academic Press.

The Therapist's Use of Metaphor

WILLIAM HURT SLEDGE, M.D.

A linguistic perspective is applied to the therapist's use of original metaphors in psychoanalytically oriented psychotherapy. I present a review of the literature along with a view of psychotherapy and metaphor from a linguistic perspective. Three examples from psychotherapy are used to illustrate properties of metaphorical interpretations. An examination of the portion of the hour that precedes the therapist's metaphor suggests the importance of context in reducing the dangers of misunderstanding inherent in the use of metaphor.

This work is an attempt, through a consideration of ideas from linguistics, to cast light on the therapist's use of metaphor in the psychotherapeutic situation. Specifically I am concerned with how metaphor conveys meaning, how metaphor may serve as an interpretative tool to facilitate patients' understanding of their experiences, and how the immediate context of the hour might influence the patient's response to the therapist's metaphor.

The literature on the therapist's use of metaphor is sparse, reflecting the peripheral position of language per se as a focus of study for psychotherapy research. There are few studies specifically devoted to a consideration of metaphor in psychotherapy despite the ubiquity of metaphor in ordinary discourse and the centrality of metaphor in the philosophy of language, poetry, and aesthetics. Those few studies content have been concerned with the patient's metaphor (Aleksandrowicz 1962, Muncie 1937, Parker 1962, Sharpe 1940, Voth 1970) and that of the therapist (Cain and Maupin 1961, Caruth and Ekstein 1966, Ekstein and Wallerstein 1956, Reider 1972). There

The author wishes to acknowledge the support and guidance of Dr. Albert Rothenberg who served as mentor and advisor during the course of this work; the influence of the faculty, especially Dr. Marshall Edelson, and students of the Behavioral Sciences Track of the Yale Medical School; and the cooperation of therapists and patients who agreed to be tape-recorded for this project.

are two broad approaches to the problem of the therapist's use of metaphor in psychotherapy: (1) the therapist's use of the patient's metaphor, so called interpretation within the metaphor, and (2) the therapist's use of his own original metaphor.

Using the patient's metaphor differs from the therapist's introduction of his own original metaphor. The use of the patient's metaphor usually represents a means of indirect discourse in which the therapist and patient speak in one realm (the metaphor), while the therapist maintains a split consciousness by talking and thinking in the metaphorical realm of indirect discourse and also thinking (consciously) in the literal realm of psychodynamic meaning. When the therapist uses an original metaphor, he may not utilize this split consciousness but attempt instead to convey a thought or interpretation by means of figurative language. Despite these differences, however, there are also similarities which rest mainly on the ability of metaphor to convey multiple meanings simultaneously, so that while what is being explicitly discussed may be some form of impersonal object, fantasy, or a story, the metaphor may also signify highly affect-laden psychodynamically meaningful material.

One example of using the patient's metaphor is Beulah Parker's account (1962) of her psychotherapy with a schizophrenic adolescent in which much of the work was carried out "within the metaphor" of machines and mechanical process. This type of discourse served as a means of indirectly talking about the patient and his attitudes and feelings. Ekstein and his coworkers (Caruth and Ekstein 1966, Ekstein and Wallerstein 1956) advocate the therapist's use of patient metaphors in the form of stories, dreams, and symbolic play in the treatment of psychotic and borderline children. These authors state that "the use of the metaphor derives its primary value from maintaining contact with patients who are constantly in danger of being inundated by a break-through of primary process material" (Caruth and Ekstein 1966, p. 35). They assert that the use of metaphor serves the "defensive" function of allowing the patient to maintain the necessary distance from conscious awareness of the content of the conflict while at the same time it serves the adaptive function of facilitating a reduction in distance between patient and therapist" (p. 37). Furthermore, they write, metaphorical communication may repeat an early preverbal type of communication arising from the mother-child symbiosis. "Interpretation within the metaphor" or "interpretation within the regression" thus permits communication beyond what is verbalized in the manifest content and permits a deeper empathic process between patient and therapist—a type of wordless communication. In discussing the use of a schizophrenic woman's metaphors in psychotherapy, Aleksandrowicz extends this approach and concludes that the technique provides a desired form of distancing and permits the therapist to enter the patient's autistic world. He warns, however, that the metaphor may be misunderstood unless employed carefully with a due consideration to context. It should be noted that this form of interpretative activity is advocated in patients with precarious ego integrity. Proponents of this approach view it as a means toward an eventually more direct representation of important material.

An example of the therapist's use of original metaphor is Reider's detailed discussion (1972) of his psychoanalysis of a phobic-hysterical woman in which his use of a metaphor seemed to serve as a turning point in the analysis. It was followed by the memory of an important childhood dream that became the focus of the remaining psychoanalysis. He questions what it is about the form of metaphor that provides the opportunity for representing in consciousness repressed, affectively charged material. He emphasizes the aspect of choice in the patient's response. Because of the multitiered meaning of his metaphor, the patient was able to choose her own depth of understanding without engaging in a defensive struggle with the analyst. He goes on to add that metaphor may be particularly attractive to some patients because of its aesthetic ambiguity and the sense of understanding conveyed by the therapist. He sees metaphor as a potentially useful therapeutic intervention because of its "economic condensation of understanding of many levels of experience" (p. 469).

Cain and Maupin (1961) discuss interpreting within the patient's metaphor with emphasis on dangers of its miscarriage. Specifically, they warn that the therapist may overvalue his metaphor and become so narcissistically involved in his clever utterances that he misses the clinical point altogether. They also warn that its use can support a defensive posture on the part of the patient by providing too much distance from affect-laden material. They point out that metaphor may be misperceived, especially by paranoid patients, who may tend to see its use as a form of veiled communication.

In the work that follows I hope to demonstrate, through a consideration of the features of metaphor from a linguistic perspective, how the therapist's use of metaphor provides the opportunity for choice in the level of patient response and how the context of the hour influences the impact of a metaphorical interpretation. I will present a brief concept of psychotherapy from a linguistic perspective, review some central linguistic concepts, and finally, discuss examples.

PSYCHOTHERAPY

Although there is some disagreement about this among the schools of therapy, I suggest that psychotherapy is not an enterprise that undertakes to discover causal relationships, at least in any physical or biological sense. Instead, much of the work of psychotherapy concerns itself with the elucidation and extension of meanings, an idea emphasized by Edelson (1971, 1972, 1975) and others (Leavy 1973, Rosen 1969, 1974, Rothenberg 1972, and Spence 1968). In the context of the patient-therapist relationship the meaning of events, relationships, thoughts, fantasies, dreams, symptoms and feelings are discovered, clarified, and worked through in terms of how these meanings affect the patient and the therapist-patient relationship. Freud pointed in this direction early in his psychoanalytic career when he discovered that it was not factually correct that many of his hysterical patients had undergone some form of childhood seduction which caused their hysteria. Instead of abandoning his theory of the etiology of hysteria, he modified it by postulating that these patients believed they had been seduced; thus the notion of psychic reality was put into the context of a comprehensive theory of psychopathology. Likewise, his emphasis on what dreams mean, the intention of parapraxes, the sense of symptoms, and his development of techniques of free association all point toward a concern with the efficacy of meaning rather than with cause and effect relationships (Edelson 1971, 1972, Freud 1963, and Rosen 1969, 1974).

There are, of course, several different kinds of meanings of interest to psychotherapists (Edelson 1971, 1975, and Spence 1968). When our patients talk to us, we not only listen for the denotative meaning evoked by the words and rules of language; we also read between the lines. We listen for the intentions of the speaker toward himself, his message, and the listener as well as for his attitudes, values, and the significance of a particular symbolic or real item.

Interpretation is one tool the therapist has at his disposal to convey and clarify meaning. Although other types of interventions or remarks are an important part of his therapeutic repertoire, interpretation is the mainstay. In fact, noninterpretive remarks such as confrontation, information requests, and clarification involve some kind of interpretative activity. By interpretation, I mean here a broad generic category of therapist activity that includes some decision on his part as to what is important, what needs attention and naming, and what an event, behavior, interaction, or thought may mean for the patient. Interpretation is the active search for meanings that are unavailable to the patient because of repression.

Interpretations are therapeutic to the extent that unconscious fantasies, conflicts, and mental expressions are identified, related to the reality context of the patient's present experience and behavior, and presented in such a manner and time that the patient is able to hear the interpretation, integrate it, and work through the material. Interpretations work to relieve repression, bring the unconscious into consciousness, provide insight, and ultimately to facilitate symptom relief (Langs 1973). Hence, interpretations call attention to some aspect of the patient's experience (both conscious and unconscious) and provide an opportunity to place the formless, dimly perceived and, at times, chaotic experiences of the patient into some perspective more manageable (Hammer 1968, Leavy 1973). Psychotherapy aided by the interpretive process enriches experience by intensifying and extending meaning as it relates to anxiety and unconscious mental conflict. Interpretations name what has previously been unnamable because of repression.

Concerning how interpretations should be delivered, there is an extensive literature addressing itself to issues of depth, timing, frequency, and style. Generally, there is agreement that interpretations should be molded by conceptual economy and precision, and should be "translated into the patient's concrete experience" (Hammer 1968, p. 35). Truax and Carkhuff (1964) pointed to the importance of concreteness when they found concreteness on the therapist's part correlated highly with effective psychotherapy. They conclude that concreteness or specificity seems to function to (a) insure emotional proximity, (b) enhance the accuracy of the therapist's response, and (c) encourage specificity in the client's efforts.

LINGUISTICS

Inasmuch as psychotherapy is a process involving the explication of meaning, one might wonder how linguistics may be helpful in understanding features of psychotherapy. Linguistics is, after all, the study of the system of representation of meanings and the rule governed patterns for combination of these representations. I would like to focus on what linguistics informs us about the transference of meaning to elucidate how metaphor transfers meaning. Before detailing this process, however, I will briefly examine language as meaning conveyer. Although such an examination is of necessity oversimplified, one can say in general that meaning is the relationship between a signifier (such as a word or symbol) and the mental representation of what is signified or evoked by the signifier (Rosen 1974). Meaning is conveyed by signals, signs, and/or symbols and their rule-governed patterns as embodied in language. The relationship between signifier and its mental representations are reciprocal in that one evokes the other.

There are, of course, different kinds of *meaning* (Leech 1969, Edelson 1975). *Meaning* may be used in the narrow sense of cognitive or denotative, the kind of meaning in which the dictionary maker is interested. This is to be differentiated from psychological meaning which I will refer to as *significance*, which includes emotive and attitudinal considerations. Technical language (as in legal and scientific writing) attempts to convey only cognitive meaning, whereas in a communicative enterprise like poetry or psychotherapy, in which complex emotional and attitudinal states are represented, cognitive meaning is only one aspect of total significance.

When multiple meanings are represented simultaneously by one signifier, we have ambiguity. Ambiguity is a universal property of language. One depends on the linguistic context (how the words are combined in phrases, sentences, etc.) and the psychological context to interpret any single ambiguous utterance. In linguistics, ambiguity usually entails the multiple simultaneous presence of cognitive meanings; the literary critic, on the other hand, may view ambiguity as the capacity to convey multiple significances at once. In ordinary discourse and technical language, ambiguity is anathema; however, in a literary text, ambiguity contributes to the richness of its significance (Leech 1969).

Psychotherapists are interested in the ambiguity of a patient's speech in much the same way as the literary critic is interested in the ambiguity of a work of poetry. How a person talks about something is an important clue as to what his attitude toward it or the listener may be. Patterns of ambiguity may be unconsciously motivated. Our awareness and understanding of a patient's ambiguous utterances enriches our knowledge of the patient and contributes to his own understanding of himself.

Ambiguity makes possible indeterminacy of meaning. This concept embraces the notion that the meanings of a given utterance cannot be fully or exhaustively specified or limited. Just as with the limitlessness of the latent ideas alluded to by the manifest content of a dream, so it is (at least theoretically) with the meaning of a poem, a patient's speech, or a metaphor. Indeterminacy is a class of ambiguity, but a particular linguistic act can be ambiguous without being indeterminate.

Any utterance in the psychotherapeutic situation must be interpreted both in terms of cognitive meaning and significance. The guidelines for interpreting cognitive meaning in speech or writing are the rule-governed patterns of language. Grammar functions in this manner at the level of the sentence. There are rhetorical rules that govern the interpretation of significance and cognitive meaning in discourse or communicative acts more complex than sentences. These rhetorical rules can be considered an element of the linguistic context. One aspect of rhetorical interpretation is foregrounding—the departure from accepted norms (linguistic, psychological, etc.) that gives interest and a sense of surprise to a particular communicative act and calls attention to it. When an artist paints a picture, he does not simply give a photographic rendition, but emphasizes or highlights some aspect of what he represents in his painting—that is, he foregrounds it. In poetry, as in psychotherapy, the foreground figure is a linguistic entity that is deviant in its departure from an expected or automatic pattern (be it linguistic or psychological).

A particular item may be deviant because it violates rule-governed patterns of linguistic structure; it is, thereby, a *qualitative* deviance. Another form of deviance is the matter of frequency of use (the phenomenon may be very frequent or very infrequent). In this case the violation is *quantitative* and no rules concerning the actual construction or understanding of language are violated. In poetry, the extraregularity of a particular linguistic unit which causes an obtrusive repetition is called *parallelism*; it is manifested by the repetition of sentences, phrases, and words, as well as by certain sound repetitions such as alliteration, rhyming, and assonance. In psychotherapy, parallelism might exist verbally in the repetition of words, phrases, expressions, or themes. The consideration of deviation from linguistic rules, which constitutes a form of qualitative deviation, now brings us to a fuller consideration of metaphor.[1]

Metaphor is a member of a broader class, figurative language—departure from usual rules of language so that literal meaning is rejected as nonsensical. For a communicative act to make sense under such conditions, the meaning must be filled in or interpreted. "The human mind deplores a vacuum of sense" (Leech 1969, p. 220). Meaning (both significance and cognitive meaning) is transferred or filled in depending on the kind of figure of speech. Metaphor, according to Aristotle, consists of "giving the things a name that belongs to something else; the transference being either from genus to species, or from species to genus or from species to species or on the grounds of analogy" (Nowottny 1962, p. 49). In terms of the discussion about qualitative deviances, one can think of metaphor as the equation of two or more things, events, concepts, or meanings in such a way that the rules of regular language-use are violated. Metaphor itself is not a thing, but a process of interpretation of a linguistic event.[2] For the person confronting a metaphoric utterance, there are at least three stages of understanding: (1) recognition of the violation of some rule of language-use (deviance from some rule-governed pattern of language-use), (2) the decision that this utterance is not meaningless, and (3) the attempt to make sense of or interpret this deviant utterance. For example, in the sentence *He is a human elephant*,[3] one will immediately recognize this as being deviant since *he* cannot be both *human* and *elephant* simultaneously. One may decide it is nonsense and there is nothing more to say about it, or one may decide it is meaningful in which case it must be interpreted.

One way of analyzing a metaphor is to divide it into a literal component and a figurative or nonsensical component (Leech 1969). The meaning of the metaphor arises from the similarities between the literal and figurative elements. The literal component is called the *tenor*; the figurative component, the *vehicle*. The literal part of *He is a human elephant* (where *he* refers to a human being) is simply *He is a human*. The figurative component is *He is an elephant*. The basis for comparison between the two depends on how these two concepts (human and elephant) are similar or alike. For most people interpreting this sentence out of context, the basis for comparison will likely be size, since this is the attribute most commonly associated with elephants. The context, however, will also guide our interpretation. For example, one may dwell instead on such common attributes as big ears, long noses, huge appetites, burden bearing capacities, loyalty, irritability, etc. This depends on what is known of the person to whom *he* refers and how elephants are viewed. This comparison between the literal and figurative elements of a metaphor is called the *ground*; the term refers to the metaphor's meaning (both cognitive meaning and significance). Since metaphors convey meaning ambiguously (multiple meanings may be present at once), the ground of a metaphor may by indeterminate.[4]

Metaphor as a meaning conveyor has many functions (Beardsley 1962, Black 1955, Nowottny 1962, Rubenstein 1972 and Tucker). For example, it can extend the reach of ordinary language (Rubenstein 1972), in that it provides the potential to construct new concepts, to express something otherwise inexpressible (for instance, to emphasize characteristics that warrant special attention), and to make up for deficiencies in ordinary language. Metaphor can provide a concrete model that implies abstract properties and also guide the affective response to the meaning (Nowottny 1962).

We see then that the use of metaphor by the therapist presents (theoretically, at least) a special situation by virtue of some of its linguistic features. Metaphor is ambiguous, implicative, and allusive; it can convey many different meanings simultaneously. The patient must interpret the metaphor; he must search for the meaning it has for him. A metaphor may function therapeutically by providing a means for expressing unconscious material unavailable for expression through literal language because of the effects of repression. Furthermore, the patient must choose an interpretation of the metaphor based on the context of his experience (both within and outside the psychotherapeutic situation) and his present state of mind. He must apply the metaphor to himself and interpret its meaning for himself.

Inasmuch as an interpretation from the therapist should provide clarity and meaning, does metaphor fail? Metaphor can indeed provide an organization, a model or paradigm, for understanding obscure and confusing experience, including unconscious processes. As noted, metaphor can make up for deficiencies in the language as a system and in the individual's language. Metaphor can be a means for talking about the unspeakable. But the question remains: When the therapist speaks metaphorically, what keeps the patient from being bewildered, confused and groping for the apt meaning?

CLINICAL DISCUSSION

The therapist using a metaphor as an interpretation must still follow the principles of good interpretative technique. Frequently, the elements of the metaphor derive from unconscious processes within the therapist. After all, it is the therapist who thinks of and speaks the metaphor. In doing so he is, of course, influenced by the patient both consciously and unconsciously. Because metaphor is allusive, implicative, and ambiguous, its construction and interpretation are more susceptible to unconscious processes. It is likely that unconscious elements will be expressed in metaphorical interpretation. Of the three clinical examples below two were taken from an unpublished report of preliminary research conducted by myself which attempted to compare the efficacy of metaphorical and literal interpretations. The sessions involved were audio-tape recorded and transcribed. One example (Case 1) is taken from my own psychotherapeutic work with a patient, was not part of a research effort, and was not tape-recorded.

Case 1

The first example, the one not tape-recorded, is technically speaking not a metaphor; however, the process of transfer of meaning discussed above and the subsequent necessity for the patient to interpret the figurative image and apply it to himself is the same as for metaphor. This example illustrates how a figurative intervention carries meaning by implication and allusion—a largely unconscious process. The patient, a homosexual male, had entered psychotherapy considering a transsexual operation. During the psychotherapy one problem was his provocative behavior in relation to the local police. The patient would dress himself in a bizarre drag outfit and, by parading in front of the police, manage to get them to harass him with repeated arrests, verbal assaults, and on occasion, physical assaults. He was proud of his ability to anger the police. He saw their response however, as a problem for which he denied responsibility. The psychotherapy had largely been unsuccessful in getting him to see that he provocatively invited the response he received.

On one occasion he related a recurrent childhood episode in which he would enter a department store, make sure the security system guard saw him stealing, and then covertly return the merchandise. When he attempted to leave the store, he would naturally be stopped. He drew great satisfaction from the surprise of the "stupid cop" when he was searched and no merchandise was found. By this act, he felt he had made a fool of the security guard. As he related this story, I had a strong mental image of a matador working a bull, provoking the bull to charge with the movement of his cape only to step out of the way at the last moment. I shared this image with my patient and noted that he, like the matador, tempted fate and stood a chance of being gored. This comparison between him and the matador gratified him greatly. Indeed, the masterful, provocative, effeminate figure of the matador was expecially appealing, and, I suspect, the image of being gored held a specific sexual fascination. He reflected on this image for a while, clearly absorbed in its implications; then he told me that was an "interesting" idea but there was another aspect to it. In his relationship to people in authority, he felt like the charging bull, completely out of control, senseless, and compulsively performing irrational and self-destructive acts.

At this point, I felt I understood his neurotic behavior in relationship to the local police and me in a new way. The above interchange marked the beginning of a new treatment phase during which the patient became more able and interested in examining how his behavior in relation to people in authority was self-destructive and whether he had the capacity to act differently. In the next session his dress was less bizarre, and he began to deal with the self-destructive elements in his interpersonal relationships in a much less defensive manner.

In this instance the patient, absorbed in the concrete image of himself as a bull fighter, applied to himself the metaphor as formulated by his therapist. Indeed, he saw aspects of himself in both the main actors of the image—the matador and the bull. He was deeply gratified with the idea of himself as the matador. This gratification seemed to permit him to see himself as the bull as well as the matador. He was able to interpret the figurative comparison in two ways at once and to make use of both simultaneously. In the process, he communicated unconsciously but in a manner accessible to treatment. He emphasized features of his behavior that had been previously recognized (his rage toward authority figures). In the act of interpreting the concrete image, a patient finds abstract qualities particularly pertinent to his intrapsychic life. In this instance some of the abstract qualities of the image pertained to his psychosexual identification, his organization of aggression, and his relationship to oedipal figures. Through its concrete representation, the image of these processes not only organized the unconscious material but also provided a means for talking about what the patient had been unable to acknowledge before—his provocative, self-destructive behavior toward authority figures.

In the above example, the patient took an ambiguous image produced by his therapist and chose at least two implications from this image and applied them to his particular experience. Metaphors are ambiguous also. When used as an interpretation by the therapist, a metaphor must be interpreted by the patient. This situation of the patient interpreting an ambiguous statement by the therapist may initially seem undesirable. Generally therapists want to make clear, precise interventions. However, the use of the metaphor in psychotherapy may not be so dangerously ambiguous in reality as in theory. Both therapist and patient have the immediate and broad context of the psychotherapy to guide them in formulating and interpreting the metaphor.

Case 2

The next example illustrates the patient's choosing one meaning from an ambiguous metaphorical interpretation. This example was taken from a psychotherapy recorded for research purposes. The patient, a young man in his early twenties, was referred for long-term psychotherapy with complaints of depression and an inability to complete the required work to receive a college degree. The once a week therapy proceeded for eight months before this session was recorded. During the hour, the patient had been talking about his hope that his therapist was going to give him something to "hold him up." Prominent themes in the hour were that he was coming to therapy for his therapist's benefit, that he felt guilty because he believed he had not satisfied the therapist's demands for improvement, and that he must "go out on a limb" for his therapist. Just before the metaphorical interpretation, the patient had given an account of a recurrent mental image from childhood in which he saw himself and other people walking toward the edge of a cliff; the other people were able to fly but he was not, although the others urged him to try.

The metaphor itself consisted of "So part of your experience of coming here is the fear that I will ask you to do something—ask you to fly when you can't, and that I will kick you out of the nest." Actually, there are two figurative statements ("I will ask you to fly" and "I will kick you out of the nest") based on the central metaphor that the patient is a baby bird in a nest. The cognitive meaning might be expressed as "if you do not perform I will make you leave psychotherapy."

More, however, is implied in the comparison between the therapist-patient relationship and a mother bird-nestling relationship. With this vivid image, the therapist stated that the patient has seen the therapist as a nurturing figure, perhaps somewhat misguided, with severe and inappropriate expectations of those he nurtures. The patient has been depicted as totally dependent on the therapist and without resources for independent life. The psychotherapy situation was viewed as potentially nurturing, but also forbidding and threatening. The equation of performance and flying suggested a special kind of autonomy for the patient. But being made to fly when he lacked the capacity also suggested a particularly cruel and disastrous fate. An ambiguous aspect of the metaphor was whether the therapist (mother bird) expected too much from the patient, whether the patient's expectations of psychotherapy and the therapist were inappropriate, or whether the patient underestimated his own capacities. The central notion, however, was that the therapist ought to "care" for the patient. The meaning of "care" was ambiguous.

How did the patient interpret this metaphor? Which of the possible implications did he choose for himself? He responded immediately with the idea that perhaps he had "wings" he had not discovered. He went on to talk about how this view of himself contrasted with his usual view, in which the "outside world" was seen as the source of all of his failures. In this instance, the therapist's metaphor had an organizing effect; the metaphor produced an ambiguous model in the form of a concrete image. The patient chose from the different potential abstract features those most applicable to his own situation. The patient had been in a maternal transference relationship expressing the wish to be nourished and supported by the therapist. His angry, guilty sense of depression that this wish went ungratified was expressed as the projection that his therapist was using him, did not understand him, and wanted him to "go out on a limb." The image in the therapist's metaphor of a nestling-mother bird relationship addressed the maternal transference while the literal meaning of the metaphor (If you do not perform I will make you leave psychotherapy) addressed the defense of projection. The patient's response of acknowledging the existence of "wings" suggested some awareness of the maternal transference (Perhaps I can fly). His subsequent talk about his sense of the outside causes for his failure was an attempt to integrate his use of externalization. Following this interpretation, the patient was able to acknowledge his anger toward his therapist over a change in appointment time. Previously he had denied feeling anything about the change.

The material that preceded the metaphor (the wish to be "held up," and the childhood dream of not being able to fly) provided the basis for the formulation of the figurative element of the metaphor and perhaps guided the patient's interpretation of the metaphor.

Case 3

The phenomenon of the therapist's metaphor having been suggested by material immediately preceding is highlighted by another example taken from a published account (Gottshalk 1961) of a psychotherapy recorded for research purposes. The patient, a thirty-four-year-old, married father of five children, had recently received a Ph.D. in psychology. His work in the mental health field frequently required him to perform as a psychotherapist. He was intelligent, energetic, and ambitious, but earned a salary considerably below his level of education, and the needs of his family. He had chronic difficulty with underachievement and underproduction. "Though superficially bold and sophisticated, he was covertly fearful of the world seen by him as hostile" (Gottshalk 1961, p. 16). Impulses were poorly integrated; he was preoccupied with sex and unable to experience sexual pleasure. He was seen as an anxious, uncomfortable person whose facade of achievements was quite remarkable in view of the limitations imposed by his inner struggles.

The patient began the eighth hour by recounting his fantasy that he was an object of special interest to his therapist; then he talked about leaving psychotherapy to take a job in another city. He also mentioned having stood up his therapist for the session before (after the therapist had been away) because the patient went to a professional meeting in order to seek employment. He made a slip at this point and said he missed "a few beatings"; while he had intended to say "a few business meetings." The therapist called his attention to the slip when the patient ignored it. The patient made another slip in hearing the therapist say "Is that why you decided not to come in?" when the therapist actually said, "Is that why you decided not to comment?" During the next thirty-three minutes[5] of the hour, the patient talked about his fear of failure, his inability to produce in his work, his sense of desertion by his family of origin, and his troubles in therapy, specifically his tendency to avoid problems by intellectualizing. He related a history of taking low paying jobs and failure to perform well to the idea that these experiences are like beatings to him and reminiscent of childhood beatings. He explicitly rejected a literal interpretation by his therapist to the effect that the two slips made earlier were related to feelings about his therapist being away, and a sense of abandonment by his parents.

During this half-hour, themes of anger and hatred were quite prominent. He talked about being angry with his parents for being away, his mother's being angry with her doctor, his and his sister's hatred of his mother, and his own anger at his therapist for being interested in him merely as a research object. A striking feature of this part of the hour was the number of times he mentioned the word *beating*. During one ten-minute stretch, he used *beatings* ten times; and during the time after that, there were many references to "painful" feelings and "discomfort" experienced at the hands of others. Before the therapist made his metaphorical comment, the patient had been wondering aloud whether or not the therapist had the ability and experience to deal with a patient like him. The final patient comment before the metaphor was: "Well, I'm almost waiting for the bell, that's all, like you're on the rope" (Gottschalk, p. 36).

The metaphorical comment by the therapist was: "You're on the ropes taking a beating." The comparison here was between the patient and a boxer being cornered and humiliated. The implications of this metaphor were that the patient as a boxer was a willing participant, a professional fighter; and at the moment he was suffering a public humiliation at the hands of a more powerful and skillful foe. All avenues of escape were closed off; the situation was hopeless; the patient was being overwhelmed after an initial resistance.

Themes of attack, resistance, and acquiescence, were quite prominent in the patient's speech before the therapist used the metaphor under study. The patient had rejected, explicitly at least, a transference interpretation made by the therapist and had wondered if the therapist could handle him. These themes then had been foregrounded on the basis of their repetition and frequency. This type of foregrounding is much like the quantitative foregrounding noted above. The emphasis or highlighting came about through the extraregularity or obtrusive repetition of these particular ideas.

But another type of quantitative foregrounding also occurred. Not only had the concepts implied by the metaphor been foregrounded by repetition, but also some of the actual words used in the metaphor. The abstract properties of the cognitive meaning of the metaphor and the actual words used in the metaphor itself have both been foregrounded. The word *beating*, for example, was used by the patient during a ten-minute segment prior to the therapist's metaphor at the rate of once per minute. Furthermore, the patient used the words *rope* and *bell* in the immediate utterance before the therapist spoke the metaphor. *Rope*, of course, was part of the metaphor. While the word *bell* was not actually part of the metaphor its use here together with *rope* suggested the image of a boxing match.

One final element of foregrounding in this case was the phrase "taking a beating" which occurred in the patient's parapraxis early in the hour when he substituted *beating* for *business meeting*. By making the parapraxis the patient had foregrounded (by deviance) this phrase and idea.

The patient responded to the metaphor by acknowledging the appropriateness of the analogy, and began to talk about boxing matches he had witnessed, imagining himself in the difficult (for him) position of someone "moving in for the kill." He paused, then talked about how he would like the therapist to "close in for the kill," and how he would like to stick out his jaw and have his therapist hit him. He then talked about a previous confrontation in which his own aggression had been expressed only indirectly. Associatively, he linked his own aggression to the wish to be hit on the jaw. He finished this segment of the hour by mentioning how he would like the other person in the confrontation he had described earlier in the hour to get the mumps and a painful orchitis. Allusions to indirect aggression and themes of sadomasochism were very prominent.

In this third example, the patient addressed aspects of the transference he had stubbornly resisted before the metaphorical interpretation. He elaborated a new fantasy of a masochistic relationship to the therapist and his conflict over the expression of aggression. The concrete image of him as a boxer "taking a beating" linked his present transference situation with the material presented in the first part of the hour concerning his aggressive impulses toward members of his family.

As psychotherapists, we are interested in our patients' patterns of ambiguity. The patient speaks and in the process of so doing he wittingly and unwittingly manifests patterns of meaning within his speech. The patterns are unconscious to the extent the patient is unaware of possible meanings. One of the functions of the therapist's interpretation is to bring these patterns into consciousness. A metaphorical interpretation by the therapist exploiting this ambiguity involves a concrete, figurative statement (hence deviant by the rules of language) that implies abstract qualities in the form of its literal or cognitive meanings. As discussed above, this figurative, linguistically deviant statement carries a meaning based upon similarities and differences between the figurative and literal elements. But because all metaphors are ambiguous the patient, when confronted with the therapist's metaphor, must interpret its meaning as it relates to himself. An important consideration is how the interpretation (metaphor) helps the patient in the psychotherapeutic work.

HYPOTHESIS

When both the abstract and concrete (literal and figurative, respectively) elements of a therapist's metaphor have been taken from the preceding patient speech (when they have been foregrounded there), this type of interaction comprises an organic whole within the process of the psychotherapy and is more likely to be helpful in facilitating the patient's understanding of his own ambiguity. I hasten to point out, however, that the content and timing of the cognitive meaning of the metaphor must be relevant and appropriate to the patient. Grounding the metaphor in the patient's speech cannot be mechanically applied and must conform to the principles of any interpretative intervention from the therapist.

Of course, it is nothing new to state that an interpretation must be based on something the patient has done or indicated through his speech. And it is not startling to propose that effective interpretations, those that facilitate the patient's understanding of himself, must be firmly grounded in what the patient has said about himself. The extra dimension here is that not only must the abstract, literal meaning of the metaphor be foregrounded in the antecedent patient speech, but also the figurative or concrete component. Why should this make a difference?

As noted above, all metaphors are ambiguous in that several different abstract meanings are implied. Because metaphors are ambiguous and require interpretation, there is an increased risk that a therapist's metaphorical interpretation will be misunderstood. What disambiguates a metaphor (or any ambiguous segment of language) is the context. If the metaphorical interpretation is constructed from the patient's preceding speech, then these foreground elements serve as guides for the patient to understand the metaphor in his own concrete particularized terms—that is, to relate how the figurative elements of the metaphor pertain to him.[6] The apparent theoretical indeterminacy of the metaphor is reduced by the context of the patient's speech. The patient is encouraged to examine his own experience; the task of understanding the patient's experience is emphasized.

Furthermore, by conceiving the metaphor in the patient's words, the therapist minimizes countertransference effects. There can be no denial that the construction of the metaphor by the therapist represents his own unconscious processes. Inasmuch as the therapist is prone to conceive the metaphor in the patient's own language, it seems likely that the therapist is responding unconsciously to the patient rather than to some inner need within himself. This tendency may correlate with empathic responsiveness in the therapist.[7] Hence the likelihood that metaphor is a narcissistic adventure on the part of the therapist is diminished.

Metaphorical interpretations delivered sensitively and under the conditions of foregrounding may have special value. All metaphorical interpretations are ambiguous. The patient must select some aspect of this ambiguity in his response. The patient is permitted to choose his own level of response and in doing so reveals more about what in the metaphor is important and meaningful for him at the moment. Moreover, the metaphor through its figurative, concrete representation of meaning may permit the bypassing of repression attached to abstract literal meanings. Inasmuch as repression represents an inability to understand unconscious meaning in abstract literal terms, a metaphorical statement may represent this unconscious meaning in concrete figurative language. When the patient's own words are used, the patient is guided in interpreting and understanding his own experience as well as the therapist's metaphor. Insight is enhanced and the unconscious meaning of what he had previously represented ambiguously becomes conscious. The metaphor is a new means of representing the meaning of the interpretation—a means that is more likely to be heard by the patient.

The therapist, formulating metaphorically with the patient's words, conveys to the patient in a wordless communication that he understands the patient beyond the literal meaning of what the patient says and that he is in tune to unconsciously motivated patterns of ambiguity.

The special value of metaphor, however, depends on its appropriate use. Metaphorical interpretations for their own sake or metaphors with their figurative content derived from some other source than the patient stand at risk for being misperceived. Such a metaphor may be more an expression of unconscious countertransference trends than a therapeutic interaction.

CONCLUSION

Metaphor, as a representation of meaning, is ambiguous in that it can represent multiple meanings simultaneously. Metaphor extends the range of language by expressing ideas that cannot be expressed in ordinary language and frequently does so in a vivid yet concrete manner. Metaphor, as an interpretive instrument in psychotherapy, can function to name events, ideas, and relationships not otherwise namable (including unconscious processes). It can provide a model or paradigm for structuring patient's experiences. It can be attention-getting and provide an affective immediacy perhaps not otherwise available, and in this manner facilitate patients' talking more explicitly about themselves. It lends itself to using the patient's own language. Also, how a patient responds can be quite useful. He reveals something of himself when he chooses from among different meanings of the metaphor. He may extend the implications of the metaphor and elaborate on aspects unsuspected by the therapist.

Because the understanding of metaphor depends on the context, an important aspect of the use of metaphor as an interpretation in psychotherapy is the immediate verbal context of the hour. Metaphor represents meaning ambiguously and may be misunderstood or misapplied by the patient. The context of the hour not only provides a means to reduce the risk of ambiguity, but also serves to enrich the patient's understanding of the therapist's metaphor. Another risk in the use of metaphor is the therapist's narcissistic overevaluation of his clever utterances, a risk reduced by closely relating the metaphor to the context of the hour and the patient's words. These considerations demonstrate a possible application of linguistics to psychotherapy research and technique.

NOTES

1. I am indebted to Dr. Marshall Edelson (personal communication) for calling my attention to this distinction between qualitative and quantitative deviance (see also Edelson 1975).

2. Dr. Marshall Edelson (personal communication).

3. This example is taken from Leech, 1969, p. 147.

4. This approach to metaphor is only one of many. See also Beardsley (1962), Black (1955), Nowottny (1962), Rubinstein (1972), and Shibles (1971). Indeed some theorists (Nowottny 1962), maintain that it is how tenor and vehicle *differ* that matters in conveying meaning.

5. Time measures were recorded.

6. Nowottny (1962) has noted that in addition to naming the innominate and providing a model for understanding, metaphors also provide an affective response or portray a private emotion as part of the understanding (p. 60).

7. The idea that linguistic competence is a cornerstone to psychotherapeutic skills has been stated by Edelson (1975).

REFERENCES

Aleksandrowicz, D. (1962).The meaning of metaphor. *Bulletin of the Menninger Clinic* 26:92- 101.
Beardsley, M. (1962). The metaphor. *Philosophy and Phenomenological Research* 22:293-307.

Black, M. (1955). Metaphor. *Proceedings of the Aristotelian Society* 55:273-294.

Cain, A. C., and Maupin, B. M. (1961). Interpretation within the metaphor. *Bulletin of the Menninger Clinic* 25:307-311.

Caruth, E., and Ekstein, R. (1966). Interpretation within the metaphor: further considerations. *Journal of Child Psychiatry* 5:35-45.

Edelson, M. (1971). *The Idea of a Mental Illness.* New Haven: Yale University Press.

────── (1972). Language and dreams: the interpretation of dreams revisited. *Psychoanalytic Study of the Child* 27:203-278.

────── (1975). *Language and Interpretation in Psychoanalysis.* Yale University Press.

Ekstein, R., and Wallerstein, J. (1956). Choice of interpretation in the treatment of borderline and psychotic children. *Bulletin of the Menninger Clinic* 2:199-207.

Freud, S. (1963). Introductory lectures on psycho-analysis. *Standard Edition* 15/16.

Gottschalk, L. (1961). *Comparative Psycholinguistic Analysis of Two Psychotherapeutic Interviews.* New York: International Universities Press.

Hammer, E. F. ed. (1968). *Use of Interpretation in Treatment: Technique and Art.* New York: Grune and Stratton.

Langs, R. (1973). *The Technique of Psychoanalytic Psychotherapy.* New York: Jason Aronson.

Leavy, S. A. (1973). Psychoanalytic interpretation. *Psychoanalytic Study of the Child* 28:305-330.

Leech, G. N. (1969). *A Linguistic Guide to English Poetry.* London: Longman.

Muncie, W. (1937). The psychopathology of metaphor. *Archives of Neurology and Psychiatry* 37:797-804.

Nowottny, W. (1962). *The Language Poets Use.* London: Athlone.

Parker, B. (1962). *My Language Is Me.* New York: Basic Books.

Reider, N. (1972). Metaphor as interpretation. *International Journal of Psycho-Analysis* 53:463-469.

Rosen, V. H. (1969). Introduction to panel on language and psychoanalysis. *International Journal of Psycho-Analysis* 50:113-116.

────── (1974). The nature of verbal intervention in psychoanalysis. *Psychoanalysis and Contemporary Science*, vol. 3, pp. 189-209. New York: International Universities Press.

Rothenberg, A. (1972). Poetic process and psychotherapy. *Psychiatry* 35:238-254.

────── (1976). Homospatial thinking in creativity. *Archives of General Psychiatry* 33:17-26.

Rubenstein, B. B. (1972). On metaphor and related phenomena. In *Psychoanalysis and Contemporary Science*, vol. 1, pp. 70-108. New York: Macmillan.

Shibles, W. A. (1971). *Metaphor: An Annotated Bibliography and History.* Whitewater, Wisconsin: Language Press.

Spence, D. P. (1968). The processing of meaning in psychotherapy: some links with psycholinguistics and information theory. *Behavioral Sciences* 13:349-361.

Truax, C. B., and Carkhuff, R. R. (1964). Concreteness: a neglected variable in research in psychotherapy. *Journal of Clinical Psychology* 20:264-267.

Tucker, G. J. *Metaphors, Models and Myths.* Unpublished manuscript.

Voth, H. M. (1970). The analysis of metaphor. *Journal of the American Psychoanalytic Association* 18:599-621.

Symbiotic Block
with Psychotic Patients

DAVID B. FEINSILVER, M.D.

An impasse, which I term *symbiotic block*, occurs commonly in psychoanalytic psychotherapy with psychotic patients. Three cases, representing different levels of psychotic transference relatedness, are chosen to exemplify this phenomenon. This impasse is defined in terms of undifferentiated symbiotic transference-countertransference phenomena which interfere with the separation-individuation process. The resolution process is defined in terms of concretizing issues of self-object differentiation and causality. A brief review of the literature is presented, along with discussion of the nature of the phenomenon and some key technical points.

Symbiotic block arises when a patient develops a relatedness to a therapist based on undifferentiated symbiotic transference phenomena involving primitive projections and introjections which engulf the observing ego and when the therapist similarly becomes entangled in symbiotic countertransference expectations of the patient. The impasse is resolved as the therapist identifies for himself his own symbiotic participation and then translates this for the patient into concrete issues of self-object differentiation and causality. The resolution seems to produce in the patient a sense of independence and taking charge of himself, which includes mobilization of ego functions, appreciation of the therapist as a separate entity, and particularly, appreciation of the therapeutic task at hand. I will illustrate this with three case vignettes from my own experience. The three patients manifest different degrees of psychotic disturbance and, therefore, different levels of symbiotic block.

An earlier version of this paper was presented at the Chestnut Lodge Symposium on October 4, 1974. I would like to express my appreciation to the many colleagues associated with Chestnut Lodge who have shared their experiences with me, and also to those who have critically reviewed earlier drafts of this paper.

Case 1

I had been working approximately two years with Miss A , a schizophrenic woman hospitalized at Chestnut Lodge many years previous. Throughout this time she remained in a chronically fixed psychotic state on high doses of antipsychotic medication. Initially, we had gone through a prolonged period in which I clarified to both of us her need to see me as responsible for her in various ways. For example, she felt I was always somehow around her, controlling the unit staff, her sleep, and her dreams. During the sessions, her stream of primary process chatter would create a vague oceanic sense of grandeur and oneness. Soon, however, I began to sense she was utilizing this mode in a defensive manner. I began to have an undefined feeling that I was permitting her to wallow needlessly in a state of regressed, symbiotic, psychotic subsistence, when she was really capable of living a more organized, more fully human existence. I began to understand that I was acceding to a symbiotic demand, which she was using as a defense against seeing herself as a separate entity—a separate entity responsible for her own wishes and the affects associated with them.

Initially, at moments of separation—that is, at the beginning and ending of the hour, before and after holidays and vacations—she would often express in various ways the wish to eat me or for me to eat her. She would work herself into a frenzied rage and bemoan her fate that in "not getting rid of her," "they" were not taking proper care of her. She would bite herself repeatedly, and this would finally bring the paroxysm to an end.

At first, this usually left me feeling helplessly sympathetic with her plight, or vaguely guilty. During this period, on one occasion, I had a nightmare of being invaded bodily by a vague spirit, and I gradually became aware of the intrusive rage involved in her symbiotic demand. On another occasion, somewhat later, I dreamt I was attending a grand ball and trying to escort her into a large bus into which I could not fit her. Gradually, I became aware of my own countertransference participation and began to interpret more precisely her demands for oneness.

She responded by expressing in various ways more explicit, realistic, direct feelings of wanting to have me with her, but then would suddenly replace this by the undifferentiated rageful demand to be destroyed and incorporated. It seemed as if she were trying to ward-off continued direct expression of the actuality of her rage by reverting to a psychological state in which there would be no difference between subject and object. This soon reached a repetitive cycle of response and reversion. When she therefore walked in one day and began once again to go on with her characteristic harangue, "Oh, I don't want to be around. I want to be gotten rid of. I won't state [her favorite way of negating all discussion]. Why don't they [the ever present 'they'] do something for me. They make me come here, drug me, sleep me," I responded like a parent telling a child that she simply couldn't have her seventeenth cookie, to the effect: "Look, if you don't want to be around I can't help you. I can't do anything for you if you don't tell me what you want. You and I both know that 'they' are a way of negating responsibility for your own feelings. Nobody is making you come here to see me if you yourself don't want to; and if you don't want to, I can't help you. As far as I am concerned, you are free to talk or not, come here or not, depending on whether you want to or not. This is up to you. If you want to forget that, it is also up to you. This is your right and privilege. But it should be clear that as far as I am concerned, whether or not you come here and talk to me is up to you." Although I felt angry at the patient, I felt I had a fairly clear appreciation of what was setting it off, namely, a demand which seemed clearly unnecessary. I was able to spell out to her just what I would no longer accept any responsibility for and what I would consider her responsibility.

Her initial response was to leave the office, but at the time of the next hour she came in and began to talk as never before in clear, coherent English, "I get it, you are trying to tell me that I have to take care of myself. It's up to me. [Going on somewhat angrily.] O.K.—if that's the way it has to be—O.K." She then launched into a very clear, coherent string of associations and memories not previously expressed, stating that she never really got what she wanted from her psychotically intrusive mother, who always blamed her and wanted to get rid of her, and finally related this to her feelings toward me. She seemed suddenly able to talk about the rage which, up to then, she had only been able to put into action. In subsequent hours, she continued to show slow, steady signs of increasing individuation, including looking for ways to actually live independently outside the hospital, although, of course, frequently she would revert back to her symbiotic modes.

Case 2

Mr. B was a young man in his early thirties with a long history of drug addiction, alcoholism, and various illegal activities characterized by exploitation of others, all of which led to numerous arrests and hospitalizations prior to admission to Chestnut Lodge. I had been seeing him for over two years, and he remained rather rigidly fixed in a completely impervious, narcissistic transference relationship, characterized by two opposing and incompatible attitudes. On the other hand, he showed prolonged periods of narcissistic mirroring and overidealization, and on the other he would often devalue me and the treatment. This seemed very similar to processes described by Heinz Kohut (1971). During this period, the very tenuous basis for our relationship was readily threatened by anything that might bring out Mr. B.'s intense underlying dependency and associated envy, frustration, and rage. This seemed very similar to processes described by Kernberg (1970). A comment about our relationship—for example, an indication that I might be heading the conversation toward something about his feelings toward me— would set off tirades of contemptuous devaluation, projection of blame, and sometimes degenerating into overt paranoia. Whenever I simply provided him with a receptive, noncritical audience for his endless speeches about his vaguely defined sense of greatness, however, he would stay in it and elaborate on daily interactions with patients and staff, indicating his own ultimate superiority and the consequent inferiority of all others. I was, of course, referred to in similar terms and, therefore, as far as he was concerned I was of no importance to him. From time to time he would remind us that, of course, he had no need to be in the hospital, no need for treatment, and certainly no need for me. His defenses would slip from time to time, and he might, for example, refer in glowing terms to an idealized image of my therapeutic abilities with very difficult patients. At moments of separation, he would suddenly launch into tirades about my incompetence and worthlessness, often progressing to completely paranoid views about my trying to attack him or influence him in some way. This would often culminate in his walking out of my office. He would also storm at me whenever I tried to discuss any meaningful topic with him, and as a result no discussion of issues could take place. Often, I experienced a sense of complete frustration at not being able to make any meaningful comment and fulfill my role as therapist; sometimes I experienced a bodily sensation of suffocation, as if there were not enough oxygen in the room to meet both his needs and my basic narcissistic needs.

During this period, however, he made remarkable symptomatic improvement. As far as we could tell from all primary and secondary sources, he completely gave up his drug usage, drinking, and antisocial activities. Complete reversal and reform took place and he became a self-righteous paragon of good behavior. His efforts were now channeled into taking care of other patients. This he explained as trying to develop a vague sense of inner, dormant, creativity within himself. He seemed desirous of giving to other patients what he wanted from me, but he could never begin to acknowledge this need. He described what he was giving as a vague kind of help and guidance through a very special, sensitive, empathic understanding whereby needs and wants could be known implicitly without having to be spoken about. He soon reached a point at which he began to talk to me in a contemptuous, devaluating way about moving out of the hospital and not wanting anything more to do with the hospital or me. My attempts to ask for elaboration or to interpret this flight in any way were simply scoffed at and ridiculed, and he would finish by launching into another tirade about my worthlessness to him and then storm out of the office. Attempts at any discussion were impossible. He would repeatedly bring up in the hours, in a diffuse and vaguely demanding way, questions about his outpatiency, in a manner that would imply, You know what I want and why don't you just do it for me. I initially responded by stating repeatedly in various ways that, since he was indeed feeling better, it certainly made sense for him to begin working toward becoming an outpatient; but I did not see any sense in my continuing as his therapist in an outpatient situation, in which he and I would have to share responsibility for his being on his own, as long as he felt I was no good, my therapy worthless, and he did not want to work with me.

He puzzled over this for several months, bringing the subject up repeatedly from various angles, but always with the same contemptuous demand that I make something happen for him. My response was always the same. Gradually his attacks softened, and he presented dreams of beginning to achieve a special kind of warmness and closeness with some vague authority (teacher, doctor). Although these dreams were offered without any associations, seemingly as a gift, it seemed clear that he experienced repeated reaffirmation that he was receiving the special kind of understanding and guidance he had been giving others. He began to verbalize directly to me newly found feelings of liking and feeling close to me after all. He guessed that he really did want me as his therapist and would feel bad if I would not continue with him. He quickly added somewhat ironically that he was beginning to realize he was not sure he wanted to move out of the hospital so quickly; that he felt he now had some things he wanted to discuss, clarify, and straighten out before he proceeded.

He was beginning to acknowledge more directly that he did indeed have a need for me. It was clear that now the split-off, walled-off wishes for a special closeness with me were emerging. Consequently, what was an impervious wall began to crack; it now served more as a simple narcissistic facade, and was no longer a basic narcissistic need to completely deny the existence of the other.

Case 3

In the next case the same issues were addressed, but in a healthier borderline patient, earlier in the therapy, and with much less confrontation. Miss C, a bright young girl in her early twenties, had become chronically depressed as the result of the doubly traumatic loss of her stepfather and her mother within a month of eath other. Her depression had reached near delusional proportions. The stepfather had unexpectedly suicided by stepping in front of a train. Within a month Miss C had gone away to begin college, frequently calling home and asking anxiously about her mother's welfare. One day her mother picked up the phone, gasped, and died. No cause of death was ever determined.

Initially, in my work with her, I felt intense sympathy for her tragic plight, and there was rapport as she told me her history and symptoms. She confessed her convictions that she caused people to die and was therfore unworthy to live and that she was determined to some day succeed in killing herself. In fact, she had a secret plan to do so and considered it just a matter of time. She quickly became negativistic and silent during the hour. She hinted at there being something missing from my style of therapy, that I was trying to impose an undefined something on her, while refusing to elaborate. She began demanding a new therapist, a new hospital, special drug treatments, and made several suicide gestures. She continued to come regularly to her hours and gradually began to respond to my attempts to gently prod and coax her into discussion. I was noticing, however, that no matter how much I tried to accept her silent withdrawal as a warranted need or to coax her as gently as possible, I always had the uncomfortable feeling that I was forcing something upon her which she had to fight against. I associated my feeling to her complaint about my style of therapy and what might be coming across to her. I then developed a regular habit of always peeling off this projection by preceding any statement with a reminder that she should appreciate that it was her right and privilege to respond however she wanted to whatever I said to her. For example, if she wanted to be silent, that was up to her. I was not interested in trying to force her into anything and as far as I was concerned it was her right and privilege to do whatever she wanted.

This went on for some time until one day she suddenly demanded that I stop saying that. She didn't know why, but it bothered her. As far as she was concerned she had no problem in knowing her rights and privileges, but—by the way—what was my thought about why this might be such a problem for her? At that point, I explained to her more fully that I thought she was being reminded of something that made her feel she did not deserve to get better, but also that she was trying to make me the villain in order to get me to do something about it. She was silent immediately, but obviously thoughtful and the next day came in saying that she was feeling now, suddenly, that she wanted to talk to me, and reported the following dream: "Solzhenitsyn, the great spokesman for the oppressed masses, was wearing a special contact lens and had come across the ocean to join her at school, to help her crusade to free the oppressed masses and political prisoners of the U.S."

She began to associate to this dream in a fairly useful and productive manner for the first time in the six months that we had worked together. The patient's thoughts concerned how good she felt, although she was still very anxious. She was embarrassed about getting the privilege at a unit meeting the previous afternoon to go off the unit on a trip. This reminded her of a second dream in which she was a bird in a cage defecating on a particular patient who had teased her for her silent unresponsiveness at the meeting by saying that he would cut off her head if she did not speak. She was obviously holding back tears as she said how angry she felt toward this particular patient. She also said how she needed to wall herself off from all such people who seemed to be all around her. She then became more openly tearful as she spoke of having to cut herself off from life and of having erected such a wall between us. This was a part of her need to renounce all things in life, previously meaningful and pleasurable.

DELINEATION OF THE PHENOMENON

The preceding case vignettes, spanning the diagnostic spectrum from chronically regressed schizophrenia to a fairly well integrated borderline syndrome, share the following four characteristics.

1. The patient develops a transference relatedness, characterized predominantly by object relatedness of an undifferentiated type, in which ambivalent and preambivalent symbiotic transference phenomena are experienced in a split-off, unintegrated, and projected manner. Positive and negative aspects may be interpreted and acknowledged to some extent, but they remain essentially split-off and unintegrated. A negative aspect of the relationship becomes more prominent and unmanageable at the same time and therapeutic progress comes to an impasse.

2. The patient begins to use the negative aspect of the ambivalent symbiotic relatedness defensively against a positive attachment of a more differentiated object relatedness (including ambivalent aspects). This more mature positive attachment is split-off and repressed in favor of the fantasied ambivalent symbiotic wishes. It is as if the patient were substituting, 'If you don't give me what I want, then I will get rid of you and get what I want, for the more mature, differentiated statement, I am angry at you because I love you and I cannot get what I want from you. Please give me what I want.

3. The intervention by the therapist demonstrates to the patient that his ambivalent symbiotic wishes are unrealizable as such, and can only be dealt with if the positive, more differentiated split-off sector is recognized and taken into account, noting the following three central features.

- Self-Object Differentiation (Who's Who and What's What). The therapist spells out in very concrete terms how the patient's ambivalence and its consequences are under his own sphere of responsibility and how the therapist, as a separate entity with a separate sphere of responsibility, simply cannot, as a matter of fact, have any control over the patient's hateful activity. He describes what is up to the patient and what is up to the therapist, and how the analyst cannot do for the patient what the patient must do for himself.

- Causality (Action-Reaction Principle). The therpist interprets in very concrete, realistic, matter-of-fact terms where a causal relationship might exist between the patient's hateful activity and his repressed attachment to the therapist. In effect, the therapist says, Your hating me and getting rid of me is taking you away from obtaining what you really want. The unsuspecting patient then suddenly begins to realize he cares about this. The therapist makes clear that he cannot respond effectively to the patient's hateful activity, with particular care to present this simply as a matter of fact, that his statement is not out of any vindictiveness, and this also serves to reassure the patient of his not having a destructive effect.

• Timing. This is of course, as always, a critical matter, which necessarily involves a great deal of intuition and about which only rough guidelines can be given. The therapist times and doses his intervention, given as a whole or in parts, when he senses the progression of the patient's underlying positive attachment and working relationship becoming increasingly thwarted and threatened by an increasingly prominent ambivalent symbiotic mode. The therapist must make an implicit judgment of the strength of the underlying positive attachment so that the interpretation will be delivered sometime after it might be taken only as a rejection, but before the intensity of the ambivalence thwarts all communication.

4. If all goes well, the patient responds by becoming aware of his own independence as well as the therapist's. He becomes aware of his positive attachment to the therapist and the futility of pursuing his desires on the symbiotic level, as well as of his need to take responsibility for his ambivalence—that is, to experience the analyst as a separated, whole object toward whom he wants to direct his differentiated hateful feelings in order to satisfy his desires. Concurrently, the patient then seems to develop a more differentiated capacity for appreciating the role of the therapist as a partner in the therapeutic venture and the capacity for observing internal aspects of himself.

DISCUSSION

I shall limit my focus in this discussion to highlighting the relevant literature, briefly examining the nature of the phenomenon, and concluding with a discussion of some key technical points. For the time being, I will defer further elaboration on many very interesting issues raised; such as, development of observing ego, limit setting, splitting, differentiation from negative therapeutic reaction, and, particularly, concepts of therapeutic alliance.

Many people have, of course, written about the problem of dealing with the struggles of the psychotic patient in the basic transference position of symbiotic relatedness, though it was not always referred to in these particular terms. These writers include Tausk (1919), Klein (1946), Winnicott (1949), Federn (1952), Rosenfeld (1952), Bion (1959), Searles (1961 and 1963), Jacobson (1964), Mahler (1968), and Khan (1969). No one to my knowledge defined this particular phenomenon as a characteristic way of moving toward differentiation and individuation, nor delineated the particular elements. Several people have, however, referred to related issues. The first, of course, was probably Freud (1914) when he explained how he came to set an arbitrary termination date for the Wolf-Man: "[He] remained for a long time unassailably entrenched behind an attitude of obliging apathy. He listened, understood, and remained unapproachable.... His shrinking from a self-sufficient existence was so great as to outweigh all the vexations of his illness. Only one way was to be found of overcoming it. I was obliged to wait until his attachment to myself had become strong enough to counterbalance his shrinking and then played off this one factor against the other" (p. 11). Although it is not clear precisely how Freud then presented this to the Wolf-Man, it seems that he used the setting of a termination date as a way of letting the Wolf-Man know that, beyond a certain point, he could not expect to receive continuing gratification from the entrenched relationship. This, then, mobilized the positive transference in the service of apparently useful analytic work, which led to a seemingly successful completion of the analysis.

It should be noted, however, that the subsequent history of the Wolf-Man, as described by Ruth Mack Brunswick (Gardiner 1971), in her analysis of him, suggests very strongly that he continued in a state of negative transference to Freud, which served as the basis for a paranoid illness and returned him to treatment.

In addition, several authors have written that gratification derived from the analyst becomes accessible only after faced with termination and the anticipated loss of it (Nunberg 1955 and Orens 1955).

August Aichorn (1925), in *Wayward Youth* described how he tried to establish a relationship with a highly narcissistic delinquent boy by provoking him to run away from his hospital. Unfortunately, he does not say anything about how he did this, but it is clear that he had the expectation, which later proved correct, that the boy would then realize how much he liked being with Aichorn, compare life in the institution to life in the outside world, and thereby become accessible to therapy.

Winnicott (1949), focusing on "objective countertransference" in working with psychotic patients in "Hate in the Countertransference" describes an interchange with a nine-year-old boy from a broken home who had previously run away from any attempt to engage him in treatment. After making contact with him by interpreting his running away as actually preserving his mother, Winnicott took him into his home and soon ran into difficulty as he struggled

with the boy's assaultive attacks. Winnicott describes finding it useful to tell
the boy what had happened to make Winnicott hate him as he would put him
out the door. When his attack had subsided, the boy would ring a bell and ask
to return. Although Winnicott is focusing on the usefulness of making explicit
one's anger and on describing a real life situation, clearly, he describes a
process very similar to that above.

Harold Searles, formerly at Chestnut Lodge, in his paper on phases of
treatment (1961), was probably the first to refer specifically to these issues in
relation to work with psychotic patients. He takes up the issues of symbiosis
and self-object differentiation, and my own work extends most directly from
his presentation. Searles focuses on the need for the therapist to tease out
countertransference issues which, at times, lead to a sense of outrage on the
sudden appreciation of the full brunt of the patient's symbiotic demands. He
describes how the therapist then begins to hold the patient highly responsible
for his symptoms and to "stew in his own juice." He emphasizes how, in
contrast, as far as he is concerned, whether the patient gives up his position or
not is all the same to him. Searles gives a very vivid description of a complex,
slowly evolving process in which delineation of self from object by the
therapist parallels resolution of the symbiosis by the patient. He does not,
however, focus on clarifying the sequences involved in the process; nor does
he delineate it any further.

John Cameron, presently on the staff at Chestnut Lodge, in his book,
Studies in Psychosis (1966) and in personal communication, refers to this
phenomenon as a kind of interlocking which he calls *narcissistic block*,
resulting from problems of countertransference. He does not, however,
delineate this further. Many other colleagues at Chestnut Lodge in
discussions of clinical cases presented instances of this phenomenon.
However, it is usually described as a spontaneously arising event which
happens to work out, though sometimes not, and about which the therapist
experiences considerable uneasiness and embarrassment. In any event, this
phenomenon has been touched upon in the literature and probably is widely
encountered clinically. Because the phenomenon brings into focus elements
involved in elucidating a critical step in psychoanalytic work with patients, it
seems to deserve delineation as a separate entity.

What is the nature of the phenomenon? Why does the impasse arise and
what is involved in its resolution? The transference position that evolves with
patients functioning on a psychotic level is essentially reflective of the need to
relive an arrested developmental stage because of fears associated with higher
levels, as it is for all patients. For the psychotic patient, however, fixations
involve a regression to a symbiotic level of functioning at which the need is to
relate to an object seen as the omnipotent parent. This means that, to the
extent to which a patient functions on this level, he has a basic need to

somehow see the omnipotent parental object as a causative agent. The symbiotic level of fixation involves attributing causation to the omnipotent parental object, and this therefore, interferes with appreciation of causality on higher levels of mental functioning. The integrative and synthesizing ego functions are consumed by the need to exist on a symbiotic level.

The technical problem in dealing with such a patient becomes how the analyst can help him appreciate the irrational aspects of his symbiotic expectations, if the patient cannot think about them rationally and if he is irrationally convinced the analyst as the omnipotent early maternal object is involved in causing his emotional well-being (or pain). In this situation, conventionally correct interpretations cannot have any lasting impact. The patient may even demonstrate some response to reconstructed genetic aspects and interpretations of his need for symbiotic relatednes and of his fear and need to defend against ambivalence, but he will return quickly to the basic symbiotic position.

If, however, the source of the patient's causal expectations, the analyst, at a moment when the patient is maximally involved in omnipotent symbiotic expectations, demonstrates very concretely that he will not and cannot respond to the patient's expectations, then his symbiotic wishes will be frustrated, thereby creating a need to find other pathways. This enhances the likelihood of integration. Initially, the patient may experience this as a threat, but to the extent that the patient is in a very threatened position to begin with, he will welcome new pathways that serve to decrease anxiety and tension. Timing is very critical and probably depends very much on the moment of "immediacy and urgency" as described by Strachey (1934). The unattainabiligy of the patient's desires is therefore brought home by focusing on the three basic elements described above—causality, self-object differentiation, and timing.

This realization seems to strengthen the ego, and to effect particularly a more differentiated appreciation of what the analyst stands for in the analytic work. It seems the development of this favorable situation in work with psychotic patients might be compared to the process described in classical analytic work with neurotic patients, whereby, in the course of the work, a therapeutic alliance develops through a splitting of the patient's ego into an observing and an experiencing aspect as the initial transference resistance is dealt with (Sterba 1934, Zetzel 1956, Greenson 1954, and Olinick 1969). If, however, the factors involved in creating this impasse are not recognized, the work may continue in a stalemated condition indefinitely, or the ambivalence of the patient or therapist may lead to a sudden assaultive disruption of the relationship, or to a further regressed condition.

What is the nature of the intervention? First, what it is not: clearly, it is not a classical transference interpretation. No repressed historical material is referred to, nor in most cases has much relevant historical data come to light at this stage of the work. Only after the impasse is dealt with can the pertinent genetic data begin to emerge from the patient. The assumption of symbiotic level phenomena must be inferred according to our theories from the basic historical facts and clinical data. Also, the usual conception of the terms clarification and confrontation do not seem to apply. Can the intervention be dismissed as merely a kind of countertransference response with a fortuitous reaction? Although it is clear that at the point of impasse in each case I was experiencing significant countertransference anger contributive to the impasse, I believe the interventions were delivered as an outgrowth, first, of a studied appreciation of my response and the contribution from the patient, and, second of addressing these issues through the intervention. Certainly the countertransference rage in such an impasse must be dealt with before any effective intervention can occur, as discussed by Searles and Cameron above and as will be discussed below.

I believe, however, that the intervention can be usefully described in several ways. It can be seen as a declaration of intention by the therapist to cease countertransference participation contributory to the patient's symbiotic desires, thereby providing for the patient a kind of limit-setting, which then causes him to find some other way to deal with his frustrated desires. The intervention can also be seen as posing a threat to the patient, as described above, and it therefore might be argued that the patient is simply complying to appease the therapist. Another view might be that the therapist is simply abandoning the patient, thereby forcing him to develop his own resources. The therapist can also be seen as functioning in the role of an auxiliary ego, or ego support, providing necessary reality testing. Another major factor seen propelling the patient toward resolution of the impasse is the emergence of the idealized object as channels for positive transference become opened. All of these explanations contain some truth, but it seems they do not adequately account for the sudden emergence of the patient's ability to function as an independent entity on higher levels of integration.

This realization of new found independence could stem from specific issues addressed in the intervention, and it seems to me that probably the most useful way to consider this process is in terms of the therapist's becoming for the patient a new object who provides an essential growth experience which the previous cumulative developmental experience with the parents was unable to achieve. Therefore, because of entanglement in symbiotic fixations, these patients can be seen as being prevented from independent functioning. They can be seen as craving the opportunity for independence if only shown the way. It is comparable to the familiar developmental situation of children who make difficult separation from their parents in new situations, such as school, by continuing a big show of nagging and clinging at the point of separation, while the parent is present, but as soon as the parent leaves, becoming enthusiastically involved with their new surroundings.

However one views the intervention, it seems important to note that it falls into the class of interventions most properly considered as parameters (Eissler 1953), or deviations in psychoanalytic technique (Greenson 1958). It must be kept in mind that the total impact of the intervention on the patient may have meaning on other levels, some of which may not be immediately apparent, but must be dealt with later in the therapy (Langs 1975). For example, Mr. B and Miss C clearly indicated that they began experiencing me as their idealized object, Mr. B experiencing me as an authority figure who provided the special kind of understanding and guidance he craved and Miss C experiencing me as the great liberator, Solzhenitsyn. While at this point in the treatment it need only be noted that a powerful aspect of the transference is mobilized and motivates the patient, this is clearly a trend with many implications to be attended to in later phases.

I will now focus on a few key technical points in the handling of the issues involved. First, it must be emphasized that the setting under which the clinical examples occur is Chestnut Lodge. Obviously, the kind of regression and loss of observing ego function that these very sick patients manifested, demonstrates how much the patients required for their survival the auxiliary ego support provided by our staff, all highly experienced in handling the needs of the other twenty-three hours. Of course, this does not necessarily imply this phenomenon takes place only in patients with impaired ego functions requiring hospitalization; in fact, it most certainly can occur in healthier patients. Matters will be complicated in these patients, however, by other levels of meaningful, negativistic patterns which must be understood and technically handled quite differently, as for example in the "negative therapeutic reaction." For the most part, however, there seems to be a correlation between impaired ego strength and the potential for the symbiotic block and its intensity.

At the risk of overstating the obvious, it should be emphasized that the technique delineated here is not a precise recipe randomly applicable to a psychotic patient needing individuation, but rather a process of beginning individuation which is only part of another highly complex, slowly evolving therapeutic process—one in which much work has been previously done during the initial and symbiotic phases and which will require much more in the working through of the individuation process. It should also be emphasized that because of the highly individualized nature of the work, the particular way in which this phenomenon may occur will vary considerably, depending on the particular style of the therapist involved, as well as the individualities of particular patients.

Probably, the single most important technical problem is the handling of countertransference ambivalence. The therapist must be aware of his anger and his own wishes for symbiosis and omnipotence. Difficulties occur mainly if this anger is either suppressed by the therapist in favor of maintaining his own symbiotic wishes or overreacted to with a sense of blind frustration out of a need to deny his own symbiotic wishes. Blind frustration can lead to the analyst's being too vindictive or too much in the position of threatening and issuing ultimatums, which, of course, puts him simply into the position of omnipotence in relation to the patient. This, of course, becomes a mere reenactment of the omnipotent symbiotic transference and defeats the whole purpose of the therapy.

In doing psychoanalytic psychotherapy with psychotic patients, a therapist must be alert to the possible development of symbiotic block, the symbiotic transference and countertransference issues involved, and the process of resolution which involves concretizing issues of self-object differentiation and causality.

REFERENCES

Aichorn, A. (1925). *Wayward Youth*. Viking, 1965.

Bion, W. R. (1959). Attacks on linking. *International Journal of Psycho-Analysis* 40:308-315.

Cameron, J. L. (1966). *Studies on Psychosis*. New York: International Universities Press.

Eissler, K. R. (1953). The effect of the structure of the ego on psychoanalytic technique. *Journal of the American Psychoanalytic Association* 1:104-143.

Federn, P. (1952). *Ego Psychology and the Psychoses*. Ed. E. Weiss. New York: Basic Books.

Freud, S. (1914). From the history of an infantile neurosis. *Standard Edition* 17:3-124.

Gardiner, M. (1971). *The Wolf-Man, by the Wolf-Man*. New York: Basic Books.

Greenson, R. (1954). The role of transference, practical considerations in relation to therapy. *Journal of the American Psychoanalytic Association* 34:155-181.

—— (1958). Variations in classical psycho-analytic technique: an introduction. *International Journal of Psycho-Analysis* 39:200-201.

Jacobson, E. C. (1964). *The Self and the Object World*. New York: International Universities Press.

Kernberg, O. F. (1970). Factors in the treatment of narcissistic personalities. *Journal of the American Psychoanalytic Association* 18:51-85.

Khan, M. R. (1969). On symbiotic omnipotence. In *Privacy of the Self*. New York: International Universities Press.

Klein, M. (1946). Notes on some schizoid mechanisms. *International Journal of Psycho-Analysis* 27:99-110.

Kohut, H. (1971). *The Analysis of the Self*. New York: International Universities Press.

Langs, R. (1975). The therapeutic relationship and deviations in technique. *International Journal of Psychoanalytic Psychotherapy* 4:106-141.

Mahler, M. (1968). *On Human Symbiosis and the Vicissitudes of Individuation*. New York: International Universities Press.

Nunberg, H. (1955). The will to recovery. In *Practice and Theory of Psychoanalysis*. New York: International Universities Press.

Olinick, S. (1969). On empathy and regression in the service of the other. *British Journal of Medical Psychology* 42:41-49.

Orens, M. (1955). Setting a termination date—an impetus to analysis. *Journal of the American Psychoanalytic Association* 3:651-665.

Rosenfeld, H. (1952). Transference-phenomena and transference-analysis in an acute catatonic schizophrenic patient. *International Journal of Psycho-Analysis* 33:457-464.

Searles, H. F. (1961). Phases of patient-therapist interaction in the psychotherapy of chronic schizophrenics. In *Collected Papers on Schizophrenia and Related Subjects*. London: Hogarth, 1965.

——— (1963). Transference psychoses in the psychotherapy of schizophrenia. In *Collected Papers on Schizophrenia and Related Subjects*. London: Hogarth, 1965.

Sterba, R. (1934). State of the ego in analytic therapy. *International Journal of Psycho-Analysis* 15:117-126.

Strachey, J. (1934). The nature of the therapeutic action of psycho-analysis. *International Journal of Psycho-Analysis* 15:127-159.

Tausk, V. (1919). On the origin of the "influencing machine" in schizophrenia. In *The Psychoanalytic Reader*, ed. R. Fliess. New York: International Universities Press, 1948.

Winnicott, D. W. (1949). Hate in the countertransference. *International Journal of Psycho-Analysis* 30:69-74.

Zetzel, E. (1956). The current concepts of transference. *International Journal of Psycho-Analysis* 33:369-376.

Transitional Phenomena in the Treatment of a Psychotic Adolescent

RICHARD P. FOX, M.D.

The clinical history and the initial phase of the psychotherapy of a hospitalized psychotic adolescent are presented to demonstrate the loss of "transitional capabilities" coinciding with the onset of a psychotic regression and their subsequent restoration as the patient reemerged from overt psychosis. Winnicott's concept of transitional phenomena is reexamined, highlighting its function in the capacity for illusion, its internalization as psychic structure, and its interpersonal dimension in the establishment of a "transitional mode of relatedness" within the psychotherapeutic situation.

In the twenty-five years since Winnicott presented his paper on transitional objects (1953) to the British Psycho-Analytical Society, this concept has found a place of increasing importance in developmental and clinical studies. The scope of its application is reflected in the wide range of work in which the transitional concept has been utilized. In addition to its use in clinical studies (Fintzy 1971, Volkan 1973, Horton 1974, Fisher 1975), the transitional concept has been taken as a point of reference in developmental studies (Busch et al. 1973), in descriptions of ego development (Coppolillo 1967, Tolpin 1971), and in the construction of theoretical models of therapy (Greenbaum 1974, Fox 1973).

In the course of its development, however, the transitional concept moved a long way from its observed basis, the "first not-me possession." Winnicott in his original paper (1953) laid the foundation for these extensions when he suggested a developmental line of transitional phenomena extending from the blanket through play to religious and cultural experiences. From a review of the diversity of papers stemming from this productive concept (including Winnicott's own *Playing and Reality* 1971), it is evident that it has grown to include a variety of interpersonal as well as intrapsychic phenomena.

Attempting to lend clarity and precision to the use of the transitional object concept, Tolpin (1971) applied Kohut's idea of transmuting internalization (1971) to describe how the transitional object's function becomes part of an inner psychological structure much as, according to Freud (1923), the character of the ego results from a precipitate of abandoned ego cathexes. In descibing the internalized function of the transitional object, Tolpin emphasized its role as a self-soothing psychic structure.

Making use of this developmental formulation, Horton (1974) has applied the transitional concept to an understanding of the mystical experience of a schizoid and psychotic late adolescent college student. In a fascinating clinical study, he demonstrated that this experience emerged as a transitional phenomenon as the patient began to sever the symbiotic tie with her mother. He described how the mystical experience as transitional phenomenon was accepted and not challenged, which allowed the therapist to discover its unique adaptive and defensive functions. According to Horton, the mystical experience proved to serve the same function as that of the teddy bear or blanket for the younger child, namely a self-applied soother in the face of separation anxiety, depressive affect, and feelings of loneliness.

I will explore here another aspect of the transitional concept in the treatment of a psychotic late adolescent. I hope to demonstrate that the importance of transitional phenomena is not limited to the function of self-soothing, but that its function also remains closely linked with the capacity for illusion, as Winnicott described in his original contribution (1953). The clinical history of the patient is briefly recapitulated to demonstrate that the loss of transitional capabilities heralded the onset of a psychotic regression and that the subsequent reestablishment of these capabilities in the early months of psychotherapy occurred as the patient gradually reemerged from overt psychosis. In my discussion I will place less emphasis on the transitional object simply as soother and will emphasize instead its more general role in bridging the gap between subjective and objective experience.

Clinical History

The patient, a twenty-year-old girl, was hospitalized after an acute psychotic regression which culminated in her retreat to the attic of her college dormitory where she was found mute and incontinent. Although she responded well to her mother's subsequent arrival at the college and was able to return home with her, she then physically attacked her mother and again adopted a position of mute resistance to all movememt.

The patient's early development was relatively unremarkable except for a school refusal at the time she was to begin kindergarten. With her father's intervention the problem abated and she became an outstanding student. She was seen as a precocious, intelligent, talented child but also as obstinate and something of a tomboy.

When she was thirteen, her parents felt there was a marked shift in the patient's disposition. She became more willful and provocatively defiant—most notably in her use of drugs and in her choice of boyfriends. There were almost daily mother-daughter fights which often lasted until the father's arrival home for dinner. An unsuccessful attempt at family therapy led to a psychiatric recommendation that she accept an early admission to a distant college.

During this first year away from home, her mother became preoccupied with the patient's long standing problem of intermittent amenorrhea. The patient's own gynecologist felt the problem was functional and was pursuing a conservative course, but the mother insisted on a consultation with her own gynecologist. The mother's doctor diagnosed polycystic ovarian disease and recommended surgery, which was postponed until the conclusion of the summer college quarter.

When the mother described this consultation during my diagnostic interview with the parents, she quickly added that she herself had had a series of miscarriages and a single stillbirth between the birth of her older son and that of the patient ten years later. She also reported that during this time she suffered recurrent episodes of depression, one of which led to a brief hospitalization.

During the summer prior to the scheduled surgery the patient experienced her first acute regressive episode. In a dance class, she was told to improvise a dance, imagining herself as a reptile. She was unable to conclude the improvisation and had to be taken to a hospital emergency room where she was sedated to interrupt an acutely agitated state.

The patient returned home for surgery and made a rapid postoperative recovery, prompted, as she later acknowledged, by her intense fear of being physically cared for by her nurse-mother. She remained at home for the next academic year and was seen by another psychiatrist in twice-a-week psychotherapy.

On her return to school the next summer, she alternated between bursts of manic-like activity and depressive withdrawal and made daily phone calls to her mother. She was hospitalized briefly but reconstituted immediately upon her mother's arrival at the college. Finally, her mother was able to return home after establishing the patient in a psychotherapy with a new therapist, and coincident with the patient's involvement with a new boyfriend.

The next few months saw the patient develop an intense dependent tie to this boyfriend who escorted her to and from her twice weekly psychotherapy sessions. Later, as this relationship began to show signs of strain and eventual breakup, the patient had another burst of manic-like activity, again marked by transient dissociative reactions during dance rehearsals. Finally, as the relationship with the boyfriend came to a close, the patient discovered she had lost her capacity to dance and to use physical movement as a mode of discharge and tension release. She became overtly paranoid. At one point, she hid in the back of her van for two days, terrified of the hostility outside and convinced that the black students on campus planned to kill her.

She stopped attending therapy sessions and began to walk aimlessly around the campus or sit motionless for hours, often outdoors on the ground. She later described one incident in which she imagined an elderly woman fed her putrid milk and another in which a woman student seduced her and then tried to scald her in a hot shower. She became more and more withdrawn and immobile; finally she reached the condition in which she was found in the dormitory attic.

Discussion

Before describing my initial contacts with the patient, I would like to highlight aspects of the clinical history particularly relevant in the subsequent unfolding of the therapeutic process.

Although there were evidences of oedipal configurations in the presenting history and certainly in the subsequent psychotherapeutic material, the problem which accounted for the psychotic manifestations of this patient seemed to reside primarily in the mother-daughter relationship. Further, this problem seemed to represent a defect in the patient's capacity for internalization; she appeared incapable of establishing an identification with her mother—especially when separated from her—but instead seemed to require an actual ongoing dependent relationship with her. Her mother, who had never fully separated from her own mother, contributed to her daughter's difficulties. She seemed incapable of allowing her daughter to grow up and leave home and, in particular, seemed unable to deal with the depression which might be consequent to this separation.

Early manifestations of this problem in the mother-daughter relationship were suggested by the turmoil that surrounded the patient's development into puberty and her subsequent intermittent amenorrhea. Mother, who had maintained considerable interest in the patient's menstrual difficulties, became preoccupied with the problem when her daughter left home to attend a distant college. In this area, mother seemed incapable of differentiating her daughter's problems from her own earlier gynecologic and obstetrical difficulties. At mother's insistence the patient had a consultation with the mother's gynecologist who recommended surgical intervention.

The scheduled surgery raised the possibility of a return to the situation in which the nurse-mother would be taking physical care of her postoperative daughter. This prospect, in turn, mobilized the patient's regressive tendency to become more dependent, clinging, and child-like along with her angry struggles against this dependency. In addition this resulted in a regression in ego-functioning which affected her thought processes, her relationship to reality, and eventually her capacity for physical activity, including locomotion.

The regression reached the level of psychological organization which Melanie Klein (1946) has called the paranoid-schizoid position, in which projective and introjective modes of thought and defense predominate and the capacity for differentiation between subjective and objective experience eventually is lost. Such incapacity to keep inner and outer reality related but potentially separable was evident in the episode in which the patient was unable to terminate a dance improvisation.

As the situation deteriorated with further loss of external support, a kind of topographic regression (a form of regression in ego-functioning, see Freud 1900) occurred which included a reversal within the psychic apparatus away from motor activity and toward visual fantasy, projective perception, and eventually hallucination. The transition was characterized by a shift from activity toward passivity: Aggression could no longer find motor expression but was merely elaborated in fantasy, then projected outward. Prior to hospitalization she had reached the point of immobility bordering on catatonia; this improved transiently with her mother's arrival and presence. Later, upon return home, she attacked her mother but retreated once more into her immobility and catatonia.

This report will not elaborate in any detail on the relationship of adolescent psychosis to the earlier problems of separation and individuation. I think it notable, however, that what is being described in the clinical history, in some ways, represents a reversal of the processes described by Margaret Mahler (1968) in her studies of the early mother-child pair and of the child's movement toward autonomy and object constancy. In the history as recorded, we see a reversal of this developmental process and a regression toward the level of mother-child paired functioning characteristic of the symbiotic stage of infantile development.

THE TRANSITIONAL OBJECT

Out of his pioneering studies on the mother-infant dyad, Donald Winnicott evolved a theory about the emergence of self-object discrimination in young children. According to Winnicott, the starting point of early object relationships is not simply gratification or frustration of oral instinctual needs. Winnicott assumed as a biological given a primitive relationship characterized by dependence on the part of the newborn infant, and its biological reciprocal on the part of the mother, which he referred to as *primary maternal preoccupation* (1956). From the infant's point of view this state of total helplessness or absolute dependence is psychologically preobject—that is, the interaction is personalized (suited to his needs), but not yet personal (involving whole persons, self and mother). Winnicott suggested that the most important feature of this interaction is that the quality and quantity of maternal caring remain relatively consistent and that the reciprocity between the infant and caretaker remain essentially undisturbed— a situation he described as *good enough mothering* (1960).

During this phase of development, the crucial issue is one of the adequacy of maternal care; with adequate or good enough mothering, the developmental thrust is toward the emergence of a psychologically dyadic relationship out of the as yet undifferentiated matrix of the mother-infant situation. One aspect of this beginning psychological polarization, which will eventuate in the differentiation between subject and object, is the emergence of transitional objects and transitional phenomena (1953).

In developing his concept of the infant's beginning relationship to the outside world and reality, Winnicott emphasized the role of illusion. He suggested that in a state of need, the infant imagines or fantasies in some primitive way that which is needed. With good enough mothering the fantasy coincides with the satisfaction—with the provision supplied by the mother at the right time, of the right type, and in the proper amount. The result of this simultaneity is that the infant has the illusion that he has created what he wants. In other words, with the almost complete adaptational fit of the mother's provisions to the infant's needs, the infant develops the illusion of magical, omnipotent control of the environment—the first bridge between an inner reality of fantasy and the outer reality of maternal care. It is only at this point that the mother's frustrations of the infant's needs allows for his gradual disillusionment and recognition of the limitations of his own infantile omnipotent control (1950).

It is precisely in this period of the gradual emergence of self-object discrimination that the transitional object emerges. This transitional object, or the first not-me possession stands at the border between "inside and outside, between instinct and object relationship, between primary creative activity and a projection of what already has been incorporated, between an inner-reality and reality testing, or between a primary creativity and an objective perception based on reality testing" (1953, p. 230).

The Third or Intermediate Area. In his later work, Winnicott (1971) developed the concept of a third or intermediate area which is neither fully inside nor fully outside and which develops in the potential space between the infant and the mother. Winnicott notes that "from the beginning the baby has maximally intense experiences in the potential space between the subjective object and the object objectively perceived, between me-extensions and the not-me. This potential space is at the interplay between there being nothing but me and there being nothing but objects and phenomena outside omnipotent control" (p. 100). This space develops as a consequence of the successful negotiation of the illusion-disillusionment experience between mother and infant. In a sense, the development of the potential space or the intermediate area represents the maintenance of the capacity for illusion at the time when the illusion of magical omnipotent control of the maternal environment is being relinquished.

The transitional object, then, may be seen as the first inhabitant of this intermediate area and hence as reflecting the infant's capacity to utilize illusion in his relationship with the objective world. Winnicott (1971) demonstrated the developmental elaboration of this intermediate area as the area of playing and the location of cultural experience, suggesting that this intermediate area of experience constitutes an essential aspect of creativity and a crucial ingredient in the capacity to participate in a psychotherapeutic relationship.

In this presentation of the transitional object and the intermediate area of experience, I emphasize a somewhat different aspect of the transitional object and its developmental fate from that which Tolpin (1971) described in her paper on the beginning of a cohesive self. My focus is on that which made the creation (or the discovery) of the transitional object possible and which finds its developmental continuity in the capacity for playing and for participation in cultural experience.

The concept of the transitional object, although it has proven to be an extremely productive starting point, has not been noted for its clarity. I would like to define my use of the following terms:

- *Transitional Phenomena.* A generic term which includes all aspects of the intermediate area of experiencing (the potential space between mother and infant) and its developmental sequelae
- *Transitional Object.* The first not-me possession and the first inhabitant of the intermediate area of experiencing (the potential space between mother and infant)
- *Transitional Capability.* The ego function responsible for the intermediate area of experiencing—the experiencing ego's capacity to move between the worlds of fantasy and reality via illusion
- *Transitional Mode of Relatedness.* An interpersonal concept which reflects the overlap of the intermediate areas of experiencing between or among separate individuals—for example, playing together, shared cultural experience, and psychotherapy

In this chapter I hope to demonstrate that such transitional capabilities make it possible for certain patients to remain in contact with reality in the face of primitive conflicts involving symbiosis and separation-individuation and that the loss of such transitional capabilities may coincide with the emergence of frankly psychotic experience. It is as if the transitional capabilities allow the patient an area for introjective-projective experience without the psychotic regressive loss of the capacity for differentiation between subjective and objective reality.

Although I have not emphasized this aspect of the patient's functioning in my brief clinical presentation, there was indication that the patient, prior to her decompensation, had well developed transitional capabilities. She was a creative and talented dancer, musician, and actress. I later was to learn that she often used these abilities to deal with inner states of conflict or tension. By her report, she would dance or play in lieu of thinking about her problems. She claimed that the end result was some sense of resolution although she was incapable of conceptualizing how these activities helped.

It appeared that an early sign of the patient's eventual regression into overt psychosis was the transient loss of the intermediate area of experiencing. The resulting incapacity to keep inner and outer realities related but potentially separable, as a consequence of the loss of this transitional capability, is suggested in the episode in which the patient was unable to terminate a dance improvisation. Her incapacity to reemerge from the transitional mode of dance improvisation presaged the subsequent psychosis during which she became more permanently bound to a subjectively distorted reality. With a gradual deterioration in her general functioning, dissociative episodes while dancing became more frequent (though less dramatic); finally she stopped dancing altogether.

I hope to demonstrate that the restoration of these transitional capabilities in the course of the psychotherapeutic work coincided with the patient's reemergence from overt psychosis.

Treatment Narrative

Following the recurrence of the patient's symptoms on her return home, she was hospitalized and I began to see her in individual psychotherapy three times a week. During the first several weeks she took no initiative in coming to the sessions but with some insistence on my part she would follow me to the office. She usually remained silent throughout the hour and when told the session had ended. During meetings, I would comment that the time was for her use, but mainly I attempted to await her spontaneous participation.

During the initial session the patient made motions of glancing through an old magazine which she had brought with her. Thinking of the concept of the transitional object, I suggested that she should feel free to bring to the hours whatever she wished. In response she put down the magazine and turned away for the remainder of the hour. Before the session ended I apologized for my interference with her use of the magazine. I was concerned that my comment might be experienced as intrusive and that it might interfere with her spontaneous use of such items.

In the following session and through the first several weeks of treatment, the patient wore a rubber band around her fingers. During the session she would begin to stretch, twist, and play with the rubber band. Forewarned by my experience in the first session, I made no comment and allowed her to continue. I was surprised by my own fascination with her play during the otherwise eventless hour. It seemed that while she was playing with the rubber band, we were in some kind of nonverbal contact. It also appeared that if my preoccupation with her activity became too intense, she would set aside the rubber band and turn away from me.

This initial phase of treatment came to a close in the fourth week, when her parents took an unexpected trip. In response to their leaving, the patient became more rigidly uncooperative, negativistic, and withdrawn. As this happened the rubber band disappeared and the modicum of cooperation that it had come to represent was lost. She had to be physically assisted by the nursing staff into and out of the sessions, some of which she spent lying on the floor.

When her parents returned, there was a gradual emergence from this depressed, negativistic state into a more playful use of the treatment situation. She became unsteady on her feet and walked hesitantly, appearing in imminent danger of falling and looking very much like a child learning to walk. In the midst of one of these sessions, she balanced precariously before gracefully falling to the floor where she remained for several minutes before she looked up and broke her accustomed silence by asking, "Who is Isaac Newton?" I attempted, without success, to explore her inquiry. She merely stated that she had planned to look him up in the encyclopedia but wondered if I knew who he was. I then stated what had occurred to me when she first mentioned Isaac Newton, namely that he was "someone who had something to say about falling bodies." She then told me about an evening male nurse named Isaacs, who, she said, was "crueler" than I. She claimed that he threw her to the ground or caused her to fall. I asked what she was doing lying on the floor and she replied, "You know." She repeated "You know and you aren't telling me." As I tried to explore this she mumbled the word "burned" and then what I believed was the word "dead." She then proceeded to dramatize being dead. She lay dead for several minutes on the floor, and then went through a kind of resurrection. She haltingly rose, rolled over to her side, and turned her back to me while remaining silent. I asked what was happening, and she responded that it was like being back at her grandmother's house. She briefly described the setting of her grandmother's house but would not elaborate further. At the end of the hour, she continued to lie on the floor, and after five minutes, I enlisted the aid of the nursing staff to help her leave the room.

During another extended trip by the parents, the patient became increasingly preoccupied with her hostile, dependent, and sadistic master-slave relationship with me and the hospital staff. The evolution of these concerns took a predominantly paranoid cast in which she saw me as the master of her slavehood or as her potential attacker (*therapist* became *the rapist*). She made futile attempts to escape. She hid from me at times of our appointment, ran away from the hospital on several occasions, and later made a request (which I turned down) to leave treatment to return to college. The life and death aspects of this struggle were reflected in concern about her aging mother and about the death of a grandmother when she was five, as well as in her concern about having been put to sleep for her recent surgery and for a tonsillectomy, again at the age of five.

When I refused to allow her to leave the hospital, she became more openly angry with me. Later, reflecting on this period, she felt one incident which occurred at this time constituted a significant turning point in her reemergence from psychosis. On Halloween evening she organized and led a minirebellion on the adolescent ward. Apparently this was one of the first times she had felt capable of acknowledging and acting upon her destructiveness and shedding the passive (introjected) role of victim.

The next morning I arrived to find a remarkable little old lady playing the piano in the lobby near my office. It required some effort on my part to identify my patient beneath her clever disguise. This marked the beginning of a period of intense musical preoccupation during which the patient spent many hours a day at the piano.

During her sessions, she spoke of her music as the one thing that really helped her during the day but said that the music returned during sleep as nightmares. Once again the issue of control was paramount: at night she did not know where the music came from and could not control it.

She spoke of how until she stopped playing the piano at fourteen, she had been helped with her music by her mother, a talented pianist. As she told of mother's help, she became nauseated. She described how the piano had ceased to be something for herself but became something expected of her and therefore forced upon her. At fourteen she gave it up, and took up horseback riding, her father's avocation. (Interestingly, her first act on discharge from the hospital was the purchase of a horse which she named "Momma.")

In the course of treatment, it became clear that music had become a vehicle for self-expression which she felt was denied her in the sessions themselves (that is, by my insistence she not return to college). During this time she began showing me poems she had written and collected during early adolescence (her first prolonged separation from her parents). She noted, however, that her music was more personally her own and that she was less interested in my thoughts and opinions of that. She described how prior to her psychosis, she had withdrawn from music and dancing, after dancing took on a compulsive character linked with her fear of going to sleep and dying. She feared if she stopped dancing she might die. She also explained that there were feelings about me that she was incapable of discussing but which she felt could be expressed on the piano. A few days later, after a session in which she remained silent throughout the hour, she went to the piano and played the Chopin Sonata movement popularly known as "The Funeral March." When I confronted her with this she denied knowledge of such a melody but later acknowledged concern about what might slip out in her music.

In anticipation of a brief trip she had planned, she began to acknowledge some of her concerns about separation from her mother and from me and the hospital. She associated these concerns with fears of her mother's or her own death. She acknowledged her intense rage and claimed that she was by far the angriest person on the ward, much angrier than a young man who had threatened to kill me.

From this time until her discharge from the hospital a few weeks later, she reported a series of dreams, many clearly linked to the treatment situation. For example, on the night after I had hung a new print of sailing vessels in my office, she dreamed of an adventure with pirates.

As she began to speak more of her dreams, she reported some bizarre dreams which had coincided with the onset of her psychosis the previous year. As she reported her earlier dreams, it became very unclear where the dreaming experience left off and her recollection of her waking subjective experience began. For example, she described a dream in which a seventy-foot woman was lying in a bed of leaves on top of some kittens which might be either dead or alive. Later in the hour she spoke of wandering about the college campus confused and frightened and of lying beneath a tree for many hours during the night.

On the evening before her discharge from the hospital, she dreamed she had won the Academy Award for writing the best teen-age murder mystery of the year. In it she recalled the face of a wolf, a wolf-man, who was shot through the face in many places and was bleeding.

COMMENT

In the course of a research project on the primary transitional object, Busch and McKnight (Busch et al. 1973) discovered that conscious parental expectation did not influence an infant's attachment to a primary transitional object. In the sense that the transitional object is the first inhabitant of the intermediate area of experiencing, it must be discovered or created by the child himself; it cannot be introduced from the outside.

Busch and McKnight (1973) found that the major parental role in attachment was one of facilitation, that is, allowing the availability of such an object with the recognition of its importance to the child's feeling of well being. The parents not only recognized but also reinforced the special qualities of this object once it had been discovered by the child by providing it at times of the child's distress. Although they did not stress this point in their description, the transitional object, having been discovered by the child, thus achieves an acquired meaning to both the parents and the child. This parent-child consensus is a form of shared illusion and is the prototype for what I have called the *transitional mode of relatedness*.

During my initial session with this mute, somewhat negativistic patient, I attempted to seize upon her use of a magazine to encourage her to engage in such an interaction. As with Busch's parents who attempted to assign their children a transitional object, my suggestion and the magazine were turned aside. Her subsequent use of a rubber band, however, suggests that there was a spontaneous step toward the restoration of transitional capabilites.

At this point, it may be helpful to contrast the use of a psychotic fetish with my conceptualization of transitional phenomena. Mahler (1968) and especially Furer (1964), in their work with psychotic youngsters, described these children's preoccupation with fetish objects. Their use of such objects in some ways resembles the small child's use of a transitional object. In following Furer's clinical description, it would appear, however, that there are some notable differences. The fetish object appears more directly involved with the child's instinctual activities; it appears to have a more concrete relevance to the child (it appeared, to my reading, more a substitute for mother-child fusion than a symbol of it); and, perhaps most importantly, it seemed more an object for compulsive behaviors than for playing. For example, Furer (1964), in his description of the treatment of a psychotic boy, noted that the child did not play with toys, but instead seemed to use them as a kind of externalization of body sensation.

Winnicott suggested that "psychotherapy takes place in the overlap of two areas of playing, that of the patient and that of the therapist. Psychotherapy has to do with two people playing together. The corollary of this is that where playing is not possible then the work done by the therapist is directed toward bringing the patient from a state of not being able to play into a state of being able to play" (1971, p. 38).

Winnicott (1971, pp. 51-52) noted also that playing is inherently exciting and precarious because it belongs to the interplay in the child's mind between that which is subjective (near hallucination) and that which is objectively perceived (actual or shared reality). The child gathers objects or phenomena from the external world into this play area where they are used in the service of some theme derived from inner or personal reality.

The child's employment of a transitional object represents not only his first use of a symbol but also a significant development in his capacity to play. There is a direct development from transitional phenomena to playing, from playing to shared playing, and from this to cultural experiences and the type of playing which Winnicott sees as the core of the psychotherapeutic experience.

I would like to trace a similar development in the clinical material presented, namely the progression from playing with an object, to playing in the treatment situation (development of a "play space"), to the type of shared playing involved in psychotherapy (the possibility for a nonpsychotic transference-countertransference).

In making his observations on playing, Winnicott noted that he was directing his attention away from the content of play to its form. In attempting to trace the development of transitional phenomena in the clinical vignette I presented, I likewise will focus on the nature of the patient's experience and her mode of presentation of this experience in the psychotherapeutic situation, with less emphasis on content.

From what I could gather from my patient's subsequent reports and my direct experience in the psychotherapy, the issues involved in her frankly psychotic experience and those which she presented in the therapy were essentially the same. Briefly, she felt herself caught as a hostile-dependent in a master-slave relationship with her mother (at times the parental couple, later the therapist). She conceptualized this relationship as a life and death struggle for existence. The unresolved remnants of a symbiotic relationship with her mother and the faulty completion of the separation-individuation processes were reactivated by her physical separation from her mother and by ovarian surgery. Her major mode of conceptualizing this life and death struggle involved projective-introjective mechanisms in which she alternately anticipated her mother's aging and death (bursts of manic or aggressive activity) and her own being put to sleep or killed (depression, immobility, catatonia).

From this perspective, I will trace the form of these concerns in the patient's experience. In her descriptions of her psychosis's onset, she located the hostile intent outside of herself and assumed the role of its victim. The dream experience of a seventy-foot woman lying on top of possibly dead kittens became an actual fear of destructive women (the old woman who fed her putrid milk and the woman who attempted to scald her).

During this time, her experience of external reality was grossly distorted by subjective interpretations of this experience. Her distorted experience had a real quality similar to the psychotic child's experience of the fetish object: it was rooted in derivatives of instinctual processes; it was a substitute for (not symbolic of) mental conflict; and it lacked access to creative playing.

These concerns were carried over into her hospitalization and into the beginning phases of psychotherapy. It is conjecture on my part, but I would suggest that her use of the rubber band during the initial silent hours of treatment may have reflected a tentative restoration of the transitional capability responsible for playing—the incipient establishment of an intermediate area of experiencing as the forerunner of the development of a play space.

At this point in the treatment, however, an external event (the brief departure of her parents) led to a further regression and an apparent deterioration in the therapeutic situation. In fact, from the patient's subsequent description of this period, it would appear that the concerns and conflicts I summarized earlier were merely carried over and found reflection in the therapy and the hospital situation. She felt in imminent danger of attack or murder, and I emerged as her persecutor or the leader of her persecutors on the hospital staff. Again, this experience had the subjective quality of reality as in her earlier psychotic decompensation—only the cast of characters and the setting had been changed.

The Isaac Newton session suggested, however, that these frightening concerns were beginning to be reflected in another form. With her developing capacity for humor, there appeared another perspective on the same experience. It was in this session that the play space, which I had suggested had its origins in her earlier use of the rubber band, became the vehicle for her expression of and work with these underlying concerns.

For the sake of discussion, I will separate two aspects of the development of the play space. In terms of the patient's ego functioning, I believe the development of the play space reflected the restoration of her transitional capabilities—that is, her experiencing ego's capacity to move between the worlds of fantasy and reality via illusion. The restoration of these capacities marked a crucial turning point in her recovery from the overt psychosis just as their loss heralded the onset of the psychotic regression.

From the vantage point of the therapeutic relationship, the creation of a play space represented the beginning of a transitional mode of relatedness opening up the possibility, in Winnicott's words, for psychotherapy to occur in the overlapping area of two people playing. In this regard, the accuracy of my response about Isaac Newton is secondary to its playful, yet serious, nature.

I would like to add a few comments on the patient's piano playing within the dual framework of the transitional capabilities and the transitional mode of relatedness. In the former sense, the way the patient returned to the piano suggests some of the issues being reworked in this playing. She continued to struggle with her relationship with her mother and through her impersonation she was able to play with her ambivalent identification with her mother without becoming the mother who had to be tortured or destroyed.

But there was another aspect of the piano playing as viewed from the vantage point of the transitional mode of relatedness and the overlapping areas of shared playing. Her impersonation and her preoccupation with the piano came shortly after I refused her request for discharge from the hospital to return to school. Her request to leave appeared to reflect a defense against anxieties being mobilized by the intimacy of the developing therapeutic play space. My refusal of her request also represented an intrusion (albeit a necessary one) into the shared area of playing. In fact, I was exercising a significant degree of control over her life; in this sense I was her master. In response to these partial disruptions of the therapeutic play space, the patient found another play space for the expression of aspects of her relationship with me. She returned to the piano, which she had left years earlier because she felt it had been invaded by her mother's expectations and control.

During the remainder of her hospital stay, the transitional mode of relatedness became more firmly established within the psychotherapeutic situation as the patient's creativity and capacity to use a previously well-established play space became an integral part of the therapeutic relationship. In this context, the patient began to present me with poems, scrapbooks, and extended serenades on the piano. In addition she began to report dreams for the first time in the treatment.

Winnicott (1971) attempted with the transitional concept to differentiate dreaming from fantasying. He emphasized that dreaming is associated with object-relating in the real world and that living in the real world fits into the dream world. In other words, the dream bridges the gap between an inner world of fantasy and an outer world of reality and, in this sense, is another reflection of a transitional capability. In contrast, fantasy remains an isolated phenomenon representing (in Winnicott's construction) a withdrawal from reality. An example of a dream as a bridge between reality and fantasy was the patient's dream about an adventure with pirates which occurred the evening after a print of sailing vessels was hung in my office.

As the patient described the dreaming and waking experiences which had occurred at the onset of her acute psychotic episode, it appeared that the boundaries that usually exist between dream reality and waking reality had become blurred as the transitional capability, or in Winnicott's terms, the intermediate area of experiencing was lost.

Before I conclude my discussion of this beginning phase of the psychotherapy (which continued for a year after her hospitalization), I would like to add a few words about the dream which occurred on the evening before she left the hospital (her dream of winning the Academy Award for writing the best teenage murder mystery of the year in which a wolf, a wolf-man, was shot through the face and was bleeding). Although the patient did not associate to the dream, the link between a wolf and a fox (the therapist) does not seem farfetched. I also had some evidence that the fairy tale "Little Red Riding Hood" was one of the underlying fantasies drawn into her concern: After dying and resurrecting in the Isaac Newton session, she reported being at her grandmother's house. A few weeks prior to discharge she passed my office wearing a red cape and carrying a basket of fruit. We both laughed as she made some reference to looking out for wolves. This interweaving of aspects of inner fantasy and outer reality into the intermediate area of dreaming underlines the importance of transitional capabilities in the creative aspects of the dream work.

CONCLUSION

To conclude I will place some of the observations from this study within the framework of an overview of adolescent psychosis. This conceptualization of adolescent psychosis is drawn from a number of sources:

1. As Blos (1967) has suggested adolescence frequently entails a second individuation process.
2. In some susceptible young people, the reworking of the individuation process may precipitate a psychotic regression if at the time they are unable to separate themselves successfully from the nuclear family.
3. The regressive aspects of these psychoses tend to remobilize earlier conflicts and concerns along the symbiosis-separation-individuation developmental line. This frequently includes an interpersonal component involving one or both parents.
4. The regression tends to proceed to the level of psychological organization prior to the delineation of *self-images* from *object images*. This is the level of organization at which projective and introjective modes of experience (and thought) predominate.
5. If the patient maintains the transitional capability to sustain an intermediate area, these projective-introjective experiences may find a play space (perhaps another way of viewing Erickson's concept of a moratorium (1950). Within such a play space these projective-introjective experiences may be elaborated upon and worked toward resolution without leading to a psychotic distortion of objective reality.

6. If in the regressive process, however, this way station (the intermediate area) is by-passed, the projective-introjective experiences may totally infiltrate and psychotically distort the adolescent's view of objective reality.

7. In the process of recovery from such a psychotic episode, the three aspects of the regression may have to be reversed:

—The transitional capability or the intermediate area of experience must be restored.

—The delineation of self- from object-images must be reestablished.

—The issues related to separation-individuation must be reworked.

This latter aspect often includes a significant interpersonal component reflecting concerns about dependence versus independence and control versus autonomy.

In this presentation of the initial phases of the treatment of a hospitalized psychotic late adolescent, I have attempted to demonstrate the restoration of the patient's transitional capabilities and the establishment of a transitional mode of relatedness in the treatment situation. While aspects of self-object differentiation and issues related to separation-individuation were reflected in the early therapeutic material, the major work on these aspects of the regression occurred in the posthospital phase of the psychotherapy.

The clinical material I have presented highlights an aspect of the therapeutic relationship which involves, in part, the patient's experiencing ego's capacity to move between the worlds of fantasy and reality via illusion. Such a capacity is necessary for what Winnicott refers to as a play space in the treatment situation. I believe that such a play space constitutes the vehicle for the elaboration of a non-psychotic transference-countertransference experience which is the core of a psychoanalytically oriented psychotherapy.

REFERENCES

Blos, P. (1967). The second individuation process of adolescence. *Psychoanalytic Study of the Child* 22:162-186.

Busch, F., and McKnight, J. (1973). Parental attitudes and the development of the primary transitional object. *Child Psychiatry and Human Development* 4:12-20.

Busch, F., Nagera, H., McKnight, J., and Pezzarossi, G. (1973). Primary transitional objects. *Journal of the American Academy of Child Psychiatry* 12:193-214.

Coppolillo, H. P. (1967). Maturational aspects of the transitional phenomenon. *International Journal of Psycho-Analysis* 48:237-114.

——— (1976). The transitional phenomenon revisited. *Journal of the American Academy of Child Psychiatry* 15:36-48.

Erikson, E. H. (1950). *Childhood and Society.* New York: Norton.

Fintzy, R. T. (1971). Vicissitudes of the transitional object in a borderline child. *International Journal of Psycho-Analysis* 52:107-114.

Fisher, S. M. (1975). On the development of the capacity to use transitional objects. *Journal of the American Academy of Child Psychiatry* 14:114-124.

Fox, R. P. (1973). Therapeutic environments. *Archives of General Psychiatry* 29:514-517.

Freud, S. (1900). The interpretation of dreams, chapter 7. *Standard Edition* 5:509-621.

—— (1923). The ego and the id. *Standard Edition* 19:3-66.

Greenbaum, T. (1974). "The Analyzing Instrument" and the "Transitional Object": A discussion of the Psychoanalytic Process. A paper presented to the American Psychoanalytic Association, New York, December 1974. (To be published in *Between Fantasy and Reality*, ed. L. Barkin, S. Grolnick, and W. Muensterberger. New York: Jason Aronson, in press.)

Horton, P. C. (1974). The mystical experience: substance of an illusion. *Journal of the American Psychoanalytic Association* 22:364-380.

Klein, M. (1946). Notes on some schizoid mechanisms. In *Developments in Psychoanalysis*, ed. M. Klein, P. Heimann, S. Isaacs, and J. Riviere, pp. 292-320. London: Hogarth, 1970.

Kohut, H. (1971). *The Analysis of the Self: A Systematic Approach to the Psychoanalytic Treatment of Narcissistic Personality Disorders*. New York: International Universities Press.

Mahler, M. (1968). *On Human Symbiosis and the Vicissitudes of Individuation*. New York: International Universities Press.

Tolpin, M. (1971). On the beginnings of a cohesive self: an application of the concept of the transmuting internalization to the study of the transitional object and signal anxiety. *Psychoanalytic Study of the Child* 26:316-354.

Winnicott, D. W. (1950). Aggression in relation to emotional development. In *Collected Papers: Through Paediatrics to Psycho-Analysis*. London: Tavistock, 1958.

—— (1953). Transitional objects and transitional phenomena. In *Collected Papers: Through Paediatrics to Psycho-Analysis*. London: Tavistock, 1958.

—— (1956). Primary maternal preoccupation. In *Collected Papers: Through Paediatrics to Psycho-Analysis*. London: Tavistock, 1958.

—— (1960). Ego distortion in terms of true and false self. In *The Maturational Processes and the Facilitating Environment*. New York: International Universities Press, 1965.

—— (1971). *Playing and Reality*. New York: Basic Books.

Volkan, V. (1973). Transitional fantasies in the analysis of a narcissistic personality. *Journal of the American Psychoanalytic Association* 21:351-376.

The Treatment of
a Narcissistic Disturbance
in Childhood

STEVEN A. FRANKEL, M.D.

This paper surveys four years of psychotherapy, beginning at age eight and a half, of a boy whose psychopathology appears to be a precursor of the narcissistic character disorder described by Kernberg (1975). The vicissitudes of the transference related chiefly to the patient's underlying narcissistic vulnerability. Interventions were generally aimed at demonstrating the relation of the patient's narcissistic (grandiose) defense to his underlying concern about devaluation by the therapist. The advantages of focusing on such a patient's current needs and reactions are emphasized. The speed and success of the treatment of this child vis-a-vis adults with similar psychopathology is attributed to the relative ease with which his underlying needs (and related pathological envy, rage, and fear of retaliation) could be mobilized within the therapeutic relationship. This probably reflects the fact that his character defense was not yet fully entrenched. The contribution of normal development to the therapeutic process is also identified, as is the importance of both the real relationship and times of direct gratification of the patient by the therapist.

Most psychopathology can be examined from at least three points of view: the patient's drives, his object relations, and his narcissism—that is, his sense of self or self-esteem (Eisnitz 1974). It is my impression that the latter factor, the narcissistic, has often been accorded secondary significance in the clinical literature. However, with the recent growth of interest in narcissism, it has become clear that issues related to the sense of self or self-esteem can be viewed as a central focus of psychopathology. Further, psychopathology of this sort may call for the introduction of special techniques into the treatment situation (Kohut 1971; Kernberg 1975).

Kernberg (1975) defines the term narcissism as "the libidinal investment of the self." He points out that this "does not simply stem from an instinctual source of libidinal energy, but from many relationships between the self and other intrapsychic structures." He distinguishes *self-feeling* (Jacobson 1964) which derives from "the individual's awareness of an integrated self," from *self-esteem* which "indicates the extent to which there is a narcissistic investment of the self." The self is defined as consisting of "multiple self-representations and their related affect dispositions." These self-representations can exist at "various stages of depersonification, abstraction and integration."[1]

The degree of integration of the self, together with the complex intrapsychic factors which influence the libidinal investment of the self, determines the nature and extent of narcissistic pathology. A rough developmental continuum can be charted. On a very primitive level, the sense of self is intimately bound up with the presence and interest of the object. When the object is absent or withdraws its interest, the subject's *cohesive self* may be threatened by some degree of dissolution. The object in these cases literally functions as an extension of the self (*self-object*, see Kohut 1971). On a more advanced level, the object is perceived as separate from the self, but the subject's sense of self-esteem is highly dependent upon the interest and approval of the object (*secondary narcissism*, see A. Freud 1962). With additional development, self-esteem becomes more dependent on internal regulatory agencies such as the superego.

Both Kohut (1971, 1972) and Kernberg (1970, 1974, 1975) write about instances of severe narcissistic pathology: the narcissistic character disorder. The conceptual schema of the two authors, however, are strikingly different. Kohut views severe narcissistic disturbances as reflecting an arrest in the course of the normal development of narcissism. Kernberg, on the other hand, describes a pathological narcissistic defense characterized by coldness, aloofness, an inability to depend on others, and devaluation of others. This defensive posture represents "a pathological condensation of the real self, the grandiose self and the idealized object" and is erected against more primitive, pathological object relations centered around "narcissistic rage and envy, fear and guilt because of this rage, and yet a desperate longing for a relationship that will not be destroyed by hatred" (Kernberg 1975). It is also erected against "deep convictions of unworthiness and an image of a world devoid of (food and) love" (Kernberg 1975).

The patient described in this report showed features of severe narcissistic disturbance which, on examination, are better understood on the basis of Kernberg's formulations than Kohut's. He exhibited an aloof and, at times, exploitative surface beneath which lay an extraordinary susceptibility to narcissistic injury.

Presenting Problems

Jim A was seen by the author in exploratory psychotherapy for four years, for the first three years, once a week, and during the fourth year, twice weekly.

During the second and third years of treatment, he also attended a children's activities therapy group once a week. The author entered this same group as coleader after six months. The therapy proper began when Jim was eight years, six months.

Jim was referred for treatment by the school system for "restlessness and hyperactivity" which seriously interfered with his learning. These symptoms began about four months after Jim started prekindergarten at four years, four months. From the time of his entry into prekindergarten, he had strenuously resisted going to school. In addition, up to the time of referral, he had never shown any interest in peers but was inclined to spend his time close to his mother at home.

Jim also manifested pervasive fears of attack; that is, he constantly worried that he could get "beaten up" or "shot." These fears could be exacerbated by any threat of separation from important objects, especially his mother. He also expressed fears of being left and of traveling. He worried that he could get lost and might never find his way home again.

Development

Throughout Jim's development, Mrs. A attempted to foster a unique and intimate relationship with him: Even up to the time of referral, Jim frequently found his way into his mother's bed. When he refused to eat, Mrs. A, with disguised pleasure, would spoon feed him.

Mrs. A found caring for Jim totally gratifying up to about his eighteenth month, the time when his early gestures toward autonomy began to distress her. Their ensuing struggles over eating and toileting became a model of inconsistency. Mrs. A would initially try to ignore the problems she had with Jim, hoping they would go away. But as her exasperation mounted, she would shift abruptly and insist on Jim's doing things her way, lose her temper, and finally beat him.

Jim's development was further complicated by two dramatic events which occurred at the height of his early difficulties with his mother. When Jim was two years, three months, Mrs. A was operated on for thyroid cancer. Mrs. A was anxious and depressed and distinctly less tolerant of Jim's demands for about a year following her surgery. Then two and a half months following Mrs. A's initial hospitalization, Jim's paternal grandfather died after having been gravely ill with cancer since Jim was about one. The family perceived this event in combination with Mrs. A's illness and depression as highly significant to Jim. Mrs. A recalled that for about a year thereafter, Jim "worried a great deal," was more clinging, and asked many questions about his grandfather.

Jim's entry into school (prekindergarten) was problematic. He was intially supported by his mother's remaining with him for several hours a day, but after six weeks Mrs. A became "frustrated" and refused to stay. Two months later, she took her first job since the birth of her first child nine years previous. From this point on, Jim's distractibility increased markedly.

Mrs. A's combined indulgence and punitiveness toward Jim made him overly attached to and dependent on her. Simultaneously, he became fiercely insistent on his prerogatives and was characterized as "strongwilled and demanding." Finally, Jim harbored a pervasive underlying fear that his mother would reject and even abandon him. In part, this explains his need to stick so closely to her.[2]

Family Constellation and History

Except for his paternal grandfather whose lineage was Irish, Jim's grandparents were first generation Mexican-Americans. His family lived in a lower-middle-class neighborhood of a large city, across the street from both the maternal grandmother and the paternal grandfather. The paternal grandfather had been a skilled laborer, the father was employed as a commercial salesman, and the mother worked as a doctor's receptionist.

The mother, the youngest of ten children, perceived her own mother as critical and self-involved, and as having been even more detached after the death of her husband from tuberculosis when Mrs. A was fourteen. She remembered her father as warm and caring, but too much absent during her childhood. He had entered the hospital just before she was hospitalized for the same disease at age eleven, and he died just before her release three years later.

Mrs. A saw herself as nurturing and supportive of her own mother following the father's death. She seemed to conceal a profound wish to be cared for beneath a facade of competence and secretly held to an idealized image of her father as the one to whom she had been special and as a model for someone who would later care for her. I felt that she attempted to act out this wish, first with her husband, then with Jim, her only male child, and indirectly with doctors (her employer and then me). When any of these males disappointed her, she reacted by withdrawing emotionally and depreciating that person.

I saw the mother approximately monthly during Jim's therapy. At her request, I referred her for individual therapy several months before termination with Jim.

Jim's father, whom I saw with his mother irregularly during the first and last years of Jim's therapy, confined his parental role to that of provider and appeared to distrust and often resent his wife. His own family had been abandoned by the mother between his third and eleventh year. He continued to live with his father and sister during most of this period, although he was sent to live with an uncle between age eight and ten. His single, albeit blunted, emotional attachment was to his father and later to men reminiscent of him. He worked hard for his boss and spent a great deal of time drinking in bars, usually with older men. He showed almost no interest in his children.

Jim had two sisters, five and three years older than he. Both girls seemed reasonably well adjusted, and the oldest was impressive for her academic achievements and service activities at school—traits especially valued and encouraged by her mother.

The implications of Mr. and Mrs. A's personal histories and difficulties for Jim were as follows: Mrs. A attempted to use Jim as a substitute for her husband. She conspicuously gave Jim more time and interest than she gave her husband. This caused Mr. A to regard Jim as a rival and to treat him severely. He was quick to punish Jim and regarded Jim's stubborn and angry behavior, as well as his confusion and anxiety, as defiance. Second, when Jim challenged or disappointed Mrs. A, he became the target for her vengeful feelings as well. On the other hand, Jim's difficulties with his father were somewhat offset by the fact that he was the only male child. Mr. A somewhat regretted his hostility toward Jim and had some latent interest in building a relationship with him. This must have been communicated to Jim and may have been one factor in his intense wish, which became apparent during treatment, to have his father like him.

Although both Mr. and Mrs. A were intelligent and well-intentioned, neither was particularly psychologically minded. Mrs. A's manifest reason for bringing Jim to treatment was to get help for him. Her latent motive was to force him to conform more closely to her wishes. She also wanted to expose and punish her husband for his neglect of her and rationalized this through her manifest interest in wanting him to become a better father. It was only as Mrs. A began to gain some distance from Jim over several years of contact with me that she began to recognize that she had strong needs of her own to be cared for. It was this recognition that caused her to briefly seek more contact with me and then therapy for herself.

Work with Mr. A might have been a useful adjunct to Jim's treatment. However, my efforts to enlist him in our regular meetings were progressively unsuccessful. His reluctance to become involved in our work paralleled his lack of family involvement and unfortunately proved just as intractable.

Phase 1—Mistrust

As early as the first few weeks of treatment, Jim was making strenuous efforts to ascertain how fully I was committed to him. When he sensed that I would fail him, for example, by not bringing him a toy he asked for, he withdrew into long periods of silence, isolated play, or frenzied activity from which I was totally excluded.

Jim's effort to determine what my commitment to him would be began in the first hour when Jim cased the office and questioned me closely about whether I would have toys as the evaluator did. In the second hour, he wanted details of how I got toys, and he insisted that I would forget to get the flashlight he asked me for. I told him that it would take some time for me to know what kind of toys we would use in our therapy and suggested that perhaps he didn't quite trust me yet. I received no direct reply, but he soon introduced a puppet game in which a tiger ate a father who then killed the tiger. In the next hour, Jim was distant and tended to play by himself. Toward the end of that hour, his tiger attacked me. For the next several hours, he communicated with me only when I was willing to play as an accessory in his game—holding props while he shot at enemy cars.

The pattern of his attempt to engage followed by fury at a perceived rebuff is clear in the following sequence at the fourth month of treatment. Jim began the hour by cataloging our toys. He played by himself until, suddenly, he asked me whether I worked on Saturdays. I had hardly begun to ask what he had in mind when he told me he wanted me to come to his birthday party on the next Saturday, adding in the same statement, that he didn't think I would come. I was in the midst of replying that it was too bad he felt that way because it might be harder for him to understand why I would not be able to come, when I noticed him beginning to climb on the cupboard. I restrained him and tried to reassure him that I knew my answer must be upsetting, but to no avail. Soon rubber darts were flying all over the room. A bit later, his tiger puppet hilariously devoured everything in sight. The grand finale came when Jim pulled the entire contents of the toy cabinet onto the floor. Once again, I told him that he "must be very upset and angry with me." He mumbled something about being "miserable," refused to talk more, and tried to leave the hour early. In the next hour, he said very little to me, except to ask briefly whether I would tell his mother that it would be okay for him to get a rifle for his birthday. When I asked whether he would tell me more about his interest in a rifle, he responded only by turning away and crashing toy cars together.

It was a full two months before some reengagement occurred. During that period, Jim spent much of his time in our hours playing with my dictaphone and much of this play consisted of repetitively and endlessly running the machine back and forth. At times, he played dictaphone tapes he found in my drawers saying he wanted to hear what was on them. In conjunction with this, he used my toy stethoscope to listen to our walls. Both activities seemed directed at detecting secrets which he appeared to think I was keeping from him. He also began to search my files. Direct information about his thinking was rare. On one occasion, he suggested that I might be planning to leave him as the evaluator had. On two other occasions in the midst of isolated and disorganized play, he asked if I saw other kids. I acknowledged that he seemed interested and curious and told him I would like to better understand what he thought. His response was to turn back to his play and to shut me out further.

This was a difficult period for me as well as for Jim. Often, and for periods of many weeks, my existence went essentially unacknowledged. At other times, Jim imperiously controlled me and my responses. That is, he either failed to respond to my queries or would tell me to "shut up, you ask too many questions." It became clear that he expected direct and immediate gratification in the form of answers to his questions or immediate agreement that I would do what he requested, such as to go to his birthday party. Other responses—such as exploration or reassurance that I appreciated his distress or anger—amounted to a frustration. I found myself feeling ineffectual and unappreciated. At times, I caught myself drifting off into my own thoughts. At other times, I found myself trying to take a controlling stance (setting limits), or an educative stance (insisting to Jim that I thought he was angry at me and that we could, and implicitly should talk about his feelings).

In retrospect, only two features of my behavior seem to have been important in establishing the beginnings of an alliance: I remained committed to him in spite of the fact that he was convinced I would not; and overall, I seemed to convey that I wanted to help with things that bothered him.

Phase 2—Coercion

Six months into treatment, Jim became significantly more coercive in his dealings with me. He would order me around and demand that I give him information and, at times, small items from the office. His play and his interaction with me also became more organized and sustained.

During one session in the seventh month of treatment, Jim introduced the theme of robbing. He suggested we play a game in which he was a robber. He tied me up, held a rubber knife at my head and pretended to put me to sleep with a syringe. He then stole my treasures which alternately were diamonds and money. He also used the stethoscope to check if I was okay. (Associated with this game again was the use of the stethoscope to listen to the walls and periodic searches through my files.)

Eventually, in the ninth month of treatment, as Jim was becoming frustrated in his efforts to insure my exclusive devotion to him and in direct reaction to being told by his parents that he would be going to summer school, Jim stole a valued play thing from my office—a set of magnets. He liked the magnets because they could draw other items to themselves. This seemed to reflect Jim's wish to draw others to himself and control them. (Just prior to the introduction of the robbing game, Jim had hit on another game of control where he would tie a string onto a rubber dart which he shot out of a gun. Later in the therapy, he would also tie small figures of people onto this string.) He had wanted to stay home that summer and be with his mother and sisters and felt that he was being excluded by being sent to school. He also had the idea that I should spend more time with him, for example, by going fishing.

Several sessions following the theft, Jim made his first verbal effort to communicate his frustration to me. For three sessions after I observed that the magnets were missing, Jim withdrew into solitary play. (At the time, I did not implicate Jim in the theft.) He began the fourth session by telling me about a fire in a local warehouse and how a cat and bird had been caught inside. He then related this to a time when he had stolen locks from a warehouse to protect his cat, who often entered the warehouse and whom he could not let out if the door were locked. He was furious with the management for locking the place and planned, in retaliation, the destruction of some of their equipment. We talked about his feelings and his empathy with the trapped animal. I reminded him that we had been talking about stealing in earlier sessions and that he had once suggested someone might have stolen our magnets. I wondered why he thought that person might have done that. He answered that kids steal because they feel someone "isn't telling them everything." He then proceeded to crash cars together. After about ten minutes, he looked up and asked whether he could take home another prized toy, a truck, which he said he wanted because his father was in the trucking business. I again had to refuse, although I told him I could understand his wish to have it.

Several sessions later, after the resurgence of robbing play and the disappearance of a few more small items (presumably a reaction to my denying his request for the truck), I suggested that maybe it was he that had been taking these items, and as he had suggested earlier, he might have done it because he felt I was holding out on him in some way. His response was immediate and sharp, "Okay, that's right, and I wanted the truck to remind me of my father's work, and you said we had to keep it here. I felt sad." From this point on, it was also possible to talk with him about his anger at having to go to summer school and how it made him feel like getting back at his parents, and at me, because he felt I had encouraged his parents to send him.

This was the first time my efforts to identify Jim's subjective experience with him evoked direct verbal confirmation. Previously, my statements had been disregarded or treated as if they were intended to frustrate his efforts to have his needs met. Jim was apparently beginning to see some positive value in our verbal interchange and this must have reflected (at least momentarily) an improved view on his part of my intentions.

Phase 3—Evolution of Trust

The next two years were characterized by the waxing and waning of Jim's feeling that he could trust me and that I really cared. Further, he steadily progressed toward the recognition that I had a life that did not include him, and that he was in competition for my attention with the other people and commitments in my life. This represented a significant progression in Jim's realistic appreciation of me as an individual.

Except for a period of discouragement upon learning about my summer vacation, the autumn of the next year (one year into treatment) ushered in a period of calm. Jim seemed pleased and quite relieved when I returned from my vacation. He soon introduced the game of checkers into our play. This was the first in a series of skills he developed and used in treatment. Jim's intent in playing was to beat me. He especially liked taking my pieces and would count his plunder over and over. When I lost, he would treat me with contempt. In the beginning when he lost, he would change the rules so he could jump as many of my men as he wanted to. Essentially, checkers was a more sublimated version of his robbing play, and provided a more organized focus for our interaction. It also had the secondary effect of bolstering Jim's self-esteem, since he became a very good player.

This period of calm began to end when Jim was started in a boys' activities therapy group at the clinic, one year and seven months into treatment. This was done because Jim was totally without social peer relationship. He objected strenuously to the decision, and his indirect associations suggested that he imagined that I might be planning to get rid of him by involving him in another therapy. These associations also reflected the rage and concomitant fear of attack brought on by this notion.

Our first several hours after he started in the group were characterized by resurgence of the suspicion that I had secrets. Jim seemed less trustful, began to use the dictaphone, and noticed a number of small changes in the play room. In one of our sessions, he had his animal puppet attack mine and bitterly accused my animal of having tricked him. Soon after this, my puppet was instructed to attack Jim's puppet.

His play also suggested that being placed in the group caused him to feel devalued. In one game, his puppet stated that all the other puppets had called him "stupid and dumb" and had done "it in front of the other toys." At another time, he confided that kids at school didn't find him interesting: "They don't want to play with me because I don't make up good enough games."

This period lasted for about three months and as usual my efforts to explore Jim's feelings about being placed in the play group went unacknowledged. He simply wanted me to discontinue him in the play group. It was only when I finally replaced a broken knife, one which he assumed had been broken by another child, that he relaxed and seemed tentatively reassured of my commitment to him. (Jim had become preoccupied with this knife and repeatedly said he did not think I would replace it.)

At this point, Jim again brought up the subject of his cats and talked about how two were sick and one had been killed several years ago by a man driving a car. He also talked about how his mother would have to get rid of the cats because Jim had allergies. Using this displacement, we talked about feelings of being "given up." Jim said he thought that the cats who were to be given up would feel "lost and sad," and that since it was because of his allergies they they would be given away, it was therefore his fault. This notion particularly upset him. With my help, Jim could also acknowledge that kids often had similar sad and even angry feelings when people left or disappointed them. He could not, however, tolerate making the step to talking directly about his own related fears that he might be abandoned by me to the play group and the possibility that something about him (analogous to allergies in our talks about his cats) could cause me to do that. Still, I found his willingness to talk through the vehicle of the cats most encouraging.

Although this period of rapport between Jim and myself was short-lived, there did seem afterward a new foundation of intimacy in our relationship. Just prior to my vacation that year, one year and eleven months into treatment, Jim began to question me repeatedly about my family. (This was the first time he acknowledged that I might have a family.) My efforts to explore his interest rather than provide direct answers frustrated him immensely. The ensuing subperiod, characterized by Jim's intense curiosity about my family and my other patients and by the waxing and waning of Jim's conviction about the genuineness of my interest in him, lasted for a year and a half. During this time, there was recurrent evidence from Jim of a tenacious underlying fear I would abandon him for another patient or family member.

Selections from key periods during this subphase follow. They illustrate Jim's reaction to small ambiguities and disappointments and the interventions useful in helping him revise his distorted view of my intentions.

In April of that year, one year and eight months into treatment, Jim underwent implantation of small drainage tubes into his ear because of recurrent middle ear infections. This frightened him tremendously, and my persistent interest in talking about it paid off. For several sessions, he told me that he didn't want to talk about the tube implantation because he would then have a "hard time getting thoughts about it out of his head." He made associations to the death of his cat and other instances of death. He seemed relieved, however, when he could finally recount the details of the operation. For several sessions thereafter, Jim seemed much more open and talked more generally about his problems. He particularly expressed sadness about not having more friends, implying once more that it must be he who drove people away. He played a revised version of our robbing game in which he was now the bad guy and got hanged for "stealing something, cheating at cards, and committing ten other crimes." When, during these sessions, I told him I was going on vacation (my second vacation during treatment), he seemed stunned and immediately asked me if I had a wife. This was his first reference to my family. When I wondered what he had on his mind and said that I was glad he wanted to know more about me, his response was simply to warn me that it would be dangerous for me to leave because "hurricanes might come up." He then scattered our toys.

In the next session, he noticed changes in the office and was soon asking about my wife and wanted to know the names and ages of my children. I again put him off, telling him I knew he was very anxious to know about those facts, but that I thought I could help him more if we spent some time talking about his ideas about them first. The next two sessions were downhill. He became insistent that I give him the answers. At first, he argued with me and told me, "You tell my mother things, so why won't you tell me." He then tried to tease me into telling him by saying that maybe I was embarrassed to tell him. Finally, he accused me of not wanting to tell him. I told him that I had explained why I didn't tell him (that is, that we needed first to know his ideas), but he didn't seem to believe me. Rather, I said he seemed to feel that I didn't want to tell him. He agreed and continued to press me. I then wondered if he had had experiences with others not telling him things. He answered that he once asked his mother if his father owned a gun. She replied no, but he then found out that she had lied to him when he discovered a rifle his father had hidden in the closet. (Note the shift to imagery of danger, an apparent reflection of a fear on Jim's part that I had a powerful and dangerous secret.) His next act was to string a male figure from a dart and shoot the dart at the ceiling. He began the next session by sarcastically saying, "How's your family?" I again tried to talk with him about how upset he was about my not answering his questions and the importance of his sense that I was going away with my family and not with him. He followed this by stringing the male figure up and shooting at it.

The conviction that I preferred others was exacerbated again during the next fall and winter (the beginning of Jim's third year of treatment), when I became a leader in his group. He had been in the group for about six months, and since he was making some progress, it was decided that he should remain in spite of the possible contamination of our treatment by, among other things, his constant observation of me interacting with other boys. From September through November, prior to my taking the leadership, Jim warned me persistently that he did not want me to become involved in the group. He claimed repeatedly that he would lose his temper and said, "You might not like me if you see this." This referred both to his anticipated jealousy at my interacting equally with other children, and the already mentioned concern that myself and others would dislike him if we saw how nasty he could be.

During these and the ensuing months, Jim became less accessible in the treatment. He also began to come late and seemed to want to leave early. In response, I often found myself being more talkative than usual. I was trying, I think, to persuade him to hear my point of view, that he was afraid he would be uncomfortable in the group with me and the other kids, but that we could try to understand those feelings.

The full content of Jim's thinking was revealed in a November session, when he suddenly said, "Did you get [Christmas] presents for your kids yet?" He went on to say that he had "thought about my kids all during the last vacation." After trying to explore this, I reminded him that he also seemed to have a lot of thoughts about the kids I would be working with in the activities group. He immediately asked if I saw any other patients in the group. When I asked him for his thinking, he strung up a male figure, shot at it, and laughed. Shortly after this response, he suddenly and disjointedly said, "I'm still afraid of the dark because I once saw from my window two men attack another man." He also said that "gangs wander through the city and throw grenades in windows." Again, as a result of the immense anger elicited by his thinking about other people in my life whom I might favor, and in response to my not giving him a direct answer, his thoughts shifted to an impressively aggressive theme—this time reflecting his projected aggression.

During this time, Jim also began an impressive crusade to enlist his father in a relationship. He would wait every weekend to see whether his father would take him fishing on their boat in a nearby town. Usually, he was disappointed. It appeared that, in anticipation of the sense of loss and jealousy that he would experience in having to share me with the other boys, he had turned toward his father for a hoped for substitute relationship.

Over the next several months following the inception of my role as group coleader, Jim's latenesses increased and he missed several sessions and engaged in more puppet play in which his puppet was attacked and tricked by other puppets. In March (two years and eight months into treatment), he reverted to a generally hostile and teasing posture, frequently calling me such names as "chicken." In the group he functioned well, but he remained aloof from me and repeatedly threatened to quit. At times, he acted out his threat by coming late and by even staying away from the group on a few occasions. His frustration continued to build and was reinforced by his father's lack of interest in him.

Toward the end of April, he began to ask me, this time with exasperation, how many patients I saw, how many hours I worked, and what my salary was. In response to my inquiries, he also told me that he wanted to know the same thing from his father, but never obtained answers. Several sessions later after his playing out a theme of attacking a male figure and then attempting in play to attack me directly, the subject again arose. This time, after some exploration, I decided to give him some direct information. (I had not yet answered any of his questions about my wife and children.) I told him that I worked from eight until six and that my salary was more than ten thousand dollars. He immediately relaxed and became talkative, telling me again about his disappointment that his father didn't talk more with him.

However, by July, Jim again became distrustful of me and implicated me in his parents' decision to make him attend day camp. At that time, he stole some money from his mother and bought a knife with it. He also developed two new methods for dealing with his anger. One was to travel and walk long distances by himself. If his father and I wouldn't take him places, he would go without us. The second was to climb onto the roof of his house, a place from which he could see the bar at which his father drank. During that summer, he went fishing alone almost every day. Following this, he began to find odd jobs with men in the neighborhood.

The final step in his slow movement toward being able to trust me came during October and November, three years and two months into treatment, when Jim accidently discovered that I was treating a girl who was also in his special reading class. He again became insistent that I give him things and grew distant when they were not immediately forthcoming. He grew more domineering, acting as if he had very little need for me, and finally began missing appointments.

I again found myself becoming forceful and instructive, trying to get him to see that he was afraid that I preferred my other patient to him. After a while, I also found myself feeling discouraged and caught myself occasionally coming a few minutes late for our appointments.

Finally, on one occasion, when Jim said he felt particularly discouraged by his inability to engage his father and also lonely on his walking trips, I told him that I thought he was feeling a similar loneliness and discouragement with me and that it seemed to have started when he learned I was seeing his classmate. A flood of questions followed: "How often does she come? How long has she been coming?" I again decided to answer some of these directly, in part because I knew he already knew the answers. I told him, "I see Jeannie twice a week on Tuesday and Friday. She has been coming to therapy for a long while." Jim seemed tremendously relieved. He didn't want to leave that hour and spent the next several hours reviewing why he had become so discouraged with me. We agreed on the idea that he was often suspicious of me and that my not directly answering his questions made it worse. He said it made him feel I was keeping something from him. He also said he felt his mother and father rarely answered his question, and that made him feel bad. Jim agreed with my suggestion that, maybe, we could use therapy to answer a lot of questions he had, such as why he currently felt so disappointed with his father. I suggested that we might have to look into the past for some of the answers.

Within a month, Jim and I found ourselves talking about his problems for the entirety of our sessions. The whole quality of our interaction changed. Jim no longer grew suspicious of me, seemed eager to talk, and only expressed feelings of sadness that we couldn't spend more time together. He also, for the first time, began playing spontaneously with peers, and by the time of termination, eight months later, had an active social life which was persisting at the last followup two years after the end of treatment.

Phase 4—Commitment to Psychotherapy

In the final segment of the treatment, the last eight months of the fourth year, Jim produced and processed an enormous amount of historical material. He first tried to understand his relationship with his father. Through shooting games, he brought into focus an interest in the Civil War, about which he had spoken sporadically since the beginning of treatment. This interest was related to Jim's notion that his paternal grandfather might have fought in that war. He imagined some resemblance between Lincoln and his grandfather. At times, when Jim felt frustrated in his efforts to engage his father, he liked to play out the theme of the assassination of Lincoln and pretend that he, John Wilkes Booth, was acting valiantly to get the vice-president, whom he identified with his father, into office. The point of this game was that by assassinating Lincoln, he could be rid of his greatest competition—the image of his grandfather. Implicitly, he could then have his father to himself. Once we understood the meaning of his play, we went on to explore Jim's ideas about his father's much idealized early relationship with his grandfather. For example, it turned out that one reason Jim wanted a rifle so badly was that his grandfather had bought his father one when his father was twelve. Also, Jim's fanatical interest in going fishing with his father derived from the knowledge that fishing had been a favorite activity of his grandfather and father. Jim continued to review in detail the disappointments experienced in trying to engage his father, and was finally able to understand that, in part, they were attributable to his father's personality and not to some deficiency of his own. At this point, Jim's ability to look at details of the past contrasted dramatically with his previous inability to look at any of his current or past experiences in detail.

Four months before the end of treatment, I told Jim I would be leaving the city and would therefore have to terminate treatment. Jim's immediate response was to wonder whether he would be able to visit me. As the hour progressed, however, he grew suspicious and questioned me about my other patients, and I felt that he suspected that I might not leave them behind. In the next hour, he told me a story about a doctor who had not responded to an emergency call. I was able then to suggest that he might worry about having problems and not being able to contact me after I left. This led Jim to talk about communicating with me after I was gone. He suggested we use a walkie-talkie. His worries continued over the next several hours as he talked about pollution killing fish and animals. Again, it was easy for him to see the connection between these images and his feelings of vulnerability deriving from my leaving. The most severe reaction to the impending termination followed in the next two sessions when he became distant, claimed he wanted to work his problems out by himself, and developed headaches and the fear that he was losing his vision. As we tried to understand these reactions, Jim made a tentative link between the fear of losing his vision and early fears of the dark and being left alone. He also recalled being made anxious at that time about the thought of what it would be like to become blind. He speculated that he had imagined it as making him feel totally lost and helpless.

For the next two months, Jim's conversation alternated between talking about his continuous efforts to engage his father, expressing bitterness when his father was moody or showed more attention to others, and expressing sadness that I was leaving. (He was aware that he wanted to substitute a relationship with his father for the one he would lose with me.) At times, he told me that he felt that things "just wouldn't be the same afterwards." Again in association, he told me that "the environment is being destroyed by pollution."

A month and a half before termination, Jim came home with a walkie-talkie. He claimed he had found it, but his parents felt he had stolen it. In therapy, as we discussed the walkie-talkie, Jim inadvertently referred to his father's unwillingness to buy him a dog and then a gun, and his anger about that. The implication was that he might have stolen the walkie-talkie to compensate. Jim's interest in the walkie-talkie was soon tied to his wish to communicate with me after my departure. In two weeks, that interest spontaneously generalized into a full-fledged interest in electronics.

The final development during the last several months, and seemingly tied to the loss of me and lack of availability of his father, was an abrupt turning toward peers. Increasingly, during the last few months of treatment, his feelings of sadness at my going led to his thinking about his new friends and optimistically describing their exploits together.

During the last several sessions of treatment, Jim again talked with feeling about a wish to visit me and even to resume therapy with me in several years if I returned to the city. In the sixth from last session, the balance between old anxieties and hopefulness about the future were poignantly expressed. Jim began by animatedly describing his new friends and a game they played together. He then said that the only person who spoiled their fun was his maternal grandmother, who characteristically reminded Jim of his mother and was very strict. Suddenly, he again said that he was afraid that "things won't be the same after you leave. They won't be as much fun." Jim began to review the treatment and reminded me about one of our early games, the shooting of animals in the dark. This led him to recall a dream and associated fears which he placed at around age seven. The dream, as he remembered it, was as follows:

> He was tied up by a witch who placed him over a large pot filled with man-eating piranha fish. He was tied by a rope. A candle was burning under this rope and when it burned through the rope, a knife would be released. The knife would then cut the rope, and he would drop into the pot.
> Everything went as the witch planned, but just as he was about to be dropped into the pot, he squirmed free, grabbed hold of the rope above him and scrambled out of a window. The piranhas were already biting at his feet when he made his escape. When he got out of the window, he ran as fast as he could because he was still afraid that the witch would follow and catch him. He also remembered having an image of the piranhas eating the rope and even the pot.

Jim said that following this dream, he had terrible night fears for about a year of a witch who would "come in the night" and might "take him away." He felt that she could disguise herself and change into an animal. She also had an assemblage of followers, all of whom were aggressive "bad" animals. He had also been afraid that this witch and her animals might come and take his "new things" away from him. As a result, he had kept his stuffed animals on his bed in order to protect himself against these other "bad animals." His animals were "good animals."

Jim then said that the dream had followed a trip to an aquarium where he saw a man feeding piranhas. He was amazed at the speed with which they devoured the meat. He also said the dream had occurred just following his move from sleeping in a room with his sister to sleeping on a convertible bed in the living room. It was the first time in his life he had slept alone. He said that he had at first been frightened and lonely in the new room. I suggested that he "might *also* be worried about being lonely and even of some of the old fears coming back after I left." Jim agreed. At this point, the hour was up.

The dream was never directly discussed again, but in the next hour, Jim brought the family picture album, and, after looking at pictures of him as a child, we spent the remainder of the session talking about how upset and frightened he had been as a child when his mother was angry at him. He said she usually instructed his father to hit or whip him. I told him that my leaving might be making him afraid that "old problems with his mother's anger might come up again and that he might also be concerned that he would have no one to talk to about it." He agreed, but soon, thoughtfully said that his mother "really wasn't as much of a problem now as she had been earlier." (This, in part, was an accurate perception of Mrs. A.) He then shifted the topic and spoke optimistically about his new friends. (Shortly after the hour in which Jim told me the dream, Mrs. A reported a dramatic improvement in Jim's mood, his socialization, and even his appetite).

In our last session, Jim gave me a gift. It was a statue of a boy and his dog. Jim told me that he had chosen this statue because the boy was wearing the same kind of hat he always wore and that he thought the statue would "help you to remember me." He added that he liked the dog's presence on the statue because "you know I like animals." He also gave me pictures he had drawn of his cats. I took the opportunity to ask him if he was concerned about my remembering him. He didn't answer directly, but turned to look through the file of his drawings he kept in my office. Following this, he made a detailed comparison between my current office and my old one and talked about how much he had changed over the past four years. He then said he hoped he could visit me sometime, but "we can at least write."

DIAGNOSTIC CONSIDERATIONS

It is tempting to formulate Jim's problems within a framework of fixation at preoedipal levels and conflict over unacceptable preoedipal and oedipal level instinctual strivings. For example, Jim's problems at the time of his referral could be framed partially in oedipal terms with Jim in the role of a potential oedipal victor. He had an intimate and seductive involvement with his mother, while he seemed particulary distrustful of his father. Symptoms, including school difficulties and a preoccupation with being attacked could be formulated as resulting from projected death wishes (Cooledge et al. 1962). In addition, Jim clearly manifested preoedipal fixations which significantly colored his thinking. Early in the treatment, for example, Jim constantly worried about deprivation, especially at the hands of his mother and was harassed by fears of destruction and annihilation often coupled with imagery of frightening, devouring animals. However, in spite of the obvious significance of these factors in determining Jim's difficulties, they do not seem sufficient to fully explain its nature or extent.

The position taken in this paper is that a central focus of Jim's difficulty was in the area of his narcissism. In itself, this requries clarification since, on close inspection, Jim showed two different narcissistic features. The first, the core of Jim's pathology, was his narcissistic vulnerability. The second was Jim's narcissistic defense. These two narcissistic features were interrelated in that Jim's icy detachment and tendency to exploit served to compensate for and defend against his narcissistic vulnerability. A narcissistic injury regularly led to Jim's becoming detached.

The clinical section demonstrates how the single underlying focus of Jim's life was his desire to engage a key object in an exclusive relationship. Most often during therapy, this object was the therapist; later it was also Jim's father. The features of this relationship are significant.

First, Jim could not tolerate the possibility that the therapist might have an interest in anyone other than him. Jim fundamentally distrusted the therapist and with the slightest hint of a disappointment would frantically look for clues that the therapist's involvement with him was declining. This easily magnified into the notion that the therapist would abandon him—for example, at the time when Jim entered the activities therapy group.

Second, Jim reacted with enormous rage to these perceived breeches of relationship. Indications that he felt neglected by the therapist were regularly followed by destructive activities (the scattering of toys, games in which Jim's play character would trick and kill other play figures) or by associations to death and injury. Rage was also projected so that when Jim became angry, his mind filled with terrifying thoughts of devouring animals, and previously trusted objects became threatening. During the third year of therapy, for example, in response to his anger about the therapist's participation in the activities group, Jim began to treat the therapist as if he were a threatening object, counterphobically provoking him and calling him "chicken." Indeed, an immense terror about the world at large characterized Jim during the early phases of his treatment.

Third, it became clear at the end of the second year of treatment that Jim perceived his rage as dangerous and as the real reason that others withdrew from him. In his games, Jim progressively became the bad guy and asked that he be put in jail. Later, he could talk about his temper and how he thought other boys and his teacher didn't like him because of it. Finally, Jim was prone to devastating feelings of devaluation when he felt that a valued person was losing interest in him. At these times, he might describe himself as "dumb."

Since the responses just elaborated resulted from his beginning to count on another person, Jim needed to guard against emotional involvements. Jim's narcissistic defense, that of withdrawal into virtual self-sufficiency, served this purpose. In therapy, Jim would play by himself and only acknowledge the therapist's presence when he felt the therapist could do something for him, for example, bring him a new toy. He became domineering at times, and engaged the therapist in activities as a kind of servant. Finally, when he didn't get what he wanted, he was inclined to take it (see Manaker 1973).

The psychopathological features just elaborated are those of the narcissistic character disorder described by Kernberg (1975). Jim departs from Kernberg's description of this syndrome in the ease with which his intense primitive needs and vulnerabilities surfaced in the therapeutic relationship. A major reason for this may be Jim's age. It seems probable that over time, Jim's defensive narcissism (character defense) would have become entrenched and more difficult to overcome. He would have become progressively more aloof and exploitative. A second point of departure from Kernberg's description is the speed with which Jim progressed. One possible explanation for this is that the therapy was conducted simultaneously with Jim's normal development and that it removed intrapsychic obstacles which had interfered with this process. That is, the working through of Jim's distorted object relationships allowed the normal building of positive and realistic object relationships to resume. (As a result, the relationship to the therapist cannot strictly be conceptualized as transference. The work in the relationship was not simply referable to the past, and current relationships outside of the therapy, but included also a current developmental aspect.) A related feature of Jim's developmental situation, which may also have contributed to his ability to change so rapidly, was the continued and increasingly constructive presence of his parents, the objects with whom his difficulties had originated. Jim's mother especially benefited from her collateral work in the therapy. She became less intimately and seductively involved with Jim and less punitive when disappointed by him.

The fact of Jim's age also affected the way in which the therapy was conducted. There was more emphasis on explaining the therapist's intent and on producing tangible evidence of the therapist's interest and good will. There was always a sense of providing a developmental experience for Jim as well as helping him understand his needs and reactions. Apart from this, the therapy bears out Kernberg's (1975) emphasis on the need to analyze the underlying experiences of envy and rage in response to perceived rejection and devaluation by the therapist, and on the need for much treatment to focus on the patient's current needs and reactions as opposed to past experiences.

Treatment

Overall, the therapy can be viewed as a series of tests of the therapist's involvement and reliability by Jim. The first progression was Jim's movement from accepting only action which would gratify his needs, such as the replacement of a toy, to his accepting empathic statements. By the third year, it was possible to go a step further and explore in detail with Jim the nature of his reactions to the therapist, for example, to talk about his sad or angry feelings that the therapist had disappointed him and possibly favored someone else. It was only at the beginning of the fourth year, when Jim seemed finally to trust the therapist's commitment to him, that he could use the therapy to view his defensive behavior and to explore the origins of his distortions by looking at their precursors in his past.

This suggests a close and sharp focus on the patient's current reactions as the hallmark of the early phases of this kind of treatment. It also highlights the enormous importance of the therapeutic relationship and the events within it. It confirms Kernberg's suggestion (1975) that much of these treatments must focus on the nature of the patient's current experience within the therapy.

The intensity of Jim's needs and reactions also accounts for the personal difficulties encountered by the therapist in conducting this treatment. These mainly derived from Jim's narcissistic defense, that is, his withdrawals and domineering behavior. As illustrated in the clinical section, the countertransference reactions mainly consisted of anger in response to Jim's seeming lack of appreciation of my efforts and a sense of impotence when none of my actions or comments seemed to reach Jim. This was manifested either as discouragement, or more often, as efforts to force Jim to hear me and respond. At times, I also noticed myself becoming angry in response to feeling depreciated. This occurred when Jim repeatedly treated my ideas and suggestions as if they were worthless. This was often a subtle feature of Jim's attitude at times when I disappointed him. He would turn away from me and reject as insignificant any statement I made. Characteristically, at the end of such sessions, he would leave the room abruptly and without a trace of emotion. During the beginning and middle phases of treatment, I also recognized myself feeling hopelessness in reaction to the recognition that Jim's need for me was so starkly egocentric. He behaved as though I should have no existence beyond the functions I served for him. Perhaps, through my empathy with him, Jim had evoked in me some of my own deeply buried fears of narcissistic isolation. Without the ongoing self-evaluation of these feelings, they could have conceivably caused me to withdraw in discouragement from Jim and to rationalize this by considering Jim too disturbed for an explanatory psychotherapy. These experiences are in agreement with both Kohut's (1971) and Kernberg's (1975) more formal treatment of typical countertransference paradigms encountered in working with patients with narcissistic character disturbances.

The discussion of Jim's immense needs and marked tendency to mistrust and distort the intentions of important persons in his life points to the issue of how open and, in addition, how directly gratifying the therapist should be in work with these patients. Jim constantly pushed me to assume a major gratifying role in his life. My reluctance to do this led to the anger and withdrawals repeatedly illustrated in the clinical section. Clearly, it proved helpful to maintain an exploratory and somewhat detached posture, and wait patiently until Jim and I could understand the exaggerated nature of his needs and reactions, and eventually find a historical basis for them. Too much direct gratification would have obstructed this work because the full extent of Jim's mistrust, envy, and rage would never have become manifest and understood (see Kernberg 1970, 1974, 1975).

At the same time the author's firm conviction that a major feature in the success of this case was the existence of a significant (albeit attenuated and controlled) real relationship. During the early and middle phases of treatment, Jim did not care to hear my often correct clarifications of his state of mind. Jim's progressive movement into a therapeutic relationship during this part of the treatment, it seems, is mainly attributable to the genuine interest in understanding and helping him that I repeatedly conveyed. This was conveyed in words, in tone of voice, and in such gestures as replacing broken toys. Later, it was conveyed in my recognition that empathic statements identifying of Jim's needs and frustration (communicated through a well-timed response or the labeling of his needs and feelings) was an important gratification for him. Finally, at appropriate times, I indicated my empathy by more direct gratifications such as the straightforward answering of questions. This was done only after the etiology of Jim's frustrations was reasonably clear to me and when I judged that the distortion in Jim's view of me was causing Jim to withdraw from the therapy to such a degree that he was completely unavailable for an interpretive intervention. In the case of answering questions, for example, an important precursor was Jim's parents' tendency to be secretive. My willingness to answer certain of his questions not only helped Jim revise his assumptions about the therapist, but also led, for the first time, to a profitable discussion of his immense frustration with his parents when he thought they withheld information from him.

Implicit in this discussion is the notion that in child psychotherapy and in psychotherapy with children like Jim in particular, there is a significant element of a developmental experience. The relationship with the therapist is a new relationship upon which the patient continues to build, as well as revise, his internalized object relations. This is particularly significant with children whose internalized object relations tend to be so lacking in positive elements.

SUMMARY

Jim's disturbance is seen as a childhood precursor of the narcissistic character disorder described by Kernberg. The vicissitudes of the therapy are almost all referable to events within Jim's relationship with the therapist. He was exquisitely sensitive to any indication that the therapist might be less than exclusively devoted to him. When he felt betrayed, he would typically become furious and retreat into narcissistic isolation. The progress in the treatment consisted of stepwise improvement in Jim's confidence in the therapist's commitment to him and in the fourth year of treatment, in Jim's ability to explore usefully the antecedents of his current difficulties. It is the author's contention that the real relationship with the therapist is an especially important component of treatment of children with this disorder. Progress occurs not only because the distortions in the child's conceptions of objects become identified and understood, but also because of a simultaneous experience of a helpful concerned relationship at a time when the child is normally in the process of revising and developing his object relationships.

NOTES

1. For a more complete discussion of the complexities and absence of clarity in the use of the term narcissism, the reader is referred to Pulver (1970).

2. Mahler (1966, 1971) and Settlage (1971) provide a framework for understanding the development of these traits in the context of the difficulties between Jim and his mother which began at his eighteenth month.

REFERENCES

Cooledge, J., Tessman, E., Waldfogel, S., and Willer, M. (1962). Patterns of aggression in school phobia. *Psychoanalytic Study of the Child* 17:219-383.

Eisnitz, A. (1974). On the metapsychology of narcissistic pathology. *Journal of the American Psychoanalytic Association* 22:279-291.

Freud, A., Nagera, H., and Bolland J. (1962). Developmental profile—modifications and present form (Draft of Diagnostic Profile), unpublished, pp. 11-18

Jacobson, E. (1964). *The Self and the Object World*. New York: International Universities Press.

Kernberg, O. (1966). Structural derivatives of object relationship. *International Journal of Psycho-Analysis* 47:236-253

——— (1970). Factors in the psychoanalytic treatment of narcissistic personality. *Journal of the American Psychoanalytic Association* 18:51-85.

——— (1974). Contrasting viewpoints regarding the nature and psychoanalytic treatment of narcissistic personalities. *Journal of the American Psychoanalytic Association* 22:255-267.

——— (1975). *Borderline Conditions and Pathological Narcissism*. New York: Jason Aronson.

Kohut, H. (1971). *The Analysis of the Self*. New York: International Universities Press.

——— (1972). Thoughts on narcissism and narcissistic rage. *Psychoanalystic Study of the Child* 27:360-400.

Manaker, E. (1973). A contribution to the study of the neurotic stealing symptom. *American Journal of Orthopsychiatry* 9:368-378.

Mahler, M. (1966). Notes on the development of basic moods: the depressive affect. In *Psychoanalysis: A General Psychology*, ed. R. Lowenstein, L. Newman, M. Schur, and A. Solnit. New York: International Universities Press.

——— (1971). A study of the separation-individuation process and its possible application to borderline phenomena. *Psychoanalytic Study of the Child* 26:402-424.

——— (1972). The rapprochement subphase of the separation-individuation process. *Psychoanalytic Quarterly* 41:457-506.

Pulver, S. (1970). Narcissism, the term and the concept. *Journal of the American Psychoanalytic Association* 18:319-341.

Settlage, C. (1971). On the libidinal aspect of early psychic development and the genesis of infantile neurosis. In *Separation-Individuation*, ed. J. McDevitt and C. Settlage, pp. 131-165. New York: International Universities Press.

Depersonalization
in a Female Adolescent

RICHARD L. MUNICH, M.D.

This paper demonstrates the relationship between the onset and persistent manifestation of the depersonalization phenomenon in a female adolescent. On the basis of a case report it is postulated that certain external stimuli coinciding with anxiety lead to a physiologically induced altered state of consciousness which defends against the maintenance or repetition of these events. If the state functions effectively, as in the presented case, a symptom pattern develops which resembles very closely that altered state of consciousness. The particular form of the altered state is postulated to depend upon the personality configuration of the individual patient.

Then all the charm is broken—all that phantom world so fair vanishes, and a thousand circlets spread, and each mis-shape the other. —Coleridge

Understanding depersonalization is complicated by several factors: First, this ubiquitous phenomenon not only has a high incidence in many specific mental disorders (Shorvon 1945) and is prevalent as a transient experience in the normal population (Sedman 1966), but it is also, after anxiety and depression, the most common complaint of hospitalized psychiatric patients (Stewart 1964). Second, there is confusion in the literature as to whether or not depersonalization represents an entity or symptom unto itself (Bellak 1958), a defense mechanism (Jacobsen 1959), a precursor to various psychotic states (Galdston 1947), a pathological ego state (Federn 1952), a result of cerebral dysfunction (Mayer-Gross 1935), or a disordered attention state (McGhie and Chapman 1961, Silverman 1968). Third, differentiation in the literature between phenomenological and genetic-dynamic formulations is rather unclear. And finally, differences in definition of the phenomenon itself range from regarding depersonalization as autoscopic sensation (I feel like I am looking at myself) to a change in the subjective experience of one's sense of self so as to feel distant and detached. In addition to these autoscopic

The author thanks Jean Schimek, Ph.D. and Theodore Lidz, M.D. for their assistance in the preparation of this material.

sensations, the depersonalization syndrome includes perceived changes in the environment so that everything seems unreal (derealization) and other emotional events such as disturbances of mood and affect, difficulty in organizing thoughts, sensations of numbness, and feelings of emptiness in the head (Bellak 1958, Schilder 1950). It is not difficult therefore to imagine such notions as not being in touch with feelings and not getting it all together, and feelings of emptiness, alienation, and death as being in some way related to aspects of depersonalization.

One can usefully organize the diverse ways of looking at depersonalization by thinking of it as an altered state of consciousness (ASC). The definition of an altered state of consciousness, as derived by Ludwig and maintained by various writers, is: "Any mental state, induced by various physiological, psychological, or pharmacological maneuvers or agents, which can be recognized subjectively by the individual himself (or by an objective observer of the individual) as representing a sufficient deviation in subjective experience or psychological functioning from certain general norms for the individual during alert waking consciousness (Ludwig 1966). Initially conceived in terms of and in connection with trance states and hypnotic and mystical experiences, the concept of ASC became more sophisticated as knowledge of sleep states increased and the investigation of the effects of hallucinogenic drugs became more careful. Recently, the understanding of ASCs has proceeded through research directed toward attention states, proprioceptive and exteroceptive regulatory and perceptual systems, and response mechanisms. Although ASCs may manifest themselves in many ways, most writers agree that common elements include alterations in thinking, a disturbed sense of time, loss of control, emotional lability, changes in body image, perceptual distortions, and changes in meaning and significance. Finally, those factors which either precede or produce an altered state of consciousness are formally categorized as follows: (1) extreme variation in sensory input, either a marked increase or decrease, (2) extreme variation in level of awareness, again either a marked increase or decrease, and (3) alterations in physiologic and/or neurophysiologic systems, either endogenous or exogenous (McGhie 1961, Silverman 1968).

The purpose of this clinical material is to demonstrate the relationship between the onset and persistent manifestation of the depersonalization phenomenon in a female adolescent.

CLINICAL MATERIAL

Edie K, a seventeen-year-old, white, high school girl, had been referred at sixteen for long term residential hospitalization after three hospitalizations during the previous year had failed to ameliorate her persistent depersonalized state and high suicidal potential. During the previous hospitalizations, Edie had received phenothiazines and antidepressant medications in high doses, a course of 20 ECTs, and a trial of Lithium Carbonate—all without success. During her early years she controlled her high level of anxiety by rigid social and religious appropriateness, compulsive intellectual and athletic overachievement, and an extensive and complex fantasy life. Like the gothic novels she now read assiduously, this fantasy world alternated between being frightening and uncomfortable on the one hand and otherwise admitting of positive and romanticized resolutions on the other. Nonetheless, except for an almost constant nervous giggle, the patient was described as an attractive, happy, active, and personable girl.

The onset of any observable difficulty occurred just prior to Edie's fourteenth birthday. During the preceding year the patient began menstruating and became aware of increased tension and a vague feeling that something was wrong. She related those feelings to the pressure she felt to do well enough academically to be admitted to preparatory school. Near the end of the summer, she spent a very troubled week at the beach with a friend, during which she discovered that many girls her age were drinking and "fooling around" with boys. Feeling unprepared for such activities, she returned home earlier than planned. A few days after her return, she attended the wedding of one of her brother's best friends, at which she became intoxicated from drinking too much champagne. She remembers walking outside, struggling to keep from being taken home, and finally passing out at home for about three hours. Upon awakening everything seemed distant and unreal to her; she felt "detached, as if I were on a pedestal and the rest of the world were below me." This frightening condition persisted for several days so that Edie was taken to a neurologist whose examination, including an electroencephalogram, revealed nothing. Over the next year there were at least three more episodes during which she felt detached: following general anesthesia for a dental extraction; when losing control on a ski slope; and following a bee sting. During these detached states, Edie not only felt that everything was distant and unreal, but was also quite frightened, confused, and perplexed as to where she was ("I kept asking people if I had just been there") and unsure of the passage of time ("I would look at the clock after a couple of minutes only to find that two hours had passed"). Soon the "out of it" feeling came to be associated with social situations, usually ones in which she felt rejected. Whereas a retreat to her fantasy world had formerly been effective in ameliorating most difficult situations, this no longer worked; and Edie noticed that the new feelings would "crowd the good things out" of her mind, leaving her feeling empty and hopeless. The feelings became more persistent and severe following a particularly traumatic rejection by her boyfriend after a college weekend during which she came very close to having intercourse.

Upon returning to boarding school, Edie was alternately suicidal and depersonalized. By this time the patient's concerns about herself and her frequent depersonalized states had produced considerable secondary anxiety, which Edie herself attempted to alleviate by a series of minor wrist scratchings and ingestions of pills, as well as by small doses of different poisons. After five months at boarding school, Edie returned home and began seeing a psychiatrist who hospitalized her after a brief and unsuccessful office treatment.

The patient is the only daughter and youngest of four children whose paternal grandfather committed suicide and whose father suffered an acute depressive reaction when the patient was eight, becoming distraught. During Edie's first hospitalization and in the midst of her course of ECT, he committed suicide by jumping from Edie's window at their home. The patient's mother is described as intrusive and controlling, with a frightening temper. She remembers very few details of her daughter's early years. Edie's parents' disturbed marriage was complicated by the fact that they lived in a social situation well beyond their economic means—a situation which the mother angrily resented but nonetheless participated in vigorously. Edie remembers that when her mother would get angry at her father and begin yelling at him, he would simply fall silent and get a distant look in his eye. "I really felt sorry for him at those times, and wished he would fight back," she said. Edie's earliest memories of her older brothers was of their frightening and teasing her a great deal. She recalls how her brothers took care of her during the evenings when the parents went out. "They would let me watch half of a horror movie, then make me go to bed and close me in the room. Then from the next room they would beat on the walls and make funny noises." Nevertheless, Edie wept bitterly as each left for preparatory school and would call their names for several days after they left. Edie and her father would often escape the tense atmosphere of the home by taking long walks together, going horseback riding, and playing tennis. Often they spent several hours playing with Edie's large antique doll house and making up elaborate stories. Since he never liked to be alone and furthermore had some difficulty with his memory, Mr. K would occasionally take his daughter with him on business trips. Edie did not always find these times of being together comfortable, especially following difficult and tense times in the house: "As I got older, there was something about him that was scary. When he touched me or put his arm around me, I just felt like running away, . . . but I used to promise him that I would never get angry like my mother did." Mr. K constantly placed rigorous athletic and intellectual demands on Edie, and even though she was quite afraid of horses, he made her take riding lessons. Furthermore, he used to stand over Edie for long periods to make sure that she understood her math and science work. Tears were unavailing: "My mother always used to tell him that he would drive me crazy."

At no time during two hundred and fifty psychotherapeutic interviews did the patient demonstrate evidence of a formal thought disorder. Similarly, extensive psychological testing, four times in two different settings over two years, showed no evidence of disorganized or psychotic thinking; rather it showed a repressed, impulsive, anxious, and highly distractable character who experienced moments of emptiness especially in relation to her father's absence. She revealed that she often had an image of her dead father's face before her; and although she sometimes regarded this phenomenon as silly and sometimes as frightening, she knew it was not real. Usually this image occurred in the context of a desperate wish to join or rejoin her dead father in some way: "I think about him all the time. I think about being with him when I am about to hurt myself. It just couldn't end and there be nothing afterward." At times during a depersonalized state, the room or hallway seemed to change dimensions, her own body parts did not seem related to her, and she was frightened of being with people. Rather than a paranoid delusion, this latter appeared to be more a fear that people would find out how and what she is thinking, or that she appeared "crazy," or that they would expect her to be able to relate to them. Even before her father's death, Edie used to experience something like these perceptual distortions around her horse. The horse would change shape, its head often seeming to change into a picture of her father's face: "I haven't ridden her since he died. . . . She was just as much his horse as mine, he really loved her."

As might be expected, the patient's fearfulness around people constituted a major resistance in her psychotherapy. Each minute revelation was immediately followed by denial and each glimmer of intimacy by retreat. Often it was difficult to discern whether she was talking about the depersonalized state or the anxiety associated with her fear of being overwhelmed by it. It was only with great pain and obvious embarrassment that she recounted some of the details of her early years and gave more substance to what she meant by feeling "out of it." From at least age eight, Edie was often preoccupied with thoughts of harming herself; more specifically, she had a fascination for heights and would often attempt jumping down whole flights of stairs, from trees, and from the roof of the barn. Ostensibly these jumps were to test whether or not she could break her legs. In addition to its being her father's favorite sport, her fascination with skiing had to do with climbing up and "falling" from the top of a mountain. The combination of self-destructive and sexual themes in this was thinly veiled, and was to become clearer in later behavior during which she experimented with various poisons and pills, and held onto large kitchen knives whenever her parents left her alone in the evenings. She was terrified, feeling certain that an unknown intruder would force his way into the house and assault her. She often conveyed that she experienced the psychotherapy as a similar intrusion and assault.

Edie was often observed in the midst of a depersonalized state, but on those occasions, she was too anxious and apparently disorganized to talk about it. Her regular response at these times was, "I don't know." Her recall of details of the altered state was also uniformly poor. A regularly observable phenomenon was the patient's obvious disturbance following a visit with her mother. As reported by the patient, these visits were comfortable as long as she and her mother were talking about or shopping for clothes and discussing trips or the activities of Edie's brothers. When the conversation moved to more personal matters, however, a fight between them inevitably ensued; afterward Edie always felt "out of it" for the next several hours. Once, when her mother had a temper tantrum on the ward, Edie was noted to be giggling uncontrollably and staring vacantly all around her. Three times during a high fever, she appeared so agitated and depersonalized as to convince those around her that she was having a psychotic reaction of some sort. However, when her fever fell she rapidly became more organized and could not remember many details of the previous hours. Suicidal gestures usually terminated periods of great anxiety. Later events made it seem that her depersonalized state might more properly be called a *dissociative trance state* (West 1967). For example, after a new boyfriend told her she still dressed like a prep school girl, she returned to her room and two hours later suddenly noticed that all of her clothes had been ripped from her closet and strewn all over her room. Or, twice, when she visited a nearby cemetery, she found herself locked in, having spent an unknown amount of time at a grave daydreaming and crying. She said, "I'm not sure how I got there, but I must have been thinking about death, or my father." She described encounters with her boyfriend as if she were not herself. "When we are alone, it's like I lose myself; I become like an animal, ripping clothes off and becoming very passionate." Her most recent suicide attempt came immediately after having sexual intercourse for the first time. The only details she can remember were her lack of feeling and the picture of her father hovering above her. However, when asked why she had taken a large overdose of medication, she replied that she wanted to lessen the impact of an anticipated fall: "I was afraid it would hurt, but I have always wanted to know what Daddy felt when he jumped. I could never imagine it." During the period of this latest altered state, the fusion of sexual and self-destructive themes was never more obvious.

DISCUSSION

This case raises several interesting questions: For example, has this patient's picture over the past several years suggested an intermediate step in the genesis of what earlier writers called a hysterical psychosis? And furthermore, what is the relationship here between depersonalization phenomena and dissociative reactions in general? If we assume that altered states of consciousness arise de novo from random neurophysiological events, then we are forced to ignore the expressive, symbolic, and defensive functions of the contents of these stages which otherwise seem related to many aspects of the patient's development. This paper suggests that a way of linking the essentially physiological notion of ASC and more functional aspects of personality development is to consider the altered state as a reactivation of some previously organized way of thinking and feeling, a view which corresponds closely to that held by such ego psychologists as Rapaport (1967).

The relationship between depersonalization and disorders of consciousness has been alluded to in previous writings (Federn 1952, McGhie 1961, Silverman 1968, Ludwig 1966, Waltzer 1968, West 1967). In this complicated example of the depersonalization phenomenon it is postulated that the onset of Edie's puberty contributed to a significant increase in already high levels of precariously defended anxiety. Just at the same time when her defensive pattern was under its most severe strain, she experienced a series of stresses which led to an altered state of consciousness. At first this altered state of consciousness served to mitigate her anxiety significantly enough to become a welcomed and useful addition to her defensive structure. Since the time of admission this complicated altered state of consciousness has served as a primary defensive operation and patterned response to somatic, intrapsychic, and interpersonal stresses. The principal questions to be answered in developing this hypothesis are: (1) How is this clinical state an altered state of consciousness? (2) Why was this phenomenon so rapidly incorporated into the patient's defensive structure? (3) What is the relation of this particular defensive retreat to a depersonalized state and altered states of consciousness?

As we have defined altered states of consciousness, the patient's state is congruent not only with the definition but with the manifestations. Several writers have commented on the association of onset with accidental or induced change in consciousness or the period following an acute trauma (Roth 1959). Others have commented on the frequency with which depersonalization begins during a period of fatigue following prolonged physical or psychological stress (Shorvon 1945). Psychoanalytic studies of the phenomenon suggest that abrupt changes in environment, even in pleasurable instances, can be reacted to during the first days or weeks with episodes of depersonalization (Jacobson 1959). The close temporal associations of depersonalization with alcoholic intoxication, and general anesthesia in this patient, are strongly suggestive of a connection with, and the patient's dramatic responses to, the bee sting and various febrile illnesses. Unusual hypersensitivity appears to be a precondition for an altered state of consciousness experience (Silverman 1968).

In answering the second question we must attempt to relate the patient's depersonalized state to her earlier and more pleasurable fantasy world so that we can see how this could so readily be incorporated into the defensive structure. First, both states represent a symbolic withdrawal from the exigencies of the external world. In the first case withdrawal is from the complex relationships and social stresses of early adolescence; in the second case, from the sad and frightening aspect of her earlier family interactions. Second, during both kinds of withdrawal, the patient eschewed personal contact, experiencing people as intrusive and frightening. Third, during both states, Edie was relatively unresponsive to the cues of the environment; she was perceived in younger years to be preoccupied, spending hours alone, and in later years to be out of it. Finally, the content of both states appears to be global and highly symbolic, with self-destructive and sexual themes predominating.

The third question is more complicated. Many writers stress the role of depersonalization as a defensive operation against anxiety; it has been variously suggested that this anxiety is related to the generating of unconscious hostile feelings, feelings of rejection, loss of love, or other unacceptable impulses or feelings (Oberndorf 1950, Blank 1954, Rosenfeld 1947, Peto 1955, Berman 1948, and Bergler 1950). The critical point in the development of these theories is the notion that anxiety catalyzes a splitting within the ego so that one part is viewing another in such a way as to create distance between viewer and viewed. Unable to contain the anxiety by normal repressive tactics, the individual retreats to earlier identifications, and a struggle develops between that part which has and that part which has not accepted these negative parts of the self. Thus an aggressive, or unloved, or exhibitionistic, or sadistic part of the self is temporarily detached from the overall self-image a person may have. Put another way, a person's feeling of unity in regard to the continuity, contiguity, and causality of experience is changed. In ego psychological terms, the ego or ego boundaries have lost some of their strength. These descriptions relate closely to sleep and dream states, hypnotic and other trance states, and dissociative phenomenon in general, the common denominator being an alteration in the state of consciousness (Ludwig 1966).

In the case presented, for example, when the patient found herself in a difficult situation with, or aware of, negative feelings toward her mother, she felt guilty and there usually ensued an attempt to withdraw from the unpleasant stimuli. The clinical material suggested that in withdrawing, Edie appeared then to regress to a state of negative identification with her mother and an attendant wish to be reunited with her father. For example, she would vigorously refuse any contact with nurses or other female patients, and would only sit with her therapist in virtual silence. At these times, when asked what was happening, she might reply that she was thinking of dying or that she had the "old feeling" again. Instead of defending against the impulses, she either thought of her own death, or the defense became directed against a bad self *in toto*, which then became split off and put out of existence. Or when Edie experienced a rejection from her boyfriend following a weekend or more recently from her therapist (she experienced the elucidating or stimulating of negative feelings as rejection), the retreat might be to an identification with the picture of her depressed father upon whose love and smile she depended. This, of course, would stimulate the latent incestuous impulses which, in Edie's development, appear to have been reciprocated. The unloved or incestuous self then became detached from the intact self-image and viewed as distant. Although these narcissistic identifications were far more complicated than presented, the significant point is made that during the altered state of consciousness the stimulus was reduced, and early and more primitive symbols became more important factors in conscious awareness. Another way of looking at the situation is to think of attention being focused on the stimulus in such a way as to minimize any information pertaining to it. That is, the purposeful manipulation of internal images and ideas required in normal thinking becomes altered through distractability and a global reaction (McGhie 1961; Silverman 1968).

A final area of the clinical picture that requires comment is the secondary anxiety generated by the depersonalized state and the resulting suicidal gestures. Although, as several writers have commented, the altered state of consciousness is designed to ward off painful affect and anxiety, it may of itself lead to a severe and overwhelming panic, secondary to the feelings of unreality and fragmentation (Shorvon 1945; Waltzer 1968). Several writers have commented on how anticipation of or eventual disorganization of the perceptual matrix can lead to crippling anxiety (Goldstein 1942). As noted with the patient, the fear is specific and conscious, and it is noteworthy that she conceives of this as her primary battle. As with other patients, part of this panic is motivated by her fear of becoming insane and losing control. A good part of the patient's reluctance even to speak of these matters is related to the same factor. Although suicidal ideation may be related to thoughts of joining her dead father or to defending against death wishes toward her mother, and although a gesture itself may serve to convince her that she truly is real and has feelings, the suicidal thought also functions to relieve the mounting tension and provide escape from the overwhelming panic.

CONCLUSION

A hypothetical mechanism for the instigation, development, and maintenance of an altered state of consciousness has been described in a psychiatric patient who presented with persistent depersonalization. The clinical material suggests that the effects of certain physiologic responses provided a model which the patient used for certain psychological ends. These ends included such expressive functions as identifying with her father and aggression toward her mother. They also included defensive functions against noxious internal stimuli, including the affect associated with these drives. Reactions to the altered state itself and some aspects of the psychotherapeutic process were also discussed.

Questions for further investigation include discerning what kind of development predisposes to such a state, what symbols are expressed by it, and what aspects of a person's history and character development may lead to a recurrent use of this pattern of defense and conflict resolution.

It is a general impression that more young patients referred for inpatient treatment complain of similar phenomena, very often with a concomitant and severe drug history. Although many individuals unconsciously seek and achieve temporary withdrawal from stressful stimuli by the use of psychotomimetic drugs, a paradoxical effect of the widespread usage of such drugs may be the instigation of ongoing and seriously pathological altered states of consciousness at a time when learning other defenses may be more useful. This would be particularly true when, as in the case presented here, the altered state of consciousness generalizes to become a patterned response to all stresses.

REFERENCES

Bellak, L. (1958). *Schizophrenia: A Review of the Syndrome.* New York: Logos Press.

Bergler, E. (1950). Further studies on depersonalization. *Psychiatric Quarterly* 24:268.

Berman, L. (1948). Depersonalization and the body-ego with special reference to the genital representation. *Psychoanalytic Quarterly* 17:433.

Blank, H. R. (1954). Depression, hypomania and depersonalization. *Psychoanalytic Quarterly* 23:20-37.

Federn, P. (1952). *Ego Psychology and the Psychoses.* New York: Basic Books.

Galdston, I. (1947). On the etiology of depersonalization. *Journal of Nervous and Mental Diseases* 105:25-39.

Goldstein, K. (1942). *After Effects of Brain Injuries in War.* New York: Grune and Stratton.

Jacobson, E. (1959). Depersonalization. *Journal of the American Psychoanalytic Association* 7:581-609.

Ludwig, A. (1966). Altered states of consciousness. *Archives of General Psychiatry* 5:225-234.

Mayer-Gross, W. (1935). On depersonalization. *British Journal of Medical Psychology* 15:103-122.

McGhie, A., and Chapman, J. (1961). Disorders of attention and perception in early schizophrenia. *British Journal of Medical Psychology* 34:103-116.

Oberndorf, L. P. (1950). The role of anxiety in depersonalization. *International Journal of Psycho-Analysis* 31:1-5.

Peto, A. (1955). On so-called depersonalization. *International Journal of Psycho-Analysis* 36:379-386.

Rapaport, D. (1967). States of consciousness. In *The Collected Papers of David Rapaport*, ed. Merton Gill, pp. 385-404. New York: Basic Books.

Rosenfeld, H. (1947). Analysis of a schizophrenic state with depersonalization. *International Journal of Psycho-Analysis* 28:13-19.

Roth, M. (1959). The phobic-anxiety-depersonalization syndrome. *Proceedings of the Royal Society of Medicine* 52:587-595.

Schilder, P. (1950). *The Image and Appearance of the Human body*. New York: International Universities Press.

Sedman, G. (1966). Depersonalization in a group of normal subjects. *British Journal of Psychiatry* 112:907-912.

Shorvon, H. J. (1945). The depersonalization syndrome. *Proceedings of the Royal Society of Medicine* 39:37-50.

Silverman, J. (1968). A paradigm for the study of altered states of consciousness. *British Journal of Psychiatry* 114:1201-1218.

Stewart, W. A. (1964). Panel discussion of depersonalization. *Journal of the American Psychoanalytic Association* 12:171-186.

Waltzer, H. (1968). Depersonalization and self-destruction. *American Journal of Psychiatry* 125:155-157.

West, L. J. (1967). Dissociative reaction. *Comprehensive Textbook of Psychiatry*, ed. A. H. Freedman, and H. I. Kaplan, pp. 890-891. Baltimore: Williams and Wilkins.

Impotence, Frigidity, and Depersonalization

WAYNE A. MYERS, M.D.

A review of important psychoanalytic literature in the perplexing area of depersonalization focuses primarily on its phenomenology and genesis. Case material from two patients elucidates a relatively neglected, specific substate. These two analyses center about prominent complaints of impotence and frigidity which are seen as equivalents of, or screens for, underlying depersonalization. Only by understanding and working through the genesis of the masked depersonalization could these sexual dysfunctions be adequately treated. Depersonalization was also manifest outside the sexual sphere, but its presence there led to a more thorough elucidation of its etiology, in which actual childhood observations of the primal scene were of paramount importance. A comprehensive description of depersonalization phenomenology is offered which considers this state as a compromise formulation with contributions from each structure of the mental apparatus. Normal and pathological determinants of the sensation of a split within the self into observing and participating aspects are described, as is the genesis of feelings of alienation and estrangement.

There is no universally accepted definition of depersonalization. Most authors offer descriptive definitions based upon subjective accounts of the phenomena related to them by their patients. Perhaps the most generally accepted distinction (though by no means a definition) is that phenomena related to one's own body are referred to as *depersonalization*, whereas similar phenomena occurring with respect to objects in the outside world are included under the heading *derealization*.

REVIEW OF LITERATURE

Freud (1936), in "A Disturbance of Memory on the Acropolis," refers to his incredulity and feelings of derealization on finally viewing the Acropolis. He notes that such "phenomena are to be observed in two forms: the subject feels either that a piece of reality or that a piece of his own self is strange to him. In the latter case we speak of 'depersonalization'; derealizations and depersonalizations are intimately connected." He sees derealization as a defense in which his sense of incredulity was both displaced in time to past events and was also aimed at "keeping something away from the ego, at disavowing it" (p. 245). He notes that the disavowal involved in his derealization feelings on the Acropolis had been directed against the threatened emergence of an unresolved, guilty oedipal wish to undervalue and surpass the oedipal father. In relating derealization to an oedipal level conflict, Freud differs from a number of other authors who see depersonalization as related to preoedipal conflicts. Unfortunately, Freud offers no further thoughts on the choice of this particular defense.

A number of authors, including Fenichel (1945), Nunberg (1948), Federn (1952), and Schilder (1953), attempt to explain the phenomenology of depersonalization in economic terms utilizing libido theory. They reason that object loss in reality leads to narcissistic regression, diminishing object libidinal investment and heightening narcissistic libidinal cathexis of the mental processes. They see this intensified cathexis as the basis of the discomfort and estrangement found in depersonalization. Their individual contributions are of interest and are worthy of exploration in greater detail.

Fenichel notes, "Experiences of estrangement and depersonalization are due to a special type of defense ... a countercathexis against one's own feelings which had been altered and intensified by a preceding increase in narcissism. The results of this increase are perceived as unpleasant by the ego which therefore undertakes defensive measures against them ... by a countercathexis. The augmented self-observation and the feeling that the missing sensations are still in existence ... are clinical manifestations of this countercathexis" (1945, p. 419). Although he bases his discussion primarily on feelings of depersonalization in schizophrenics, Fenichel related early disturbance in body image formation to later depersonalization, a point I wish to underscore for subsequent consideration.

Nunberg limits his definition of depersonalization to "those states in which the ego and the external world appear different, changed and foreign to the patient" (1948, p. 60). Considerable emphasis (in terms of the genesis of the later states of depersonalization) is in one case put on a traumatic weaning experience which led to increased childhood masturbation and to a heightening of castration anxiety. Nunberg sees the loss of the breast and the subsequent fears of the loss of the penis as equivalent in this patient's mind to a "loss of a part of the ego" (p. 64), and as predisposing to the shift in libidinal cathexis from external objects to mental processes. He too comments on heightened self-observation (p. 67) and notes the similarity between sleeping and depersonalization. Again, his clinical data raise the connection between problems in early object relationships and later states of depersonalization.

Federn also emphasizes a sense of unfamiliarity with respect to one's own body and the outside world. He mentions the split between what he refers to as the body ego and the mental ego (1952, p. 250), but does not see depersonalization as a defense mechanism, despite mentioning that patients suffering from it often become aware of extreme sexual and aggressive fantasies (to my mind, evidence of the failure of the defense). His limited dynamic considerations are stated in terms of castration fears leading to the detachment of that portion of the object libido which gives the object its sense of familiarity. Needless to say, this last sentence could be easily restated in terms of depersonalization as a defense against castration fears.

Schilder (1953) describes depersonalization as the patients' feelings that their own bodies or objects in the external world no longer appear the same. Depersonalization here defends against perceptions being experienced fully. Schilder notes that such patients experience things as originating "not in their center but on their periphery" (p. 305)—another manner of describing the sensation of being split into observing and participating aspects (self-representations). He explicitly comments on the compulsive self-observation in such patients.

One major objection to the specific economic explanations described above has been advanced by Arlow (1966). He reasons that such explanations merely restate the phenomena of depersonalization in different terms, without delineating which specific ego functions are affected or why such cathectic shifts lead to depersonalization and not to hypochondriasis.

Another group of authors, including Oberndorf (1933, 1934, 1939, 1950), Greenson (1954), Sarlin (1962), Rosen(1955), and Jacobson (1959), view the phenomenology of depersonalization as resulting from intrasystemic conflicts over identifications within the structures of the mental apparatus. Arlow pointedly criticizes this explanation on the grounds that the ego and superego are comprised of many identifications which only gain dynamic, and hence conflictual, significance when the "specific identifications represent derivaties of an id or of a superego demand" (1966, pp. 459-460). Despite this criticism, we should look deeper into the valuable contributions these individual authors have to offer.

Oberndorf (1933, 1934, 1939, 1950), believed depersonalization occurred when intellectual activity, specifically the pattern of thinking, had previously been erotized. He saw a superego identification with the parent of the opposite sex (in the sense of possessing similar thought patterns). When these patients, becoming aware of their conflicting bisexual identifications, attempted to modify them and their attendant thought patterns, they experienced sensations of unreality and self-estrangement. One could equally well characterize this state as an intersystemic conflict between id wishes and superego demands, resolved by the ego through depersonalization. Still, the observation of intense bisexual conflict is frequently made in articles on depersonalization. In addition to the frequently mentioned sense of heightened self-observation and of being split in two, Oberndorf also notes the repeated genital surgery which one of his patients underwent during early latency. In my own clinical data, such early surgical traumata are not uncommon in patients with depersonalization.

Greenson (1954) describes cases of early parental deprivation who felt prominent longings for oral gratification from objects in later life. These longings unconsciously seemed to threaten merger with a hated parental figure, which led to defensive denial during depersonalization. Again we see the emphasis on early deprivation, but here this raises the issues of the developmental levels at which early traumata occur and of the depth of regression involved in the depersonalized state. Of interest also, are his description of body image disturbances and his mention of primal scene observations as related to later episodes of depersonalization.

Sarlin (1962) like Greenson sees depersonalization and derealization as resulting from a struggle against wishes to merge with equally detested parental figures. His economic explanation of the phenomenology involves both a defensive withdrawal of cathexis from the self-representations, with a resultant feeling of self-estrangement and a subsequent narcissistic regression to a primitive undifferentiated state. Sarlin's patient exhibited, in his depersonalized states, an identification with his aggressor parents, in that his denial of his feelings mimicked the early parental attitudes toward him. Once more, the emphasis is on early parental deprivation.

Rosen's patient described feelings of fragmentation of the self and of strangeness and unreality toward external objects (1955). Rosen conceptualizes the derealization as resulting from a struggle within the ego to repudiate a degraded object image. Peculiar bodily sensations were also prominent and the patient's acute illness had been precipitated by an object loss in reality. The salutory outcome of the case hinged on the reconstruction of object losses during early childhood. Adult feelings of unreality were again seen as an identification with aggressor adults, in this case parents and a nurse who all had denied the reality of the patient's childhood perceptions of the mother's suicide attempt. Rosen views a deficiency in the patient's capacity for repression as predisposing to his use of derealization as a defense. The derealization involved narcissistic regression to a state in which self- and object-boundaries were blurred so that painful affects, unmasterable in present day reality, were dealt with as somatic sensations referrable to this primitive self-concept. Rosen adds, interestingly, that real traumatic events occurring in childhood, at a time when the distinction between reality and fantasy is still vague, are of importance in the genesis of later episodes of depersonalization, a point well illustrated in my clinical data.

Jacobson defined depersonalization as "an experience pertaining either to the bodily or mental self . . . The person will complain that his body or . . . parts of the body do not feel like his own. . . . He may describe them as being estranged from himself or as being dead. . . . [This] may go along with subjective sensations of numbness and of change of size and volume of the estranged body parts" (1959, p. 581). She also mentions the "frightening experience of becoming suddenly the outside observer of the performing part of the self" (p. 583). She observes that the body parts perceived as estranged were those involved in aggressive fantasies. In her psychoanalytic case material, she notes the narcissistic quality of her patients' object relationships. The sudden loss in reality of an object or its love, or the sudden degradation of a narcissistically loved object, led to a revival, in the ego of the patient, of such degraded self-images as being castrated or unacceptably aggressive. These had to be disavowed by the defensive depersonalization. She sees depersonalization as a defense mobilized when repression fails to handle the anxiety aroused by the threatened disruption of object relationships—a threat seen when intense, aggressive drive derivative wishes toward the objects arise during rapid states of drive defusion. Jacobson also stresses the importance of early parental deprivation and early traumata, such as traumatic weaning, primal scenes, and the observation of miscarriages, as important factors in the development of later depersonalization. Jacobson's observations on the change in size and volume of estranged body parts, closely parallels my own in one patient presented in this paper (Case 2) as does her focus on early traumata (primal scene) leading to a disavowal of unacceptable aspects of self- and object-representations.

Peto's patients with depersonalization described experiences of feeling surrounded by a mist or of feeling strange, empty, lost, and dead. His clinical data focuses on disturbances in the mother-child relationship prior to self-object differentiation. In this regression splitting is utilized as a prominent mechanism of defense. In theorizing on depersonalization experienced in latency and puberty on looking into a mirror (see Case 2), he speaks of the unexpected self-confrontation as loosening ego controls and leading to a splitting off and reemergence of repressed parental imagos, with the integrated ego observing this splitting phenomena. Peto views depersonalization as neither a defense nor a symptom, but as a by-product of instinctual defusion. In his view, if defusion and the consequent release of aggression is not quickly followed by a recathecting of the ego with libido, the ego perceives itself as empty and strange. He cites the infant's loss of the nipple as the prototypical traumatic experience of object loss, to be dealt with by an integration of the lost object into the ego with the help of some archaic defense mechanism (1955, p. 385). It is, of course, difficult to validate the economic hypotheses Peto offers, and once more we must question why drive defusion and recathecting of the ego with libido lead to depersonalization, as opposed to hypochondriasis or grandiosity. I would agree with his suggestion of a prototypical early splitting experience predisposing to later depersonalization even though dating it to the infant's loss of the nipple makes it impossible to validate.

Bird (1957) describes an adolesent boy whose first episode of depersonalization was subsequent to primal scene observation. The patient experienced changes in bodily perception as well as the sensation of being split into two people. All subsequent episodes of depersonalization occurred after traumatic visual experiences and are viewed as defending against an overwhelming upsurge of aggressive impulses. Bird sees the sensation of being split in two as symbolically representing the two parents from the primal scene observation and sees the loss of the patient's sense of reality as representing castration. Concern about genital differences and castration are viewed as displaced by a narcissistic regression onto concerns about the system consciousness, seen as being libidinized and then treated as if it "were an object. . . . As a result of this hypercathexis the normal function of consciousness came under inhibition, and the system consciousness, instead of recording the impulses, attempted to represent them—to represent various shocking experiences of loss and a longing to be reunited with all lost objects, particularly with the mother. The symptom is thus to be regarded as a hysterical conversion" (p. 262). I am in accord with many of Bird's ideas and with the genetic importance he ascribes to primal scene observation. I further agree that in the subjective experience of the patient we see a representation of the early traumata.

Greenacre, in her paper on screen memories, comments on the frequently evident sensation of being the detached onlooker. "The detached onlooker quality characteristic of the typical screen memory may be due not only to the paralysis and temporary depersonalization caused by fright or panic and carried over to the substitute remembered experiences, but further and perhaps chiefly to the arousal of the superego function whose force influences decisively the need to deny and the feeling of general intensity, and which is represented by an actual watchfulness in the screen memory" (1949, p. 76). The case cited involved a young woman who had slept in the parental bedroom until the age of four. The patient's screen memory of a primal scene observation at the age of eight was seen to screen off even earlier confusing and traumatic sexual observations. Greenacre unfortunately does not include any particulars as to whether the patient experienced frigidity or depersonalization in sexual situations.

In a later paper on the primal scene, Greenacre emphasizes the traumatagenic potential of early, *actual* observations of the primal scene. She feels that witnessing the primal scene before the age of three (prior to significant verbal facility) seems to leave an especially strong impression. "The impression of the primal scene must be deposited more in the physical components of the emotional reactions than would be true at a later age. These early body memories may be absorbed into later symptoms and often reappear in direct or converted forms in the course of treatment. They may also be absorbed into, and fixated in, peculiarly distorted forms by traumatically experienced revisions, notably in the phallic phase and especially in pre-puberty" (1973, p. 13). She sees exposure to the primal scene as influencing perceptions of reality and as leading to such changes in the state of consciousness as confusion and also notes that repeated enemas in the first two years of life cause body image confusion in children. Regarding the persistent walls of denial precipitated by early primal scene exposure, she sees the strongest denials as those "that have been re-enforced by operation on, or induced painful manipulation of the genitals themselves" (p. 26). In describing this female patient, Greenacre refers to the symptomatic veil of denial which Freud (1914) mentioned as afflicting the Wolfman. Though she does not mention the term depersonalization, as such, her reference to the Wolfman's veil and to walls of denial, altered bodily sensations, and changes in the state of consciousness, to my mind implies that she sees depersonalization as one of the sequelae of early, actual primal scene exposure.

Arlow sees the core experience in depersonalization as "a dissociation of two ego functions which ordinarily operate in an integrated fashion, the function of self-observation and the function of experiencing or participating. The participating self (and the instinctual wishes displaced onto it) are . . . partially . . . repudiated . . . by dissociating oneself from the self-representation or from reality or by considering the participating self or reality alien and estranged or both" (1966, p. 474). To restate this: By a mechanism of denial in fantasy, the threatening drive derivative wishes, which he sees as being primarily aggressive in nature, are displaced onto the external world, then disavowed. Although he also refers to impairment in the sense of reality in depersonalization, reality testing is seen to remain intact. In his clinical data, he does not see the regression to a total loss of personal identity which other authors have observed. One of his more interesting observations is that regressive reactivation of function from four early phases of ego activity appear genetically related to later states of depersonalization.

- *Dreaming.* The split into observing and participating self-representations and the sense of estrangement from bodily organs is similar to that experienced in depersonalization.
- *The transitional object phase.* Self and other are not clearly demarcated.
- *The child's anal phase relation.* The fecal matter, once extruded into the outside world, is still seen as connected to the self.

• *The self-discovery phase before the mirror.* The "self-image may be treated as an object existing in the external world" (p. 476).

He notes this latter phenomenon as characteristic of the psychology of twins, the double, and the imaginary companion and felt this mechanism considerably significant for the later development of depersonalization. From his clinical data, he too emphasizes the actual exposure to the primal scene as predisposing to later depersonalization. I agree particularly with Arlow's formulations involving prototypical splitting experiences as of genetic importance.

W. Stewart, in his published work in this field (1964), but even more so in an extensive unpublished monograph (1976) on the subject I was privileged to see, discusses depersonalization from a different viewpoint—in terms of feeling a lack of familiarity with what should be familiar, meaning one's own body or objects in the outside world. He specifically differentiates this from what he refers to as *pathological objectivity* and defines as a marked increase in self-observation at the expense of the registration of affect. This experience he sees at the core of the definitions of depersonalization employed by such authors as Jacobson (1959) and Arlow (1966). In Stewart's view, pathological objectivity does not contain either the sense of unfamiliarity with the familiar or the feelings of mental anguish he associates with true depersonalization. He further observes that whereas most articles about depersonalization deal with the presumed nature of the underlying conflicts, he views the crucial problem as involving the choice of depersonalization as the particular form of solution for such conflicts. In his own conceptualization, he expands upon Bird's ideas (1957) and sees the denial of the affectual impact of the outside world as achieved by a hypercathexis of the function of consciousness, with a consequent overemphasis on the apperception of perception. In this manner, concerns about object loss, castration, primal scene, etc. are converted into concern about the loss of an ego function, that of meaningful apperception. He also hypothesizes, from his own clinical data, that the fundamental predisposition to depersonalization is generated by repeated episodes which lack any expectation of satisfaction from the early object. Without this expectation the investment of the body and of the external world is devoid of emotional meaning. Thus, a variety of later stimuli, which trigger off visual and aggressive memories, possibly reevoking the original early traumatic experiences, are defended against by the defensive withdrawal of depersonalization.

Stewart's demarcation of pathological objectivity from states of true depersonalization runs counter to most other phenomenological descriptions, and is contrary to my own clinical experience. Stewart's fundamentally economic explanation (involving the familiar narcissistic regression and hypercathexis of an ego function) is saved from the criticism referable to earlier economic explanations inasmuch as Stewart takes great pains in clinical descriptions to differentiate feelings of unfamiliarity from hypochondriacal sensations and attempts to account explicitly for the specific form of the experience. Focussing on the function consciousness at the expense of registration of outer or inner visual percepts (imagery) seems to me another manner of describing the sensation of being split in two which others emphasize.

I will briefly mention some of my own previous formulations regarding depersonalization. In one paper (Myers 1973), I described a patient with chronic, verified primal scene exposure and depersonalization. The sensation of a splitting within the self into observing and participating aspects, apparent in the manifest content of certain dreams and in episodes of depersonalization, related to conflicting passive and active wishes emanating from the earlier primal scenes and to the presence of a mirror in the parental bedroom. In that paper, I refer to the early visual primal scene experiences as prototypical splitting episodes predisposing to later depersonalization. The patient suffered from erratic mothering and from prominent bisexual conflicts, and his feeling of abandonment by his mother during the primal scene experiences was genetically connected to his sense of separation from the participating aspect of himself in depersonalization episodes.

In a more recent publication (1976), I presented material from the analyses of four young women with imaginary companions, or fantasy twins, and extensive mirror play during childhood, and who in adolescence and adulthood had mirror dreams and depersonalization. In so doing, I attempted to show that early prototypical experiences involving a sense of participant-observer splitting within the self were genetically linked to later episodes of depersonalization. While my material clearly exhibited early maternal deprivation, the turning away of the father during the oedipal period (usually after the birth of a favored male sibling) was seen as a narcissistic mortification which enhanced the patient's sense of castration and led to the creation of the imaginary companions, who served as idealized phallic self-representations. Primal scene experiences were also prominent in these patients. I allude here to visualization of prototypical splitting experiences as predisposing factors to later episodes of depersonalization. In the concluding section of this paper I will return to these conceptualizations.

Summary

Most authors stress the defensive function of depersonalization. It is seen as a second line of defense, after repression has failed, against either libidinal or aggressive drive derivative wishes. The nature of the threat posed by these drive derivative wishes has been viewed differently by different authors. Some stress the possible disruption in important object relationships which might arise if intense aggressive and libidinal wishes are not defended against by depersonalization. Others view the underlying wishes as threatening the sense of total self (personal identity) or see the anxieties defended against as pertaining to such specific aspects of the self as the penis (castration anxiety).

Authors have described the mode of operation of the defensive depersonalization in quite varied ways. Some view the state as involving a massive regression to a state of dedifferentiation of the ego. In such a state, primitive splitting mechanisms are seen as being revived, involving all good and all bad self- and object-representations. Implied in this type of profound regression, is the expulsion of bad self- and object-representations from the ego, with a concomitant mitigation of the anxieties aroused by threats to the self and to important objects. Others see the regression as not proceeding so far, and view the hyperfocusing on some aspect of self as a means of defense— for example, depending against fears of castration by an unconscious displacement from the penis to this aspect of self. Still other authors conceive of depersonalization arising through the defense mechanism of denial in fantasy. By this means, unacceptable drive derivative wishes attached to aspects of the self and the objects are split off from the rest of the ego and disavowed. The denial in fantasy just described, whereby one aspect of the self is disavowed and treated as if it did not belong to the self, is seen by some authors as paralleling a problem suffered by such patients in their early object relationships, in which they had been treated by their parents as if they, or their feelings did not exist. These authors see the mechanism of identification with the aggressor as an important component of the denial in fantasy. The ego here is seen as modifying itself (its own functions) in the service of defense.

Many writers in this field focus on very early experiences of oral (maternal) deprivation as genetically important. They see such experiences as failure of expected satisfaction from objects as predisposing the ego to the later utilization of the primitive splitting mechanisms. They couple this hypothesis with the clinical observation that many episodes of depersonalization appear triggered by experiences of object loss, which they see as invoking these massive regressive mechanisms.

Other writers see later traumata as being of greater genetic relevance. Body image disturbances arising from early febrile illnesses or surgical and anesthetic experiences are frequently mentioned as predisposing to later episodes of depersonalization. In a number of articles, a high degree of emphasis is put on early, frightening traumatic experiences of a visual nature, such as the primal scene. Such scenes are viewed as arousing, among other things, conflicting passive and active wishes to be both distanced from and actively engaged in the parental sexual acts. Here again a type of splitting mechanism is implied, but at a higher level of ego development. In line with this viewpoint, some authors describe a developmental series of phenomena involving splitting mechanisms as genetically linked to the subsequent appearance of depersonalization.

CLINICAL MATERIAL

Case 1

Mr. A, a forty-four-year-old businessman, entered a four-session-a-week analysis nearly four years ago. His marriage was dissolving because of an affair with a younger woman, L, who both physically and emotionally reminded him of his mother. While he felt guilty about the idea of leaving his wife and daughters, he did so shortly after the analysis commenced.

The patient spent the first three years of his life in the parental bedroom. After moving to a separate room, he developed osteomyelitis and had to be hospitalized several times between the ages of three and six. While in the hospital, he was operated on twice under general anesthesia. During, and shortly after the phase of hospital treatment, there were brief periods of return to the parental bedroom. After the hospitalizations, Mr. A became quite isolated from his feelings and began to immerse himself in his studies as he would later in his jobs. From the beginning of his marriage, in his early twenties, he was emotionally distant from his wife. In their sexual life, his performance was adequate, but he felt mechanical and derived little pleasure from intercourse. He resorted to casual affairs and to masturbation, with fantasies of subjugating women and treating like "shits." With L, however, he was very active sexually, and from the onset of their relationship, he derived great orgastic satisfaction from intercourse with her, feeling a sense of union he had never experienced before.

During the first year on the couch, he was intensely anxious, as the couch reminded him of the operating room table and the beds of the early hospitalizations. He verbalized fears of my being angry with him or hurting him in some way, as the surgeons had hurt him in his early life. The most striking feature of this period in the analysis, however, was the patient's ability to recall the most minute details of the early hospital years which he had not remembered prior to analysis. The early memories generally emerged in association to his frequent dreams, many of which involved the colors black and white. He would dream, for example, of his automobile being wrecked and draped in a white tent from which a black man emerged. In associating to this particular dream, he related the white tent to sheets draped over the osteomyelitic leg and the black man to a particular aide who had wheeled him into surgery.

He felt a sense of excitement during the sessions in which these recollections emerged, and I found myself sharing in that feeling. When he expressed the wish to be my best analytic patient ever, I thought to myself that he probably was. I initially interpreted the dreams and memories as given as gifts to me so that I would not abandon him, as he had felt abandoned by his mother and father during the early hospitalizations. As he began increasingly to verbalize his feelings of having been damaged by surgery, I interpreted his exhibiting his phenomenal memory to me as a defense against his feeling damaged (castrated), via an upward displacement from his leg (penis) to his mental processes. Mr. A would readily agree with such interpretations, adding confirmatory details and feelings stemming from the early hospital period.

After a considerable period of time, probably lengthened by the gratification of my own wishes to finally realize the analytic fantasy of being able to remember everything from one's early childhood, I began to wonder if the hospital memories might be screening off other important experiences in this man's life. The continued recollections of beds and of the sense of having been attacked and damaged by the surgery led me to inquire as to any memories he might have about the early years in the parental bedroom. Though he was intrigued with my question, an uncharacteristic sparsity of recollection ensued. Instead, he once more focused his attention on the period of hospitalization and reexperienced painful feelings of isolation and humiliation, recalling a scene in which his parents peered at him through a glass window into a room where he had been left alone in order to maintain asepsis. In response to my comment that this scene involved looking at, and being looked at by, the parents, he spoke of wanting to look at me when he felt lonely on the couch and of my looking at him as being reassuring, in the sense that I cared about him. In other words, no details about the parental bedroom emerged at that time.

Toward the end of the first year of the treatment, his relationship with L began to deteriorate. He began to verbalize fears that her severe mood swings and her intense symbiotic need for closeness would lead to his destruction, as would her inability to manage money in a responsible fashion. He found himself feeling less involved with her, detached as with his wife. When she responded with angry, suicidal outbursts, he felt increasingly justified in his fears about her. Anxieties about his ability to perform sexually with her ensued, and he suffered from episodes of erectile impotence and premature ejaculation, which made him feel inadequate as a man and raised questions in his mind about his being a homosexual. With the rapid deterioration of the sexual interaction, the relationship was broken off for several months.

Following the break off with L, he entered on a prolonged period of casual affairs and a resumption of masturbation with fantasies of subjugating women, which helped to bolster his sagging sense of masculinity. He was deeply disturbed by his impotency and concentrated his discussions on feelings of anxiety and humiliation such episodes produced in him. Initially, few details about the actual sexual encounters were revealed. Further fears of homosexuality and of anal assault appeared in associations to dreams in which men, whom he associated to the analyst, embraced or attacked him from the rear. These dreams were followed by other memories of the hospital stay, and he embellished on the details of the glass room episode, adding the recollection of the feeling that his father was "tearing" his mother away from the glass and from his longing gaze at her. He angrily perceived the analysis, and analyst, as having torn him away from L. She, too, was not spared from his rage, which he related to his mother's not having informed him in advance of the extent of the surgery he would undergo, and to his shock on awakening from one procedure to find himself encased in a full body cast. The cast had led to the use of enemas, to shame-provoking episodes of soiling himself in bed, to a humiliating sense of himself as "shitty" for being so dependent on the nurses, and finally to his desire to revenge himself on women and to treat them as "shits."

During sessions in which this material emerged, he would go on in an excited fashion, then would feel himself becoming confused as to whether he had told me specific details just mentioned, or as to the meaning of his feelings during his hospital stay—feelings he had eloquently and insightfully described just a moment before. For a period of weeks, his confusion was paralleled by my own, as I wondered why memories, reconstructions, and insights he recalled or grasped so clearly, were so quickly and totally obliterated. I initially interpreted the sense of confusion as a defense against the rage he was feeling, but later wondered if it were not also a concomitant of what he must have felt during the early period in the hospital. I saw the reactivation of the confusion as a means of avoiding integration of the early traumatic experiences which had been too painful to look at in the past. He corroborated these interpretations by recalling his disbelief and confusion when the full body cast was removed and he saw how thin and shriveled his operated leg appeared. He recalled his wishes to deny that the leg belonged to him and the feeling that it belonged to someone else, in other words the wish to disavow the painful perceptions.

As the episodes of confusion became less frequent, Mr. A experienced increasing feelings of anger toward his mother. He also felt an increasing sense of rage toward me, relating this to his feeling that he had to please me with his hypermnesic productions in order to prevent my losing interest (love) in him or my abandoning or castrating him. When in a dream he saw me as allowing him in a white sailboat in black, fecal seas to run aground, he brought out the idea that I was giving him enemas, as the nurses in the hospital had, in order to make him "shit out" memories for me. We were also able to reconstruct the early toilet-training struggle with the mother in which he had felt he had to passively produce his feces for her, or be given enemas, in order to avert the possibility of her abandoning him or of his losing her love. Periods of sexual acting out were viewed by him as expressing defiance to me (the mother-analyst) and as "shitting all over the analysis."

As the third year of analysis began, he resumed the relationship with L. On one level, this was interpreted as a defense against the anxiety caused by his passive, homosexual wishes toward me. On another level, it was seen as an acting out of his incestuous wishes toward his mother. The sexual relationship, however, was far from idyllic, and episodes of premature ejaculation and erectile impotence occurred frequently. The two partners resorted to the use of pornographic films and books in order to arouse themselves. Tumultuous arguments followed bouts of unsatisfactory love-making, and dreams were brought into the analysis in which he would observe, or be observed by, other men having intercourse with L and then would be attacked by, or attack, the other men with knives and guns. These dreams took place in strangely lit rooms, and the figures involved (the other men and L) seemed very large to him.

The looking/being-looked-at quality in the above dreams, and the patient's need to look at pornographic films and books in order to arouse himself, finally led me to press for further details about his sensations during impotency and premature ejaculation. He spoke of painful feelings of "numbness" and of being "glassy eyed," as if "drugged," as he strove to will his erections and to hold back on his ejaculations. He also referred to sensations of being "split off" from himself and from his penis, which was seen as "not belonging" to him, and of observing his sexual performance from a distance, as if he were watching another person participating in a sexual act. In other words, he described what I would label depersonalization, manifest in these instances as sexual performance difficulties. In his associations to such episodes, he related his limp penis to the shriveled up osteomyelitic leg he had also wished to disavow. The sensations of being "drugged" and "glassy eyed" he related to early anesthetic experiences and to his mother's being "torn away" from the glass windowed room by his father. When I focused on the quality of the lighting and the distorted size of the figures in the dreams, we were led back to the early parental bedroom. This occurred via associations to longstanding feelings of anxiety in darkened movie theaters while watching "larger than life" figures on the screen and through considering his need to view pornographic films to arouse himself. He began to feel an increasing sense of conviction in my reconstruction of his having observed his parents having intercourse. He then began to recall minute details (corroborated by his parents) of objects in the early parental bedroom, such as the color of the figures on his crib. Shortly thereafter, painful feelings of isolation and of emasculation at having been abandoned by his mother, and father, during the sexual act began to emerge, and he wondered if he had soiled himself at such times in order to receive attention and to avoid the perception of the mother's having chosen the father over him.

As this material emerged, the patient once more experienced episodes of confusion. I related these feelings to the confusion he must have felt as to what occurred in the parental sexual acts and interpreted them as a wish to deny the external perceptions of the acts and the internal feelings then aroused. Following these interpretations, the patient dimly recalled observing the parents having intercourse. He was uncertain about the veracity of his recall, but was unable to deny the ensuing feelings of rage and sexual arousal.

Mr. A then began to fully comprehend his choice of L as incestuous and saw his sexual performance problems as relating to a need to disavow his forbidden wishes toward his mother. The feelings of being split in two during depersonalization (a heightened sense of observation of the performing aspect of himself as if it were another person) were also associated to the need to disavow the incestuous longings. He began to contemplate truly breaking off with L and felt saddened by the impending loss. He likened this feeling to others experienced during depersonalization episodes. As we worked through this material, his sexual performance improved with L as later it would with other women. As the analysis nears termination now, he is endeavoring to find a less conflictual and more satisfying object relationship.

One point I wish to underscore from Mr. A's case history is the influence of the early anal, surgical-anesthetic and primal scene traumata on the developing tendency toward splitting off (disavowal) of unwanted aspects of the self. I see these prototypical splitting experiences, dating from the anal and oedipal periods, as of crucial significance toward the later development of self-representation splitting seen in adult episodes of depersonalization.

Case 2

Miss B entered a four-session-a-week analysis at the age of thirty-five because of chronic depression. Her treatment ended five years later with considerable improvement in her condition. Her parents had separated before she was born, and her mother, who suffered from quasi-delusional ideas about her face being distorted and swollen, spent little time with her. She was abandoned to the care of the maternal grandparents until she was four and her mother remarried. The patient became attached to her stepfather but felt that she could never measure up to his perfectionistic standards. When the patient was six, a half-brother was born and the stepfather's attentions shifted to his son. The half-brother was lodged in the patient's room for a number of years, thereby infringing on her privacy.

After the half-brother's birth, the real father, whom the patient barely knew, reappeared for one last visit, then vanished. At this time, the stepfather was hospitalized for some months with tuberculosis, and shortly thereafter, the patient underwent surgery for mastoiditis. The surgery and ether anesthesia terrified her. The parents rarely visited during the hospital stay. There were several more surgical anesthetic procedures for this condition in the next few years.

As with Mr A, lying on the couch initially evoked terrifying memories of early surgery and hospitalization. In dreams, I was seen as a surgeon mutilating her, and she complained of increasing depression. On awakening, she experienced feelings of depersonalization which persisted into her morning analytic hours, when she would voice ideas that her thoughts were "unreal" and crazy" and that her arms and legs felt "numb" and "tingling." During such sessions, she also spoke of herself as feeling "cut in two," as if she were very far away from the aspect of herself which was talking to me. She perceived her face as "immobile" and "masked" and likened her complaints both to her feelings during the surgery and ether anesthesia experiences and to the mother's complaints about her own face.

As the analysis progressed, she frequently dreamt she saw herself, or other characters and scenes, reflected in mirrors. In one such dream, she criticized the mother for being "dirty" after seeing, reflected in a bathroom mirror, the mother's hand extended into a roach infested crevice in a wall. Her associations revived her anger at the mother for enemas administered to her as a child when she had been "naughty" and "dirty." She also felt angry at the mother for having given birth to and placing the "roach" half-brother in her room—both experiences being seen as rejections. Although the idea that looking at her mother involved in doing something "dirty" might have other connections did not occur to the patient at this time, it did cross my mind in listening to her, because of prior experiences with patients with similar dreams.

As the second year of the analysis drew to a close, Miss B's relationship with men became the central focus of treatment. The few men she desired most (sexually and emotionally) were unattainable, both because they were married and because they lived at great distances from New York, making frequent visits impractical. When I pointed out how little she knew about these men and how scant her actual satisfactions were with them in reality, she would become resistant and tenaciously maintain that they were wonderful and were the only men who could really make her happy. Men who found her desirable, were regarded as inadequate: the patient maintained the stance that no man could be worthwhile who was interested in anyone as "shitty" as she. During sexual intercourse with any man, she was almost totally anesthetic and had never experienced orgasm. Although this lack of sexual satisfaction was recognized as one of her central complaints, few actual details of her sexual encounters emerged at this point.

In another dream, in the third year of the analysis, she saw her face receding into the depths of a mirror. This led her to recall having received, after the half-brother's birth, a book from her mother about a girl with a dollhouse inhabited by a tiny human being. At that time, Miss B had created a tiny imaginary companion. In her childhood fantasies, she visualized the tiny person as an idealized version of herself, adored by both parents, thereby undoing the rejection she felt from them. She remembered, as well, lifelong play and fantasies involving attempts to will herself through mirrors into better worlds where she would be reunited with people who loved her, her grandparents, for example. She saw the surgery as having deformed (castrated) her and as having rendered her unlovable and bad. Her real father was mentioned at this time as one whom she had imagined as having loved her only to be driven away from her by the mother and stepfather.

When I inquired whether she knew anything about where her real father was, she became silent and finally said she thought her mother had once told her, he lived in the far west—the area where the married men she was involved with lived. She refused to consider my suggestion that there might be fantasies about the real father connecting him with these men, referring to my thoughts as "analytic oedipal garbage."

A brief time later, she began to describe her sexual difficulties with men in greater detail. She spoke of herself as being "cut off" from herself and as "cut in two," with "no feelings below the waist." She spoke of being aware during sex both of herself as she actually was and of a tiny observed self, "like the little girl in my childhood." She felt she (her vagina) was "too small" and that she would be destroyed by men's penises. I attempted to explore these feelings further, tentatively interpreting the projection of her own castrative rage toward men onto the feelings of being destroyed. My efforts were followed some days later by two dreams in one evening. In one, she was once more mutilated in an operating room, by a man she associated to me. In the second, she briefly glimpsed an older couple having intercourse.

She offered no spontaneous associations to the dream until I asked if she had ever witnessed her parents having intercourse and she said that she had. The primal scene observations had occurred at home in the recovery period following the first mastoid surgery. She recalled her stepfather's anger at her intrusion on the parents' privacy. There was also a vague, anxiety provoking recall of having seen his penis and a sense of awe at its size, which she readily related to her fears of being destroyed by the man's penis in intercourse. She felt an increased sense of abandonment and anger at the mother's, once more, having abandoned her, though she saw that in this instance (as opposed to the enemas as recalled through the roach dream) she was the one intruding on the mother's privacy. Feelings of sex as "bad and dirty" became clearer to her, and she realized that she had condensed her feelings about herself concerning the "dirty" surgery with her feelings about sex, as related to the primal scene observation. Episodes of depersonalization during intercourse became infrequent, though she was still unable to achieve orgasm.

A peculiar fact began to impinge on my awareness late in the fourth year of analysis. The patient had long since told me that she made all her own clothing. I was curious why she always chose brown or black material. When I inquired about this, I received little response. When I further observed that she often complained about how difficult it was to get herself to make new clothing, and that she often wore her clothes when they were dirty, new information emerged. She spoke of hating to be seen by people, especially men, though she secretly desired to be admired by them. She fetl acutely embarrassed at being seen naked before intercourse. She felt "fat and flabby" and spoke of seeing her body as "deficient." She then unveiled a character never mentioned before, a black maid, who had been the person responsible for her actual rearing, after the loss of the grandparents. The maid had been discharged shortly after the half-brother's birth. When I inquired as to why the maid was discharged, Miss B was uncertain at first; all she could recall was that the maid used to tenderly bathe (clean) her and was warm and loving. Some time later, when Miss B observed a black female patient leaving my office, she had a dream of a black couple having intercourse. When she offered few associations, I suggested that the dream was a response to seeing the black woman leave my office and that she might have wondered if I were having intercourse with the black woman, since she had expressed wishes herself to have intercourse with me in the past. She became anxious and finally revealed having seen the maid having intercourse at about the same time as having observed her parents in the primal scene. In her associations to the dream, Miss B once more connected sex and dirt (the black couple). She also saw her own wearing dirty clothes of black and brown as a means of holding onto the good mother who had loved her.

In the period following recovery of the second primal scene experience, I was able to connect her frigidity and her depersonalization with the primal scene experiences. These formulations were based on ideas she had expressed that if she had an orgasm, she would dirty herself and be abandoned by her mother and by the maid. She also began to realize her wishes to replace the mother in the primal scene, both incestuously and as a means of achieving closeness (union) with the mother, previously impossible in any other way. She feared, however, that in so doing she would become a "fat blob" (like her mother) and that this would destroy her sense of individuality, as she felt the mother had attempted to do with the enema violations. The idea of being one with the delusional, defective (castrated) mother upset her greatly, as did the thought of the mother's (and my) wrath at her expression of incestuous desires toward the stepfather.

On returning home from the session in which she voiced her wishes to replace the mother in the primal scene, Miss B observed her face in the mirror and felt that it looked like her mother's; she again experienced depersonalization. Shortly thereafter, her lover from the far west was in New York. During intercourse with him, she nearly achieved an orgasm for the first time. When she related this to me, she said, "I came so close, I only had a little farther to go." Because of the material which had recently emerged about the wish to replace the mother in the primal scene, I linked the words *farther* and *father* and inquired whether she thought that by replacing her mother, she might regain her real father. She began to cry and related a longstanding fantasy that if she were clean and good, her father would come back and reclaim her from the "shitty" life and "shitty" parents she had been left with. At times she envisioned him living alone and at other times she imagined him with the black maid. During latency and adolescence, she had utilized the fantasy (in different variations) for masturbatory purposes. In one such variant, her father was the Lone Ranger (the man of the west) who found her as an orphan child and sent her off to school in the east. When she grew up, he reclaimed her and married her. In a transference reactivation of the fantasy, she imagined that I had a western drawl and was in charge of her schooling in the east, cleansing her of "dirty" sexual and aggressive thoughts. When treatment was finished, I would claim her as my wife.

In speaking further of her orgastic problems, she saw losing control of herself in intercourse as a realization of her incestuous fantasies about the father. Yet at the same time, she saw the orgasm as a renunciation of her wishes for the father, as she knew the lovers were not her real father. As we worked through this material, she began to experience orgasms and to look for less incestuous object choices. Thus her depersonalization during intercourse was seen as a disavowal of an aspect of herself, which had once been split off and idealized during childhood (the tiny imaginary companion). In adulthood, this aspect of herself had to be disavowed because she was now capable of actually having intercourse with men (seen as the father and stepfather), thereby realizing (in fantasy) her incestuous longings.

One final note I wish to emphasize here is that in Miss B's case, as in that of Mr. A, anal, oedipal, and latency traumata, again centering around toilet training, surgical-anesthetic experiences, and actual primal scene observations, helped crystallyze earlier tendencies toward splitting off (disavowal) of unwanted aspects of the self. These early prototypical splitting episodes, predispose in my opinion, to the later adolescent and adult episodes of depersonalization.

SEXUAL DYSFUNCTION AND DEPERSONALIZATION

Review of Literature

While there are a large number of papers on the subject of depersonalization, per se, there are relatively few analytic case reports which specifically refer to the occurrence of depersonalization (or descriptions of states which I would define as depersonalization) in conjunction with sexual dysfunction or during sexual intercourse.

A. Reich (1940), in writing on extreme submissiveness in women, cites material from a case in which hostility to the preoedipal mother was unconsciously displaced onto the husband. So that the object tie might be maintained, however, the aggression was discharged upon the self in fantasies accompanying intercourse, in which the patient identified with a brutal, sadistic man. Reich goes on to say: "At these times, she would . . . experience a . . . split of her personality. At the same time that she was feeling sexual pleasure as a woman she would also feel like a bystander watching the conquest of a woman. She frequently had the fantasy of being a man and doing the same thing to a young girl. Likewise some of her masturbation fantasies revealed . . . active and passive attitudes; first, a boy is castrated by his father; then the grandfather performs the same operation upon the father" (p. 476). It is not possible from Reich's clinical data to conclusively determine if her patient was suffering from depersonalization. The excerpted material describes the sensation of a split of the sense of self into observing and participating aspects, which I see as one criteria of depersonalization. In addition, this splitting mechanism clearly defended the patient from the anxiety aroused by her rage toward the object. The patient was not frigid, however, as Miss B was. Reich stresses early maternal deprivation in her formulation. She also describes oedipal castration fantasies as well as intense wishes to possess the phallus. The fantasy of playing both roles in the sexual act is typically seen in patients, such as those I have described, who have been exposed to the primal scene.

Nunberg (1948), in his previously described paper on depersonalization, briefly mentions a patient with impotency problems (pp. 70-71). The man appeared at an analytic hour following an unsuccessful attempt at intercourse, complaining of feelings of depersonalization-derealization in which objects in the external world seemed devoid of feelings; similarly, his own body felt peculiar, as if it did not belong to him. He located the sensations of estrangement in his legs and saw them as having begun in his testicles. The patient then fell asleep on the couch and dreamed of flying. When awakened by Nunberg, he spoke of feeling burning and pulling sensations, once more perceived as emanating from his testicles. The patient had long been attracted to women with slim legs and had suffered from castration dreams about his own legs being amputated. In this man's masturbation, he pressed his thighs together and exerted pressure on his testicles and on the back of his penis, while fantasizing himself to be a woman. Nunberg mentions that the patient was told that he was probably operated on in his first year of life for a phimosis, though he did not consciously recall the experience. During the analysis, the patient repeatedly mentioned the surgery and the prolonged period of nursing following it. No mention is made of primal scene experiences in Nunberg's data on this case, and unfortunately little further discussion of the psychodynamics of the case is offered. In this context, it seems unprofitable to speculate further. I simply insert it here, as it is one of the few analytic case reports which show an episode of depersonalization in juxtaposition with a sexual performance problem.

Jacobson (1959), in her paper on depersonalization referred to earlier, does describe episodes of depersonalization occurring during intercourse. She says, "Not rarely ... we detect states of depersonalization pertaining to the genitals and to the sexual act, which at first sight may impress us as cases of impotence or frigidity. When carefully questioned, such patients will report ... their genital as ... estranged. ... Male patients of this type may suffer from psychic impotence, but ... may have erective potency, be able to perform the sexual act, have an ejaculation, and even some kind of orgastic experience. But in this case they perceive themselves as going through the act without being 'present.' ... The depersonalized patient['s] ... experience is that of a detached spectator who is observing another person's performance" (pp. 581-582). In another section of her depersonalization paper, she refers to a patient whom she had described in her paper on denial and repression (1957) who liked to observe the woman's delighted facial expression during intercourse. His watching was intended to undo and deny female castration but his sadistic desire to expose the defect would occasionally break through. During actual intercourse, he rarely gratified his "desire" but "would become depersonalized and 'watch' himself perform. Here we can see that the self-observation ... absorbs and transforms the original sadistic voyeuristic impulse toward the woman and, turning it to the self, employs it for a denial of the identification with this castrated object" (1959, p. 607). Her observations are very similar to my own, in that initially the patient focuses on the sexual dysfunctions and only under careful questioning regarding the episodes of impotence and frigidity are the underlying states of depersonalization uncovered. As I noted earlier, Jacobson ascribes considerable importance to primal scene fantasies (she does not mention actual observations), and to early traumatic visual experiences in the genesis of later episodes of depersonalization.

Bychowski (1963), like Reich, emphasizes preoedipal hostilities to the mother in such patients in a paper on frigidity and object relationships. He mentions the loss of a parent at an early age as an important factor in later frigidity in women, because of the displacement of feelings of hostile clinging and fears of object loss to the later sexual partners. He notes this attitude is not conducive to the abandonment required for full sexual enjoyment. In this regard, he says, "Rather than permit 'the abandonment' by the lover, the ego withdraws its cathexis from the sexual act so that it can watch and observe, wait for the inevitable 'loss' of the love object" (p. 58). In this manner, the self is protected from becoming aware of its rage toward the object and from the feared retaliation. In amplifying his remarks on the loss of a parent at an early age, he speaks of a constant watchful attitude by the observing aspect of the self, so that the longed for lost parent may not be missed in the wished for reunion. Such fantasies are identical with the ones described in the case of Miss B. In one patient he cites in the paper the self-observation in intercourse served to affirm an object tie to the parents—a fantasied identification with them expressed as "They are watching me; I am watching myself" (p. 59). He explicitly states that "these patients have an attitude of partial depersonalization at least in the area of sexuality" (p. 60). Though Bychowski mentions the primal scene, his clinical data is insufficient to tell whether he is referring to fantasies or to actual observations.

In a previous publication, I have related a patient's episodes of depersonalization to his chronic, verified primal scene exposure (Myers 1973). In homosexual relationships, he experienced no sexual performance problems. In heterosexual activity, however, he often had erectile impotence and ejaculatio retardata, as well as depersonalization. At such times, he perceived his penis as "dead." He also experienced splitting of his sense of self into observing and participating aspects. Earlier, during adolescence, he had been fearful of heterosexual activities on dates because of a fantasy of being observed by his parents. In the splitting of the sense of self in the adult heterosexual relations, as in the adolescent fantasy, the watching/being-watched was both a wish to reverse and a desire to be actively engaged in the exciting/terrifying scenes.

Masters and Johnson (1970) comment extensively on the split into observing and participating roles in premature ejaculation and frigidity. About the former, they note, "There is a . . . transition from the role of physical self-distraction during coition to that of a fear ridden spectator at his own sexual performance" (p. 100). Their material, however, contains little of psychodynamic interest to us in this context.

Clinical Discussion

Both of the cases described in this paper and four additional patients (two male and two female) whom I analyzed and whose symptoms of impotence and frigidity during intercourse masked underlying states of depersonalization, suffered from severe early maternal deprivation. In all of these patients, the use of splitting of self- and object-representations into good and bad selves and objects was present (to the greatest degree in Miss B), but never very pronounced. This was understood as a defense against intense feelings of rage toward important objects, with an attendant threat to the stability of the object relationships. The discovery of early maternal deprivation and the employment of splitting mechanisms is described in a number of articles in the survey of literature on depersonalization at the beginning of this paper. Whether such early splitting mechanisms serve as an anlage for later tendencies toward ego-splitting in the service of defense is a subject I will discuss in greater detail in my concluding remarks.

Traumatic toilet training experiences, as evidenced in both the patients described in this paper, damaged their sense of bodily integrity and intensified earlier tendencies toward splitting of self into good and bad aspects. The body image disturbances were markedly augmented in both patients by the profound surgical-anesthetic traumata suffered during the oedipal and latency periods.

In both patients, actual observations of the primal scene seemed to serve as the organizing experience for all of the aforementioned traumata. Primal scene observations are well suited for this role, in that they serve as a mnemonic shorthand, by which various libidinal, aggressive and ego developmental traumata may be rendered:

1. Early abandonment traumata
2. Anxieties concerning genital differences between the sexes and the disparity in the size between infantile and adult genitalia
3. Oedipal incestuous, (bi)sexual feelings toward objects, with attendant inclinations toward passivity and activity (another form of splitting)
4. Feelings of aggression toward and fears of aggression from objects (the surgical-anesthetic experiences were most intensely felt in this area, though several other of the areas now mentioned were also included in the ramifications of those experiences in Mr. A and Miss B)
5. Heightened voyeurism and exhibitionism (a splitting of component instincts)
6. Experiences of confusion and of unreality (with respect to objects and to the feelings and wishes arising within the self)

In my patients, the overstimulation of the actual primal scene observations were handled by a variety of mechanisms. Initially, the patients utilized denial and alterations of ego functions, such as those involved in determining the sense of experiential reality (an example of this was the confusion seen in Mr. A). As ego maturation proceeded, during the oedipal and latency periods, primal scene observations became integrated into oedipal and latency masturbatory fantasies, which were evoked or acted out during the analyses of these patients. These fantasies centered on wishes to watch and be watched, and to actively or passively engage in both parental roles in the primal scene. Watching and being watched and the choice of an active, masculine versus passive, feminine role in such fantasies again involved splitting mechanisms. When these individuals reached puberty, further problems ensued. With the enormous upsurge in the intensity of the drives (and consequently in the impetus attached to the desire to gratify the revived oedipal and preoedipal drive derivative wishes toward old incestuous love objects), the earlier mechanisms were inadequate to deal with the anxiety aroused by the possibility of actually (in reality, not simply in fantasy) committing incest, or of really having the strength to murder the objects. It is for this reason that I see the later splitting mechanism, evident in the defensive alteration of ego functions seen in depersonalization, as needing to be invoked. That the depersonalization occurs in the sexual setting in certain patients, and may be manifest as sexual dysfunctions, (impotence and frigidity) seems related to the actual (versus fantasied) observations of the primal scenes at an early age— especially in individuals where the distinction between fantasy and reality is not well demarcated. Depersonalization is also related to perceptions of the genitals as being disturbed, as a result of the symbolic representations of the genitals as other body parts which are seen as having been attacked in the early traumatic surgical experiences.

CONCLUSIONS

At this juncture, I will return to some questions about depersonalization which arose from the review of literature. I will endeavor to provide some answers derived from my clinical experience with patients suffering from depersonalization.

In proceeding now with some of my own thoughts on depersonalization, I would initially like to offer a brief comment on the phenomenology of this state. From the descriptive viewpoint, the patients' subjective experiences encompass one or the other (and usually both) of the two following phenomena: (1) a sense of unfamiliarity (alienation, estrangement) from the self or with objects in the external world and (2) a feeling of a split within the self (self-representations) into a portion which is observing and a portion which is seen as participating in actions. This participating aspect of the self is seen as distanced or estranged from the other, more central core aspect of the self, the aspect engaged in intensive self-scrutiny.

To theorize about depersonalization, one must keep in mind the patient's subjective descriptions of the experience itself. Through the understanding of the unconscious meanings of this experience, as revealed in the analysis, we may be better able to arrive at a more comprehensive theoretical explanation of the phenomenon of depersonalization. As in the analysis of a dream, it is not simply through the patient's associations to the specific elements in the manifest content of the dream that we arrive at an understanding of its latent contents, but also through the analysis of the specific words utilized by the patient (the subjective description) to depict those elements.

If we return to the economic theories of depersonalization, in which the phenomenology of the condition is explained in terms of a decathexis of object libido and a subsequent hypercathexis of the self (the mental processes), one major problem becomes readily apparent. In such theories, unconscious fantasy formation is seen as a byproduct of the depersonalized state, rather than as the generative force leading to the formation of this state. In other words, for defensive reasons the economic shifts occur and then the unconscious is conceived of as elaborating fantasies about the state so developed. I cannot subscribe to this view, which seems to me little more than a restatement of the old *actual neuroses* idea, wherein a damming up of the drives was seen as leading directly to symptom formation without the intermediary mobilization of unconscious fantasies.

My viewpoint of depersonalization is that it is a *compromise formation*, much in the manner of a hysterical symptom. Through a thoroughgoing analysis of the patient's subjective description of the episodes of depersonalization, I have been able in a number of such patients to arrive at an accurate understanding of the contributions to the state from each of the structures of the psychic apparatus. Drive derivative wishes from the id, seen as threatening to important object relationships (either because of their aggressive or libidinal content), come into conflict with the superego values of the patient and arouse anxiety and a need for punishment. Both the anxiety and the need for punishment aroused are handled by the ego through a defensive alteration of specific functions of the ego itself. The specific alterations of the functions of the ego mentioned are set in motion by unconscious fantasies which have their own important genetic determinants, rooted in certain phenomena and traumata of childhood.

From the clinical material detailed in this paper, and from my work with other patients with depersonalization, I see the id wishes underlying depersonalization as generally stemming from anal and oedipal levels. Examples of such wishes, highlighted in this paper, are the voyeuristic desire to see and the actual desire to replace one or both of the copulating parents in the primal scene. I believe that the wish to see is largely derived from the patient's actual primal scene observations and is symbolically represented in the patient's descriptions of a split within themselves into a portion observing and a portion participating in actions. In this paper, these actions were sexual relations unconsciously viewed as being incestuous in nature. Hence, as expected, the compromise formation itself contains an element, albeit displaced, of gratification for the original id impulses.

While both patients described in this paper, and many of those discussed in the literature, exhibited fears and wishes of merging, with the consequent threat of the loss of self and object differentiation, none of the patients included here ever actually experienced the total annihilation of the sense of self which they feared, and the fears were never that markedly pronounced. This of course touches upon the subject of the depth of the regression described by other authors and on the genesis of depersonalization, which I will return to shortly. Suffice it to say at this moment, fears and wishes about merging often, on further analysis, revealed themselves in my case material to be regressive expressions of wishes for an incestuous union with the mother on a genital, rather than on a pregenital level.

Let us turn now to the subject of the placation of the superego, which I view as being accomplished in depersonalization by the defensive alteration of specific ego functions. In expressing this viewpoint, I am in agreement with Arlow's formulations (1966), whereby he sees the mechanism of denial in fantasy as extremely significant. Essentially, he sees the ego as utilizing an unconscious fantasy of disavowal of the unacceptable drive derivative wishes attached to aspects of self-representations. These wishes, and the participatory aspect of the self-representation with which they are associated, are split off from the rest of the ego, or disavowed. It is this mechanism which accounts for a patient's feeling of a split within himself into a portion that observes and a portion as participating in actions.

The genesis of the sensation of a split within the self described above is a matter of considerable controversy. As I mentioned earlier, a number of authors view this splitting sensation as evidence of a regression to an early ego state in which primitive splitting mechanisms once utilized are now reactivated. While I believe that these primitive splitting mechanisms are genetically connected to the sense of splitting seen in depersonalization, I do not find the evidence of massive states of regression described by previous authors in my own case material. I see a developmental series of prototypical splitting experiences, some normal and some pathological in nature, as leading to the splitting sensations seen in depersonalization. When, for example, the normal sense of splitting involved in the anal experience (wherein an aspect of the self, the feces, is seen as both belonging to and disavowed from the self) becomes intensified to the point of being traumatic (as with both cases described in this paper), because of a disturbance in the mother-child interaction, the predisposition to the type of splitting seen in later depersonalization is heightened. Similarly, when the fantasied utilization of an imaginary companion as an idealized self-representation (with the attendant disavowal of degraded or unacceptable aspects of the self) is intense and prolonged, this too, tends to heighten the predisposition to the later splitting seen in depersonalization. From the viewpoint of the patients described in this paper, the splitting into active-passive, observer-observed roles (engendered by the actual observations of the primal scene in childhood) was of utmost importance in terms of intensifying their predispositions to later episodes of depersonalization.

Although I believe that my discussion of the sensation of a split within the self has considerable explanatory value with respect to subjective descriptions of patients with depersonalization, regarding their feelings of alienation, estrangement, and unfamiliarity with the self and the object world, I would like to end this paper with a few additional remarks which I feel might be of benefit here. In both my cases, conflicts regarding body image formation were engendered by the traumatic use of enemas, by the presence of physical defects, and by traumatic surgical-anesthetic experiences. It is my contention that, particularly when patients lacked the verbal facility to adequately communicate their feelings to others or even to themselves (or lacked parents able to respond to their communications), then sensations occuring during these experiences are revived in a symbolic or in a direct manner in the episodes of depersonalization. In my clinical data, and in the writings of others, such terms as *drugged, masked, glassy-eyed,* and *immobile,* which I see as derivative of the early experiences just mentioned, are commonly voiced. Hence, paying attention to the specific descriptions of patients about their feelings during episodes of depersonalization can be of considerable value. This may provide us with clues helpful in the reconstruction and working through of unremembered traumata which had direct pertinence to the genesis of later states of depersonalization.

REFERENCES

Arlow, J. (1966). Depersonalization and derealization. In *Psychoanalysis: A General Psychology,* ed. R. Loewenstein, L. Newman, M. Schur, and A. Solnit, pp. 456-478. New York: International Universities Press.

Bird, B. (1957). Feelings of unreality. *International Journal of Psycho-Analysis* 38:256-265.

Bychowski, G. (1963). Frigidity and object relationship. *International Journal of Psycho-Analysis* 44:57-62.

Federn, P. (1952). Depersonalization. In *Ego Psychology and the Psychoses,* pp. 241-260. New York: Basic Books.

Fenichel, O. (1945). *The Psychoanalytic Theory of Neurosis.* New York: Norton.

Freud, S. (1918). From the history of an infantile neurosis. *Standard Edition* 17:7-122.

——— (1936). A disturbance of memory on the Acropolis. *Standard Edition* 22:239-248.

Greenacre, P. (1949). Screen memories. *Psychoanalytic Study of the Child* 3/4:73-84.

——— (1973). The primal scene and the sense of reality. *Psychoanalytic Quarterly* 42:10-41.

Greenson. R. (1954). The struggle against identifications. *Journal of the American Psychoanalytic Association* 2:200-217

Jacobson, E. (1957). Denial and repression. *Journal of the American Psychoanalytic Association* 5:61-92.

―――― (1959). Depersonalization. *Journal of the American Psychoanalytic Association* 7:581-610.

Masters, W., and Johnson, V. (1970). *Human Sexual Inadequacy*. Boston: Little, Brown.

Myers, W. (1973). Split self-representation and the primal scene. *Psychoanalytic Quarterly* 42:525-538.

―――― (1976). Imaginary companions, fantasy twins, mirror dreams and depersonalization. *Psychoanalytic Quarterly* 45:503-524.

Nunberg, H. (1948). States of depersonalization in the light of the libido theory. In *Practice and Theory of Psychoanalysis*, vol. 1, pp. 60-74. New York: International Universities Press.

Oberndorf, C. P. (1933). A theory of depersonalization. *Transactions of the American Neurological Association* 59:150-151.

―――― (1934). Depersonalization in relation to erotization of thought. *International Journal of Psycho-Analysis* 15:271-295.

―――― (1939). On retaining the sense of reality in states of depersonalization. *International Journal of Psycho-Analysis* 20:137-147.

―――― (1950). The role of anxiety in depersonalization. *International Journal of Psycho-Analysis* 31:1-5.

Peto, A. (1955). On so-called depersonalization. *International Journal of Psycho-Analysis* 36:379-386.

Reich, A. (1940). A contribution to the psycho-analysis of extreme submissiveness in women. *Psychoanalytic Quarterly* 9:470-480.

Rosen, V. (1955). The reconstruction of a traumatic childhood event in a case of derealization. *Journal of the American Psychoanalytic Association* 2:211-221.

Sarlin, C. (1962). Depersonalization and derealization. *Journal of the American Psychoanalytic Association* 10:784-804.

Schilder, P. (1953). Depersonalization. In *Medical Psychology*, pp. 304-309. New York: International Universities Press.

Stewart, W. (1964). Depersonalization: scientific proceedings—panel report. *Journal of the American Psychoanalytic Association* 12:171-186.

―――― (1976). Unpublished monograph on depersonalization.

Adverse Response
to Neuroleptics in Schizophrenia

DONALD B. NEVINS, M.D.

Negative therapeutic reactions to neuroleptics in schizophrenic patients are examined from the psychoanalytic perspective through case examples. Intrapsychic changes resulting from this medication, ordinarily considered beneficial, are shown, in some cases, to be disruptive of schizophrenic functioning and organization and potentially to endanger the continuation of medication itself. Changes are described which effect defenses, object relations, psychotic restitution, use of external reality, body image and cognition, and the symbolic significance of medication. Alterations in narcissistic ego states and disruption in preconscious processes, superimposed upon defective ego functioning, are used as explanatory concepts. These interact with transference based responses; in some cases, important psychodynamic issues emerge amenable to transference interpretations. Further study of intrapsychic changes may be useful in delineating a previously inexplicable response, understanding symptom formation, recognizing shifts in the patient-psychotherapist relationship, and forestalling premature cessation of medication.

Neuroleptic medications are important in the treatment of schizophrenia. These medications reduce psychotic symptoms, the rate of recidivism, and the length of hospitalization (May 1968). Moreover, relapses occur more frequently when these drugs are discontinued (GAP 1975). Some patients complain, nevertheless, of side effects, not attributable to medical factors, but due to disagreeable changes in mental state. They stop medication and become overtly psychotic.

A review of the literature on adverse psychological effects accompanying neuroleptic administration in schizophrenia is noteworthy in part because of the scarcity of papers despite frequent empirical observations of patients' subjective complaints along these lines. In three recent major reference works on drug treatment (Klein and Davis 1969, Ban 1969, Kalinowsky and Hippius

I am grateful to Doctors Mardi Horowitz, Enoch Callaway III, Irwin R. Feinberg, Ames Fischer, and Stanley Steinberg for their review of the manuscript and their helpful suggestions.

1969) and in a comprehensive overview of schizophrenia (Bellak and Loeb 1969), there is little mention of negative or undesirable, nontoxic psychological responses. In contrast, there are vast numbers of investigative reports cataloguing physiologic and biochemical variations, social and descriptive alterations, and medical side effects. It seems that the psyche of the schizophrenic, which is after all the target of the psychotropic medications, has been neglected. There is, furthermore, a scarcity of articles bearing directly on the intrapsychic factors leading to discontinuation of these medications, though in clinical medicine such factors are well recognized (Blackwell 1973). Recently, Van Putten (1975) has drawn attention to manic-depressive patients who discontinue lithium during stressful life crises.[1]

According to the available reports, depressive reactions in schizophrenic patients have been noted after long-term neuroleptic medication (Cohen et al. 1964) and in approximately half the schizophrenic patients whose acute psychotic symptoms had been controlled by phenothiazines (Bowers and Astrachan 1967). Sarwer-Foner (1957, 1960, Sarwer-Foner and Ogle 1956) observed adverse "paradoxical" responses to neuroleptics and considered these as based on modifications in defensive activity. Physiologic interference with motor activity, especially when utilized as a major behavioral defense against passive feminine identifications, were psychologically threatening and accompanied by a "paradoxic" increase in anxiety. Also noted were an intensification in depression, changes in body image, and transference reactions, whereby the drug was regarded as an assault or seduction by a powerful doctor. Azima (1957, 1959, Azima and Sarwer-Foner 1960) considered drugs to primarily affect drive systems. As a result, predominantly aggressive impulses emerge: these being facilitated by inadequacies inherent in the schizophrenic's defenses—splitting, withdrawal, and projection. Kline (1956) observed a weakening of "defense mechanisms" which results in the expression and recognition of disturbing underlying emotions.

CLINICAL OBSERVATIONS

Examining case material obtained in ambulatory treatment from the psychoanalytic perspective shows that intrapsychic changes, even those that reflect apparent improvements, can in themselves be disruptive and give rise to regressive alterations in schizophrenic personality organization and functioning—alterations potentially endangering the continuation of medication itself. An appreciation of these intrapsychic changes may be useful in forestalling premature cessation of medication, as well as in understanding the more general issues of noncompliance in the patient-psychotherapist relationship. The latter is especially important in view of the increasing use of depot medication (Groves and Mandel 1975).

Changes in Defenses

Changes in defensive activities occur as an accompaniment or result of neuroleptics. This many particularly true with such primitive defenses as denial. C, a twenty-six-year-old schizophrenic man denied that he did not have a job or vocational skill and that his father, a former art teacher, was now dead. His father was replaced by his "father who art in heaven," and through a psychotic identification, the patient believed himself to be Jesus Christ. Indeed, he did then have a job and a skill, if not a mission. With medication, the sudden distressing awareness developed that he was not the Savior. He was now unlike his dead father and developed a poorly tolerated grief reaction. He felt guilty in that by not possessing a job or skill he would be a failure to his father. The subjective experience and complaint, however, were focused on the medication: it made him feel tired and depressed and caused him to become withdrawn.

As I inquired further into his objection to the medication, C expressed a desire to know me better. He wished I was his friend and thought I was unhappy and alone. Why, he asked in a sad and plaintive manner, was I "saturating [him] with Prolixin?" This, he felt, only necessitated his drinking excessive amounts of coffee to "counteract" the medication (otherwise he would "disappear") and led to memories of his father's alcoholism and to beatings he had suffered at his father's hands. During those beatings, he had longed for his father to leave, or to sober up with coffee so the alcoholic state would go away.

He began to blame me for causing him to feel fatigued, "slowed down," and withdrawn. How could I "predict" his response to medication? I was cruel for causing him to suffer. The psychotic belief emerged that the medication was an "input from the spiritual," "someone pressing on . . . squashing my skull." "Heavenly powers" were using the therapist . . . to reach him. The medication "slowed" him down and made him feel "tired and depressed," which was particularly frightening since he then became the "center of the universe: If I'm the slowest moving object . . . things circle around me." This state enabled his father to locate and make contact with him. He recalled having once "predicted" his father's death and felt that he was now being punished: "Things I've done are coming back to haunt me." He believed he was being punished for killing insects (animals) as a child and decided to become a vegetarian. With trepidation he asked whether I ate meat. If so, he was nervous about animals that I had killed. I was murderous and my own body, containing dead animals (bodies) might kill me or, in fact, I might be dead.

I interpreted his fear of being harmed and punished by the medication, his concern for my safety, and his guilt in relationship to his father's death. C became a vegetarian and initiated vocational-rehabilitation training in food preparation—rather than "waiting for another lifetime." He continued to take medication and his complaints about the medication, while they persisted, were expressed in a less punishing manner. There was improvement in his feelings of depression, lassitude, and in his fears of being slowed down.

Another schizophrenic patient, M, denied he was ill despite multiple hospitalizations. Instead, he maintained the delusional belief that he was in charge of weather control for an entire metropolitan area. Abruptly, feeling unprepared, panicky, and overwhelmed, he complained bitterly that "Thorazine makes me aware I am ill." In a similar manner, changes occur in repressive defenses, bringing about awareness of previously unconscious thoughts and fantasies. In another schizophrenic patient, R, the neuroleptics were accompanied by memories of adolescent pedophilic activities whenever he would now be in the company of younger men; medications "caused perverted thoughts" he said.

A response to medication, by virtue of reduction in motor outlet or activity, can bring about a heightening of passivity, feelings of helplessness, and an increase in feminine homosexual ideas (Sarwer-Foner 1960). This is especially a problem when motor activity has been utilized as a major behavioral defense or when passivity has been a major characterologic feature. In addition, when the drug is regarded as a magical substance, a further increase in passivity is fostered. A, a twenty-one-year-old schizophrenic man had been unemployed and dependent upon his parents for support. Unable to engage in social relationships without disorganizing panic, he maintained a withdrawn autistic existence, one in which he would "carry on my own thoughts . . . that's my life." A major portion of his day was spent actively and compulsively participating in sports and maintaining the grandiose belief he was a nightclub entertainer who awaited discovery. Toward his father, he held the paranoid psychotic identification: "He's like me, I'm like him: He's nervous around people. He can read people too much. I can feel his feelings, but don't know why he can't handle it. Dad doesn't want me to work. Dad likes to have me by him, for his security so he can have something to do. I humble myself."

Administration of Stelazine was followed by feelings of laziness, bodily fatigue, and fears of physical immobility. His body felt heavy ("can't shake it"); he shaved his moustache and stopped playing sports. He was a "lazy person anyway; this makes it worse." The medications were "killing something in my body." Furthermore, medications were a magical "crutch [to] rely on . . . not you." His thoughts felt slowed down: The medications "control me. Make me dwell—not get off [unpleasant] thoughts. All of a sudden they hit me. Don't know where from. Off the wall. Things I'm thinking aren't me." He began awakening in the morning feeling "pinned down—with nothing to do other than fight for my life. Toward evening he feared for his safety and would compulsively check his windows and closets before falling asleep for the presence of robbers. He believed he would be mugged because he was the smartest person in the world and because he intimidated others by "seeing things in them that they could not see in themselves. I stare at people and make them look at themselves." (This belief has interesting transference implications.) He had fantasies of either being pushed out a window or being commanded to jump or be shot: "Take your pick; I'd get shot." He also feared that he would be required to submit to being stabbed, tortured, crucified, and forced sexually to perform fellatio by a gang of Hell's Angels while they shit on him. He began to feel like a woman and prayed, "If you're going to take me, take me in my sleep."

Therapeutic sessions were punctuated by A's impressions of singers and movie stars. At times, he would assume their affectations and postures, or even stand up and enact a brief dance or choreography routine. His father admired show business and took him on trips to Las Vegas and Broadway and introduced him to famous people. His attempts to entertain me were a form of acting out within the transference. In response to my interpretation of his behavior, he voiced complaints that I, and the medication, forced him to "jump hoops." In association to this, he had the image of having to passively submit to being pinned up against a wall and having a man shoot arrows at him. Following a series of clarifications of his sense of reality in relationship to me and my continued presence, and following interpretations directed at his passivity, fears of being harmed by the drugs, and having to submit to my demands, A resumed athletics and moved out of his parents' home. Both his delusional fears of personal harm and complaints directly referrable to the medication subsided.

It should be emphasized that these changes in defensive structures are experienced by the schizophrenic as sudden, and as an interference with automatic modes of functioning. There are accompanying feelings of powerlessness, helplessness, and loss. In these patients, and in those described below, there are also complaints of sudden unfamiliar feelings of self and changes in the self.

Changes in Object Relations

Use of medication may lead to symptomatic improvement in the sense of reality and reality testing (Bellak and Loeb 1969, p. 41). It may also lead to decreases in hostility, belligerence, uncooperativeness, social isolation, and withdrawal; along with these changes, the use of medication may bring about a lessening of autistic behavior (Klein and Davis 1969, p. 90) and of narcissistic preoccupations. Such changes may result, however, in secondary, or subsequent, interference with areas of functioning previously nonconflictual, or not recognized.

C's characteristic style of relating to women was to be superficially involved in a number of sexual affairs at any given time. With Prolixin he would complain of a change in and loss of "sexual drive." Further examination revealed that as he developed more sustained relationships with women he began to recognize them as separate from himself. He would now, however, experience fears of merger during sexual intercourse and the subjective experience of not being involved in, or a part of, the sexual act. In addition, instinctual regression and conflict emerged, as did a more direct expression of aggressive drives. He would: "Try to get my mind in a romantic frame of mind. [Begin] stroking a girl. What comes out [is] now it's time to feel her butt up. Wasn't thinking of dirt—or of eating my dandruff, but that's what it comes down to." He feared he "might become violent—like choking [or] cremating mother" and become a woman himself: "Feel I am a witch. I'm not the only one. I'm running into other girls too." The result was an inability to have an erection, and counteravoidance of the sexual act. This same individual was no longer able to pick up male hitchhikers. Formerly, once he had picked up a hitchhiker he would be unaware of that person's physical presence and would proceed without concern or distraction. Now he became apprehensive of the desire to place his hand upon the hitchhiker's leg, stimulating the emergence of partially repressed and frightening homosexual thoughts and feelings. I interpreted his conflict over sustaining close relationships, including one with me, and his fears of submitting and being harmed by me. He developed more prolonged, passive relationships with women, who now functioned as maternal figures, and he regained his sexual potency.

In another schizophrenic male, H, the institution of Trilafon was associated with cessation of the need for compulsive autoerotic masturbation. At the same time, however, masturbatory activity was regarded as "freaky" and his penis as without feeling and not a part of himself. Since heterosexual activities had always been frightening, he now felt "sexless" and depressed.

Thus, with partial reintegration of personality organization and abandonment of a more regressive narcissistic position, previously repressed impulses, as well as the invocation of defensive depersonalization can emerge. This produces anxiety, instinctual regression and conflict, deneutralization of aggressive drives, and interference in previously unaffected drive discharge or secondarily autonomous functions.

Interference with Psychotic Restitution

Neuroleptics may interfere with psychotic restitutive symptoms. A schizophrenic man, T, attributed to medication his lack of energy and alertness, diminished awareness, and inability to relate to others. Further exploration revealed the lack of a former sense of omniscience in controlling traffic lights, clouds, and the sun. T now believed that when he approached another automobile's rear bumper or when he shifted his clutch he could no longer trigger the traffic light green. Clinically, the psychiatrist would judge this as a decrease in ideas of influence, that is, a positive therapeutic response. This was experienced by the patient, however, as a debilitating loss of energy and as an inability to influence or reestablish relationships with other persons. Similarly, being unable to bring out the sun or move the clouds meant that he was no longer the "center of the universe" nor the main authority on anything or anyone, including himself. Consequently, he felt incompetent, retarded, and depressed: "Prolixin rips off my power to open up the sky. I need to have more influence over it than it has over me."

Bodily Harm

To the patient, the use of medication may represent bodily harm with an accompanying loss of powers. J, a twenty-seven-year-old paranoid schizo-phrenic man and a former construction worker, had a history of publicly disruptive behavior, jailings, physical abuse of girlfriends, repetitive hospitalizations following discontinuation of medication, exhibitionism, and recurrent psychotic episodes involving great feats or bursts of physical activity. On one such occasion he was apprehended by the Coast Guard after swimming out two miles into the Pacific Ocean on his way to Asia in order to locate his girlfriend. Injectable Prolixin Enanthate was experienced as producing a weakened condition with subsequent diminished energy and inability to "boast" or have an erection. He was no longer able to "walk through anyone," became increasingly dependent upon his girlfriend, who opposed the medication, and had recurrent dreams in which the medication would incarcerate and kill him. He abruptly terminated treatment and eloped with his girlfriend.

K, a twenty-four-year-old schizophrenic male, through his facility with and access to primary process material, gained local notoriety as a palmreader. In a clandestine manner he taught palmistry and developed a following; at the same time he worked as a junior executive in his father's business. He sought psychiatric treatment following the birth of a son, and the development of insomnia and overt psychotic thoughts. The administration of Stelazine was followed by an inability to perform previously practiced (even in the overtly psychotic state) palm reading. This was experienced as being "absent minded," "dissipated," "forgetful," and "not having the powers I once thought I had." He became depressed.

Approximately one month later K noted that Stelazine was a pill like his wife's oral contraceptive. He believed, as a consequence, that he could no longer father a child. He feared becoming "dependent" on an "artificial" pill. He began to vomit in attempts to reduce the impact of the pills. This behavior, he remarked, was like that of his mother who suffered from chronic stomach ailments. He feared adult responsibilities and became panicky when, alone in the presence of his infant son, he felt like a child himself. At this point, he dreaded both working at his father's office and continuing his psychotherapy appointments. When his father was away, K would secretly sit at his father's desk and have a "power trip." At other times he had fantasies of blowing up corporate buildings. He feared that his thoughts and behavior would now be revealed. Similar competitive feelings emerged toward me. He recalled that when he practiced palmistry, he "would not have to draw attention" to himself directly. He possessed a "gift" which would make people come to him. Everyone, including doctors, were "awed" by his powers. "People told me you tell me more than my psychiatrist." He feared I would now condemn him for being a "witch doctor," and, as a consequence, he would be punished: "Fear whatever I do to others. [Will] have it done to me. When I open up others I'm opening up myself." He would now suffer bodily mutilation ("get blown apart into twenty pieces"). Stelazine dosage at the time was twenty milligrams. His brain would be "opened up [for a] blood letting." My interpretation of his punitive castration fears, his psychotic elaboration fantasies of body damage, and his conflicts over competitive strivings in relationship to me were followed by a reduction in his fears about medication, psychotherapy, work, and fatherhood. He did not resume palm reading but became more involved with his job and family.

Interference in the Use of External Reality

Neuroleptics may interfere with the schizophrenic's attempt to use external reality, especially interpersonal relationships, to ward off psychotic conflicts and further psychotic disintegration. An example is patient C, whose numerous sexual encounters permitted a warding off of disorganizing underlying homosexual conflicts. K, the palmist and local guru, who experienced a decreased facility in retrieval of primary process material, could no longer turn to his following and "make them come to me," and was less able to resolve conflicts in this manner. Similarly, a male schizophrenic patient, W, used absurd humor (including condensation, displacements, and fragmentation of thought) to permit relationships with women. Neuroleptics interfered with access to primary process thinking and, as a consequence, his appeal diminished. He could no longer turn to women and utilize them to prevent further psychotic disorganization.

Symbolic Significance

The medications may have major symbolic significance. S, twenty-two-year-old college coed, whose father was a chemist, had an initial response to Stelazine characterized by a clinical improvement of both schizoid withdrawal and difficulty in concentration, as well as abatement of hallucinations and delusional thoughts. Medication came to represent, however, submission to her father's influence, and her own personal failure and loss of self. She viewed herself as evil, unlovable, a peasant, and a "basket case." Soon she began to arise late in the morning and developed accusatory auditory hallucinations. That she was taking a chemical and that her father was a chemist symbolically brought her in closer contact with him, the individual against whom she measured herself. This served to increase her feelings of guilt, worthlessness, and self-punishment—feelings elaborated in a psychotic manner. She believed the medication was intended to "disrupt" and control her thinking. Cognition, an area of major importance to S's sense of self, was now threatened. She could no longer think for herself ("I don't think therefore I'm not"), and she began having feelings of dissolution. There was difficulty in both separating herself from her father and in distinguishing between father's will and her response. I became an agent of her father and the medication was seen as intended to "kill" her. Furthermore, medication became equated with her mother's alcoholism. S believed that by taking medication she would become a prostitute and defended against this concern with the paranoid belief that the medication I gave her would result in her being "crippled," like her brother's wife who was paralyzed (without feeling) from the waist down. Interpretations were directed at reality testing, ego boundaries, and autonomous functioning. While there was subsidence of overt paranoid thoughts and hallucinations, she complained the medication made her feel "empty," without feelings, and less capable in handling her studies. She terminated therapy when she left home to resume college.

Alterations in Body Image

Neuroleptics, by virtue of their direct pharmacological effects on peripheral tissues and their functioning, may cause changes in body image and distortions in the sense of reality, thus imposing added reality tasks on the schizophrenic's already defective or weakened ego. Frequently these changes are elaborated in a psychotic manner. For example, O, a schizophrenic man, complained that the medication caused him to become withdrawn. Further examination revealed this sequence: neck muscle stiffness, weightiness to the neck, God coming down on me, the fear of God, withdrawal. Blurred vision in another schizophrenic, L, was magnified into a more global problem with perception: "Something is always wrong with how I see things." Ego boundaries then became less distinct and his tears became the result of another's sadness. At the same time, his powers increased to the point of "penetrating" vision and "extrasensory perception." Muscle stiffness in another schizophrenic was felt as a being encased inside the body; it led to social isolation. To yet another, sedativeness was "brain damage."

Incorporation into Schizophrenic Cognition

Furthermore, when bodily changes are combined with idiosyncratic schizophrenic cognition, utilizing primary process thinking and predicate logic (Arieti 1955), they assume an even greater psychological meaning. A twenty-six-year-old schizophrenic man, E, while on low doses of injectable depot Prolixin Decanoate (twenty-five milligrams IM every two weeks) would complain of fatigue and incessantly requested a prescription for Ritalin to give him more energy. He believed the injectable Prolixin *Deca*noate would result in infiltration of a chemical substance into the body causing it to *decay* and age. He also feared, through a psychotic identification with his deceased alcoholic father, who had been further wasted by cancer, that he himself would, like his father, decay. He had observed that Ritalin was given to hyperactive schoolchildren who themselves were young. Through the identity of predicates, the identity of subjects emerged: receiving Ritalin became identical to the attribute of being young. To him, this youthfulness would counter the psychotic body image distortion and decay brought upon him by the Prolixin Decanoate.

DISCUSSION

Sudden intrapsychic changes brought about by chemical alterations in schizophrenic personality organization, though facilitative, can also be disruptive. Neuroleptics have characteristics that (a) pharmacologically alter peripheral somatic processes (for example, in their effects on the autonomic nervous system) and (b) psychotropically affect the functions of the central nervous system—the ongoing central program is altered. This paper is primarily concerned with this disruption of the ongoing central program. These medications alter both physiologic and psychologic frames of reference. This alteration interacts with both preexisting defective (Beres 1956) and weakened (Hartmann 1953) ego functioning; a sudden rate of change from a formerly stable, though pathologic, personality organization occurs. As a result, a disorganizing unfamiliarity is produced.

This report is not intended to describe the positive therapeutic changes in psychotic symptoms or social functioning attendant on neuroleptic usage, nor their psychophysiological effects. Nor does it refer primarily to the medical side effects of neuroleptics, such as those affecting extrapyramidally mediated motor functioning or autonomically mediated cholinergic or adrenergic changes, although any of these changes can be stressful and may be psychotically elaborated. In my opinion, however, dosages can be adjusted to deal with these problems, and most patients do not stop medication because of medical side effects alone. Finally, I am not describing those complaints which are incorporated into a preexisting delusional system and become attributed to medication—paranoid delusions, for example, that the medication is poison. Also not included in this study are complaints which serve to externalize and provide a focus for regressive behavior and schizophrenic disorganization: complaints of the medication's causing, for example, oversedativeness or difficulty in arising in the morning, which may reflect instead, a progressive state of withdrawal or the stressful ego-fragmenting transition from sleep to wakefulness. In either instance, discontinuation of medication or lowering of dosage would neither alter psychopathological changes nor decrease complaints.

These medications have been hypothesized as helpful agents in diminishing levels of disproportionate perceptual input and central nervous system arousal or activation (Lehman 1974). Furthermore, they may exert beneficial effects by reducing cognitive distortions brought about by inclusion of irrelevant stimuli, overinclusive thinking (Cameron 1946), or by the inability to maintain a major set (Shakow 1962). Adverse responses may, however, be produced, because of an interference in the adaptive value (though limited) of the organism's ongoing stabilized (though pathologic) state.

If schizophrenic interference is likened to the interruption of an ongoing computer set, with both persistence and diversion from the program (Callaway 1970), then certain parameters of functioning are aided by a medication which would reduce this interference (such as by alteration in stimulus barrier), while other parameters may be differentially and variably affected. Neuroleptics have been postulated to increase (perceptual) sensory filtering by delaying EXIT from a program. That is, a reduction of the ongoing program's vulnerability to environmental interference by delaying premature EXIT may allow an increased time for perceptual sensory filtering. However, as Callaway (1970) points out, the operation of one program may inhibit the running of other programs.

I propose that the major adverse effects of these drugs are that other personality functions, other programs, are differentially affected. What is suggested by the negative response to medication is that alterations are produced in narcissistic ego states and disruptions occur in preconscious processes, including access to primary process content. These interact with transference based responses to receiving the medication. Furthermore, in some cases, as economic and adaptive shifts occur, conflictual reactions become displaced onto the therapist and psychodynamically central issues emerge which are amenable to transference interpretations.

Affects not only signal danger but give an appraisal, of adaptive value, to the state of the organism (Rapaport 1953, Pribram 1967)—a how-am-I-doing? Medicated schizophrenics frequently complain of "feeling not myself," "zombie feeling," "I can't feel," "strange," "changed," "altered," etc. The medicated schizophrenic feels himself to be unreal; a state of depersonalization is produced.

The concept of ego feeling is relevant here. According to Federn (1950), ego feeling is the feeling of uninterrupted bodily and mental relation. This includes motor and sensory memories concerning one's own person and the somatic organization or unity of ordered perceptions of one's body, both with respect to time and content. These medications appear to produce a discontinuity of preexisting ego feeling. The ego unit or self is changed. According to Schilder (1950), the body ego is the continuing awareness of one's body. The neuroleptics produce discontinuities here as well. These discontinuities can occur independently or may precede a psychotic elaboration of body image distortion. The unique paradox of the ego is, according to Federn, that it is subject and object in one, "The ego knows itself, feels and encounters itself. . . . The ego is the feeling of it*self*" (1950, pp. 8-9, my italics). It is not surprising that when we engraft this unfamiliar feeling on to the schizophrenic's weakened ego (for example, defective synthetic functioning, Nunberg 1931)—which already has a tendency to disorganize— both the unity of the organism is stressed and other significant disturbances in functioning occur.

Neuroleptics produce narcissistic changes which are defensive in nature and result in depersonalization. As Jacobson (1971) points out these states of depersonalization "represent attempts at solution of narcissistic conflict. . . . The conflict develops within the ego and has its origin in struggles between conflicting identifications and self images" (p. 160). Furthermore, the state of depersonalization in schizophrenics is "a defense of the ego which tries to recover and to maintain its intactness by opposing, detaching, and disowning the regressed, diseased part" (p. 164). This can occur in reaction to a bodily part or be displaced onto the neuroleptic medication. The feeling of estrangement or depersonalization can then represent a rejection by the patient of the medication. It is defensive and hypochondriacal in nature and directed against further narcissistic regression.[2]

To the extent there are two elements—medication induced perceptual change in the feeling of unreality and psychotic defensive depersonalization— it may be an important task of psychotherapy to differentiate one from the other. When the two become confused and further psychotically elaborated (as for example in a grandiose, hypochondriacal, or punitive manner), a stressful state is produced which may culminate in discontinuation of medication. Moreover, neuroleptics appear to produce abrupt, massive interruption of grandiose preoccupations and of the associated pleasurable omnipotent feelings- -especially when considered in relation to the nature reconstitutive process. Concurrent psychotherapy having to do with narcissistic changes and the sense of loss may be particularly important in this phase.

Furthermore, if we examine ego functions (in contrast to feelings of self, body image, ego feeling, sense of reality, etc., Spiegel 1959), a major problem of the schizophrenic's weakened ego is the regressive alteration of ego functions, including extreme forms of defensive activities (Arlow and Brenner 1969). A medication which produces sudden substantial changes in perception, body image, and grandiosity would not only affect feelings of self, but also affect such other ego functions as object relations, regulation of drives, synthetic-integrative functioning, and defenses. The latter by their very nature in psychoses are primitive and "unreliable" (Arlow and Brenner 1969, p. 11). The disruption in K's relationship with his father—and following the panic occasioned by the emergence of his poorly tolerated aggressive ʿeelings, and the interference in his ability to continue working—is a good example.

Jacobson (1967) has drawn attention to the use of objects and reality for defensive purposes to control psychotic conflict. As a result of weaknesses in boundaries between psychic representation of objects and the self, a regressive narcissistic relationship to objects can permit an externalization of conflicts. In some of my patients this appeared to have been interrupted by medication. As an illustration, K, the palmreader could neither control his hostile impulses when he felt displaced by his newborn son, nor, due to changes in preconscious ego state, externalize conflicts toward his following by projective identification. He lost his powers, could no longer control himself, and became both agitated and depressed.

Federn (1950) described *preconscious falsification* as the process whereby preconscious ego states lose the cathexis of their boundaries and fail to function automatically; on the other hand, ideas seem imposed upon or taken away from the schizophrenic. Medications in some patients appear to enhance preconscious falsification. The occurrence of perverted thoughts in patient R is an example, as is the change in preconscious states occasioned in the palmreader, K.

In this paper, I have sought to describe a number of intrapsychic changes that occur during the administration of neuroleptic drugs. Unless these are recognized (and within the context of the therapeutic relationship), the schizophrenic patient experiences these changes as *due* to the medication and *on this basis*, may discontinue the medication or undergo considerable amounts of confusion and morbidity.

NOTES

1. Since this article was written, Van Putten, Crumpton, and Yale (1976) have described a group of chronic schizophrenics who habitually refused medication. There was a significant association of drug refusal with grandiosity. The findings were interpreted by these authors to mean that some schizophrenics may "prefer" an ego syntonic grandiose psychosis to a relative drug-induced normality.

2. Tausk (1919) has described a related phenomena in the sequential development of the *influencing machine*, though here the emphasis is on the patient's body. Hypochondriacal internal alteration is followed by rejection, experienced as estrangement, and leads to construction of the influencing machine which is a summation of these alterations projected outward as a hostile power.

REFERENCES

Arieti, S. (1955). *Interpretation of Schizophrenia*. New York: Brunner/Mazel.
Arlow, J. A., and Brenner, C. (1969). The psychopathology of the psychoses: a proposed revision. *International Journal of Psycho-Analysis* 50:5-14.
Azima, H. (1957). Psychoanalytic action of rauwolfia derivations. In *Psychopharmacology Frontiers* (International Congress of Psychiatry, Proceedings of the Psychopharmacology Symposium, Zurich, 1957), ed. N. S. Kline, pp. 281-284. Boston: Little Brown, 1959.
―――― (1959). Effects of rauwolfia derivaties on psychodynamic structures. *Psychiatric Quarterly* 33:623-635.
Azima, H., and Sarwer-Foner, G. J. (1960). Psychoanalytic formulations on the effect of drugs in pharmacotherapy. In *International Symposium on the Extrapyramidal Reactions and Neuroleptics, Montreal, 1960*, ed. J. M. Bordeleau, pp. 507-518. Montreal: Editions Psychiatrique, 1961.
Ban, T. (1969). *Psychopharmacology*. Baltimore: Williams and Wilkins.
Bellak, L., and Loeb, L. (1969). *The Schizophrenic Syndrome*. New York: Grune and Stratton.
Beres, D. (1956). Ego deviation and the concept of schizophrenia. *Psychoanalytic Study of the Child* 11:164-235.
Blackwell, B. (1973). Drug therapy: patient compliance. *New England Journal of Medicine* 289:249-252.
Bowers, M. B., Jr., and Astrachan, B. M. (1967). Depression in acute schizophrenic psychosis. *American Journal of Psychiatry* 123:976-979.
Callaway, E. (1970. Schizophrenia and interference: an analogy with a malfunctioning computer. *Archives of General Psychiatry* 22:193-708.
Cameron, N. (1946). Experimental analysis of schizophrenic thinking. In *Language and Thought in Schizophrenia*, ed. J. S. Kasanin. Berkeley: University of California Press.
Cohen, S., Leonard, C. V., Farberow, N. L., and Schneidman, E. S. (1964). Tranquilizers and suicide in the schizophrenic patient. *Archives of General Psychiatry* 11:312-321.
Federn, P. (1950). *Ego Psychology and the Psychoses*. New York: Basic Books.
Group for the Advancement of Psychiatry (1975). *Pharmacotherapy and Psychotherapy: Paradoxes, Problems and Progress*. New York: Brunner-Mazel.
Groves, J. E., and Mandel, M R. (1975). The long acting phenothiazines. *Archives of General Psychiatry* 32:893-900.
Hartmann, H. (1953). Contributions to the metapsychology of schizophrenia. *Psychoanalytic Study of the Child* 8:177-198.
Jacobson, E. (1967). *Psychotic Conflict and Reality*. New York: International Universities Press.
―――― (1971). *Depression*. New York: International Universities Press.
Kalinowsky, L. B., and Hippius, H. (1969). *Pharmacological, Convulsive and Other Somatic Treatments in Psychiatry*. New York: Grune and Stratton.
Klein, D. F., and Davis, J. M. (1969). *Diagnosis and Drug Treatment of Psychiatric Disorders*. Baltimore: Williams and Wilkins.
Kline, N. S. (1956). Pharmacology, Publication No. 42 of the American Association for the Advancement of Science, Washington, D.C., p. 87.

Lehmann, H. E. (1974). Physical therapies of schizophrenia. In *American Handbook of Psychiatry*, vol. 3, ed. S. Arieti, 2nd ed., pp. 652-675. New York: Basic Books.

May, P. R. A. (1968). *Treatment of Schizophrenia*. New York: Jason Aronson.

Nunberg, H. (1931). The synthetic function of the ego. In *Practice and Theory of Psychoanalysis*, pp. 120-136. New York: Nervous and Mental Disease Monographs, 1948.

Pribram, K. H. (1967). Emotion: steps toward a neuropsychological theory. In *Neurophysiology and Emotion*, ed. D. C. Glass, pp. 3-40. New York: Rockefeller University Press.

Rapaport, D. (1953). On the psychoanalytic theory of affects. *International Journal of Psycho-Analysis* 34:177-198.

Sarwer-Foner, G. J. (1957). Psychoanalytic theories of activity-passivity conflicts and of the continuum of ego defenses. *Archives of Neurology and Psychiatry* 78:413-418.

——— (1960). Recognition and management of drug-induced extrapyramidal reactions and "paradoxical" behavioral reactions in psychiatry. *Canadian Medical Association Journal* 83:312-318.

Sarwer-Foner, G. J., and Ogle, W. (1956). Psychosis and enhanced anxiety produced by reserpine and chlorpromazine. *Canadian Medical Association Journal* 74:526-532.

Schilder, P. (1950). *The Image and Appearance of the Human Body*. New York: International Universities Press.

Shakow, D. (1962). Segmental set. *Archives of General Psychiatry* 6:17-33.

Spiegel, L. A. (1959). The self, sense of self, and perception. *Psychoanalytic Study of the Child* 14:81-109.

Tausk, V. (1919). On the origin of the "influencing machine" in schizophrenia. In *The Psychoanalytic Reader*, ed. R. Fliess, pp. 31-64. New York: International Universities Press, 1948.

Van Putten, T. (1975). Why do patients with manic-depressive illness stop their lithium? *Comprehensive Psychiatry* 16:179-183.

Van Putten, T., Crumpton, E., and Yale, C. (1976). Drug refusal in schizophrenia and the wish to be crazy. *Archives of General Psychiatry* 33:1443-1446.

The Psychotic Character

LEON J. SAUL, M.D.
SILAS L. WARNER, M.D.

A warp in the childhood emotional pattern may involve the ego and superego enough to cause psychotic elements or coloring, which may evolve into the psychotic character or into the potential for it or for psychosis. A brief review of relevant literature and a series of clinical vignettes are presented from the perspective of Alexander's model of the neurotic character. The psychotic character is seen as showing: the dynamics of the neuroses acted out as in the neurotic character; narcissistic egocentricity and a failure of emphathetic, sympathetic identification and loving object relations; id impulses rationalized by a distortion of reality (manifested not in specific delusions, but rather, more diffusely throughout the ego); minimal or no insight into illness, as in criminality; and a failure of defenses against id impulse although the ego organization is intact. The clinical material reveals that these elements are encountered in all combinations and gradations; several types of psychotic character are discussed.

In a brilliant and now classic piece of psychodynamic exposition, Franz Alexander portrayed the *neurotic character* (1962, pp. 56-73), defining it in relation to neurosis, psychosis, criminality, addiction, and perversion. Alexander's 1930 formulation is still valid and will serve as a model for a study of the psychotic character. The relevant elements of this model are listed according to the ego's decreasing capacity for repression (addictions and perversions are omitted). These elements are, of course, rarely if ever seen in pure form.

- *Neurotic symptoms.* Unconscious impulses are displaced and manifested autoplastically by substitute gratifications.

- *The neurotic character.* Unconscious impulses are acted out alloplastically, to yield disguised but real gratification.

- *Psychosis.* Defenses fail, with ego breakdown, yielding undisguised but autoplastic gratification, usually of very regressive impulses.

- *Criminality.* Defenses fail, but with ego intact, permitting undisguised, direct, alloplastic gratification.

- *The psychotic character.* We see (a) neurotic dynamics, acted out alloplastically, as in the neurotic character; (b) a failure of defenses, with intact ego organization and uninhibited alloplastic gratification, as in criminality; (c) a usually extreme narcissistic egocentricity—one's own wishes and desires being paramount over identification, empathy, sympathy, and loving object relations with others (or with most others) so that these feelings are often minimal; (d) minimal insight into illness; and (e) the acted-out id impulses justified to the ego by a distortion of reality, as in psychosis. This distortion is not extreme, not beyond possible reality; and this defense mechanism, rather than being relatively circumscribed as in a clear-cut psychosis, is more diffused through the ego and therefore more difficult to perceive and describe. Indeed, the analyst may intuitively sense that one of his patients is a psychotic character without being able to support this feeling with solid observational facts for a considerable period.

PSYCHODYNAMICS

Every child is born with certain potentials which interact with his emotional and physical environment forming an emotional pattern of reaction, the nucleus of which is usually well established by about the age of six (Freud 1949). Generally, the younger the child, the greater the effect of environmental influences. Insofar as this effect is traumatic, through omission or commission, the child's emotional pattern of reacting to others is warped. And insofar as this warping distorts the ego, superego, and sense of reality, it produces the elements of psychosis. If the distortion is severe enough the groundwork for a lifelong psychosis is laid. In general, the earlier in life traumatic influences are exerted, the more apt they are to cause psychotic distortions. In other words, the distortions in the childhood emotional pattern (Saul 1977) create psychotic elements in the child's psychodynamics that form a psychotic character, or the potential for psychosis itself, when the child grows up and the rest of his psyche matures.

CLINICAL MATERIAL

There are many types of the psychotic character: simple, diffuse, regressive withdrawal, hostile, schizoid, paranoid, depressive, criminoid, and criminal. These types are illustrated in the following clinical vignettes.

A charming, kindly, highly intelligent man of sixty came to talk about his daughter. She had a good marriage and four children. The patient seemed quite anxious about her: at first about her physical health and then, as he revealed more, about her marriage. Was it really a happy one? He had heard fragments of talk that suggested his daughter's husband might be having an affair. In fact, maybe his daughter was also. After the gentleman was questioned in detail for three visits as to the evidence and the actual behavior of the family, it appeared that his case for worrying had evaporated. I told him that it was my impression that he had unrealistic worry about his daughter and her family and that there was really no adequate reason for his anxiety. From other sources I had received information about the family and learned that they had long recognized his extremely unrealistic concern. With my reassurance and suggestion that he have more confidence in his daughter and son-in-law, he seemed genuinely relieved and thanked me.

As he was leaving the office, however, he said, "Oh, I should have told you about my other daughter; she is the one who *really* has the problem. When can I talk to you about her?" He returned to discuss his three daughters and his son. His wife had died some years before. With his permission I contacted the psychiatrist they had both seen before her death, who told me that this behavior had been going on for twenty years. Originally the patient had been worried about his wife, who had come for help in dealing with him. His dynamics were those of the overprotective mother. They went so far, however, that he actually believed his worries justified; he had, like the paranoid or hypochondriac, constructed most of them from a small kernel of truth. This type might be called *simple* for lack of a better term. Neurotic dynamics were acted out alloplastically, with ego intact but so distorted in its sense of reality that apparently rational thinking and behavior were used for irrational acts of interference, dependence, and hostility to his children and their families.

The *paranoid* type is illustrated in the frequently-seen unreasonably critical wife. A woman of thirty-five was appealing because of her dark beauty and force of personality, combined with a contrasting little-girl element that seemed to express a plea for love. Her handsome, adoring husband worshipped her, but she usually complained so angrily about him that when she was reasonably pleasant he was grateful. There were two daughters and a son. She had been a good mother until the children began to emerge from childhood at the age of eight or ten. Then she became critical of them also: "Why did you do this? Why did you do that?"

Her endless complaints about her husband expressed two main themes: he was controlling and he gave her no time, or help. It was unmistakably clear from interviews with the husband and from the wife's own account that this was almost pure projection. She was the one who completely dominated the household, giving orders and making demands. Her husband emptied the garbage exactly her way and on her schedule, washed the dishes, hung up the laundry, and everything else. She controlled the sleeping arrangements, the love-making, and the restricted social life. Her conversation was mostly critical and hostile. If she mentioned football, an enthusiasm of her husband's, it was in terms of the players swarming out onto the field like vermin out of the woodwork. She came to me to complain about her husband, but she complained about the butcher and the baker too—their products, the neglect, the abominable service—never seeing that her regal and hostile treatment of them provoked their attitudes. Nor could she see that her husband was a saint to put up with her, let alone love her and patiently remain devoted and faithful. His reactions to her endless demands, criticisms, and hostilities she saw only as indicative of all his problems and of what an awful person he was. If he put out the garbage at the appointed hour for a year and then forgot or delayed a single time, she launched into an unending tirade. If he was driven to losing his temper, she might attack him physically, sometimes dangerously, with whatever was handy.

She did not come to me for help for herself, but to persuade her husband to come and to change. If this monster who so ill-treated her did not change, she would throw him out and get a divorce. There was a shocking absence of any sense of what he, poor man, must be feeling.

Her mother had been depriving and dominating during the patient's very early years. After the patient was five or six, the mother treated her better. There were only hints of this, but I had the opportunity of checking it with her older brother. The patient had transferred her image of her mother to her husband, friends, acquaintances—to her whole world. This was evident in her comments on plays, books and people, and in her conversations. Her outlook was mildly paranoid in a diffuse way. She was not psychotic; she was well organized and effective in the home and in any job she undertook. You could introduce her into any group. It was impossible to give her any insight into her own hostilities and provocative dynamics. Thoroughly defended against insight into illness, she was barely defended against her own unconscious demands and hostilities, which expressed the pattern of reaction to her mother. She justified these demands by a generalized distortion of reality. Just as the depressed person sees the world through dark glasses, this patient saw it in a way that was keenly perceptive and realistic so far as it went, but that selected and toned the behavior of others to make her feelings of frustration and anger seem quite natural. It was alloplastic.

This patient was physically and psychologically fit. She relished her food, was indefatigable, feel soundly asleep on hitting the pillow, had no autoplastic complaints—in fact, no complaints at all except that she had to put up with such a husband and such a world. But her ego, undamaged in structure, was so deeply colored by her id impulses as to make her thinking, sense of reality, and behavior psychotic rather than neurotic in quality. The relation to *criminality* is evident in her extreme lack of identification and empathy with her husband

and in her physical attacks upon him. He sensed a danger that sometime her id hostility might break through her defenses completely during one of these rages and he would not be safe if his back were turned at such a time.

The difficulties in determining whether certain patients can be termed psychotic characters can be seen in Bartley's case. He was almost six feet tall, beautifully proportioned and possessed of superior coordination. Bartley was handsome; one could say he had a perfect physique, looks, health, and athletic ability. His intellect was also superior and his personality most attractive. He was universally popular; girls flocked to Bartley wanting to sleep with him, live with him, marry him—anything and everything. At age sixteen he had a beautiful fifteen-year-old girl all his own and enjoyed full sexual relations with her. His pleasure was alloyed, however, by feeling that he was too dependent on her. Then Bartley got a sports car and became absorbed in tinkering with it. The girl interfered with this and he now thought her too dependent on him. He tinkered and polished the car; the relationship with the girl ended.

At twenty, Bartley felt little interest in girls. His greatest pleasure was his sports car, especially when he was driving it. But if any car were behind him he felt tense and anxious, and that spoiled his pleasure. His parents could willingly afford any schooling he wished. He had youth, health, perfect body, mind, and attractiveness, but Bartley could not be interested or enjoy these gifts; he gradually came to the conclusion that life for him was not worthwhile and that the only answer was suicide.

He met with firm resistance the idea that he have a physical exam, that his blood sugar might be low, or some other condition might exist or be found. He also refused a short trial of lithium. The central feature of his psychology seemed to be this regressive infantile quitting attitude. He seemed to say, If everything is not just as I want it (even though in reality he had everything) then I'll quit, I just will not play. This is the attitude of a small, very spoiled child. The striking absence of manhood, of fighting spirit, of the will and desire to live are all apparent. Bartley had a normal conscious wish for independence, but tried to express it only in ways certain to keep him dependent—namely, by fighting every step that might assure his physical and psychological health.

What shall we call this? Is this just a severe neurosis? Is it a psychosis? If so, is it a schizophrenic *withdrawal*? The *depressive*, suicidal elements seem much more a result rather than a basic condition. At age twenty possessed of every advantage, he could not enjoy them and was frustrated to the point of suicide. If this is psychosis, is it not *diffused* throughout his whole personality rather than a specific combination of symptoms, and therefore best labeled *psychotic character*?

This leads to the following considerations: A powerful feeling such as anger (from the id) may be blocked in a particular person by the conscience (of the superego) so that it cannot be vented in unmitigated cruelty and violence. Yet it may be so strong that it distorts ego functions, reason, memory, and the sense of reality. If these faculties are sufficiently distorted we call the condition *psychosis* and the person *psychotic*. A very fine, superior man believed that he had devised a formula of great potential good for mankind but that a gang was plotting to steal it from him. In fear of "them" he began to travel, fleeing from city to city. Apart from this delusion, his ego was intact with good memory, judgment, and sense of reality. But whatever the topic of conversation, in about fifteen minutes he would bring up his delusion and manifest a distressing combination of fear and rage. This psychosis was paranoia, and although so severe that for a time he had to be hospitalized, it was circumscribed.

In other cases the psychosis is not so sharply delineated. For one young man it was subtle and *diffuse*, permeating his whole thinking. Even the most extreme *paranoid* delusions and delusional systems are generally built up by distortions and exaggerations of a kernel of truth. Ryan was a sophomore in college, a loved child who was still overly dominated by both parents, yet was permitted and encouraged to defy them. Stereotypes and thinking in stereotypes usually mean seeing groups and categories of people as part of one's own childhood emotional pattern. Ryan typically projected his childhood pattern onto the social scene: "the establishment" was too controlling, young people today want more freedom, they do not want domination, they show spirit in defying and rebelling, and so on. He could not see that our country, while not perfect of course, had achieved a greater degree of democracy than any other in history, that police were necessary, that military preparedness was essential for survival in the world as it existed, that the university he attended was sincerely trying to do its job well. There was indeed a kernel of truth in every abuse he listed, but it was all seen from the perspective of his being controlled, as in reality he had been by his parents in early childhood. Now he saw this control as coming from all authorities, from the establishment. His early conditioning had spread (in psychoanalytic terms *transferred*) to others, to all who could be seen as having power. His emotional reaction as a child had been fear and rage. The fear and rage kept this view vital, distorting his sense of reality, his reason, his judgment, not so grossly as to call it paranoia but yet so pervasively—so saturating his views on food, dress, bathing, music, sex, politics, economics, in short on everything— that Ryan could correctly by called a *paranoid* character.

Another man might see revolutionaries everywhere. In other words, paranoid distortions can be projected on anything and are clearly evident in political extremism from right to left. In the McCarthy era, it was from the right that this paranoid distortion came, and even such great patriots as General George Marshall and President Eisenhower were publicly accused of being subversive Communists. Currently, among students, the distortion is from the other direction. Many of these extremists cannot be diagnosed as definitely paranoid but their whole outlook, including the political, while always having the kernel of truth, is so suffused with this distortion of reality that their total personality is colored. If such coloring is dark, pessimistic, and severe enough to twist reality, then it is a psychotic character of the *depressive* type. If the person acts out his feelings on the basis of a hostile, fearful, distorted view of reality then his is a psychotic character of the acting-out *hostile* type. This acting out may take various forms—personal, political, criminoid and criminal. The political form of acting out can be seen, for example, in those extremists who try to rationalize violence which achieves no real purpose but exists only for its own sake—that is, the acting out of internal feelings of hate and hostility. Acting out can, of course, occur in all variations and combinations of all these types. Generally, extremists of all sorts seem to suffer from emotional illness. To comprehend the problems of society it is important to recognize this.

In the psychotic character of the *criminoid* type (Saul 1976) injury is done to others, but though flagrant enough is within the law. The garden variety example of such behavior within the family was the husband who, after twelve years of utter devotion, decided he was no longer interested in his wife and children and asked for a divorce to marry a young girl, with no feeling for his family or their suffering at his hands. The dynamics of this case were the usual dependence upon the wife, which the husband sought to compensate for by acting as the big man with the young girl, a desire to escape from family responsibilities to play with a young girl, and spoiling and domination by the husband's mother, which apparently generated a lifelong undercover rebellion against her and against all that she emphasized as proper, including responsibility for wife and children. The husband was in full rebellion. Home meant submission, and he declared his freedom and independence; he indulged in undisguised selfishness and hostile rejection of wife, children, and of his mother, showing no sign of identification, empathy, sympathy, or object love despite their obvious anguish and the children's reactions— failures in school and a growing sullenness and misbehavior. This husband justified his hostility and egocentric indulgence as mature independence for himself at long last. He saw loyalty, love, and responsibility as arguments that his wife and friends were using to control him, just as his mother had. His ego organization remained intact, and he ruthlessly continued with his determination to satisfy himself regardless.

A patient of neurotic rather than psychotic character, possessed of an attractive family, got himself into the same position as the one described above—an affair with a young girl. But his ego was less colored and his reality sense less distorted; his love and empathetic identification remained. Feeling the pain he was causing his family and seeing the damage to his children, he was guilty and miserable. He also saw his inability to forego the gratification of the other woman. He had enough insight to recognize this as a problem and sought treatment.

An example of the psychotic character who acts out politically is the boy who was locked in a domination-submission conflict with his father from his earliest years and came to see himself as submissive. This was intolerable; it hurt his narcissism and enraged him. At other times he saw himself as sadistically dominating others, utterly crushing all opposition, and his whole inner drive was devoted to achieving this. It colored his entire outlook. His ego organization was intact, and he had a certain political genius in perception and action. But he justified his hostile drives for domination, destruction, and sadism, devoid of sympathy and empathy, by coloring and molding his view of his country and its enemies to fit these impulses. The fearsome fact is that many millions accept such distortions to justify their unrestrained indulgence of every id impulse.

We reemphasize the point that rarely is any outcome of emotional disorder seen in pure form; the differences are largely quantitative, and all combinations and gradations are seen in any given individual.

DISCUSSION AND DIFFERENTIAL DIAGNOSIS

We have arbitrarily selected the term *psychotic character* rather than *psychotic personality*, because the term *personality* seems to have a broader and less specific meaning than does *character* in the psychoanalytic literature. Hopefully there will be worked out a broad-based inclusive theory of personality which could be called *personalogy* (Brierly 1951) and which would serve as a structural base for psychoanalytic diagnosis and theory. Meanwhile, we use the more familiar term *character*, which includes the influence of early conditioning on the later fixed personality traits as well as on all other factors which lead to the development of certain fixed behavior potentials, on the concept of the world, and on characteristic emotional attitudes. Factors leading to character formation include not only early conditioning but also genetic and constitutional, as well as social and cultural, influences. To study the evolution of the term *character* is to review the history of psychoanalysis. The term has changed through the years from emphasis on traits of character to that on character structure, disorders of character, and finally, on character neurosis.

Glover characterizes the psychotic character's most striking feature as "the operation of alloplastic systems of defense, meaning thereby that abnormal patterns of reaction are displayed in object relations, whether sexual or social, the aim of which is to modify the environments to suit the fixed instinctual needs and demands of the patient. This aim corresponds to the reaction of the psychotic, with this essential difference, however, that whereas the psychotic abandons his most important object-relations and substitutes for reality a fantasy system of relations, the psychotic character maintains an extremely tenuous system of relations and persists in his attempts to modify his objects, thereby maintaining his hold on reality" (1955, p. 254).

Frosch has defined psychotic character as "a syndrome, delineated from among the borderline conditions. It is a counterpart of the neurotic character. In many respects, the features of the psychotic character resemble those seen characterizing the disturbances of the psychotic." One of the important differences is that "the capacity to test reality, while often very defective and manifesting primitive qualities, is nonetheless relatively intact. Although there is a marked proclivity for regression and de-differentiation, just as in the psychotic, in contrast to the psychotic, there is a capacity for reversibility. The nature of the object relationship in the psychotic character, although at times prone to primitivization with occasional regression to archaic objectless levels, is relatively at a higher level of psychic development. These persons can establish object relations, albeit at an infantile level. In spite of severe disturbances in relation to reality, they nonetheless manage to make an adaptation, which functions reasonably well and is at a reality-syntonic level." Frosch makes an important differential point in stating that "it is the more crystallized borderline personality that in many instances I have chosen to designate as psychotic character" (1964, pp. 94-95).

It is essential that we clearly distinguish between the psychotic character and the borderline syndrome. Grinker sees the latter as showing "fundamentally a deformity or distortion of ego-functions." He claims "the borderline is not a regressive process but a developmental defect on which a wide variety of adaptive and defensive neurotic behavior is overlaid" (1968, p. 22). He further specifies that the borderline syndrome has the following four characteristics: (1) anger as the main or only affect, (2) a defect in affectional relations, (3) an absence of self-identity, and (4) depressive loneliness (p. 176).

Some cases of the psychotic character seem to have a very distinct but too rigidly defined self-identity. However, his own self-identity and how most of the world sees him are usually distinctly different. With respect to affectional relationships, some psychotic characters seem capable of very strong and often very exclusive interpersonal relationships, albeit of a very infantile love-hate variety.

Kernberg suggests that borderline conditions have in common, "symptomatic constellations, such as diffuse anxiety, special forms of polysymptomatic neuroses, and 'prepsychotic' and 'lower level' character pathology." Most of those we call psychotic characters do not experience ego-alien symptoms per se because the alloplastic process externalizes the conflict and protects the individual from the subjective discomfort of symptoms. His main affect is usually anger at those onto whom he projects his primitive introjects. These victims feel anxious and uncomfortable whereas the psychotic character is more apt to feel righteous indignation. Kernberg's other criteria for borderline personality disorders certainly coincide with our concept of the psychotic character. This would include his "defensive constellations of the ego, namely a combination of nonspecific manifestations of ego weakness and a shift toward primary-process thinking on the one hand, and specific primitive defense mechanisms (splitting, primitive idealization, early forms of projection, denial, omnipotence), on the other." But, we would add, these are so diffused and well rationalized as to be not readily recognized. Kernberg's criteria also include "a particular pathology of internalized object relations" and "characteristic instinctual vicissitudes, namely, a particular pathological condensation of pregenital and genital aims under the overriding influence of pregenital aggressive needs" (1975, p. 44).

From our study of a series of patients, we draw certain conclusions about the nature of the *psychotic character*. It shows the dynamics of the neuroses acted out as in the neurotic character, with extreme narcissistic egocentricity and a failure of empathetic, sympathetic identification and loving object relations. These id impulses are rationalized by distortion of reality as in psychosis, less in circumscribed ways as specific delusions but more diffusely throughout the ego with minimal or no insight into illness. As in criminality, defenses fail against id impulses although ego organization is intact. We strongly believe that the psychotic character is frequently found clinically and constitutes a distinct diagnostic entity. A psychotic character's alloplastic acting out can be so devastating that careful study is mandated in the hope of modifying its destructive, adverse effects.

REFERENCES

Alexander, F. (1962). *The Scope of Psychoanalysis*. New York: Basic Books.

Brierley, M. (1951). *Trends in Psychoanalysis*. London: Hogarth.

Freud, S. (1949). *An Outline of Psycho-Analysis*. New York: Norton.

Frosch, J. (1964). The psychotic character: clinical psychiatric considerations. *Psychiatric Quarterly* 38:94-95.

Glover, E. (1955). *The Technique of Psychoanalysis*. New York: International Universities Press.

Grinker, R., Sr., Werble, B., and Drye, R. (1968). *The Borderline Syndrome*. New York: Basic Books.

Kernberg, O. (1975). *Borderline Conditons and Pathological Narcissism*. New York: Jason Aronson.

Saul, L. (1976). *Psychodynamics of Hostility*. New York: Jason Aronson.

———(1977). *The Childhood Emotional Pattern: The Key to Personality, Its Disorders and Therapy*. New York: Van Nostrand-Reinhold.

The Alcohol Induced
Hypnoid State and
Its Analytic Corollary

AUSTIN SILBER, M.D.

Alcohol can be ingested to achieve a hypnoid state. This altered awareness is actively sought by the alcoholic as part of an ongoing attempt at mastery. By this symptomatic resort to a change in consciousness, the painful affects connected with earlier assaults and seductions carried out by severely disturbed parents, are maintained in repression. At the same time this self-induced hypnoid state facilitates the gratification of both conscious and unconscious fantasies. The case history of a patient is reported who while in analysis, and on the analytic couch, evoked a hypnoid state. For this patient the analysis of his hypnoid state led to the recall and verbalization of early traumatic experiences. The similarity of early life circumstances, in regard to disturbed and inadequate parenting, in both the carefully studied analytic patient and the less frequently available data on patients treated by psychotherapy in an alcohol clinic is discussed.

This paper hypothesizes that alcohol is ingested to precipitate a hypnoid state. This state can be defined as an altered state of awareness defensively instituted to ward off the experiencing of painful affects (Dickes 1965). It is different from the hypnoid state investigated by Loewald while reviewing Freud's concept of hypnoid hysteria. This state which, in effect, "reveals itself as the equivalent of the ego state corresponding to the period of infantile sexuality" (1955, p. 205) is a much more inclusive concept than the defensively wrought condition described above. Dickes writes, "I would venture the opinion that all who suffer from this syndrome to any marked degree have encountered unusual and excessive seductions and beatings. These injurious and devastating traumata, usually inflicted by parents, were carried to such an extreme and intolerable degree as to force these unlucky children to seek

Presented at the Ninth Annual Symposium of Psychodynamic Studies of Physiological Phenomena in Psychiatry (Topic: Psychodynamic Implications of Various Studies in Alcoholism), the department of psychiatry of the Medical College of Pennsylvania, November 9, 1975.

refuge in a stupor which can be likened only to the deep trance stage of hypnosis" (p. 375).

This altered state, of varying depths, is actively sought and regularly induced by the ingestion of alcohol as part of an ongoing attempt at mastery. By this magical ingestion—and now symptomatic resort to a hypnoid state—both painful affects and the remembering and reexperiencing of memories related to early traumatic experiences are warded off. Simultaneously, this self-induced hynoid state facilitates the gratification of unconscious fantasies.

Data to support this inference comes from two very different sources: experience over the past twenty years supervising the psychotherapy of alcohol patients in a clinic setting and understanding gleaned from analyzing a hypnoid state as it occurred during the course of a lengthy analysis.

BACKGROUND

Thinking about these two areas of experience, I became impressed with a basic similarity in the otherwise different individuals who are the subjects of this report. A recent paper (Silber 1974), based on my specific supervisory role made certain observations. The parents of patients seen in individual, primarily one-session-a-week therapy, by either psychiatric residents, social work staff, or students, were found to be either psychotic or else to behave in a psychotic manner. This finding was repeatedly confirmed in case after case. It was rare for me to supervise treatment of a patient in which this behavior, on the part of a parent, was not readily apparent. The patients, as children, had to learn to cope with often uncontrolled behavior on the part of these parents, which frequently led to unprovoked assaults. This behavior occurred at the very time when, as children, there was an obligatory reliance upon these parents for literal survival.

I would assume that many of the alcoholic patients, as children, reacted to assault by psychotic parents in a manner similar to that reported by Fliess (1961) and Shengold (1967, 1971). They noted that children traumatized and overstimulated by psychotic parents resort to what they called hypnosis and what Dickes defined as a hypnoid state. Thus Dickes (1965), in speaking of the adult hypnoid state, says, "This adult state is often a repetition of a childhood hypnoid state which occurred as a means of warding off intolerable feelings due to overstimulation and abuse" (p. 397). It is this state of mind that can be reinstituted by the ingestion of alcohol. Now, however, it functions not just to ward off the painfulness and recall of the early traumatic experiences, but to foster the mechanism of denial and weave together fantasies that serve to undo, master, and overcome the early traumas. This helps the individual obtain a sense of gratification, control, and mastery while in the self-induced hypnoid state.

Not only did all the patients initially reject the possibility of unprovoked assaultive or sexual behavior on the part of their parents, but as I noted, it was only with great difficulty that the therapists could finally recognize and accept the reality of the parents' illness or bizarre behavior. It was only by encouraging the therapists to contemplate anew their patients' descriptions of their parents' present deportment, as well as intimations of past functioning, that the picture of the parents' psychotic behavior gradually emerged. Here is a brief description of a typical parent of this sort taken from my paper.

A patient reported that from childhood on his mother would hide small quantities of food in various unlikely places in the house. When occasionally these caches were discovered, the mother would remark, "The world is always so unsettled, perhaps we'll lose our money, or dad will lose his job—it's important to prepare for any eventuality." If the patient would protest about the odor or the insects attracted by the food, the mother would in a fury attack him with the statement "you want us to be unprepared, to be at the mercy of anyone with money or food, you don't want us to be a free and independent family, etc." The patient would succumb to the harangue, feel guilty because he really did not have the family's best interest in mind, and come away from the confrontation with the idea that his mother was prudent and he was thoughtless. His mother was extolled by his father, the rest of the family and many neighbors as a thoughtful, pleasant person—the patient in a general way shared their views. (1974, p. 42)

This type of observation has been made or can be inferred from reports of other authors. Chayfetz (1959), in enumerating factors contributing to the emotional deprivation of alcoholic patients, noted that as children some had psychotic mothers. He felt that "the common thread running through these patients' early relationships was the absence of a warm, giving, meaningful relationship with a mother figure during this period (early years) of development" (p. 294). Schuckit et al. (1969) stressed that "both the clinical psychiatric concomitants and the family history of the psychiatric illness are important factors in the nosological grouping of alcoholics" (p. 306). Ferenczi (1933), in discussing pathological adults, stated, "The real rape of girls who have hardly grown out of the age of infants, similar sexual acts of mature women with boys and also enforced homosexual acts, are more frequent occurrences than has hitherto been assumed" (p. 161-162). Simmel (1948) described mothers who overtly seduced and manipulated their children. When the child, as a result of this marked overstimulation responded to the seduction with a sexual response of its own, it was unmercifully attacked by the outraged parent. A few examples from Simmel (1948) follow:

The stepmother of one of my patients, considerably younger than her husband, would regularly allow her four-year-old boy to caress her leg from the foot up to near the vagina, but she would beat him and threaten him with castration when he wet his bed, or when she found him playing with his penis. The father of a woman patient, himself an alcoholic, would attack sexually all the female members of the family, including this daughter, but he beat her whenever he found her playing with her genitals. When, in adolescence, she made her first attempts to get away from him by having dates with boys, he forbade such "indecency," and punished her drastically for overstepping his prohibitions. (1948, pp. 12-13)

The loss of control manifested by this type of parent, and the resultant infliction of painful assaults of a sexual and aggressive nature upon their own children, severely traumatizes the child. In the traumatized child, it can lead to the type of behavior described below in regard to the alcoholic victim of a psychotic parent: "One can trace the vicissitudes of the parents' pathology as seen in the alcoholic patient. Frequently, these patients act out in relation to their own children certain traumata inflicted upon them as children. The action is frequently carried out in a fury, during which there may be some subtly altered state of consciousness, so that the patient gives the impression of being momentarily lost" (Silber 1974), p. 43). In this instance a hypnoid state (Dickes 1965) may defensively ward off the patient's awareness of certain of *his own* drives and affects. One response available to the child to cope with this traumatic event is its own resort to a hypnoid state which may, in this instance, evolve out of a mimicking of the parents' "absence." The fury and irrationality of the assault is psychologically denied by effecting the same manifest lost expression of the parent. I have previously mentioned a hypnotic state in children traumatized and overstimulated by psychotic parents (Fliess 1961) and Shengold (1967, 1971). Shengold noted the use of autohypnosis to facilitate repetition of past traumata in attenuation. He also stressed the impaired sense of identity of these patients.

In treating patients subject to this type of assault, the therapist must grasp the defect in the parent and his or her functioning clearly. This makes it possible, at an appropriate time, to help the patient recognize, acknowledge, and evaluate the parental abnormality. Overwhelmed by the parental assault, the child frequently resorts to the defense of denial in an effort to salvage some vestige of a relationship to the developmentally inadequate but vitally needed parent. Frequently, shared delusional ideas compromise the burgeoning sense of separateness, individuality, and identity. Very often, a primitive type of identification, based on a regression to a primary identification, takes place, making the task of separating self from object more difficult. Modell (1975) described the negative identification open to borderline patients. This identification, also modeled on an identification with the aggressor (A. Freud 1937), serves fundamentally defensive purposes.

In the alcohol clinic patient population, severe problems in the area of object relationships are a ubiquitous finding; object-relations are shallow, fragile and tenuous. As a group, alcoholics are noteworthy for the ease with which they develop seemingly new attitudes based on primitive identificatory mechanisms. They imitate readily and display a somewhat chilling as-if propensity.

Modell (1975) notes that in order for the ego to gain control over the instincts of the id, an identification with a good object is necessary. This identification in turn requires a supplementation from the human environment—that is, the fitting in of what Winnicott (1960, 1962) calls good-enough object-relations. Since he does not have "good-enough parents, the alcoholic can not use such identifications to mitigate the intensity of his instinctual demands. At the same time, this particular failure of identification interferes with his capacity to sublimate these impulses. Identifications are frequently restricted to those with an object created by the subject (quite often omnipotent or grandiose) or to identification with negative aspects of the object" (Modell 1975, p. 61). This negative identification can also be seen in the previously described identification with the hypnoid state of the attacking parent.

In the therapeutic situation, the importance of the realistic aspects of the relationship with the therapist is directly related to the degree of deprivation the patient suffered from primary objects during development. Since the group of patients seen in the clinic setting were affected by the pathological behavior of at least one parent, the actual object tie to the therapist takes on extreme importance (see Greenson and Wexler 1969). To work more effectively with this group of patients the therapist must drastically modify the usual psychotherapeutic technique (see Silber 1974).

Case History from the Clinic

An example of the evocation of the hypnoid state by ingesting alcohol follows. A therapist reported on a young male patient, in his early twenties, who would rush to a neighborhood bar immediately after work. He was aware of a sense of unease as he sat on a bar stool and looked at the bartender. Instead of asking for a drink, he would point to a bottle of bourbon (Old Grandad) and by motioning with his hand indicate that he wanted a drink. After downing this drink, he would immediately indicate the desire to have another of the same, as he paid for the initial drink. The patient described to his therapist the pleasant, peaceful feeling that supervened with the quick dispatch of the refill. He felt at ease, though somewhat foggy and not fully alert: "Not quite with it, a little drowsy but, feeling no pain." (Similar expressions have been used by many of the alcohol patients treated. This is the state they wish to attain and strive to remain in as long as possible.) The bartender now seemed pleasant and smiling, and the patient now knew that the other customers in the bar were also friendly. Once he had succeeded in reaching this pleasant fuzzy state, a state I would define as a self-induced hypnoid state, he wished that time could be suspended, he felt so at ease. As Dickes (1965) has noted, the hypnoid defense "is one of the most primitive among the ego's repertory of defenses and perhaps most closely related to denial" (p. 398).

The patient's father and grandfather were both drinkers. He remembers his father at home, drunk, screaming abuse at him and his two younger siblings. He remembers a younger brother being picked up by his father and flung onto the floor with such force that a leg was broken and had to be placed in a cast. His father was hospitalized after suffering from a nervous breakdown and spent some years in a mental institution. He recalls his father screaming in terror, fearful that a prowler in the apartment would attack him with a knife which "would be shoved up his ass." His father also felt that his own father had instigated this prowler to attack him. The patient remembers how he feared his father's shouting and cursing and how he dreaded going home after school for fear of what he would find. His father might be drunk and might even be fighting with his own father. While the patient was a child, the grandfather had lived with the family for some years. His mother was quiet, she would sit at home, looking helpless, withdrawn, and apathetic. She never intervened to protect the children. As soon as the patient finished high school, he obtained a job and moved into his own apartment, a short distance from where his mother still lived.

He became aware of being fearful of returning to his own apartment after work. He went to the neighborhood bar instead. As he bolted down the liquor, he was aware of the warm feeling in his stomach. He felt protected and safe. The alcohol made him feel comforted and secure. He realized that this was what he had always hoped his mother could do. He remembered the thought "dear mother" as he downed the drink.

It became apparent that a number of unconscious fantasies were being acted out in his bar ritual. They represented his attempt, in fantasy at least, to exert control over some area of his life. Thus choosing to go to the bar represented his attempt to set up a different home atmosphere. The bartender, who would respond to his gesture and provide the liquor that brought about the good feeling inside his stomach, was supplying the kind of satisfying substance (milk) that symbolized the comfort he wished his mother could have given him. Shortly after swallowing he would become aware of a pleasant slightly drowsy feeling, his state of awareness would change, and the sought after hypnoid state supervene. In fantasy, he was feeling protected by his mother whose advocacy he evoked magically by pointing, handling, and swallowing the liquor. As the hypnoid state induced by the alcohol began to take over, the anxiety he had initially experienced, began to dissipate. He was now no longer fearful that he would be screamed at or abused; in fact, he was able magically and silently to bring about this good feeling by having the bartender fill his glass. Thus the bartender also represented, in unconscious fantasy, a now tractable father who could, without an uproar, help make the patient feel comfortable. By ordering Old Grandad he was also magically converting his grandfather, whom he also feared, into a now palatable comforting agent magically helping to dispell his fears. As the effect of the alcohol became more apparent and as the self-induced hypnoid state deepened, he felt that his life was a comfortable one in these warm, accepting surroundings. He felt as though he were at home, the way he had always wished home would feel—safe and protected, with parents (bartender) responsive to his every whim and gesture. The hypnoid state made the environment of the bar feel friendly and these cozy conscious fantasies (surrounded by friends who were, like family, eager to please and satisfy him) took over. This was the state he magically attempted to bring about again and again with alcohol. This actively induced hypnoid state, which he could bring about at will now, substituted for the hypnoid state that in all probability had been invoked in childhood to deal with the overwhelming assault of his depraved father and depriving mother. Similar tales were reported by many patients.

Thus for many alcoholic patients, the environs of the local bar, in fantasy, is converted into a warm, cozy home, full of cheer and good spirits—in contrast to the frequently reported stark, strident home atmosphere that, in reality, had prevailed. The bartender or barmaid becomes the good parent bringing forth acceptance and love, all concentrated in the alcoholic product (which can represent milk, feces, urine, or semen in fantasy). The vessel in which the alcohol is served can, in fantasy, represent breast, penis, bladder, etc. Thus woven about the bar and its occupants and the alcohol products that are served, are many unconscious fantasies, soothing in a narcissistic way, which replace the starkness and despair of the actual home and homelife. This fantasy existence is expedited by inducing the hypnoid state with the ingestion of alcohol.

Case History from Analysis

At this point I would like to report the case history of a patient treated in analysis who was very similar in background and symptomatology to the patients treated at the clinic. With this patient it was possible to study in detail what could only be inferred from the many case histories from the clinic. The analytic patient would invoke the hypnoid state when he became anxious during his session. His growing awareness of his difficulties in dealing with reality situations developing at home and at work was reflected in his analytic sessions with me. Stress situations similar to those which would drive the clinic patients to use alcohol in order to alter consciousness and mitigate the developing anxiety, would cause my analytic patient to spontaneously invoke an altered state of consciousness.

The patient was in analysis for many years. A specific altered state of consciousness which was fully analyzed, took place during the course of an analytic session. After a considerable period of time the sequence of events leading up to the altered state, and finally the meaning of this occurrence, became clear. Similar altered states were repeated many times during his analysis before they were fully analyzed and thus resolved.

The appearance of the altered state during the analysis was always preceded by a recital of material from his current life, the significance of which he had trouble evaluating. For example, he would become aware that he consistently misinterpreted his bosses' request for information as an attack upon his character or his wife's remarks about his tendency to enjoy carpentry or reading as an aspersion on his ability to earn a livelihood. He would become increasingly physically restless on the couch in response to the painful feelings inspired by his faulty interpretation of these reality events and his inability to control this type of response. He might move his feet or shift his body; his associations would become more sparse and then suddenly cease. A silence of several seconds would supervene and then the patient would mutter some nonsequitor: "I see myself falling through a grating," or "I see myself moving a tower." He would then state that he had briefly fallen asleep and what he had muttered was the description of his dream. To complete the report of this dream, he would describe that he now felt "completely refreshed," as though all the cares he had just been so acutely distressed by had now completely disappeared. This transformation from tenseness and extreme restlessness, to somnolence, to "refreshed" alertness was extremely dramatic. An erection accompanied what we came to call his "refreshing dreams." The erection was transient, disappearing shortly after he awakened into his refreshed state.

As the patient described increasing recognition of his difficulties in handling reality situations in his life, a similar difficulty arose in his analysis. Communicating with me made him increasingly anxious. The analytic situation took on, in an affective sense, the meaning of the current life situation he had been describing. Subsequently, from his associations to the varied dream images it became possible to recognize that also transferred onto the analytic situation was his childhood involvement with his mother.

Between the ages of three and four, the patient was repeatedly the victim of his mother's sexual seductions. These encounters were experienced by him as physical assaults. He also was overwhelmingly sexually excited. The experiences constituted a "trauma" in the sense in which Freud (1926) defined it. He dealt with these traumatic events by becoming profoundly hypnoid. While in the hypnoid state and with his mind temporarily flooded by the effects of her sexual assault and his response to her seduction, he perceived various dream-like images. It was these images that he recalled during treatment.

Initially, he recalled a series of naps taken with his mother. It was the recalling from amnesia of these afternoon naps, and all the experiences attending them, that eventually led to a fuller understanding of the significance of these altered states. The series of afternoon naps with his mother were recalled in association to these altered states of consciousness—in effect short naps which took place during the session. These memories emerged over a period of years, piecemeal, against great resistance, in a relatively characteristic manner.

The usual afternoon nap of earliest childhood was modified early in his third year of life. Instead of taking a nap in his own crib, he and his mother would lie down together on her bed. At least this is the way it started. He recalled lying next to her, feeling her bodily warmth, aware of her distinctive aroma. He was usually clad in a pair of undershorts. His mother would be wearing only a slip and a bra. Sometimes his mother's slip and occasionally her bra would no longer be worn. At this point a particular game would begin. His mother would take his hand and place it upon a scar on her lower abdomen. She would tell him, "Since you made this, you are entitled to touch it." (The patient had been born by caesarean section after a prolonged and painfully unsuccessful labor. There had been many discussions about how difficult *he* had made the whole process of his birth.) She would take his hand and run it over the length of the scar. Gradually the excursions over the scar were extended so that his hand just brushed against her pubic hair, and finally it was moved over her vulva. She would begin to move his hand more vigorously over her vulva and around her introitus. At this point, she might shift his whole body from alongside her to on top of her. She would then hold his hips and begin to move his whole body, at first gently and then more forcibly over her now moistened genital. He would experience some pain and discomfort from the abrasive contact with her pubic hair over parts of his thighs, genitals, and abdomen. She might suddenly shift to using his thigh or leg more vigorously over her genital. As she rubbed parts of his body against her vulva, he began to stiffen up because he was experiencing the friction against her pubic area and especially her hair as painful. She was uttering soft cooing or chirping sounds; occasionally she might gently sing a nursery rhyme that at other times she rendered to put him to sleep. When he could manage to look up at her while all this was going on, she would gaze into the distance, he recalled, her eyes seemingly unseeing, with a vacuous smile on her face.

He would struggle more as he experienced more discomfort. This seemed to have the effect of exciting her more so that she would increase the vigor of her manipulations. He might flail out with his arms, also trying to push himself away from her body. This effort further excited her and she would intensify the stimulation of her genital area with his body. He would finally collapse—his body going limp. She would become angered by his sudden limpness, and more forcefully use his body in an even more frantic manner—apparently hoping to encourage further struggling on his part, and he would escape into a profound hypnoid state.

The hypnoid state experienced on the couch and subject to analysis was accompanied by a specific dream image. This image—"I see myself falling through a grating"—depicted the patient's observation of the process of removing himself from contact with me during the analytic session. It also dramatized his psychological removal from his mother's overstimulation, which had also provided an outlet for the discharge of his own excitement. The process of withdrawing into hypnosis was turned into visualized metaphor. The attempt at mastery of his state of mind by this kind of image formation was meant to compensate for the lack of control of his mind and body experienced during the seduction assault itself. The emphasis on mastery via fantasy construction (with fantasy gratification taking precedence over interest in realistic activity) did prove fateful for the patient's specific psychological functioning.

His association to his dream image then led to a fear he recalled having experienced as a child of being broken and thrown away like a toy soldier. As a five- to six-year-old child he played endlessly with his toy soldiers. He frequently ended up destroying them. He would also touch these toys to his penis and recalled how much pleasure this provided. Playing with the toy soldiers directly and symbolically meant playing with his penis. His fear of being broken and discarded like his toy soldiers was a manifestation of the body-phallus equation. It thus became apparent that he had expected his mother to destroy his body and/or phallus, and, in fantasy devour him in her vagina. He had thus elaborated and altered the sexual activity that had taken place with his mother during the period of naps into masturbatory fantasies that accompanied his games with his toy soldiers. Later, the fantasies dominating his adolescent and adult masturbation involved a strange woman whom he would actively seduce with variations of elaborate schemes devised to excite his reluctant, struggling female victim. There was a progression (in the service of mastery) from actual sexual activity which he experienced as a passive victim, to masturbatory sexual fantasies in which he, in effect, became the active sexual performer. From his associations it was apparent that these strange women all stood for his mother. It is clear too that he identified with his victim and thus, with his mother. His hypnoid states in analysis thus represented a masturbatory equivalent which permitted the gratification of unconscious masturbatory fantasies. These involved exhibiting his erect penis and thus exciting and seducing various reluctant women. The accompanying erection dramatically gratified his exhibitionistic wishes and boldly proclaimed his sexual excitement. His dream image represented the equivalent of a masturbatory fantasy. The hypnoid condition could also have depicted the clouding of consciousness which may accompany an orgastic state, for he associated to this state the same kind of feeling that he associated with a masturbatory climax.

The symptom complex with the altered state of consciousness can be regarded as hysterical; it fits Freud's characterization—the precipitate of a reminiscence (1916, p. 396). In this instance what was reenacted was the memory of the traumatic seduction and the related unconscious fantasies which accompanied masturbation. The altered state on the couch was not only a defense against reexperiencing the memory of the seductive assault, but also, like any hysterical symptom, permitted the possibility of gratification via the masturbatory element which was being manifested by the fantasy.

DISCUSSION

Freud (1954) called masturbation the primary addiction. The ingestion of alcohol leads to an altered state of consciousness which may have an equivalence to that associated to masturbation, to which it has been linked: "It is striking how often we find that the struggle of the alcoholic with himself or with his environment in combatting or indulging the forbidden enjoyment of drinking is an actual repetition of his original fight for or against masturbation" (Simmel 1948, p. 11). At the same time, the altered state may also be invoked as a defense against the awareness of fantasies and memories involving earlier parental assaults and indiscretions.

In the psychotherapy clinic cases, it was ascertained that one psychological consequence of the ingestion of alcohol was the *illusion* (Silber 1974) that impaired functions had consequently been restored to optimal functioning. Specifically these were certain autonomous ego functions whose intactness is essential for any psychotherapeutic situation—that is, self observation or verbalization. For the alcoholic, alcohol ingestion, and the supervening altered awareness, promoted the use of fantasy formation as a defense against the recognition of his own compromised functioning and painful life circumstances. The unwelcome reality in regard to both past and present was denied while the fantasies, which invariably involved the patient actively overcoming sexual and aggressive obstacles, provided a welcome gratification. The pleasure in fantasy formation during alcohol ingestion might have mirrored the pleasure in constructing masturbatory fantasies which became the main source of satisfaction for the patient in analysis whose brief history was reported. In the alcoholic his pleasure in handling his glass of liquor and swallowing it can be substituted for the pleasurable manipulation of his penis. (See Arlow 1953 for discussion of the two aspects of masturbation: physical manipulation of the organ involved, and the fantasy accompanying this manipulation.)

In this way alcohol—leading to a hypnoid state—encouraged the construction of fantasies capable of absorbing the interest and satisfying the libidinal longings of the individual. An important advantage of alcohol is that it permits the individual to bring about this altered state from outside his own body, and at will. So the hypnoid state, a necessary defense against experiencing too much pain or anxiety (as related to earlier assaults and seductions), is now brought about in a controlled and magical way by the effects of the ingestion of alcohol. The actively sought hypnoid state helps maintain in repression the earlier victimization. Secondarily, the process of constructing and weaving together these many fantasies can bring satisfaction in and of itself. Interest in the real world and its objects are loosened, and the fantasy life of the individual flourishes.

From the analytic case example cited, it can be seen that in fantasy, the libidinal involvement remains with the original object (parent), who was so destructive to the patient's psychological development. This parent neither functioned as a good-enough parent nor provided what Harmann (1939) would call an average expectable environment.

In the clinical example involving the alcoholic patient with his psychotic father and withdrawn mother, the induction of the hypnoid state and the evocation of the many pleasurable unconscious fantasies (in regard to the bar, the barkeeper, the alcohol, and the vessel in which it was served) also preserved his link to his inadequate, destructive parents. The induced hypnoid state removed the pain connected with the conscious awareness of a barren home life. What was consciously experienced was a sense of quietness in which the patient's body felt at ease and comfortable, his stomach felt warm and glowing, and he consciously fantasized that he was suffused with a sense of well being. His environment was a friendly one and he imagined that this was what home was really like.

For the supervised clinic patients the ingestion of alcohol and the ensuing modification of consciousness permitted an intolerable reality to be altered. Thus alcohol can, in a magical way, and at will, alter the state of consciousness. The ensuing hypnoid state then effects the perception, appreciation, meaning, and meaningfulness of the immediate external environment (in regard to people or things) as well as of the internal environment (which includes the awareness of one's body and one's sense of self). The affects related to any of these experiences are also subject to modification by the willfully induced hypnoid state.

The more the state of awareness is modified by the ingestion of alcohol, the greater the possibility of gratifying one's wishes by the construction of fantasies. Some patients will attempt to act on these fantasies in relation to their immediate environment. The other occupants of the bar are viewed as idealized members of an ideally conceived family. When the bar patron attempts to fulfill these expectations, altercations can take place. Unfortunately, one patron's fantasies will not always match those of another. Actions resulting from this discrepancy can be directed against the external environment (affecting people as well as things) or the internal environment (affecting the awareness of one's body and sense of self).

In the analytic patient studied, the hypnoid state permitted the discharge and gratification (via fantasy formation) of the pressing instinctual derivatives and the varied environmental pressures. We can see how the residues of the early seductive assaults were maintained in the masturbatory fantasy life of this patient; the content of the fantasies continually reversing the patient's role to active from the passively experienced trauma—but at the cost of impaired reality functioning.

An alcoholic can use alcohol to bring about a hypnoid state which permits him also to ward off (in a compromise of discharge and defense) affects and ideas connected with early traumatic experiences. Frequently, there can be an acting out of elements of the past traumatic experiences onto the environment. Most important, however, is the fantasy formation and resort to the mechanism of denial furthered by the hypnoid state induced in adults who were seduced and attacked as children. The hypnoid state compulsively sought out by the intake of alcohol may also unconsciously represent the subtly altered awareness that occurs with masturbatory climax (see Freud 1909, Abraham 1910, Keiser 1949, Needles 1953, 1973).

CONCLUSIONS

The hypnoid state described is broader in scope than that defined by Dickes (1965). It remains primarily a defense against painful affects and wishes, as Dickes so effectively documented, but it also defends against the perception of a painful or unpleasant reality. In addition, it promotes the possibility of gratification by encouraging the flowering of unconscious fantasies, often involving the active overcoming of passively sustained traumas. Thus, the frightened child is replaced by an omnipotent man whose gesture brings instant response. The youngster fearful of a screaming father is waited upon by a reassuring and giving barkeeper. Many of these fantasies are of a masturbatory nature. The hypnoid state being described is much like a hysterical symptom—part wish, part defense. It can also be likened to the altered awareness that occurs with masturbatory climax. It is thus a complex entity, magically brought about, at will, by the ingestion of alcohol.

The relationship between the many alcoholic patients, whose histories could be only broadly drawn due to the limited nature of the psychotherapeutic encounter (once-a-week therapy), and the analytic patient, in regard to whom intimate details were available, are similar in the following sense. They both had inadequate parenting.

The fact of the psychotic parent as a developmental reality for so many alcoholic patients, meant the exposure to unprovoked aggression and phase inappropriate behavior. This would likely lead, as reported in children attacked by psychotic parents, to the development of a hypnoid defense. It was possible to trace in detail a hypnoid state which developed during the course of an analysis. It could be defensively induced during treatment by a patient whose background was similar to that of the alcohol clinic patients. The fantasy gratification promoted under the aegis of the hypnoid state was also noted. Similar gratification alongside defense could be evoked by the ingestion of alcohol in the clinic population group.

Thus, the not good-enough mother (or father as the case may be) in a developmental sense continues to cast a shadow over the emotional life of the victim (alcoholic or otherwise). He remains bound to her (in fantasy) for his autoerotic satisfaction. She persists in thwarting his meaningful involvement with other people, long after her traumatic depredations have been forgotten.

REFERENCES

Abraham, K. (1910). Hysterical dream states. In *Selected Papers on Psychoanalysis*, pp. 90-124. New York: Basic Books.

Arlow, J. (1953). Masturbation and symptom formation. *Journal of the American Psychoanalytic Association* 1:45-58.

Chayfetz, M. E. (1959). Practical and theoretical considerations in the psychotherapy of alcoholics. *Quarterly Journal of the Study of Alcohol* 20:281-291.

Dickes, R. (1965). The defensive function of an altered state of consciousness: a hypnoid state. *Journal of the American Psychoanaltyic Association* 13:356-403.

Ferenczi, S. (1933). Confusion of tongues between adults and the child. In *Final Contributions to the Problems and Methods of Psychoanalysis*. New York: Basic Books, 1955.

Fliess, R. (1961). *Ego and Body Ego*. New York: International Universities Press.

Freud, A. (1937). *The Ego and the Mechanisms of Defense*. London: Hogarth.

Freud, S. (1909). Some general remarks on hysterical attacks. *Standard Edition* 9:229-234.

——— (1916). Introductory lectures on psychoanalysis. Part 3. *Standard Edition* 16:392-411.

———— (1926). Inhibitions, symptoms and anxiety. *Standard Edition* 20:7-74.

———— (1954). *The Origins of Psychoanalysis*, ed. M. Bonaparte, A. Freud, and E. Kris. New York: Basic Books.

Greenson, R., and Wexler, M. (1969). The non-transference relationship in the psychoanalytic situation. *International Journal of Psycho-Analysis* 50:27-39.

Hartmann, H. (1939). *Ego Psychology and the Problem of Adaptation*. New York: International Universities Press, 1958.

Keiser, S. (1949). The fear of sexual passivity in the masochist. *International Journal of Psycho-Analysis* 30:162-171.

Loewald, H. W. (1955). Hypnoid state, repression, abreaction and recollection. *Journal of the American Psychoanalytic Association* 3:201-210.

Modell, A. H. (1975). The ego and the id: fifty years later. *International Journal of Psycho-Analysis* 56:57-68.

Needles, W. (1953). A note on orgastic loss of consciousness. *Psychoanalytic Quarterly* 22:512-518.

———— (1973). Orgastic loss of consciousness: its possible relationship to Freud's theoretical nihilism. *International Journal of Psycho-Analysis* 54:315-322.

Schuckit, M., Pitts, F. N., Jr., Reich, T., King, L. J., and Wanokur, G. (1969). Alcoholism. *Archives of General Psychiatry* 20:301-306.

Shengold, L. (1967). The effects of overstimulation: rat people. *International Journal of Psycho-Analysis* 52:403-415.

———— (1971). More about rats and rat people. *International Journal of Psycho-Analysis* 52:277-288.

Silber, A. (1974). Rationale for the technique of psychotherapy with alcoholics. *International Journal of Psychotherapy* 3:28-47.

Simmel, E. (1948). Alcoholism and addiction. *Psychoanalytic Quarterly* 17:6-31.

Winnicott, D. W. (1960). The theory of the parent-infant relationship. In *Maturational Processes and the Facilitating Environment*. New York: International Universities Press, 1965.

———— (1962). Ego interaction in child development. In *Maturational Processes and the Facilitating Environment*. New York: International Universities Press, 1965.

Frightened Men:
A Wish for Intimacy
and a Fear of Closeness

K. H. BLACKER, M.D.

Men who failed to achieve an adequate separation from their mothers are particularly prone to experience serious distress with their marriages during their middle years, when the wish for intimacy, coupled with a fear of closeness never resolved during infancy, is retriggered. An onslaught of biological, social, and psychological stresses force acknowledgement of previously denied needs for succor, plunging them into battle with their wife-surrogate mother. The resulting counterphobic, hypersexual, often self-destructive behaviors are usually falsely interpreted as oedipal. Clinical material in this report strongly suggests this distress is not primarily related to genital sexual issues or fears of castration, but more often concerns issues of autonomy and independence which typically involve the mother and which arose in the toddler or anal phase. Supportive evidence for this thesis from cross-cultural observations, child developmental studies, and primatology is presented, and the usefulness of this view in facilitating clinical work with such men is described.

A middle-aged man, a physician, fled in panic from his home and marriage. An unhappy professor felt constrained and entrapped by his wife. A lawyer longed for intimacy but feared he would be controlled if he loved. These individuals and others like them appear frequently in the consulting rooms of myself and my colleagues.

The problem of distressed middle-aged men (ages thirty-five to fifty-five) has long been recognized and described in the lay press (Fried 1967, Comfort 1974) and in the professional literature. Its high frequency prompted investigators to search for biological factors that might be responsible. It was postulated that physiological changes, shifts in hormonal balance akin to those seen in women at menopause, might cause this distress. This hypothesis was explored and discarded (Prados and Ruddick 1947).

Psychoanalytic and psychiatric literature has stressed the importance of a kindling of castration fears triggered by aging. Decrease in physical powers and sexual potency has been held to foster adolescent-like hyperactivity as individuals attempt to deny castration anxiety and fears of death by a reassertion of masculinity through sexual conquest (Prosen 1976).

A typical case described in this fashion is that of a middle-aged man who sought psychoanalytic treatment because of falling in love with a prostitute (Moore 1960). Although the dynamics were complex, they were interpreted as relating to the patient's feelings that his difficulties were congenital, based on a confusion of the meaning of the word *congenital* with that of *genital*. His fears were interpreted as dealing primarily with punishment and castration, and his complex intellectual defense was seen as the attempt to deal with these fears. His fears were seen as represented in this statement, "Therefore, I do not need to fear losing my penis but may continue to enjoy myself" (p. 312).

The usual explanations, both popular and psychiatric, do not fit several patients I have recently seen in psychotherapy or psychoanalysis. Their fear of women was the *prominent* stress and the fulcrum about which their dynamics were organized. Moreover, this fear seemed to be of a particular type which, to my knowledge, was first described by Loewald (1951). He pointed out that concomitant with the narcissistic attachment to the mother, the child has a primitive fear of being sucked back into the womb. "Libidinal relation to the mother is understood as consisting of the two components: need for union with her and dread of this union" (p. 16).

Mahler et al. (1975), utilizing a series of extensive child-parent observations, recently summarized many of the issues concerning narcissism and separation-individuation. Men's fear of women has been well described in the psychiatric literature (Lederer 1968), but its possible relationships to the crisis of middle-aged males has not been stressed.

Case 1

Dr. A, a panicked forty-year-old physician, called my office seeking an immediate appointment. He stated that he was at a crisis point in his marriage and was uncertain whether to remain at home or separate. In our initial interview, he was anxious and frightened. He reported that he had been married for fifteen years, filled with unhappiness and quarreling. He did say that during several of the early years of the marriage when his wife, a foreigner, was getting acquainted with the new culture, the marriage was quiescent.

He might well have continued this unhappy pattern except that in the previous year he had almost been killed when an errant driver smashed into his car. During several months of hospitalization and the even longer period of recuperation, he became painfully aware of his unhappiness. As he lay in bed, he brooded about his marriage. The more he pondered the more consciously he recognized how controlled, stifled, and trapped he felt. His sex life had almost completely vanished; he no longer had erotic wishes or feelings for his wife. He had only desires to avoid and escape her. Although he was terrified of being alone, his narrow miss from death provided the impetus for flight and an attempt at a better life.

Although Dr. A was a highly successful professional man, he felt that his wife was more powerful. His fear of her was so great that he often felt his wife would walk into his study and stifle him. He literally trembled at the retelling of these events.

Dr. A was an only child. His father died suddenly when he was ten. He lived with his active and powerful mother until he entered medical school. She worked hard, encouraged her son to achieve, and never let him forget how much she was doing for him. Except for explosions of profanity at his mother, Dr. A was a dutiful son. The foreign girl he married was his first serious attempt at social and sexual intimacy.

The parallels between wife and mother were remarkable. With both he was desperately uncomfortable. He avoided his mother's presence. Indeed, a primary motivation for his move to the West Coast was to place 3,000 miles between himself and his mother. Despite the great physical distance, a phone conversation with his mother still gave him gastric distress; nevertheless he felt constrained to call her at weekly intervals. He was angry and resentful at his mother, although for many years, he had been preoccupied with fears of loneliness associated with thoughts of her death.

In our second and third sessions, it became clear that Dr. A had decided to leave the marriage but was concerned with the implications of his decision. Somewhat as an aside, he indicated he was having an affair with a woman some fifteen years his junior. In appearance, Dr. A was far from a confident philandering male. He was completely panicked, he did not feel he could tolerate living with his wife any longer: "I have to get out of there."

The extent of his fear seemed out of proportion to the actual events. His wife, a bright, attractive, socially adept individual, was not unduly upset or angered at him about his present affair. Indeed, his wife had indicated that an affair might be good for him. She saw the affair as a minor episode that would blow over quickly. She did not want a separation, much less a divorce, but wanted to please her husband in whatever ways she could.

Initially, I was puzzled as to the source of Dr. A's terror. His distress did not seem related to feelings of guilt over his recent affair, nor to fear of his wife's leaving. I met with the couple in a joint interview in order to obtain further information. I asked both Dr. A and his wife for an image that would describe their feelings about each other. The wife described a pleasant vista with a large tree from which she plucked fruit. Dr. A's description was also graphic but far less pleasant. He visualized a python winding about and crushing him. The wife's image denied the marital problems and described the succor the marriage provided her. Dr. A's imagery of a constricting snake portrayed his fear of women, wife and mother.

The source of Dr. A's panic became clear. He feared his wife would control him as his mother had controlled him. His fear had reached a crescendo and he was now bolting. It seemed the near-fatal accident had brought the possibility of death forcibly into his life. His helplessness in the face of death apparently recalled to him feelings of weakness before his mother. With this reactivation, the tenuous equilibrium with his wife was broken and he fled the marriage.

Dr. A's actions were in many ways counterphobic attempts to deny feelings of helplessness. The same counterphobic mechanisms had surfaced earlier in his swearing at his mother, were present in his daily life in his blustery, bombastic, interpersonal style, and appeared in the transference as he began to bring a pipe or cigar to the interviews. Despite the development of some trust in me during the course of four years of psychotherapy, he remained fearful of dependent and helpless feelings. He was not able to regress and explore important parts of his life. For example, he was not able to mourn the sudden death of his father at age ten. These and other important experiences remained sealed off, although he did demonstrate considerable improvement.

Case 2

I had the opportunity to explore these ideas in much greater depth when a somewhat younger man, Professor B, age thirty, came to me seeking psychoanalysis. His difficulties were of great intensity and had appeared early in life. While it is conceivable that Professor B's problems are not related to Dr. A's or to the other middle-aged men I have seen, the many similarities, I believe, preclude this possibility. The five years of analytic work with Professor B provided me with a more precise and indepth look at these recurring *infantile* struggles between mother and son as they are played out later in life in the interactions of adult men and their wives.

Professor B sought analysis because of depression and phobias concerning his wife. For example, when Professor B left for work in the morning, his wife insisted he kiss her goodbye. Although he could not resist her command, he cringed as she pecked him and when out of sight, wiped the kiss from his cheek as small children do. He did not allow her to touch his genitals. Although he longed for this, he felt that she was not sensitive enough and that she handled them inappropriately and roughly.

He had frequent terrifying dreams of spiders. He feared being trapped in their webs and destroyed. He often fantasized escaping from his marital predicament by making many sexual conquests, but for many reasons had not left the marriage. Ostensibly, he was afraid a divorce would offend his family. His narcissism led him to fear that his wife would not survive without him. He was also afraid of being alone.

Professor B was the youngest of four children in a tightly knit Italian family. His relative age, five years younger than his next sibling, and the organization of his family resulted in his being raised as an only child. His mother's brother, twelve years older than the patient, also lived with the family and had an important influence on him.

The patient's father was an unsuccessful business man, in stark contrast to several of his uncles who were acclaimed professional men. The family was ambitious and upwardly mobile. Although the father was physically a powerful man, the mother controlled all; she was the dominant parent. The young uncle who lived with the family, though unscrupulous in his dealings, became successful. He often terrified the family when the patient was a young child. He was frequently out of control, and died suddenly, a possible suicide, when the patient was twenty-two. From him, the patient learned to fear direct action and strong emotions.

The initial amorphous characterizations of the parents gradually crystallized as the analysis progressed. The professor had generally experienced his mother as cold, stiff, and distant. There appeared many memories of the mother remaining in bed in the morning long after the father had left for work and the patient, as a small child, had been up and about. He frequently associated to a memory of his mother sitting before her dressing-room mirror, preoccupied with trying on clothes, while he looked longingly on. On still other occasions, he reported the mother had pampered and overindulged him. The father had been experienced as warm and nurturing, but ineffective in coping with or controlling the needs and demands of the mother.

Professor B was a compliant child and an outstanding student. He was mild and self-effacing in all relationships except with his mother. At her, he would sometimes yell and scream abuses. She, and later his wife, was not disturbed by these outbursts. They both seemed to recognize them as "full of sound and fury signifying nothing."

He had several high school sweethearts. However, when he became emotionally close to them, he left them. He chose to attend a university near home. He was successful and rose rapidly in academic stature. At twenty-three, within a year of the uncle's sudden death, he married a "nice Italian girl." He married to please his parents, "to somehow make up for the loss" of the uncle. Before the marriage, the couple lived together and were sexually comfortable but not passionate. After the marriage their sexual relationship almost ceased. He felt resentful, angry, and pressured. He had intercourse every month or so but only when coerced. He vilified his wife in his mind and experienced her as stupid, ugly, inept, and incompetent. His wife, whom I had met briefly at a professional gathering, was, in reality, a moderately attractive, intelligent professional woman. He often teased her saying, "Why don't you let me go? I'm kidding." Despite the abuse, she wished to continue the marriage.

His relationship with men was distant and competitive. Frightened of homosexual advances, he could not tolerate men touching him. He feared he would be forced into a passive homosexual relationship. Behind this fear was the wish to curl up in a strong man's arms.

Presenting himself as inept and incompetent, he protested that he needed guidance regarding every decision in his life, minor and major. He was extremely talented in these efforts, for he had every female colleague and most male colleagues offering him continuous support and advice—advice which, of course, he had ambivalent feelings about and which he rarely accepted. This pattern was played out over and over in the transference. The pull on me was to aid this helpless baby; but only by not aiding his feigned helplessness and by not attacking him out of frustration with such a passive, difficult child, was I able to help him slowly recognize the problem and improve.

Transference issues can be observed in the contents and interactions of early psychoanalytic sessions. It is important to reemphasize that the man who presented himself in such a passive and socially inept fashion was, at the same time, a highly competent member of a university faculty, a Phi Beta Kappa, and the former student body president of his junior and senior high school.

Prior to our first analytic session, the professor phoned and asked for direction to my office, though I had previously given them to him. He lay on the couch in the initial analytic session, one foot on the floor and one foot on the couch. He talked of his hopes and fears for the analysis. He wanted to please me and feared rejection. He asked whether he should place his shoes on the couch or whether he should take his shoes off. I told him either way. He removed his shoes, placed them neatly on the floor, and reclined. He recalled his mother objecting to his putting his feet on the living room couch. I told him that I thought he was trying to please me by removing his shoes. He agreed and added he wanted to be as unobtrusive as possible.

In a subsequent hour, he talked of his shame at presenting himself in such a weak fashion. Again, he lay half on and half off the couch. When I inquired about his posture, he said he did not want to get the couch dirty. He explained, "shoes are dirty." He didn't want to put dirty shoes on the couch, but if he took his shoes off his socks were dirty. He didn't want to put dirty socks on the couch either. He remained perplexed. He described feeling like "a peasant girl in the presence of a nobleman." Later in the hour, he commented on this image and noted its feminine identification and passivity.

During the early phases of analysis he had frequent associations concerning his unworthiness and my nobility. In his thoughts he was Italian—a Wop and dirty. I was a Wasp and clean. Only in the middle and later portions of the analysis did he reverse the images. At that point I became inferior and inept, lacking the gifts and strengths of his ethnic background.

In one hour, after a long period of silence, he talked about his unease with a male colleague who touched him while talking to him. He thought his discomfort must be related to feelings about being a homosexual. Immediately after making the statement, he said that the statement was probably not true. He described feelings of being a "wimp" and inadequate. He recalled memories from junior high school when he had compared the size of his penis to those of the other boys. He associated to difficulties urinating in public bathrooms, and was uncomfortable talking about these things. He thought of screaming and shouting, then suddenly became aware of images of breasts in the wood paneling of the office and felt comforted. He thought perhaps psychotherapy would be better for him than psychoanalysis. He understood that in psychotherapy the therapist told you the answers. He wanted answers from me, but I didn't give him answers.

In the first month of the analysis, a series of associations further defined the nature of the developing transference. He frequently stated he wanted to remain unobtrusive, yet at the same time he worked very hard to please his students, colleagues, and analyst. Several times he reported fantasies of being carried away by a woman. He thought the fantasies indicated a very feminine posture. He wondered if perhaps he would make a good woman. He reported a tingling in his body as he talked about these matters. Another hour, he talked about his religion. He wished he could open himself to it and have a purposeful life. He felt that his mother had done this. He recalled a childhood fantasy of fainting before God. He was aware as he talked of a fullness of his bladder and of bowel pressure. In the next hour he had the idea that, maybe, what he wanted to do was to "just roll up in a little ball and have Mother say, 'there, there.' "

In his associations he offered himself like a helpless, degraded child to a powerful parent. Although the analyst was male, he frequently associated to desires to be close to his mother, or to fear of offending Mother. He also presented himself as the passive feminine victim of a powerful male, the analyst. Fantasies of mother, child, and homosexual surrender were interwoven.

Resolution of transference distortions and changes in the professor's relationship to the analyst took place through the many months of analysis. Two dreams reported in the last month of the analysis and the patient's associations to them portray some of these changes. The first dream took

place in a large university auditorium. The analyst was sitting in a row in front
of him near the bottom of the amphitheater. He was talking to the analyst
about his analysis, about what the analysis meant to him. The analyst was
facing him. Everyone was listening. In the analyst's eye he saw that the analyst
was proud of him. Time was getting short, but he kept on talking. He stopped.
The analyst was proud of his leaving the analysis with such strength.
Everybody applauded.

The professor's voice was full of emotion and he choked as he talked about
the dream. In a sensitive fashion, he interpreted the meaning of the dream and
the dream's relationship to the rapidly approaching termination of analysis.
Particularly important to the professor was the feeling of being on a par with
the analyst, sitting face to face, working together as colleagues. In actuality,
the patient remained on the couch. Physically he was still in a down position,
but his internal images had changed.

The second dream occurred the night before the professor was scheduled to
lecture at an important conference. In the dream a man with a tremendous
penis stood before a large audience. The people in the audience paid homage
to him and touched his penis. The man ejaculated. The fluid sprayed forth
over the entire audience. The semen kept coming and coming.

The professor said he was the man in the dream. In an open fashion,
interlaced with appropriate humor, he described the dream as relating to his
scheduled lecture, his ambitions, and his desires to be admired and loved. The
dream's highly charged symbolic content and the professor's pride in actively
interpreting the dream in a knowledgeable and witty fashion were markedly
different from the dull ramblings of the subservient patient of the initial
analytic hour, when colorless productions and timid demeanors had
camouflaged impulses to be bright and exciting.

Professor B developed a greater sense of self- and personal-strength. He
became active in his life and able to make decisions. His perception of me as a
distant, omnipotent, omniscient God or Goddess requiring servitude from
him, a weak small child, changed. He was able to show off, to brag of his
considerable accomplishments, and to attack me. At the same time he was
also able to recognize his fondness for me and his desire to be close to me.

He became better able to tolerate both aggressive and passive wishes. He
divorced his wife and set up bachelor's quarters. Somewhat to his surprise, his
analyst, wife, family, and he survived the separation. He found pleasure in
being able to establish his own living patterns and felt a new sense of freedom.

He began several sexual affairs. Several months later he found a steady girl
friend, but insisted on his independence. On one occasion, when she placed
some clothes in his closet, he became tremulous and fearful. He began
experiencing pleasure in his sexual activities. Another girl appeared on the

scene who was of his social and educational background and he began living with her. He enjoyed having her with him and was not frightened or dominated by her. As the analysis ended, Professor B was living with this girl, planning to marry and have children.

Professor B's changing relationship with women can also be monitored by observing changes in reported dreams. Not all of his dreams regarding women were concerned with this main theme. For example, several dreams regarding his mother toward the end of the analysis were classically oedipal. The dreams described below, however, are particularly striking in their content and are selected to illustrate the sequential changes in his view of himself and women.

At the beginning of his analysis, Professor B reported that since childhood he had suffered frequent nightmares concerning spiders. Typically, these dreams consisted of his being caught in a web and rendered helpless, while a menacing, perhaps devouring, spider came closer and closer. The spider dreams appeared in the analysis when he felt helpless and trapped in his marriage. His report of the spider and the web sounded remarkably like his view of his wife and marriage. This was the period during which, under duress, he would kiss his wife at leave-taking and then later wipe the kiss off. In his marriage he felt unable to move, smothered—a total lack of freedom, an almost total engulfment.

Later, Professor B began to describe the spider in such dreams as black, a black widow. These dreams reflected his initial protestations of helplessness and ineptness, his cry for the analyst to help him with each and every decision. He offered himself up as a helpless fly to the analyst spider. Evidence for the growing importance of the analyst was seen as the spider became black— Blacker—the name of his analyst. As the analysis progressed, the spider dream took on a more immediate and precise meaning as Professor B found himself entrapped within the analytic web by the developing transference.

During the middle third of the analysis, the patient reported another spider dream but the dream contained new elements: "I dreamt again of a spider last night. It came down from the ceiling and was close by my head. It was yellow and black. I blew it back up the web. I wasn't frightened. A woman came along and squashed it instead of admiring the beautiful web as I had thought she would." In this dream he was not terrified. He looked at the spider and played with it. In his associations, the professor identified the woman who squashed the spider as a competitive colleague, a colleague who had frightened him in the past but with whom he could now compete and work. In his associations, he also described the good qualities of his girl friend much as, in his dream, he had observed the multicoloring on the spider. His women were still powerful and could still squash, but no longer were they unidimensional. They were now interesting and colored as well as potentially powerful and black.

Several months following the dream of the multicolored spider, he dreamt of a large crab-like monster. In this dream, the professor stood on the monster's back, on one of its armored plates, and shoved his spear deep into its vitals, killing it. He was pleased with the dream and his heroic actions.

In an hour during the last third of the analysis, the patient initially reported "eminently successful sex." By this he meant that during lovemaking, his girl friend had gotten on top of him. His sexual excitement had continued and both had enjoyed intercourse very much. Although his girl friend was on top, he had not been threatened nor frightened. He was amazed that he had not felt dominated and controlled while on the bottom.

The professor went on to describe further success. During the same night he had a dream in which he successfully defended himself. In this dream he was on his way home when an old man had tried to hit him with a telescope. He easily avoided the old man's blow and continued home. This description was immediately followed by the report of a second dream. In this dream, Joan, his girl friend, stood with him on a lecture platform in a large hall. She took off all her clothes and stood in high heels. The audience admired her sensual beauty. He was proud because she was beautiful and sexy. In the dream the professor fielded comments and questions from the audience with alacrity and dazzling brilliance. He was particularly astute in his answers to the series of questions posed by a female professor. The audience, amazed and excited, whispered to one another, "That guy knows what he is about."

In his associations to the dream, he talked of an active and comfortable life with Joan. He was now able to share with her without feeling dominated or controlled. He described increasing sexual pleasure and recent academic success, Though he had always been a productive scientist, he had never felt able to hold his own in department politics. He now felt capable of defending himself, as he had in the dream, and was engaged in several political battles.

In this important hour, we can see further evidence of assurance and control: He felt comfortable being passive in intercourse. He was capable of managing a threatening old man with the telescope (the analyst). He shared the accolades and admiration of the large audience with his girl friend. Her femininity and sensuality and his brilliance were acclaimed. In several preceding dreams, his women walked behind him as in old China. Now the woman shared the same platform.

Near the end of his analysis, the patient reported the following dream: A beautiful cousin stood naked before him. From her large voluptuous breasts warm milk flowed. He became excited and made love to her. It was wonderful. In his associations it became clear the dream image of a bounteous, giving, embracing woman was of a perfect mother-goddess—the culmination of the patient's deep longings and fears. In his associations he told of Joan's warmth and of her capacity to give. He also added that she could "turn on you and tear you apart." He had been fearful to nurse from a woman, to take from a woman, to make love to a woman. Now he was able to. He could be close, nurse, and not fear. "Beautiful nursing, yea, that's the life." He also referred to a dream reported earlier in the week in which he was an astronaut returning to "Mother-Earth." In the reporting he also talked freely of his desire to sit on the analyst's lap, secure in the feeling that he could enter or leave when he wished.

Professor B's wishes for intimacy and fears of closeness found expression in his relationships with both men and women. At the beginning of analysis, he feared being touched by both. With his wife he feared being controlled and trapped as the spider in the dream had trapped him in her web. With his colleagues he feared homosexual rape, that is, control and physical penetration. Behind these fears were the wishes to be mothered in a strong person's arms.

Initially, he felt powerless to defend himself against assault or control by wife or colleagues. His reaction had been to develop an isolated pseudoindependent existence. As the analysis progressed, he gained more strength. His dreams illustrated his perception that he was now equal to, at times even superior to, his male analyst and to strong women. In his dreams, he killed monsters, sprayed semen over a large audience, loved and suckled from an earth goddess, and as an astronaut, returned to Mother Earth. Feeling strong enough to say no, he could now permit himself to say yes. Feeling a sense of strength and identity, he developed a capacity for mutuality.

Case 3

Sexual impotency and constant conflict with a wife are clearly related to issues of autonomy and control in the life of a third patient, Mr. C, a thirty-nine-year-old lawyer. The exuberant, only child of middle-class parents, he had been constantly reminded as a child not to "act up, don't be silly." As a child he had felt loved and smothered by his mother. As an adult he longed to love his wife but feared being controlled. The several clinical excerpts reported below were taken from the middle portion of his analysis.

In this hour Mr. C attempted to describe his feelings about intimacy. "It's something much greater, something much larger than sticking a pecker into a vagina." I asked for his associations. He began talking about commitment, involvement, dedication. "Somehow this all seems to be a natural and an appropriate part of intimacy and yet it has a fearful connotation. . . . It means surrender or envelopment. Part of it seems to be a kind of dues or an obligation or a requirement to pay back. The significance is getting swallowed up, that I can't get away from the person."

Later in the hour he described sexual intercourse and intimacy as equivalent. "There is a connotation to me that is unacceptable. I can feel being afraid of that. I can feel it right now as I talk. Perhaps it's the intimacy, it's a terribly, terribly intimate thing. That's what drives me away. Which at the same time is the thing that I may want. I want to belong but I don't want to belong, to anyone or anything. It's terribly, terribly intimate. There is a terribleness about the intimacy. You can't be intimate without being owned.

"I want to be loved, cuddled, and liked. But I don't want to give up. I don't want to do that. I have a stubborn sort of attachment to not doing it. In a way it signifies my identity. If I did want to, I would lose my maturity, my manhood, my identity. If I did it, I would be somebody's pawn."

Mr. C's struggles with issues of separation-individuation are expressed in his sexual difficulties. He longs for closeness and sensual pleasure; however, if he would succumb to these womanly enticements, he fears he would lose his identity. At this point, only by saying no does he feel he can maintain his separateness.

DISCUSSION

Fear of Women. References to man's fear of women have been compiled and identified by Wolfgang Lederer (1968) in a fascinating book aptly titled, *The Fear of Women.* In his introduction he stated:

> In the unashamed privacy of our consulting room we do from time to time see strong men fret, and hear them talk of women with dread and horror and awe, as if women, far from being timid creatures to be patronized, were powerful as the sea and inescapable as fate. . . . A lawyer races his sports car home, lest his wife accuse him of dawdling. A pilot cannot get married because he is nauseated by womanish toilet smells which recall his mother's sanitary napkins. A student shudders at the hair on his girl's arms and an engineer is morbidly fascinated and repelled by varicose veins. A full-sized man has nightmares that his wife, in bed, will roll on him and crush him. (p. 7)

Dr. Lederer concluded his book:

> For each of us the task is laid out from the beginning, from birth: we all run essentially the same obstacle course. We each must learn to escape her seductive embrace, and yet return to her; we must destroy the teeth in her vagina, and yet love her poignantly and tenderly; we must defeat the Amazon in order to protect her; we must drink sustenance and inspiration from her dark well, and yet not drown in it; and we must cater to her insatiable needs, and not be destroyed by them; we each must define ourselves as men in opposition to women as nature, and yet not lose our humanity in frigid isolation. (p. 23)

The feminist accusation that the physical attributes of a wife play an important role in man's defending himself against the power of a woman may be correct. "Men may marry mother figures but only if they are safely powerless. Wives are generally younger, less mobile and physically smaller than their husbands—and their husband's childhood mother. Men do not violate incest taboo. They do not recreate certain critical conditions of their childhood" (Chesler 1972, p. 138). This pattern is even more clearly evident in other contemporary and ancient cultures. For example, with the ancient Greeks there was "a tendency for males to marry barely pubescent girls, and to encourage their women to practice depilation of all body hair" (Slater 1968). This apparently diminished their fear of the dominating mother.

Developmental Issues.   How are we to understand this terror of women? A man's relationship with a woman begins at conception. Initially, male fetus and mother are one. During fetal development the two are physiologically tied together. At birth the direct physical ties are broken by the disruption of the umbilical cord. However, a complex web of physiological and behavioral attachments between the two still exists. For example, an infant's cries will produce distress or lactation in the mother. Built-in behaviors like the rooting mechanism guide the infant's mouth to the nipple. Only gradually, over months, do these physiological ties lessen, and only over years, do psychological bonds diminish.

Initially, the infant experiences himself and the world as one. Slowly he differentiates from the world; he differentiates, separates from his mother. If the process proceeds in a healthy fashion the infant emerges with a feeling of basic trust (Erikson 1963). The next developmental phase involves the issue of autonomy. This phase, the terrible twos, contains a rapid growth of cognitive structures and is often filled with many struggles. Recent work (Fraiberg and Adelson 1973; Meeks 1971) has stressed the importance of the mother's continuing influence through the anal and phobic phases, and even throughout adolescent development.

Further development continues throughout the life span, each age having its specific tasks and achievements. Each age is influenced or colored by the solutions of the preceding ages. Each age contains its pathologies as well as its victories.

It is my contention that the basis of the middle-aged crisis in some men, perhaps in many, is a failure to have achieved an adequate separation from their mothers, a failure to have developed an adequate sense of autonomy. In cases I have observed, the men were fawned on and pampered as children. They maintained a facade of independence during their late adolescence, their twenties, and early thirties by means of almost total involvement in school and profession. In this fashion they obtained a distance or a pseudoautonomy from their mothers and wives. At middle-age this delicate equilibrium was exploded by a confluence of forces, psychological, social, and biological.

Withdrawing or recoiling from the wife is a typical behavior of the men I have described and it seems, to me, its roots lie in the processes described by Mahler. "We have observed many of our normal children recoiling from mother or showing other signs that had to be interpreted as a kind of eroticized fear upon being cornered by the mother who wanted playfully to seek bodily contact with the child. . . . These behaviors, we feel, were signs of the fear of reengulfment by the narcissistically invested, yet defended against, dangerous 'mother after separation'" (Mahler et al. 1975, p. 118).

Physical illness, threat of death, failure to advance professionally, almost any event which caused them to feel weak or helpless, triggered, using Mahler's term (Mahler and Furer 1968), a new rapprochement crisis. A new battle, like the old one with the mother, was now fought with the wife-surrogate mother. Issues squashed but never resolved at ages two, three, or four—issues centering on intense conflicting desires for dependence and freedom, succorance and autonomy—were rekindled and refought. The apparent adolescent-like rebellious activities were in reality more akin to the temper tantrum of a toddler.

The men I have described are neurotic; they have obsessive character neuroses. They are not borderline. They have clearly differentiated themselves from their mothers (Mahler and Furer 1968). In their histories and fantasies and in interactions in treatment, the other person is sharply discerned. There are no fears of fusing, melting, or disappearing into the important other. There is, however, a strong mixture of narcissism, omnipotence, and negativism—a mixture which reflects important elements of the failure to resolve the rapprochement crisis.

Loewald's comments (1951) can also be helpful here. Toward the mother there is originally a positive libidinal attachment "growing out of the primary narcissistic position." There is also a negative, defensive one "of dread of the womb, dread of sinking back into the original unstructured state of identity with her" (p. 16). Both a pull and a fear are experienced by the child. Loewald states the father is of crucial importance in resolving this developmental dilemma. According to Loewald, despite the castration threat from the father there is also a positive identification, even primary to the development of the oedipus complex, which utilizes the attachment to the father as a defense and an alliance against a fear of being swallowed up by the womb. As noted in the clinical material, the fathers of Dr. A and Professor B were either physically absent (dead) or psychologically absent (ineffective); the normal development issue was therefore not resolved.

Dominance and Sexuality.   When these heterosexual men became fond of women they wished to be loved but feared being dominated. When they became fond of men (experienced wishes for tenderness and closeness) they feared being dominated by the men which they also experienced as homosexual feelings or a homosexual surrender. They consciously feared being overwhelmed and raped, and that they would be found out as latent homosexuals. Many of these concerns have been described by Ovesey (1969) as pseudohomosexual.

This transformation of the interpersonal power of the mother into its later perception as physical and sexual forces may be less confusing if we consider primate behavior where sexual behaviors are clearly used to signify power and dominance (Vangaard 1972). "An animal is said to present to another animal when it takes on the attitude of a female willing to be mounted. . . . This use of presentation as a signal of submission is found in particular among animals which are able to do each other serious harm. . . . Mounting and presentation are used as signals among baboons, regardless of sex. For instance, a young male will present to an older, stronger female, and she may mount him. Among the females presentation and mounting are used in the same way."

These men had never developed a sense of individual strength or autonomy. They feared psychological penetration by women (being mounted and dominated by women). They also feared physical penetration by men (being mounted and screwed by men). Both with strong women and strong men, they were submissive, and experienced homosexual fears. It was as if they were aware of the subjective experience of presenting themselves (presenting in the animal behavioral sense of offering their bottom to a more dominant animal).

These men experienced fears of being dominated by women and men in different ways. When they spoke of women, they described fears of being trapped and controlled. When they spoke of men, they initially made vague references to homosexuality. Careful inquiry revealed they feared men would catch them, hold them, rape them, and humiliate them. Their homosexual concerns were not built upon erotic interests but were derived from feeling weak in relationship to a strong male, from issues of dominance and control. These men reacted to other men as if humans as well as primates climbed on top of the weaker animal and used sexual physical mounting to signify dominance.

Middle-aged men frequently have sexual affairs with younger, less educated women. I view these affairs as attempts to assert dominance over women, an attempt, so to speak, of one upmanship. It is an attempt to deny feelings of weakness experienced with the wife-surrogate mother. For a male, success in sexual intercourse leads to self-assurance. Indeed, according to Abernethy (1974), primatological, ethnographic, and psychiatric data strongly suggest "male dominance facilitates male-female copulatory behavior while female dominance inhibits it" (1974, p. 813).

Abernethy's brief article produced a flurry of support and critiques. Trosman (1975) felt that "the notion of dominance seems insufficient to resolve the affective components in the relationship of such men to their sexual objects." Pitman (1974, 1975), however, suggested Freud's observations that a certain type of neurotic individual "only develops full potency when he is with a debased sexual object" lent support to Abernethy's hypothesis.

Krales (1974) was critical of the possible sexist implications of the hypothesis. Friedman (1975) criticized the hypothesis on methodological grounds feeling that it was reductionistic, its concepts too broad to be testable, and that supporting information offered was imprecise. Abernethy, in her reply (1975), felt that Friedman had missed the point in that the usefulness of a hypothesis was to organize and stimulate research. She also disagreed with Friedman's other criticisms and added that her hypothesis was, "unambiguously stated: It can be proved wrong, and it can be broken down into innumerable testable propositions."

Primatologists have generally supported Abernethy's thesis. Jensen (1974) agreed that it is apparently true that "male dominance facilitates the male's sexual behavior." He had earlier (1972) suggested that status or dominance may explain why male chimps and monkeys had never been observed mating with their mothers. Maple (1975) described recent work in which investigators changed the usual male-female dominance among primates by caging male rhesus monkeys with larger female baboons. They found that "sexual behavior may be quicker to develop when males are dominant over females, but sexual behavior is still possible when the male is subordinate, especially when there are no alternatives for sexual contact." However, Maple added, "Under natural conditions, when sexual dimorphism prevails, nonhuman primates do seem to behave accordingly to her (Abernathy's) view; . . . "Male dominance facilitates male-female copulatory behavior while female dominance inhibits it."

Gina Bari Kolata's recent review (1976) clearly points out the many pitfalls inherent in the conceptualization and measurement of dominance in primate sexual studies. Male sexual activity is related to many factors. There are many differences from species to species. For example, old world monkeys and new world monkeys differ markedly in dominance behavior. Also, species differ greatly in their sensitivity to childhood deprivations. Monkeys, for example, are much less able to recover from childhood deprivations than chimpanzees. Even the behaviors within a species will differ, depending upon whether they live in grass lands, forests, islands, city areas, or in captivity.

The above evidence suggests that within broad limits the biological underpinnings for sexual activity and sexual inhibition in humans and primates are probably derived from similar sources. When these men I described felt weak and powerless in their relationships with their wives, they became impotent. Frequently they attempted to bolster feelings of self-worth by a biological means (through sexual conquest of women). This sexual activity seemingly represented their attempts to reassert dominance over a wife-mother surrogate.

Speculations concerning parallels between man and primate behavior can be useful. Although there are similarities between the two, it is important to remember that differences are also large and that speculations can lead to distortion and false assumptions. Such comparisons are most helpful when they lead to the development of hypotheses which promote new investigations. Abernathy's suggestion, for example, seems to be a good example of such a hypothesis.

Social and Cultural Factors.   As these frightened men moved into their middle years, their fragile relationships with women came under greater pressure. In addition to increasing awareness of death and to physical changes which may be experienced as decreasing strength and potency, there were threatening social and role changes. During middle-age, across a wide variety of cultures—in East Indians, American Indians, Middle-Eastern peasantry, and middle-class Americans (Gutmann 1973)—there is a pronounced and major shift in sexual attitudes. Gutmann (1974) found that males "during their youth and adulthood, are competitive, even combative, but mainly focused toward disciplined productive achievement. They are striving to control the sources for security for themselves and their dependents." During this time most men expel from their consciousness longings for pleasure and security that might distract them from their role as provider and defender.

Later in life as the social and economic pressures shift, the psychological structures established by men and women in response to the previous situation change, and important sex role reversals occur. Men begin to live out directly the passivity, the sensuality, or the tenderness, in effect, the femininity, previously expressed in the service of production and defense. By the same token we find, across a wide range of societies, the opposite effect on women.

If, as Gutmann suggests, these shifts typically occur, it would follow that a man who is uncomfortable about his maleness would become frightened and upset. His fears would also be accentuated by the response of the woman who now, after the child-rearing years, takes a more active and aggressive role. Physical changes have also occurred so that when the husband looks across at his wife, he no longer views a nymph but sees a mature woman who may look remarkably like the woman who mothered him when he was an infant and child. Indeed, in many families in our culture, the husband, along with the children, calls his wife "Mother."

Social and psychological issues interacted to shift the balance of power in Dr. A's marriage. His wife had become more psychologically secure as she had grown attuned to and at ease with her new culture. She also had more energy available after her children had entered school. In addition, she was physically stronger than Dr. A during his period of recuperation from his auto accident. Similarly, Mr. C's wife became more energetic and aggressive as she moved into middle age. Such shifts undercut the delicate equilibrium these men had maintained, and their fears of women broke through in more primitive and psychologically disturbing forms. Subtle shifts associated with midlife changes added fuel to their unresolved conflicts.

In our American culture an almost total pursuit of material rewards or professional success had enabled some men to temporarily sidestep conflicts regarding intimacy. Often, however, the attainment in middle age of two cars, a large house, corporate success, or multiple degrees and awards fails to fill the void. The resulting disillusionment leads in turn to a new openness or awareness of a tremendous neediness. Moreover, as these men subsequently attempt to move toward intimacy with the wife and others, they become terrified, as they are again caught up in a conflict with the mother they so long struggled to avoid.

TREATMENT

These men appear for therapy at times of crisis, often marital crisis. They feel exposed, vulnerable, frightened, and panicked. They feel humiliated in asking for the help and support they desperately desire. The therapist is faced with the difficult problem of providing needed support and information in a manner that will not be misinterpreted by a patient as seductive and controlling. A helpful neutrality is essential.

Some dilemmas in treating this group are: If a patient does not experience some support and relief as he meets with a therapist, he will leave therapy. However, if he feels the therapist is overly solicitous or overly supportive, he may bolt, fearing that he will be controlled as his mother controlled him. His perception of the therapist as an overly helpful mother may also prevent him from being able to experience and examine the anger he holds toward such important others. Therapy will then consist only of a reexperiencing of the same problems without offering the possibility of new solutions.

At the beginning of treatment, Dr. A could only describe his difficulties in a confused, highly abstract, intellectual manner. He seemed to be somewhat aware of his confusion and of his need to psychologically distance himself from the immediate threatening events. To have insisted on immediate clarification would have challenged him and panicked him further. I acknowledged the pain and confusion he was feeling and indicated that as we talked further he would feel more secure, in command, and able to cogently describe and approach his problems.

Moralizing, offering simplistic solutions to these extremely complicated, long-term problems is, of course, counterproductive. It must be remembered the patient is presenting an issue which, although acute, is not new and which refers not only to the immediate wife but also to the past mother.

When such a patient enters analysis there is an immediate intense and ambivalent maternal transference. The patient will tempt the analyst to take over and control his life as his mother did. He will offer himself as a helpless individual in need of direct guidance. The analyst must not fail this test and become overly intrusive and controlling; he must maintain an interested, but cool posture if he is to identify and work with the patient's passivity without terrifying him. You will recall that Professor B offered himself up as a helpless fly to his friends and to the analyst-spider. Only by not swallowing the bait, so to speak, could analysis begin and move forward to a successful resolution.

These men elicit powerful and opposite emotions within those who become involved with them. These reactions appear, of course, in the therapist as well as in the spouse, parents, and friends. Their passivity, as mentioned, may evoke mothering responses within a therapist such as the urge to quickly aid such a helpless child. Professor B had most of his colleagues offering him support, suggestions, and aid. On the other hand, the stubbornness and thinly veiled anger of such men may also stimulate a therapist to attack and crush the rebellious child.

I experienced both reactions. I found, somewhat to my surprise, that these emotions might appear when the patient was reporting seemingly innocuous material. I learned to utilize my responses to gain a better perspective of the patient's communications.

It is important to remember the patient is struggling with simultaneously occurring opposite feelings. A most helpful image for me came from a video tape of an interaction between a twenty-eight-month-old toddler and his mother on a nursery room floor. A frustrated boy stood angrily before his mother who was kneeling on the floor, raised his arm with his fist clenched to hit her. As his arm began to descend, his gesture changed from a blow into a hug and he melted into his mother's lap.

It may be difficult for a young male therapist to think of himself as a mother as he treats a male patient who may be his senior in age. He may be tempted to overinterpret competitiveness and castration. A young woman therapist with a middle-aged male may too readily interpret material as seductive and sexual. I do not mean to say that these issues are nor present and should not be worked with. I do wish to stress, however, the importance of developing and maintaining an awareness and sensitivity to issues and to control and to fears of closeness when working with such men.

REFERENCES

Abernethy, V. (1974). Dominance and sexual behavior: a hypothesis. *American Journal of Psychiatry* 131:813.

———— (1975). Letters to the Editor. *American Journal of Psychiatry* 132:1083.

Chesler, P. (1972). *Women and Madness*. New York: Doubleday.

Comfort, A. (1974). Sexuality in a zero growth society. *Reflections*. New York: Merck.

Erikson, E. (1963). *Childhood and Society*. New York: Norton.

Fraiberg, S., and Adelson, E. (1973). Self-representation in language and play: observations and blind children. *Psychoanalytic Quarterly* 42:539-562.

Fried, B. (1967). *The Middle-Age Crisis*. New York: Harper.

Friedman, R. C. (1975). Critique of a hypothesis of dominance and sexual behavior. *American Journal of Psychiatry* 132:967.

Gutmann, D. (1973). The new mythologie and premature aging in the youth culture. *Journal of Youth and Adolescence* 2:139-155.

———— (1974). A comparative approach to parenthood. Unpublished.

Hamburg, D. A. (1974). Recent observations of chimpanzee behavior. Storer Life Sciences Lectures, University of California at Davis. March 7, 1974.

Jensen, G. D. (1972). Primate sexual behavior: its relevance to human sexual behavior. *Medical Aspects of Human Sexuality* 6:112.

———— (1974). Letters to the editor. *American Journal of Psychiatry* 131:1413.

Kolata, G. B. (1976). Primate behavior: sex and the dominant male. *Research News*, January 9, p. 55.

Krales, J. (1974). Letters to the Editor. *American Journal of Psychiatry* 131:1413.

Lederer, W. (1968). *The Fear of Women*. New York: Grune and Stratton.

Loewald, H. W. (1951). Ego and reality. *International Journal of Psycho-Analysis* 32:10-18.

Mahler, M. S., and Furer, M. (1968). *On Human Symbiosis and the Vicissitudes of Individuation*. New York: International Universities Press.

Mahler, M. S., Pine, F., and Bergman, A. (1975). *The Psychological Birth of the Human Infant*. New York: Basic Books.

Maple, T. (1975). Dominance and sexual behavior. Primate Laboratory, University of California at Davis. Unpublished.

Meeks, J. E. (1971). *The Fragile Alliance*. Baltimore: Williams and Wilkins.

Moore, B. E. (1960). Congenital versus environmental: an unconscious meaning. *Journal of the American Psychoanalytic Association* 8:312-316.

Ovesey, L. (1969). *Homosexuality and Pseudohomosexuality*. New York: Jason Aronson.

Pitman, R. K. (1974). Letters to the editor. *American Journal of Psychiatry* 131:1289.

———— (1975). Letters to the editor. *American Journal of Psychiatry* 132:568.

Prados, M., and Ruddick, B. (1947). Depressions and anxiety states of the middle-aged men. *Psychiatric Quarterly* 21:410-430.

Prosen, H. (1976). Change in sex pattern at middle age can indicate midlife crises. *Clinical Psychiatry News* 4:18-19.

Slater, P. (1968). *The Glory of Hera: Greek Mythology and the Greek Family*. Boston: Beacon Press.

Trosman, H. (1975). Letters to the Editor. *American Journal of Psychiatry* 132:568.

Vangaard, T. (1972). *Phallos: A Symbol and its History in the Male World*. New York: International Universities Press.

Weiss, J. (1971). The emergence of new themes: a contribution to the psychoanalytic theory of therapy. *International Journal of Psycho-Analysis* 52:459-467.

Alienation:
Character Neuroses
and Narcissistic Disorders

PETER L. GIOVACCHINI, M.D.

Various defensive adaptations are described that patients with structural defects involving the self-representation (character neurotics) use to adapt to the external world, often achieving an organization sufficiently stable to lead to considerable success. Externalization rather than projection is used. The differences between these two psychic processes are important for our understanding of character neurotics. Projection signifies placing impulses or parts of the self into external objects whereas externalization involves creating or finding a reality to support the defenses, including projecting. The patient externalizes his infantile traumatic environment to construct a current world after his early environment which he finds both threatening and familiar. Clinical material illustrates how the process of externalization operating within the transference context may lead to special technical problems. One type of character neurotic demonstrates a special type of externalization which supports overcompensatory feelings of self-aggrandizement, which are in effect, narcissistic defenses. To varying degrees, all character neurotics have some narcissistic defenses. Countertransference problems are also discussed.

Everyone has a character and perhaps some degree of neurosis, insofar as it is difficult to think of a human being without some defenses against intrapsychic conflict. This generalization, however, minimizes the gravity of psychopathology and the importance of character neuroses as a group.

The possibility that persons with character neuroses constitute a large segment of the population makes them more important rather than less. As is true for any group, there is a spectrum of psychopathological severity. In analytic practice, one tends to see patients whose usual adjustments have failed, but this does not necessarily mean that the patient is severely disturbed. It often does, but just as frequently, patients who from a structural viewpoint have a relatively good integration find it difficult to adapt to their environment and seek psychotherapeutic assistance.

Many clinicians find this group of patients especially intriguing because there may be a wide gap between their ability to function and the extent of their structural defects. In contrast, even some of the most primitively oriented characters have been able to achieve a stable defensive superstructure which permitted them to function adequately. The competence of some character neurotics is striking; some are eminently successful and have achieved positions of power, leadership, and prominence. It is frightening to learn how much psychopathology is covered up by successful achievement in a personage whose responsibilities involve our survival as a civilization.

DEVELOPMENTAL ASPECTS OF
CHARACTER NEUROSES AND TRAUMA

The symbiotic stage can be conceptualized as a phase of emotional development somewhere between a preobject stage and the beginning of rudimentary object relationships (Giovacchini 1972). Patients suffering from character neuroses face specific difficulties in the resolution of symbiotic fusion and this affects the very early stages of object relationships which Freud (1914) described. The narcissistic neuroses, to my mind, are a special type of character neurosis—a type distinguished by its unique and often successful defensive constellation.

I would like to avoid any nosological confusion which might be provoked by classification of the narcissistic neuroses. Freud (1914, 1915) used the term in a very specific way. He had discussed narcissism as a normal developmental stage and also its significance as a pathological vicissitude. In this latter connection, he contrasted the narcissistic neuroses with the transference neuroses and postulated that they are not good candidates for analysis because they do not form transferences whereas the transference neuroses, by definition, do. The depressions and psychoses constitute the narcissistic neuroses and supposedly the libido of these entities is primarily ego-libido, not enough being left over or sufficiently mobile to be converted into object-libido and thereby projected into a transference relationship. The nonoccurrence of transference in depressions and psychoses is no longer an issue. That transference does, indeed, occur is not arguable; it is a simple empirical fact. Nor is narcissism, as it is involved in psychopathology, confined to the adhesiveness of libido to the ego.

Kohut's designation of narcissistic personality disorders (1971, 1972) is purportedly derived from formulations based upon the developmental factors I am discussing here. He conceptualizes narcissistic personality disorders as developmental arrests. The therapist's task is to set the developmental journey in motion once again. I believe, however, that the narcissistic neuroses, which are the same as Kohut's narcissistic personality disorders, are not a primary diagnostic category. I consider them to be distinguished from other disorders by specific defensive adaptations. The developmental difficulties of these patients involve both narcissistic and symbiotic phases, and there are, therefore, disturbances of narcissistic equilibrium, but this is much more complex than fixation on a normal phase of development.

In fact, *there is no such a thing as fixation on a normal phase of development.* Traumatic relationships have interfered with the developmental process, and when forward development is halted or, more precisely, retarded, that particular stage has necessarily undergone pathological distortion. Inasmuch as trauma affects all developmental stages, there must be corresponding pathological distortions of all stages, but these distortions occur primarily, or rather with greater force, at specific psychic stages, which are the points of fixation.

Freud (1916) expressed this idea beautifully in the metaphor of the advancing army. The reader will recall that Freud viewed emotional development as an advancing army. On its way toward its objective (in Freud's psychosexual scheme this would be genital sexuality and intimacy), it has to conquer various outposts. The more difficult the battle at any particular outpost, the more havoc is wreaked and the larger the army of occupation left behind to secure it must be. Freud went on to describe how the now weakened advancing army may meet superior forces and have to retreat. This backward movement presents us with a graphic description of regression: the army will retreat back to the outpost where it left its largest number of troops. This is known as the fixation point. Freud did not, however, elaborate on what happened in this garrison where the first battle was fought. This is the subject of our particular interest.

Battles leave scars. The army of occupation is placed there not only to prevent further battle, but to maintain peace and see that the regular events of everyday living are carried on as smoothly as possible. However, to continue this metaphor briefly, a town run by an army of occupation is not the same as one with a well-functioning representative government.

The situation I have described is that of an ego state that has been damaged and thus, in order to maintain psychic equilibrium, requires certain specific defenses—characterological defenses. The forward motion of developmental forces, the flow of libido as Freud would say, differs from what it would have been, had there been no developmental disturbance.

The defensively held together ego state—one that has undergone pathological distortions—is a fixation point. It represents a developmental arrest, but it is vastly different from a corresponding phase of development that has been achieved fairly smoothly, without trauma or with relatively minimal trauma. Freud was interested most in the movements, that is the advances and retreats, of the army, whereas here, from a characterological viewpoint, our interest is in the structure, components, stability, and organization of the garrison. With such a close scrutiny of ego states in psychopathological conditions, one invariably finds structural defects, especially at the points of most intense fixation.

Returning specifically to character and narcissistic neuroses, fixation occurs chiefly during early stages of object relationships, somewhere between symbiotic fusion and the emergence of good and bad part-objects. Though this is an early developmental stage, there has been considerable psychic integration and cohesion in comparison with other types of character disorder. The part-objects involved are still very primitive and are not yet organized as the stages of psychosexual development (oral, anal, phallic) that Freud viewed as fixation points for the various psychoneuroses. Still, the ego of the character neurotic distinguishes rather well between the self and the outer world and has the capacity to form fairly stable mental representations of external objects and adaptive experiences.

When there are disturbances in early object relationships, disturbances which I believe are the essence of character neuroses, splitting is a prominent defensive mechanism. Character neurotics rely heavily on dissociation in order to keep good and bad internal object representations separate. This is amply illustrated in clinical material, especially in the transference projections of patients in analysis who suffer from character neuroses.

Disturbances in object relations indicate that these patients also have difficulty relating to the outer world. They have problems adapting. They do not, however, characteristically withdraw and feel helpless, although they are not immune to such responses during periods of regression and decompensation. On the contrary, character neurotics have sufficient structure and defensive adaptations to cope with the exigencies of reality and in a moderately satisfactory fashion gratify their needs. Occasionally, as with some narcissistic character neuroses, they make very effective adaptations.

ADAPTATION AND EXTERNALIZATION
IN CHARACTER NEUROSES

After having emerged from the symbiotic phase, those who suffer from character neuroses had to adapt to the external world. This, of course, is true for everyone because as self and object become progressively differentiated, the child must enter the external world.

For those with character neuroses, the assaultive elements of the symbiotic phase were directly deposited into the external world, and the world became a traumatic battleground, but one which could be dealt with. Character neurotics acquire techniques to deal with an environment which they have, in part, constructed much as the paranoid creates his persecutors.

Freud (1920) had a good deal to say about trauma and its effects. He postulated a repetition compulsion associated with mastery which he believed antedates the pleasure principle and, in being independent of it is "beyond the pleasure principle." He viewed the repetition compulsion as a quality of the psyche that makes its appearance before the pleasure principle, but one which operates on its own during early developmental stages and which may do so again in the instance of trauma or traumatic neuroses. I believe Freud's formulations are relevant, because patients with character neuroses often present material that can best be explained on the basis of a repetition compulsion. These patients often seem to repeat the same self-defeating or nonproductive behavior over and over again.

If the character neurotic models his world on the basis of the early trauma he has suffered, he will have to pit himself constantly against a traumatic environment. These efforts may become the basis of his survival. Such endeavors support Freud's theses that repetition and mastery belong together and that this type of mastery is different from that which is under the dominance of the pleasure principle. I believe these subtle theoretical distinctions are important aids in clarifying many puzzling aspects of the behavior of the character neuroses which, on the surface, appear paradoxical.

The character neuroses place the traumatic elements of the symbiotic phase in the external world. This is illustrated in the repetitive qualities of primitive mastery in their adaptive and defensive behavior. They keep doing what to us seem to be the same unrewarding things over and over again without pleasure. Still, one quickly senses how vital this behavior is for their equilibrium, and feels very keenly how disastrous it might be if they were prevented from behaving as they do.

The frequently observed generation of anxiety is an important activity for many patients suffering from character neuroses. This is a familiar situation. The clinician often encounters patients who are always restless and anxious. Their behavior is generally tense. Today, they are called *hyper,* in the past, *spastic,* terms referring primarily to motor reactions.

On the affective side, these patients seem to go out of their way to feel anxiety, often fomenting an endless series of crises in order to maintain tension. To feel anxiety seems vital. This makes sense if one keeps in mind Freud's thesis that anxiety is required to cathect the protective shield of the ego so that it can master the traumatic impingements of the external world.

From another related perspective, Freud (1926) viewed the production of anxiety as a necessary preparatory activity for the construction of defenses. This is the familiar signal function of anxiety which was conceptualized as dealing with intrapsychic conflict and protecting the ego from aberrant, unacceptable instinctual impulses. In the character neuroses, the *Reizschutz* model is more apt since these patients are struggling with conflicts between the ego and external reality, although this, by no means, excludes coexistent id-ego conflicts.

I once reported a patient who beautifully demonstrated anxiety's psychic-life supporting function (Giovacchini 1956). This patient had some conscious control over the generation of anxiety. She needed to feel anxious, because she had to be able to feel something. Otherwise, she would have no assurance that she existed. Not to feel represented a state of nonexistence or existential dissolution, and it was experienced as apathetic terror different from anxiety. Even though anxiety was painful, it was, nevertheless, a feeling that proved to her that she was alive, that she had some identity. Here was an instance in which the patient developed a unique method to maintain herself in what for her was a complex and dangerous world. Certain internal aspects of her psyche determined how she perceived and reacted to her particular reality.

The character neurotic's construction of, and relation to, reality has many unique qualities. He adapts to such a reality and, at the same time, feels frustrated. I wish to stress two qualities, frustration and externalization, which I have repeatedly referred to and which, I believe, are important for our understanding of patients with characterological problems. I want to elaborate on these two psychic elements.

These two reactions belong to different conceptual levels. Frustration produces a behavioral response, while externalization represents an ego mechanism that requires theoretical clarification.

Freud (1925a, 1925b) described the psychotic's conflict as being between the ego and the outer world. Not all patients who suffer from characterologi-cal defects are psychotic, but all have a more or less distorted perception of their environment. If, as they attempt to adjust to their perceptions, they fail, they may recognize they have emotional problems and seek help. The patient then attempts to recreate in the transference an environment that he believes he can cope with. In the transference, in addition to projecting affects, impulses, and attitudes, he externalizes some aspects of his inner organiza-tion. I will return later to the nuances which help make distinctions between projection and externalization after illustrating the mechanism of externaliza-tion in some clinical material. At that point, I will also bring in frustration, as I want to view it here.

Case 1

A middle-aged housewife illustrated how externalization and frustration were prominent adaptive and defensive features. Her life seemed to be nothing but a bundle of frustrations. Her husband constantly mistreated her, her children made unreasonable demands, and her friends were selfish and inconsiderate. She lacked, however, the fixity and grimness often seen in the paranoid patient. At first, it was unclear why she had sought therapy when she did; later, it became apparent that her family and friends were seeking attachments elsewhere.

The patient was feeling increasingly alienated. Her childhood had been chaotic and traumatic. Both parents beat her frequently and demanded that she shoulder the responsibility of raising her younger siblings. Her father was described as an unpredictable alcoholic. She never knew what to expect from him, a caress or a blow. She believed that her mother was more consistent for varying periods of time, although from the patient's description it seemed that her mother was suffering from periodic agitated depressions. She recalled episodes lasting months on end when her mother was warm and loving and felt very much concerned about her daughter's welfare. Paradoxically, the patient felt uncomfortable and anxious at these times. After such benevolent periods, she would find herself in physical jeopardy since the mother had violent outbursts and continuously attacked her in the midst of much agitation and tears.

I rather quickly formed the impression that in spite of all this, at least in the present, she was not seriously uncomfortable. I concluded that she wanted me to fight with her, but I did not see this as being typically sadomasochistic, despite periods of considerable masochism. It seemed she wanted to preserve the atmosphere of the battlefield rather than experience or inflict pain.

She was critical of just about everything and would spend many hours telling me how I should dress, decorate my office, and, in general, how I should conduct my life. One could easily become annoyed with this. After several months of such behavior, I interpreted that she needed to see me as an opponent since I continued doing things the way I liked instead of catering to her ideas and preferences. I emphasized that she was more interested in the battleground than the actual issues, since what she was harping upon were minor points and matters of personal taste usually not disputed. She quickly replied, calmly, to my surprise, that high-ranking military strategists had always fascinated her and she had often fantasied herself standing over a huge map, planning campaigns, while at the same time she could visualize the enemy playing the same game. She rather animatedly told me of a rather complicated game she had recently bought, one in which armies are at war with each other, a game that delighted her.

The next day she had lost all her exuberance. She had an air of wistful melancholy which she could not associate to anything in particular. She then reported her first dream.

An amorphous person (she could not distinguish whether male or female) came at her with a club, but she was not frightened. She knew that she would not be hit and enjoyed the challenge of being what she later called the "artful dodger."

She pictured me as the amorphous attacker. Since I sat behind her she did not have a clear picture of me. She said all of this spontaneously, and then added that she felt sad as she thought further about the dream. She was beginning to believe that I was not at all like the person with the club, and this upset her. She now thought of me as a warm, generous person who wanted to understand her, and this made her feel miserable.

Primitive pregenital elements now emerged, rather than associations which would have expressed the more obvious sexual implications of the dream. Instead of playfully enjoying herself as she seemed to be doing in the dream, she presented herself as anxious and desperate. True, she was begging for a fight, but, at the same time, she saw herself as falling apart. This dream was followed by many dreams of drowning and of houses crumbling. Unlike the usual dream of this type which signifies structural collapse, all of these catastrophes occurred in a pleasant setting. She then had the following dream.

She was dressed in tattered rags and walking in a dirty slum. As she continued walking, this disordered ghetto gradually changed into a well-lit, spacious, clean, rich neighborhood. She found herself facing a beautiful, large mansion, but at this precise moment, she "disappeared." She felt tremendous anxiety and awakened.

The dream was difficult to describe; she felt panic and thought of herself as a flimsy and empty shadow. After reporting this nightmare, she had an angry outburst at me, stressing the unmanageable frustration she was suffering.

I commented that in the dream, she would have felt safer and more comfortable in the slum, and that she had made me into a mansion. She quietly agreed and then pointed out that she wanted to make me into a slum, so that I would be as dirty, horrible, and angry as she was. It was my stubborn refusal to be anything but kind and understanding that made her feel so miserably frustrated. *The analytic setting was at variance with the ambience she needed to construct, one that would permit her to project infantile needs and feelings.*

She elaborated on the importance of the environment. She remembered a story she had either seen in a motion picture or heard in a soap opera on the radio during childhood, a story that had left an indelible impression. A kind and beautiful heiress brings a disheveled, deprived ragamuffin into her large, luxurious home where she has provided for the child a playroom full of toys. There is also a table, full of all kinds of candy and other delicacies. The heiress leaves the child alone, to contemplate and enjoy her miraculous good fortune. As soon as the heiress is out of sight, the little girl quietly walks to the window and climbs out, running back to the slums as fast as she can.

The patient wanted to see me just as she saw herself, she wanted to be at the same level. She had to externalize her feelings and attitudes and to perceive the outside world as she perceived her inner organization. She could not integrate her experience with me with her usual perception of the world. She reported that it was especially difficult to be with a person who was interested in her needs and wanted to understand her. This was both indulgent and perplexing.

During the course of treatment, she began to realize that there might be some hope of raising herself from the slum level to the level she attributed to me. Her view of me remained favorable, but it was primitive insofar as it had megalomanic elements. The mansion, however, was not unattainable. She had after all created it herself. If she could ascribe such qualities to me, it was possible then that they could also become part of her psyche.

The fact that the analytic relationship survived her regressive need to make it into something chaotic and degraded was also helpful. The analysis continued without any disrupting complications, though it had many difficult moments.

The patient's narcissistic balance is particularly interesting. She needed to make me part of an environment, a private reality, that was familiar to her and with which she could cope. Nevertheless, she projected omnipotent grandiosity into me. She gave me qualities that narcissistic character neuroses use as defenses in order to protect them from their basic feelings of inadequacy, vulnerability, and helplessness. These qualities could not survive in the reality she habitually created for herself so she projected them into me. In so doing, she revealed something interesting about symbiosis and fusion states.

She felt that being different can be dangerous, and I have encountered this feeling in many other patients suffering from characterological problems. She found it terrifying to fuse with someone who was different from herself, someone who was at a "different level." One could not effect a fusion without being destroyed. The person with the greater structural organization would amalgamate, swallow up, destroy the other. The reverse would be impossible because a lesser organization could not integrate a greater organization. Thus, she had to make me the way she saw herself, and this would be congruent with her private reality.

Being alike would make a symbiotic fusion safe and perhaps useful. If I were the same as she, then fusing with me would only lead to an extension of her boundaries, but it would not threaten her status as a distinct person with an autonomous organization. If good qualities were to be found outside of herself, then fusion would cause them to become part of herself. The fact that the environment she had to create was a harsh, cruel one seems, on the surface, paradoxical, but she was familiar with it and this gave her security, although she felt alienated from the world in general.

PRIVATE REALITY AND
THE THERAPEUTIC SETTING

That the environment this patient was seeking was a painful one might cause us to think of masochism. Certain features of the self-defeating behavior of patients with character problems should be distinguished from those of masochists. Masochistic behavior requires a degree of coherent organization with a well defined superego and a capacity to experience guilt, leading to considerable intrapsychic conflict. The patient here described and other patients with similar character neuroses have undergone a moderate degree of maldevelopment, and their self-defeating behavior is not functionally organized to protect them from a harsh superego. Self-defeating behavior that has a defensive purpose must be distinguished from that resulting from a faulty organization or breakdown of the personality.

My patient simply could not cope with a warm and nonthreatening environment. I have encountered other patients with character disorders who react in a similar fashion. They react to a benign situation as if it were beyond their level of comprehension. These patients do not have the adaptive techniques to interact with a reasonable environment. Their formative years were irrational and violent, and they make this chaos and upheaval a part of themselves. Thus their inner excitement may clash with surroundings that differ from their infantile environment. When the world becomes benign and generous, the patient may withdraw in panic just as my patient described herself doing during a phase of ego dissolution. This was particularly emphasized by the story of the heiress and the slum child.

This woman's requirements of the world are those often seen in persons who have suffered much trauma in childhood. Their egos have become acclimated to a frustrating environment. The person with a character neurosis expects and brings about his failure. He adapts himself to life by feeling beaten in a harsh, ungiving world. Although to the observer, this may seem an inability to adapt, the character neurotic, in his peculiar way, achieves synthesis in what seems to be a relentless, unrewarding struggle. This situation differs from a masochistic adjustment designed to effect a psychodynamic balance; the defensive constellation of my patient was vital to maintaining a total ego coherence instead of dealing with discrete conflicting disruptive impulses.

Her psychopathology can be understood in several ways. Very often she saw herself as a frightened little girl who had never known love and intimacy. As much as she wanted closeness, she could not accept it. In treatment, her provocative behavior was a defense against her libidinal attachment to me. By regarding the analysis as having little value, she need not become painfully dependent and thus expose her helplessness and vulnerability. She could maintain control by projecting the despised and weak parts of herself onto the analyst. This was a defensive stance, an alienated position which forbade her warm and receptive relations with external objects. When the analytic situation did not support such defenses, she felt traumatized.

The analyst is faced with a paradoxical situation when the patient feels frustrated, because the analyst refuses to frustrate him. The analytic setting provides consistency, the constant reliability Winnicott (1955) described, and hence is conducive to regression. It causes the patient to hope that infantile needs will be gratified, but because of past experiences, this hope cannot be trusted. Instead of risking the inevitable disappointment of megalomanic expectations, the patient prefers relating in a setting to which he has learned to adjust. His narcissistic balance is precarious. If the analyst does not frustrate or threaten him, the patient's psychic balance is upset. To reinstitute ego equilibrium, the patient attempts to make the analyst representative of the world that is familiar to him. Such a defensive endeavor must be distinguished from projection.

Freud (1896, 1911) very early described projection as the attribution of unacceptable and dangerous id impulses to an external object. In the course of time, the concept has been broadened to include not only unacceptable id impulses but also disruptive affects, as well as discrete psychic elements such as introjects (see Giovacchini 1964, 1967a).

Such primitive defenses are often employed in character neuroses, but what my patient was attempting to achieve in analysis was more than just projection. Her reconstruction of reality was not based only upon projection of unacceptable impulses and affects. She was attributing a particular level of integration to reality, a process better described as *externalization*. She had a need to be frustrated, and this is different from simple projection of hostile wishes onto an external object who is thereby transformed into a persecutor. Rather, her need to be frustrated represents a mode of adjustment that made interaction between the ego and reality possible. According to Freud (1911), the patient projects destructive inner impulses. This patient projected a frustrating environment. Externalization provided her with a setting that enabled her to use adjustive and defensive techniques that she had acquired during her early development. Although there is always some projection in every externalization (insofar as the construction will invariably involve the attributing of unacceptable impulses to external objects), there are additional factors.

Externalization can be conceptualized as the placing of *ego mechanisms* into the outer world, whereas the defense mechanism commonly called projection deals with impulses, affects, and aspects of self- and object-representations that are closer to the id than to reality. For example, if the ego's chief adjustive modality is repression, then the psyche seeks a repressive environment. But, if the ego makes its adaptation to a world perceived as full of rage and violence, then acting out may be the chief interaction with the environment. The acting out displayed by my patient, however, was not flagrant anti-social behavior. She externalized her feelings by transforming them into actions, that is by relating in an active manner to some segment of the external world. Thus, the ego seeks its adjustment, not in a vacuum, but in a reality that supports its defenses and this may be a painful and frustrating reality.

Brodey (1965) describes externalization as distancing without separation. According to him, projection also occurs but the manipulation of reality referred to as externalization has the "purpose of verifying the projection." Other aspects of reality are simply not perceived.

Externalization is not confined to persons with character defects; it occurs in normal development. In the psychoneuroses, it also helps support defenses, and as the ego develops, it is instrumental in the establishment of reality testing. The child's ego not only endopsychically registers a maternal imago, it also incorporates the setting characteristic of the object. The mother is a means by which the child becomes adapted to the environment; hence, the child, in addition to forming a maternal introject, perceives the mothering process as an adaptive technique, a natural sequence in view of its function of achieving instinctual gratification. Introjects carry out the mothering function by helping the child to establish a relationship between the inner and outer world and to develop and use subsequent experience for the acquisition of further adaptive techniques.

When my patient tried to make me representative of a specific traumatic environment, she was, at the same time, projecting parental images and hated parts of herself into me. The latter process is characteristic of transference, but with this patient, it was an uneasy and conflicting transference because she could not reconcile her projections with the analytic setting. This situation had, nevertheless, therapeutic advantages, since it did not lead to a transference fixation but made possible the understanding of irrational and infantile expectations.

Anna Freud (1965) discusses externalization as a mechanism that externalizes parts of the self, or inner-conflicts, or both. She notes that the therapist may become representative of conflicts or of a psychic agency such as the superego. Clinically, this transformation of the environment has to be described in terms of specific content. To speak of conflict and superego is to introduce a categorization that goes beyond clinical observation and description. The patient's construction of external reality can be understood only in terms of his perceptions. The psychic mechanisms involved in conflicts or in a psychic agency are elaborated into experiences, which then are reported as perceptions and feelings. Anna Freud also believes that there is a difference between projection and externalization, but she does not emphasize this difference. She furthermore believes that when the patient externalizes, the therapeutic relationship differs from one in which a transference has been established, but she does not pursue the topic further or offer explanation.

Some clinicians question whether externalization can be considered a defense. This, of course, depends on how one defines a defense. If Freud's (1894, 1896) first descriptions are retained as immutable standards, then externalization has to be classified as something else. Freud viewed defenses as reaction, that is, as psychic mechanisms designed to handle anxiety which is generated as a signal by intrapsychic conflict (Freud 1926). Externalization is turned in another direction. It is directed toward finding and constructing a special reality. Still, it is a defense in that its purpose is to establish psychic equilibrium, and, as stressed, it is a very important mechanism for the ego integrity of persons who have character neuroses, that is structural defects and the consequent disturbances of narcissistic balance.

OTHER DEFENSIVE ADAPTATIONS
AND TECHNICAL DIFFICULTIES

I have just described a mode of adjustment, externalization, which may manifest itself by frustration, struggle, and repeated failure. Patients with character neuroses display other adaptive characteristics. These may appear to others as either eminently successful or unrewarding and futile. In those character neuroses often referred to as narcissistic characters, successful adjustment is sometimes seen. These patients are frequently able to deal effectively with reality. Often they are highly successful, hard working, and very skillful at favorably impressing their associates. They seem to make their way through life easily and smoothly.

Such narcissistic characters are, however, increasingly coming to the attention of analysts. The fact that they seek analytic help belies the picture of invulnerability and self-containment that they lavishly present and which may either charm or infuriate the onlooker. Underneath a strong and arrogant exterior, the analyst is frequently confronted with a frightened, confused, helpless infantile orientation.

I emphasize that in spite of wide differences in the surface picture, these narcissistic patients, from a structural viewpoint, are not significantly different from those who use externalization as a prominent adaptive modality and who seem to be alienated and vulnerable rather than confident and successful.

Their defensive adjustments are primarily overcompensatory, and they ruthlessly find their way in a world that values success. To the degree that they create the world in which they find material rewards, attention, and praise, they are also externalizing some parts of their psyche. They hold themselves together on the basis of having megalomanic expectations fulfilled and then create a world in which they can gratify their omnipotent needs. If they succeed, one sees a picture of narcissistic fulfillment—a well-functioning integrated organism, but with a minimum of human qualities and feelings.

This type of character neurosis is commonly seen: a plastic, hard working, and perhaps unscrupulous person who achieves, usually for his self-enhancement and power, but who may significantly affect the world. In creating a world that supports his narcissistic balance, he may actually change the world we live in. The previous examples of externalization I have given related to an already existing segment of the world. The patients did not really create it; they found something that was already there. At most, they may have made manifest certain latent tendencies in the environment. The narcissistic patient usually does much more than that and in many instances has had a tremendous effect on society for better or worse. Basically, however, he is not concerned about the fate of the world he influences. He is only concerned about maintaining a certain level of self-esteem in order to prevent psychic collapse. Collapse would mean a state of helpless vulnerability; he would find himself at the mercy of external forces and assault, in other words, at the mercy of an external world that would use him for its own needs and thereby stamp out all vestiges of individuality and autonomy. The patient, therefore, has to be constantly on top of the situation by seeking total control and invulnerability. These are narcissistic defenses that lead to mastery. This view of the role of narcissism as it is involved in psychopathology is clearly different from that which sees it as the outcome of fixation on the developmental stage of primary or even secondary narcissism.

Not all patients with narcissistic character neuroses are successful. Undoubtedly, the achievement of success is the outcome of many factors, not simply a response to a psychopathologically constructed defensive need. Talent obviously is involved; no matter how pressing the need, if the person is not sufficiently gifted, he will not be able to obtain the narcissistic gratification he so badly needs.

Perhaps most of these patients are patients because they have failed to extract from the external world sufficient narcissistic supplies to avoid feeling the consequences of their ego defects and vulnerabilities. One often sees pathetic attempts to appear powerful and competent, and the more these patients fail, the greater their megalomania. The patient's adaptive and defensive attempts may establish a vicious circle. As he fails in his attempts at achieving magical control—magical because he does not have the ability to make it congruent with the external world—his feeling of basic inadequacy and vulnerability correspondingly increases. This leads to a need for further narcissistic enhancement which encounters further frustration. The more he is frustrated, the more inadequate he will feel and the greater the omnipotence he will need to protect himself from his vulnerability. Thus, the vicious circle continues.

Many patients with character neuroses present lives punctuated with failure, and they often seek treatment with a sense of pressing urgency.

In one respect, all patients with character neuroses could be considered examples of narcissistic character neuroses. These patients, as a group, have an intense need to be protected from their basic sense of vulnerability. Some achieve psychic equilibrium by being successful in obtaining narcissistic supplies. Others are not successful, but this represents a failure of defensive adaptation. They still seek narcissistic supplies, but their structural defects are closer to the surface than is the case with the well compensated narcissistic patient. Rather than the arrogant self-confidence commonly found in narcissistic patients, the character neuroses who fail to achieve often insist they are helpless, inadequate, and needful, but, in spite of their obvious and perhaps flamboyant self-depreciation, they still have a discernible, if poorly hidden, arrogance. Although frightened and intimidated, their attitude toward the external world can be sneering and contemptuous.

As is true for so many patients suffering from ego defects, identity problems are prominent in character neuroses, and their attempts to establish some cohesion to the self-representation may take several characteristic forms. I have already mentioned narcissistic overcompensation. Now, I wish to discuss several other typical constellations designed to achieve a cohesive sense of identity and narcissistic equilibrium. These are defensive and adjustive attempts which usually fail, as do those of some patients who cannot maintain an exalted position to protect them from their vulnerability. Actually, again such attempts are very similar to the search for narcissistic gratification. I am, in fact, discussing a variation of narcissism, different only in that omipotence and grandiosity are not so obviously manifest.

One commonly encountered group of patients—especially among college students and other young adults, although they are found in older age groups as well—are always engaged in some activity or project but never finish it. In some instances, they never start it, although they are constantly talking about it and planning. The student who is always writing the dissertation he will never finish is a typical example. I recall the incredible situation of a man who had been "finishing" his Ph.D. for thirty years. The fact that a ridiculous amount of time had passed never occurred to him. He still talked about it as if he were going to graduate the next week and ignored the fact that this next week had been coming for three decades.

These patients are, as one of them said, in a state of becoming. They have to be involved in something, an activity accepted by the external world as leading to the consolidation of an identity—in this case a vocational or professional identity. As long as they have such a project to fasten upon, they feel they have a mission and purpose in life. They feel they exist and this helps establish an autonomous boundary. The pathetic aspect is that it finally becomes obvious to everyone except the patient that built into their project is the condition that they will never achieve it. With the patient who had been finishing his dissertation for thirty years, there is practically a delusional quality to his belief that he would complete his project in just a few days. How he could continue being sincere in such a conviction, and it definitely comes across as a conviction, is incredible. It becomes apparent that without such a project these patients would have nothing to give meaning to their lives. The actual achievement of their goal would be frightening because it is beyond their integrative capacities.

Constant striving to define oneself seems to be typical of many persons suffering with character neuroses. This may take many forms other than those just described. Much peculiar and flamboyant behavior is the result of adaptational attempts, the outcome of a need to find oneself, to find a place in the universe. The drug culture, homosexuality, deviant life styles, often prove in analysis to be manifestations of adjustive integrations to enable the ego to feel itself as distinct and unassaulted.

Case 2

One twenty-one-year-old graduate student well illustrates some of these structural features. This patient could not tell me precisely why he sought analysis. Everything about him was vague. He considered himself a graduate student but had never graduated. He was going to bypass the bachelor's degree and proceed directly to a master's or Ph.D. He found life generally unsatisfying and unrewarding but could not focus upon anything specific.

His analysis was characterized by several themes which were manifestations of both defensive adaptation and failure of adaptation. The latter dominated the opening phases of treatment.

He went into intricate detail about all of his activities. I found it astonishing because he did not recognize that he was giving me examples of maladaptive and nonpurposeful behavior. He spoke in a calm voice of accomplishment about events that most of us would have found very sad and dismaying. For example, he owned two very expensive sports cars and a powerful motorcycle. With all these exotic modes of transportation, he still had to take public transportation to my office because the vehicles very seldom ran. He was extremely proud of his automobiles and would tell me with enthusiasm how fast and maneuverable they were, but after he had driven one of them a block or so and gone through a complex ritual of gear shifting, the auto would somehow stop running. This happened constantly, and he was usually unable to use either of his cars or his motorcycle. Once, in a whimsical mood, he referred to them as having "psychosomatic failure."

In many ways, the situation with his sports cars was typical. Nothing ever seemed to go right in his life. He did badly in school, although he tested in the upper range of intelligence. Socially, he was almost completely isolated because he had alienated most of his friends with his gauche behavior and speech.

His behavior could be bizarre. He might, for example, go downtown, even to a concert, in bermudas—this when dress habits were more formal than today. On Thanksgiving, he would eat lobster instead of turkey. The rooms in his apartment were organized in a most unique fashion. The kitchen contained a couch and was set up somehow like a living room. The living room, in turn, had a mattress on the floor and he slept there. The bedroom and dining room had other idiosyncratic functions.

This behavior had many meanings, prominent among them his driving need to find an identity of his own, one different from that which he considered conventional. If he were to be the same as everyone else, he felt that he could be submerged, crushed and swallowed up and that he would be annihilated (see Giovacchini 1964).

More important here is the fact that the patient's psychic organization did not permit him to relate realistically to the surrounding world. His ego state was organized at a different level than the external world, and his failures were the outcome of his inability to integrate the inner and outer world. Again, this is typical of the adaptive failures frequently found in character disorders.

The patient suffered from intense feelings of inadequacy but had not been able to link these feelings with the way he was living. He saw nothing unusual in his attitudes or behavior. He had very distinct opinions about right and wrong and considered almost everything he did right while he found wrong in many of the injustices of society, such as poverty and war. Still, he felt miserable.

As is typical for patients with character neuroses, he had constructed defenses to compensate for his difficulty making efficient and productive adaptations to his surrounding milieu. He constantly failed but was able to protect himself against the recognition of such failure and the devastating blow it would have been to his self-esteem.

The complex defenses he erected to protect self-esteem can be considered characteristic narcissistic defenses. He differed from other patients whose narcissistic qualities are on the surface in that he felt depleted and inadequate and in that his alienation was a part of his abysmal failure and gaucherie. He did not seem to have any of the grandiose qualities that seem intrinsic to narcissistic character types.

To repeat, his defenses were narcissistic defenses in that they had the same purpose as all narcissistic defenses, that is to preserve self-esteem and to protect the psyche from facing the desolation and misery associated with an inadequate, helpless and vulnerable self-representation.

His fairly primitive defenses were characterized by splitting processes and introjective-projective mechanisms (see Kernberg 1966). Patients with character neuroses still near the early end of the developmental scale use relatively primitive defenses. Consequently, the patient dissociated good and bad and projected bad objects into certain aspects of the external world. Unlike the paranoid, he did not feel persecuted, although the character neuroses often do have some paranoid ideation. He attached himself to good causes in order to combat the bad elements of society.

In attaching himself to good causes he was projecting and introjecting good objects. Fundamentally he was seeking magical rescuing and trying to find omnipotence to protect himself against a basic self-representation of weakness and inadequacy.

He sought omnipotence in movements and projects. He affiliated himself with many fads, various health diets, astrology, encounter groups, yoga, the drug culture, and many fringe groups as quickly as they sprung up. I regret to add that he had placed psychoanalysis in the same category as these groups and was expecting the same kind of benefit from it as he did from them. At the beginning of treatment, however, this was not obvious to either of us, and he would have claimed different motivation. His eager participation in such groups helped compartmentalize the world into two factions, one of evangelical goodness and the other bad. The bad was not so in the moral sense of fundamental evil; rather it was misguided and ignorant and could be destructive and dangerous. It was his mission to correct such ignorance, and this was extremely important.

In fact, everything he did had momentous significance, though it was very difficult to ascertain exactly what he was doing. He was quite busy and his schedule was so packed that he often found it difficult to keep his appointments. He was in the habit of canceling many of them because of the pressing urgency of something that simply could not wait. He created a world in which he appeared to be very busy indeed.

As this picture became increasingly clear to me, I became more aware of what could be considered narcissistic elements in the patient's character, elements that were not at all evident when he first presented himself in his humble self-deprecatory clumsiness. The importance of what he was doing and the total lack of accomplishment presented such a striking contrast that one could not help but be amazed by the incongruity of what came across as supreme self-assurance. This was in spite of the fact that he also considered himself inadequate. This was lost sight of as he proselytized for the cause of the moment. He was contemptuous, superior, and arrogant, and this was clearly self-bolstering and compensatory when considered in the context of the transitory nature of his enthusiasm and its absolute lack of results. Others frequently became infuriated with him and rejected him socially.

It was fortunate for his defenses that he was attending a university that, at the time, was very flexible in its demands as to when dissertations had to be completed. The patient officially identified himself as a graduate student and had been working on his master's thesis for four years. He remained in treatment with me for three years and did not progress one page further during that time. Nevertheless, he kept himself extremely busy—most of his activity consisting of actions designed to postpone getting down to work. For example, before he could start writing, he had to clear his desk, which, according to his description, was cluttered with all sorts of pamphlets, books, reprints and correspondence. After arduous effort, he might succeed in putting away or throwing out most of these. But then he would be exhausted and have to rest in order to "await inspiration." In the meantime, papers would once more start accumulating, and by the time he was ready to begin work on his thesis, his desk would again be unmanageably cluttered. This process seemed to be repeated endlessly.

The patient was never daunted by the fact that he never completed anything. His friends, the few he had, were quite similar in this respect. They were authors who never wrote, painters who never painted, and others who were always intensely preoccupied, often displayed enthusiasm, but accomplished nothing. I finally learned that the completion of a task was an irrelevant side issue. What really mattered was dedication to some activity which conferred an identity, not the carrying out of that activity. The patient had to be in a *state of becoming*. He had to have a project, a purpose, and a mission in life and that would be sufficient to make him feel worthwhile. Certainly it was a precarious and tenuous balance, but as long as he could feel he was heading in a certain direction, he was able to maintain some cohesion to the self-representation.

The therapy was difficult, at least for me. The patient constantly idealized what to me seemed a totally worthless existence and most of the time proved himself shallow, gauche, and in bad taste. He saw himself, on the contrary, as sensitive, intuitive, and profound. I was careful never to challenge his position during the first six months of analysis. This gave him ample time to project his sense of mediocrity into me, and he began comparing psychoanalysis unfavorably with other systems. He attributed all kinds of wisdoms and power to astrology, chiropractic, dianetics, yoga, extrasensory perception, and many other movements, some of which have been proven to be without basis. Even when he knew about scientific refutations, he continued to cling to his beliefs and to what I learned were magical expectations.

He turned to these fringe groups, these outskirts of reality, for omnipotent salvation and projected his negative orientation into me. The latter consisted of bad internal objects and hated aspects of the self. Clearly, he was using splitting mechanisms.

I had the very definite feeling that he would have liked to place me in his omnipotent category rather than in his despised one. The results of splitting were not absolute. He had put some omnipotence into me, but, apparently, I had not reinforced it.

Nevertheless, in a limited way, I was useful to him. Even though he frequently missed appointments, he was quite disconcerted on the rare occasions when I had to cancel one. He often asked for extra sessions, and whenever possible I gave them to him. I was serving a function by being a receptacle for the badness he felt within himself.

Perhaps, he preferred me as the negative target of his dissociative defenses rather than as the positive one, which I am now certain he was eager to attribute to me at the beginning of treatment. He could not do this because, as he later described, I had not become engaged with him, I had not given him any feedback, and he had to be intuitively "locked in" with someone. This could even mean telepathic communication. The latter, and many of his other bizarre ideas did not, however, seem part of a psychosis. In any case, he continued attacking my analytic orientation although he was always pleasant and polite. He depreciated analysis, usually indirectly by extolling the virtues of what he considered a rival system.

My attempts at interpretation were rebuffed, at first by being ignored. I tried to point out how he had a need to compartmentalize the world on the basis of how he saw himself. I had been made into that part which caused him to fail and which failed him. I stressed also the adaptive aspects of his ability to achieve this. The patient would allow me to say what I wanted and then proceed as if I had said nothing.

He had to believe I had said nothing and indicated in many subtle and not so subtle ways that if I would not join him in an omnipotent relationship, really a symbiotic fusion, then it was best I remain silent. That way, I would not interfere with his hostile projections into me, projections which characterized the transference. An interpretation in this instance would have made it more difficult for him to continue projecting.

Apparently I was not content to remain a receptacle indefinitely. When, after about a year, I tried to gently interject some of my ideas about what was happening between us, he started arguing with me. He felt that I was being critical and that fundamentally I did not approve of his life-style. He believed that although I found him likeable, basically I considered him a freak. I realized that what he was saying was partially true and admitted that his customs were different than mine. I also pointed out that I had no inclination to make value judgments about his ideologies and his behavior. I was devoted to helping him understand why he had to pursue these various movements and how his involvements left him functionally paralyzed.

Again the patient seemed to ignore what I said. He continued arguing against psychoanalysis and still felt that I disapproved of him. I believed he was projecting, but I also realized that there was some truth to his accusations. In spite of my desire to function as an analyst and to view his material in a calm and objective fashion, I, nevertheless, found him irksome. I kept reacting to what I considered to be incredible arrogance—his superior all-knowing attitude that contrasted so sharply with his inability to do anything, even drive an automobile, which had become an agonizing experience. Though I tried to control my feelings and not express them overtly, they somehow seeped out and made our relationship uncomfortable and tense.

This patient just did not respond to my attempts to analyze him. He remained with me for three years and was more or less content to use me as a receptacle. To a degree, he found the negative transference useful; it helped relieve him of the burden of his helplessness and low self-esteem. Still, since the essence of this transference was that I was useless, he was getting nothing out of analysis. He left treatment feeling that I had failed him, but he was polite and friendly.

I found it interesting that he harbored no bitterness. Our parting was most amicable. I now realize that I felt as if I had been relieved of a burden and was grateful to him for wanting to terminate.

The patient still keeps in touch with me. Every year he sends me a very imaginative Christmas card, something that he has made himself. As far as I can gather, he lives as he always has. I do not know if he is still working on his dissertation, but I would not be surprised if he were. He has affiliated himself with a group that holds workshops and engages in some type of group therapy. He is one of their practitioners. He has also privately published several books of poetry which he has given me as presents.

There are many facets of this man's personality that I have not discussed, I have not explored here in any depth this patient's functional paralysis. Elsewhere, I have attributed this problem to what I called a frozen introject (Giovacchini 1967a), a maternal imago that did not permit him to be effective. Here, I simply wish to point out that we are confronted with an ego defect which characterizes the patient's adaptation or maladaptation to reality. The patient had constructed rather complex defenses, and these were elaborated in the therapeutic setting.

As is true for the character neuroses in general, this patient made elaborate use of splitting mechanisms. He placed the inadequate and hateful parts of himself into the external world and then tried to transcend them. He maintained the magical good object within himself though he also found elements of reality which he could imbue with omnipotence.

Thus, the patient saw reality in two fashions which corresponded to the way he split objects into good and bad. He attached himself to fringe groups and saw them as omnipotent. These he then introjected and made part of his omnipotent self-representation—another example of pathological narcissism. He also projected reality as incompetent, immoral, and full of injustice.

The patient's introjected elements then attempted to deal with his projections. He was going to rid the world of all of its destructive and self-destructive aspects, a classical example of what Melanie Klein (1935) called making reparation. He was totally unsuccessful for many reasons.

Inasmuch as his resources were based upon spurious systems that only dealt with magic, he was not, in fact, able to change anything in a nonmagical reality. His inner fantasy world trespassed on a secondary-process-oriented external world. For example, one may dream of banquets, but this does not allay hunger. He continued dreaming and not working.

He had to protect himself from work. If he worked, matters would be put on a reality basis and taken out of the realm of omnipotent fantasy. Furthermore, he had a need to keep the reality world bad in order to be able to project continuously. If he were able to transform the world into something good, he could no longer construct internal objects on the basis of splitting mechanisms. His intrapsychic balance depended upon keeping the internal world good and viewing the external world as part good, the world of magical systems, and part bad, the world of concrete reality. In order to maintain this constellation, he had to appear as if he were involved in productive activities, but he could not sustain involvement to complete the activity.

Other patients succeed in effecting changes, which at deeper levels of the personality signify omnipotent rescuing. How do they differ from this patient? Here, we encounter differences in specific elements of the traumatic background and varying degrees of structural defect. Innate abilities also come into play. I believe that my patient may have had considerable talent but could not get in touch with it. He had to keep various aspects of himself separate and as a result he became functionally paralyzed.

The patient's identity sense was tenuous and to regress from object relationships based upon splitting to symbiotic unity would have threatened the integrity of his self-representation. To discuss this fully, I would have to present a history of his early development; here, I simply wish to emphasize how he had to compartmentalize the external world and do nothing to change the status quo while at the same time he had to appear as if he were exerting superhuman efforts to achieve such a change in order to maintain a grandiose self-representation.

This patient did not respond to psychoanalytic treatment; at least nothing seemed to be resolved. Does something intrinsic about this type of patient's psychopathology make analysis impossible? On the developmental scale, he is further along than many other patients, and yet his response was the least satisfactory. There are several factors that may explain this young man's inaccessibility to psychoanalysis.

Immediately, one's attention is captured by the similarity between his response to analysis and his life pattern of general non-productivity. The analysis certainly seems to be an example of another task not done. Still, would it not be possible to analyze this defensive adaptation? Often defenses are so vital that the patient cannot relax them and seek other modes of adaptation, and that may have occurred here. I believe that this contributed to the dissolution of the analytic relationship. At best, one could say that the patient had decided how long he wanted to continue the therapeutic relationship and he had experienced as much analysis as he cared to. Nevertheless, I felt that our relationship had not ended well and that other factors were involved beyond the patient's psychopathology.

I am, of course, referring to countertransference. Recall, when I described the patient's relationships to reality, I chose to refer to his external world, that segment from which he extracted narcissistic supplies and omnipotence, as a fringe reality. That must mean there are two types of reality, a reasonable, acceptable reality and one that is on its fringes. No matter how objective I may have tried to remain, this was still a value judgment and as such antianalytic. I had decided that my reality was better than his, and this must have had deleterious effects on the analytic relationship.

The patient needed to ignore and devalue me. I believe that I do not usually have much difficulty with such needs as they determine the transference. I treated this patient some years ago, however, and I may not have been as keenly aware of how adaptive it is for patients suffering from characterological defects to make the analyst the receptable of the painful, inadequate, hateful parts of the self. Still, this patient also affected me in such a fashion that made it especially difficult for me to bear his projections.

The patient was quite flamboyant in showing me how superior his beliefs were to mine and often enough his arguments had some semblance of logic. However, they were spurious arguments, and if one responded to him, as I sometimes did, his defense was weak and naive. After such an exchange, I felt guilty or angry, as he still stubbornly clung to his position.

This combination of devaluing, sometimes in a seemingly rational and coherent fashion, something I valued, psychoanalysis, plus his projection of his vulnerability, disquieted me. My resentment was intensified when he repeatedly demonstrated how ineffectual he was or how everything he glorified always ended in a cul-de-sac. I found it extremely difficult to keep my personal reactions of dislike separate from my analytic orientation. In contrast to him, who constantly compartmentalized, I was unable to stop these two contradictory orientations from coming together. This undoubtedly had a profound effect on the analytic interaction and must have been largely responsible for its lack of success. Perhaps it would have been different with another analyst.

CONCLUDING PERSPECTIVES

The prevalence of character neuroses have forced analysts to reconsider their ideas about treatability, an issue that is always foremost in the mind of the clinician. I believe much of the current interest in the so-called widening scope of psychoanalysis centers around this group. It forces us to examine further our value systems and our view of reality and the bearing they have on our attitudes toward patients in general.

Our orientations and value systems may hinder our efforts at analyzing some of these patients, and I offer my experience with the last patient as an example. I was strongly convinced that my reality was better than his and this had deleterious effects on the analytic relationship. I do not wish to be self-effacing. I still think my reality is better than his, and I have not modified my sense of values. I simply want to point out that these factors should have been irrelevant in an analytic context.

I believe this awareness is important because one hears of so many therapeutic approaches that are aimed at strengthening the patient's relationship to reality. But whose reality? The therapist's, of course, and there is no consideration whether the way the therapist construes the world is consonant with the patient's value system, background, orientation, and with his character structure in general. I often hear of a realistic, limit-setting, no-nonsense approach to these patients, one aimed at controlling acting out. Again, these are the therapist's limits and more likely than not *acting out is defined as behavior he cannot stand.* The character neuroses, because of their need to externalize, that is to construct an environment which replicates that of the traumatic infancy, seem to call into play our need to control. Perhaps to be faced with other realities, other value systems, is inherently threatening and may be the basis for many of our countertransference difficulties.

Some of these struggles in therapy resemble the conflicts more generally seen between generations. One cannot but wonder whether the prevalence of character neuroses means that we are confronted with a new type of psychopathology or with the same basic types of emotional problems but with different manifestations. Reichard (1956) reexamined descriptions of some of Freud's classical patients and concluded that they were also suffering from severe structural problems. I am inclined to believe that the manifestations of psychopathology have changed but not the underlying psychopathology itself, and that these changes are reflections of differences between our contemporary social-cultural milieu and that of Freud's. The processes involved in the relationship between culture and the construction of psychopathology, processes which are bidirectional, are beyond the scope of a clinically oriented study and extend beyond the realm of psychoanalysis.

The character neuroses may be especially threatening to therapists, much in the same way adolescents are threatening to adults. The age of the patient does not matter; it is the nature of his adaptations that upsets the analyst's, and sometimes society's, equilibrium and which cause both to react in a fashion aimed at gaining control of behavior. Not all of this behavior is basically anti-social in that it is criminal or destructive. Most of the time, it is anti-current ideology, as my young patient so well demonstrated. Society's response, however, up until recently has been suppressive, and therapists have conducted themselves in a similar fashion. Many of them have, nevertheless, considered what they were doing as sensible, reality-oriented psychoanalysis.

I believe that the equation of control and limit-setting is a mistake, and I am willing to admit I made that mistake with my patient. I do not know, even now, if I could have avoided it, or if I can fully avoid it in the future. I do not know whether I want to avoid it, but I believe it is important to know what I am doing. What I was doing was not analysis.

As analysts, we have to face the fact that sometimes we do not want to be analysts. This may be inevitable and determined by our innate values and orientations, by the nature of our externalizations, by the world we construct for ourselves. The character neuroses cause us to reflect on basic issues about emotional problems since they present us with conflicting realities rather than with intrapsychic conflicts. If there has to be change, where does it begin?

Not all patients can or should be analyzed, and this may help explain why other therapeutic approaches are so popular. I regret that they are often confused with analysis and sometimes they are described in such a fashion that they appear to be analytic. They are disguised as analysis, the focus ostensibly being on intrapsychic factors and transference issues.

I repeat, not all patients can or should be analyzed. Many patients with character neuroses have been successfully analyzed; in terms of their psychopathology, they do not, as a group, present us with problems that are intrinsic contraindications to analysis. They threaten our beliefs and they challenge our most cherished principles and *modus operandi*, our striving for the achievement of maximum autonomy, and our methods for attaining this goal. The latter define psychoanalysis. The character neuroses test to the utmost our analytic dedication and inasmuch as they do, we pronounce them to be difficult cases. True, they are difficult, because they force us to examine what is going on within ourselves. This is an intrinsic consequence of the unfolding of the transference and occurs in every analysis. It occurs more with

314   PETER L. GIOVACCHINI

the character neuroses because they demand that we reexamine our values, the same implicit demand we make of all our patients. If we balk from this task, we should not be surprised that patients do the same. Should we demand that patients do what we refuse to do? The question then is not one of analyzability in the fundamental sense; it is related to how much we tolerate the autonomy of both ourselves and our patients, and to how much we really believe in what we profess.

REFERENCES

Brodey, W. (1965). On the dynamics of narcissism. *Psychoanalytic Study of the Child* 20:165-193.
Freud, A. (1965). *Normality and Pathology in Childhood.* New York: International Universities Press.
Freud, S. (1894). The neuro-psychoses of defence. *Standard Edition* 3:41-62.
———— (1896). Further remarks on the defence neuro-psychoses. *Standard Edition* 3:157-187.
———— (1911). Psycho-analytic notes on an autobiographical account of a case of paranoia (dementia paranoides). *Standard Edition* 12:1085.
———— (1914). On narcissism: an introduction. *Standard Edition* 14:67-105.
———— (1915). Instincts and their vicissitudes. *Standard Edition* 14:109-141.
———— (1916). Introductory lectures on psycho-analysis. *Standard Edition* 16:241-478.
———— (1920). Beyond the pleasure principle. *Standard Edition* 18:1-65.
———— (1925a). The loss of reality in neurosis and psychosis. *Standard Edition* 19:183-191.
———— (1925b). Neurosis and psychosis. *Standard Edition* 19:149-155.
———— (1926). Inhibitions, symptoms and anxiety. *Standard Edition* 20:75-175.
Giovacchini, P. L. (1956). Defensive meaning of a specific anxiety syndrome. *The Psychoanalytic Review* 43:373-380.
———— (1964). The submerged ego. *Journal of the American Academy of Child Psychiatry* 4:279-292.
———— (1967a). The frozen introject. *International Journal of Psycho-Analysis* 48:61-68.
———— (1967b). Frustration and externalization. *Psychoanalytic Quarterly* 36:571-584.
———— (1972). The symbiotic phase. In *Tactics and Techniques in Psychoanalytic Treatment,* ed. P. Giovacchini, pp. 137-170. New York: Jason Aronson.
Kernberg, O. (1966). Structural derivatives of object relations. *International Journal of Psycho-Analysis* 47:236-253.
Klein, M. (1935). A contribution to the psychogenesis of manic-depressive states. *International Journal of Psycho-Analysis* 27:145-174.
Kohut, H. (1971). *The Analysis of the Self.* New York: International Universities Press.
———— (1972). Thoughts on narcissism and narcissistic rage. *Psychoanalytic Study of the Child* 27:360-400.
Reichard, S. (1956). A re-examination of "Studies in Hysteria." *Psychoanalytic Quarterly* 25:155-177.
Winnicott, D. W. (1955). Clinical varieties of transference. In *Collected Papers,* pp. 295-300. New York: Basic Books, 1958.

Lack of Timing
and *Ejaculatio Praecox*

ENRIQUE GUARNER, M.D.

Underlying factors in *ejaculatio praecox* are investigated through excerpts from the analysis of a man who suffered from this symptom for many years. The literature is reviewed, and the symptom complex is related both to the patient's character structure and to the difficult resistances that he presented in analysis. The roles of the concept of time and of an inability to conceive completion are studied, as is the type of prevailing anxiety seen in these patients.

In *Inhibitions, Symptoms and Anxiety*, Freud said: "The sexual function is liable to a great number of disturbances, most of which exhibit the characteristics of simple inhibitions. These are classed together as psychical impotence. The normal performance of the sexual function can only come about as the result of a very complicated process, and disturbances may appear at any point in it. In men the chief stages at which inhibition occurs are shown by: a turning away of the libido at the very beginning of the process (psychical unpleasure); an absence of the physical preparation for it (lack of erection); an abridgement of the sexual act (*ejaculatio praecox*), an occurrence which might equally well be regarded as a symptom; an arrest of the act before it has reached its natural conclusion (absence of ejaculation); or a non-appearance of the psychical outcome (lack of the feeling of pleasure in orgasm)" (1926, pp. 87-88).

Sexuality depends on the interrelationship of psychic stimulation and physiological response. Any alteration of these coordinated reflexes may cause impotency in men; for this reason psychosomatic considerations are extremely important in regard to the sexual function.

I will present an unusual case—unusual in view of the difficulties from which the patient suffered and because he had defeated a great number of analysts in their therapeutic endeavors—and try to formulate a theory about *ejaculatio praecox*.

CASE HISTORY

When the patient called for his first appointment, his voice was shrill and he spoke rapidly. My secretary, who first answered the telephone, was unable to determine whether he was a man or a woman. The patient is short and robust with a spheroidal abdomen. His neck is short. His face is fair and round and he blushes easily. He wears a well-trimmed beard. His forehead is broad and his cheeks hang. He is almost bald, although he tries to disguise it with his side hair. His blue eyes are sunken under his eyebrows. He dresses well, without luxury; he has a certain imposing quality which provokes respect. What was most striking was that in spite of what seemed to be rather definitive characteristics, he still seemed nondescript.

He told me that he had suffered from absolute impotency since his marriage four years ago and that he had been unable, up to that moment, to deflower his wife. He added, however, that he loved her very much and did not want to lose her. He said that he knew his case was extremely difficult, insofar as he had seen many therapists. He acknowledged that he had never completed any treatment, but he hoped that I would be able to help him finally resolve his problems and relieve him of the burden of his tragedy.

He was forty-nine years old. Born in a small town in Germany, he came from a moderately wealthy Jewish family that had had to emigrate to South America in 1938 because of the Nazi persecution. The father was forty when the patient was born. He was described as having been able to achieve a modicum of financial success, but apparently he was a man who never found himself. He was also considered to be unaffectionate and distant from his family. Upon his arrival in South America, he stopped working. He was able to live off his investment in his brother's business. He stayed home reading, and punctually every day went for a walk in the park near the house he lived in. At the age of sixty-two, he suffered a coronary and died a few days later. The patient keeps very few remembrances of him. The father did not pay too much attention to his son and was concerned only that his homework be done well. Very seldom did he play with his children.

The mother was one year younger than the father. She had a strong, exaggerated, and domineering character. She always worried about feeding the children properly; she seldom let them go out on the street, and for that reason the patient was fearful of and cowardly in his relations with other children. He never participated in sports and even now has no interest in them. The mother died three years after the father, when the patient was twenty-five.

His childhood and adolescent memories in Germany are scarce although he had been fourteen when he left. He remembered anti-Semitism at school, on the part of schoolmates and some teachers. He received lower marks than children with lesser capacities, but he had felt it futile to compete. In the beginning, there were still a few Jewish children, but when he arrived at the Gymnasium he was the only one left, because the other Semites had fled the country. His father was one of the last to leave Germany and did not do so until 1938.

From the sexual history, it is important to say that the patient has never masturbated. When he touches his genitals he feels fear and immediately washes his hands. He had his first sexual relation at twenty-one, an almost ritualistic act with a prostitute. His brother-in-law arranged everything, and although the patient experienced great anxiety, he also felt pleasure in his first sexual contact. When he returned to his home, there was a celebration because, at last, he was a man, and he felt a sense of completion.

The patient had occasional but infrequent relationships with prostitutes when he went to college. He did well in school and was able to win a scholarship to continue his studies at the postgraduate level. He went to two institutions in different countries, the last one in the United States. Although he was a very good student, he never succeeded in obtaining his doctorate, a fact that has haunted him up to the present time. During his graduate years, he first experienced *ejaculatio praecox* with prostitutes, a pattern which continues to persist.

He remained just a year in the United States and returned to South America to a job previously held and to his monotonous existence. Being a very peculiar and shy person, he had almost no friends and dedicated hundreds of lonely hours to reading. On holidays he had lunch with his sister and brother-in-law. Once in a while he found a prostitute, but she did not satisfy him.

One of his friends suggested to him that he go into personal psychoanalysis. He went to a therapist who at first helped him, but after three years, the sessions became monotonous and he decided to abandon the treatment. Later he started treatment with another doctor who gave him six LSD treatments, and he attended group therapy for two years. Deep inside, he does not have good memories of his experience and considers the therapist a "gabbler."

At the end of 1965, he met a very attractive prostitute and decided to establish a close relationship. He invited her once or twice a week to have dinner and they had sexual relations in his apartment. Nevertheless, he felt blackmailed by her, because she demanded great amounts of money. (He thinks that he gave her a third of his income.) His sexual relations were rudimentary because his erection did not last and he experienced premature ejaculation. He felt deceived, but with this woman, in contrast with previous ones, he felt the pleasure of possessing a beautiful body.

It is interesting to notice that the patient had never had a girlfriend although he was over forty years old. He had been in love with a librarian to whom he never talked. Some years later he dated a colleague, but she soon married another man.

In his present position, he met a girl eighteen years younger who worked for the same organization. After a somewhat whirlwind courtship, they married. Yet, the marriage was never consummated. The patient could not maintain an erection. All attempts at intercourse failed because he ejaculated before he could penetrate.

Manifestations of his impotency varied from one occasion to another. Most frequently, he had premature emissions. With each unsuccessful attempt at intercourse his feelings of inadequacy intensified. For long periods of time, he would not be able to have an erection. If he were able to, he would ejaculate immediately, soiling his wife with his seminal fluid. At other times, his orgasm would be so rapid that it would occur without an erection.

Both the patient and his wife grew desperate. He sought all types of therapies, varying from hypnosis to such drugs as benzedrine and nupercaine. He felt dissatisfied with all of them and abruptly terminated each treatment attempt. Several years ago he was transferred to Mexico City. When he arrived he visited three analysts recommended to him, but he stayed with me because, as he stated, my office was just one block from his home.

In general, he is a very difficult patient, and shows practically no affect. He constantly compares me to his last analyst, saying that my interpretations would never have been made by him. When I confront him with his negative feelings toward me, he states that he is not certain he will continue with his therapy because he does not see any results. When I remind him that he is not my prisoner, he immediately pulls back and says that he will try for another six months, and that the same situation occurred with his last psychoanalyst.

He talks in a diffuse manner and almost completely ignores my existence, reducing all the sessions to the recitation of actual events. The tricks this patient plays on me are also noteworthy. Once in a while he introduces a new character into the therapy to see if I am listening, and if I ask about this person he states that he has mentioned him before on several occasions. Other times he brings a dream, which by the way are scarce, and when I start investigating it, he suddenly gives me clues that he had hidden from me to see if I were capable of interpreting his dream without them. Another typical characteristic is his constant questioning; he always asks about the origin of things.

His inability to differentiate between impulses, affects, body sensations, and his incapacity to postpone discharge causes a bizarre transference reaction. It seems to me that he has submitted to analysis because he is unable to break off treatment. Coming punctually to the appointed hour magically avoids a crisis. He does not respond to any interpretation, but tries to carry out his role as a patient, never developing an observing ego. His prolonged dependency on a parent has facilitated this situation. He does not want to remember his dependency on his mother; at the same time we can infer that a profound hostility toward her took place in childhood. A major resistance in transference feelings is the denial of the hate he felt for his mother, the analyst acting as a surrogate.

A defect in the development of basic ego functions stems from a disturbance of early object relationships and thus of early identifications. The Nazis were frightening and he could not establish any close relationships in Germany. All these factors make any working alliance impossible. On a conscious level, this patient has no realistic hope of alleviating his neurotic misery and shows a lack of mobility of cathexis for displacement, which makes him mistrustful of all therapists. He clung tenaciously to a number of psychoanalysts in the past but had tremendous difficulty sustaining a transference relationship. Although in certain areas he seems to function reasonably well, he maintained only a fragile equilibrium with all his previous analysts.

Each session is similar to the previous one. He spends considerable time in superficial monologue. There is a marked absence of dreams and much silence. The only difference between my technique and that of his other therapists is that I focus upon his seemingly defensive lack of emotions.

When the patient talks about real events, he habitually brings up problems with his wife. Very often he presents an "emergency." Because of the lack of sexual activity, his wife flirts with several men. At the beginning of treatment, it was her painting teacher; on another occasion, an attractive neighbor. In general these emergencies are minor because, at nonsexual levels, he believes his relationship with his wife is good. However, he suffers intense anxiety due to his general insecurity. He lives depending on his wife's arrival at home. He watches her constantly and feels persecuted if any man comes close to her.

At the same time, the continuous demands made on the therapist, and the bizarre transference manifestations, provoke a disturbed countertransference reaction. This patient, whom we could call either a severe character disorder or a borderline, is in a way a heavy emotional burden for anyone who cares about him. I feel that almost none of my interpretations are accepted because he cannot identify with me. He provokes a great deal of frustration on my part, since I have no satisfaction or sense of accomplishment. On the other hand, I feel that I can understand this patient in a better way than his previous therapists, because I suffered a certain persecution in my own childhood and also had to leave the country I was born in.

In all, this patient creates a most difficult analytic experience for himself and his analyst; there is a persistent sense of frustration and disappointment in both participants. An inner state that appears related to his *ejaculatio praecox* creates a comparable interaction between himself and his wife. The basic factors in this symptom appear clinically as his impaired masculine identification, his unresolved aggression toward his mother, and a number of ego dysfunctions which make it difficult for him to deal with his underlying primitive sexual and aggressive fantasies.

DISCUSSION

Abraham postulated (1917) three mutually dependent causes for impotency: (1) a basic feminine orientation, (2) a sadistic attitude toward women, and (3) an increase in urethral eroticism that makes the patient equate urine with sperm as children do.

Wilhelm Reich (1928) related *ejaculatio praecox* to certain forms of hysteria. The emission would be a reaction to the prohibition to masturbate: The penis should not be touched. According to this author such cases would have a more favorable prognosis than those stemming from pregenital problems.

Stekel (1927) wrote of the desire "to become impotent," a last effort to make sexual relations impossible. This could be provoked by: (1) fear of losing independence (patients would equate sexual relations with marriage and loss of freedom), (2) fear of venereal disease (this is equated to castration panic, but he also mentions vaginismus and the captive penis), and (3) fear of death (this can be related to guilt about the committed sexual act).

Gutheil (1959) emphasizes pregenital elements in which oral and urethral phases are predominant; at the same time he emphasizes a passive, feminine orientation toward sex. This author describes the frequency of enuresis in patients with *ejaculatio praecox* as the result of an infantile attitude that substitutes urine for the depositing of semen.

Other pregenital zones are occasionally referred to in the literature, but I would like to discuss an aspect of *ejaculatio praecox* not previously mentioned. During orgasm one discharges a substance and simultaneously feels excitation. In general, there is a close relationship between semen and excitation. The prolongation of the sensation of pleasure is important. In the majority of animals precopulatory patterns are brief, and so is copulation itself. In baboons, for instance, the time from mounting to ejaculation is no more than seven to eight seconds, with less than fifteen pelvic thrusts, often fewer. The human being, however, has a copulatory phase of several minutes before the male reaches the consummatory act of sperm ejaculation. In humans, the aim of sexual activity is to prolong the act as long as possible in order to achieve maximum excitation with the emission of semen. *Ejaculatio praecox* would cut off the mounting excitatory crescendo by interrupting the process of summation of erotic sensations. Emission occurs before completion and semen is ejaculated with a relative lack of sensation or feeling. Thus, the sex act does not progress along its natural course. It is incomplete.

In *The Self and the Object World*, Jacobson (1964) states that in the second year the changes in the nature of the relations of the child with the object world, introduce in the psychic organization a new category: time. She is obviously referring to the maturity of the locomotor apparatus, sphincter control, and the ego's capacity to discharge instincts in a graduated fashion. One acquires the ability to make judgments in terms of *now* or *after*. In contrast to the oral stage, the *now* is not the instant of satisfaction, and the acceptance of delay can bring the pleasure *after*. We see therefore the importance time acquires during anal and urethral phases.

My patient was always preoccupied with time. He was constantly concerned with his wife not coming home on time. He persistently focused upon being punctual, early, or tardy. His sexual development took place rather late, and up to this day he has never masturbated, being unable to discharge instinctual excitation. He married at forty-five; again his timing was late. He has never completed any treatment, and he has never been able to consummate the sexual act with his wife. His life has been punctuated by imperfect timing, being late in his sexual development, or being early within the confines of sexual activity as in *ejaculatio praecox*. The latter is associated with his inability to achieve completion.

The following orientation seems characteristic of this patient's *ejaculatio praecox*, one which may be fairly common in patients suffering from structural problems.

First, as stressed, he could not bring any act to completion and this extended into the sexual area. Completion was equated with commitment, and the patient was terrified of a close relationship. The latter could lead to dissolution of his identity sense, or at a deeper level, to annihilation.

Next, the patient's anxiety was primitive; more precisely it was an anxiety characteristic of early phases of development. This type of ego constellation antedates the firm establishment of the sense of time and continuity which is part of a good time differentiation. He demonstrates how such poorly developed functions manifested themselves in the sexual act and contributed to the formation of the symptom of *ejaculatio praecox*.

CONCLUSIONS

The analysis of this patient appears to confirm the importance of pregenital traumas and problems in the development of *ejaculatio praecox*. Other pertinent factors, some of which have been described in the previous literature, include a feminine orientation, a variety of ego dysfunction, a dread of closeness and a fear of losing one's independence, incestuous fixations, and extensive unresolved aggressive conflicts. Of particular additional importance is the patient's dread of the passing of time and of the completion experience. Underlying these factors was a primitive anxiety with fears of annihilation and dread of merger, anxieties intensified by the patient's failure to establish a firm sense of time.

REFERENCES

Abraham, K. (1917). Ejaculatio praecox. In *Selected Papers on Psycho-Analysis*, pp. 280-298 New York: Basic Books, 1957.

Agoston, T. (1949). Horror vacui. *Psychoanalytic Review* 37:438.

Erikson, E. (1963). *Childhood and Society*. New York: Basic Books.

Federn, P. (1953). *Ego Psychology and the Psychoses*. New York: Basic Books.

Freud, S. (1926). Inhibitions, symptoms and anxiety. *Standard Edition* 20:77-175.

Gutheil, E. (1959). Sexual dysfunctions in men. In *American Handbook of Psychiatry*, ed. S. Arieti, chapter 36. New York: Basic Books.

Jacobson, E. (1964). *The Self and the Object World*. New York: International Universities Press.

Morris, D. (1967). *Primate Ethology*. London: Weidenfeld and Nicolson.

Reich, W. (1928). The genital character and the neurotic character. In *The Psychoanalytic Reader*, ed. R. Fliess. New York: International Universities Press, 1948.

Stekel, W. (1927). *Impotence in the Male*. New York: Liveright.

Solomon, J. (1964). *A Synthesis of Human Behavior*. New York: Grune and Stratton.

The Evolution
of a Shoe Fetish

JAMES W. HAMILTON, M.D.

This paper deals with clinical material gathered from the long-term, psychoanalytically-oriented treatment of a patient with a shoe fetish. Genetic and dynamic aspects of this problem are emphasized. The combination of a dominating mother and a passive and absent father, the sharing of a bed with an older sister until age eleven, and the receipt of frequent enemas contributed directly to the development of the fetish, the most crucial determinant being the cumulative traumatic effect of the enemas. During adolescence, the patient also resorted to transvestism to deal with the intensification of castration fears. Becoming a husband and father threatened to disrupt his tenuous defenses and forced him to seek therapy for two years, during which he was able to gain sufficient insight to forego the fetish and to engage in heterosexual activity in a reasonably conflict-free manner. Previous theoretical contributions on the subject are included and theoretical issues are dealt with, particularly the role of the core fantasy of the phallic woman in the perversions.

In his first reference to fetishism, Freud (1905) observed that "No other variation of the sexual instinct that borders on the pathological can lay so much claim to our interest as this one, such is the peculiarity of the phenomenon to which it gives rise." In his later paper on the subject, Freud (1927) stressed the importance of the defense mechanisms of denial and splitting to support the possibility of the female phallus and thereby alleviate castration anxiety.

Greenacre (1963) has defined fetishism as the obligatory use, as part of the sexual act, of some nongenital objects without which gratification cannot be obtained. "The object may be some other body part, or some article of clothing, or less frequently some more impersonal object. In most instances the need is for possession of the object so that it can be seen, touched, or smelled during or in preparation for the sexual act whether this be masturbatory or some form of intercourse. In some instances, it is not only the possession of the object but a ritualistic use of it which is essential."

Bak (1953) emphasized not only the significance of castration from without in fetishism, but the inner wish to identify with the female as well. Later (1968), after affirming that the principle defensive function of the perversion is "the reinvestment of the fantasy of the phallic woman" and that fetishism is "the basic perversion," he went on to question the fetishist's reliance upon ego splitting, feeling that Freud and others overestimated its role. "It seems more accurate to assume that due to the equivocal perceptions and the lack of intimate knowledge of the female genital, the child's ego suspends the decision about the presence or absence of the penis and leaves it uncertain, defensively mistrusting his own perception, neither denying it or accepting it. The ego, rather than incurring a split, attempts a tentative synthesis by upholding an 'uncertainty' as a 'maybe' . . . This uncertainty helps maintain an oscillatory identification with either parent, prevents the clear demarcation of the two sexes that would lead to certainty of sexual identity, and sustains a bisexual position by fused self representations."

Payne (1939) and Gillespie (1940) drew attention to preoedipal factors in the development of fetishism, especially oral sadism and the impulse to kill the love object against which the fetish, because of its indestructibility, helps to defend. Greenacre (1955) amplified the contribution of early trauma, which creates "an enormous stimulation of aggression," thus complicating the oedipal phase. In this same paper she observed, "It is the traumatic disturbance of the phallic period, however, which leaves, I believe, the deposit of the specific content, compulsively repetitive or ritualistically acted out in the search for sexual relief in fetishists. In this connection it is to be noted that the perverse fetishist may have a real problem of establishing a tender sexual relation with his loved one. He may feel tenderness for her and the wish for an active yet tender consummation; yet the sexual act, once approached, is too aggressivized, and the fear of castration fits too readily with the identification through vision and with the fantasy of punishment for killing, so that continuation of intercourse becomes a struggle for relief and to preserve some sense of body integrity rather than to achieve a high degree of object relationship with their partners, who are used rather for narcissistic than for mutual gratification, especially at the genital-sexual level."

In offering an overview about the development of perversions, Greenacre (1968) postulates that "due to early disturbances in the mother-infant relationship there is a severe impairment of object relationships which combines with a specifically determined weakness of the body and self images, especially involving the genitals. This becomes most significant during the phallic and oedipal periods when castration anxiety is extraordinarily acute, due to the quality of the aggression aroused at these times. The maturing sexual drives are distorted in the interest of bolstering the body image. There is then a vicious circle of recurring castration panic for which the fetish or the ritualized behavior serve almost literally as a stopgap permitting the semblance of a more nearly adequate sexual performance or relationship." Few detailed cases of fetishism, however, have been reported in the literature. This is in part because individuals having such problems seldom present in psychiatric settings, since the symptom is generally ego-syntonic. Further, those who do enter treatment usually have great difficulty establishing and maintaining a therapeutic alliance (Romm 1949).

Developmental History

The patient to be discussed here was a twenty-one-year-old white male whose fetishistic rituals, with which he had been quite comfortable, gave way to chronic anxiety during his three-year marriage. He had become progressively more angry with his wife, being concerned that he might hit or kill her, especially after intercourse, in which he could participate only if he fantasized another woman wearing a particular kind of shoe. He had separated from his wife abruptly and returned to live with his parents. He asked her to dress in a pair of his jeans, one of his T-shirts and a pair of her shoes; when she became distressed at the request and refused to comply, he left her enraged and shortly thereafter sought psychotherapy.

He had become interested in female shoes at the age of four to five, when he would cut up those belonging to his playmates and then expect these girls to continue wearing them. From five to seven, he played with his mother's shoes and his older sister's drum majorette boots and obtained intense erotic pleasure from getting them wet. Throughout latency, he was concerned exclusively with men's shoes, especially cowboy and work boots, again being stimulated by soaking them in water, after which he would oil them and douse them again. During this period, he once got an erection while looking at a male friend wearing cowboy boots. At twelve to thirteen, after buying a new pair of loafers for himself, he became preoccupied once more with women's shoes. He would steal, wear, destroy, and throw them away. Over the years, he stole thirty-five to forty pairs and later, in adolescence, broke into several houses to get such footwear. When he started driving, he would carry at least one pair of women's shoes in the trunk of his car at all times.

In order to appeal to him, these shoes had to be of a particular low-cut type and fit in such a manner so as to produce a special symmetry, fullness, and "connection" with the foot. He was unable to describe this connection precisely. He had his first masturbatory experience at thirteen. While running away after stealing some shoes, he suddenly got an erection, noted a tingling sensation in his penis, and ejaculated without any manual stimulation. His greatest pleasure was associated with getting the shoes wet. Later, while masturbating, he would fantasize ("like turning on a TV screen") various unidentifiable women with the shoes. He obtained the maximum pleasure from the shoes' destruction and could not ejaculate until he had found a way of immersing them in water. When dating, during adolescence, if the girl wore shoes which attracted him, he would playfully try to push her in mud puddles, and if unsuccessful, would lose all interest and drop her. In early adolescence he began to dress in women's clothing and continued to do so at irregular intervals, until he became involved in therapy.

He was the younger of two children, having a sister eight years older. His mother was an overbearing, domineering, controlling woman, who had always tried to run his life; his father was extremely passive and seldom around the house during the patient's younger years, as he worked the afternoon shift regularly. He felt that he never had any relationship with his father and resented that he had not been exposed to such "manly pursuits" as hunting and fishing. He slept with his sister until he was eleven, when she married, which came as a profound disappointment. He was "close" to her but never saw her naked, "at least nothing that sticks out." He had always felt more feminine than masculine and preferred playing with girls rather than with boys. He had been much concerned about the size of his buttocks at age eleven to twelve, which he attempted to conceal by dressing in a certain fashion. He experienced constant concern about the size of his penis and had a pronounced fear of stripping in front of other men and of urinating in public toilets.

His early memories were extremely significant. At age three to four, he was beaten by his mother for running naked on the front lawn. At five, he and a girl playmate urinated behind a bush together, at which time he was sure she had a penis. From that time on, he thought all girls had penises and that the only means of differentiating between the sexes was by the length of hair, which stirred considerable anxiety whenever he was forced to visit a barber. Around five, he also remembered being escorted to a wading pool by his mother, and when he had to have a bowel movement, being taken by her to a clump of bushes where he was able to defecate. At seven to eight, he began surreptitiously to study an anatomy book belonging to his parents, thought that several of the female drawings looked like his mother, and wondered if she might not have a penis after concluding that the sigmoid colon of one specimen looked like an inverted penis. He denied any primal scene experiences, emphasizing that his parents were extremely puritanical about sex and slept in separate beds, and that he did not witness intercourse until thirteen, when he observed a pair of dogs (Peto 1975).

He had always been terrified of snakes and spiders. As a child, he was cruel to animals, yet often wished he could have been a cat himself. Before becoming interested in dousing shoes, he took particular delight in removing pet turtles from water, "drying them out" for prolonged periods, and getting them wet again. He would go through the same routine with house plants, failing to water them until they started to wither, then saturating them. During latency, he was fascinated by the concept of perpetual energy and assembled an apparatus consisting of a battery, motor, and generator where one component continually "fed the other."

He met his wife at seventeen, having been attracted to her because she reminded him of his sister. He was forced to marry her a year later when she became pregnant, and to leave high school in the middle of his senior year. He sought work in a hospital, first as an orderly and then as a surgical scrub nurse, the position he held upon entering therapy.

Dynamic and Genetic Factors

The patient was in therapy for almost two years, initially on a once-a-week basis, increasing to twice a week at the end of the first year. As treatment progressed, he would attempt to forego the shoe fantasy while masturbating or having intercourse, only to experience varying degrees of impotence which made it necessary for him to resort once again to the fantasy.

During the fourteenth month, in a particular session, he became extremely angry with me and was uncertain whether I was trying "to get" his penis, or he, mine. He related that on the previous weekend, he had been stimulated by caressing the buttocks of his girlfriend, had masturbated her without having intercourse, and then had had the urge "to shit all over her." He became preoccupied with defecating on people generally and with drawing the digestive system with an unknown object underneath the anus. The object, he thought, could represent either a toilet, his girlfriend, his mother, or his therapist. He was much more aggressive toward his mother whenever she attempted to dominate him and was gratified by this turn of events: "Got results. I flexed my muscles."

He reported seeing "the shoes" without feet of late ("dirty, old, muddy shoes") and had been therefore able to inspect their insides, only to discover that the lining was torn. He then remembered that at age ten, he had seen his mother sitting on the toilet defecating and, though unable to view her genitalia clearly, thought she had a penis. This recollection was followed by: sudden, spontaneous outbursts of "fuck, shit, fuck, shit"; the wish again to shit on his girlfriend, whom he had nicknamed "Grabdick"; the recall of a fantasy of killing his wife; and the reassurance that he had never behaved violently at any time, though he had forced his wife to have anal intercourse once when she was pregnant and later licked her anus and blew in it.

During the ensuing month, he was unable to get an erection without the shoe fantasy. The fantasy returned, although the shoes were now "battered" and he could see the girl's foot through a defect in the sole. He was masturbating infrequently and had actually perceived the vagina, while making love, "as a nice, warm place to be" but had not had intercourse because he thought he felt "a roughness" at the introitus. For the first time, his masturbatory fantasy became that of a naked girl who was not wearing shoes, but who was also without feet, arms, or head and whose torso was bent to the same angle that his penis made with his body, and whom he referred to as "a little prick" (Lewin 1933, Fenichel 1936).

During the next hour, after mentioning that his erections while with his girlfriend had been unusually firm though he still hesitated to have intercourse with her, he remembered vividly that he had been given enemas by his mother when four or five; that she used an orange-brown bag with a hose and nozzle; that he was always positioned on his right side with his left leg drawn up; and that, while he did not like the experience, there were some pleasurable feelings associated with it. He could see clearly the wallpaper in the room where the enemas took place and was sure that his father "was somewhere in the picture." He went on to talk about an incident, from which he achieved much sadistic gratification: while he was working as a hospital orderly, he had administered twenty-six consecutive soap suds enemas to a male patient, after being told to be sure the man was "cleaned out." He proceeded to describe a black Corvette sports car that he was interested in purchasing, and, after a period of silence, exclaimed suddenly, "Bang! Red, black. Enema bag and nozzle. My favorite colors of shoes and cars. Always red and black. Nozzle, fuck. Enema, shit. My mother stuck her penis in my ass." He visualized himself giving himself an enema, wondered if "the roughness" he felt at the introitus while making love previously might be similar to the anal valves he observed while assisting at sigmoidoscopies and hemorrhoidectomies, and said that his "main delight" whenever he had intercourse came from inserting and reinserting his penis in the vagina like an enema.

In the immediately following session, he stated that he had gone from my office to a used car lot where he purchased a Corvette and that he had thought about nothing else since, refusing to show it even to his girlfriend, which angered her, and constantly taking apart and repairing it in his fantasies. He remembered that when he was given enemas by his mother, his father would be standing off to one side holding the enema bag. He related that the three cars that he had owned were red, black, and brown, adding that there had been much prudishness about sexual and bowel function in his family.

Two weeks later, he spoke of having a good time with a girl on New Year's Eve, two days previous. He had suddenly become quite sarcastic toward her for no obvious reason. As he thought about his reaction during the hour, he decided that he would like "to fuck the shit out of her" and then give her an enema.

In reconstructing this clinical case material, it is clear that the shoe fetish represented the female phallus, and that, while vastly overdetermined, the most important genetic trauma in the development of this symptom was the enemas administered to the patient by his mother. The attendant helplessness and vulnerability of this experience, he sought to master in his later fetishistic rituals, a forerunner of which was the practice of depriving plants and turtles of water, then suddenly rehydrating them. He displayed many anal characterological traits such as neatness, parsimony, stubbornness, persistent lateness, and an intense need to control every situation in which he was involved.

His interest in women's shoes began at the age of four to five, receded during latency and returned with adolescence when he had started to steal these articles and incorporate them in his masturbatory fantasies. The fetish later allowed him to perform heterosexually and to defend against passive homosexual conflicts, especially anal rape—such fears being intensified during therapy whenever he would relinquish, even temporarily, the fetish (Freud 1927).

The overexposure to his sister, due to the fact that they shared the same bed until ᴜe was eleven, was another crucial determinant of his perversion (Greenacre 1953). Although he claimed never to have seen her naked, he qualified this by adding "at least nothing that sticks out." In his early memories, he was convinced that his female playmate had a penis as did all women. After the first year of therapy, he stated that he knew on one level that his girlfriend did not have one, but was not sure and doubted later that his playmate was so endowed. Such memories might lend support to Bak's assumption that it is synthesis with "maybe" replacing "uncertainty" about the possibility of the female phallus, rather than splitting, which occurs within the ego of the fᴜishist.

Unresolved oral issues were also significant contributing factors in the perversion. The patient had an inordinate dread of snakes and spiders, generally considered a displacement from the terror of the devouring mother (Little 1968).

This latter conflict was expressed quite directly when he became sexually aroused and got an erection while reading a passage in a World War II novel, describing how nuns on Tarawa forced the native women to wear brassieres so as to not excite the Marines. He then visualized a pair of breasts, experienced a sensation of "being sucked in" and said: "I'm afraid. I can see myself sucking. It looks like a penis. I can see myself as a little boy crying. Now the breast is in the mouth. It belongs there. Now it's gone and I'm crying." Previously, he had become very distrustful of one woman who had bitten his breast during foreplay and "almost drawn blood," causing him to wonder what she would do if she ever got her teeth on his penis.

His relationships with women were narcissistically structured to insure against any displays of affect which were threatening due to his inability to differentiate aggressive from libidinal impulses. His fear of genital sexuality and the fear that he might lose control and hurt his partner during or after love-making may have been due, in addition to the above factors, to the confusion between the explosiveness of the enema discharge and orgasm (fuck, shit), thus causing a blurring of anal and phallic conflicts and combining the fear of bodily disintegration with that of castration (Brodsky 1959). At one point in therapy, he had a dream in which he threw "the shoes" in a toilet which then erupted, splattering him with feces and causing him to awaken with much anxiety (Payne 1939, Gillespie 1940). On another occasion, while talking about his fear of having intercourse, he thought of a friend whose penis had "turned blue" due to a hematoma resulting from a hernia repair. At still another time, after an episode of foreplay, he suddenly took his pulse and announced jokingly, "I'm dead!" He then remembered several patients observed while doing hospital work. The first sustained a myocardial infarct during intercourse; one died in bed after urinating; another defecated postmortem when turned over by attendants; and a fourth expired after burping. The patient's fascination with perpetual energy machines may have been an attempt to deal with fears of death stemming directly from the enema experience.

During many sessions, when anxious, he would pull on one thumb or the other. On one such occasion, he declared: "I don't want to lose it." He then felt faint, which recalled two instances while he was working as a surgical scrub nurse—one in which he had nearly fainted during the second operation in which he participated, a mastectomy, when he was asked to hold one of the retractors; and another in which he had actually fainted sometime later while assisting on a hydrocelectomy.

He had unusually large thumbs about which he was self-conscious, and he was kidded by male associates who claimed that women preferred his thumb to his penis. He referred often to his interaction with women as "keeping them under my thumb." Once, after accidentally cutting a thumb, he remembered a dream he had presented during the first hour in which a chicken was pulling at his thumb. The animal then became half-chicken and half-dog, although he could not be sure which end was which.

Utilizing Greenacre's (1968) concepts, it would seem that when deficits of early maternal care lead to problems of separation-individuation and a persistence of primary identification along with projective and introjective mechanisms, the unresolved oral rage under certain circumstances such as premature and repeated exposure to the naked female body, as could well have happened to the patient through his relationship with his sister until he was eleven, may be transposed into a fear that the mother will retaliate by castration, which at the genital-phallic level is expressed symbolically through concerns about the dentate vagina. As he was recovering memories of the enemas, he had a dream involving himself, his mother, his girlfriend, and another man. He was five and "getting smaller and smaller" until he became an infant wearing a blue sweater and white booties "with a tube hanging out my ass. I'm happy. My mouth is open and I've got whiskers like a cat." He then bit an electric cord and was killed. His associations were that he had had a pet cat who died in the same manner and that he often used the slang term "pussy" for the female genitalia. During his younger years, he had wished repeatedly he were a cat.

Given this anlage, a severe castrating type of trauma such as repeated enemas (especially at the ages of two or four which Greenacre 1968 feels are "times of special sensitivity to body injuries") is sufficient to precipitate or crystallize the development of "pronounced" fetishism.

While a perversion may be found with varying degrees of generalized psychopathology, in this instance it was part of a borderline personality organization characterized by poorly-structured object relations, chaotic sexual identity and body image, pronounced ego and superego deficits with poor impulse control, and a predisposition toward acting out (Kernberg 1967).

Why is it that the foot and shoe happen to be the commonest objects chosen as fetishes (Greenacre 1953, 1960)? Besides the fact that the foot is paired, has multiple appendages, and is constantly growing during childhood (as evidenced by the continuous need for larger shoes), it may also be cast in bas relief to the penis should the young boy look down while standing to urinate, and therefore be even more likely to become a displacement for castration conflicts. This particular contrast might well have been further accentuated in the patient described in this paper, due to his having been placed on his right side whenever he received an enema with his left leg retracted toward his chest, bringing the left foot into greater prominence in his visual field. Feet and shoes are employed in many familiar sayings having phallic overtones: filling the old man's shoes, following in father's footsteps, putting a foot down, receiving a boot or kick in the rear, getting a leg up on someone, dying with one's boots on.

Since mid-adolescence, the patient had relied upon automobiles to reinforce his masculine strivings and sense of bodily intactness and to gain reassurance about castration fears. These needs can best be appreciated in his associations to various sports cars immediately after the recollection of being given enemas. Here an important consideration might be the function of the foot in controlling the power of the vehicle via the accelerator and brakes. It will be recalled that the patient was in the habit of carrying a pair of female shoes in the trunk of his car at all times. He would drive in a reckless, counterphobic manner and was involved in two serious accidents while in treatment. Luckily he emerged without injury, reacting later to the damage of his cars "as if a part of me was missing." At one point during therapy, his interest in cars shifted to the Beatles who, with their long hair and guitars suspended from the waist, offered a concrete externalization for the fantasy of the phallic woman. He let his hair grow, thought of taking singing lessons and becoming a Beatle-like entertainer. He decided against this possibility and then named his sports car "my Beatle."

As an additional means of coping with castration anxiety, the patient resorted to transvestism in mid-adolescence. He would dress as a woman "from the waist down" with nylons, high-heeled shoes and jeans, and then go out and urinate in bushes, recapitulating his early experience with his female playmate.

While there is much controversy about the relationship between transitional objects and both infantile and adult fetishes, it was not possible to determine what part the former may have played in this case (Greenacre 1970, Bak 1974). The patient did have a teddy bear named Bruno during his early childhood but could remember nothing precisely about his relationship with it. Shortly after beginning treatment, he had a dream of being chased by a large bear which he wanted to shoot, but could not as he had no gun and therefore awakened.

Therapeutic Considerations

The patient had a difficult time developing a working alliance, and the therapeutic relationship throughout the first year was both tenuous and stormy with basic trust being a central issue. He declined a suggested twice weekly schedule, was continuously late, would miss sessions, and was extremely negativistic, often expressing his anger in toilet terms such as "I'm pissed off" or "You aren't worth a shit." There were long periods of stubborn silence, the result of his reluctance to perform and "do the talking." Payment of the fee was always an area of contention, with the patient feeling that he should not be expected to pay for anything. As he became more comfortable with this aspect, he bought a gift for his girlfriend, the first time in his life that he had ever done so for anyone.

During the early phases, whenever he would forego the fetish even momentarily, passive fears would emerge in the form of concerns over being homosexual and over being attacked from behind. He responded initially to an interpretation as if he were being penetrated anally and would vehemently deny any possible validity to such interventions. Later, the most meaningful interpretations dealt with his need for the fantasy of the phallic woman and his fear of loss of control. Prior to therapy, he claimed never to have had positive feelings for anyone, but gradually he realized that he relied on the shoe fantasy to avoid any awareness of such affectual bonds.

The quality and character of the transference are conveyed by a series of fantasies he would elaborate upon before falling asleep. Around the time of the first anniversary of treatment, he became very discouraged about the progess being made, thought seriously of quitting, but agreed to continue with an increase in the frequency of visits to twice weekly. He remembered that his father had once taken flying lessons but had stopped when a sparkplug in the plane did not function properly and had never flown again. Shortly thereafter, he presented a dream of having intercourse with a woman who reminded him of me; the intercourse was interrupted by the alarm ringing. This was the first time he had ever dreamt of a girl, and he proceeded to talk about a fantasy of the previous night in which he was a wartime army surgeon. An enemy doctor asked him to perform a caesarean section on his wife since all the enemy's colleagues had been killed. He agreed, gave the woman a spinal, became worried about the risk of infection since the operation was carried out in a basement using nonsterile water, and was elated when the procedure turned out successfully. He and the other doctor subsequently became friendly. "We were aware of each other as humans despite being enemies." The patient then confessed that he had been having such "surgical fantasies" for the past year, but had been unable to bring them up in therapy until this juncture.

In the following hour, he related a fantasy of having repaired a uterus that had perforated due to a self-induced abortion. Another surgeon had wanted to do a hysterectomy but he objected to this plan, wanting the woman to be able to have children. When she recovered from the operation, he referred her to a psychiatrist because of a previous history of multiple abortions. He recalled that his girlfriend had recently joked about "amputating" his penis, which caused him to be quite anxious. He had thought about his mother, at that time, and myself, later, while relating this material in the session, as potential castrators. The next week he fantasied doing a mitral commissurotomy on a friend with whose wife he was infatuated. When the friend did not survive the operation, he told the wife that his death was due to a septal defect. The patient realized that he was attracted to women who belonged to other men and was pleased whenever he could lure them away.

In the midst of recounting the enema experience, he described two fantasies. In the first he used a polyethylene graft to restore circulation to the right leg of a man run over by a train and then went on to repair torn mesenteric arteries. The victim was a friend married to one of the patient's former girlfriends. During various sessions, he would complain of his right leg "falling asleep" because of the way he positioned himself in his chair. In the second fantasy, he operated on John Kennedy after he had been shot in Dallas and saved his life by inserting a graft in the carotid artery and reconstructing the injured nerves and muscles. He was not a surgeon in this fantasy but had simply walked in off the street and taken over the case.

During the sixteenth month, he had a fantasy in which he removed a piece of glass from the heart of a young girl injured in an automobile accident. For the first time, he was a staff man and not a resident, and was congratulated after the operation by a colleague "Dr. H" which made him feel "good," although he realized "that the heart wouldn't be itself again until it had more time to heal." He had been angry with his father of late and was deliberately avoiding him—these feelings being a reaction to his awareness of the latter's passive role when he was given enemas. A few days afterwards, he fantasied that he was assisting me with a nephrectomy and proceeded to discuss anatomical sexual differences, being curious if the clitoris could be a female penis and if stimulating a woman's breasts during foreplay would cause the clitoris to enlarge. A week later, while sucking on his girl's breasts during foreplay, he momentarily thought that her breast might be a penis. He considered asking her to wear "the shoes" but was not sure how this would affect him if she were to let others see them and entertained fleeting thoughts of stealing a pair of shoes. He had a fantasy the previous evening of being a resident again and listening to a lecture given by a female surgeon. "A Dr. G, but that's too close to H. So I changed it to W for Williams" (my middle name).

During the next two weeks he reported obtaining much pleasure from fondling his girlfriend's breasts and using them in his masturbatory fantasies. He then "saw the girl next door" when he had been four to five. "It's like a moving picture. I don't think she had a penis." They were together in his crib having an afternoon nap and he actually gave her his shoes which were small and brown. This incident he was certain took place after the one when they urinated in the bushes. He wondered where this girl might be as of that moment and felt an urge to find her and "pull down her drawers and check." He admitted to considerable difficulty differentiating between the sexes and a preference for masturbation over intercourse. He stressed that "a naked woman is nothing. Without the shoes, she isn't stimulated" which he corrected to "stimulating." He next realized that the woman in a particular fantasy was himself and that he was actually giving himself an enema and that the shoes in his fantasies were always "dirty and muddy" since they would become so if they were introduced into the rectum. He had "an image" of the shoes entering the rectum, immediately felt his "ass tightening" and then fantasied that he had an extralarge penis and was having anal intercourse with himself, adding "all my fantasies are dirty!"

In the twentieth month, having gone three weeks without any surgical fantasies, he removed the appendix of a well-known millionaire. The scene was a ski lodge which had become "snowed-in," and he was not a physician.

His patient, on whom he used a low spinal anesthetic, reminded him of me, and he was pleased with the completeness of the surgical set-up, especially the intravenous bottles of saline. At one point, during the procedure, he asked one of his patient's bodyguards to leave the operating theater because the latter refused to wear a mask. Out of gratitude, his patient gave his entire fortune to him. After this fantasy, he went to sleep.

These fantasies, the manifest contents of which contained many derivatives of the enema experience (low spinal anesthetics, bottles of intravenous saline, concerns over contamination, the receipt of large sums of money, etc.) played a crucial role in his efforts to master sadistic impulses, castration fears, and passivity and to begin to consolidate a more adequate self-representation and sexual identity. Identification with the aggressor was an important mechanism in these fantasies, particularly in his attempt to deal with various aspects of transference. As noted, he did not introduce the fantasies in therapy until after he had dreamt of having intercourse with a woman who resembled me. Prior to that time, he had inquired if the hospital where my office was located ever performed surgery on out-patients and, if so, what types of procedures were done. Around the sixth month, he mentioned that he would like to become a surgeon and to model himself after a cardio-vascular surgeon whom he had worked with and begun to idealize. He emphasized, "I respect him tremendously like you would your father." He preferred orthopedic surgery to the other subspecialities because of the opportunity it offered to repair broken bones.

Working as a scrub nurse implied a primary identification with the castrating mother who had given him the enemas. His greatest anxiety in this role was associated with doing preps in the groin area. After being in therapy for nine months, he gave up hospital work and took a job in the automobile factory in which his father had always been employed, suggesting that he was beginning to develop a more consistent sense of himself as a man.

After he was able to perform heterosexually without the fetish and at a time when he had decided to remarry and become engaged, he asked to terminate and did so despite my repeated suggestions that such action was premature. He rationalized that he would not be able to remain in treatment because he was taking on a second job in order to support two families, and was already making a round trip of forty miles for each session. This action, however, may have been based upon fears of having to deal with negative aspects of the transference and of losing his potency if he were to continue in therapy (Tarachow 1963, p. 84). While this hypothesis could not be confirmed directly, he developed a slight fear of his future father-in-law following his engagement. He then had several fantasies of the latter having a brain tumor but would fall asleep without performing any surgery, having assessed the overall situation as "hopeful."

As a result of therapy, certain definite gains were made. In the sphere of object relations, he was able to be more assertive with his mother and not allow her to dominate him. He had gotten close to his father consistently and could express affection and respect for him openly for the first time in his life. He was able to achieve a measure of autonomous heterosexual capability after a protracted struggle. Without the fetish, he was hesitant at first to go beyond foreplay. He then assumed the female position in intercourse, where he could gain additional reassurance against castration fears by seeing his partner's breasts, before shifting to being on top. His transvestite behavior ceased during the first year of therapy and did not recur.

He completed his high school education, interrupted by his first marriage, earning high grades. As mentioned, he had given up his position as a scrub nurse for one in an automobile plant where he was able to be appropriately aggressive, stressing "I'm not a pussy at work anymore." His job was driving a hi-lo pick-up machine, and he was later promoted and placed in charge of four older men, an arrangement he could not have handled in the past.

REFERENCES

Bak, R. C. (1953). Fetishism. *Journal of the American Psychoanalytic Association* 1:285-298.
——— (1968). The phallic woman: the ubiquitous fantasy in perversions. *Psychoanalytic Study of the Child* 23:15-36.
——— (1974). Distortions of the concept of fetishism. *Psychoanalytic Study of the Child* 29:191-214.
Brodsky, B. (1959). The self-representation, anality and the fear of dying. *Journal of the American Psychoanalytic Association* 7:95-108.
Fenichel, O. (1936). The symbolic equation: girl-phallus. *The Collected Papers of Otto Fenichel*, vol. 2, pp. 3-18. New York: Norton.
Freud, S. (1905). Three essays on the theory of sexuality. *Standard Edition* 7:125-243.
——— (1927). Fetishism. *Standard Edition* 21:149-157.
Gillespie, W. H. (1940). A contribution to the study of fetishism. *International Journal of Psycho-Analysis* 21:401-415.
Greenacre, P. (1953). Certain relationships between fetishism and the faulty development of the body image. *Psychoanalytic Study of the Child* 6:180-205.
——— (1955). Further considerations regarding fetishism. *Psychoanalytic Study of the Child* 10:187-195.
——— (1960). Further notes on fetishism. *Psychoanalytic Study of the Child* 15:191-207.
——— (1968). Perversions: general considerations regarding their genetic and dynamic background. *Psychoanalytic Study of the Child* 23:47-62.
——— (1970). The transitional object and the fetish: with special reference to the role of illusion. *International Journal of Psycho-Analysis* 51:442-456.
Kernberg, O. (1967). Borderline personality organization. *Journal of the American Psychoanalytic Association* 15:641-685.
Lewin, B. D. (1933). The body as phallus. *Psychoanalytic Quarterly* 2:24-47.
Little, R. B. (1968). The resolution of oral conflicts in spider phobia. *International Journal of Psycho-Analysis* 49:492-494.

Payne, S. M. (1939). Some observations on the ego development of the fetishist. *International Journal of Psycho-Analysis* 20:161-170.

Peto, A. (1975). The etiological significance of the primal scene in perversions. *Psychoanalytic Quarterly* 44:177-190.

Romm, M. (1949). Some dynamics and fetishism. *Psychoanalytic Quarterly* 18:137-153.

Tarachow, S. (1963). *An Introduction to Psychotherapy.* New York: International Universities Press.

Prevention, Infant Therapy, and the Treatment of Adults
1. Toward Understanding Mutuality

JUDITH S. KESTENBERG, M.D.
with ARNHILT BUELTE

This is the first in a series of papers about the relevance of infant therapy to the treatment of adults. A description of maternal and infantile movement patterns is used to substantiate our thesis that not only does the mother hold the child, but the child holds the mother. A good-enough holding environment is maintained when the mother's adult patterns of effort and shaping dovetail with the infant's inborn reflexes to make mutual holding possible. Mutual support enables mother and child to attune in tension-flow rhythms (used for need satisfaction) and to adjust in shape-flow rhythms (used for intake and output). Attunement is the physical core of empathy, and adjustment is the cradle of trust. Empathy and trust between therapist and patient develop in a good-enough holding environment which is derived from mutual holding in early infancy. Not only does the therapist provide a holding environment for the patient, but the patient does his share to support the therapist in his aims.

Winnicott (1963, 1965) introduced the term *holding environment* to describe a therapeutic setting modeled after the early caretaking functions. The term *holding* denotes not only actual physical holding, but also the total environmental provision for the child's well being—such as a crib, proper room- and bath-temperature, fresh air and other necessary environmental objects (Balint 1960). Mother's presence is felt everywhere, in a cot, a pram, or the general atmosphere of the immediate environment. Thus, the relationship between two people continues even if they are separated (Winnicott 1958, p. 30). The capacity to be alone is based on the experience of being alone in the presence of someone else. Winnicott considered it the "stuff out of which friendship is made" and thought that it probably is the matrix of transference

From the Center for Parents and Children, Port Washington, New York, sponsored by Child Development Research, Sands Point, New York.

(1958, p. 33). Neither Winnicott himself nor Anna Freud (1976) believed that analysis can bring the patient back to the stage of infancy, but there are certain features of treatment reminiscent of the caretaking activities in early childhood. Modell (1976) referred to the *holding environment* as a metaphor modeled after certain aspects of the mother-infant relationship, and he extended this metaphor from its derivation in the infantile period to the broader caretaking functions concerned with the older child. In the treatment of transference neuroses, the extended holding environment functions silently. It is taken for granted as it constitutes part of the confidence the patient feels toward the therapist.

In most discussions of infant care and its derivations in patient care, the onus is put on the caretaker (the good-enough mother or the good-enough therapist), and the infant or patient is pictured as unable to contribute his share to the holding environment. Modell's conceptualization clearly implies that in therapy this occurs only in cases of ego distortion, but is not necessary where the patient becomes actively engaged in "curing himself" (Freud 1920).

Erikson (1950) preferred not to speak of *confidence* (Benedek 1949) in the early stages of infancy. He chose the word *trust* because there is more mutuality in it. He added, "The general state of trust, furthermore, implies not only that one has learned to rely on the sameness and continuity of the outer providers, but also that one may trust oneself and the capacity of one's own organs to cope with urges; and that one is able to consider oneself trustworthy enough so that the providers will not need to be on guard lest they be nipped" (p. 220).

This suggests that mutuality is based on the infant's developing trust in the mother and the mother's developing trust in him, from which a sense of trustworthiness (in the sense of self-trust) arises. Mother and infant rely on each other's ability to fulfill the appropriate share of their cofunctioning (Call 1968). The infant's sense of trustworthiness evolves from the experience of trusting and being trusted. Searles (1976) went a step further when he spoke of the infant's curative efforts toward his mother. In such cases, the child not only functions for himself, but also for his mother; at least the child facilitates the awakening of maternal abilities by virtue of his trust-inspiring behavior. Mothers have a word for such children. They are *good* babies, easy to rear. Guntrip (1975) quoted Winnicott as saying that he, the analyst, was good for his patient, Guntrip, but that Guntrip was also good for him, the analyst. The quotation suggested that Guntrip was capable of raising Winnicott's self-esteem while another patient might lower it.

According to Winnicott (1960) good-enough holding gives the infant a feeling of continuity of being which is the beginning of psychic structure. The mother develops her sense of holding during pregnancy and continues this maternal action after delivery; she becomes able to interpret the external world to the infant. The analyst's understanding is equivalent to that of the holding mother who understands her child. In these passages Winnicott referred to two essential functions of the caretaker and the therapist— understanding and the ability to convey that understanding to another. Greenson (1960) looked upon empathic understanding as sharing, a two-way relationship. There are patients who can be easily understood and others who resist being understood and do not explain themselves. The same is true of analysts who may understand empathically but are unable to couch an interpretation so that the patient can respond to it.

When we speak of empathy, trust, and holding, we are dealing with those aspects of psychic functioning which cannot be easily separated from physical experience. Empathy is based on attunement to another's needs and wishes; trust is an adjustment of responses to make them coordinated and predictable. Neither can flourish without the primary ingredient of mutual holding, which constitutes a protection against bodily and psychic insult. This triad constitutes the core setting which facilitates the development of psychic structure in infancy. An analogous triad provides the setting for the restructuralization expected to take place during analysis. The patient's capacity to be alone in the presence of the analyst seems to be derived from his early relationship with an empathic and trustworthy mother. The same applies to the analyst's capacity to be alone in the presence of the patient.

In this paper we hope to demonstrate mutuality between mother and child from the start. Through a description of maternal and infantile movements and positions we shall show how each of them contributes to the creation of a holding environment in which empathy and trust can be generated. Using the same method, we shall illustrate how some early holding failures originate. Furthermore, we shall present examples to show that patient and analyst intuit the degree to which they can empathize, trust, and rely on each other from the way they move and from the way they hold themselves up. This type of mutuality enables them, more than words do, to reconstruct early holding failures which have left their traces in the adult's feelings about himself and others.

Without equating therapy with child-care, Winnicott (1960) maintained that three experiences—having been a child, a parent, and an observer of infants—sensitize us to the hidden meanings in patients' and in our own communications. To these sensitizing experiences we can add the practice of prevention through mother-infant therapy.

In our work with infants and mothers, we encounter the average maternal and infantile failures which stimulate differentiation and separation. We are also mindful of the many chances the child has to recuperate from previous failures, especially when his earlier needs, regressively revived, are met by new and more adaptive responses. Yet, we have seen that many early failures in mutual holding, which may have originated in the mother's or the child's lagging development, or in both, persist and burden later developmental phases. To prevent such consequences of early failure as fear of collapsing instead of *holding-oneself-up,* lack of self-confidence, and despair at not being understood, we have developed a nonverbal method of retraining mothers and children. (For a description of this method see Kestenberg and Buelte in this volume.) Our observations and method of treatment are based on a detailed exploration of movement patterns in the mother and the child. It is necessary therefore to introduce here those movement patterns relevant to our theme.

MOVEMENT PATTERNS

There are many ways to observe and classify movement. From the countless combinations of motion factors, observers can focus on developing skills and functions (Gesell 1940), on gestures and postures (Lamb 1965), on tension states (Reich 1927, Lowen 1958), on distancing (Hall 1959), or on the symbolic use of positions and directions (F. Deutsch 1953). In the special study on which our infant therapy is built, we devised a movement notation supplementing the effort-shape system that relies on the classification of movement styles originated by Laban and Lawrence (1947) and Lamb (1965). Our observations are drawn from normal development, from the progressive recovery of functions during infant therapy, from personally retraining mothers and children, and from the vicissitudes of patients' movements.

In the following sections we describe patterns of *mobility* present at birth and used for attunement and mutual adjustment. We distinguish them from those which mature later and are used to cope with environmental forces and objects. Both are intrinsic to the infant's holding environment. The advanced patterns can be noted in such caretaker-activities as picking up, carrying, and supporting the baby. The infant's inborn reflexes are used in conjunction with maternal functions, not only to facilitate them but also to hold and support the mother. Two examples of mutual holding will be given under the heading of *stability*—the nursing and the upright embrace. At the end of each subsection we shall give examples from or discuss aspects of therapy designed to show the relevance of our insights to the treatment of adults.[1] To facilitate understanding of the movement terms used, we include two tables defining them. More detailed descriptions of interest only to some readers are given in notes.

Table 1. Classification and Definition of Movement Patterns

Tension

Rhythms of tension-flow
Repeated alternations of tension change
Serves need-satisfaction and drive-discharge

Qualities of tension-flow
Free or uninhibited flow
Bound or inhibited flow
Intensity factors
Maintenance of adjustment of tension levels
High or low intensity
Abrupt or gradual tension change

Tension-flow, mediated by the gamma system, underlies basic affects of feeling anxious or safe and their variations. Tension-flow is coordinated with shape-flow as seen in tension- and shape-changes in respiration.

Efforts (Laban)

These patterns control tension-flow and make it subservient to the exigencies of reality by
Approaching space directly or indirectly
Serves attention
Dealing with weight via strength or lightness
Serves intention
Coping with time via acceleration or deceleration
Serves decision making

Body-Shape

Rhythms of shape-flow
Repeated alternations of shape changes
Serves self-expression

Qualities of symmetrical or asymmetrical shape-flow
Growing: Enlarging the shape of the body
Inhaling or opening the mouth
Shrinking: Diminishing the shape of the body
Exhaling or shutting the mouth
Three dimensions of growing or shrinking
Narrowing or widening
Lengthening or shortening
Hollowing or bulging

Shape-flow underlies affects of discomfort or comfort, repulsion or attraction, and their variations.

Shaping of Space in Directions and Planes

These patterns control shape-flow and make it subservient to their aims
Body dimensions projected into space create directions to be used as bridges to objects
Across the body or sideways
Downward or upward
Backward or forward
Shaping in planes creates multidimensional closed or open shapes in space which bar or expose to contact with others
Enclosing or spreading in the horizontal plane
Descending or ascending in the vertical plane
Retreating or advancing in the sagital plane

Table 1. Tension- and shape-flow are qualities of all living tissue. Available to the newborn, they diminish in frequency of alternation and repetition when the more advanced effort-and shaping-patterns emerge.

Based on Kestenberg, 1965 a, 1965 b, 1967

I. MOBILITY

Tension Flow

Rhythmic changes of tension are the basic qualities of living tissue. Rhythmicity serves need and drive satisfaction. For example, in sucking, free (uninhibited) and bound (inhibited) flow alternately repeat themselves. When sucking- and milk-flow-rhythms are synchronized, the influx of milk is inhibited during swallowing and released when the oral cavity is emptied and the infant resumes sucking in free flow. Not only the lactation rhythms but the majority of the mother's tension-flow rhythms are attuned with those of the infant. He, in turn, is capable of attuning to her rhythms. Intrinsic to these rhythms are qualities of tension which change in intensity, frequency, and rate of repetition according to needs (table 1). While maintaining the basic maternal ego-attitudes, the mother regresses with the baby in the service of child care. During nursing, she may rock or tap the baby in an oral type rhythm. If he gulps and chokes, her own rhythmic tapping will reintroduce a lower intensity and a less abrupt manner into his nursing activity. The better he sucks and the more easily he can attune to maternal rhythms, the easier it is for the mother to maintain her regression without losing sight of her role as a mother. At the end of feeding, she will readily change her tension-flow rhythms to serve other needs of the baby, such as diapering him. After she puts him into his crib, she will devote herself to other activities which do not necessitate regression to infantile rhythms.

When mother and baby attune to each other's needs, *empathy* develops. A similar process occurs in analysis as well, except that both patient and therapist regress in the service of therapy. A controlled regression facilitates the flow of associations, freeing and binding them rhythmically. Speaking with "free floating attention," one must inhibit some interfering associations in order to select ideas which can be expressed comprehensively. The analyst's empathic understanding is more sensitive when his patient's and his own flow of associations are synchronized, or attuned. However, when the patient stumbles and cannot resume the flow of his thoughts or verbalizations, the analyst may help him restore an acceptable rhythm by freeing him from an excessive inhibition. The analyst will help lower the patient's intensity and reduce his impetuosity when his associations become unduly free and an excess of primary process material makes his productions incomprehensible and frightening. Not only the therapist but also the patient must maintain certain controls during the session. The patient is not free to jump and run or destroy furnishings. The good-enough patient is not only a self-caretaker (Winnicott 1972) but also takes care not to injure the analyst. Under these conditions mutual empathy and trust can develop and deepen. At the end of each session, empathy is reduced considerably when the partially suspended ego-controls are resumed and both patient and therapist assume a new nonanalytic attitude in which the normally prevailing secondary process thinking replaces free associations.

Efforts

We have discussed the rhythmic changes in tension used for need- and drive-discharge in the infant and the adult and have drawn attention to a similar rhythmicity which pervades free associations in analysis. Through this tension-flow medium, babies reveal their needs to the attuned mother and patients disclose their feelings to the attuned analyst. The ensuing empathy is not one-sided. Attuning to the mother, the baby learns to understand her, as the attuned patient develops an understanding of the analyst's communications. Overlaying these processes are advanced ego-functions which are instrumental in creating an organized holding environment. Adults are in control of these functions; the baby is not. The caretaker of the child uses the ego-controlled patterns, called efforts, which safeguard the child against the hazards of the environment.

Efforts are motion factors suitable for coping with environmental forces of space, gravity, and time (table 1). A mother must be capable of approaching the space in which childcare is transacted directly (with precision) or indirectly (trying out variations). She must be able to evaluate relative weights and use strong or light efforts to lift her own weight, the child's, and that of objects around her. She must know how to accelerate to catch a child's fall or decelerate in order not to rush the child. A stable holding environment is the result of efforts executed in the creation of the child's immediate environment. The overuse of efforts, however, implies that this task is never accomplished and that continuous work is involved to achieve it.

Mothers greatly concerned with the external details of the environment frequently suffer from a lack of empathy with the child. They may be efficient and dependable caretakers but they often treat the baby as if he were one of the items in the room. They will use steady strength in picking him up instead of rhythmic tension changes which synchronize with the baby's attempts to climb up as he is being picked up. They will accelerate to catch the baby's fall, but may give him no opportunity to do his share in restoring his equilibrium. They may place him in the crib with precision without attuning to his need to stretch, twist, and change tension in various parts of his body, as he settles himself in his new location. On the other end of the maternal spectrum are the careless mothers whose effort control is deficient. They may drop the baby, fail to pick him up in time, or put him down every which way. However, once the child incurs an injury, they may quickly attune to his distress and soothe him with empathy.

In therapy we encounter intellectual, efficient patients who are afraid to regress and equally dependable therapists, who do not allow their empathy to unfold. For instance, they explain all time changes and vacations at certain set specific time intervals and will interrupt the patient's associations to do so. There are also careless patients and lax therapists. Careless patients do not come on time, drop their belongings, and frequently change their position on the couch. Careless therapists may think they are flexible when they are late, change their mind frequently, and readjust their own positions in a conspicuous way. Careless patients may let their feelings overflow and often have an uncanny ability to understand what the analyst feels. They are especially sensitive to losses of ego control in others. They may disrupt the holding environment of the average therapeutic setting to such a degree that their therapists are prevented from maintaining their habitual constancy in time, space, and weight (Kestenberg 1977a).[2]

In the ordinary child-care or therapy setting, we do not usually encounter such extremes of efficiency or carelessness. Each individual is characterized by specific lags in empathy on the one hand and effectiveness on the other.

At first, the infant uses his inborn reflexes as an aid in the creation of his own holding environment. Once his tension-flow rhythms come under the control of efforts, he can begin to establish a proper balance between affectivity and reality-oriented achievement. Through periods of regression and progression, he assists his mother in organizing an optimal ratio between empathy and reason which allows for commensurate changes in the holding environment.

Shape-Flow

We have discussed attunement in tension-flow from which empathy arises and the use of efforts to create external safeguards for a good holding environment. In this section we describe shape-flow rhythms: the patterns of mutual relatedness from which *trust* arises.

As the body takes in substances its shape grows; as it expels waste its shape shrinks. The foremost example of this flow of shape is symmetrical growing and shrinking in inhalation and exhalation (Kestenberg 1967). An asymmetrical form of shape-flow rhythms consists of growing toward and shrinking from localized, attractive and repulsive stimuli. In a good-enough nursing embrace, mother and baby come close to one another when they inhale and separate when they exhale. This contact regulates the baby's immature breathing and creates a balance between states of comfort and discomfort. When the baby dozes off and ceases nursing, his mother can "grow" toward him and, in this manner, stimulate a renewal of alertness and resuscitate nursing. She may herself shrink away from the baby prematurely, giving him a sign that she has become uncomfortable and would like to terminate contact. Breathing toward her, the baby invites a renewal of contact and may reinstitute maternal comfort and interest.

In harmonizing shape-flow rhythms within all the body dimensions, babies and mothers widen and narrow their chests during nursing, lengthen and shorten during upright support, and bulge and hollow as they approach or separate (table 1). In this manner, they give one another comfortable breathing space. The *trustworthy* baby does not lean on the mother so heavily that she cannot breathe in comfort, nor does the *trustworthy* mother hold him in a rigid embrace which interferes with his respiration. The same is true of shape-flow rhythms, which further growing into pleasant stimuli and shrinking away from unpleasant contact. When the baby's mouth bulges to seize the nipple, it meets an erect, bulging form which yields the pleasure-giving milk. When his lips withdraw to avoid an overflow of milk and choking, the nipple shrinks a bit also. Pushing the nipple (and later the spoon) into the baby's mouth before he has swallowed the last mouthful, disrupts the inborn, preformed connection between pleasure and growing toward the source of food. The intrusion into the body of the child becomes a source of displeasure from which he shrinks. The result is a loss of trust on the part of the baby. Similarly, a mother may not develop, or may lose, her trust in a baby who digs into her breast when she feels empty or responds to her loving touch by shrinking away. In either case, mother and child are not sure what to expect from one another, and the feeling of primary relatedness is shattered. The *Isakower phenomenon* (1938) depicts the terror of the pressing breast which prevents breathing. The fear of engulfment and of being swallowed up is a frequent sequel to early failures in shape-flow adjustment. In average development, shape-flow adjustments lead to mirroring and identification, while slight misalliances in shape-flow enhance differentiation.

Similar fine adjustments and failures occur in therapy when patient and therapist react to each other's signs of growing and shrinking. The patient may become dimly aware that the analyst breathes shallowly or has changed his position to veer away from the patient. He may react with an unconscious fantasy of being betrayed and rejected, and this can lead to breath holding or silence. There may be hesitation in his voice when he talks, or a sigh may reveal his feeling of dejection and his loss of trust. In a full circle of such interaction, the therapist feels that the patient is moving away from him and may in turn become reserved as if he distrusted the patient. Mutual trust can be restored, however, either through very fine readjustments of relatedness or through drawing the patient's attention to the estrangement.

Via frequent adjustments of shape-flow rhythms and harmonizing them with their maternal counterparts, the child becomes acquainted with the dimensions and shapes of both bodies. Outer and inner stimuli provide the external and internal sources for the structuring of images of fullness versus emptiness, of expansion versus constriction, and of growing bigger versus becoming smaller. Through corresponding changes in tension, the outlines of these shapes vary from overflowing (free flow) to becoming fixed (bound flow). The outlines give the affective overtones to early psychic representation.

The proximity of the mother enhances the incorporation of maternal body boundaries and shapes into the baby's own. Prolonged separations impoverish these aggrandizing features and depress vital functions. The vascularization and turgor of body surfaces may diminish; breathing may become shallow and irregular; the whole body of the child may look drawn in and shapeless. Regular, phase-adequate, short separations, however, promote differentiation and enhance the practice of projecting body dimensions and shapes into space, in search of the absent mother.

Shaping in Space

Touching mother and self is an aid in differentiating body surfaces. Looking and listening facilitate the bridging of distances to find the object. Growing toward the distant object brings no contact, but extending the arm in the direction of the object and taking its shape in visually provides the illusion of togetherness. Orientation in spatial directions is the structural mainstay of the interpersonal holding environment. Seeing mother, seeing one's hand, and remembering the direction in which they can be found transforms spatial bridges into *holding lines*.

An eight-year-old boy who suffered in his infancy from asthma and feeding problems used to invite his mother into the analyst's office and tie her up to the furniture. As soon as he was able to transfer his feelings to the analyst, he tied her up and took the spool of thread with him to the car. In his fantasy, he could pull the spool and thus locate the analyst while away from her. He thus created the holding environment he could not achieve in his infancy.

The manner in which analyst and patient use spatial structure evolves in part from the early period during which locations and directions served to create a lasting tie between child and mother. Patients and analyst have their assigned locations in the office. Patients tend to occupy the same chair in the waiting room, and they expect the analyst to come in at the same spot each day. One adolescent patient put it to me very succinctly: "You have no business coming all the way into the waiting room when you have never done it before." She had to remain standing in my office until I sat down. Only then could she lie down and talk. Only when the proper *holding distance* was established could she engage in the therapeutic process.

When shape-flow becomes subordinated to a directional framework, trust and distrust become object-directed. A mother who can integrate the baby's and her own shape-flow rhythms, vision, and hearing through her own direction-giving movement helps convert early stimulus-related patterns into object-seeking mechanisms. In this she is aided by the baby's inborn reflexes which help direct the child's movement toward objects (table 2). When the mother ignores or suppresses the child's rooting or following movements (Wolff 1966), he has to rely solely on her directions. He may still develop a sense of trust, but there is the danger that he will become unduly dependent on the anaclitic object and lose the feeling of trust when left alone. When a mother relies too heavily on adult patterns of spatial orientation, she may show the baby her breast to guide him or may push the nipple into his mouth. She may be primarily interested in maintaining the attachment to the nipple and thus allow the rest of the child's body to remain unsupported. Unable to elicit or give support the baby may stiffen and cling to his mother. His developing trust is disturbed by the experience of simultaneous gratification and discomfort.

Some patients lie rigidly on the couch, hold on to themselves, and assume uncomfortable positions, all along speaking incessantly. They do not allow the analyst to interrupt for fear they will lose contact when they cease speaking. Like sucking infants, they seem to cling to the analyst with their mouth and enjoy it. It becomes very apparent to the observer of infants that early positions and directions, imposed upon the infant, can become embedded in individual body attitudes which intensify during analysis (Kestenberg 1975, chapter 10). When this theme comes to the fore in analysis, verbal intervention must be brief and address itself to the core of the problem in order to be understood. Such succinct remarks as, You don't seem to be comfortable, You hold on to yourself, You want me to say something, or You feel you must go on, give these patients the minimal directions they need to function without undue loss of trust in themselves and the analyst.

The average mother uses directions consistently to structure the holding environment in such a way that biphasic and multiphasic shape-flow patterns can merge and separate in a meaningful way. When the baby turns to the mother's breast, her sense of direction helps her to contact him in the right place, where mouth and nipple meet. When she adjusts to his breathing and aids him in adjusting to hers, she will not turn her head in another direction, but will react to his turning away from her at the end of the feeding, by moving back and allowing him to maintain a distance from her. Carrying him, she will coordinate changes in his and her body dimensions with the direction she takes and will help him project his newly acquired dimensional self-feelings into spatial directions. By the way she approaches, supports, and embraces the baby, the mother provides models of spatial configurations into which he can fit and which he can emulate. He can thus become an active participant in the creation of an object-filled holding environment. In it, the shapes of the nursing embrace and its disengagement are externalized in such shaping patterns as enclosing and spreading in the horizontal plane; the shapes of the mutual upright support and let-go positions are reproduced in the shaping of ascent and descent in the vertical plane; and the shapes of approach and withdrawal form the basis for the shaping of advancing and retreating in the sagittal plane (table 1). Through shaping of his space in spatial planes, the older child communicates his wishes, shows his understanding of other people, and anticipates their actions. By shaping the holding-space in coordination with the child's vision and his inborn reflexes, parents model for the baby how objects fit into cradling embraces, into *holds*, and into less constricted forms which permeate the outer limits of the horizon. Long after internalization has been accomplished, these spatial forms provide a framework to relationships which persist as an external referent to the memory of the concrete shape of the object. Shaping of space is an adjunct of speech (Birdwhistell 1970). Language retains the traces of its origin in the shape of things and in the shaping of relationships. Within the context of such well-known combinations of words and movement as, How big is the baby?, I love you so much, or Come to Mommy, the holding environment combines multisensory experiences into integrated permanent structures.

Maternal shape-flow responses contribute to the harmony between mother and child as she rocks him, stoops to him, picks him up, and walks with him. From such stuff trust is made, but this source of trust must be secured by the delineation of directions and spatial planes which constitutes the three-dimensional structure of our space.

When directions and shaping patterns are used excessively, at the expense of harmonizing with the baby's shape-flow rhythms, relationships are isolated from feelings of comfort and discomfort and trust is supplanted by reasonable expectations. Some parents are incapable of directing and shaping sufficiently, and they look to their young children for the structure they themselves lack. Under normal conditions, spatial boundaries which expand and limit relationships are not just gifts from the mother or contributions from the inborn and maturing systems of the child; they are created by both, under the guidance of maternal ego functions.

Difficulties in the beginning of treatment often arise because the analyst, the patient, or both, overdirect and overexplain at the expense of developing harmony in the therapeutic relationship. Some therapists and patients can develop confidence only when a rigid structure is imposed upon them and inflexible rules of therapy guide their conduct. Less often a therapist will look up to his patients expecting him to organize the treatment. In a good-enough therapeutic alliance, the therapist guides the patient so that together they can create a good-enough holding structure—one which can withstand the impact of regressive repetitions of infantile failures.

Table 2. Inborn Reflexes of the Newborn and Young Infant

Rooting or Search Reflex
When the cheek or perioral area is touched the head turns toward the stimulated side and the mouth opens.

Rooting and Spontaneous Creeping
In prone position, the infant pulls one or two of his legs under the pelvis, and one or both arms extend. The head may rise or burrow on the surface of the sheet or turn sideways as the cheek touches the sheet and the mouth opens. Through the thrust of the leg-flexion and arm extension, the infant propels himself in an irregular fashion, rooting like a puppy in search of the breast (See note 3).

Stepping Reflex
Supported in an erect position with the soles of the feet resting upon the edge of a table top, the infant extends the legs upon contact and makes alternate stepping movements. Loss of contact results in flexion, which makes for variations in the infant's attempt to climb up on the mother.

Startle Responses
Extension and flexion, abduction and adduction, of limbs, in response to loss of support or jarring, sudden noises; rotating the head and tapping of the abdomen. In spontaneous startles the stimulus is not known.

Scratch Reflexes
When one foot is scratched at the sole the leg flexes. When the leg is flexed at the time of the stimulus, it is thrust into extension. When one leg is flexed and the other extended and the foot sole stimulus is applied to the sole of the flexed leg, it will flex the other leg, and vice versa.

Tonic Neck Reflexes
When the head of the baby is passively turned to one side, the whole side of the body on the chin side of the turned head assumes a heightened extensor tonus and the other side assumes a heightened flexor tonus. If the head is extended passively (dorsiflexed), there ensues a bilateral extensor tonus in the upper limbs and a bilateral flexor tonus in the lower.

Righting Reactions
Rotation of head induces body rotation as a whole.

Table 2. All these inborn reflexes and reactions can be seen at birth or a few weeks after. They underlie the infant's stable positioning which facilitates *the mobility* necessary for gratification and relief from discomfort.

Compiled from Pratt (1954), Fiorentino (1963), Bartenieff (1977), and personal observation.

II. STABILITY
INBORN REFLEXES AND HOLDING

Since a young baby is not yet capable of using efforts or shaping, one is tempted to assume that he has no share in creating the holding environment but must rely solely on his caretaker's stability to maintain his body integrity. Robbins and Soodak (1972) discovered that the newborn's inborn reflexes are the mechanisms by which he can hold his mother (table 2). Through these reflexes the baby can, in contact with his nurturing mother, assume positions in space which help maintain his stability during nursing. Intrinsic changes in the flexor and extensor tonus enable the infant to practice rudimentary antigravity patterns. He has inborn mechanisms of attachment and disengagement timed in accordance with his needs. These primitive inborn reflexes, which he uses to contribute his share to the holding environment, contain rudiments of the much later maturing patterns of effort and shaping (Bartenieff and Davis 1972, Bartenieff 1977). When, during early care, reflexes such as the tonic neck reflex and the creeping or stepping reflexes (table 2) are allowed to function in harmony with the mother's shaping and direction-giving actions, they become the stable core on which identification with the mother and thus relationships are built. Holding and being held, mother and baby respond by forming a bond between them. At the same time, the mutuality of holding in the first days and weeks of life becomes the mainstay of future holding-oneself-up and feeling self-reliant.

Our preliminary investigations suggest that holding modes become engrained in the psychosomatic memory and are used again and again over generations so that certain holding habits are ritualized in specific cultures (Mead and Bateson 1942). Some cultures make good use of the infant's inborn holding mechanisms; others assign the principal task of holding to the caretaker and suppress the use of early infantile holding reflexes. Correspondingly, whole generations of children tend to become self-reliant and others dependent.

We will confine ourselves here to the description of two basic holding positions: the nursing embrace and the upright embrace with shoulder-chest contact. One promotes intake of nurturing and provides the optimal environment for filling the child's body; the other facilitates output of waste and aids in the emptying of the body. One is a model setting for gratification-pleasure and the other for relief-pleasure.

The Nursing Embrace

There are a great many ways of holding an infant for nursing, in addition to those established by custom. They depend on the mother's and child's physiques, the position of the breast, the maturity of the baby, and individual preferences. The following description presents an abridged model of holding which promotes an optimal interaction and fits with the child's inborn holding reflexes.[3]

During nursing, the mother supports the baby's head and spine, providing the necessary stability to counteract startling and disengagement from the nipple. To do so, without tiring, she needs good back- and arm-support herself; and she functions much better when she crosses her legs. Together with the torso her limbs provide a concave cradle for the baby, allowing him to extend and flex to the degree that he is capable of changing his recent cramped intrauterine balling. The cradle is characterized by (a) the firm support given by the mother's arm and leg, which extends from the baby's head (in the nook of the maternal elbow) through his spine, pelvis and legs, and (b) the more flexible contact between the front of the baby's body and the maternal chest. As an external counterpart of the placenta, the upper front of mother's body provides an elastic and plastic cushion for feeding and breathing. Her warm and pulsating tissue is shaped to fit the baby's shape.

The baby not only sucks and breathes when the nutritive supplies of milk and oxygen are offered to him, but also follows his own attachment and holding procedures, which are designed to fit in with analogous maternal behavior. Through rooting (Spitz 1965), a rotation of the head is accomplished and the nipple is seized; this is a synchronous attachment behavior of mother and child (Bowlby 1958). Through the tonic neck reflex, evoked by head turning, tension is distributed so that the baby can hold his mother, almost duplicating the way she embraces him (Robbins and Soodak 1972). The high intensity of bound flow in the embracing limbs is a counterpart of the firmness through which mother gives support to the baby. The turning of the baby's body toward the mother and the adjustments of turning before the nipple is found (Spitz 1965) are analogues of maternal ways of approaching space in conjunction with enclosing the baby's body with her own. The latter, a shaping pattern, is preformed in the baby's tonic neck reflex, which positions his limbs and body to make an enclosing of the mother possible. In addition, mother and child stimulate each other's skin by gentle, stroking or dabbing actions. The child's hand and fingers knead the breast or clutch it; mother may help him with similar actions. From time to time, the baby's fingers play on the mother's side back, and toes contribute their share to the self-stimulating and mother-arousing behavior. Especially when sucking slackens or the baby seems uncomfortable, maternal hands move and stroke him. Both the child's and the mother's rhythmic play is attuned to the prevailing nursing rhythm.

During a good-enough mutual nursing embrace, many mothers feel strong uterus contractions. Nursing mothers are rarely conscious of the slight, gradually rising and falling tension waves which emanate from their inner genitalia, radiate upward, and become transformed into sinus rhythms. The latter are identical with the synchronized oral rhythms of milk-ejection and sucking which are coordinated with corresponding breathing rhythms. The mutual attunement in tension-flow and adjustment in shape-flow rhythms form the psychophysical base of mutual empathy and trust. When responses abated in the child or mother, digit-play acts as restorer of attunement and harmony. The experienced mother and mature baby attain this type of mutuality in functioning during the first day of the baby's life. The novice mother and the immature baby take longer and need more help to establish comfortable and secure patterns of holding one another for nursing.

What are the direct consequences and further developments of a good-enough mutual holding? Foremost, it provides a basis for a balanced ratio between stability and mobility which, in turn, prepares for differentiation between basic functions, beginning in the first days of infancy.

A division is initiated between the two hands: one assisting the nursing process by kneading the breast and the other holding the mother. Both the doing and holding hand and the corresponding toes play as well. We see here the origin of work and play and their relationship to one another (Kestenberg 1977b).

The firm support of the back of the body enhances extensor tonus and a delineation of body boundaries. The frontal region of the body is less stabilized and its boundaries have considerable leeway. Their elasticity and plasticity provide the tension- and shape-flow base for gradations of basic, intimate relationships between people. The feeling of being enveloped by the maternal embrace becomes the affective core of the child's body-image. The mother, whose shape and self-image have undergone a change during pregnancy, is helped by the child's embrace and support to build a new one. Moreover, the child's fingerplay seems to activate the child's and the maternal gamma system in such a way that a redistribution and reintegration of tension, breathing, circulation, and temperature is initiated (Kestenberg 1977c, Kestenberg and Weinstein 1977). This physiological mechanism which originates the primary relatedness called *transsensus-outgoingness* by Glaser (1970) ceases to operate smoothly when the mutual embrace is disturbed by such mishaps as dropping the baby's head, or swaddling him (immobilizing the body),[4] or by his breath-holding, limping, or becoming rigid. In such instances, restorative finger play is either abolished or becomes ineffective.

Thus, three functions which evolve from the mutuality of the nursing embrace of the nursling can be singled out:

1. The beginning of differentiation between the holding and the "doing" hand, specific to the human species.

2. The differentiation between the supporting and supported back and the more mobile, elastic front of the body
3. The vitalizing function of finger and toe play which seems to act as a subtle trigger for the restoration of function through the reestablishment of lost unity between mother and child

These three functions are basic to the formation of the kinesthetic and tactile body image (Schilder 1935)—the first rudimentary psychic structure, from which self- and object-representations will emerge. Through the increasing influence of vision and hearing (via long distance receptors), the child begins to stare and listen attentively. These patterns enlarge the baby's horizon and become another source of stabilization. The mutual embrace can be now dominated by visual fixation (Spitz 1965). The increasing mobility of coordinated eye and hand movements is experienced as freedom from confinement while the pleasure of nursing diminishes in proportion to the need for voluntary self-support and independent exploration through movement.

Failures of the early holding environment lead to early clashes between mother and child. Sometimes both make valiant efforts to overcome the estrangement. When a mother lets the baby's head drop, his neck sink between his shoulders, or his legs dangle (Mead and Bateson 1942, p. 125, picture 7), she may try to overcome his discomfort by becoming rigid or by leaning over him to secure the nipple to his mouth. The baby may try repeatedly to lift his head to become more securely attached to the nipple. In trying not to slip further away from the source of his satisfaction, he too may become rigid or his holding arm and leg may fall limply and cease to embrace his mother.

As indicated by Winnicott (1972), the adult patient does not remember what happened to him in his early infancy. However, the early holding failure becomes embedded in his manner of holding himself and in the ways he resettles to achieve more comfort. A patient feels deprived, makes demands on the analyst and is unable to find ways to soothe himself when he is anxious, or comfort himself when he feels a loss. We deduce from his demeanor that he is fixated in the oral phase and we anticipate material that will explain the nature of his oral deprivation. Sometimes, we can detect in the patient's use of words that he has little faith in his own capacity to hold himself up and wants to be picked up and held. He looks to the analyst as someone who will restore his functioning, but he also scrutinizes him for signs of weakness. In some instances he engages in an *acting in* (Zeligs 1957) which repeats in analysis the early holding failure.[3] The analyst himself may tend to activate such acting in by providing a pillow or chair which does not allow sufficient flexion in the neck. The patient may try to resettle and, in so doing, will slide upward and meet the gaze of the analyst. He may want to substitute the lack of neck support by visual contact. He may want to come closer to the analyst. A confident analyst will acknowledge the patient's lack of comfort and his need to establish himself more securely in the analytic situation. A beginner, intent on keeping to rules, may become uncomfortable when the patient looks at him. Through his reproving gaze he may engage in what Langs (1975) calls a misalliance with the maladjusted patient. He may become rigid to combat an urge to readjust his own position into a more comfortable one.

The analyst habitually settles into his most comfortable position while the patient settles himself. There is a silent understanding that changes are perceived and have a meaning in the therapeutic context. A defensive turning away or slumping by the therapist may be interpreted by the patient as a rejection. The transition from the perception of the analyst's movement to the patient's ensuing feeling that he is being abandoned or dropped may be quickly repressed, but can recur in dreams of losing support or getting lost. The therapist often takes a deep breath or resettles before he makes an interpretation. A sensitive, empathic patient becomes immediately attentive, giving the analyst support through his stable listening stance. A patient will resettle on the couch or in the chair when, either on his own or through the therapist's intervention, he becomes capable of making a substantial change in his self-representation. His new position reflects his new ability to support himself.

Instead of resettling, some patients begin to move their fingers, toes, or ankles in involuntary fashion. These rhythmic motions serve to revitalize the patient, especially when visual separation threatens his integrity. Such movements contain rudiments of early infantile modes used to reestablish kinesthetic contact with the mother. On a different level, they represent unconscious confessions of autoerotic play concealed from the analyst (Kestenberg 1966), the patient himself, or both. When a therapist draws the patient's attention to these involuntary rhythmic movements early in treatment, he may be rebuffing the patient's attempts to restore the holding environment or unwittingly scolding him for autoerotic practices. When the patient becomes aware of feelings that the analyst does not understand him, he may be more receptive to the analyst's interpretation of his rhythmic movements as attempts to revitalize himself and the analyst so that a milieu of mutual empathy can be established or renewed.

Mr. X, a compulsive patient, began his second analysis by complaining incessantly about aches and fears of becoming sick and dying. When the analyst drew attention to the rhythmic movements of his ankles and feet (Kestenberg 1966), a crucial point in the analysis occurred. He confessed that he had began to masturbate anally during his first analysis, when he replaced genital masturbation with perianal rubbing. The confession opened up transference manifestations which allowed us to analyze and work through the anal struggles of his toddlerhood, to which he had regressed.

Despite the good results of the analysis, Mr. X would come periodically to talk things over which bothered him. He was sitting up in these sessions and I could see much better than before that he held his neck and shoulders stiffly and could not perform enclosing motions. He suffered from a cervical disk compression and was not allowed to arch his neck backward. It became evident that many of his aches and pains, which had been only partially relieved during the analysis, were caused by a cervical radiculopathy. He aggravated this condition by periodically arching his neck when he looked away from me. He did not allow his neck to drop backward, but merely released his habitual stiffness a bit while arching. When I drew his attention to this habit, he denied it at first, but could readily understand that he was repeating a failure in his early holding relationship with his mother and substitute caretakers. He became tearful when he thought that his neck had not been supported and he could not relax and enjoy the pursuit of gratification without aches and fears. It was clear that temper tantrums and struggles over toilet training which had been worked through in analysis, had not been linked with the experiences of holding failure in the oral phase.

Upright Embrace

The nursing embrace promotes enough flexion in mother and child to allow for mutual gazing and to initiate an integration between kinesthetic and visual perceptions. Carrying the baby upright promotes vertical extension of the spine and face-to-face confrontation or looking in opposite directions. The transition from maternal arms during nursing to lying supinely in the crib contrasts with the transition from mother's shoulder to a prone position. Creeping, pulling oneself up, stooping, and walking all evolve from practicing in the prone and the upright postions.[5] The child's ability to hold, strain, push, and relinquish voluntarily are the essential ingredients of bowel control, which can be accomplished only when the child is no longer afraid of losing equilibrium and falling. It is not surprising to discover that the upright shoulder-chest-pelvis support is most conducive to burping which brings relief by eliminating gas trapped in the bowels. Neither is it surprising to discover that the child's early participation in getting to, and remaining in, the upright position initiates the kind of self-reliance and autonomy which peaks in the second year of life (Erikson 1959, Kestenberg et al. 1971, Kestenberg and Buelte 1977, in this issue).

To pick up a young baby, the caretaker places one hand under the child's neck and head and the other hand under his rump. She lifts him in this position, maintaining the support of his head until he can rest on her shoulder. To pat the baby's back and facilitate burping, the mother makes sure that the baby's head remains supported and will not sink or wobble. If she is skilful in utilizing the baby's spontaneous rooting (Spitz 1965), she helps him creep up on her and will place his arms around her neck or on her shoulder—a horizontal surface he can push his head away from, using his arms as support. He can rest his head or raise it and turn it as he does in the prone position in his crib. Leaning against her chest, he feels her breathing and her heart beat. When he feels discomfort in his stomach or intestines, he can press against her and he may clutch her hair or clothing. When mother feels his discomfort she presses also. The child's flexed legs, conforming to the mother's supporting forearm will flex more and more and become bound in response to an abdominal cramp. The release of gas in either direction is experienced in synchrony with the relief-bringing extension of the body in free flow. These alternations between shortening and lengthening (table 1) add their share to the climbing reactions of the baby. A mother, attuned to the baby's tensions-flow rhythms will change her own rhythm to serve his needs. She will also shorten a bit when he shortens and will lengthen at the time the child begins to feel relief (table 1). Their attunement and adjustment become more refined and modulated when they feel a good mutual support. There is a mutual embrace not only in the nursing but also in the upright position. Mother's embracing arm supports the child's pelvis; the child's embracing arm holds the mother's neck or shoulder. Together they form a holding unit which remains a model for mutual soothing, relief bringing, comforting, and reliance from infancy through adulthood.

What are the consequences and further developments of a good-enough upright mutual holding in early infancy? The rudimentary support patterns (at first subcortically controlled) become the basis for the latter cortically regulated creeping, standing, and walking. These are dependent on the development of a firm middle and a stable extension from the pelvic area through the back and neck. Combatting gravity through maturation of antigravity patterns (table 1) is facilitated by psychosomatic memories of holding, being held, and gaining support in an upright position.

In the nursing embrace, mouth, hands, feet, and digits (the periphery of the body) are mobile, and support is experienced primarily in the curved back. In the upright embrace, head, neck, the lower proximal joints and later the shoulders become more mobile, and stability is felt primarily in the extended trunk. A differentiation between the upper and lower part of the body seems to evolve from such motions as turning and clutching in the shoulder-arm-hand area and twisting and turning in the pelvis. Maternal rubbing and pressing and the child's responsive squirming and counterpressing facilitate elimination. these relief-bringing patterns presage the kind of play which makes hard work easier to bear. Whereas the digit play of the nursling seems to restore continuity, this type of upright play eases strain and pain. During flexing and stretching in the upright position, the baby begins to feel the differences between the inside and the outside of the body. The emergence of a solid middle which holds the upper and lower parts of the body together adds to the stability of neck and back support, from which self-holding develops.

Thus, three functions, which evolve from the early supporting environment of the upright infant can be singled out:

1. The beginning of differentiation between the upper and lower part of the body, the former more involved in holding on and the latter in holding-oneself-up.
2. The beginning differentiation between inside and outside pressures with a focus on the body-middle as a solid, holding-in structure and on the neck and back as pillars of self-support
3. The relief-bringing function of squirming, twisting, and holding play which begins to be distinguished from the peripheral play that maintains or reestablishes gratification pleasure

These three functions supplement those which emerge from the nursing embrace (p. 354) and contribute their share to the formation of the body-image in depth. The upright position brings the baby's face closer to that of his mother. When held high enough he plays with her hair, neck, and ears. His mother's voice resonates and vibrates and his vision comes and goes as he raises and lowers his head. He is more alert and perceptive in the upright position (Prechtl 1958) and begins to become acquainted with rudiments of sound-volume and spatial depth. When he pushes himself away from his mother's body and resumes contact, he practices antecedents of separation and rapprochement (Mahler et al. 1975), and these become associated with painful discomfort and comfort-restoring relief. All these experiences combine to help him initiate a multisensory image of himself and his mother.

If a mother picks up baby by his armpits, she immobilizes his body and pulls up his shoulders in such a way that he seems to hang on them. His head sinks between his tense shoulders and his arms hang by his side. In this position he cannot attach himself to his mother. His primitive rooting reflexes are abolished and he cannot lean or hold on to his mother's shoulder or neck. His head will either arch backwards or slide down on her chest. The mother may respond by holding her chest to create a nook for him or she may lean and arch backwards to give in to his weight. She may touch the baby's feet stimulating reflexes which promote extension of his body, and reestablish good support. However, when this motion frightens her, she may immobilize him again or let him slide down once more.

The sliding child, who loses support and fails in supporting himself, will grow up in fear of falling and will not feel safe holding himself up (Kestenberg and Buelte 1977). As an adult he may still draw on the kinesthetic memory of being held and dropped. When standing up, he may frequently feel that his stomach is sinking or his knees are giving out. A most frequent sequel of a mutual holding failure is the fear of heights. Traces of old holding failures can be observed in the way patients carry their own weight whent they come to the office and leave. Subtler effects of holding failures lead to a persistence of the need to use all senses as a safeguard against object-loss.

Looking ahead or letting his gaze wander, listening to small noises, a patient may lift his head a bit, tense his shoulders, rest an arm on the wall or put one hand on top of the other, cross and uncross his legs in silence. He may be trying to use a multisensory approach to establish a mutual holding-situation. He may act as if he had lost the analyst and has no one to talk to. In a way, each silence is a parting and each parting is a loss which connotes a breakdown in mutual support. When the time is up and the support of the couch is being withdrawn, it is incumbent upon the patient to support himself. His self-support bridges over the ensuing separation and each separation becomes a practice in holding-himself-up. a flicker of sadness may be discovered in the slumping of the head or wobbliness of legs when he leaves the session. He may overcome it by raising himself up to feel bug and in control. The therapist's ability to carry his own weight securely and his steadying gaze constitute a supportive meansure which fosters the mutuality of holding-each-other-up for the sake of therapy. When the therapist himself feels a loss of support and cannot participate in the uplifting process, he may stiffen, avert his gaze, pull up his houlders, slump or hold on to his chair. The patient will leave with this image of the therapist. He will become discouraged or will muster his strength further to support the failing therapist. Each situation is different, depending on the patient, the therapist, the phase of treatment, and the holding failure which plagues one or both participants in the therapeutic process.

During his analysis, Mr. X complained about chest pain, a fear of falling, and about a seemingly unrelated obsessive thought that he would soil himself. The latter became prominent in transference. Whenever he returned to see the analyst, the old idea of soiling her would reappear on the way to, and in, her office. He would end each session with a compulsive act. He would confront the analyst on his way out and, to do so, would turn his whole body rather than the neck and torso. His shoulders and neck would remain stiff as he complained that he had been scolded or put down instead of receiving the support he came for. At one time, the immediate cause for his return was not an external practical event which he wanted to discuss, but a recurrence, in a new form, of his fear of heights. He was angry at the analyst and denigrated her, trying to make her fall from the pedestal on which she seemed to stand. It became apparent that his soiling obsession was connected with a fear of falling. If he were to collapse because I could not hold him up, he could no longer hold on to his feces and we would both get dirty. When I finally understood that he wanted me to lift and hold him so he could relax, enjoy himself, and find relief from his aches and pains, he left the session feeling better. He felt dizzy and his fear of falling was activated in the interval between sessions. His defenses against falling included a turning of passivity into activity which expressed itself in a need to look down at me and shoot me with his feces (see Kestenberg and Buelte 1977, p. 388 in this issue).

DISCUSSION

During the observation and treatment of infants one can study the nature and origin of empathy and trust. These develop from attunement and adjustment of maternal and infantile rhythms. Under optimal conditions, sucking and milk ejection are synchronized and the coordinated breathing patterns harnonize to assure good nurturing. To bring relief for intestinal pain and discomfort, maternal patting and back-rubbing are attuned with the child's gastrointestinal rhythms, and the mother and child breathing harmonizes with holding and releasing. These mobile patterns (tension- and shape-flow rhythms, table 1) cannot proceed undisturbed unless there is a stable framework which protects the child against loss of contact and falling. The adult caretaker uses ego-controlled coping patterns (called efforts and shaping, table 1) which are instrumental in erecting such a framework. By providing a holding space for the child, combatting gravity, controlling the timing of contact, and arranging the child's total environment to secure his survival, the parents create the early holding environment. The infant has no relation to external reality and can neither use efforts nor shape the environment. However, he has at his command inborn inflexes, which are the core of later reality-oriented mechanisms (table 2).

Not only the mother holds the infant, but the infant holds the mother (Soodak 1971, Robbins and Soodak 1972). The rooting reflex is the baby's response to the stimulation by the maternal breast. The tonic neck reflex provides the framework for the child'd embrace of his mother. Spontaneous rooting in the upright position combines with the stepping reflex and, if need be, with scratch reflexes to allow the baby to creep up, or climb, on his mother and hold her, supporting himself on her shoulder (table 2). The early reactions, used in mutual holding, are met by mother's effort and shaping, which she uses to embrace and support the child. Through primary, kinesthetic identification with the mother, the child begins early in life to transform primitive reflexes into ego-controlled modes of coping with the external environment. His ego development is guided by the developing stable structures, which evolve from repeated experiences of holding, being held, supporting, and being supported. Through the mutuality of the nursing and the upright embrace, the child begins to build his boundaries and the feeling of volume and solidity in the weight-bearing middle of the body. The foundation is laid for future creeping, standing, sitting, and walking, which rely on an adequate ratio between stability and mobility. The early reflexes and reactions "do not altogether disappear. They continue to serve as a basis of our various adaptations to the environment. Though overlaid by conscious selective modes of action, they are a facilitating, stabilizing factor in all our daily postural adjustment" (Bartenieff 1977).

Efforts and shaping leave permanent traces in the stable body attitudes which provide a solid core for the formation of the ego. This ego-core evolves from the experience of mutual holding which facilitates the processing of mobile, rhythmic patterns on which empathy (versus alienation) and trust (versus distrust) are built. Not only does the good-enough mother feel empathy for the child and evoke trust in him, but the good-enough child begins to feel empathy for his mother and becomes a trustworthy member of the mother-child team.

Insight gained from observations of good-enough early holding environments and from experiences in devising and using methods of treatment for holding failures, has a high degree of relevance to the treatment of adults. The therapeutic holding environment need not be considered a metaphor, but rather an adult model for a stable environment which facilitates mobility of thought processes. While the emphasis remains on verbal communication, empathy and trust based on mutual attunement in tension-flow and mutual adjustment in shape-flow are the basic ingredients of a therapeutic relationship. In this paper, examples were given of the manner in which patient and therapist move, but it must not be forgotten that tension-changes in the vocal apparatus and their correlation to breathing patterns are responsible for intonations, melody, and changing volume of speech. These elements of paralanguage (Birdwhistell 1970) convey feelings which may reinforce or contradict the content of speech. Within the stream of associations, we detect changing ratios of secondary and primary processes and the transitions are marked by corresponding changes in movement and body attitude.

To a degree, each patient suffers from a holding failure and presents us with a history of his attempts to secure or reinstate self-support, autonomy, and mutuality of response to objects. Analyzing defenses and transferences brings on an imbalance and regression through which analyst and patient can recognize individual sources of anxiety and depression. They can go beyond the analysis of fantasies and extend into the somatomotor sphere which underlies psychic phenomena.

This presentation is meant to be a bridge between our understanding of the infant's first ways of establishing psychic structure and our views of the adult's rebuilding of old and building of new structures within the therapeutic process. In a detailed case history of holding failure and treatment of an infant and his mother, A. Buelte and the author (1977, in this issue) illustrate how the first roots of structure formation are not lost, but become gradually incorporated into the developing patterns of feelings and thought.

NOTES

1. Every therapy relies on a mutuality between doctor and patient. However, psychoanalysis, more than any other form of psychotherapy, derives its special features from a modified repetition of the early holding environment. In discussing the therapeutic milieu, we have addressed ourselves principally to psychoanalysis, but much of what we say is applicable to other forms of therapy as well. It would take us too far afield to examine which basic derivatives of the early holding environment show up more clearly when the patient lies down and when he sits during treatment. It is to be hoped that future research will uncover these differences.

2. In studying Freud's technique with the "Rat-Man," I discovered that Freud's capacity to maintain these constancies (time, space, weight) allowed him to achieve success despite the many mistakes he made during Mr. Lorenz's treatment. Constancy in weight in the analytic holding environment refers to the analyst's and patient's ability to attach significance to items which promote the analytic process and suspend judgments based on conventional values. In child care, constancy in weight not only refers to the mother's ability to lift the child in accordance with his weight, but also to the mutual strategies through which they hold each other up (see pp. 352-357). In this paper attention is drawn also to the analyst's and patient's carriage through which they reveal their ability to support one another.

3. When the mother puts the child to the breast, the breast-cheek is stimulated and the rooting reflex evokes opening of the mouth and turning to the side of the stimulus. The mouth seizes the nipple in free flow and pulls on it in bound flow, followed by a pause during deglutition. Coordinated with the sucking rhythms is the baby's breathing, the child's body coming closer to the mother during inhaling (growing) and seizing of the nipple and shrinking away while exhaling, pausing, and swallowing. During the pause the nipple is partially released, to be seized again in its entirety in preparation for the next pumping action. The maternal holding must not be lax or the baby may lose the nipple, but it must not be rigid either because it might not leave room enough for sucking excursions and breathing.

When the baby's head rotates to the breast, the ensuing tonic neck reflex evokes an increased extensor tonus on the same side. As a result the baby's arm and leg stretch and embrace the mother. On the opposite side, the whole body assumes a heightened flexor tonus. One arm slips under the mother's holding arm, and the other flexes and turns to the breast. One leg comes closer to the mother's leg and pelvis, and the other flexes and crosses over stimulating the lateral abdominal area. Within the first few weeks of life, the rotation of the head induces body rotation as a whole, so that maternal and infantile fronts of the body meet. This righting reflex is anticipated by the mother who helps the baby's body to rotate toward her rather than be left behind with only the head attached to her. With his slightly flexed head safely ensconced in the nook of her elbow and his spine supported by her arm, the baby can make use of the symmetrical tonic neck reflex which responds to head-ventroflexion with bilateral upper limb flexion and lower limb extension. This modifies the assymmetrical, neck reflex by reinforcing the flexion of the breast-limbs and diminishing the extension of the other side of the child's body, rounding out the mutual embrace. The baby's embracing arm crosses under the mother's embracing arm. On the other side of the body, the baby's embracing leg crosses over the mother's embracing leg. For the mutuality to encompass the total body, mother must cross her leg over to the same side on which she holds the baby. The baby moves his breast-arm alongside mother's breast; he may clutch her brassiere strap or put his own thumb into his mouth. With her free hand, mother may pat the baby, help pump her own breast or help support the baby's legs. The baby fingers the breast and the back or side of his mother in irregular intervals. His toes move in a similar fashion.

4. The consequences of head-dropping are not only related to physical danger but also to emotional estrangement between baby and mother. During nursing, the child's head may drop and extend over the arm of the mother with the child's neck arching around it. The head extension evokes a symmetrical tonic neck reflex which brings on a bilateral extensor tonus in the upper limbs and a flexor tonus in the lower. Both arms stretch out, but especially the already somewhat extended embracing arm, which now loses contact with the maternal body. The lower part of the body shrinks away from the mother's leg. Mother feels that the child is slipping away from her, and her embrace may become rigid so that she can better hold the baby. She may lift her shoulder and hollow her chest to create a nook for the baby. Her reactions may be due, not only to her own anxiety, but also to the baby's defect or lag in inborn tonic or righting reflexes. Some intuitive mothers will use whatever reflexes are available to the baby at the moment to effect a physical rapprochement. If the mother puts her hand on the shrinking-away (escaping) sole of the child's foot, she makes use of the spinal scratch reflex and is rewarded by an extension of the leg, which she may interpret as a return of the escaping limb. If he then pushes himself away from the mother's leg, mother, acting in synchrony with the reflex, can raise her elbow a bit and bring the child's head safely back into the elbow nook. A novice mother may continue to nurse the child in an uncomfortable position. She may have to bend sideways and forward, directing her torso and the breast to the child's mouth and putting more weight on his cervical spine. Trying to reach the hanging neck she sometimes acts as if she needed a visual communication to be sure that baby is still there and nursing.

A hazard compounded by habits of newborn nurseries arises from an immobilization of the arms which does not allow the child to embrace his mother. The immobilization of hand and fingers prevents finger play. The mother is frequently taught to attach a swaddled, inert baby to the breast rather than make use of the baby's own attaching equipment. The discomfort arising from this failure in mutual holding may lead to a dislike of breast feeding, as if it were a chore, and bottle feeding may be preferred. Bottle feeding is more prone to enhance symmetrical responses than breast feeding. It frequently deprives mother and baby of the frontal contact during which their early relatedness grows. Sometimes, the bottle-fed baby is dropped lower and lower until he rests on his mother's legs and hardly receives arm support. His face is averted from his mother and his hand may clutch the bottle. The mother does not receive support from the baby, as he cannot embrace her; finger play is precluded as both hands are inert or engaged in holding the bottle. When the child's head drops backward, he cannot hold the bottle any longer and he must rely solely on his mother to hold it. The end result of this holding failure can be seen in patients who need intermediate objects to establish contact and need to be fed, feted, and given presents before they can feel they have something to hold on to.

5. Lying prone in his crib, the young infant will push himself away from any hard surface which his sole touches. His legs flex and they get under his buttocks. His head will burrow into the surface of the sheet and his arms extend. Moving his head sideways, up and down, with his arms sliding in the cephalad direction or pushing themselves away, he behaves like a rooting puppy in search of the nipple. Extension of his head (dorsiflexion) reinforces the flexion of the lower limbs and produces bilateral upper limb extension. Ventroflexion produces the opposite reaction. The symmetrical and assymmetrical tonic neck reflexes combine in such a way that the baby's

spontaneous rooting appears to be an irregular creeping. Unless he is swaddled or rigidly blanketed he will locomote in his crib and can be found at its head after a period of time. These creeping reactions are used in the upright position to climb up on the mother. They are reinforced by scratch and stepping reflexes (Mead and Bateson 1942, p. 97, picture 8). The better the baby's head-control, the more efficient his climbing reactions and the less control he needs from his mother. The more she holds him in a rigid grip, the more immobilized he is and cannot make use of growing and shrinking in the vertical dimension which ordinarily enhance his peristalsis.

REFERENCES

Balint, M. (1960). Primary narcissism and primary love. *Psychoanalytic Quarterly* 24:6-43.

Bartenieff, I. (1977). *The Art of Movement: A Key to Perception*. Unpublished.

Bartenieff, I., and Davis, M. (1972). Effort-shape analysis of movement: the unity of expression and function. In *Research Approaches to Movement Analysis*. New York: Arno.

Benedek, T. (1949). The psychosomatic implications of the primary unit: mother-child. *American Journal of Orthopsychiatry* 19:642-656.

Birdwhistell, R. L. (1970). *Kinesics and Context*. Philadelphia: University of Pennsylvania Press.

Bowlby, J. (1958). The nature of the child's tie to the mother. *International Journal of Psycho-Analysis* 39:350-373.

Call, J. D. (1968). Lap and finger play in infancy: implications for ego development. *International Journal of Psycho-Analysis* 49:375-379.

Deutsch, F. (1953). Analytic posturology. In *The Yearbook of Psychoanalysis*, ed. Lorand, pp. 234-249. New York: International Universities Press.

Erikson, E. H. (1950). *Childhood and Society*. New York: Norton.

——— (1959). *Identity and the Life Cycle*. New York: International Universities Press.

Fiorentino, M. (1963). *Reflex Testing Methods for Evaluating CNS Development*. Springfield, Illinois: Charles C Thomas.

Freud, A. (1976). Changes in psychoanalytic practice and experience. *International Journal of Psycho-Analysis* 57:257-260.

Freud, S. (1920). Beyond the pleasure principle. *Standard Edition* 18:3-64.

Gesell, A. (1940). *The First Five Years of Life*. New York: Harper.

Glaser, V. (1970). Das Gamma-Nervenfaser System (GNS) als Psycho-Somatischer Bindeglied. In *Atemschulung als Element der Psychotherapie*, pp. 210-221. Darmstadt: Wissenschaftliche Buchgesellschaft.

Greenson, R. R. (1960). Empathy and its vicissitudes. *International Journal of Psycho-Analysis* 41:418-424.

Guntrip, H. (1975). My experience of analysis with Fairbairn and Winnicott. *International Review of Psycho-Analysis* 2:145-156.

Hall, E. T. (1959). *The Silent Language*. New York: Doubleday.

Isakower, O. (1938). A contribution to the pathopsychology of phenomena associated with falling asleep. *International Journal of Psycho-Analysis* 19:331-345.

Kestenberg, J. S. (1965a). The role of movement patterns in development: 1. rythms of movement. *Psychoanalytic Quarterly* 34:1-36.

——— (1965b). The role of movement patterns in development: 2. flow of tension and effort. *Psychoanalytic Quarterly* 34:517-563.

——— (1966). Rhythm and organization in obsessive-compulsive development. *International Journal of Psycho-Analysis* 47:151-159.

——— (1967). The role of movement patterns in development: 3. the control of shape. *Psychoanalytic Quarterly* 36:356-409.

——— (1975). *Children and Parents: Psychoanalytic Studies in Development.* New York: Jason Aronson.

——— (1977a). Ego organization in obsessive-compulsive development in the Rat-Man. In *Freud and His Patients,* ed. Kanzer and Glenn. New York: Jason Aronson, in press.

——— (1977b). The multiple facets of work. Expanded version of a discussion of Arlow's paper "Some Psychoanalytic Reflections on Work," presented at annual conference of the Council of Psychoanalytic Therapists, 1976. To be published in *Psychoanalytic Quarterly.*

——— (1977c). Transsensus-outgoingness. In *Between Reality and Fantasy,* ed. Grolnick, Barlin, and Muensterberger. New York: Jason Aronson.

Kestenberg, J. S., and Buelte, A. (1977). Prevention, infant therapy, and the treatment of adults. 2. mutual holding and holding-oneself-up. In this issue, pp. 369-396.

Kestenberg, J. S., Marcus, M., Robbins, E., Berlowe, J., and Buelte, A. (1971). Development of the young child as expressed through bodily movement. *Journal of the American Psychoanalytic Association* 19:746-764.

Kestenberg, J. S., and Weinstein, J. (1977). Notes on the function and origin of the transitional object. In *Between Reality and Fantasy,* ed. Grolnick, Barkin, and Muensterberger. New York: Jason Aronson.

Laban, R., and Lawrence, F. C. (1947). *Effort.* London: MacDonald and Evans.

Lamb, W. (1965). *Posture and Gesture.* London: Gerald Duckworth.

Lamb, W., and Turner, D. (1969). *Management Behavior.* New York: International Universities Press.

Langs, R. (1975). *The Technique of Psychoanalytic Psychotherapy.* New York: Jason Aronson.

Lowen, A. (1958). *The Language of the Body.* New York: Grune and Stratton.

Mahler, M., Pine, F., and Bergman, A. (1975). *The Psychological Birth of the Human Infant.* New York: Basic Books.

Mead, M., and Bateson, G. (1942). *Balinese Character: A Photographic Analysis.* New York: Academy of Sciences.

Modell, A. H. (1976). The holding environment and the therapeutic action of psychoanalysis. Journal of the American Psychoanalytic Association 24:285-306.

Pratt, K. C. (1954). The neonate. In *Manual of Child Psychology,* ed. L. Carmichael, pp. 190-254. New York: Wiley.

Prechtl, H. F. (1958). The directed head-turning response and allied movements of the human baby. *Behavior* 13:212-242.

Reich, W. (1927). *Die Funktion des Orgasmus.* Vienna: Int. Psa. Verlag.

Robbins, E., and Soodak, M. (1972). *Personal Communication.*

Schilder, P. (1935). *Image and Appearance of the Human Body.* New York: International Universities Press.

Searles, H. (1976). The patient as therapist to the analyst. In *Tactics and Techniques in Psychoanalytic Therapy,* vol. 2, ed. Giovacchini. New York: Jason Aronson.

Soodak, M. (1971). Movement training for parents. Presented at the Fall meetings of the American Psychoanalytic Association (Group Studies in Progress: Movement Patterns: Diagnostic and Therapeutic Considerations) 1971. Unpublished.

Spitz, R. A. (1965). *The First Year of Life.* New York: International Universities Press.

Winnicott, D. W. (1958). The capacity to be alone. In *The Maturational Processes and the Facilitating Environment,* pp. 29-36. New York: International Universities Press.

——— (1960). The theory of parent-infant relationship. *International Journal of Psycho-Analysis* 41:585-595.

——— (1963). Dependence in infant-care, in child-care and in the psychoanalytic setting. *International Journal of Psycho-Analysis* 44:339-344.

——— (1965). *The Maturational Process and the Facilitating Environment.* London: Hogarth.

——— (1972). Split off male and female elements found clinically in men and women: theoretical inferences. *Psychoanalytic Forum* 4:362-379.
Wolff, P. H. (1966). *The Causes, Controls, and Organization of Behavior in the Neonate.* Psychological Issues, monograph 17. New York: International Universities Press.
Zeligs, M. (1957). Acting-in. *Journal of the American Psychoanalytic Association* 5:685-706.

Prevention, Infant Therapy, and the Treatment of Adults: 2. Mutual Holding and Holding-Oneself-Up

JUDITH S. KESTENBERG, M.D.
ARNHILT BUELTE

This is the second paper in a series of papers concerned with the relevance of infant therapy to the treatment of adults. The detailed presentation of a case of infant therapy illustrates our thesis that (1) early failures in mutual holding lead to a distortion of the body image, to an insufficient development of trust and empathy, and to a difficulty in holding-oneself-up and becoming self-reliant; (2) movement retraining of mother and infant is a method of choice to prevent the sequelae of holding failures; (3) insight gained from infant-therapy through movement retraining helps us understand adult patients whose body attitudes reveal their attempts to hold themselves up by putting strain on their neck, back, or shoulders; (4) the analysis of the defensive use of certain parts of the body for self-support reveals the underlying fear of falling, collapsing or falling apart.

Infant observers are increasingly convinced that traces of nonverbal experiences in early infancy are embedded in the growing child's psyche and thus are not lost to the adult. An adult cannot remember how he held his mother and was held by her when he was a baby, but he can report "a sensation of infinite falling" which can be used imaginatively by the analyst to explain that the feeling was a sequel of an early holding failure (Winnicott 1957, p. 113). Feeling understood by the analyst, the patient may react by asking to be picked up. The analyst's compassion must not allow him to grant the patient's wish. Analysis cannot transform the adult patient into an infant

Presented in an abbreviated version at the International Congress of Child Psychiatry, Philadelphia, 1974. The accompanying film is available for showing in the Center for Parents and Children, Port Washington, N.Y., which is sponsored by Child Development Research, Sands Point, N.Y.

and the analyst into his mother (A. Freud 1976). Once, however, the origin of the patient's sensation has been uncovered, one can link up the early holding failure with later failures in holding-himself-up and their end result. Disencumbered of a crippling fear of falling, the patient can find new ways of supporting himself and becoming independent.

Working in the Center for Parents and Children, we have seen that a holding failure prevents the child from holding the mother with a resulting disturbance of mutuality (Erikson 1959), empathy, and trust. Analyzing the mother at this time is not a practical method to alleviate early holding failures. Their source in the mother's infancy cannot be discovered quickly enough to alter maternal behavior while the child is still an infant. Verbal counseling neither improves holding nor does it teach the mother how to help the infant hold her and become capable of holding himself up. With this in mind we have included in our preventive interventions *movement retraining* designed to supplant defensive modes of holding with adaptive patterns best suited to create a holding environment in which the child can participate. (For a detailed description of the movement patterns and holding modes we study and utilize in retraining see Kestenberg and Buelte 1977, in this issue.)

We present a case of mother-child retraining to give therapists of older children and adults a longitudinal view of a type of infant therapy which reveals the nature of an early holding failure and its consequences. As the history unfolds one gains insight into the way in which early anxieties and defenses evolve from holding failures. Through a modification of certain basic body attitudes in mother and baby, they become capable of empathy and trust. Through identification with the retrainer, the young child becomes capable of problem solving, especially in the transition from nonverbal to verbal communication. By identification with the retrainer, the mother, and indirectly the father, may further progress through the developmental phase of parenthood and benefit the child (Kestenberg 1977b).

The review of Candy's development and retraining in the first two years of life will help highlight some rarely mentioned aspects of psychotherapy. These include the consequences of early holding failures, the influence of a good social holding environment on therapy, the derivation of fears of disintegration from changes in the body-image, the unity of fantasy and body attitude, and others.

CANDY

A Communal Holding Environment

Parents and their infants or toddlers come to the Center for Parents and Children twice a week for two hours. While the children play, parents and staff observe, care for them, and talk to them and about them. The sameness of environment and time and the mutual support of the participants constitute the core of the Center's stabilizing influence.

Candy began regular attendance at the Center when she was ten weeks old. Since she was their first child, her parents were not prepared for infant care and were eager to exchange information with others in the same position. Alicia, Candy's mother, used the Center to overcome her social isolation and gain reassurance as to her parental role.

Candy was sensitive to noises and would fret and fuss after the family had company. To relieve the burdened mother and save her the embarrassment of an unconsolable child, JK would carry Candy in the Center to calm her. The baby was able to settle down resting her head on JK's shoulder and holding both arms around her neck. When the baby fell asleep, she was placed prone in the play pen, where she invariably stretched out her arms and held them Yoga fashion (palms up) by her side. She would not tolerate the prone position while awake.

Candy's parents are long, lanky, and tall, narrow in their shoulders, and hollow in the chest region (see table 1 in Kestenberg and Buelte 1977, in this issue). Baby Candy felt slippery in their arms. To hold her up, Alicia would forshorten and raise her shoulder, narrowing it further, bringing it forward and tensing it until there was no room left on it for Candy to rest her head. Candy would slide her neck between her shoulders, and her waist would sag as she curled up like a small, limp ball in a hollow nook of her mother's chest. To hold her there, Alicia had to support her head with the other hand and was thus incapable of carrying out any other task while she held the baby.

One of our film sequences illustrates the way Alicia—in keeping with prevalent customs—picked up Candy by her arm pits; the impression is that she was carrying a limp body hanging by the shoulders. Candy, then four months old, recovered from her limpness when mother placed her high up to kiss her. However, when she was dropped to a level below her mother's chin, Candy made an attempt to embrace her neck with her right arm, but soon allowed it once more to fall by her side. Then her left arm reached for mother's face and shoulder, but could not maintain itself there comfortably and slid down her mother's holding arm (figure 1).

Even though only partially engaged in the nursing embrace, Candy seemed more comfortable while sucking from the breast (figure 2). Alicia gave her good back support but allowed her head to retroflex a bit. Dorsiflexion usually stimulates arm extension and leg flexion (see table 2 in Kestenberg and Buelte 1977, p. 351, in this issue), but Candy's legs could not flex. Instead they dangled down the sloping maternal leg (figure 2). Candy would extend her right arm to reach her mother's face which resulted in an increase of retroflexion of the head. The left arm which would have ordinarily embraced

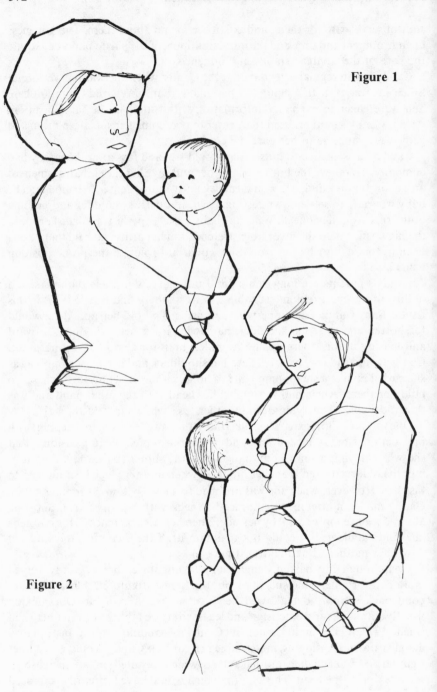

Figure 1

Figure 2

the maternal back, hung limply by the side.[1] At first we thought Candy's arm was paralyzed, but then we discovered that, when she was held on the other side, her right arm extended and limped as well.

No doubt our concern conveyed itself to Alicia, for she gradually developed insight into the difficulties she encountered holding her child. She was still, however, much more concerned with Candy's crying, especially since the original quality of her sounds had changed into an arrhythmic, harsh screeching.

Anxiety Relieving Measures

Candy's sensitivity to noise seemed connected with the disturbance of her tension-reducing rhythms brought about by her sliding or being dropped or immobilized. When mothers and babies congregated at the piano, Candy never cried and was the first child to extend her arms to reach the keys. Her intolerable screeching was especially noticeable during snack time. It may have been a defensive mirroring of arrhythmic, jarring sounds and movements which occurred when utensils were banged and dropped.

By the time Candy was four and a half months, she developed a technique of stabilizing herself through staring. She also manifested a premature stranger anxiety which prevented us from holding her. We began to soothe her with tapping rhythms which were attuned to hers and mirrored the shape of her movements. By five months, she could be calmed by a musical jack-in-the-box which popped out in synchrony with her leg movement, a rhythm she had learned at home when placed in a bouncer. The bouncer held her upright and moved with a steady rhythmic spring action. AB could now hold Candy's waist while the child sat on her lap and kicked.

Having grown in size, Candy could almost sit up during nursing, which reduced the retroflexion of her head, but her arm would still fall limply by her mother's side. When held in an upright position she began to push herself away from her mother's chest, which babies usually do in preparation for creeping. Alicia became more anxious and tightened her grip; she would feel much better holding Candy by the waist and facing her the same direction as herself. Candy's lack of success with early creeping reactions and with attempts to push herself away made her feel limp and inert in the middle of the body; however, in the new tight waist-holding position she was never in danger of being dropped or of falling. When sitting on the floor and leaning against her mother, she began to use her extended arm for self-support. In this manner, Candy and her parents (father held her the same way as mother) established a security system based on a rigid division of Candy's body into upper and lower. During the day Candy cried much less now, but at night she cried out in her sleep as if she had nightmares.

Mother's Periodic Attempts to Get Help

At five months, Candy developed a fear of the bath. We visited the home and witnessed its preparation. Mother undressed her on a wobbly surface and would rub her down with the towel on top of the same unsteady appliance. We wondered whether Candy became fearful when her own rhythms were interfered with and her mother could not hold her tightly as she did in the sitting position. This gave mother food for thought.

One day when she was alone with AB, she requested help in getting Candy to reach for toys in the prone position. After two successful attempts to help Candy remain prone, supported by her flexed arms, mother became fearful lest the arching of the baby's back (when she reached for toys) would put too much strain on it. She paradoxically recalled the doctor's warning that she must not let the baby sit up too early. Perhaps she held Candy's waist in such a hard grip because she wanted to make sure that she received the support she considered safe. She herself liked to lie supinely, stretch out her arms fully and bounce the baby on her knees. When she stood up, she leaned on her own shoulder blades and stiffened her neck so that her chest sunk and hollowed. This stance must have felt safe to her, and maybe for that reason, she systematically trained her child to hollow instead of arch (figure 1). When she sat on the floor with Candy, we could see how difficult it would be for Candy to embrace and playfully finger her mother's back as babies do during nursing. Alicia not only immobilized and stiffened her back to exclude it from breathing until it hurt, she was also unable to respond to touch or stroking in this region. Candy continued to drop one arm during nursing and would sag in her mother's arms or in the front-carrier suspended from her mother's neck. Since it became increasingly difficult and painful to hold a child, who did not hold her, Alicia tried to release her tension and widen her shoulders, but serious motivation for a systematic retraining was still to come.

Unfolding of Trust

By the time Candy was seven months old, her separation anxiety became so acute that she could not be left in a room alone without her mother. On hearing her mother's voice, she would get excited and try to get to her, but could not. Just at that time, the mother was advised to give up nursing for her own health. She looked upon weaning as an abandonment, especially since Candy was already anxious enough now and was not skilled in drinking from a cup. After consulting specialists, we could reassure Alicia that she could continue nursing without detriment to her health. We became her allies in the last ditch attempt to make Candy's infancy a happy one, and we gave equal support to the mother's desire that Candy advance in motor development and become independent.

By six and a half months, Candy began to pivot in the supine position and made an abortive attempt at crawling. A month later she learned to turn from supine to prone. She started to travel by rolling from one side to another, but her peculiar locomotion did not keep pace with her increasing need to follow her mother around. Alicia became concerned about what she thought was Candy's retardation and felt sorry for Candy who was so distressed at such a young age. She began to understand in a nonintellectual way that Candy's dropping and stretching her arm during nursing, her inability to cuddle and embrace her mother, her dislike of the prone position, and her inability to push herself away from the floor to creep were all part of the same syndrome—one which might have begun when mother and child could not find a way to hold each other with ease. She focused on her shoulders as too narrow and too tense to give support to the child and that became the theme of the opening phase of her retraining, which began on a regular basis when Candy was about seven and a half months.

Mother's Retraining Begins (7.5-10 months)

We began Alicia's retraining to give her and Candy another chance to embrace one another and thus enable them to generate mutual trust and empathy more successfully. We showed mother how she limped and dropped her shoulders, keeping them very narrow at the same time and how, as a countermeasure against limping and dropping, she locked her shoulder-joints and immobilized them. All she could do when she held Candy was to raise the shoulder, stiffen it and narrow it still further. To prevent Candy from sliding down her arm, she hollowed her chest and leaned on her shoulder blade for support. She learned that except for her shoulders she was able to widen throughout her body, especially in the pelvis. This made her understand why she liked to sit on the floor and hold Candy on her lap. Her shoulders began to feel different as she began to unlock her joints and move about in free flow when she widened and in bound flow when she narrowed (see table 1, Kestenberg and Buelte 1977, p. 343, in this issue). When she learned to breathe frontally and toward the back, the hollowing of her chest reduced, and she felt a keen sense of relief. Gleefully she discovered that Candy responded to her growing-toward her by mirroring the deepening of her breath. They began to hold each other with their chests, go out to each other, and feel a mutual support.

Even though Candy at nine months could hold her mother and feel her support, she was not yet able to climb up on her or pull herself up on an object. When put in a standing position her legs stiffened, but there was no stability in her pelvis and waist. Despite the improvement she felt and her growing trust in us, in her eagerness to help Candy, Alicia introduced a walker in which the child could propel herself from one room to another and find her mother. Her self-confidence was not developed enough to enable her to help Candy become more independent without an external prop. At the same time, she felt at odds with the transitional object Candy had chosen to comfort herself while she was being weaned from the breast. The child's blanket was left in the crib, and she was not allowed to be there during the day. This gave Candy no opportunity to pull herself up on the bars of the crib to practice. At the same time it deprived her of her baby (her blanket) to whom she could cling instead of holding on to her mother. Her anthropomorphization of the blanket conveyed itself through her demands that it be given a cracker each time she received one.

During a home visit, Alicia was helped to see with her own eyes how the walker threw Candy every which way, frightening her and making her long even more for the stability of the crib and the comfort of her blanket. Alicia quickly understood that the blanket was a substitute for the nursing embrace and a reminder of mother, and she became more relaxed about its use. We showed her how to exercise with Candy to strengthen her pelvis and legs so that she could learn to advance on her own power during the summer vacation. With the walker removed and with the initiation of sitting up exercises, Candy immediately invented a locomotion of her own. She hitched on one side of her buttocks, propelling herself forward at a rapid jerky pace without abandoning the sitting position.

A New Pregnancy Reinforces Motivation (10.5-13 months)

When the family returned to the Center in the fall, we learned that Alicia was now in the third month of pregnancy. She had been sad about losing her nursling and wanted another one, but had not planned on it quite so soon. She worried about having two babies on her hands and was eager to resume her retraining and advance Candy's development as well. The new pregnancy brought on a widening in her chest and a new fullness of the breasts, which had just run dry. Alicia found it easier to practice widening now and endeavoured to make her embrace as roomy as possible by spreading her arms out instead of dropping them by her side. She did not fare well in helping Candy walk. Since neither she nor her husband liked to bend and flex and their hands did not reach down to the level of Candy's fingers, they pulled her arm up to support her. Candy hung up on one side and still sagging in the middle, she was shoved circularly sideways and backward—an experience familiar to her from the walker. The whole family was united in its aim to pull Candy up and this preoccupation overshadowed and distorted their effort to help Candy become independent and stable. We were reminded how Alicia used to pick the baby up by her armpits and how she would pull her own shoulder up to raise Candy when she slipped. When her own retraining resumed, however,

Alicia understood quickly that her hand could be a lever on which Candy might pull herself up, rather than a puller.

Candy, eager to walk, would leave her mother and walk from her to the father. In the Center, she tried the same technique. After tottering a few steps forward, she would turn as if in search of someone, perhaps the father, to catch her, even though another step was needed to reach the waiting teacher. She could turn back sometimes and fall into her arms, but more frequently she would sag and plop into sitting. As she slumped, her face would lose all tension and become shapeless; only her wide eyes betrayed the terror she felt. The falls stunned her and seemed to make her weary of adults who did not hold her up or catch her.

We explained to Alicia that Candy's holding power had to be developed and her middle strengthened. Alicia was just then becoming aware of her own need to establish connection between the upper and lower part of the body. No doubt her enlarging girth aided her in this undertaking. We noted her tendency to support herself on her own shoulder blades and heels. She seemed to feel a pull and tension in those parts of the body. We conjectured that she had become used to receiving support from someone who pulled her upward and backward, holding her armpits and wondered whether she had been picked up and supported in this manner as a baby and had retained the kinesthetic memory into adulthood.[2] This would make it understandable why she had pulled herself and the baby up to gain support and why she needed to hollow and hold Candy's back to her chest. We speculated that, unconsciously, she still felt her mother's support and pull in her back while she provided a similar support for her child.[3]

Alicia gained considerable relief from being able to breathe more freely in front and in back, but she would reinstate her previous tenseness, narrowing and hollowing her shoulders when she was asked to put her weight forward. We assured her that we would hold her up if she lost her footing, but she paled and became afraid of falling. The fear reinstated her shoulder and back support, and she would also lock her knees, put her weight on her heels, and walk stiffly. Gradually she learned to lean forward without undue fear and use her antigravity muscles for holding herself up instead.

In the meantime, Candy, watching her mother exercise, understood rather quickly that AB would help her stand without exposing her to the danger of falling. Perhaps she had a kinesthetic memory of the time AB supported her waist—at five months—in a manner quite different from her mother's. AB helped her in both instances to establish a connection between the upper and lower parts of her body. Thus, even though Candy had been pulled up and caught by her parents, she still wanted to walk by herself and was pleased with AB's efforts to steady her until she could respond with counterpressure. Tensing and releasing tension in attunement with another, AB's hands and Candy's waist seemed to hold on to each other. They fit together especially as

Candy learned to shorten and broaden her middle by widening and bringing chest and pelvis closer together. Through attunement in tension-flow and mirroring of shape-flow, retrainer and child began to empathize with and trust one another. By identification with the holder, Candy not only held AB but held herself up. She developed a new feeling about herself when she realized that her legs and pelvis supported her chest and that the chest could lean on them or pull away a bit without a loss of connection between them.[4]

The retraining of mother and child was supplemented by the new way they interacted. It is doubtful whether Candy could have kept up her self-support if her parents had continued to pull her up by an arm. Alicia understood from her own fear of falling that she should not make Candy dependent on her pulling action but should allow her to learn to support herself without fear. She was just beginning to feel that when she leaned forward, she could be given support by someone smaller and less strong than herself, that is, provided she supported the supporter. She would stoop or sit down now and allow Candy to pull herself up by holding on to her fingers. At the same time, when she carried the child, she gave her more room within the confines of her arms and allowed her to move up and down. In the meantime, Candy, at the age of thirteen and a half months, had stopped walking altogether and was relentlessly practicing pulling herself up and letting herself down. Not until she was fifteen months could she stand up from lying prone or sitting. During this period, she began to cry with every bowel movement. Her mother suggested that her abdominal muscles were sore from exercising.[5]

Progression, Regression and Working Through (15-17 months)

When Candy developed a dependable center of gravity and felt pride in her independence, she also began to employ more successful defenses, turning for the most part from passive to active. Whereas she formerly had shown fear or stared defensively and looked away, she now used movement to ask questions. When upset by noises, she would, for instance, turn to her mother with a questioning look as if she were saying What's that?

Capable of using strength now, Candy developed rages when thwarted and would stiffen her whole body until her mother slapped her. No doubt Candy cherished her new capacity to resist, but she could also mellow. Mother and child were rewarded for their work when at last, at the age of fifteen and a half months, Candy put her head on mother's shoulder, embraced her, and melted into her. They both relaxed; they were holding one another and experiencing the good feeling of mutual support.

For a brief time Candy's verbal ability did not keep pace with her rapidly progressing cognitive development, but she made up for it by behaving like one of the mothers or the staff in relation to other children. Her empathy blossomed out. She became solicitous and protective of children (mostly older than herself) who were shy and hesitated before entering the play room. She guided them into the room with a light touch, prodding them softly and supporting their back. She was distressed when her efforts were not met with success. At the age of sixteen and a half months she discovered her genitalia and at the same time became maternal with dolls and babies. She still cooed to her blanket and kissed it; she developed an endearing vocabulary when addressing it. It was remarkable that she could now release a variety of finely modulated feelings and could so generously and trustingly give of herself. Yet, she was by no means free of fear. In the midst of all the advances she would shriek on hearing a sound she dreaded. Each progression contained regressive features or was interrupted by a brief relapse.

Candy who had become well coordinated, would become clumsy with each new regression and would fall again. At times her arm would drop limply by her side as if she lost control over it. Each time this happened, AB would help her to regain her equilibrium, and become self-supporting once more. Restoring her progress was particularly important because Alicia was threatened by each set-back and would follow suit, regressing herself and renewing her defensive backward leaning on her heels. We were dealing here with the motor substrate of phobic attitudes, and we used a repetition of old and an initiation of new exercises to help mother and child regain the feeling of self- and mutual-support. Another source of regression was Alicia's tendency during her middle pregnancy to become more angry and intolerant than usual (Kestenberg 1977c). When Candy pulled on her, expressing her obvious need to be picked up and held, mother would distort her face in rage, yank the child's arm away, or hit her. Observing such incidents enabled us to institute retraining procedures through which Alicia experienced how she increased her tension and became abrupt, especially when she felt burdened by the weight of the fetus and did not know how to deal with the added burden of carrying Candy.

As her pregnancy progressed into the third trimester, Alicia's focus shifted to what the baby was doing inside her and how it would come out. Our aim was to help her adjust to the older child *and* the new baby. Becoming aware of the way she carried the fetus and notating the tension-flow changes in the fetal movements, Alicia had been attuning to the baby inside of her for some time. With the increase in fetal weight and the tendency of the fetus to descend, Alicia practiced making room for the growing baby by active self-stretching. This helped her carry the weight rather than feel pulled down by it. As she prepared herself for holding both children by widening her chest and by spreading her arms to make room for them, she became more aware of her back and its relation to the front of the body. She realized that she tended to tense and stretch her arms and become limp in her waist like Candy. In identification with her retrainers, she resolved to help Candy catch up on her development and teach her to climb and creep.

Both in the Center and at home, Alicia practiced with Candy, teaching her how to ascend and descend steps by creeping up and down. She and her husband constructed a low cardboard box and enticed Candy to get into it to retrieve toys she wanted. Neither walking nor hitching could get her there. Playing cat or dog or racing on all fours, both parents crawled with Candy. Holding the child in her arms, mother now experienced what it felt like to have a child creep up on her body. Candy would push herself away while sitting on the mother's arm and would lean back to cuddle on mother's shoulder. Since Candy proved that she could support herself on her mother's shoulder, Alicia no longer acted as if she were afraid the child would fall out of her arms. Conversely, Candy gained self-confidence through identification with her mother.

Integrating Verbal and Nonverbal Interventions (16-20 months)

Candy's and her mother's individual retraining was supplemented by regular music-and-movement sessions in which the whole group participated. During those times, we tried to integrate various sensory, motor, and verbal modalities while taking into consideration individual needs. For instance, when Candy was learning to crawl we played and sang about snakes. To incorporate longer themes into the program we created books as stepping stones for mother-child discussions. In the last months of Alicia's pregnancy, we frequently read two books, one about the young child himself, how it came out of the mother and grew, and another about the separation from the mother when a new baby is born. At the time we were reading about progress in development from being a nursling to creeping, standing, and walking, Candy had just about mastered the locomotor advances she had missed in her first year. Both books were designed to allow the young listener to identify himself or herself with the child in the book. They gave incentives for mothers to identify with the book-mother. When we pointed to the invisible fetus that made mother bigger and bigger as it grew, Candy invariably pointed to her own flat belly indicating that she had a baby inside. At first, Candy seemed confused about the boundaries between herself and her mother; they seemed to share the pregnancy and the baby would be theirs. Soon, however, her new ability to hold herself up and climb allowed her to become more aware of herself as an individual, and she began to show signs of wanting to take mother's place and be a mother instead of her. Her mother supported the illusion of pregnancy-sharing by such actions as letting Candy wear a dress cut like a maternity garment. When Candy could not fall asleep at night, but neither called for her mother nor mentioned her in her endless recitations of the baby's and her own name, Alicia wrote in her journal that she felt guilty about "putting such a heavy burden on one so young" (see p. 383). No doubt she needed at that time to rid herself of the heavy fetal burden, and she may have encouraged or welcomed Candy's offer to take her place and carry it.

Candy would stuff a doll under her dress and come into the playroom pregnant, but soon the baby would drop out without her seeming to notice it. Mother, on the other hand, felt that the fetus was pulling her down. With each new change of fetal weight and position, we showed her how she could carry the fetus without losing her balance and without having to lean back more and more. She exercised pulling in and letting go and was getting the feel of rhythmic changes from passivity to activity and vice versa (Kestenberg and Marcus 1977). All these exercises eased her fear that she would be stretched and torn in the transition phase of her delivery. Almost out of nowhere, Candy's father appeared as a supporter who would be present during the delivery and literally stand behind Alicia and hold her in the back when she would have to bear down. (Note here the similarity to the way Alicia, as a baby, must have received her support from her mother, see note 2). Attending the Lamaze childbirth exercises with her husband, Alicia felt a rapprochement to her husband. She used the Lamaze instructions creatively rather than mechanically, choosing from them what was good for her and her husband. The concentration on herself, the new baby, and the husband helped her gain a new distance from Candy and expect less maternal support from her. She smiled when she reported that Candy now addressed her as "me-me" (the term she had reserved for herself) and referred to herself as "mom."

The new distance enabled Alicia to help JK in her efforts to convince Candy that she was not pregnant and would not deliver a baby when her mother went to the hospital. Candy became visibly depressed and stopped being helpful and solicitous of other children. She still played with dolls but seemed to drop them more often than before. Two weeks before the delivery, when she was eighteen and a half months, she regressed to stumbling and falling. Once more it seemed that her lack of coordination and inability to hold herself up was organic, but our anticipation that Candy would recover as soon as she felt better, proved correct. Despite the separation from her retrainer during a short vacation, Candy held up well and accepted her mother's departure for the hospital without anxiety. However, when Alicia returned from the hospital, Candy would not look at the baby when mother nursed her and every morning she cried inconsolably without being able to explain the reason for her distress.

Mother and JK Fail Candy

When JK visited Candy shortly after the mother's return from the hospital, Candy was busy putting a bottle in a doll's mouth while her mother breast-fed the new baby, Ellen. She readjusted herself, the doll, and the bottle several times trying to get into a more comfortable position, but tended to hold the doll at arms' length (see p. 375). Alicia on the other hand found it easy to hold the new baby, who embraced and held her securely from the start. Ellen was an easy baby, easy to hold and content, not vulnerable as Candy had been. It seemed as if mother had forgotten all her retraining and did not appreciate that she held Ellen differently than Candy. All she could see now was that, at last, she had an easy child to bring up. Candy finished the feeding of the doll before mother stopped nursing Ellen. She brought her own pottie-chair and placed the doll on it in an obvious attempt to train her. Unable to control the stiff doll she became distressed when the doll's head fell into the pottie and her legs were sticking out. Only when her mother stopped holding Ellen, did Candy turn to her for help with the doll. We learned then that Candy was trying desperately to train herself but did not succeed because of her loose bowels.[5] Alicia willingly helped Candy with the positioning of the doll on the pottie and was pleased that Candy was trying to grow up and did not interfere with her nursing of the baby. When she resumed Ellen's nursing, Candy lay down on the floor in a supine position and felt quite comfortable holding up her doll the way mother used to do with her when she was a young baby.

Candy's feeding of the doll was only tangentially concerned with an imitation of her mother. She seemed more concerned with the fact that she had not been properly held and fed as a baby, and complained through the pottie-play that her toilet training could not succeed either. She was displaying her own version of the past, but she was "bigger now"[6] and still needed to be held properly to support herself on the pottie. If there was any doubt about Candy's attempt to reproduce her own past and link it up with the present, her next action dispelled it completely. As soon as mother relinquished the new baby to the grandmother and was ready to play with Candy, Candy fetched the family album and insisted that mother show JK pictures of the whole family. She found her parents' wedding picture, pointed to the image of the mother in her first pregnancy, and singled out several pictures of herself as a baby. Moreover, she addressed the doll by her own name expressing clearly that she wanted to relive her past; she complained that, now as then, she did not receive adequate support. In her play, Candy not only identified with the mother of her infancy, but most probably also with JK who used dramatization to help even the very young express their feelings.[7] To make this assumption more understandable, such an early intervention is described below.

At ten months, Candy reverted to screaming whenever mother tried to bathe her. Alicia informed us that Candy was last bathed on a day she had developed an ear-ache. Might it be that water had gotten into Candy's aching ear? How were we to know since Candy could not tell us? We decided to act out such a scene and await Candy's reaction. JK put a doll into the bathtub and enacted its screaming when the ears were hurt by the water. We took the doll out and reassured it that the water would not get into her ears at this time and that her ear-ache was over. Candy allowed Alicia to bring her closer to the bathtub. She was very interested in the dramatization of the reluctant doll, who cried and fought all attempts to put her into the water. When we promised that her mother would hold her securely above the water, Candy consented to stand in the tub. It seemed that our dramatization not only reassured Candy but also alerted the mother that Candy must be held securely to prevent slipping. Our display of actions and words had served as a problem-solving model. In this instance, as in many others that followed, we confronted Candy and her mother with the child's distrust of the adults in her environment and suggested what could be done to reinstate trust and keep the child free of anxiety. Thus we gradually developed a *working alliance* through which Candy gained trust in us and in her mother. Alicia, trusting our judgment, learned to empathize with Candy's needs. Candy also learned to empathize with her mother. As soon as she was able to express herself in words, she began to ask her mother "You angry?" or "You sad?", detecting such feelings in her mother's face before mother became aware of them herself.

Appraising Candy's play when Ellen was born in the light of this background, we are inclined to think that Candy not only reenacted her past and current feelings but also the past and current feelings of her mother. In her play, she showed how her mother had failed her and had become exasperated with her. She also mirrored what she felt was her mother's current rejection of her, by ignoring the new mother-child unit. Candy's plea for support and attention did not reach her mother; engrossed as she was in her new baby, she temporarily withdrew from Candy. She held Ellen and Ellen held her. Especially pleasing was the fact that the baby, being long and lean, fitted just right on top of her thighs and between her long arms. She had temporarily relinquished Candy's care to her own mother and reinforced the latter's stress on Candy's role as a big sister.[8] In this spirit, she would help Candy position the doll on the pottie but did not respond to Candy's plea for support for herself. JK empathized with Candy, but could not, at that point, intervene on her behalf..

The Center as Good Holding Environment (19-22 months)

In the center, Candy ignored JK and sought support from AB. Accompanied by her grandmother, Candy came to the Center and announced "Ellen" so that all would hear that she had a sister. Away from mother and baby she displayed a special awareness and an ability to make herself understood with an astounding economy of facial and verbal expression. She knew all the children and mothers by name and adopted a new baby, Rosann, as her own. At home she still ignored mother and baby when they were together and continued to cry every morning.

At twenty months, Candy came to the Center with her mother and baby-sister. She would interrupt her own meal when Ellen cried and mother did not respond. Very likely she had resumed her old fantasy that she was Ellen's mother. In addition, reaction formation against her anger helped her overcome the desire to ignore the baby. Still, every morning she was gripped by a fear for which she had no defense.

Despite our failure to understand Candy's morning fear, the Center—as a beneficial social structure which facilitated a better home-holding-environment for Candy—was now reinstated. Candy gained in prestige because she was the sister-owner and protector of a coveted baby. Center staff watched over Ellen so that Alicia could make herself more available to her older daughter. Under those circumstances Candy was able to devise an ingenious method to formulate the crucial question which preoccupied her. Retaining her trust in AB from the time of her retraining for secure standing, she acted now as if she knew that she would receive support again, albeit on another level.

When Candy turned to AB and asked "Book, baby," AB produced the book which had been used to prepare Candy for the baby's birth. Candy stood by AB leaning on her while the story was read. She identified all figures in the book and patted the picture of the grandma affectionately. On reaching the next page which showed mommy and daddy entering the car on the way to the hospital, Candy called out "Car, car" and did not want to proceed further. We reviewed the day of the delivery and were not able to come up with a solution until Candy repeated the same performance several times. As anticipated in the book, mother said good-bye to Candy before she left for the hospital. However, her labor proved false and she returned the same day without a baby, but this did not seem to surprise Candy. No one had alerted Candy beforehand that her mother would leave again at night. When Candy awoke in the morning, her parents were gone. AB regretfully apologized to Candy because the book-mommy had gone to the hospital once, not twice like Alicia. Candy had been given a great deal of stability from reading the book, a stability in more sense than one. Her trust must have been shaken once more when she discovered that the book had misled her. Despite AB's explanations, she was not sure whether her mother would be there each morning when she woke up, and she continued to cry. Not until her mother held Candy in her lap at home and promised she would never leave again without telling her about it did Candy feel a renewal of trust and stop crying. Encouraged by our advocacy of Candy's rights and by our suggestions as to how to include her, mother was now able to invite Candy to sit by her and feed her doll while she

Figure 3

Figure 4

was feeding Ellen. She put one arm around Ellen and the other around Candy. She knew now that she was the only one who could allay Candy's fear of abandonment. This insight brought her closer to Candy so that she could now include her as a participant in the unity she felt with Ellen (Mahler et al. 1975).

Regression and Progression During Vacation (23-24 months)

Alicia found it very easy to care for Ellen. Even though like Candy she was a slippery baby, she could be helped to get on her mother's shoulder (figure 3) and could give support to her mother while she was in a secure embrace for nursing (figure 4). She lifted her head at the age of four days. At eight weeks she rolled from stomach to back and started to gaze at her fists. By three months her dialogue with her mother was impressive. Candy did not fare as well. As Ellen reached the height of her symbiotic phase, an intense *transsensus*, or growing toward each other (Glaser 1970, Kestenberg and Buelte 1977, in this issue), developed between mother and baby. At this time, Candy had to be put on a milk-free diet and she was also burdened by excessive restrictions which hampered her developing autonomy.

Both parents came to JK during the summer months to view a film we had made from the nearly two years of our contact. The film reawakened the memory of Alicia's retraining which had become hazy in her mind. Although she had blossomed out as a mother and an individual, she had also regressed to the point that the old pain in her neck and shoulders returned. Tired and achy, she would become impatient and parry most of Candy's requests and actions with a no. Candy had become subdued but developed a disquieting neck-tic. This made both parents feel guilty and made them search for the cause of the symptom. Alicia described how all at once the kinesthetic memory of her own *no* movements flashed through her mind. She knew with certainty that the tic represented a *no* gesture. Both she and her husband resolved to be more patient and permissive and to allow Candy to develop the stamina of a two-year-old. They were rewarded when Candy's feces became more solid and she was able to train herself with great pride.

The family's ability to progress through insight derived from observations of the children and of themselves remained as a solid parental trait which enabled them to cope with developmentally or environmentally triggered regressions.

DISCUSSION

Our narration of Candy's development from the age of ten weeks to two years focused (a) on the vicissitudes and sequels of an early holding failure, and (b) on the resistances and progression and regression which could be observed in the course of our preventive interventions, among which physical retraining was the most important method.

The Holding Failure and Its Consequences

Alicia, Candy's mother, did not utilize Candy's inborn reflexes to facilitate a mutually satisfactory nursing embrace. Nor was she able to hold Candy on her shoulder in such a way that Candy could hold herself up there. Since we did not see Candy as a neonate we can only surmise that she had weak tonic neck reflexes and creeping reactions, so that her mother had to rely primarily on previously established methods of holding herself up to hold the baby. When the baby could be put in a sitting position—tensely held by the mother's arm in front and in contact with the mother's abdomen in back—mother and child established a *false security system*. With her waist either sagging or immobilized, Candy did not receive the necessary priming for future creeping and standing up.

As a young infant, Candy suffered from frequent crying spells and was easily overstimulated and distressed by arrhythmic stimuli. We assume that her inborn sensitivity to noises (Bergman and Escalona 1949) was reinforced by the holding failure, causing her to be easily jarred out of her natural flow of body rhythms. Alicia gave her enough back support to ensure continuity of sucking, but the rest of her body was positioned in such a way that her head dorsiflexed, and one of her arms and two legs dangled or were suspended. This prevented a free passage of rhythmic tension changes from the oral region to other parts of the body. The rhythmic changes in the shape of the body which regulate intake and output could not be coordinated with tension changes. This dysrhythmia was compounded by mother's inhibition of rhythms in her own back, neck, and legs. The result was a limited attunement and an insufficient body-adjustment between mother and child.

In contrast to the difficulty they experienced in nearness, mother and child had an especially good visual rapport. Stretching their arms, looking, smiling or bouncing, they enjoyed one another. When they established the secure back-to-front sitting position, they looked ahead at the same things which seemed to give them additional stability. It was not surprising that Candy learned to gaze intently when she was held in the upright position and developed an early defense of staring or looking away. Her sensitivity to noises seemed to merge with a very early distrust of strangers. Her separation anxiety and clinging to the mother reached a peak at ten to thirteen months. During her practicing phase (Mahler et al. 1975) she was torn by a conflict between her need to develop independent locomotion and conquer gravity and her fear of being dropped (left alone). She could not tell us that she was afraid of falling, but we could see her terrified facial expression when she tried to pull herself up or actually fell.

It was interesting to note that Alicia provided Candy with inanimate substitutes for her deficits. Candy learned to attune to a bouncer which held her securely and did not let her fall. Later, when she needed to be near her mother and could neither creep nor walk, mother provided her with a walker. On the other hand, when Candy developed an attachment to her blanket, mother became apprehensive lest she withdraw with her blanket and stop developing. The mechanical devices kept mother and child together without the necessity of holding each other. A transitional object seemed threatening because it facilitated separation from the mother and closeness with a mother-substitute.

No doubt Candy could become attached to the blanket because sitting in her crib and sucking and rubbing the soft material combined for her the good feelings of being by the breast and of sitting with her mother in a safe position. What we saw develop was not a disturbed relationship to the mother in the sense of a weakening of the bond between mother and child, but a defensive clinging to the sight of the mother. Lacking the self-trust which ordinarily develops in the setting of good mutual holding, Candy was afraid to be alone. Neither could she develop the confident expectation that her mother would come when she needed her, even when she was out of sight.

Both mother and baby experienced a partial failure in the first year. The oral phase was ending, and owing to an insufficient preparation for autonomy and training, the developmental task of the next phase was endangered by phobic attitudes. Very likely Candy's loose bowel movement, which she had suffered from since birth, was, at least partially, a result of an early inhibition of transmission of rhythms from above to below. No doubt, the sagging in her middle and the limpness that befell her and made her slide or fall had a kinship with an internal sagging and limping of the bowel.[9]

Our interpretation of Candy's development suggests that the early holding environment encompasses definite preparatory steps for the fulfillment of developmental tasks to emerge at a later date. An impairment in mutual holding not only interferes with the evolution of empathy and trust, it also impedes the development of holding-oneself-up without support, a requisite for autonomy and self-control. It may have a lasting effect on the body image especially as far as distribution of weight and support in different body parts is concerned.

These considerations alert us to the not infrequent failures in analysis which go unnoticed because of the success brought about by the disappearance of flamboyant symptoms. A case in point (described in Kestenberg and Buelte 1977, in this issue) is that of Mr. X whose obsessive characteristics and symptoms disappeared in analysis, but whose need for support went unnoticed until he came back to discuss his new fear of falling. His body attitude betrayed his attempts to hold himself up by stiffening the neck and shoulders. When he was confronted with his wish to be picked up and held, he became tearful and subsequently regressed to a state in which an unclear fear of falling was coupled with a renewal of his preoccupation with feces. Now, the feces did not assume the central role they had held at the height of his obsessions, but were primarily related to the image of himself as loose, collapsing, falling apart (that is, unable to control himself). He looked upon the therapist as equally incapable of holding him up or unwilling to do so. He became tearful again when his jerky intense movements were described and the suggestion was made that he might have been an infant, difficult to hold and perhaps adjudged as bad from the start. We were dealing here with self-feelings submerged in a loud obsessive symptomatology: self-feelings which were the precursors of Mr. X's inexorable superego. Even though analysis freed him from the excessive need for self-punishment, the tense feeling of having to hold himself up by himself and his despair because he was doomed to be "bad" had gone unrecognized until his subsequent return for help.

The Social Holding Environment

The Center can be looked upon as a holding environment because of its unchangeable surroundings, the regularity of time of attendance, the sameness of location, and the constancy of the staff. Staff members are united in their goal to provide understanding and safety for all participants. Going to the Center becomes an important routine for mothers and children. They talk about it in a proprietary way, similar to that of patients who refer to "my analytic hour." The sense of having a constant place and time and steadiness of support is a requisite for a good therapeutic setting (Kestenberg 1977a).

From another point of view, the center-setting is comparable to such stable holding environments as are provided by good schools and good working conditions which give incentives for individual development. Inasmuch as its influence extends into the home, the Center helps change the home environment so that it can sustain periods of togetherness, separation, and the inbetween—time of being-alone-in-the-presence of another (Winnicott 1958). Once more we note a parallel to treatment. The better the patient's social holding environment, the more he can endure separation and the more he can engage in being alone with the analyst during his sessions.

The Humpty Dumpty Syndrome

It is interesting to note that the same social forces which increase patients' unwillingness to cooperate in analysis also alienate parents from children and depreciate parental aspirations. Under pressure from media and institutions, even those parents who attend the Center become unsure about the value of preventive methods which are based on psychoanalytic principles. However, they are even more fearful and resistant when innovative interventions such as retraining are advocated.

Candy's mother took her time before she requested aid in helping Candy support herself in the prone position. As soon as she saw initial signs of progress, she was overcome by a resistance based on a fear of disintegration of the ideal image of the child's body which she modeled after her own, and her mother's.

We encounter similar fears in child-analysis when parents are afraid that their child will be changed and will lose the qualities they had imbued him with. Fears of disintegration become especially prominent in adults when defensive body attitudes come under the scrutiny of analysis. Sometimes dreams reveal the underlying Humpty Dumpty Syndrome, a fear that the patient will fall apart and will never be put together again.

Candy's mother clung tenaciously to holding patterns which she must have acquired in infancy to hold herself up.[2] She abetted and sustained a similar development in her child. No doubt, Candy represented an intrinsic part of Alicia's body, but over and above it she was destined to perpetuate qualities fostered by Alicia's mother, whose early image was to be preserved in her first grandchild.

When we deal with patients' resistances to change, we not only have to cope with the usual anxieties of body injury but also with the fear that traces of maternal handling, left in the patient's body-image, will be abolished and the patient will forget the mother of his infancy (Kestenberg 1971).

Alliance with Developmental Forces of Parenthood

Throughout the developmental phase of parenthood (Benedek 1959, Kestenberg 1977b), parents tend to regress and relive the childhood phase through which their children are passing at the time. They may fail in some aspects of phase-specific childcare, but their desire to give the child his due is supported by their identification with the child and by their aspirations to be good parents.

By allying ourselves with Alicia in her wish to continue nursing her baby without damage to herself, we won her confidence. In addition, her wish to do better with a second nursling and especially the need to be a good mother to both children helped her overcome the resistance to changes in her body-image. Accordingly, her first interest in retraining centered on becoming wide enough so that she would give Candy enough room to embrace her. It was important at that time to leave the child's retraining in the hands of the mother and not to interfere with her maternal aspirations. This allowed her to feel that the child would not change more than she and her husband could tolerate.

A mother who cannot relinquish her child to the analyst is often much more willing to receive help in improving her mothering methods. In the treatment of a parent, one must not only ally oneself with the parent in regard to curing him, but also in regard to improving his image of himself as a parent.

As is so often the case, vacation brought about the contradictory feelings of a greater need to function without help and of a regressive need to identify with her own mother, who had rushed Alicia's development in preparation for the birth of her brother. Added to this were the regressive trends of early pregnancy which reinforced dependency and allowed Alicia to transfer these feelings to the Center staff when Center sessions were resumed. She could now entrust Candy's advancement to AB. At the same time she became inventive in supplementing the child's retraining by teaching her to creep and climb. Her own retraining proceeded well, especially because it converged with the reformation of her body-image due to pregnancy.

The study of several analyses during pregnancy (Dewald 1972, Kestenberg 1977b) revealed a lack of focus on the current reorganization of the patient's body-image. This process seemed hidden or ignored via a silent agreement of patient and analyst to let the pregnancy changes run their course without interference. It may well be that the patients' fear that analysis will disturb their pregnancy was shared by the therapists.

The Unity of Fantasy and Body Attitude

As Alicia's pregnancy progressed and became more burdensome, she and her daughter began to share a fantasy, first of a common burden and later of a takeover by Candy of the maternal role. This was revealed in words, actions, and body attitudes. The pregnancy fantasy reinforced Candy's newly won independence and helped advance her ego development beyond her years. When she was brought back to reality, she regressed and once more needed retraining to help her stand up without hazard to her safety. We could better understand the unity of self-holding, holding the baby, and the fantasy of pregnancy and becoming a mother when all of these factors collapsed simultaneously through the failure of one.

Miss Y, who prided herself in being independent and more self-reliant than her older siblings, began to realize in her analysis that she was still dependent on her mother. In the next session she displayed a rigid, painful neck. She was obviously putting too much strain on it by keeping it very erect and stiff. This constituted a last ditch attempt to hold herself up instead of shrinking like a baby who needed to be held and supported. The not infrequent phenomenon of simultaneous regression to dependency and to a body-feeling related to an early holding failure is sometimes explained as somatization or hysteria; its origin in early infancy is either unrecognized or ignored.

Failure and Recovery

When her sister was born Candy enacted her current needs, which contained a somatic memory of her early holding failure. This would have required a verbal intervention to explain Candy's feelings to mother who, on her own, could not intuit what Candy meant to convey. JK's failure to do so was motivated in part by her empathy with Alicia who was so involved with the new baby that she could not be easily reached. Candy felt abandoned, was afraid to lose her mother, and defended herself by ignoring the mother-baby pair. We understood much later that Candy was glad when Alicia did not bring a baby home after returning from her first visit to the hospital. The current alienation between Candy and Alicia reinforced the earlier trauma which occurred when Alicia left for the hospital at night (to deliver a baby after all) and Candy did not find her home in the morning.

Candy attended the Center another two years, and throughout this time, she would make a point of telling JK not to talk to her mother. This was Candy's way of conveying that she did not trust JK to properly interpret her feelings to her mother, although she would approach her to seek help and ask questions. At the time of her return to the Center with Ellen, she singled out AB, her retrainer, to help her solve the problem of her morning distress. When this was accomplished, Candy's trust in the Center as a holding environment which facilitated a rapprochement to her mother was vindicated. The failure of the Center's book to prepare Candy for mother's leaving the house twice to deliver the baby and JK's failure to reach her mother on Candy's behalf after the baby came home were overcome by Candy's ingenuity and perseverance in expressing her concerns and formulating her question to AB.

It is remarkable how often a patient is able to stand the feeling, that the analyst does not understand him or her and can continue to rely on trustworthy features which outweigh failures. M. X looked upon me as a combination of figures, comparable to Candy's mother, JK, grandmother, and AB. He came back to treatment repeatedly, hoping to get the support he needed because he trusted me as the therapist who had assisted him in overcoming his obsessions. The factors which helped him to make himself better understood than before and aided me in the reconstruction of his holding failure were (a) the fact that he was about to become a grandfather which brought back the vision of his own infancy, and (b) the therapist's new insights about holding failures which made it possible for her to verbalize appropriately what the patient felt now and as a baby (Winnicott 1957).

Miss Q was continuously preoccupied with the possibility that the analyst would throw her out for bad behavior or lack of cooperation. One day she complained that the analyst had been angry with her at the end of the preceding session. Confirming that her impression was correct, the analyst discussed the nature of the behavior which evoked her anger. Miss Q responded with a resolve to leave treatment. This was in line with her behavior in childhood when she had left the house whenever her mother was dissatisfied with her. The realization that despite her lapse into anger the analyst had empathy for her and trusted her prompted her to stay in treatment.

Both patients had overcome the failures of their early holding environment through an exaggerated need to be self-supporting and self-reliant. This gave them a false sense of security which was not easy to give up. Without it, they would fall prey to utter helplessness and an infantile need to be carried. Even before Miss Q and Mr. X discovered their dependency needs, they were afraid of collapsing and maintained the treatment because they recognized the dependability of the analytic holding environment. Both patients maintained a defensive holding-themselves-up structure which resulted in a defensive self-reliance and in physical symptoms, related to an undue stress on the spine.

Alicia's identical problems were improved through retraining. Candy could not develop self-reliance from visual mastery alone. True self-reliance became evident when she learned to hold herself up without collapsing. From then on mother and child gave each other support not only in holding one another but also in terms of emotional coacting. They went through a series of progressions and regressions, but despite occasional failures they were both able to utilize the Center's holding environment to resolve conflicts and progress again. While mother developed insight into Candy's emotional state, Candy learned to integrate a variety of media of expression (movement, intonation, words, and pictures) to make herself understood. She seemed to realize that it was up to her to elicit the adult's understanding, and she trusted that the Center staff would assist her in her undertaking. This insight facilitated the transition from nonverbal to verbal modes of communication.

Notes About Retraining

Infant-mother retraining is an innovative method being developed in the Center. We learn from each case about the possibilities and limitations of the method. When Candy used to regress we felt a keen sense of disappointment, but we learned from each regression. We experimented with new safer ways to hold babies and with new ways of helping mothers to hold themselves up. We reexamined our own holding patterns and improved our techniques of observation. We developed a feel for connections between nonverbal and verbal communication which came in good stead when Candy changed her sign language into speech and could be reached by interventions modeled after some of the methods used in psychoanalysis of very young children (Kestenberg 1969). We learned how mother's new emotional and intellectual insight would follow in the footsteps of body-image changes which resulted from retraining. Candy and her mother were helping us to become better infant-therapists and each new experience aided the formulation of better rules to guide our verbal and nonverbal interventions.

One fundamental rule of retraining, which must be impressed upon all students of this method, is to avoid verbal intepretations and accept without comment new insights which emerge during or after retraining sessions. They may serve as guides for programming future sessions, but must not entice infant therapists to engage in adultomorphic conversions of retraining into psychotherapy. Verbal interventions (based on a knowledge of psychoanalytic techniques) are adapted to fit preventive measures and should be used within the framework of parent-child education, not in physical retraining. They must be clearly distinguished from nonverbal retraining methods even though insight derived from the latter does pave the way toward a better verbal understanding between parent and child.

Mother-infant retraining is a method of choice for the prevention of sequels of early holding failures, but it is not a panacea for all maternal and infantile problems. Retraining of the mother is an integral part of nonverbal infant therapy, but by no means can it replace the verbal types of therapy used to alleviate neurotic conflicts of adults.

SUMMARY

We presented a case of mother-infant retraining which covered the span of nearly two years. We observed how a failure in mutual holding in early infancy led to the child's failure in holding herself up, creeping, and standing. The Center which mother and child attended regularly provided a setting for retraining. Through it mother and child gained a feeling of mutual- and self-trust and empathy that withstood the strains of developmental and environmentally induced regressions.

The detailed description of our method of infant therapy served to highlight selected problems in the treatment of older children and adults. We suggested that these problems can be understood better when seen through the spectrum of early failures in mutual holding. This and similar studies of early holding failures alert the therapist to body attitudes which give the adult a false sense of security. The analysis of the defensive manner by which a patient holds himself up confronts him with the underlying fear of falling or collapsing.

NOTES

1. How this interplay was initiated by a failure or by a maternal inhibition of the tonic neck reflex and how the symmetric tonic neck reflex in response to head retroflexion produced the extension of the upper limbs, can be understood better by perusing Kestenberg and Buelte 1977, table 2 and pages 363-366, in this issue.

2. Our speculation proved to be correct; some years later we saw photographs of Alicia as a baby being held by her mother.

3. Note a painting by Leonardo da Vinci showing Ann, Mary, and little Jesus in that kind of a dual back support position (Freud 1910, p. 187).

4. No doubt hanging on had given her an opposite feeling: With her arm stretched up and forward and her shoulder raised, her chest was being pulled away from what was to become her center of gravity so that she was more in a position to get ready to fly than to stand or walk. This fly-walk depended on her lengthening and tensing at the same time. When this clashing combination of patterns would cease for a moment, Candy sagged in the middle and collapsed.

5. Only by comparing Candy's bowel movement with that of her second child did Alicia discover that Candy's stool had been loose since birth, so that she had never had to strain to defecate.

6. *Your Are Bigger Now* is the title of one of the books we read to Candy to prepare her for the arrival of the sibling.

7. We are familiar with children's spontaneous reproduction of past events in play. No doubt Candy was able to show in the play how she felt now and may have been able, without any external model, to reproduce early holding failure. We are inclined to think that at nineteen months a child would not ordinarily express herself with the clarity Candy exhibited in her play if there were not an early acquisition of understanding through dramatization.

8. Grandmother treated Candy as she had treated Alicia in her childhood. She demanded good and responsible behavior from the older child and did not tolerate regression. When Ellen was born, the grandmother told us stories about Alicia's bad behavior with her eighteen months younger baby brother.

9. We have observed that toddlers who develop strong antigravity muscles and are able to stoop early are in better control of their bowel movement than those who lag in autonomy and feel weak and compliant.

REFERENCES

Benedek, T. (1959). Parenthood as a developmental phase. *Journal of the American Psychoanalytic Association* 7:389-47.

Bergman, P., and Escalona, S. K. (1949). Unusual sensitivities in very young children. *Psychoanalytic Study of the Child* 3/4:333-352.

Dewald, P. A. (1972). *The Psychoanalytic Process: A Case Illustration.* New York: Basic Books.

Erikson, E. H. (1959). *Identity and the Life Cycle.* New York: International Universities Press.

Freud, A. (1976). Changes in psychoanalytic practice and experience. *International Journal of Psycho-Analysis* 57:257-260.

Freud, S. (1910). Eine Kindheitserinnerung des Leonardo da Vinci. *Gesammelte Werke* 8:128-211. London: Imago, 1943.

Glaser, V. (1970). Das Gamma-Nervenfaser System (GNS) als Psycho-Somatisches Bindeglied. *Atemschulung als Element der Psychotherapie*, pp. 210-221. Darmstadt: Wissenschaftliche Buchgesellschaft.

Kestenberg, J. S. (1969). Problems of technique of child analysis in relation to the various developmental stages: pre-latency. *Psychoanalytic Study of the Child* 24:358-383.

——— (1971). From organ-object imagery to self- and object-representation. In *Separation-Individuation*, ed. J. B. McDevitt and C. F. Settlage, pp. 75-99. New York: International Universities Press.

——— (1976). Regression and reintegration in pregnancy. In *Female Psychology, Journal of the American Psychoanalytic Association.* 24 (Suppl.)213-250

——— (1977a). Ego organization in obsessive-compulsive development in the Rat-Man. In *Freud and His Patients,* ed. Kanzer and Glenn. New York: Jason Aronson, In press.

——— (1977b). Notes on parenthood as a developmental phase. In *Clinical Psychoanalysis,* ed. Orgel and Five. New York: Jason Aronson, in press.

Kestenberg, J. S., and Buelte, A. (1977). Prevention, infant therapy, and the treatment of adults: 1. toward understanding mutuality. In this issue, pp. 339-367.

Kestenberg, J. S., and Marcus, H. (1977). Hypothetical monosex and bisexuality. *The Self In Process Series.* New York: Behavioral Publications. In press.

Mahler, M., Pine, F., and Bergman, A. (1975). *The Psychological Birth of the Human Infant.* New York: Basic Books.

Winnicott, D. W. (1957). On the contribution of direct child observation to psycho-analysis. In *The Maturational Processes and the Facilitating Environment,* pp. 109-114. New York: International Universities Press, 1965.

——— (1958). The capacity to be alone. In *The Maturational Processes and the Facilitating Environment,* pp. 29-36. New York: International Universities Press, 1965.

On Lying Fallow:
An Aspect of Leisure

M. MASUD R. KHAN, M.A.

The capacity for lying fallow is discussed as a nonconflictual affective state and as a function of the process of personalization and growth. The qualities and achievements of the fallow mood are indicated, as are the factors on which this state is dependent.

Writing to Countess M on March 10, 1921, Rainer Maria Rilke expressed a sentiment which in a humbler way is true of all of us. Rilke said, "Ultimately each one of us experiences only *one* conflict in life which constantly reappears under a different guise."

What for Rilke was "*one* conflict," has been, in my life experience, a preoccupation with a person's relation to himself. Here I shall focus on a rather private, nonconflictional and personalized area of self-experience, namely *lying fallow*. The noun *fallow* is defined by the Oxford English Dictionary as: Ground that is well-ploughed and harrowed, but left uncropped for a whole year or more.

Through the metaphor of an active verb I wish to indicate that the mood I am trying to discuss is not one of

inertia

    listless vacancy

        or idle quietism of soul

nor is it a flight from

    harassed purposiveness

        and pragmatic action.

Lying fallow is a transitional state of experience, a mode of being that is

    alerted quietude

        and receptive wakeful lambent consciousness.

It is indeed difficult to define positive nonconflictual moods and affective emotional states. Language bears a very long and complex relation to conflictual states, be they vis-a-vis external reality or inner psychic reality. Over a long period of time, it has evolved an expertise and competence in defining these conflictual states of angst and fear, hope and despair, elation and depression.

For centuries, writers, sages, and priests have cultivated and perfected the instrumentality of the spoken and written word as a way of regulating and organizing human experience, purposiveness and action. The latest arrivals on this scene are the psychoanalysts, and over the some seventy years that they have been active, guided by the researches of Freud, a lot has been said and established about the human being in a state of conflict. What I shall discuss is not a neurotic, conflictual, or distress state. Quite the contrary: I am talking about what we call in our jargon, an ego-capacity. By this we mean a healthy function of the ego in the service of the individual.

In recent years both in psychoanalysis and in other disciplines, the need to view the whole human being as an existential entity has been stressed more frequently. Winnicott and Heinz Hartmann have contributed a great deal toward an understanding of those intractably silent states which we associate with the human individual in health. The most effective and persuasive plea on this score, however, has been made by Pierre Teilhard de Chardin. After accounting for the long and complex evaluation of human consciousness over thousands of years, Teilhard de Chardin came to the conclusion: "It is not possible that in our theories and in our acts we have neglected to give due place to the person and the forces of *personalization*."

My argument is that the capacity for lying fallow is a function of the process of personalization in the human individual. This process of personalization achieves its sentient wholeness over a slow period of growth, development, and acculturation in the human individual and its true matrix is a hierarchy of relationships of

the mother looking after the infant;
the father supporting the mother;
the family nurturing the parents;
and society maintaining the family in a living and nutrient ambience for the individuating person.

This is a long process and is waylaid by many a traumata—personal, familial and social. But if all goes well, and it does more often than not, what crystallizes and differentiates into the separate status of adult selfhood is a personalized individual with his own privacy, inner reality, and sense of relatedness to his social environment.

Today we live in excessively pragmatic and ruthlessly evangelical societies, where everything is being done for the *individual* through the instrumentality of the state and politicians, sociologists and psychiatrists, psychoanalysts and entertainers. In this excessive zeal to rescue and comfort the individual, perhaps we have overlooked some of the basic needs of the person to be private, unintegrated, and to lie fallow. The welfare state, whether idealistically socialist, traditionally conservative, or militantly Marxist, has evolved an intrusive concern for the individual's well-being, which, instead of promoting his personal growth is turning him into a depersonalized parasite, as well as a victim, with ready-to-hand rescue measures of skills and programed endeavours.

I am not jeering at the true virtues of modern civilizations and that civic concern for the well-being of the individual which is one of the great achievements of the Christian cultures. Through my nurture I am able to evaluate the nihilism built-in by centuries of the spiritual inertia of the Eastern cultures, with their obsession with rarified purity of the soul and their utter disregard for the human being as a civic organism. In my early years, I saw such body-misery, poverty, and destituteness of existence in the Hindu-Muslim culture of India that nothing will ever convince me that a civilization that does not look after the ordinary welfare of its citizens, no matter how excellent it is with the metaphysics of the soul, is not worth a bean. It is precisely because in Western cultures and civilizations, the civic dignity, freedom, and well-being of the individual became firmly established, that we should try and look at the more subtle aspects of the private and silent human psychic experiences and their value for human existence.

Let me say it outright that the soul has meaning only in a well-cared for individual. In abject poverty no person can lie fallow.

*   *   *

Let us try and make a phenomenological statement about lying fallow. To define it by a negative dimension: it is not a state of tension either instinctual or environmental. We all experience it frequently in fleeting patches. Quite often what we register consciously is a mellow disinclination to apply ourselves to something that we should be doing. We nag at ourselves with admonitory rigor, but somehow we fail to move or harass our executive faculties to the task. We sense a need to be somewhat idle and feel our way out of this benignly languid passive mood. If we are forced out of it by either our own conscience or by the environment, we feel irritable and grumpy. Quite often we are only too ready to pick on some external factor to blame our incapacity to hold and sustain this fallow mood.

Another aspect of this fallow mood is that though it is essentially and inherently private and personal, it needs an ambience of companionship in order to be held and sustained. In isolation or deprivation one can neither arrive at this mood nor sustain it. Someone—a friend, a wife, a neighbor— sitting around unobtrusively, guarantees that the psychic process does not get out of hand, that is, become morbid, introspective, or sullenly doleful. There are endless variations of the failure of the fallow mood: One extreme is the rigorous self-immolating bleakness of a mystical retreat from life and the imprisonment of self by a rationalized idealistic apologia for such states of being. There are all the exotic ranges of experience that some persons strive after and achieve through narcotics, alcohol, and other drugs.

The question that arises here is What does the fallow mood achieve for us? The answer is a paradox: a great deal and nothing. It is a nutrient of the ego and a preparatory state. It supplies the energic substratum for most of our creative efforts, and through its unintegrated, psychic suspended animation (which is the obverse of organized mentation) allows for that larval inner experience which distinguishes true psychic creativity from obsessional productiveness.

So the fallow state is
1. A transitional and transient mood
2. Nonconflictual and noninstinctual, and an uncritical intellectual state
3. A capacity of the ego
4. An alert wakeful mood—unintegrated, receptive and labile
5. Largely nonverbal and imagistic—kinaesthetic in expression
I would even go further and state that the fallow mood is largely experienced or expressed only in silence, even with oneself. It is however more amenable to pictorial expression than verbal articulation. Doodling, etc., can be quite an adequate vehicle for it.

It is perhaps one of the few genuine achievements of modern art between 1900 and 1940 that it divested the pictorial activity of painting of its too close alliance with thematic representation. The cubists (Picasso, Braque, Leger, Gris, etc.) staked a claim for expressing transitional states of visual experience—a claim which derived from lying fallow rather than from dream states. The enchanting exponent of painting as a vehicle of the fallow mood is Miro, with his wayward somnambulant doodles and blotches of color, which are so playful in their stillness.

By relating the fallow mood to creative artistic productions, I wish to establish an important value coefficient of this mood—its discipline and relation to *will*. It is not an idle moronic state of being. It is a cogent capacity in a well-established, disciplined, and personalized individual. We may all make-believe that we can doodle like Miro, but the strength and vigor of sensibility needed to sustain that state of free-floating animation and to capture its innate aliveness through imagery is no small achievement of the ego. Compare to it the nostalgic escapist efforts of the Sunday painters, and it is not difficult to establish the difference. Lying fallow is a way of being that is above all the proof that a person can be with himself unpurposefully.

*   *   *

In my subtitle I have related lying fallow to leisure. On reflection I have found that lying fallow is in some ways the obverse of leisure, particularly as it has become known today. It is a strange and uncanny result of urban civilization and the impact of technology on human experience that leisure has become a pursuit and an end in itself. It has gradually become an industry, a profession, and an imperative social need of the individuals in modern societies. Everyone strives for more and more leisure and knows less and less what to do with it. Hence the emergence of a colossal trade in organizing people's leisure. This need is perhaps one of the real absurdities of our existence today. And it reflects the decay of some crucial value-systems that the wisdom of religions sponsored for ages, in all types and kinds of human beings. The pursuit of frantic leisure, with little capacity to make a personalized experience of it, is perhaps one of the most dissipating qualities of the technical cultures. The individual on whom leisure has been imposed in massive doses, and who has little capacity to deal with it, then searches for distractions that will fill this vacuum. A vast amount of the energy of modern man is spent in searching for these distractions, and when he fails to be assuaged by distractions, he concocts states of ill-health and morbidity which then occupy his leisure. A great deal of distress and psychic conflict that we see clinically today in our patients is the result of a warped and erroneous expectancy of what human nature and existence should be like. It is the omnipresent fallacy of our age that all life should be fun and that all time should be made available to enjoy this fun. The result is apathy, discontent and pseudoneurosis. It may be rather odd that a psychoanalyst should treat human conflict with this irony. But I think unless we are honest and distinguish between true conflict and illness and illusory faked neuroses which derive from misconceptions of human nature, we only confuse our task as therapists and confuse our patients.

A craving for leisure, and the concomitant yearnings for distractions to fill the void of given-leisure, is the result of our failure to understand the role and function of the need to lie fallow in the human psyche and personality. Over the past six or seven decades we have industriously misinformed ourselves about the essentials of human nature. We have confused the necessity to relieve human poverty and misery as a demand that all life should be fun and kicks. The entertainment media of modern cultures have further exploited this leisure void for commercial gain, and flooded the citizens with ready-made switchable distractions so that no awareness of the need to develop personal resources to cope with fallow states can actualize as private experience.

A pathetic consequences of this is that we have a style of personality development emerging which is overdemanding in its claims on the environment, on others, and its need to be related to by others, but has little comprehension of the necessity of the responsibility of an inner relation to its own self. Even a superficial acquaintance with our contemporary theater and literature will show how dramatically and vociferously the isolation, misery, loneliness, bereftness, etc. of the individual is portrayed with no inkling of insight into the primary human responsibility for a person's commitment to sustain and nourish himself.

It has often been said that the failure to find a true relation to the self is the major symptom of our times, and the blame for it has been overgenerously apportioned to parents, society, and the scientific revolution. What has not been stressed enough is that very few individuals today regard it as their own responsibility to relate to themselves. We have replaced effort with labor, and lying fallow with idle leisure.

The capacity to lie fallow is dependent upon
1. acceptance of self as a separate person
2. toleration of noncommunication
3. and putting up with reduced relatedness to and from the environment

*   *   *

The present discussion is a homage to the genius of Donald Winnicott. Therefore, lastly, I would like to say that one of my debts to him is that he taught me how to enable a patient as a person to find, when he needed to in the analytic situation, his own capacity to lie fallow, without feeling a silent coercive demand from my presence to fill the session with a debris of facts or to berate himself for not free-associating. Language and relating are only creative when the person speaks from himself in order to relate both to himself and the other, and thus actualize himself for himself and the other. For this to happen the capacity to lie fallow in a quiescent aloneness with the other is an inevitable prerequisite.

Notes on
Ibsen's *Peer Gynt*

MARGARET I. LITTLE, M.R.C.S.,
L.R.C.P., M.R.C.PSYCH.

A short account of the verse drama *Peer Gynt* is given, showing its setting in Ibsen's life and work, and its content. The paper relates what the poem tells us about Ibsen to what I know of him from elsewhere, specifically to certain conflicts and the search for his "true self." It also relates the poem to the experience of psychoanalysts and psychiatrists (illustrating this with clinical material), and, finally, to aspects of the world today.

My interest in *Peer Gynt* was first aroused in 1944, when I saw it in London, staged by the Old Vic Company; Ralph Richardson, Sybil Thorndike, and Laurence Olivier played Peer, Aase, and the Button Molder. Its impact made me read, in translation, almost all of Ibsen's plays (*Emperor and Galilean* defeated me), as much of his poetry as I could find, and many bits of writing about him.

My interest then centered round the personality change in Peer when his mother died, apparently from pathological liar to psychotic. Later, I came to regard it rather as the breakdown of a psychopath into a psychosis, against which psychopathy had been a defence, for I had seen this happen both in patients and acquaintances.

I am limiting these notes to two main themes: (1) relating what the verse play tells us of its author to what I know about him otherwise and (2) relating it more fully both to my own experience and to aspects of the modern world. I am also limiting myself in the matter of quotation, crossreferences, or comparison to a few plays—to *Brand*, to Ibsen's last play, *When We Dead Awaken*, and to brief quotations from other authors.

Contributed to a Festschrift in honour of Dr. Richard Sterba, May 1973. Revised 1976.

Ibsen himself was most insistent that *Peer Gynt* is poetry: "Everything I have produced as a poet had its origins in a state of mind and a real life situation." Though he denied that *Peer Gynt* was autobiographical, or a self-portrait (he called it a "caprice"), he did acknowledge that both Peer's mother and his father were something like his own parents: the ambivalent and rather helpless woman taking refuge in a world of dreams, myths, and fairy tales from the difficulties of life with an overambitious, irresponsible, spendthrift husband. He considered what kind of man the child of such a marriage could grow to be.

He wrote many poems, and most of his earliest plays (which were historical and nationalistic in tone) were written in verse. Three of the most striking poems are perhaps one describing the miner who delves into the caverns of the earth, striking "hammer blow on hammer blow" into the heart of the rock, one on living and writing ("to live is to war with the troll, in caverns of heart and brain; to write—that is to hold doomsession [to sit in judgment] on one's self"), and one titled "On the Vidda" (the wide open mountain plateau). This third poem tells how a young man leaves his mother and his betrothed to hunt in the mountains, at the call of a strange hunter—a call to action, not dreams. He stays there through summer and winter, and then finds he has grown away from his former love and former way of life. He mourns their loss, but finds that he is now free, and can live a life of action. The hunter had been an unknown part of himself.

This poem was published a few months after Ibsen's marriage. Three years later he toured Norway collecting myths and folklore to use in his later work, and two years after this, in 1864, he left Norway in a mood of dispair and disillusionment, having never been successful in his life or work there. He had struggled to establish himself academically and as a writer. Moreover, he carried for fourteen years the burden of supporting an illegitimate son whom he had begotten at the age of seventeen. He identified himself closely with the struggles of his country to become independent of Denmark, and later, of Sweden, which was only achieved in 1905, and to establish the freedom of the Norwegian language.

He was deeply affected by the failure of his country to support Denmark in the war with Prussia when Schleswig-Holstein was annexed. On his journey toward Italy, Ibsen saw in Berlin the victory parade of the Prussians in which the Danish guns captured at Dybbol were displayed and spat upon by the crowds. He returned to Norway after twenty-seven years, to ensure that the son of his marriage could retain Norwegian nationality.

Brand was written a year after he left Norway, and with its publication and performance came success. *Peer Gynt* followed *Brand*; he described it as having "come through by itself," and also as "a victor's song of triumph." The verse play shows all the characteristics of dreams—the apparent inconsequence of changing scenes, hallucinations, recall of memories, condensation, displacement, etc. As in a dream all the people who appear are aspects of the dreamer, so all the characters in *Peer Gynt*, I believe, represent aspects of Ibsen, known or unknown.

In *Brand* and *Peer Gynt*, we can see Ibsen's growing self-recognition, maturation, and integration in the logical development from the omnipotent dreamer, through the mourner, to the free man of action, decision, and reality sense.

After *Brand* and *Peer Gynt* he wrote very little poetry, saying that poetry actually hindered drama. He chose instead "the incomparably more difficult art of writing in the straightforward language of reality." His next play, *Emperor and Galilean* (which seems long, rambling, and moralistic, though he spoke of it as his masterpiece) was followed by the series of great plays— *Pillars of Society, A Doll's House, Ghosts,* etc., ending with *When We Dead Awaken*, which he subtitled *An Epilogue*. These dealt with the moral or ethical problems of his time and country, but gradually tended more and more to return to poetic or lyrical ideas. *When We Dead Awaken* is not about death, but rather about the realization that "when we dead awaken we find what we have lost. We find that we have never lived," and the inalienable right of every person to live, and to be his true self, which is impossible without love. (Edith Weigert 1960 has spoken of "the horror of non-being.")

Brand ("fire" or "sword") Ibsen says at one point is his own best self. He is a man of immense courage, strength of will, and trust in his God; but he is a fanatic, without insight, and without compassion. His God's love is truly hate (this is said, in as many words). *Brand* demands the sacrifice of everything "All or nothing" and seeks to force his own will on others as the will of God.

He refuses to visit and give the Sacraments to his dying mother unless she gives all she has to build a new church. He insists that his wife give away to a beggar all the clothes of their dead child; she may not even keep back one small cap. The child, and later the wife, too, dies because of the demands of Brand's God that he (Brand) and they, should give all or nothing, living and working in a cold, unfriendly, and sunless village on a remote fjord.

After his wife and mother die, Brand goes into the mountains, led by a crazy peasant girl, in search of the Ice Church of his dreams and visions, only to be swallowed up in an avalanche. A voice proclaims, "God is Love."

Brand is what we would now see as a primitive, sadistic superego, showing clearly its roots in the id. Ibsen was to write later a good deal on the subject of conscience and the conflict that is associated with it. Brand is free from *inner* conflict; his conflict is with the outside world—first, with storm and tides, when he risks his life to visit a dying man on a distant island and, later, with his family and his flock.

Peer Gynt is a ne'er-do-well, cowardly and destructive, and an "incurable romancer," telling the deeds of others as his own. He abducts his neighbor's daughter at her wedding, and for that becomes an outlaw, a "wolf's head," with every man's hand against him and all his goods forfeit. He is, in turn, seduced by cowgirls who are looking for Trolls as mates, and then by the Troll King's daughter. He is trapped by the Trolls, forced to adopt their way of life and seeing. Their motto "To thyself be enough," replaces the human "To thyself be true." He refuses to let his eyes be cut, which would make him a Troll for ever, and escapes after a violent struggle with the Trolls, during which the church bells are rung by his mother and the little girl, Solveig, with whom he has fallen in love for the first time and idealizes and who loves him in spite of her fears.

He encounters, fights with, and tries to destroy the invisible Troll—the great Bøyg, something immovable, unknowable, which will not let him pass and answers the question "Who are you?" only with "I am myself."

Up to this point Peer has known that he was lying, that such dreams as flying or being emperor were lies; now he is aware of his plight and that he must fend for himself. He builds a hut in the forest. He sees a boy, due for army service, deliberately chop off his right forefinger with a sickle to avoid the draft. Peer marvels that the boy could do it: "To have the idea, the wish, yes—but to *do* it, No! that is beyond me."

He dreams of living in his hut with Solveig, but finds that the Troll King's daughter and her child, malformed, and misbegotten by his *desire* alone are setting up house next door. He runs away, promising himself that Solveig will wait till he comes back.

He hears that his mother, Åase, is dying, and is asking for him. At known risk he goes to her. In a most moving scene he comforts her by playing the sleigh-ride game that she had played with him. With Blackie the cat as the horse Granë, they journey to heaven's gate, where God the Father welcomes her. The journey ends, he closes her eyes and kisses her. "Thank you, dear, for all you gave me, the thrashings and kisses too. But now you must thank me also." His kiss is her "fare for the drive." At this point he *knows* he must get away and goes "to sea, and farther still." Until the end there is little of reality.

We follow his journey through a long series of fantastic dream scenes, in which comedy predominates at first. Ibsen mocks at his own dreams, his wish to be rich, to be emperor, to live without commitment to family and others, to be promiscuous without the binding responsibility of relationship. In the desert Peer hob-nobs with other psychopaths, who leave him in a ship that "miraculously" explodes. This he sees as an act of God on his behalf. He meets the singing statue of Memnon, and the Sphinx (which closely resembles the Bøyg). Then we see him in an asylum, crowned with straw as the "Emperor of Self." Finally we see him returning, an old man, to Norway; and moving toward his death at the hut in the mountains where Solveig waits.

Ibsen's "war with the Troll" is very clearly defined, in the antithesis between the human who is *true* to himself and the Troll who is *enough* to himself, who lives without commitment or relationship, and who may have an idea, but dare not carry it over into action unless he balance it with its opposite, keeping a bridge by which he can go back. Peer sends idols to China and then missionaries. He offers money to the crew of a sinking ship, until he finds that they are married men with families waiting to welcome them. Then he will give only enough to buy drink, to wreck their homecoming, since he is alone.

Peer comes to a village where there is a funeral. The Pastor speaks of the dead man, who had come as a stranger among them, and who always kept his right hand hidden; the forefinger was missing, he had chopped it off. He had worked and striven, built a home, and raised a family in spite of endless adversities. He had been *himself*, always, *within his limits*, and now they could pray that God in His mercy would make him no longer a cripple. (How unlike Brand.)

Peer eats wild onions, peeling them and finding them onion all through, "no heart." He reaches the hut, and hearing Solveig sing, he dimly remembers her and realizes "My Empire was here."

Out of the mist and darkness he hears "the sound of children weeping, weeping that is half a song," and finds threadballs on the ground at his feet. These are the thoughts he never thought or gave life to, the words he never spoke, the songs he stifled, the tears unwept, the deeds undone.

The Button Molder comes out of the wood looking for Peer, whose grave is dug with the coffin ready. He is to be melted down in the casting ladle (Peer's own childhood toy); he has lost his loop. He who had dreamed of being emperor had thrown away his real empire, a woman's love; he who had prided himself on always being *himself and nothing else* had never really been himself in the positive sense of commitment and relationship, but only negatively, avoiding all that would have made demands on him. He had never even been a great sinner; he could not be all Troll. He must now lose the hope of being a real person, in his own right—the person that he should have been—and be melted down with all the other insignificant people.

At last, having tried every way to avoid his fate, he becomes still. "I was dead long before my death," or, as in another translation, "I fear to die before my death."

So a soul can go back, so wretchedly poor
Into the grey mists of nothingness.
Beautiful earth, do not be angry
That I have trod you and left no mark.
Beautiful sun, you have squandered your light,
Your glorious light, on an empty house.
There was no-one within to be heartened and cheered;

The owner had gone. You beautiful sun,
You beautiful earth who wasted your warmth
And sustenance on my mother's womb!
How mean is the spirit, how lavish is nature!
How costly to pay with one's life for one's birth!
I will climb to the top of the highest peak,
I will see the sun rise once again,
I will gaze on the promised land till my eyes
Are tired out. Then let the snow pile over me,
And above my tomb write "Here No-one is buried"
And afterwards, well — let come what will.

Again the Button Molder comes, and Peer realizes that the Bøyg's "Go round about" is no longer for him; "this time it's straight through no matter how narrow the path." Once more he hears Solveig singing, and he begs her forgiveness. He asks her, "Where has Peer Gynt been all this while?, since, with the mark of destiny on his brow, he first sprang forth as a thought newly born in the mind of God? Where was I, my real self, my whole self, my true self, with God's seal upon my brow?"

She answers "as a mother speaks of her child": "In my faith and in my hope and in my love. But who is his father? He who forgives in answer to a mother's prayers. Sleep and dream, my own dear love." The Button Molder would have the last word, "to the last cross-roads, Peer," but Solveig sings again. Perhaps, for the first time, in his death, Peer is alive and is, within his limits, his true self.

In a speech to students in 1874 Ibsen said "in the straightforward language of reality":

It was a long time before I realized that to write is essentially to see, but . . . to see in such a way that what is seen comes into the possession of the beholder as the poet saw it. But only that which is *lived through* is seen and beheld in this fashion. And this living through is the real secret of the literature of this modern age. Everything I have written in the last ten years I have lived through in spirit. . . . And now . . . a few words . . . that also have a connection with something lived through. When Emperor Julian reaches the end of his career, and everything is collapsing about him, there is nothing that depresses him so profoundly as the thought that his total achievement was this: to be remembered with respectful acknowledgment by certain cold and clear minds, whilst his opponents were lodged in warm living hearts, rich in love.

In both *Brand* and *Peer Gynt* the mother's death is a point of climax, after which there is a lasting loss of contact with reality. This loss differs from that in such previous episodes as Peer's hallucinatory meeting with the Trolls, from which the thoughts of his mother and of Solveig recalled him, like the sound of church bells.

Ibsen's mother was still alive until two years after Peer Gynt was published; his father lived another twenty-five years. He remained estranged from them, though he wrote affectionately of both after their deaths.

Ibsen shows us the importance of the loss of the mother(through weaning or the birth of a younger child), the lack of a loving father, and the cold hate that is aroused. Ibsen himself was the eldest of five children, and he left home at the age of fifteen, henceforth to support and educate himself entirely, but he never "lost his loop."

Ibsen knew a great deal about mental processes and mental illness, and although this comes out in all his poems and plays, I think it is shown perhaps most clearly in *Peer Gynt*. There are Trolls in many of his other plays, *Hedda Gabler, Gregers Werle, Hilda Wangel, The Rat Wife, Rubek*, and even *Brand*; through lack of love they wreck the lives of those around them. There are also many like Peer, whose proper fate is to reach the casting ladle.

In Rome, Ibsen found that he understood "Michael Angelo, Bernini and his school better than many modern sculptors . . . who continue to create heroic ballads in clay and marble." The former were "the kind of men with the courage to do something crazy now and then." Certainly he thought of writing *Peer Gynt* as "doing something crazy," and in writing to Grieg about the music he said "there must be some devilment in it."

The more serious aspects are there too. He wrote earlier that year of "the intellectual discipline and training that is needed to understand the nature of delusion." Later, he wrote of "the conflict . . . between reality and the claims of idealism; . . . the clash of ability and aspirations, of will and possibility, at once the tragedy and comedy of mankind and the individual." Ibsen was before his time in understanding the nature of delusion, and in *seeing* the search for the self, with which psychoanalysts and others have become so familiar.

In the years when he was writing his verse plays, *Brand, Peer Gynt*, and *Emperor and Galilean*, Ibsen resolved these clashes and conflicts in his own life and found himself. His marriage and the close and warm relationships between himself and his wife and son (his real empire) were fully developed, even though this was a time of great hardship, poverty and isolation. He *might* have become Brand, Peer, or Julian, but none would have been his "real, whole, true self, with God's seal upon his brow." His love saved him from becoming a Troll.

In Peer we see the clash and search; we see his growing loss of ability to distinguish "truth" from "lies" (dreams, psychic or poetic, from factual truth) and his intolerance of the separation between them. Simultaneously, we watch the struggle of the psychotic to remain "true to himself" in face of the impossibility of being "enough" to himself.

Ibsen's own ability to distinguish was in him to the last. When he was dying, after his last stroke, his wife saw him open his eyes, and said "Look he is better." He said: "Not at all," and died. He could *assert* his death, because he was alive and was himself, within his own limits.

Such struggles as Peer's are seen by psychoanalysts who treat psychotic and borderline psychotic patients whom Freud would have considered inaccessible because of their failure to develop a transference neurosis. (Transference psychosis was only recognized later.) In the histories of these patients we often find elements such as those shown in Peer's.

Case 1

On an Atlantic crossing in a freighter, I was called to see a young engineer who had broken down. He was threatening to damage the steering gear and had to be restrained. This was his second voyage and we were approaching his homeland.

His first voyage had been very long, and on returning he had found that his mother had died more than a year before, soon after he had left home, and no one had told him. Now, he feared that he would find his sister dead. His father had left the mother when he was a child; and at fifteen he had had to identify the body of his elder brother, killed in a motorcycle crash.

When I first saw him he was plainly psychotic, paranoid and out of contact with all reality. I told him that on landing he should be admitted to hospital. Within a few days he became, instead, an aggressive psychopath—defying authority, denying his fears, unloving, and unlovable; still out of touch with his feelings, but sane.

Case 2

I was asked to see a man who was in trouble, threatened with law proceedings and suspended from his job. He was a psychotherapist who had seduced (or been seduced by) an adolescent boy, one of his patients. He was said to be depressed.

At consultation, I could find no depression. Again, what I saw was a psychotic patient with flights of ideas, talking incoherently and with no reality sense. It seemed impossible to establish contact. I offered analysis, which he would only accept if his wife were willing; and he spoke so extravagantly of her, and of his enormous love for her and for his children, that I feared he might commit multiple murder and suicide. He and his wife finally agreed to hospitalization and analysis for him, and I visited him.

The acute psychotic state lasted only a few days and did not recur during the year that I attempted analysis with him. He demanded arrogantly to be allowed to practice as a psychotherapist again; he pursued both his former patient and other boys, and some of his seductions were actually incestuous. He asserted that only as a psychotherapist and active homosexual could he be truly "himself." He incessantly played records of Mahler's Kindertotenlieder.

Both parents were alive, but apparently ineffectual. His elder sister had died when he was six, and his elder brother when he was fifteen; he felt that his parents had cared only for them.

He broke off treatment when told that he would not be prosecuted and when I made it clear that I would not treat him if he were practicing as a psychotherapist. I was not attempting to cure his homosexuality or to prevent its consequences, except in so far as the ethical aspect of the therapist-patient relationship was involved, a relationship he rejected.

Case 3

After some years of analysis, in which modifications in classical technique had been necessary, owing to the extent of the disturbances, a borderline patient needed short hospitalization during a psychotic episode. This proved to be the beginning of the terminal phase of her analysis, which still laster another two years, but ended quite dramatically.

The material throughout this time was concerned with her search for her identity and with the separation of herself from me.

I could have been the Bøyg. She screamed repeatedly "Who are you?" and no obvious response or interpretation brought relief. What *did* was a whole series of such answers as, "I am your pain, your unhappiness; I am your love, your hate, your headache; I am the tree you bashed your head on. I am the parents who could let you be an extension of them, the person who has hurt you, who has listened to you, cared for you, held you; and you are my headache, *my* love, *my* hate," etc. I had to accept *being* these things, not representing them, thus I had to accept her delusion as true.

Later her question was, "Who am I?" And she answered herself, "I am your patient, for whom you have cared; and you are my analyst, *not me*."

After that came the real sorting-out, intensely painful and difficult for us both. "You breathe. I didn't know. And you have *your own* feelings, which I don't feel." Eventually she fixed a date for ending which I felt unsuitable, but she insisted on. She would sit facing me and move her chair till she was nearly touching me, at which point I moved mine back. She was furious, "Why? Why? Why?" I would point out our separateness, and that I had a right to refuse something I did not want. I had allowed her her rights, including the choice of date for finishing.

Finally, on the day before we were to finish, she announced that we would go on, and I firmly said No. This precipitated a violent temper-tantrum, in which she behaved like a child of three or four. I sat and said nothing, even though she screamed and threw herself on the floor, and clutched my legs, *imploring* me to say Yes. At the end of the hour I said only that it was time for her to go and that she had been reliving an actual experience from childhood. Next day, she came, calm and friendly. She thanked me for all the years of our work together, and said goodbye.

Her recovery has been complete. She is a whole person in her own right, and knows it. And she is free, as never before; she has known loss, and mourned for it; she has accepted both her limitations, and her Troll-self, and is able to love and to create.

Ibsen's relevance to aspects of the modern world is shown again in *Peer Gynt*. What the Trolls demanded of Peer, under pressure and threats, was that he should support their lies; and it was their lies that divided him form "his real self, his true self" and from the world of men. The lie that he could be "enough" to himself—not "true to himself"—drove him to give up involvement with, or commitment to, all that is human and so avoid conflict and conscience.

The tyranny of totalitarianism (arising out of earlier tyrannies) with increasing bureaucracy, indoctrination, secrecy, censorship, and denial of the importance of individual human beings with their right to be true to themselves is of the essence of the Trolls' ideology and way of life.

In a speech, in 1885, Ibsen said "An element of nobility must find its way into our public life, into our government, among our representatives and into our press. Of course I am not thinking of nobility of birth, nor of money, nor even of ability or talent. What I am thinking of is a nobility of character, of mind, and of will. That alone can liberate us. This aristocracy . . . will come to us from . . . [those] which so far have not suffered any irreparable damage under party pressure."

Commenting on *Rosmersholm*, Strindberg wrote of "modern mind murderer":

> From having once been purely physical (imprisonment, torture, death), the fight for power has gradually developed into something more psychological, though no less cruel for that. . . . In previous ages one killed one's opponent without having changed his convictions; now one creates a majority against him, 'persuades' him . . . ascribes to him

different intentions from those that he has, deprives him of his livelihood, denies him social respect, makes him look ridiculous, in a word tortures him to death by lies or drives him insane instead of killing him.

Here, again, is a reference to the power of the lie—the Troll's chief weapon, brain-washing. And today, even in the world of psychiatry we are seeing this very use of the lie for mind murder and the destruction of the true selves of those who dissent or resist it. Other authors writing of recent happenings support Ibsen implicitly in his clear distinction between Trolls, whose motto is "To thyself be enough" and humans whose motto is "To thyself be true."

In his book *Licensed Mass Murder*, H. V. Dicks portrays one of the Nazis he interviewed as a norm-setter: "He still wanted some powerful daddy to come and tell the world he was a good chap. I have seldom, if ever, experienced such pain at the depth of degradation of, or non-arrival at, a human level as with this man. This may be the nature of fiends; that they, needing to love, must needs love those like themselves—the fellowship of the damned who hate lucky sissies and softies who can love and create."

Hanna Arendt, in *Eichmann in Jerusalem*, writes of "the banality of evil," describing people like Dicks's norm-setter. She comments, "How few people have the resources needed to resist authority." The Dean of Johannesburg (The Very Reverend Gonville ffrench-Beytagh), in *Encountering Darkness*, has written of his discovery that the root of apartheid is the "real belief that 'blacks' are animals, *not* men."

Finally, some time ago Alexander Solzhenitsyn's oration to be given in Sweden on receiving the Nobel Peace prize, was read in translation over the radio, and the next day similar words of Mikos Theodorakis were quoted in the London *Observer*. "Violence cannot continue to exist without the lie. Violence does not take people by the throat and strangle them; it demands only that they support the lie.... A lie can resist many things, but it cannot resist art.... There is a special relation between art, especially that of the writer, and truth. It is the only real force which can unite men and not divide them."

What the Trolls demanded of Peer was that he should support their lies, and it was the Trolls, with their lies, that divided him from his real self, his true self, and from the world of men. The lie that he could be enough to himself drove him to give up involvement with, or commitment to, all that is human, and so to avoid conflict, and conscience.

Ibsen's spectrum is far richer and wider than I could hope to show. I will end just by wondering if it is not significant that, while Solzhenitsyn has been honoured in Sweden, it was the Society of Norwegian Writers and Artists that offered him a home if he were exiled by force.

REFERENCES

Arendt, H. (1963). *Eichman in Jerusalem*. London: Faber.
Bradbrook, M. C. (1946). *Ibsen the Norwegian: A Reevaluation*. London: Chatto and Windus.
Dicks, H. V. (1972). *Licensed Mass Murder*. London: Sussex University Press (Chatto and Heinemann).
ffrench-Beytagh, G. (1973). *Encountering Darkness*. London: Collins.
Ibsen, B. (1951). *The Three Ibsens*. London: Hutchinson.
Ibsen, H. (1866). *Brand*. Trans. F. E. Garrett. London: Dent, 1894.
——— (1867). *Peer Gynt*. Trans. N. Ginsbury. London: Hammond, Hammond, and Company, 1945.
——— (1899). *When We Dead Awaken*. Trans. M. Meyer. London: Rupert Hart-Davis, 1960.
Koht, H. (1931). *The Life of Ibsen*, 2 vols. Trans. R. McMahon and H. Larsen. London: Allen and Unwin.
McFarlane, J., ed. (1970). *Henrik Ibsen: A Critical Anthology*. Harmondsworth, England: Penguin.
Meyer, M. (1967). *Henrik Ibsen: The Making of a Dramatist. 1828-1864*. London: Hart-Davis.
Weigert, E. (1960). Loneliness and trust: basic factors of human existence. *Psychiatry* 23:121-131.

Psychoanalytic Notes on Suicide

W. W. MEISSNER, S.J., M.D.

The typology of and theories on suicidal behavior are reviewed to integrate various points of view in terms of the paranoid process. Freud's theory of internalized aggression, the relation of suicidal impulses to depression, the operation of narcissistic components in the complex motivation of suicide are related to the concept of the victim-introject as central to the pathology of suicide. Suicidal patterns play out the dynamics inherent in the victim-introject and its correlative component the aggressor-introject. The victim-introject serves as the core internalization around which a false-self system is organized; the suicide represents the attempt to destroy the false-self as a means of realizing the dynamic purposes of the victim-introject. The concept of the victim-introject integrates previous psychoanalytic formulations of suicide and provides a template for the development of a therapeutic rationale. Implications for therapeutic response are considered, particularly in terms of the need to undermine the patient's attempts to maintain and reinforce his victimization.

There is perhaps no enigma more perplexing and more confounding than suicide. The motivations of the suicidal impulse have escaped our capacity to understand, and consequently frustrated our ability to predict and prevent the suicidal event. Suicide has been defined as "a human act of self-inflicted, self-intentioned cessation" (Shneidman 1973). As a human act, suicide embraces a multitude of underlying motivational states, both conscious and unconscious, and is influenced by multiple factors, no one of which can be regarded exclusively as the basic cause. Factors which come into play and which influence suicidal behavior are, at a most critical level, certainly intrapsychic and psychological, but they also are strongly influenced by interpersonal events, social forces, economic crises, cultural influences, and a host of other determinants which exhaust the capacity of scientific thinking to detail and integrate.

Our purpose in this study is to indicate the basic typology of suicidal behavior, discuss briefly the basic sociological orientations toward suicide, and then focus more particularly on the psychoanalytic understanding of suicidal phenomena.

TYPES OF SUICIDE

Descriptive categories of suicidal behavior have been broken down in a variety of ways. The first important distinction is that between committed suicide and attempted suicide. *Committed suicide* refers to one of the general recognized modes of death—natural, accidental, suicidal, or homicidal—involved in the certification of actual deaths. In this usage, the term generally implies that the victim consciously intended the lethal act to result in his own death. *Attempted suicide*, however, is complicated by the issue of intent. Stengel (1968) defines the suicide attempt as "any nonfatal act of self-damage inflicted with a self-destructive intention, however vague and ambiguous."

A second important distinction involves the seriousness of the suicide attempt. Other than cases of successfully completed suicide, *serious attempts* may be regarded as those in which the individuals express a definite intention to die, but the suicide act is aborted through some unforeseen circumstance. In other less serious attempts, such as cases in which attempters gamble with death or in which the suicidal intent is uncertain even to themselves, the act must still be regarded as serious enough to pose a definite risk to life. Even attempts which involve a minimum of suicidal intent and are perpetrated for consciously or unconsciously manipulative motives cannot be regarded lightly. We will return to this aspect of suicide later, in regard to the question of intentionality.

An area of consideration important to the understanding of suicide is *subsuicidal phenomena*. Menninger (1938) described subsuicidal phenomena in terms of *chronic suicide*, which includes ascetism, martyrdom, addiction, invalidism, and psychosis; *focal suicide* which involves acts of self-mutilation, malingering, polysurgery, multiple accidents, and impotence and frigidity; and finally, *organic suicide* which refers to the operation of psychological factors in organic disease states, particularly self-punitive, aggressive, and erotic components. Moreover, the role of self-destructive impulses in alcoholism and drug addiction; the neglect of medical care for such chronic and debilitating diseases as hypertension and diabetes; and even the role of suicidal impulses in the victims of homicides, have been carefully studied.

Seen in the broader context of subsuicidal phenomena and *suicidal equivalents*, the incidence of suicidal behavior and of the suicidal impulse in the human race is by no means minimal, nor is its significance to be underestimated. The questions raised by this self-destructive dimension of human existence are indeed profound and perplexing. They touch on some of the most basic theological, philosophical, social, psychological, and moral questions about human nature and human existence. We can wonder indeed whether the suicidal impulse and the incidence of serious committed suicide can ever be meaningfully reduced beyond a certain level.

Suicide Risk

The most serious psychiatric aspect of dealing with suicide is the recognition of suicidal patients and the prevention of suicidal behavior. There are a number of indices pointing to the increased, serious suicide risk. Association with psychiatric illness, particularly severe depression, psychotic (unipolar) depression and bipolar affective disease, otherwise known as manic-depressive psychosis, and also association with schizophrenia—all increase the potential for suicide. The period of apparent recovery from severe depression has been described as a period of increased suicide risk (Shneidman and Faberow 1957). Clinical improvement may frequently be a sign that the patient has decided on a suicidal solution to his difficulties. Other important indicators of suicide risk include alcoholism, drug addiction, and previous attempts. Almost three-fourths of all suicide victims previously threatened or attempted suicide (Shneidman and Faberow 1957). More than two-thirds of the patients who attempt suicide communicate their suicidal intent in one way or another, and 41 percent have specifically stated they intended to commit suicide. The most common expressions take the form of a desire to die, or the thought that they would be better off dead, or an explicit statement of an intent to commit suicide, or the feeling that their families would be better off if the patient were dead. The risk of suicide is highest in white males over fifty. The rate of attempted suicide is higher among females; the rate of committed suicide higher among males. Incidence increases with age in both sexes and is highest in those who are separated, divorced, or widowed. Consequently, your chances of dying by suicide are best if you are male, white, over fifty, if you are separated, divorced, or widowed, and if you live alone.

In the attempt to bring more specific understanding to the dynamics of suicide and avoid oversimplistic, if easy, generalization, there has been an attempt to divide suicidal behavior into a variety of subcategories. Surveying a fair amount of this literature, Beall (1969) concluded that there seem to be three main suicidal syndromes, two having to do with attempted suicide and one with completed suicide. In the first form of suicide attempt, the syndrome is characterized by psychopathic acting out, in which the behavior is more or less impulsive and aggressive and in which there is little evidence of guilt. The suicide attempt itself tends to adopt a more passive form and usually comes without much advance warning. This form of suicide attempt is usually not very harmful and tends to occur among men. A second form of suicide attempt occurs primarily among women with a hysterical personality style. Again, the mode is primarily passive, but there is an increased amount of guilt manipulation and the method tends to be dramatic. The attempt comes with a clear and definite warning to elicit rescuing maneuvers from important figures. This pattern is closer to that of manipulative suicide, as described by Sifneos (1966).

In contrast, completed suicides tend to occur more frequently among the professional and managerial classes. In these cases, the conflict is more internal, the behavior is restricted rather than impulsive or aggressive, and the personality tends to be obsessive and compulsive, with a good deal of guilt over dependency wishes. Generally, if a warning is given, it is not dramatic and the method chosen for suicide tends to be more painful. The suicide attempt, when it occurs, is serious and the result is usually fatal. The interaction of socioeconomic determinants and personality style in these descriptive types of suicide reflects once more the interplay of social and psychological factors in the determination of patterns of suicidal behavior.

Another important aspect of the suicide action is that it can be regarded as a form of communication. There is a cry for help which is implicit in every suicidal action (Faberow and Shneidman 1961). While the cry for help plays a prominent role in many suicide actions, particularly attempts of a less serious and manipulative nature, there are also other cases in which the cry for help is too implicit to play a very observable role. The basic issue is the extent to which the suicidal individual has resolved the underlying dilemmas of life and death, and the extent to which the balance has been tipped in favor of the forces of life as opposed to those of death.

An important and critical notion more recently added to the vocabulary of suicide is *lethality*. Lethality was originally described by Shneidman (1969) as the probability of an individual's killing himself in the present or immediate future, or as the *deathfulness* of the act. Weisman (1971) had gone on to distinguish three basic forms of lethality: (1) lethality of intentionality, pertaining to ideation and involvement, (2) lethality of implementation, pertaining to factors of risk and rescue, and finally (3) lethality of intercession, in connection with available resources, relief, and reorientation. Weisman comments:

> No one attempts suicide in a vacuum, and no one investigates suicide without an implicit concept of lethality. Clinicians who treat suicide attempts tend to define lethality according to the damage inflicted. Psychiatrists and psychologists who deal with demographic and psychosocial factors are apt to emphasize ideas, moods, and cultural and

social involvements. This is the lethality of intentionality. Workers who are engaged in preventive activities view lethality in terms of the person's available resources and supports. This is the lethality of intercession, or, more properly, nonintercession. (p. 228)

Thus lethality must be distinguished from the degree of discomfort or distress in the patient. It rather concerns the probability of the patient's committing suicide. Any given adult, at any given time, may have more than one aspect of this lethality. there may be a more or less long-range, chronic, pervasive, and characterological orientation toward death or suicide, which functions as an integral part of his psychosocial make-up and affects his philosophy of life and other aspects of his general functioning. At the same time, he is capable of a more acute, relatively short-term exacerbation of lethality. Clinically, this is in fact what is meant by saying that a patient has become suicidal. Both aspects are crucial for the clinical evaluation of the suicide risk in any patient. A patient may be highly disturbed and distressed, caught up in the acute turmoil of a schizophrenic episode, and not necessarily be suicidal. The opposite is in fact all too often true, that a patient may not manifest any noteworthy degree of distress, but may indeed go on to kill himself. It is specifically the increase in lethality that kills the patient. The identification of lethality and the preventive protection of patients during periods of exacerbated lethality are the major problems in dealing with suicide behavior.

The issue of intentionality is related to lethality. In this regard, deaths may be regarded as intentioned, subintentioned, or unintentioned (Shneidman 1973). In this sense, the death is intentioned or intentional when the subject plays a direct and conscious role in bringing it about. Death is unintentioned when the subject plays no effective role in it and where the death results from independent physical events whether traumatic or biological. Between these polar categories lies the large and relatively unchartered area of subintentioned deaths. These are cases in which the subject plays some partial, implicit, or unconscious role in bringing about his own death. We have discussed this category already, particularly in regard to Menninger's concepts of chronic, focal, and organic suicide. Suicidal intent can vary from the more or less nonserious and manipulative suicidal gesture (Sifneos 1966) to the most serious, severe, and unalterable commitment to death. Even here, one must be cautious. The terms *manipulative* and *gesture* are unfortunate, since they often lead clinicians to minimize the inherent suicide potential of these patients. Frequently enough, such patients do end up committing suicide, some unintentionally, some perhaps subintentionally, and a few even finally intentionally.

THE SOCIOLOGICAL APPROACH TO SUICIDE

At this point, we can turn our attention to a consideration of some major theories of suicidal behavior. The major sociological theorist of suicide was Emile Durkheim (1897). In his classic treatise, Durkheim proposed three categories of suicide: egoistic, altruistic, and anomic.

Egoistic suicide results from the individual's failure to integrate into his own social structure. Thus, the suicide rate tends to be low in Catholic countries because religion integrates the individual into the collective life of the Chuch, while it tends to be higher in Protestant countries where the stress is on individualism. Similarly, suicide rates drop in periods of political crisis, since in such periods society is more strongly integrated and individuals become more actively involved in social life and are thus less subject to egoistic suicide.

Altruistic suicide is more or less the antithesis of egoistic suicide in that it represents instances in which the individual is excessively integrated with his society. Thus a suicide becomes the fruit or price of religious sacrifice or fanatical allegiance (Japanese suicides in World War II). On the other hand, *anomic suicide* occurs in situations in which the accustomed relationship between the individual and his society is suddenly shattered, radically altered, or shifted in some significant manner. The sudden loss of a job, a close friend, or a fortune could be the precipitating factors for an anomic suicide.

Critics of Durkheim's work have found fault with his collection of data and with frequently unexplained "exceptions" (for example, the high suicide rate in Catholic Austria). His general approach to statistics was to employ them as explanatory rather than as descriptive devices. For Durkheim, sociology was the positive science of social facts, the extrinsic social forces that determine human behavior. Durkheim's study of suicide rates as regularities of social behavior concluded that such regularities must mean that social forces outside the individual were at work causing the observed regularities.

The problem with much of Durkheim's approach—and with it a considerable body of subsequent sociological interpretation—was that in the search for relevant means to understand social behavior, Durkheim was continually forced to supply commonsense meanings to interpret suicidal actions. Thus Durkheim committed a two-fold error, first in trying to explain social behavior by merely extrinsic factors, and second in explaining meaning by the implication of the observer's own commonsense understandings. The methodological weakness is critical and points to the fact that suicide action and the meaning of suicide are sufficiently complex and difficult to exceed the grasp of any single methodology, even one as far reaching as that of sociology (Douglas 1968). As Beall (1969) has commented:

The inadequacy of statistical or actuarial correlations (whether with age, occupation, or residential area) have been pointed out by many investigators....Such correlations are too simple and mechanical. Suicide is not a simple variable that can be correlated directly with another single feature of society. It involves much more than simply being detached from or integrated with society. Social attitudes, feelings of belonging, evaluation of self according to group mores, competitive interpersonal struggles, and identification of one's welfare with that of other people are important, but they are not the entire story. To attribute an increase in suicides to the development of civilization, to economic depressions, anomie, or social disorganization, and then to attempt a purely sociological explantation omits the basic internal struggle that these environmental situations produce. It also fails to explain why, in these circumstances, only *some* individuals commit suicide. An examination of psychological explanation is needed to fill this gap. (p.4)

FREUD

When we enter the realm of the psychology of suicide, we encounter considerable diversity and complexity. In fact, we enter a quite divergent realm of study since the sociological phenomena of suicide are, to some extent, different from those of the psychological approach. Sociological studies are based primarily on the statistics of actual suicides, while psychological studies deal primarily with attempted and unsuccessful suicides. These are quite divergent phenomena, not only descriptively but dynamically as well.

As in so many other areas of psychodynamic understanding, it is Freud's thinking which has given primary direction to our understanding of the dynamics of suicide. Freud's (1901) attention was drawn in the early stages of his work to the occurrence of accidents. He suggested that these apparently accidental and unintentioned instances of self-injury are in fact manifestations of an impulse to self-punishment, which normally finds its expression in self-reproach or symptom formation, but in these instances take advantage of the external situation to bring about the injurious effect. Freud reported that his own son made a temperamental threat to kill himself one day when he was made to stay in bed. Later on he banged himself against a door handle and developed a swelling on one side of his chest. When Freud asked why he had done this, the eleven-year-old child replied that that was his attempt at suicide. Freud proceeds to comment:

Anyone who believes in the occurrence of half-intentional self-*injury*—if I may use a clumsy expression—would be prepared also to assume that in addition to consciously intentional suicide there is such a thing as half-intentional self-*destruction* (self-destruction with an unconscious intent), capable of making skillful use of a threat to life and of disguising it as a chance mishap. There is no need to think such self-destruction rare. For the trend to self-destruction is present to a certain degree in very many more human beings than those in whom it is carried out; self-injuries are as a rule a compromise between this instinct and the forces that are still working against it, and even where suicide actually results, the inclination to suicide will have been present for a long time before in lesser strength or in the form of an unconscious and suppressed trend. (pp. 80-81)

Freud added a further note in the analysis of the Rat-Man (1909) in which he established that the suicidal impulse is itself a form of punishment for a murderous wish directed against an external object.

These views received greater crystallization in Freud's classic paper "Mourning and Melancholia" (1917b). In thinking about self-destructive sadism, Freud pondered how the ego can consent to its own destruction in the suicidal act. Freud answered that the suicidal impulse is equivalent to a turning against the self of murderous impulses originally directed against a loved object. Thus, the depressive mechanism is equivalent to a taking-in of the ambivalently cathected object in a form of internalization which represents a regression from a basically narcissistic form of object choice. Consequently, the self is the receptacle of impulses previously directed against the object, including the destructive impulses. Subsequent to Freud's formulation, thinking about suicide was dominated by concepts of identification with the ambivalently held object, both loved and hated, and the turning of aggression against the self as a result of murderous hostility against the introjected ambivalent loved object. Suicide was thus viewed equivalently as murder turned inside-out. Freud (1917b) himself observed: "The analysis of melancholia now shows that the ego can kill itself only if, owing to the return of the object-cathexis, it can treat itself as an object—if it is able to direct against itself the hostility which relates to an object and which represents the ego's original reaction to objects in the external world" (p. 252). Thus the suicidal impulse at one and the same time strikes a blow against the ego itself as well as against the loved and hated object (Freud 1917a, p. 427).

Freud's understanding of suicide kept pace with his evolving views on aggression. After his formulation of the death instinct (1920a) the suicidal impulse was regarded as a turning of the death instinct against the self. Hence in his analysis of the suicidal impulse in a homosexual woman (1920b), the motive was ascribed to the turning of the death instinct against the patient's self in the form of self-punishment for a death wish originally directed against the parents. Freud explained the enigma of suicide in the following terms:

"Probably no one finds the mental energy required to kill himself unless, in the first place, in doing so he is at the same time killing an object with whom he has identified himself, and, in the second place, is turning against himself a death-wish which had been directed against someone else" (p. 162). Freud went on to insist that such death wishes inhabit the unconscious of every human being.

The next step in the argument came with the transition to the structural theory and the crystallization of Freud's thinking about the superego (1923). Behind the phenomenon of guilt, Freud saw the sadism of the superego turned against the ego. He turned again to his original analysis of melancholia:

> If we turn to melancholia first, we find that the excessively strong super-ego which has obtained a hold upon consciousness rages against the ego with merciless violence, as if it had taken possession of the whole of the sadism available in the person concerned. Following our view of sadism, we should say that the destructive component had entrenched itself in the super-ego and turned against the ego. What is now holding sway in the super-ego is, as it were, a pure culture of the death instinct, and in fact it often enough succeeds in driving the ego into death. (p. 53)

Freud then noted that the manic or obsessional defense may serve to preserve the ego from the threat of self-destruction. The obsessional regression to pregenital levels makes possible the transformation of impulses of love into hate directed against the object; the ego is consequently forced to struggle against these destructive impulses. The obsessional ego is thus trapped between the murderous impulses on the one hand and the reproaches of a punishing conscience on the other.

Freud's last statement in these matters, his unfinished *Outline* (1940), emphasized the notion of a primitive aggressiveness, a form of self-destructiveness within the human psyche. Thus, impulses to self-destruction, the death impulse, are countered and balanced by the instincts to self-preservation. When the normal constraining fusion of these instincts is undone, the defusion results in the liberation of the destructive instinct which is directed inward and thus brings about the reversal of the impulse to self-preservation, the suicidal intention.

The basic Freudian notion of superego aggression directed against the self has held first place as the predominant model for the understanding of suicidal behavior.

Post-Freudian Developments

Perhaps the best known development of Freud's view was presented by Karl Menninger in *Man Against Himself* (1938). Menninger amplified the psychodynamics of hostility and divided the murderous wish in suicide into the wish to kill, the wish to be killed, and the wish to die. Gregory Zilboorg (1936, 1937) added that not only does every suicidal case contain strong unconscious hostility, but it also reflects an unusual lack of the capacity to relate to and love others. He similarly maintained that the role of the broken home in the tendency to suicide demonstrates that suicide is the result of both intrapsychic and external causal developments. The danger of suicide, or its correlative homicide, can thus be increased by a regression which activates underlying oedipal conflicts and related internalizations based on an essentially sadomasochistic relationship between the parents. As we shall see later, the internalization of such sadomasochistic components derived from parental object relations may play a considerable role in the dynamics of suicide. Zilboorg also added the important point that suicide is motivated by the need to oppose frustrating external forces, but even more specifically the need to achieve immortality and thus extend the existence of the ego rather than terminate it.

Some important contributions were added by Melanie Klein (1934), building on Freud's original formulations. She specifically viewed suicide as an expression of the death instinct turned against the introjected object. She envisioned a further objective in the suicidal act, namely unification with the loved object.

But, while in commiting suicide the ego tends to murder its bad objects, in my view at the same time it also always aims at saving its loved objects, internal or external. To put it shortly: in some cases the fantasies underlying suicide aim at preserving the internalized good objects and that part of the ego which is identified with good objects, and also at destroying the other part of the ego which is identified with the bad objects and the id. Thus the ego is enabled to become united with its loved objects. (p. 296)

Suicide in Klein's view may also take the form of an attempt to preserve the good external objects by ridding the world or the loved objects of that part of the ego identified with the bad objects and the inherent, id-related destructive instinct. Thus the depressive suicide is equivalently an attempt to save the external loved object from the uncontrollable destructiveness of the death instinct. From a more developed object-relations perspective, such inwardly directed aggression is, in the normal course of development, neutralized by its integration with relatively stable structural formations derived from the relatively nonambivalent internalization of object relations. The failure of this process and the consequent ready mobilization of self-destructive impulses is often dramatically seen in the borderline syndrome (Kernberg 1967, Blanck 1974).

Suicide and Depression

Also as a consequence of Freud's earlier formulations there was a general trend toward linking suicide with the dynamics of depression, particularly in terms of the superego model. This trend was more or less brought into question by Edward Bibring's important study of depression (1953), in which he regards depression as an ego state in which the feeling of helplessness and hopelessness is the basic underlying dynamic. Bibring's view did not envision depression simply in terms of the turning of hostility against the self, but rather as an independent primary affect. Thus, at least in some cases, the pathogenesis of clinical depression may be independent of aggressive vicissitudes.

Recent studies (Gershon et al. 1968, Friedman 1970) have lent support to this view. A comparison, for example, between acutely depressed and suicidal patients suggests that manifest hostility is the most important distinguishing characteristic of suicide attempters in contrast to depressives who are considerably more compliant and passively accepting (Weisman et al. 1973). One would expect from the classic model that the increase of the intensity of the suicidal impulse would be accompanied by diminished hostility.

Subsequently, the role of feelings of helplessness and hopelessness has been highlighted in the suicidal syndrome (Appelbaum 1963, Stengel 1964), but the association between suicidal behavior and depression cannot be taken as absolute. Stotland's review of the concept of helplessness (1969) defined it in terms of a cognitive schema whose basic characteristic is negative expectations about the future. This cognitive distortion results in a pessimistic or hopeless view that nothing can turn out right, important goals are unattainable, and the worst problems are incapable of solution. Recent evidence (Minkoff et al. 1973) suggested that such negative expectations as a component of helplessness may be more closely related to the seriousness of suicidal intent than the depressive affect.

Narcissistic Issues

The analytic view of suicide, particularly in recent years, has not limited itself to the perspective of superego dynamics or the vicissitudes of depression. The gradual differentiation of the dynamics of suicide from the dynamics of depression has found its counterparts in analytic thinking as well. In his summary statement on analytic thinking regarding suicide, Fenichel (1945) discussed two major forms of suicide dynamics: the classic model of superego aggression turned against the ego (depressive suicide), and a second form based on hopeful illusions leading to some form of alternative gratification.

Thus the aim in the suicide attempt is not destruction of the ego as a murderous equivalent, but rather fulfillment of libidinal aims associated with the ideas of death. These hopeful fantasies may take the form of joining a lost, dead loved one, an identification with a loved, dead person, or even the longing for reunion with the mother. Such hopeful illusions may also play themselves out in the form of depressive suicide in terms of the attainment of forgiveness and reconciliation—this representing a form of reunion with the living protective superego, a reunion that puts an end to the inner evil and re-creates the original narcissistic omnipotence of symbiotic union. Fenichel pointed out that such a narcissistic union with the loving superego is achieved in fact in mania, so that the manic state serves as a defense against underlying suicidal impulses.

Subsequent literature has emphasized the libidinal and regressive aspects of suicide. The libidinal aspect and the inherent symbiotic wish have been particularly emphasized in borderline personalities (Blanck and Blanck 1974). The suicide attempt may represent a wish for fusion with the maternal breast, a wish to achieve the illusion of an objectless stage of narcissistic satisfaction. In this stage, objects are no longer needed for purposes of need satisfaction, and thus can neither be lost nor destroyed (Modell 1961). Such suicidal attempts may be associated with severe regressive states involving loss of ego boundaries and a wish for fusion with the mother (Socarides 1962). Suicidal fantasies have thus been linked to early infantile fantasies of falling asleep at the breast and seem to reflect the complex issues of union with and separation from the mother in the early undifferentiated state of object relationship (Lewin 1950).

The link between the oral triad and the regressive wish for symbiotic union with the mother have been related to the suicidal tendencies in fugue states (Luparello 1970). It may be that in some of these cases the threat of separation or abandonment gives rise to a murderous rage, so that the regressive symbiotic wish may avert this murderous impulse. This dynamic would seem to come closer to the original depressive model. A similar point was recently made by Pollock (1975), citing Zilboorg's (1938) earlier view that the sense of guilt which relates to the repressed wish for the death of the parents underlies and motivates the self-destructive wish for immortality—this represents a return to the earliest symbiotic state. In suicidal regression, intrapsychic structures and ego boundaries are de-differentiated and the suicidal victim immerses himself in a narcissistically blissful state of reunion—a form of personal utopia.

Similar motivation may express itself in the longing for death found in many older people for whom life offers more suffering and less pleasure. Loewenstein (1957) speculated that diminution of genital gratification brings about a regression to pregenital libidinal stages which carries with it the wish for reunion with the symbiotic mother. These powerful wishes for undifferentiated narcissistic symbiotic union with the archaic mother underlies the powerful wishes for union with the dead loved object and the achievement of immortality. As Pollock (1975) observes: "The merger of the grandiose self with the idealized object explains the regressive solution of re-establishing earliest narcissistic equilibrium and cohesion. Regressive merging with the god-figure results in an immortal, blissful, pregenital existence" (p. 343). In a similar case suicide served the function of reestablishing narcissistic equilibrium, thus contributing to the cohesiveness of the self; at a higher level of narcissistic development, however, it pointed toward reunion with the ego ideal. Hendrick (1940) presented the case of a young woman who attempted suicide as a form of regression to an erotic and idealized relationship with her brother, in which the suicide represented the fulfillment of her wish for identification with him rather than a consequence of such an identification. The brother had been an aviator-hero in the First World War who had achieved his moment of highest phallic achievement in a flaming death over the fields of France. As Hendrick comments: "This suicidal attempt, in contrast to depressive suicides, represents a different escape for aggression, libidinal frustration, and anxiety, rather than an act of self-punishment. It is not a consequence of identification, but an effort to fulfill the need to solve this terrible crisis in the patient's life by achieving an identification with the act of a hero."

In a later comment, Hendrick (1964) adds that the patient's destiny was ruled by an imperative need to be like her dead, hero brother, who formed her ego-ideal since childhood. In this case the ego-ideal was of a special type represented externally by the person of the brother. Thus this external ego-ideal which Hendrick refers to as a *prepuberty ego-ideal* was a necessary component for the maintenance of the cohesion of the patient's self. Thus, "ego failure and regression to primitive and unsocializable narcissism resulted from the traumatic impact of the death (or its equivalent) of the real person who represented the ego-ideal" (p. 525).

Suicidal Motivation

In the light of such cases it becomes abundantly clear that the suicidal intention is various and variously motivated. In some cases it may express the dynamics of self-punitive, self-destructive impulses—along the lines of the more classical Freudian analysis—while in other cases it may express the deepest and unconscious wishes and needs for narcissistic self-fulfillment and self-expression. It was Weisman (1971) who pointed out that intentionality is not equivalent to the wish to kill oneself or the suicidal intent. Motives for attempting suicide are as obscure, if not more obscure, than motives for any behavior. The expression of suicidal intent is often a reliable clue to a high degree of lethality. But they are by no means related. More commonly, suicide attempters try to deny their wishes or to mask them by presenting their ambivalence and equivocation. Intentionality, even in the suicide act, is concerned with the organization and direction of purposeful activity. Intentionality is thus a form of consciousness by which we distinguish purposeful human activity from merely reflexive or stereotype forms of behavior. Human intentionality is related to the capacity we possess to make sense out of our experience and the ambiguities of life. Consequently, lethal intentions must be seen as reflecting and expressing "transient belief-systems that impel people to anticipate greater pain and to terminate existence" (p. 229).

In the light of these theoretical considerations we can approach a clearer appreciation of the role of precipitants in the suicide act. Frequently enough, object-loss of one kind or another lies behind the suicidal behavior. The loss of the object sets in motion a mourning process, which is incomplete and is prevented from moving forward to achieve detachment from the lost object. The current loss seems to revive and symbolize repressed or denied reactions to previous childhood losses.[1] In addtion, these patients demonstrate a strong dependency on the lost object for the maintenance of narcissistic integrity and equilibrium (Dorpat 1973). Generally, suicide attempters show a higher rate of childhood separations (Levi et al. 1966) and a higher number of precipitating life events (Paykel et al. 1975). The incidence of such events in suicide attempters in the six months prior to the attempt was four times that in controls and one-and-a-half times that in depressed patients. Precipitating life events seemed to peak in the month preceding the suicide attempt.

The dynamics of object-loss and mourning as precipitating factors in suicidal behavior must be related to the problem of anniversary suicides, which take place in the period close to the anniversary of a parent's death. The incidence of such suicides far exceeds statistically expectable rates (Bunch and Barraclough 1971). Anniversary reactions must be taken as manifesting incomplete or partial mourning of the lost objects. Suicidal acts, then, can be motivated in varying degrees by the need to restore narcissistic equilibrium in the face of narcissistic loss and the need to compensate for resulting narcissistic rage and guilt (Pollock 1970).

Adolescent Suicide

Perhaps the area in which these dynamics express themselves with the greatest vividness is that of adolescent suicide. Winnicott (1971) has made some telling comments in this regard:

If the child is to become adult, then this move is achieved over the dead body of an adult. . . . In the total unconscious fantasy belonging to growth at puberty and in adolescence, there is *the death of someone*. A great deal can be managed in play and by displacement, and on the basis of cross-identifications; but, in the psychotherapy of the individual adolescent . . . there is to be found death and personal triumph as something inherent in the process of maturation and in the acquisition of adult status. This makes it difficult enough for parents and guardians. Be sure it makes it difficult also for the individual adolescents who come with shyness to the murder and the triumph that belong to maturation at this crucial stage. The unconscious theme may become manifest as the experience of suicidal impulse, or as actual suicide. Parents can help only a little; the best they can do is to *survive*, to survive intact, and without changing color, without relinquishment of any important principle. This is not to say they may not themselves grow. A proportion at adolescence will become casualties or will attain to a kind of maturity in terms of sex and marriage, perhaps becoming parents like the parents themselves. This may do. But somewhere in the background is a life-and-death struggle. The situation lacks its full richness if there is a too easy and successful avoidance of the clash of arms. (p. 145)

In this regard, Friedman et al. (1972) noted that the impulse to destroy or mutilate one's own body occurs rarely before adolescence. They suggested that the changes of adolescence make it possible for these aggressive impulses to be directed against the adolescent's self in such extreme ways. One of the crucial tasks of adolescence is the detachment of the libidinal cathexis to the original object. Suicidal adolescents, however, are unable to make this detachment, have great difficulty in giving up the libidinal tie particularly to their mothers, and react as though the breaking of this tie were an intolerable loss that could not be faced.

Instead of the normal developmental mourning processes associated with adolescent movement away from parental ties, these subjects seem to develop a state more akin to melancholia (Toolan 1975). The ties to the mother are markedly ambivalent, involving intense hostile, even murderous feelings existing side by side with intense feelings of loving dependency. Thus separation from parents, particularly the mother, seems to represent a threat to vital libidinal supplies and, we would also suggest, a threat to narcissistic integrity. The reluctance to surrender and mourn the object results in introjection, "narcissistic identification," as described by Freud (1917b). Thus the suicide attack may be seen as a hostile and destructive attack launched against the internal object, usually the internalized mother introject. The authors discuss the case of an eighteen-year-old girl who overdosed because she could not stand anything in herself which resembled her mother.

Adolescent girls may feel a need not to give in to their mothers. Such rebelliousness may serve as a defense against regressive, often masochistic or homosexual wishes related to the mother who is somehow seen as powerful, overwhelming, and castrating. Defensive aggression, however, in my own experience, is often related to an attempt to counter and mask the underlying feelings of dependency, longing for closeness, and nurturance from the mother. Thus even where such rebellious and aggressive attitudes are manifest, there are often identifiable elements of a strong maternal introject. This defensive aggression and the underlying aggressive wishes tend to intensify the difficulties and conflicts over aggression which is a typical adolescent problem. For the young woman the emergence of secondary sex characteristics tends to increase the implicit identification with the mother.

The internalization of aggression in such patients has often been noted; many suffer from depression, guilt, low self-esteem, and even psychosomatic difficulties. However, although the tendency to introject and thus identify with the more vulnerable and weak, susceptible aspects of the parents may be less discernible, it is of no less significance in the dynamics of the suicide. This is particularly important in terms of the identification of suicidal adolescent girls with victimized, vulnerable, and castrated maternal imagos. Thus, while the suicide attempt may from one perspective represent an attempt to destroy one's own body as the instrument of murderous aggression, it may also represent an attempt to achieve in some maximal sense that inner vulnerability by which the adolescent feels most attuned to and identified with the parental object.

It should be remembered, however, that in the suicide act, the subject is both the destructive aggressor and the passive victim. Friedman et al. (1972) suggested that such suicide attempts or self-mutilatory acts reflect the dynamics of primal scene fantasy. As we have suggested elsewhere (1977a, 1977b), although primal scene fantasies influence to some extent, they also reflect the sadomasochistic organization of introjects. Thus, primal scene fantasies may be influenced strongly by other aspects of the sadomasochistic relationship between the parents or other aspects of the family situation.

While the dynamics of adult suicide reflect residues of family dynamics in an internalized form, it must be appreciated that suicidal dynamics in adolescents themselves are much more immediately responsive to the ongoing patterns of influence from the adolescent's family. Adolescent suicide attempts may often come as the culmination of progressive disorganization, disruption, and social maladaptation within the family (Barter et al. 1968). As Sabbath (1969) pointed out, the adolescent suicide is often enough an "expendable child," that is, the object of a parental wish to be rid of the child or for the child to die. In such cases, the child's growth conflicts stir unresolved adolescent conflicts in the parents themselves. Often such children were unplanned and unwanted, and the history of ambivalence in the parent-child relationship reaches a crisis during the developmental stresses of adolescence. The parents come to regard the child's emerging sexuality and aggression as threatening to themselves, to their own marital stability, sanity, and even existence. Correspondingly, the parents are seen increasingly as oppressive and persecuting. The suicide becomes a matter of compliance with an implicit parental. wish. Hendin (1975b) described similar circumstances in which the suicidal wish seems to express a compliance with parental wishes. For these adolescents death becomes a way of life. Their family milieux have been permeated with depression and their lifelessness has been required to sustain the family emotional matrix. Hendin (1975a) observes, "Suicide is a way of life for the many students I saw who continually killed their enthusiasm, their hope, their freedom, and finally attempted to kill themselves. It is the climax of the ongoing drama they play out with parents in which emotional death is seen as the price of domestic peace" (pp. 253-254). Obviously similar dynamics as those previously described are operative here as well, and reflect a pattern of what I elsewhere described as "adolescent paranoia" (1977a). An additional note must be added that the adolescent suicide often reflects and expresses dynamics within the family such that the suicidal act restores an intolerable tension in the family emotional system.

THE DYNAMICS OF SUICIDE

I would like to link some of these elements of the dynamics of suicide to a more general frame of reference described elsewhere in terms of the *paranoid process* (1977a). The paranoid process is envisioned as a fundamental process in the organization of developmental experience and defensive-adaptive functioning—one which underlies the experiential continuum reflected at one extreme in the mature and integrated functioning of a stable human identity and at the other extreme in the most severe and pathological forms of human dysfunction. The paranoid process is essentially based on the mechanisms of introjection and its correlative projections and on the elaboration of a cognitive frame of reference, the paranoid construction, which serves to sustain and integrate the rest.

Victim Introject

The organization of the pathogenic introjects is central to understanding the dynamics of suicide and, in fact, serves as the focal point of derivation for the other aspects of the paranoid process. Introjection refers to the aspect of the paranoid process through which the subject's inner world and the organization of a sense of self is achieved. That organization takes place specifically through the internalization of objects in such a way as to provide the nucleus of the sense of self. These internal objects carry with them into the subject's inner experience of himself all of the defenses and developmental vicissitudes embedded in the original external object relationships. An understanding of the basic introjective mechanism of the paranoid process is crucial, since, as we shall see, it underlies some of the basic dynamics of the suicidal impulse.

One of the central and most critical aspects of the pathogenic organization of introjects concerns the victim-introject. We are already familiar through the work of Anna Freud (1936) with a related but quite different aspect of introjective economy in terms of her description of *identification with the aggressor*. Identification with the aggressor is in fact an introjective function which serves very specific developmental and defensive purposes. The victim-introject, however, is a necessary precursor and correlative component of the introjective dynamics of the aggressor-introject.

If we return for a moment to the Freudian superego model of suicide dynamics, it is the turning of aggression against the ambivalently held and internalized object that provides the basic mechanism. This makes sense in terms of the internalization of the victim aspects of the object—the victim introject. The victim is the recipient of destructive aggression. The aggression, however, is the subject's own. When this model is transferred to the superego, the aggression in question is somehow that of the object—through identification with the aggressor. This early model thus contains certain inconsistencies and failed to provide an adequate explanation for other aspects of the internalization.

More current views have come to appreciate the considerable significance of narcissism in the dynamics of internalizations. Freud had hinted earlier at this significance by pointing out that the object relationship in cases of melancholia was of a narcissistic type. He labeled the internalization associated with melancholia *narcissistic identification*. Our current view would infer that the rage against the lost object concerns a narcissistic injury or trauma due to the loss. In many such cases, the object was important to the maintenance of narcissistic equilibrium and to the integrity of the affected individual. The object may have served as an idealized object—Hendrick's (1964) prepuberty ego-ideal or the other forms of self-object described by Kohut (1971)—or, at a more primitive level, may have been required to sustain the subject's inner integrity or cohesiveness. Thus the suicide may also reflect the need to reconstitute narcissistic integrity by reunion with the lost, but necessary, object.

In the present formulation, the suggestion is made that it is the victim-introject through which these dynamics are expressed. Internalization of and adherence to the victim-introject are motivated by the narcissistic need to cling to and even fuse with the object. The victim-introject is equivalently the internalization of a self-object. The ultimate realization of that identification comes through the suicide act, by which the individual becomes the ultimate victim, thereby gaining fusion with the required victim-object. The organization of the victim-introject, then, serves as the vehicle of the defensive absorption of superego aggression, of sadomasochistic introjections (particularly those underlying the dynamics of a masochistic-depressive posture), and of union or fusion with the victim-object. Thus it is the focus for feelings of helplessness and hopelessness. While the dynamics of the victim-introject are primarily expressible in terms of the vicissitudes of aggression, it must not be overlooked that these interactions ride on a substratum of narcissistic concerns and investments. Consequently, introjection of the victim-introject is simultaneously a matter of continuing relatedness to the needed object and maintenance of the integrity of the self. The same necessity underlies the compliance with the implicit demands of the family system. Thus, the suicide's victimization may be required for the securing of the psychic integration of the parents and the equilibrium of the family system.

Aggressor Introject

In a developmental perspective, the purpose of identification with the aggressor is to ward off aggressive impulses by externalizing them and identifying with the aggressive external source. The mechanism consequently implies the defensive ability to separate self- and object-images by projection of these aggressive drives onto external objects, while at the same time a portion of these same drives is temporarily taken into the self. Consequently, the externalization partially spares the immature and vulnerable ego from the destructive effects of unneutralized aggression. As Orgel (1974) commented in this connection:

True morality begins when the internalized criticism, now embodied in the standards exacted by the superego (whose contents include aggression of varying degrees of neutralization compatible with the ego's ability to mediate discharge or countercathexis), coincides with the ego's perception of its own default. True morality also implies a stable retention of self-object differentiation, and maintains the object relationship even in the face of threatened aggression by the object of the self. A structured superego is, thus, a barrier against suicide, maintaining a balance between identification and projective elements compatible with normal empathy, preventing both object loss and regressive self-object fusion. (p. 531)

Orgel went on to describe what he called fusion with the victim as a regressive vicissitude of identification with the aggressor. Fusion with the victim is equivalent in this concept to what I have called the victim-introject. Where this aspect of the introjective economy is prominent, one can see the failure of the subject's capacity to maintain stable aggressive feelings toward objects. This may range all the way from simple self-assertiveness to sadomasochistic relationships to outright hatred of aggressive others. Thus the victim-introject is the exact opposite of identification with the aggressor, although the defenses against it may take either the form of shifting to the position of the aggressor-introject itself or the form of explicitly paranoid reactions.

In the course of development, when a fixation takes place at the level of the victim-introject, it serves to impede the capacity to proceed into and beyond the stage of identification with the aggressor, and thus creates conditions under which the organization and functioning of the superego are impeded. The basic postulate underlying this view of introjective development holds that when the infant's primary love object, particularly the mother, fails to provide a reliable aggressive resonance—particularly from about six to fifteen months—Mahler's (1965) practicing phase—conditions are set up by which it becomes relatively impossible for the immature ego of the infant to neutralize these aggressive drives and to discharge them in a sufficiently fused form against the mothering object in such a way as to provide a safe area of projection away from the child's own threatened and fragile ego.

The manner in which the child works through the interlocking processes of introjection and projection is, in some degree at any rate, a function of the interaction between himself and the mothering figure. In discussing the relationship of aggression to the growth of the child's internal world, Winnicott (1958) made the following comments:

> The psychology of the infant from now on becomes more complicated. The individual child becomes concerned not only with the effect on his mother of his impulses, but he also notes the results of his experiences in his own self. Instinctual satisfactions make him feel good, and he perceives intake and output in a psychological as well as in a physical sense. He becomes filled with what he feels to be good, and this initiates and maintains his confidence in himself and in what he feels he may expect from life. At the same time he has to reckon with his angry attacks, as a result of which he feels he becomes filled with what is bad or malign or persecuting. These evil things or forces, being inside him as he feels, form a threat from within to his own person, and to the good which forms the basis of his trust in life. (p. 207)

The child deals with these inner forces of evil or destruction by projecting them onto the significant figures in his environment. The capacity to project these aggressive and destructive impulses becomes a matter of vital concern to the emerging development of the child's inner world. These impulses, left awash in the child's inner world, threaten to fragment and destroy his emerging sense of self. As long as they persist, he is in the position of ultimate self-victimization and dissolution. Projection provides the mechanism of escape. Orgel (1974) comments: "Restitutional attempts are made, to a greater or lesser extent, to create counteraggression in the sought-for objects. Such a relationship, even if it is with someone who can safely be hated or an aggressor with whom one can safely identify, or to whom one can masochistically submit, provides an external object upon whom one may rid oneself of quantities of aggression that threaten ego fragmentation and self-destruction" (p. 532).

The question, then, is whether the significant objects, the objects of the child's dependence and love, can allow themselves to be the adequate object for the discharge of the child's destructive impulses. This is a difficult matter, but nonetheless crucial. This can only be accomplished to the degree that the mothering figure particularly is capable of tolerating and absorbing the child's aggressive impulses without being destroyed by them and without allowing the loving relationship with the child to suffer dissolution or distortion. The critical element here is the extent to which the mother can tolerate her own aggressive destructiveness, her own feelings of hate generated in response to the child's aggressive initiatives. According to Winnicott, "A mother has to be able to tolerate hating her baby without doing anything about it. She cannot express it to him. If, for fear of what she may do, she cannot hate appropriately when hurt by her child she must fall back on masochism, and I think it is this that gives rise to the false theory of a natural masochism in women. The most remarkable thing about a mother is her ability to be hurt so much by her baby and to hate so much without paying the child out, and her ability to wait for rewards that may or may not come at a later date" (p. 202).

Consequently, it is to some extent the mother's capacity to be a good hater of her child that provides the context within which the child can emerge from a state of passive victimhood to a position of being able to discharge noxious and threatening aggressive impulses. This discharge provides the matrix within which he can make the important developmental step toward identification with the aggressor. As we have already noted, this developmental progression is critical in the formation and integration of a more stable superego and the institution of more consistent structural barriers to regressive pulls.

False Self System

I will return to this issue in more pragmatic terms in a few moments, but I would like to shift the ground at this point to another aspect of Winnicott's view of the development of the child. Winnicott addressed himself to the formation of what he calls a *false self* (1960). Where the dynamics we have been describing fail, the consequence is the emergence of a false self, usually based on the child's compliance as a defense against undischarged and unneutralized aggression. This forces a split in the child's emerging sense of self, between the true self and the false self, and forces the child's development in the direction of an evolving and progressively adaptive elaboration of the false self. The price is the frustration and strangling of any true worth of the inner and real sense of self.

The child's compliance is of course sought for and reinforced by many forces around him. It brings immediate rewards from the adults on whom the child is so dependent for love and sustenance; these adults very easily mistake the child's compliance with their wishes for real growth. True inner development, then, can be bypassed by a series of introjections so that what becomes manifest is a false-acting self, a copy of the significant objects with whom the child relates and complies. This compliance, however, serves inherent narcissistic needs in the child. The introjections form the core around which the false-self configuration is organized. Compliance with parental wishes becomes an integral part of the shaping of the self—even when those wishes are implicitly destructive.

The true or essential self, however, is hidden and deprived of the roots of meaningful living experience. Those who are caught in this destructive web may seem to function well and adaptively and to lead normal and healthy lives, yet at some point they may attempt to actually end those lives which have become so false and unreal. It is worth considering the extent to which our child-rearing practices, our social and cultural mores, our socially reinforced expectations, and even our systems of morality and religious belief, contribute to this inner undermining and splitting of the child's emerging personality and to the erection and enforcement of the false self.

From another point of view, the false self can be seen in part as a struggle to cope with the dangers and difficulties of the outer world. It thus serves often quite specific and important defensive needs. At times, it can represent an often heroic struggle to stay alive. The price that it pays is the sacrifice of creativity, vitality, and originality to the more pressing needs for safety and insuring external supports. To pick up the thread of our earlier observations, if the important caretaking objects cannot tolerate and respond meaningfully and lovingly to the child's emergent aggression, the child is forced into a position of compliance and internal division which leads to the formation of the false self.

It is the persistence of this false self that can have a powerful impact in setting the stage for suicidal acting out. This implication was clearly stated by Winnicott (1971):

> As I have already indicated, one has to allow for the possibility that there cannot be a complete destruction of a human individual's capacity for creative living and that, even in the most extreme case of compliance and the establishment of a false personality, hidden away somewhere there exists a secret life that is satisfactory because of its being creative or original to that human being. Its unsatisfactoriness must be measured in terms of its being hidden, its lack of enrichment through living experience.
>
> Let us say that in the severe case all that is real and all that matters and all that is personal and original and creative is hidden, and gives no sign of its existence. The individual in such an extreme case would not really mind whether he or she were alive or dead. Suicide is of small importance when such a state of affairs is powerfully organized in an individual, and even the individual himself or herself has no awareness of what might have been or of what has been lost or is missing. (pp. 68-69)

I am reminded at this juncture of a case in my own recent experience of a young woman whose early experience was one of constant rejection and devaluation from a hostile and rejecting mother. The whole pattern of her life was carried out around the internalization of that malignant and devaluing maternal figure. My patient felt that nothing was good, nothing strong, nothing worthwhile in herself. Her constant complaint to me was that there was no hope, no future for her, and that it would have been better had she not been born. Moreover, the whole pattern of her external life had been carried out in such a way as to try to appease the mother's expectations and gain some measure of acceptance from her. She had turned to nursing as a career as a result of her mother's suggestion that she do so, since mother felt that she did not have the brains or ability for much of anything else. The false self-pattern was of course considerably more extensive than simply a matter of career choice. My patient reviled the whole pattern; she was disgusted and caught up in hopeless despair over almost every aspect of it. Her only alternative as she saw it was suicide. It seemed clear to me at this juncture that a suicide action on her part would have had two clear implications: the first was that it would have destroyed the false self built upon her lifelong compliance to her mother's wishes and her seeking for her mother's acceptance, and second it would have realized in the fullest measure the sense of victimhood that she sensed within herself and within her life experience.

My patient represents many of the aspects of what Guntrip, building on the basic notion of the false self, has called *schizoid suicide*. The schizoid suicide differs somewhat from the depressive suicide in which the impulse to self-destruction is angry and hostile. Rather it is the result of an apathy toward real life which can be accepted no longer. There is a quiet but tenacious determination to fade from the scene and give up the struggle. The death of the false self carries with it the hope of a rebirth of what is more authentic and creative in the subject's own existence. Guntrip (1969) writes:

> Schizoid suicide is not really a wish for death as such, except in cases where the patient has utterly lost all hope of being understood and helped. Even then there is a deep unconscious secret wish that death should prove to be a pathway to rebirth. . . . Whereas in depressive suicide the driving force is anger, aggression, hate and a destructive impulse aimed at the self to divert it from the hated love-object, i.e. self-murder, schizoid suicide is at bottom a longing to escape from a situation that one just does not feel strong enough to cope with, so as in some sense to return to the womb and be reborn later with a second chance to live. (pp. 217-218)

In my patient, as in others of this sort, it was a rebirth with the hope of experiencing a meaningful accepting and loving relationship with the mother that lay at the root of these impulses. It was a relationship of loving closeness and acceptance that had been constantly desired, constantly frustrated, and never attained.

The idea that I am proposing here in a more theoretical vein is that the false self is in fact organized around the introjects that we have been describing (Meissner 1977a). In suicidal patients, it, in particular, is the forming of a false self clustering around a central introject of the victim that forms the basic root and underlying motivation of the suicidal tendency. The suicide impulse, then, becomes the expression of the inner unneutralized and unresolved aggressive impulses which have been solidified and embedded in the victim-introject, and which form an essential aspect of the core of the individual's sense of self.[2] It is the unresolved aggression which cannot be adequately discharged and absorbed by the significant love-objects, which must be projected onto those objects and subsequently reintrojected and internalized to become the permanent possession of the child's emerging sense of self. It is in this context, then, that the self-hate and self-loathing of such individuals takes on a particular meaning. It reflects not only their inner sense of guilt and shame because of the inner hatefulness and evil they sense in themselves; it also reflects the unresolved and unassimilated hatred in their significant love-objects (more often unconscious that conscious).

It is worth noting that the interplay between the dynamics of the victim-introject and victimization on the one hand, and the dynamics of hatred on the other, play themselves out not only in the developmental experience of the child but in the living experience of the adult as well. It is not merely that the suicidal patient is fixated at a point of victimization; there is also a commitment to victimization and an adherence and clinging to the victim-introject. The clinging to the victim-introject has strong narcissistic underpinnings, the discussion of which would carry us far afield, but it can be noted that this becomes a powerful force in the suicidal patient's unconscious motivation and represents a clinging to the original, intensely ambivalent object of infantile dependence. The point that I wish to focus on here, however, is that the patient's commitment to victimhood leads him to attempt to elicit and provoke the conditions of victimhood in many of his adult relationships. An understanding of these dynamics provides some insight into not only the child's developmental experience, but also into the patterning of the suicidal patient's life experience which draws him to the brink of suicidal behavior.

THERAPEUTIC IMPLICATIONS

If the suicidal patient carries out these dynamic processes at large in many contexts of his living experience, it is expected that the same dynamics can come into operation in an even more intense and provocative way in the therapeutic encounter. In a sense, the patient re-creates the dynamics and interplay of destructive and ambivalent impulses that were at work in the original relationship to the primary love-objects. It is essentially the undischarged and unneutralized aggressive destructive impulses which the patient projects onto the figure of the caring object and which are experienced, then, as hate.

This maneuver has the obvious unconscious advantage of reinforcing and consolidating the patient's position as victim. The patient reacts with a sense of inner evil, worthlessness, and primitive guilt. The defensive gain through this projective maneuver is of sufficient importance that the patient must attempt to validate it by various forms of provocative behavior. The patient then tries to arouse hatred and destructive feelings in the caring objects in a variety of behavioral and verbal attacks. The patient will discredit, devalue, criticize, and disparage his therapist. Any least sign of irritation or anger in the doctor's response will be taken as confirmation and validation of the projection. The provocations may take the form of direct physical action, involving physical assault or destruction of personal property. There may be telephone calls at particularly inconvenient and annoying times. They may take the form of mutinous rebellion and withdrawal within the therapeutic situation.

Generally there is the abiding accusation that the therapist is inadequate, is not being helpful, is doing little or nothing to alleviate the patient's pain—in general, the constant, direct, and implicit assertion of the therapist's incompetence. Thus the resistance to any therapeutic inroads or effective progress can be quite rigid and intense and may frequently take the form of a profoundly negative therapeutic response. If we remind ourselves that the suicidal patient carries out this behavior in many facets of his life experience, it is not difficult to understand how the constant reinforcement of these dynamics can lead progressively closer to a suicidal resolution.

The dynamics of this interaction were carefully delineated in a recent contribution by Maltsberger and Buie (1974). They described in some detail the patterns of defense which therapists mobilize in one or other degree to deal with the distressing experience of hatred elicited by the patient. Such countertransference hatred may be repressed, so that the therapist finds himself daydreaming or thinking of something else besides what is happening in the therapy. He may find himself restless or bored or drowsy. The countertransference hatred may instead be turned against the therapist's own self, and begin to fill him with doubts as to his capacity to help the patient; he may begin to experience feelings of guilt, degradation, and a sense of inadequacy, helplessness, and hopelessness. He may even begin to experience suicidal impulses and feelings himself. This masochistic and penitential stance on the part of the therapist further impedes any possibility of the patient's unleashing directly aggressive impulses on him and only intensifies the suicidal dynamics.

A third way of dealing with countertransference hatred is to turn it into its opposite. The therapist finds himself preoccupied with trying to be helpful to the patient, being excessively solicitous about his welfare and well-being. There is an anxious urgency to cure and help. The therapist may be drawn into an excessive fear of the patient's suicide and resort to the excessive use of restrictions and even hospitalization when it may not be particularly called for. Such a therapist cannot take the necessary reasonable risks in dealing with the patient's suicidal impulses and rage and, in general, cannot help the patient with these feelings.

Countertransference hatred can also take the form of counterprojection onto the patient's own projective operations: "I do not wish to kill you; you wish to kill yourself." A subjective sense of anxious dread might accompany this, and the therapist become preoccupied with fantasies about the patient's potential for acting out the suicidal impulses. Thus the therapist often may tend to feel helpless and have considerable difficulty deciding how much of his concern comes from the objective possibilities and how much from his own hostile feelings. There are a number of risks that operate in this position. The therapist may act out his countertransference hostility by imposing unnecessary external controls such as hospitalization; these will serve to disrupt the therapeutic alliance and possibly provoke suicidal acting out. The therapist may also run the risk of failing to recognize the objective need for protective measures out of fear of such acting out. Or the therapist may run the risk of giving up the case and rejecting the patient, feeling that the situation is hopeless when in fact it is not so. The projection may at times also take the form "I do not wish to kill you; you wish to kill me." This may be in part a recognition of the patient's own hatred, but it runs the risk of the therapist's responding to his sense of frustration with further rejection and abandonment of the patient.

Lastly, the therapist may resort to distortion and denial of the objective reality as a way of validating the countertransference hatred. Under these circumstances, the therapist tends to devalue the patient and is prepared to see the patient as a hopeless or bad or dangerous case. He may then interrupt the therapy prematurely or transfer the patient to other therapists or other institutions or discharge him prematurely from the protective environment of the hospital.

Maltsberger and Buie concluded their discussion of these patterns of defensive interaction in the dynamics of countertransference hate by making the following observations which resonate strongly with the previous comments of Winnicott regarding the hatred of the mother for her child:

> The best protection from antitherapeutic acting-out is the ability to keep such impulses in consciousness. Full protection, however, requires that the therapist also gain comfort with his countertransference hate through the process of acknowledging it, bearing it, and putting it into perspective. Guilt then has no place in his feelings, and the therapist is free to exert a conscious loving self-restraint, in which he places a higher value on the emotional growth of his patient than he does on his own tension discharge. At the proper time, the patient can be shown how his behavior leads to an attacking or rejecting response in others. In other words, the suicidal patient's repetition compulsion to involve others in relationships of malice and ultimately to be rejected is signaled in the therapist's countertransference hate. In time it can be interpreted and worked at, provided the therapist, by accepting, tolerating, and containing the countertransference, does not join the patient in repeating his past instead of remembering it. (p. 632)

These elements played themselves out in a vivid manner in a stylish woman of fifty in whom suicidal feelings persisted in an intense and agonizing manner over several years of treatment. She was the only child of well-to-do, socially prominent, but indifferent parents. The father particularly was subject to recurrent depressions and often felt suicidal. The parents were poorly matched, constantly fought, and were chronically on the brink of divorce. When the patient was five, an older orphaned cousin was taken in by the family. The patient felt pushed aside, as if her wishes did not count—while the cousin became increasingly demanding and difficult. The cousin became increasingly a source of difficulty and discord in the family, but my patient continually felt that it was her lot to act as peacemaker between her parents and the cousin. When finally the parents had both died, the patient turned over her inheritance (a substantial amount) to the cousin on the grounds that the cousin had nothing and no one, while the patient herself could make her own way—a repetition of the childhood pattern.

This masochistic pattern of repeated victimization played itself out in recurrent contexts throughout the patient's life. In each instance, she would make a critical decision putting herself at considerable disadvantage, usually in relation to an older male figure whom she devoted herself self-sacrificingly, and always with the feeling that she was doing the better thing and that she could take care of herself. She never married and repeatedly fended off opportunities that presented themselves. In this way, she repeatedly put herself in the position of victim, at each step building a reservoir of bitter resentment and murderous rage. In this process, she was capable of working at a high level of competence and resourcefulness. The immediate precipitant of her depression and suicidal wishes was the retirement of her boss, an older high level executive, who then moved out of town. The patient was offered another position, but abruptly quit the company and entered her downhill course.

The oedipal components of this picture were transparent. She was once again the helpful support of a faltering father figure—her own father had been withdrawn and unable to work in his depressive periods. The patient cherished the illusion that her boss cared for her and would one day ask her to marry him. His departure and abandonment dashed her illusions, propelled her into exquisite victimization, and stirred her unconscious rage. She stopped working, spent her savings, withdrew from friends, even moved to another city. She progressively created the circumstances of increasingly desperate victimization in every aspect of her life. She was alone, without family or friends, without work, and was inexorably eroding her financial resources. The hole she was digging was getting deeper and deeper. At this point, she entered treatment with me.

Gradually, in the face of considerable resistance, we were able to establish and clarify this pattern of victimization. We related it to the little girl in her who desperately sought love and caring from a good father-figure (and by degrees from me as well) but who felt hurt, enraged and abandoned when she did not receive it. The little girl then responded with a sort of intrapsychic temper-tantrum, turning her frustrated rage against herself and plunging herself deeper into the pit of victimization. Each stage was a renewed cry for help which she hoped would come from her illusory father-substitute. Each disappointment reinforced her hurt, rage, and guilt. Underlying this pattern was an intense stubborn degree of primitive narcissism: the little girl demanded that her expectations be satisfied, her frustrations and deprivations made up, without any effort or responsibility on her part. Her guilt floated on an underlying stratum of envy which dictated that any good possessed by others must be seen as her deprivation (as in her childhood interaction with the cousin) along with the contradictory conviction that she deserved nothing. These opposite polarities of envious entitlement and self-deprivation are readily recognizable as expressions of pathogenic narcissism in the introjective configuration.

The patient had integrated a false-self system around a victim-introject which expressed itself in compliant submission to important figures, but whose self-sacrificing, masochistic self-denigration served only to feed the intensity of self-destructive components embedded in her aggressor-introject. The victim-introject clearly was based on the depressive, nonfunctional victim she recognized in her father in conjunction with her somewhat masochistic, self-sacrificing mother. The victim-introject was reinforced by critical internalizations from both parents and was lived out in her pathology—particularly her identification with her depressed, suicidal father.

The therapy turned into a recurrent saga of playing out these elements in relation to me. The invitation was constantly at work for me to feel sorry for her, to sympathize, to try to be helpful and reassuring, to make exceptions in her treatment because she was so helpless and disadvantaged. In response to these pressures, I maintained a therapeutic middle road, being simultaneously sympathetic and responsive to her pain, but yielding hardly at all from a firm therapeutic stance that insisted on exploring the dynamic aspects of her feelings, constantly focused the aspects of victimization in her behavior, in her life, her therapy, her history; and insisted on the need for her to take hold, accept responsibility for her life and her behavior, and resist the regressive pulls that tempted her to give in to her suicidal impulses. My tack was constantly to insist that she was not a helpless victim of the past, of her parents, of her life circumstances, or of her impulses and feelings, but that for specific reasons she chose to adopt and cling to her victimhood. Her resentment and anger at my making her responsible for what she felt and did—for undermining her victimization—had to be vigorously confronted and the responsibility thrust back on her, without guilt on my part.

The countertransference risks with such resistant and suicidal patients are well known to experienced therapists. The patient seems intent on defeating the therapeutic process and intent at all points. In this patient, no combination of medication seemed to bring relief, any medication elicited bothersome side effects that required stopping or changing it, any interpretations or insights were accepted compliantly without apparent effect. In such a case, for the therapist there is continual frustration, self-doubt, guilt, and anger. His therapeutic skills are on the line, his narcissism under attack, his impatience and frustration ready to shift into irritation or hopelessness regarding the patient. The interaction is set up as a constant inducement to play the counterpart to the patient's victim. My patient constantly confronted my limitations as a therapist and the inherent limitations of the therapeutic process.

The central task for the therapist is to keep these countertransference elements in constant focus so that he does not inadvertently take up the patient's invitation to play into and reinforce the victim-introject. This calls for a consistent effort to sustain the crucial elements of the therapeutic alliance, a persistent effort to explore the dimensions of the victim introject, particularly as they display themselves in the therapeutic interaction, and a willingness to confront the patient's unwillingness to accept responsibility for his suicidal wishes. The schema for this approach has been detailed elsewhere (Meissner 1976). It is particularly important for the therapist in dealing with the suicidal victim-introject *not* to take responsibility for the patient's need to kill himself; at the same time, he must accept full responsibility for helping the patient to explore, understand, and manage these impulses—even to the point of hospitalizing such a patient as a means of protecting him from these impulses when they become overwhelming. Such an approach is never easy to follow, but success lies in constant self-monitoring of inevitable deviations and a collaborative focusing of the reasons for them with the patient. This can be the most effective opportunity for clarifying the operation of the victim-introject in the therapy with correlative therapeutic gains. Hopefully, as the victim-introject is gradually eroded, space is created for a more positive organization of the patient's self—one more authentically lived and felt and more congruent with the patient's own inner purposes rather than the fallacious dichotomies of his or her false-self organization.

It is in this fashion then, however difficult it may be to attain, that the therapist undermines the dynamics of the victim-introject and avoids the reinforcement of the false-self configuration. To the extent that the therapist can acknowledge, tolerate, and deal with his own countertransference hatred, he will not be victimized by the patient's inherently aggressive and destructive impulses. A way will be open for the patient to begin to deal with those earlier issues of identification with the aggressor which have been previously thwarted and which in regressive fashion have been impeded by the persistence and domination of the victim-introject.

NOTES

1. Evidence suggests that a broken home in the suicidal patient's childhood is a significant factor. Dorpat et al. (1965) found that 50 percent of completed and 64 percent of attempted suicides come from broken homes. The death of a parent was the most common cause of broken home for completed suicides, while divorcing was the most common cause for attempted suicides.

2. The victim-introject thus becomes the core around which is organized a *negative identity*. In discussing adolescent suicide, Erikson (1956) suggests that "the 'wish to die' is only in those rare cases a really suicidal wish, where 'to be a suicide' becomes an inescapable identity choice in itself" (p. 82).

REFERENCES

Appelbaum, S. A. (1963). The problem-solving aspect of suicide. *Journal of Projective Techniques and Personality Assessment* 27:259-268.

Barter, J. T., Swaback, D. O., and Todd, D. (1968). Adolescent suicide attempts: a follow-up study of hospitalized patients. *Archives of General Psychiatry* 19:523-527.

Beall, L. (1969). The dynamics of suicide: a review of the literature: 1897-1965. *Bulletin of Suicidology*, March, pp. 2-16.

Bibring, E. (1953). The mechanism of depression. In *Affect Disorders*, ed. P. Greenacre. New York: Wiley.

Blanck, G., and Blanck, R. (1974). *Ego Psychology: Theory and Practice*. New York: Columbia University Press.

Bunch, J., and Barraclough, B. (1971). The influence of parental death anniversaries upon suicide dates. *British Journal of Psychiatry* 118:621-626.

Dorpat, T. L. (1973). Suicide, loss, and mourning. *Life-Threatening Behavior* 3:213-224.

Dorpat, T. L., Jackson, J. K., and Ripley, H. S. (1965). Broken homes and attempted and completed suicide. *Archives of General Psychiatry* 12:213-216.

Douglas, J. (1968). *The Social Meanings of Suicide*. Princeton: Princeton University Press.

Durkheim, E. (1897). *Suicide: A Study in Sociology*. Glencoe, Illinois: Free Press, 1951.

Erikson, E. H. (1956). The problem of ego identity. *Journal of the American Psychoanalytic Association* 4:56-121.

Faberow, N. L., and Shneidman, E. S. (1961). *The Cry for Help*. New York: McGraw-Hill.

Fenichel, O. (1945). *The Psychoanalytic Theory of Neurosis*. New York: Norton.

Freud, A. (1936). *The Ego and the Mechanisms of Defense*. New York: International Universities Press.

Freud, S. (1901). The psychopathology of everyday life. *Standard Edition* 6.

——— (1909). Notes upon a case of obsessional neurosis. *Standard Edition* 10:153-318.

——— (1917a). Introductory lectures on psycho-analysis. *Standard Edition* 15/16.

——— (1917b). Mourning and melancholia. *Standard Edition* 14:237-260.

——— (1920a). Beyond the pleasure principle. *Standard Edition* 18:3-66.

——— (1920b). The psychogenesis of a case of homosexuality in a woman. *Standard Edition* 18:146-174.

——— (1923). The ego and the id. *Standard Edition* 19:3-68.

——— (1940). An outline of psycho-analysis. *Standard Edition* 23:141-208.

Friedman, A. S. (1970). Hostility factors and clinical improvement in depressed patients. *Archives of General Psychiatry* 23:524-537.

Friedman, M., Glasser, M., Laufer, E., Laufer, M., and Wohl, M. (1972). Attempted suicide and self-mutilation in adolescence: some observations from a psychoanalytic research project. *International Journal of Psycho-Analysis* 53:179-183.

Gershon, E. S., Gromer, M., and Klerman, G. L. (1968). Hostility and depression. *Psychiatry* 31:224-235.

Guntrip, H. (1969). *Schizoid Phenomena, Object Relations and the Self.* New York: International Universities Press.

Hendin, H. (1975a). *The Age of Sensation: A Psychoanalytic Exploration.* New York: Norton.

—— (1975b). Student suicide: death as a life style. *Journal of Nervous and Mental Diseases* 160:204-219.

Hendrick, I. (1940). Suicide as wish-fulfillment. *Psychiatric Quarterly* 14:30-42.

—— (1964). Narcissism and the prepuberty ego ideal. *Journal of the American Psychoanalytic Association* 12:522-528.

Kernberg, O. (1967). Borderline personality organization. *Journal of the American Psychoanalytic Association* 15:641-685.

Klein, M. (1934). A contribution to the psychogenesis of manic-depressive states. *Contributions to Psycho-Analysis: 1921-1945.* New York: McGraw-Hill, 1964.

Kohut, H. (1971). *The Analysis of the Self.* New York: International Universities Press.

Levi, D. L., Fales, C. H., Stein, M., and Sharp, V. H. (1966). Separation and attempted suicide. *Archives of General Psychiatry* 15:158-164.

Lewin, B. D. (1950). *The Psychoanalysis of Elation.* New York: Norton.

Loewenstein, R. M. (1957). A contribution to the psychoanalytic theory of masochism. *Journal of the American Psychoanalytic Association* 5:197-234.

Luparello, T. J. (1970). Features of fugue: a unified hypothesis of regression. *Journal of the American Psychoanalytic Association* 18:379-398.

Mahler, M. S. (1965). On the significance of the normal separation-individuation phase. In *Drives, Affects, Behavior,* vol. 2, ed. M. Schur. New York: International Universities Press.

Maltsberger, J. T., and Buie, D. H. (1974). Countertransference hate in the treatment of suicidal patients. *Archives of General Psychiatry* 30:625-633.

Meissner, S. J., W. W. (1976). Psychotherapeutic schema based on the paranoid process. *International Journal of Psychoanalytic Psychotherapy* 5:87-114.

—— (1977a). *The Paranoid Process.* New York: Jason Aronson.

—— (1977b). The Wolf-Man and the paranoid process.

Menninger, K. A. (1938). *Man Against Himself.* New York: Harcourt Brace.

Minkoff, K., Bergman, E., Beck, A. T., adn Beck, R. (1973). Hopelessness, depression, and attempted suicide. *American Journal of Psychiatry* 130:455-459.

Modell, A. H. (1961). Denial and the sense of separateness. *Journal of the American Psychoanalytic Association* 9:533-547.

Orgel, S. (1974). Fusion with the victim and suicide. *International Journal of Psycho-analysis* 55:531-538.

Paykel, E. S., Prusoff, B. A., and Myers, J. K. (1975). Suicide attempts and recent life events: a controlled comparison. *Archives of General Psychiatry* 32:327-333.

Pollock, G. H. (1970). Anniversary reactions, trauma and mourning. *Psychoanalytic Quarterly* 39:347-371.

—— (1975). On mourning, immortality, and utopia. *Journal of the American Psychoanalytic Association* 23:334-362.

Sabbath, J. C. (1969). The suicidal adolescent—the expendable child. *Journal of the American Academy of Child Psychiatry* 8:272-285.

Shneidman, E. S. (1969). Suicide, lethality, and the psychological autopsy. In *Aspects of Depression,* ed., E. S. Shneidman and M. Ortega. Boston: Little, Brown.

—— (1973). *Deaths of Man.* New York: Quadrangle.

Shneidman, E. S., and Faberow, N. L. (1957). Clues to suicide. In *Clues to Suicide.* New York: McGraw-Hill.

Sifneos, P. E. (1966). Manipulative suicide. *Psychiatric Quarterly* 40:525-537.

Socarides, C. W. (1962). Theoretical and clinical aspects of overt female homosexuality. Panel Report. *Journal of the American Psychoanalytic Association* 10:579-592.

Stengel, E. (1964). *Suicide and Attempted Suicide*. Baltimore: Penguin.

—— (1968). Attempted suicides. In *Suicidal Behaviors: Diagnosis and Management*, ed. H. Resnick. Boston: Little, Brown.

Stotland, E. (1969). *The Psychology of Hope*. San Francisco: Jossey-Bass.

Toolan, J. M. (1975). Suicide in children and adolescents. *American Journal of Psychotherapy* 29:339-344.

Weisman, A. D. (1971). Is suicide a disease? *Life-Threatening Behavior* 1:219-231.

Weissman, M., Fox, K., and Klerman, G. L. (1973). Hostility and depression associated with suicide attempts. *American Journal of Psychiatry* 130:450-455.

Winnicott, D. W. (1958). *Collected Papers: Through Paediatrics to Psycho-Analysis*. New York: Basic Books.

—— (1960). Ego distortion in terms of true and false self. In *The Maturational Processes and the Facilitating Environment*, pp. 140-152. New York: International Universities Press.

—— (1971). *Playing and Reality*. New York: Basic Books.

Zilboorg, G. (1936). Suicide among civilized and primitive races. *American Journal of Psychiatry* 92:1347-1369.

—— (1937). Considerations on suicide with particular reference to that of the young. *American Journal of Orthopsychiatry* 7:15-31.

—— (1938). The sense of immortality. *Psychoanalytic Quarterly* 7:171-199.

Obsessional Phenomena and the Concept of Intentionality

JOSEPH E. SCHWARTZ, M.D.

Obsessional phenomena exist in a variety of character types. The particular phenomena may be of limited value in total personality assessment. Some speculative links are made between obsessional phenomena and preanal developmental steps. It is suggested that the concept of intentionality of thought and action be examined in these patients to distinguish obsessionals with core conflicts that are primarily neurotic and triadic, from those with more significant, earlier difficulty in the oral period. The concept of intentionality is related to self-object distinction, the use of projections, the sense of self, pathologic ego-superego condensation, and the existence of the ability to tolerate and recognize aggressiveness within. More accurate and rapid diagnostic distinction among obsessionals has implications for different treatment approaches.

My involvement with the training of psychiatric residents over the past few years has convinced me of a certain ambiguity of available formulations concerning obsessional and compulsive symptoms. The experience of hearing cases of obsessionals presented in conference, followed by the opportunity to personally evaluate the patients, only to discover a psychotic or a borderline personality or an hysteric, is a striking one. The great frequency with which obsessional phenomena appear imply much more than a simple diagnosis, even if one appreciates that a psychodynamic diagnosis is merely a rough approximation of human experience. In this paper, I shall briefly outline some contributions to present formulations, and then reexamine obsessional phenomena from a different vantage point. I will attempt to demonstrate the usefulness of the concept of intentionality to the understanding of obsessional phenomena.

It is an understatement to say that the obsessive-compulsive has occupied the minds of psychiatrists for many years. Obsessional neurosis, one of Freud's early interests, was classified by him as one of the defense neuroses, along with hysteria and phobias (Freud 1894). He distinguished between obsessional and hysterical neurosis in that obsessionals develop "false connections" between ideas and affects (p. 52). He saw such false connections as secondary to problems in sexual life. He further tried to distinguish between obsessionalism and hysteria in his hypothesis that the hysteric had passively been involved in sexual scenes in childhood; very similar but active involvement in such scenes could lead to obsessional neurosis. Freud also discovered that passive experiences preceded such active ones (1896). Obsessional thoughts were considered "transformed self reproaches" with layers of defense elaborated over the basic sexual etiology (p. 169). He, himself, later repudiated the seduction hypothesis (1905a). While exploring the libidinal life of neurotics, he acknowledged that as concered obsessional neurosis, we needed to know more about "phases of the development of the ego" (p. 324). He postulated that in obsessionals the ego had developed in a way to outstrip libidinal life and that premature libidinal closure had occurred (1913). This idea has also received recent attention (Sandler and Joffe 1965). In the further development of libido theory, component instincts of sexuality were outlined, among which were the anal impulses (Freud 1905a). Neurotic symptoms were seen as inverses or substitutions for infantile sexual impulses. Implicit in this idea was the connection between instincutal life, and seemingly nonsexual, conscious mental life. The leap from seuxality to character was bridged (Freud 1908). Freud described the character traits of orderliness, parsimony, and obstinacy as evolving from anal impulses and reactions to them. Abraham (1921) also described such character traits. In the Rat-Man (Freud 1909), the case of an obsessional was described at length and it is from this we obtain a synthesis of many of Freud's views on this topic. The formulation is essentially that under the stress of oedipal level anxiety, there is a libidinal regression to an earlier pregenital mode, the anal. Anal impulses involve sadism and ambivalence. Secondary defenses against anal sadistic impulses are elaborated—that is, isolation, displacement, and undoing. The original regression itself is defensive against anxiety on an oedipal level.

The full value of an extensive case report is that it enables the reader to decide certain things himself. Freud, as a keen observer, tells us of the Rat-Man's great sexual inhibitions (he masturbated and had his first sexual intercourse only after his father's death). We are also told of the patient's incapacity to work for a number of years. Freud's formulation, while accurate, was in his own words incomplete. He struggled with the meaning of his observations on many fronts, distinguishing hallucinations from ideas, obsessional thinking from delirium, delusions from obsessional thinking. He noted the withdrawal of the patient into himself and his own omnipotent wishes, and away from the world. He concluded the case report with comments about the patient's apparent multiple personalities and with the statement that the "psychological field," not the instinctual, separate the obsessional from the hysterical (p. 248).

With the recognition that libido theory alone is incomplete as an explanation of obsessional psychopathology, and with the development of ego psychology, attention was shifted to other psychic structures. Wilhelm Reich (1949) magnificently described the compulsive character as having a pedantic concern for orderliness, a tendency to collect things, .. indecision, doubt, distrust, ... and the strength for complete or partial affect block (pp. 193-195). Fenichel (1945), in agreement with Freud on the libidinal aspects of obsessions (that is, on the roles of sadomasochism and ambivalence), also discussed aspects of the ego and superego. He described the role of the superego as differing in hysteria. That is, in obsessional neurosis, the obsession, felt as a command from within, is akin to the superego. Furthermore, he stated that in obsessional neurosis the ego is dependent upon the superego or ambivalent in regard to it. In obsessionalism the instincts can feel like a superego command. In discussing the loss of feces, which can represent castration as well as loss of the breast, Fenichel implied the important contribution of the ego's incapacity to sustain a loss toward vulnerability to obsessional neurosis. He stated that in the regression associated with obsessional neurosis, narcissistic elements may come to the fore or severe compulsive neurosis "may terminate in states in which the conscious ego, having become a football for the contradictory impulses of id and superego, is eliminated completely as an effective agent" (p. 292). Fenichel wrote of the "transitional states between compulsion neuroses, manic-depressive psychoses, or schizophrenia" (p. 278). He discussed the "ego cleavage" made possible by the mechanism of isolation—one part logical, another part magical and omnipotent (p. 300). He felt that the obsessive-compulsive neurosis is closer to psychosis than hysteria, because there is a turning away from reality, from real objects, toward images of infantile objects. He also wrote that full escalation of the neurosis can lead to the feared final states of paralysis of conscious will. I will return to these issues again. As concerns psychoanalytic treatment, Fenichel advocated it be tried, albeit with some reservations. He commented on problems in the analysis of the compulsive, in that the analyst is seen as the patient's superego and as a seducer to be fought.

Shapiro (1965) offered a vivid description of the style of the obsessional character. Focusing upon the "selective inattention" (p. 30) seen in such patients (that is, the seemingly willful inability to attend to a full and rich cognitive field), he stated that there is decreased volitional mobility of attention. Furthermore, there is a general distortion of volition and will. He, too, discussed an ego split (according to Fenichel this almost obviates the need for repression) in that any willfulness exerted is against one's own impulses.

The ungenuine posture of playing to a fantasied audience described by Fenichel was described by Shapiro as role playing. Shapiro, too, addressed problems in the experiencing of free will when he stated that the obsessional does not feel like a free man and is never without an overseer.

Schur (1953) applied the dynamic hypothesis explicit in the concept of regression, and pointed out that the recognition of a threat to the phallus, and the attendant anxiety, represent an ego regression in both the perception of danger and the reaction to it. Important in ego regression is under what circumstances, how readily, and in what ways it occurs. Implicit here is the idea of the unevenness of the development of various ego capacities. We must further distinguish the regression in ego functions inherent in neurosis from regression in ego structure as seen in psychosis. A psychic structure is an ever-present integrated and integrating mental agency with an organized series of functions to perform. In the obsessional neurotic the reality testing function appears intact, but how then do we understand that the ego can be "eliminated completely as an effective agent"? (Fenichel 1945, p. 292). In the obsessional symptom, where ego strivings and instincts are felt as superego commands and where the ego is ambivalent or dependent upon the superego, the usefulness of the structural theory is, I believe, cast into doubt unless we return to the concept of some kind of ego split, that is one between a logical, cognitive, remembering structure, and a feeling, experiential one.

In clinical life, a total picture of the person is needed before an assessment of psychopathology can be made. Nowhere is this more true than with obsessional neurosis, with its links to both psychosis and to neurotic oedipal conflicts. It would appear that the human organism has a limited capacity to express and deal with psychic pain and conflict; thus, obsessional phenomena are typically present in people with heterogeneous diagnoses. Common clinical experience demonstrates this ubiquity. The obsessional symptoms, however, may serve a variety of functions, difficult to elucidate. The very nature of the controlled, affect-inhibited demeanor can make clarification troublesome. This lack of affective landmarks may cause the clinician to fall back upon the classical neurotic formulation and to presume the presence of firm ego boundaries, reasonably successful negotiation of the separation-individuation phase, and the presence of struggles around anal, sadomaso-chistic impulses regressively revived as a defense against castration anxiety attached to oedipal conflicts. Perhaps in resonance with the patient's obsessional mantle, we prematurely exclude other possibilities. Similarities in obsessional phenomenology arising from different sources may mask its use in a person's dealing with a variety of somewhat different developmental, genetic, dynamic, and adaptive problems. Some of these need to be recognized early in a clinical encounter for a rational decision to be made concerning psychotherapeutic approach. For some patients obsessional symptomatology is regressive from oedipal anxiety, but for some it may represent the highest developmental level achieved.

EGO SPLITTING IN THE OBSESSIONAL

Another common clinical observation in obsessional neurosis, confirming the presence of an ego split, is that obsessionals have ready access to memories, notably in the absence of affects. What is generally said is that obsessionals tend not to repress memories, but to repress and isolate affects from ideational content. In such a discussion, stress is often placed on defensive maneuvering, which is taken as indicative of a kind of ego strength, albeit rigid and at times brittle. We could say, however, from a memory or ideational standpoint, that there has been a failure of repression, and from an affective standpoint, that there is an incapacity to tolerate affects. Stated in such a manner, the neurotic obsessional sounds more primitive than one would anticipate in neurosis. I do not mean to imply that obsessionals do not repress, but that perhaps repression is only partially achieved and some form of earlier defensive functioning, especially splitting, is utilized.

Example. A young man reports the recurrent thought to "pick up" many women and engage in "rampant sexual activities" with them. These thoughts have little affective charge. The topic of the therapy session is seemingly changed, and the therapist wonders why the thoughts were mentioned in the first place. The patient associates to the therapy fees, which he feels makes the therapist wealthy and the patient poor. This has been a recurrent refrain in the treatment. Later he states he could never leave his wife (something about which he has been thinking for some time) as long as he lacks sufficient money. He feels the therapist wants him to remain with his wife, despite his own view that she treats him badly and demeans him. Only as long as he stays with his wife, and does not have to financially sustain two households, can he afford to pay for psychotherapy. The following session the patient returns and resumes his associations.

One way to understand this example is that the individual can allow himself to have overtly sexual obsessive thoughts (and the attendant gratification) as long as feelings are attributed to someone else (the wife and the therapist wish to dominate and demean him), and as long as the connecting links between thoughts and feelings are obscured. One could add that the thoughts are defensive against, and a displaced expression of, the sadomasochistic interaction with his wife. There is covert gratification in playing out this same interaction with the therapist. Another way to view this example is that the person cannot repress his thoughts and as a result of such failure, fears loss of

454 JOSEPH E. SCHWARTZ

control and requires an outside person for control. He remembers his thoughts clearly, but his feelings are isolated, displaced, and projected.

Looking at the relationship with the therapist in this example, we can understand the observation often made that obsessionals have difficulty in tolerating closeness. The fear of loss of control of anal-sadistic impulses prevents intimacy on the one hand, while its projection onto another person contributes to it on the other. A type of splitting in the above example is evident in that the person may feel that the other wishes to hurt him, but thoughtfully knows this is not so. Affectively, outside objects can be seen as malevolent and persecutory while the obsessional wallows in self-moralism. This is a different kind of splitting than that described in borderline personalities (Kernberg 1967) where the object is split into good and bad, while the ego's experience of the object is similarly split into good and bad.

Returning to the vignette, we must ask why the patient returns if the therapist is seen as keeping him helplessly stuck in a painful marriage. When the patient is asked if he really believes the therapist wishes to get rich at the patient's emotional and financial expense, he becomes annoyed with the question. He reacts as though this is a totally unreasonable thing to say. He irritably replies, "Of course, not. I'm not crazy." It is as though the linking of a thoughtful reality with feelings about the therapist is simply not to be done. He reacts similarly when asked if he intends to act upon his sexual impulses. The thoughts of the patient are not particularly reasonable, nor are they psychotic. Perhaps they are best regarded as illusions, with varying degrees of belief in the illusion, but with a great deal of conviction on the patient's part of his right to retain the illusion. I believe that the illusion represents the ambivalent introjection of an earlier object with both omnipotent and comforting properties. These properties, attributed to the therapist, also contribute to the patient's return.

There is a striking similarity between obsessional thoughts and transitional objects. We owe to Winnicott (1953) the concept of the transitional object (the first me-not-me possession) and its relationship to illusion. The obsessional thought, like a transitional object and like an illusion, is treated as though it were not to be questioned or challenged. The transitional object's significance is not to be challenged as the child struggles with issues of omnipotent control over it at the same time attributing to it magical, soothing properties. The obsessional character plays out maybe-this-maybe-that scenarios in his mind, over which he attempts omnipotent control. Developmentally the first me-not-me possession has great significance for self-object distinctions, ego boundaries, separation, and reality testing. Phenomenologically, the distinction between the obsessional magical thought and the borderline overvalued idea is often unclear. Briefly, my point is that the obsessional has difficulty with intimacy not only because of concerns around anal sadistic impulses, but because of concerns about an omnipotent position from which he feels he could really play them out or from which he feels others could play such impulses out upon him. Another way to say this is that he is concerned with boundary loss as it relates to his affective life. In psychotherapy, the therapist can sense both the patient's passive aquiescence to the work, his awaiting the magic of the therapist, and at the same time his on-going struggles over control of time, money, words, and other things shared in the therapy.

STRUCTURALIZATION IN THE OBSESSIONAL

This combination of aquiescence and struggle can also be termed compliance and defiance. It is often viewed as ambivalence centering around anal sadistic impulses and reaction formations to them. If the therapist should interpret the patient's compliance as a resistance to the recognition of feelings within himself, I have found it quite common to see the patient react with feelings of inner emptiness, a feeling that nothing is truly his own, but that everything is just compliance with and defiance to others. The question of What is me? vs. What is not me? is very disturbing. Compatible with the feeling that nothing is truly his own (the obsessional character always feels poor) is the feeling of living life for others out of duty and always being constrained by reality so that one never does what one might want. Of course, in the obsessive symptom the person feels his thoughts are not what he wants to think. The sense of personal intentionality is often absent or stunted. One possible conclusion is that a conscious sense of self, part of the ego's self-representation, is impoverished. In place of a personal sense of self may be a mosaic of introjects which never seem quite like oneself but rather, always a little like an outside dictum or constraint. The difference between this and a sense of self can be phrased as I am versus I ought to be. I believe this distorted experience of oneself is related to failures of identification and a corresponding fullness of introjects. As Loewald (1962) said, introjects do not exist at the central ego core, but exist as objects around it.

Meissner (1971) thoroughly reviewed processes of internalization and distinguished incorporation, introjection, and identification. He stated that while primitive incorporation destroys the outside world function of the object, introjection preserves it but "involves a replacement of a relationship to an external object by a relation to an internal object" (p. 294). Perhaps emphasis should be placed upon the "replacement" as a moving away from the reality of the outside object, while retaining earlier objects psychically from which separation has not been fully achieved and over which omnipotent control has not been relinquished. This is very different experientially and structurally from the most metabolized and intimate concept of identification. As relates to internal stability, the introject is more vulnerable to regressive pulls and projections than are identifications.

Example. A person returns an extra dollar refunded to him erroneously by a cashier in a store. When asked why he did this he may simply answer that he was given the extra dollar. Only with laborious questioning about his action does he finally make the statement, "I guess I must be honest." That is, there are identifications made with earlier persons who were seen as honest. The returning of the dollar was supplely and automatically done.

Another person is asked why he returned the extra dollar given him, he readily answers "I really ought to give the dollar back to be honest. The cashier would have to account for the dollar at the end of the business day." This is the introjected experience of feeling a discernible presence within. One can readily imagine this person not returning the dollar when no one would be directly penalized for his dishonesty, or when he was not being observed. This person, though, might return the dollar even when unobserved, with the thought, "I had better give the dollar back," as though failure to be honest would encur wrath from within, that is, the wrath of an introjected object who's displeasure would be equivalent to the loss of that object.

I am attempting to demonstrate some ways in which obsessional neurosis and the introjected experience can be seen to bridge the zone between psychosis and neurosis. While some obsessional pathologies are regressive from oedipal castration anxiety and some may, therefore, be seen in the traditional mode, others may represent the highest point of development of a person. Obsessional symptoms appear in people with other basic diagnoses and oftentimes the level of obsessionalism is difficult to discern. I suggest there is an obsessional continuum.

INTENTIONALITY AND STRUCTURALIZATION

I would like to discuss the concept of intentionality and suggest that various levels of obsessionalism may be distinguished using this concept. That is, obsessionals with conflicts primarily around oedipal and anal areas will experience more intentionality than those with more poorly resolved conflicts whose problems center around separation and autonomy. I am using the word *intentionality* to denote a personal feeling of purposiveness. Intrinsic is the emotional experience of a wish that is or might be played out in relation to the real world. The concept rests on subjective, as opposed to outside observation.[1] No doubt, it falls into normal range for people to feel, at times, the constraints of the outside world and either to compromise wishes (this too, can be felt as intentional and represents the internalization of the reality principle, an adaptive ego mode) or to comply with the outside world because of superego pressure. This latter activity can be seen as due to the internalization of superego functions. However, the internalization may not be of the supple identification kind, but may be more the introject kind, not fully felt as self. This compliance may carry with it the potential for the generation of aggression and subsequently defiance, albeit at times displaced and disguised. We could add that problems with aggression in the first place, on a variety of levels, lead to reactive compliance. The aggression, reflecting unconscious anal sadistic and other ambivalent impulses and reflecting an omnipotent position, is often defended against by reaction formation, seen as compliance and passivity, which in itself can express aggression in its serving passive-aggressive functions. This struggle of compliance and defiance, often seen in obsessionals as doing and undoing, may be the result of psychic structures in conflict. That is, the aggression censured by the superego structure is dealt with by the ego structure through reaction formation.

The possibility exists, however, that such seemingly obsessional conflict may not represent conflict between structures, but the failure of structure formation. The conflict may have varying degrees to which it is felt as an internal problem or as personally real. Can we refer to psychic structures as such in a person always prepared to disavow or project an impulse, a defense, and a prohibition? Do structures exist, in such people, who are always ready to break and run from any aspect of themselves which threatens to declare itself as part of themselves? If there are structures in such cases, how do they regulate and integrate? How structured is the introjected experience with feelings and thoughts perceived as someone else's (at least) partial presence within? Someone taken in so peripherally can be expelled readily. The veneer of sameness may mask internal chaos.

CLINICAL EXAMPLES

The following case material is presented to demonstrate the usefulness of the concept of intentionality in diagnosis. While diagnosis can certainly be made in other ways, I believe the level of intentionality experienced distinguishes most clearly the diagnoses and the developmental problems inherent in them.

Case 1

A nineteen-year-old office messenger is admitted to the in-patient unit of a psychiatric hospital because of increasing agitation. He is noted to make and remake his bed "compulsively." When asked about this, he states that his activity revolves around his religious feelings. If he makes his bed, an unholy object, just once, then the singular God might be offended. If the bed were made just twice, then God and Jesus would be offended. Three times would offend the Holy Trinity. If the bed were made four times, "four" sounds like "whore," and whores go to hell. He could, therefore, not stop at four. The number "five" sounds like the word "hive." That word begins with h, just like the word "hell," etc.

The diagnosis in this case, from other data as well, was schizophrenia. This person's entire life centered around his constant contact with God. He felt all activities were dictated to him by God. He was, therefore, never alone and separate, and never aggressive. He could not feel even the intention or wish to please God, for that also, was felt as too aggressive. He simply wanted to avoid displeasing Him.

Case 2

The patient was a twenty-one-year-old single man when he presented for psychotherapy. He described doing some graduate work at a local university, while actually biding his time until a professional school entrance exam was to be given. He said he had taken that exam several times, each time performing only slightly more satisfactorily than the time before, because he felt "mental interference." This meant that he felt unable to think. It was similar to the feeling of "freezing up." He told me he had just graduated from a good college the previous June and that he was now taking one or two courses, and "taking it easy." In college he felt reasonably well until his senior year when two things happened. First, a girlfriend had turned him down for a date and had another man in her room that night. Second, at about the same time, he had taken the entrance exam and done poorly. The "interference" became progressively more intense and frequent.

While no other problems were offered at the time therapy was initiated, it was learned later that the patient had one close friend, had never had intercourse, had not defecated on a toilet for years (he crouched over it), ruminated over the possibility of having a brain tumor (he had consulted several neurologists and had received an EEG), repetitively feared ending up penniless on "skid row," ruminated over the perceived ugly contours of his nose and "scrawny body," and generally felt his head was "packed with shit." Further, it was learned that he imagined he would complete therapy in several months. He wanted to feel like a self-contained machine needing a minor adjustment, like a potentially great man with one small encumbrance on the way to the top. It was indicative of his behavior to be demanding of waitresses in restaurants to convey to them the demeanor of a man used to having great deference paid him. While studying in a library, if an attractive woman was in sight, he would at times stretch his arms (as if while yawning) with the thought that this would bring the girl to him.

History revealed he was the elder of two boys in his family, having a brother two years his junior. His mother was described as cruel. He, himself, was the "bain of her existence." He described himself and his mother locked in combat, each one demanding the other one change. The patient also described genuinely warmer times with his mother during which she helped him with school work. The father was described as the poor brother among his wealthy ones. He was viewed as frightening and pathetic simultaneously. He would lavish sporting equipment on the patient and roughhouse with him, and at times he would beat the patient, railing against the patient as his "own worst enemy," and calling him dumb. The patient would often seem to provoke such treatment. Once his father held his head under water at the beach, while they were playing. The patient remembered thinking his father wished to kill him; he himself would passively allow it to happen if his father wanted it so. The interaction between the parents was described as defiant and constantly argumentative. The patient was often assaultive to his own brother who was compliant with the parents' expectations.

As a little boy the patient had the fantasy of accosting women in the street, taking them underground, cutting off their breasts, and inserting broomsticks in their genitals. When the patient was thirteen, after a confusional period on the part of his mother, she died of a brain tumor. Afterwards, the patient became fastidious about housework (he assumed it his duty) hoping to get closer to his father. He was sent to a structured boarding school to "learn discipline" and, in fact, did well. He was known as a "stickler" for the rules as concerned others, but he himself broke rules. During his junior year at school, he was informed his father had been killed in an accident. The patient continued to do well in school and became more protective toward his brother, as he also had after his mother's death.

Mental Status examination revealed a casually but stylishly dressed young man who spoke in a somewhat stilted fashion. His use of language was near perfect. He had, at first, little affect and appeared very controlled. His facial muscles were taut as well. He quickly told me that my name was one of two psychiatrist's names he had been given, and that he had chosen me because my office was closer to his living quarters. Seeing me, therefore, was more efficient. He described a master plan of proving me incompetent in therapy so that he could feel justified in leaving me.

It was learned in therapy that the patient felt like a self-contained unit, apart from the world. Yet almost all feeling the patient experienced was perceived as coming from someone else's controlling expectation of him. At times these expectations were to be met, or thwarted, or most safely, not to be reacted to. Success in life meant proving his deceased parents wrong (he felt they thought poorly of him), but success was also complying with them and their demands. Failure in life was teaching them a lesson for their treatment of him, while it simultaneously "played into their hands," proving them right in their low opinion of him. While these feelings were alive to the point that he believed his parents had died as desperate ways to hurt him, he could intellectually see the flaw in this thinking. Much of the therapy then concerned reviewing feelings and thoughts such as the above, and testing the reality of them. The work focused upon the ego, successively allowing opportunities for the patient to cognitively understand the dilemmas inherent in his feelings. An early alliance was formed around the overcoming of the primary symptom of "mental interference," while the therapist also encouraged further psychotherapeutic work before the entrance exam was again attempted. After approximately a year, a therapeutic alliance had formed somewhat, as demonstrated in a dream in which the patient was late for a session and was anxiously looking for me. He found me either reading or being read to. The tone of the dream was that my presence was "OK."

In the first two years of work we began to explore the "mental interference." The presence of this feeling, experienced as an incapacity to read, could be detected by the patient's getting a certain feeling when he blinked his eyes. Initially, the symptom was discovered as stimulus barrier, a way of distinguishing self from object. In this period of time, feelings of being united with his dead parents were great. Headaches occurred in sessions accompanied by the statement, "I feel like my head will crack open and my mother's skull will roll to the floor." During this same period of time, therapy was marked by the expression of great sadness and anger, often toward the therapist, and often after an intervention designed to remind the patient of the difference between what he felt and what he knew.

After two years of psychotherapy, during a session in which the patient again expressed anger toward me, he stopped. He began crying and asking if he could really say these things to me. The next session he was upset, because he felt better having ventilated the session before. He was concerned he was somehow weakening, because if ventilation helped, that meant he was no longer insisting that I "change." In that same session he discussed his having recently masturbated for the first time in his recollection, and that it had felt good. The above material indicated enough separateness and sense of self so that he could now begin to take himself or something in himself as a comforting object.

In the next segment of therapy further exploration of the presenting symptom was achieved. The reading material was discernible as representing his fears of being overwhelmed by the demanding mother and his fears of destroying her by taking her inside. The patient took graduate work in another field than his original interest, and while having difficulty at times, was also successful in his work. From the beginning of therapy his relationships with people improved both gradually and markedly. Success in heterosexual functioning was achieved in the context of ever improving relationships. During this period of time the patient saw me as his "power supply." The transference was significantly of a narcissistic type, based on the relationship with his father. In fantasy, he and I had each other's goodness and success in our hands. The patient's intentionality developed over time, at first in this context, and later more autonomously. Coincident with the completion of his graduate work was a sense of accomplishment and maturity. The patient was anxious in the treatment relationship, but with no sense of desperateness about his very survival. He could look at his wishes as separate from mine. A more typical neurotic transference developed in which the relationship to the ambivalently held father was experienced. In addition to the sadomasochistic quality of this relationship, evident were many tender and competitive aspects. The regressive and defensive refusion with the mother figure became less necessary.

Of note in this case is the coexistence of what some would consider a borderline affective life, side by side with many higher level functions—that is, the existence of feelings of rage, fear, sadness, and badness in connection with objects seen as destructive or idealized, simultaneous with more advanced ego functioning. Throughout the therapy the patient reliably appeared for appointments, and while affectively seeing me at times as malevolent, he could also see the therapy as helpful to him. His relationships as they developed gained in depth, distinctions, and stability far more than do the chaotic ones, so familiar to us in borderline personalities. At first, his relationships were marked by passive dependency on his part, in conjunction with struggles for omnipotent control. Much of the work in therapy involved linking affective and cognitive ego functions which were split, except in the symptom of mental interference. The fantasies of fusion with the overwhelming mother defended against acknowledgement of sadomasochistic ones toward the father and simultaneously justified sadomasochistic fantasies toward the mother. In this way, an ambivalent introjection with the defiant father was achieved, but without acknowledgment of a separate self. Without this separate self, a sense of intentionality had not developed, and therapy in the early phases could be felt by the patient only as a series of compliances and defiances to the therapist.

In the early phases of treatment, the therapist was not distinguished from the world at large, which was seen as infinitely demanding. There was no experiencing by the patient of himself as an active participant in his life in any way. After painstakingly defining areas of himself as other than malevolent, the patient could tolerate experiencing himself as not simply a machine of evil (the "bain"). Until then the worlds outside and inside, poorly distinguished from one another, were totally demanding. Much work was necessary to define outside from inside.

Early in therapy, the therapist's feelings of being alone and being concerned about making "one false move" needed to be understood as reflecting the patient's life experience. I wondered at times if the therapy, felt as "my therapy," really wasn't sadistic and exploitative toward a person who could not benefit. With the patient's discovery of himself and his separateness, I felt proud as if I had just had a child, a feeling which resonated with the narcissistic transference which had developed. As intentionality developed at first in the context of this transference relationship, increasing gradients of aggression could be tolerated by him.

Case 3

The patient was a young man in professional school who presented to therapy with the obsessive thought that he might kill himself. The described symptom, ("as though I might fly out the window and die when I fall") was of several weeks duration. The patient initially told his girlfriend of the problem and he thereby elicited a more protective, yet more guarded and distant reaction from her. Shortly after the above thought began, he wondered if he could kill his girlfriend, and noticed himself sleeping on his hands, as if to defend against such a possibility. The symptoms had not interfered with his life in any other way, but he was made anxious by them. At this same period in his life, he had been refused summer employment in his field and had been angered by this. The patient described being half way through professional school, and parenthetically added that his father had attended a similar school years ago. His father, however, because of financial reasons around the time of the patient's birth, had had to discontinue his studies and return home. The current relationship with his girlfriend represented the patient's first, on-going, sexual, and intimate relationship with a woman.

When inquiries were made into his sexual life, he added he had begun to masturbate more since being in school this year, and for the first time, had ejaculated. He had had to "talk himself into it." As an early adolescent, he used to confess his wrongs to his mother, but could never talk about masturbation. Throughout his childhood, when troubled by his thoughts, generally "dirty ones," he would confess to mother. After such confessions he would immediately feel relief. In puberty, after reading a newspaper article, he became concerned that he might kill himself while wearing women's clothes, and this too was confessed.

His childhood history included surgical procedures at ages six and fourteen. He had been an anxious child with short lived phobias. In fact, his current obsessional thoughts of suicide and homicide were not his first clear cut experience of thoughts or actions alien to himself. In his life he had been troubled by his use of obscene language, by his masturbation using his father's sex magazines, and by his occasional homosexual play in puberty. These activities were felt as wrongdoings which had caused him shame; he would confess some of them to his mother and swear to never engage in them again. In addition to his confessional relationship with his mother, he recalled their arguing together, following which he would sulk on his bed. His mother would often come into his room tearfully, and while she sat on his bed they would "make up."

His father, a well-respected business man in their city, was described as somewhat fearsome, but "a nice guy." He recalled his father's expecting exemplary behavior from him because of his reputation. His father was described as compliant in business, but simply for sound business reasons. He was often seen sleeping off a headache on the couch.

The patient was the older of two children, having a sister two years his junior who had recently become engaged. He and his sister had always had a playful, teasing relationship. The patient had never tried to get dates for his sister with any of his friends, but had never thought much about his reluctance.

Mental Status examination revealed an animated, attractive, casual and mildly effeminate young man with flowing hair. He was mildly anxious, yet related warmly and somewhat flamboyantly. After his first therapy session he felt a warm, good, full feeling of relief. His obsessional thoughts diminished significantly. In early sessions, he struggled with questions of reality versus dreams, and mentioned how he liked stories about the mystical. He also wanted to know about the rules of psychotherapy. He wanted to understand more about his symptoms, but questioned if he would rather do that on his own, without therapy. Within a few weeks he wanted to "test" himself and his "cure." He was concerned about becoming too dependent upon therapy. He ambivalently agreed to twice weekly therapy meetings, in the context of fantasies that if he gave me what (he thought) I wanted, I would allow him to keep his cure permanently. The next session he discussed a fear that he could be a tyrant if allowed to be.

Compliance and defiance fantasies became major themes in the transference. The compliance aspect included seeing his father and himself as passive, and was accompanied by associations to homosexuals, looking at homosexual magazines, and fantasies of masturbating in female garments. Compliance infiltrated his thoughts about his career, feeling it to be his father's idea. "Settling down" and getting married was felt too as compliant, as was heterosexual activity. He saw his girlfriend's nightly interest in sex as demanding.

The defiance aspects involved seeing his father as "an asskisser" to people. In the transference he became afraid of losing my approval, especially when, during interruptions in therapy, he allowed himself to masturbate with attendant fellatio fantasies. He longed to change careers and go into the performing arts. He became angry with me for not supplying him with a panacea, and as the therapy deepened he had the obsessive thought that he could kill me. In the context of defiance also, women were seen as devalued creatures whose demands should be thwarted. At the heights of both compliance and defiance he feared "flipping out, going crazy, losing control," and encouraged the therapist to control him. Defiance aspects also included increased sexual thoughts about women. In this context, an intermittent symptom was discovered. He periodically experienced "grainy vision," meaning that he saw his visual field as if it were composed of fine dots. Associations led somewhat compliantly to his father's sexual pictures, and to his earlier shameful masturbation.

In this case, the working alliance was never overwhelmed by transference fantasies. At no point did the patient seriously doubt my interest in helping him. He was able, after briefly jousting with differences between reality and fantasy, to know affectively what he was doing, what I was doing, and what we were trying to accomplish together. He had a reasonably high level of intentionality. He was troubled by what his intentions were saying about himself. I was never concerned that the patient would act on his obsessions, and I felt that we had that certain anticipatable luxury of time together while we tried to understand things better. Countertransference reactions centered upon feeling fatherly toward the patient, and at times feeling frustrated at the fixity of his cycles (compliance and defiance) and defenses. Like his father, I believe, I thought he could "do better," and I was aware of my own angry and defensive tendency to not take the patient's flamboyant discomfort seriously at times. This was in resonance with the patient's not "taking seriously" what his intentions meant in terms of his oedipal position.

INTENTIONALITY

A cursory examination of what is necessary for the feeling of intentionality, a composite feeling, might be helpful. All of the following have to do with ego functions.

Self-Object Distinction. Certain reality constraints may thwart one's intentions. Also, intentions may be kept from consciousness because of conflicts attached to them Both reality and conflict can prevent intentions from becoming evident. Nevertheless, the recognition of separateness of self from object is necessary in order to recognize personally intending something out of personal desire.

Sense of Self.   Clearly related to the self-object distinction is the sense of self as a somewhat known and anticipatable presence within. Sense of self, of course, may vary within individuals so that one may feel "I surprised myself" or "I did not act like myself," but it is the presence of a self as a referent that is the issue. Sense of self as a referent is related to stable identifications existent over time.

Use of Projection.   Projection as a mechanism is well known in a variety of character types. The defense allows the ego to disavow unacceptable ideas or affects. With the failure of full self-object distinction and development of a sense of self, projections can occur with fluidity. Intention too, can be attributed to others.

Ego-Super-Ego Condensation.   This is a concept to which Kernberg (1970) referred in his discussion of the narcissistic character. He referred to the inability of the person to discern a "wish" from an "ought to." I believe this is present as a result of identification with the aggressor as a model of premature superego development. It is believed that archaic superego precursors serve both as attempts to deal with the frightening maternal imago (by taking her inside and trying to keep the outside object good) and also to bolster drive control in the oral period. This condensation seems to occur in schizoid and borderline personalities, as well as in narcissistic character types. Such a condensation interferes with a sense of intentionality. Borderline and narcissistic characters can feel a sense of personal intentionality only at times of sexually perverse or addictive or self-mutilative behavior, when they are "bad" or aggressive. What may be pleasurable is that they are being themselves with some sense of intention to be so. Often, however, even such pressing and self-destructive behavior feels externally driven to them.

Aggression.   Obsessionals are typically described as having active-passive struggles, which are traditionally viewed as playing out regressively both positive and negative oedipal constellations. The aggression, described as organized in an anal-sadistic mode, is inhibited, and reaction formations occur as well. Obsessionals, however, with such struggles are capable of aggressive behavior in certain areas, most often in work. In work, the ethic and duty to work assist the drive in being acted upon. Examination of the obsessional's overt activity level, such as work, generally reveals a combination of grumbling passive submission to the boss-parent, a childlike pleasure in the strength necessary to do all that work (activity pleasure, although masochistic and with exhibitionistic features), and an anxious and veiled or repressed recognition of the assertiveness of the competitive aspects. In other areas of life, the obsessional may be less able to feel and act with intentional aggression in an adaptive way. No matter how disguised, he is able to feel intention somewhere. Patients with more borderline, schizoid, and narcissistic pathologies have more difficulty in feeling intention anywhere. Activity pleasure, lacking in these more primitive pathologies, and in the more primitive obsessionals, may be related to the lack of pleasure, or anhedonia, as described in psychotics.

CONCLUSIONS

The above ego capabilities can, of course, be useful in the assessment of psychopathology in a general way. In many clinical situations the ego deficits are reasonably clear. Where obsessional phenomena, felt as ego alien, are manifest, the distinction needs to be made between discrete, ego-alien symptoms, and the more total life experience of living in an ego-alien, split off way—one which resembles an inner totalitarian state devoid of personal intentionality. I believe the clinical material illustrates the multifaceted functions of obsessional phenomena, and the usefulness of the concept of intentionality in distinguishing the higher level neurotic obsessional from the obsessional with more significant ego defects.

Ramifications of the distinction between these two differing life experiences are many as concerns psychotherapy. The working alliance deserves special attention and nurturance, and in some situations may not develop spontaneously as an extension of the patient's earliest dyadic relationship. Perhaps inadequate attention to preanal factors partly accounts for the reputation that obsessionals have of being difficult to treat, and in their often seen intellectual flight into some semblance of a transference, which masks the absence of an alliance (that is, a real relationship) with the therapist and an intention to use the therapy for an intentional purpose.

I know of no simple way to assess the feeling of intentionality in the obsessional patient. In my experience, the use of passive reflexive verbs, used to intone that all things occur to the person and that the person himself intends nothing coupled with a sense of perplexity about how things happen, should draw one's attention to this feeling. In particular, expressions of passivity of mental function, that is, expressions such as "the thought occurred to me" or "an idea ran through my mind," may indicate a paucity of intentionality. An impoverished experience of intentionality must be distinguished from other problems in which a person can feel acted upon, but has more than a dream-like and perplexed way of understanding events. A careful history should be taken to discern to what degree intentionality is felt anywhere in life. The quality and clarity of objects described in one's life is especially helpful, in that clarity of the perception of objects and their separateness generally reflects a clarity of self and its uniqueness.

Early feeling-responses the therapist may experience are helpful in seeing problems of this composite function. When one finds oneself agreeing to a course of therapy, the goals of which are unclear, coupled with the sensation that, in some way, the patient has been left behind somewhere, one should be attuned to problems with intentionality. Passive patients may not readily say what they want, but the therapist may feel the patient's need for some kind of feeding experience. As concerns early therapy with patients with impoverished senses of intentionality, I have felt my inability to console the patient, feeling quite helplessly an onlooker, while also feeling that I was being scrutinized and that with one false move, I could upset the person.

Considering the components of intentionality outlined earlier, my contention is that where this is poorly felt, the therapist must be active early in therapy. The activity level is not designed to bring insight into neurotic conflict, but to help the patient to define himself, his problems, the therapist, and the nature of the therapy more clearly. Such therapeutic activity may approach assisting the patient with reality testing despite a presumptive diagnosis of neurosis. This seeming contradiction between technique and diagnosis is, however, simply an acknowledgment of the unevenness of ego development seen conspicuously in obsessional neurosis and character. Such activity acknowledges that while the obsessional may give up intentionality in an effort to disavow aggressive impulses, the aggressive impulses expressed by the patient in his struggles with the therapist may in themselves derive from the patient's inability to experience intentionality. This inability may cause him to feel that whatever the therapist says must not be applicable to him and can only lead him astray. The therapist's interventions, therefore, must be fought against.

SUMMARY

In this paper I have presented material from three cases in which obsessional or compulsive features were evident. In each case there were problems in the subjective experiencing of intentionality, ranging from apparently none in case one to intentionality more commonly experienced, except in the presenting symptom in case three. I attempted to demonstrate the presence of precipitating events which appear oedipal in nature in the two cases described at some length. The results of the triadic and competitive conflicts were different in these cases, inducing in case two an intensification of the mechanism of isolation (that is, a splitting of affective from cognitive life) to the extent of a loss of a conscious sense of self. In keeping with this, intentionality was impoverished, and psychotherapy, in recognition of the patient's fears of what was outside and inside himself, required a prolonged period in which careful attention was paid to defining aspects of himself, the therapist, and the nature of the therapy. In case three intentionality was also an issue, but to a lesser extent. The struggles around it seemed almost whimsical at times, and disavowal of intentionality was itself a defense against acknowledgment of oedipal impulses. That is, it was primarily an issue of the transference, where in case two it was more an issue in the therapeutic alliance. It appears that the composite function of intentionality can be used as an indicator of the successes or failures in the negotiation of preanal tasks described herein, and therefore, as an indicator of core areas of conflict that lie behind obsessional presentation.

NOTE

1. Schafer (1968) links intentionality to stable identifications and the lack of intentionality to archaic introjects. He does, however, state that lack of intentionality does not occur solely on the basis of archaic introjects. While I agree, I believe that in some cases this factor is a necessary part of the explanation of the lack of intentionality.

REFERENCES

Abraham, K. (1921). Contributions to the theory of the anal character. *Selected Papers on Psychoanalysis*. London: Hogarth, 1927.

Fenichel, O. (1945). *The Psychoanalytic Theory of Neurosis*. New York: Norton.

―――― (1896). Further remarks on the neuropsychoses of defense. Standard Edition 3:162-186.

―――― (1905a). My views on the part played by sexuality in the aetiology of the neuroses. *Standard Edition* 7:271-279.

―――― (1905b). Three essays on the theory of sexuality. *Standard Edition* 7:135-243.

―――― (1908). Character and anal erotism. *Standard Edition* 9:167-175.

―――― (1909). Notes upon a case of obsessional neurosis. *Standard Edition* 10:155-249.

―――― (1913). The disposition to obsessional neurosis. *Standard Edition* 12:317-326.

Kernberg, O. (1967). Borderline personality organization. *Journal of the American Psychoanalytic Association* 15:641-685.

―――― (1970). Factors in the psychoanalytic treatment of narcissistic personalities. *Journal of the American Psychoanalytic Association* 18:51-85.

Loewald, H. W. (1962). Internalization, separation, mourning and the superego. *Psychoanalytic Quarterly* 31:483-504.

Meissner, W. W. (1971). Notes on identification: 2. Clarification of related concepts. *Psychoanalytic Quarterly* 40:277-302.

Reich, W. (1949). *Character Analysis*. New York: Farrar, Straus, Giroux.

Sandler, J., and Joffe, W. G. (1965). Notes on obsessional manifestations in children. *Psychoanalytic Study of the Child* 20:425-438.

Schafer, R. (1968). On the theoretical and technical conceptualization of activity and passivity. *Psychoanalytic Quarterly* 37:173-198.

Schur, M. (1953). The ego in anxiety. In *Drives, Affects and Behavior*, vol. 1, ed. R. Loewenstein, pp. 67-103. New York: International Universities Press.

Shapiro, D. (1965). *Neurotic Styles*. New York: Basic Books.

Winnicott, D. W. (1953). Transitional objects and transitional phenomena. *International Journal of Psycho-Analysis* 34:89-97.

The Eroding Concept
of Intrapsychic Conflict

JOSEPH W. SLAP, M.D.

With the increased interest in borderline and psychotic patients, concepts are being introduced which erode the concept of intrapsychic conflict between the ego and the other macrostructures. In particular, the drive derivative as source of danger is being lost sight of as expressions such as fear of the loss of ego boundaries and struggles against identification are introduced. Some authors who use these expressions, judging from their clinical material, do uncover their patients' fantasies and the drive derivatives and defenses they reflect. Nonetheless, they contribute to the problem by introducing inaccurate new terms. Other authors, having embraced recent innovations in theory, seem to disregard intrapsychic conflict.

In the foreword to a series of books devoted to basic psychoanalytic concepts, Anna Freud (1969) notes that there are instances in which concepts have started out as well-defined descriptions of circumscribed psychic events, but in the course of time have become increasingly vague and imprecise. One of the aims of the series is to "induce psychoanalytic authors to use their terms and concepts more precisely with regard for the theoretical framework to which they owe their origin, and to reduce thereby the many sources of misunderstanding and confusion which govern the psychoanalytic literature at present." The purpose of this paper is to call attention to the erosion of the concept of intrapsychic conflict which has accompanied increased psychoanalytic interest in patients whose pathology goes beyond psychoneurosis.

We frequently hear and read, in relation to patients who avoid intimacy through distancing and withdrawal, that they fear the loss of their ego boundaries or of their selves, or that they fear engulfment, merger, or fusion, or that they are struggling against an identification. With the widespread attention paid to Mahler's work on the symbiotic and separation-individuation phases and to Kohut's work on the self, the use of these expressions has become prevalent. The trend has been established despite the alarm sounded by Arlow in a Congress paper (1963); he calls attention to misconceptions which blur the role of conflict in symptom formation by removing the specified danger from the realm of the drives and their derivatives. Among the formulations he objects to are the threat of the loss of ego boundaries and the struggle against identifications. He has returned to this theme time and again (Arlow 1970, 1971; Slap 1974a).

In the 1963 paper, Arlow reviews the changes Freud made in Psychoanalytic theory during the 1920s which are subsumed under the designation of structural theory. Arlow stresses that defenses are mobilized in response to anxiety associated with the threatened emergence of an instinctual wish perceived as forbidden or dangerous. He seeks to demonstrate that the concepts *conflicts among the agencies of the mind* and *signal anxiety* apply to the situations which have evoked from many authors the divers formulations he objected to as unwarranted. He conceded that "some of the misconceptions referred to concerning symptom formation may result from an attempt to use inaccurate shorthand expressions for more complicated phenomena" (p. 15a).

In effect, he divides those who use the objectionable expressions into two groups. One group, while understanding symptom formation in terms of structural theory, uses, to designate types or aspects of conflict situations, expressions which contribute to the erosion of the concept of intrapsychic conflict. The clinical material these authors offer reveals that each clinical instance is studied for the specific fantasies elaborated and the drive derivatives and defenses they reflect. The other group has lost sight of what constitutes danger to the ego and of the role of conflict in symptom formation.

Group 1

Greenson (1954), Modell (1975), and Socarides (1973a) exemplify the first group. Greenson writes of the struggle against identification. In each of the four cases offered as illustrations for this concept, it is clear that basic to the struggle against identification is a conflict between drive and defense. About the first case Greenson writes, "Her struggle against the introjected mother and ... against the identification ... seems to me to have been a struggle against oral libidinal and sadistic strivings which were involved in this identification."

The second case was that of a woman who came to analysis because of chronic and severe boredom; the most torturesome aspect of her boredom was a terrible empty feeling. Greenson writes, "Analysis of this empty feeling was very complicated but very rewarding. The emptiness was in the first place a consequence of the inhibition of fantasies due to a repression of forbidden instinctual aims and objects. Furthermore, the emptiness represented hunger. It was a substitution of a sensation for a fantasy, a primitivation of an ego function. Finally. and I believe most important in this case, the feeling of emptiness was an attempt to deny that the mother had been introjected" (p. 205).

Earlier (p. 201), Greenson had written, "If one compares introjection with identification, it can be seen that introjection is an instinctual aim toward an object, while identification is a process which may result after the aim of introjection has taken place." Accordingly, the symptom of emptiness can be understood as the outcome of a conflict between defense (denial) and instinctual aim (introjection).

Greenson says of the third case: "He tried to remain unaware of this internalized father imago because he wanted to remain oblivious of the oral libidinal and sadistic impulses which he felt toward his father." And of the fourth: "On a still deeper level, however, for this patient to be identified with his father meant to submit to his father in an oral, sexual, and passive way. At this time the vagina meant for him the father's mouth. . . . It became clear that the father's visit had remobilized a very primitive identification with the father which still retained strong oral, sexual, passive and aggressive instinctual components."

In each of the cases, defense was exerted against anxiety associated with instinctual aims. Greenson, having analyzed the patients in these terms, goes on to coin the expression *the struggle against identification* to designate a particular clinical situation, one in which the patient disavows the object as part of a defense against an instinctual aim involving the object. Understood in this way, the term is valid; nonetheless it has the effect of lending support to concepts which, as Arlow put it, blur the role of intrapsychic conflict in symptom formation.

In a recent contribution, Modell (1975) introduces the concept of a narcissistic *defense against affects*.[1] The affects he refers to "signify object seeking and object hunger" and therefore are not meant to include anxiety, guilt, and other painful affects which do evoke defensive activity from the ego. Modell differentiates the narcissistic character disorder from borderline states by noting that in the former condition there is a fear that the fragile sense of self will disintegrate if the object is permitted to intrude. This fear, it is postulated, derives from the patient's childhood need to defend against the intrusiveness of the mother. Stated in this way, the conflict is not intrapsychic but interpersonal and, if the defense is against closeness or intrusion, *the concept of the instinctual drive is superfluous.*

Except for a cursory allusion to two patients, Modell provides little clinical material as evidence for his assertions. He does characterize people suffering with narcissistic character disorder as follows: "These people have an accurate endopsychic perception of their relationship to objects. They describe themselves as encased in a 'plastic bubble' or feel they are really not 'in the world'—they are in a cocoon: a cocoon provides sustenance for its occupant and protects it from the dangers of the environment; it is like a fortress which nothing leaves and nothing enters. A cocoon, no matter how well insulated, needs to be attached to something, and these people who may deny their dependent needs usually crave admiration" (p. 276a).

Actually the plastic bubble or cocoon is a waking screen and, as such, is akin to Sylvia Plath's bell jar and the Wolf Man's veil. In a previous study (1974), I have shown that waking screen symptomatology is indicative of fantasies of being asleep, often in the maternal claustrum. As a symptom it is expressive of both drive and defense. Insofar as there is a physiological need for sleep and it is pleasurable, comforting, and replicative of falling asleep in mother's arms, it is instincutal, Insofar as sleep involves withdrawal and unawareness: it may be used as a defense expressing such ideas as, I am not here and What I am observing is not real, it is but a dream.

A case of my own is instructive. An unmarried man in his late thirties came into analysis with the complaint that his feelings were dead and that he could form no lasting attachments. His affect was bland. At the end of a previous, long, and unsuccessful analysis he told the analyst that if he did not find himself in the next few years he would shoot himself in the head with a silver bullet. He did not understand the meaning of this remark at the time. When in his second analysis his defenses began to loosen, he became able to feel such affects as tenderness and anger, and he demonstrated a clever sense of humor not in evidence before. He reported a dream in which Mickey Mantle or John Kennedy was lying in state in a glass casket. The casket had a bullet hole in it. The corpse began to move. He said the body was himself; he slept in that position. He went on to say that earlier in the day a fellow worker expressed surprise when the patient showed anger at some bureaucratic demand; he didn't realize the patient ever became angry. To the bullet hole the patient associated the silver bullet required to kill the werewolf in a movie he had seen in childhood.

The dream was expressive of a conflict over phallic-oedipal strivings. He had the fantasy that this part of his personality, represented in the dream by Mickey Mantle or John Kennedy, was dead, or at least asleep, but was coming alive as with a werewolf. The deadness of his feelings are explained by this fantasy. The glass case is analogous to Modell's plastic bubble or cocoon and helps account for the lifeless facade the patient showed the world. Yet it is clear that the defense was against drive derivatives.

Modell would probably agree. He introduces the concept of a narcissistic defense against affects. He explains that these affects "signify object seeking and object hunger." If these two ideas are treated logically it can be derived that the defense is exerted against libidinal, and possibly aggressive, impulses directed at objects, a formulation consistent with the currently accepted concept of intrapsychic conflict.

Socarides (1973a) published a case history of a thirty-two-year-old unmarried businessman who, he asserts, from early childhood had an intense feminine identification with his mother which produced regressive episodes representing "a wish for and dread of merging with her and which were experienced as a threat of loss of self and fear of engulfment" (p. 432). The patient was the oldest of five siblings, the youngest being twelve years his junior; thus, four times he had the experience of seeing his mother go through a pregnancy. The clinical data indicates that he responded to these experiences in a variety of ways. There is evidence that he identified with his pregnant mother and that he wished to be in the place of the envied fetus.

This evidence is scattered throughout the paper. He had waking screen symptomatology (Slap 1974b) which implies a fantasy of sleeping within the maternal claustrum: "He complained that he felt the air around him in the consultation room very 'heavy and round' and he could sometimes feel or see 'curved forms,' could even almost taste them, 'a heavy, oppressive feeling all about'" (p. 438). He experienced dread and horror as dusk approached and night fell. "This fear of nightfall was shown to be his wish for and dread of engulfment by the maternal body. 'I would even run home after school to get there before dark, to be where there was light'" (p. 440). When he could not maintain "the optimal distance from and closeness to his mother," he described an alteration in consciousness "like I am in a black room floating for such a length of time that I cannot find myself anymore" (p. 441). And lower on the same page: "He is being whirled into a vortex, a whirlpool, the mother's body, and feels as if parts of his body are disappearing (body disintegration anxiety and loss of body ego)." Here Socarides eschews a dynamic account of the conflict situation, namely that the patient's ego reacts with anxiety to a wishful fantasy (drive derivative) of replacing a sibling in the maternal claustrum. Still, in the clinical situation Socarides (1973b) declares that it is necessary to uncover the specific fantasies of patients and that terms such as "fear of engulfment" are generalizations of types of fantasies.

Group 2

Examples of the second group, characterized above as having lost sight of what constitutes danger to the ego and of the role of conflict in symptom formation, may be found among the adherents of Kohut's recent work on narcissism and the narcissistic personality. Kernberg (1974) has contrasted his view of the narcissistic personality with that of Kohut. Kohut believes that narcissistic personalities are fixated on archaic grandiose self-configurations and overestimated, narcissistically cathected objects. These fixations, as the term implies, represent normal stages of development which the narcissistic personality has failed to grow past because of traumatic loss or disappointment in an idealized object. Kohut's treatment strategy is to allow the reactivation of the grandiose self and the idealized self-object so that they may be worked through and development resume toward a more realistic view of the self and toward true object relations.

While there is agreement about the descriptive clinical characteristics which indicates that Kohut and Kernberg are addressing themselves to the same patients, they regard the grandiose self differently. Kohut views it as a fixation of an archaic "normal" primitive self and Kernberg feels it "reflects a pathological condensation of some aspects of the real self (i.e., the 'specialness' of the child that was reinforced by early experience), the ideal self (i.e., the fantasies and self-images of power, wealth, and beauty that compensated the small child for the experience of severe oral frustration, rage, and envy), and the ideal object (i.e., the fantasy of an ever-giving, ever-loving, and accepting mother, in contrast to their experience in reality—a replacement of the devalued real parental object)" (p. 256).

Kernberg asserts that splitting, the regressive division of self and objects into all good and all bad self-object identificatory systems, is predominant in the defensive organization of the narcissistic personality. The grandiose self constitutes a positively toned identificatory system, the all good self in relationship with the all good object. Analysis of the components of the grandiose self reveals "its defensive function against the emergence of direct oral rage and envy, against paranoid fears related to projection of sadistic trends onto the analyst (representing a primitive, hated, and sadistically perceived mother image), and against basic feelings of terrifying empty loneliness, hunger for love, and guilt over aggression directed against the frustrating parental images" (p. 261).

Thus Kernberg sees the grandiose self as a structure deriving from intrapsychic conflict. It provides gratification and serves an important defensive function primarily against oral rage. In Kohut's view, it is a point in a line of development, normal in early life but anachronistic in the adult.

Kohut's clinical material fails to convincingly demonstrate the validity of his formulations. As Loewald has observed, his "passion and superior ability for comprehensive and precise formulations tends to interfere with his presentation of the case material and to pre-empt the reader's own judgment" (p. 447). Goldberg (1974, 1975), an advocate of Kohut's point of view, has offered clinical data in recent articles. His material leaves the impression that symptoms are not analyzed; they are taken to be reflections of the variety of feeling states subsumed under the concepts of the grandiose self and the idealized object.

His premature ejaculation was seen to be a reflection of his fragile and vulnerable self: a symptom that denoted sexual activity as a performance he felt demanded greatness, was sometimes too exciting, and an arena for possible painful humiliation. (p. 250)

One of the patient's early dreams concerned his being confronted by robots or mechanical men, and this filled him with anxiety. The associations were to the men he knew (father, friends, and the analyst) who responded to him without feeling and who frightened him. The dream reflected an empathic failure: a failure of the analyst to understand the patient. The patient experiences such failure as a loss or absence of the analyst. (p. 251)

The dream appears to be unanalyzed. It is possible that Goldberg felt no necessity to present an analysis of the dream and that criticism on that score is unfair; nonetheless, this essay is concerned not with Goldberg but with the fate of an important psychoanalytic concept. Therefore, it is the effect of the article rather than the author's intent that is important. The writer presents us with no day residue. Why on this particular night did the patient dream of robots? If these people affected him in the way the author claims why did the patient not dream of robots every night? Why the confrontation? Why the anxiety?

My own feel for this material is as follows. The patient was slighted on the dream day. He was enraged and, consciously or unconsciously, thought of the person or persons who offended him as belonging to the class of robots or mechanical men. However, he resisted the impulse to confront the source of his distress and this impulse provoked the dream. His tormentors are represented as robots or mechanical men. Instead of his confronting them, they confront him; his aggression is projected onto them. The source of the anxiety is the danger created by his aggressive impulses. However, in the dream as in waking life, the aggression having been projected, he is afraid of them. Such an interpretation takes into account the drive derivative as a source of danger which needs to be defended against, in short intrapsychic conflict.

He presented another dream: "Later, he had a dream of rushing up to a man at a church wedding to introduce himself; the man was slightly amused at his enthusiasm, and the patient felt hurt and deflated. This was associated to the patient's feeling that the analyst had not been properly enthusiastic in welcoming him after a vacation—another failure of the analyst as a narcissistic object" (1974, p. 251).

Once more, it appears the dream has not been analyzed. An association was made between a dream element (enthusiasm) and an event in the analytic situation. However, it is not clear by whom the association was made nor are the other dream elements accounted for. The 1975 article follows the same pattern. Clinical material is cited. From this data feeling states are picked out and explained on the basis of the vicissitudes of the idealizing and mirror transferences; many details are ignored, there is no mention of instinctual levels, nor of intrapsychic conflict. The application of theory to this data seems mechanical and procrustean.

A claim of those who set aside structural theory and the concept of intrapsychic conflict in dealing with preoedipal problems is that psychic structure is lacking in the preoedipal period and therefore intrapsychic conflict cannot be an important factor. The premise of this line of reasoning runs counter to the teachings of the principal researchers and theoreticians of the early infantile period. Fairbairn, Freud, Glover, Jacobson, Kernberg, M. Klein, Mahler, and Sandler have all written on early structure formation. This list is not intended to be exhaustive but to indicate how basic it is to psychoanalytic theory that structure exists from the beginnings of life. Further, no matter what one infers or believes about psychic structure in the first several months of life, it is clear that by the time a child or an adult becomes a patient there has necessarily occurred considerable development of psychic structure.

It may be conceded that there are instances of pathology in early life which are not attributable to intrapsychic conflict. Hospitalism is one example; another is provided by Stoller (1974) who described a type of male transvestism which in his view does not derive from intrapsychic conflict. These conditions derive from severe deviations from usual child rearing practices. Aside from such rare and special conditions conflicts over aggressive drive derivatives abound in preoedipal pathology.

DISCUSSION

It is both conceivable and desirable that theories superior to those central to current psychoanalytic understanding should some day evolve. Accordingly, one should be prepared to examine new hypotheses with an open mind and to integrate them into one's theoretical position when they organize and explain clinical data better than existing theory. Yet, when theoretical innovations are introduced, it should be clear that a change is being made, and the reasons for the change and the changes themselves should be explicitly stated. What I object to in the group-one writers is the subtle erosion and attenuation of theory through the use of inaccurate shorthand expressions or through carelessness of thought. We can only know our theory, test its validity, and seek to improve it if individual practitioners and writers use it with precision.

The writers of group two are another matter. Kohut makes it clear that he is offering new theoretical concepts. His reasons for his innovations and what the innovations consisted of have been extensively stated. They have been the subject of much study and much discussion and their place in psychoanalytic theory has yet to be determined. This article is not the place for an assessment of Kohut's work on narcissism. It does appear, however, that authors who enthusiastically embrace his work do at times dispense with the concept of intrapsychic conflict through a narrow, selective treatment of clinical material.

NOTE

1. Defense against affects is included on Arlow's list of incorrect formulations: "A brief enumeration of some of the more common misconceptions follows. Symptoms have been described as representing defense against affects or . . ." (1963, p. 14b)

REFERENCES

Arlow, J. A. (1963). Conflict, regression, and symptom formation. *International Journal of Psycho-Analysis* 44:12-22.

—— (1970). Some problems in current psychoanalytic thought. In *World Biennial of Psychiatry and Psychotherapy* 1:34-54.

—— (1971). The dehumanization of psychoanalysis. *Psychoanalytic Quarterly* 41:485-486.

Freud, A. (1969). Foreword to Hampstead Clinic Library. In *Basic Psychoanalytic Concepts on the Libido Theory*, ed. H. Nagera, pp. 9-11. New York: Basic Books.

Goldberg, A. I. (1974). On the prognosis and treatment of narcissism. *Journal of the American Psychoanalytic Association* 22:243-254.

—— (1975). A fresh look at perverse behavior. *International Journal of Psycho-Analysis* 56:335-342.

Greenson, R. R. (1954). The struggle against identification. *Journal of the American Psychoanalytic Association* 2:200-217.

Kernberg, O. F. (1974). Contrasting viewpoints regarding the nature and psychoanalytic treatment of narcissistic personalities: a preliminary communication. *Journal of the American Psychoanalytic Association* 22:255-267.

Loewald, H. W. (1973). Review of *The Analysis of the Self* by Heinz Kohut. *Psychoanalytic Quarterly* 42:441-451.

Modell, A. H. (1975). A narcissistic defense against affects. *International Journal of Psycho-Analysis* 56:275-282.

Slap, J.W. (1974a). *The Ego and the Mechanisms of Defence:* A Review. *Journal of the Philadelphia Association for Psychoanalysis* 1:36-43.

—— (1974b). On waking screens. *Journal of the American Psychoanalytic Association* 22:844-853.

Socarides, C. W. (1973a). Sexual perversion and the fear of engulfment. *International Journal of Psychoanalytic Psychotherapy* 2:432-448

—— (1973b). Personal communication.

Stoller, R. (1974). Does sexual perversion exist? *John Hopkins Medical Journal* 134:43-57.

Name Index

Subject Index

Author Index
Volumes 1-5